CREATIVE
HOMEOWNER®

1&2-STORY
HOME PLANS

CREATIVE HOMEOWNER®, Upper Saddle River, New Jersey

COPYRIGHT © 2005

CRE▲TIVE
HOMEOWNER®

A Division of Federal Marketing Corp.
Upper Saddle River, NJ

VP/ Business Development: Brian H. Toolan
VP/ Editorial Director: Timothy O. Bakke
Production Manager: Rose Sullivan

Home Plans Publishing Consultant: James D. McNair III
Editorial Assistants: Nicole Porto, Evan Lambert,
    Lauren Manoy

Design and Layout: Arrowhead Direct (David Kroha,
    Cindy DiPierdomenico, Judith Kroha)

Cover Design: David Geer

Current Printing (last digit)
10 9 8 7 6 5 4 3 2 1

1 & 2 Story Home Plans
Library of Congress Control Number: 2004116405
ISBN: 1-58011-250-1

CREATIVE HOMEOWNER®
A Division of Federal Marketing Corp.
24 Park Way
Upper Saddle River, NJ 07458
www.creativehomeowner.com

Printed In China

Note: The homes as shown in the photographs and renderings in this book may differ from the actual blueprints. When studying the house of your choice, please check the floor plans carefully.

PHOTO CREDITS

Front cover: *center* plan 131005, page 12; *bottom row* (from left to right) plan 131014, page 99; plan 161002, page 20; page 131006, page 28; plan 271080, page 155
back cover: *top* plan 271076, page 56; *center* plan 271081, page 180; *bottom row* (from left to right) plan 111004, page 8; plan 161002, page 21; plan 161002, page 21
page 1: plan 121007, page 307
page 5: courtesy of Western Wood Products
page 6: *top* Freeze Frame Studio/CH; *bottom* courtesy of Trus Joist MacMillan
page 7: Timothy O. Bakke/CH
page 68: courtesy of Merillat Industries
page 69: courtesy of Kraftmaid Cabinetry
pages 70–71: *left* courtesy of Kraftmaid Cabinetry; *center* courtesy of Jenn-Air; *right* courtesy of Wood-Mode Cabinetry
page 72: *top* courtesy of Kohler; bottom right courtesy of Ann Sacks Tile; *bottom left* courtesy of Wilsonart International
page 73: *top row* courtesy of Kraftmaid Cabinetry; bottom courtesy of Armstrong Floors
page 134: courtesy of Mannington Floors
page 135: courtesy of Congoleum
page 136: *top* courtesy of Congoleum; *bottom* courtesy of Mannington Floors
page 137: courtesy of Dal-Tile
page 138: *left* courtesy of Mannington Floors; *right* courtesy of Congoleum
page 139: left courtesy of Mannington Floors; *right* courtesy of Dal-Tile
page 202: *top* courtesy of Trex Decks; *bottom* courtesy of the Hickson Corp.
page 203: courtesy of Arch Wood Protection
page 204: both courtesy of the California Redwood Association
page 205: courtesy of Trex Decks
pages 270–271: both George Ross/CH
page 272: Christine Elasigue/CH
page 273: *top* George Ross/CH; *bottom all* Christine Elasigue/CH
page 274: *left* George Ross/CH; *right (top to bottom)* Christine Elasigue/CH
pages 275–277: all Christine Elasigue/CH

Contents

Getting Started

Maybe you can't wait to bang the first nail. Or you may be just as happy leaving town until the windows are cleaned. The extent of your involvement with the construction phase is up to you. Your time, interests, and abilities can help you decide how to get the project from lines on paper to reality. But building a house requires more than putting pieces together. Whoever is in charge of the process must competently manage people as well as supplies, materials, and construction. He or she will have to

- Make a project schedule to plan the orderly progress of the work. This can be a bar chart that shows the time period of activity by each trade.
- Establish a budget for each category of work, such as foundation, framing, and finish carpentry.
- Arrange for a source of construction financing.
- Get a building permit and post it conspicuously at the construction site.
- Line up supply sources and order materials.
- Find subcontractors and negotiate their contracts.
- Coordinate the work so that it progresses smoothly with the fewest conflicts.
- Notify inspectors at the appropriate milestones.
- Make payments to suppliers and subcontractors.

You as the Builder

You'll have to take care of every logistical detail yourself if you decide to act as your own builder or general contractor. But along with the responsibilities of managing the project, you gain the flexibility to do as much of your own work as you want and subcontract out the rest. Before taking this path, however, be sure you have the time and capabilities. Do you also have the

time and ability to schedule the work, hire and coordinate subs, order materials, and keep ahead of the accounting required to manage the project successfully? If you do, you stand to save the amount that a general contractor would charge to take on these responsibilities, normally 15 to 30 percent of the construction cost. If you take this responsibility on but mismanage the project, the potential savings will erode and may even cost you more than if you had hired a builder in the first place. A subcontractor might charge extra for hav-

Acting as the builder, above, requires the ability to hire and manage subcontractors.

Building a home, opposite, includes the need to schedule building inspections, at the appropriate milestones.

ing to return to the site to complete work that was originally scheduled for an earlier date. Or perhaps because you didn't order the windows at the beginning, you now have to pay for a recent cost increase. (If you had hired a builder in the first place he or she would absorb the increase.)

Hiring a Builder to Handle Construction

A builder or general contractor will manage every aspect of the construction process. Your role after signing the construction contract will be to make regular progress payments and ensure that the work for which you are paying has been completed. You will also consult with the builder and agree to any changes that may have to be made along the way.

Leads for finding builders might come from friends or neighbors who have had contractors build, remodel, or add to their homes. Real-estate agents and bankers may have some names handy but are more likely familiar with the builder's ability to complete projects on time and budget than the quality of the work itself.

The next step is to narrow your list of candidates to three or four who you think can do a quality job and work harmoniously with you. Phone each builder to see whether he or she is interested in being considered for your project. If so, invite the builder to an interview at your home. The meeting will serve two purposes. You'll be able to ask the candidate about his or her experience, and you'll be able to see whether or not your personalities are compatible. Go over the plans with the builder to make certain that he or she understands the scope of the project. Ask if they have constructed similar houses. Get references, and check the builder's standing with the Better Business Bureau. Develop a short list of builders, say three, and ask them to submit bids for the project.

Contracts

Lump-Sum Contracts

A lump-sum, or fixed-fee, contract lets you know from the beginning just what the project will cost, barring any changes made because of your requests or unforeseen conditions. This form works well for projects that promise few surprises and are well defined from the outset by a complete set of contract documents. You can enter into a fixed-price contract by negotiating with a single builder on your short list or by obtaining bids from three or four builders. If you go the latter route, give each bidder a set of documents and allow at least two weeks for them to submit their bids. When you get the bids, decide who you want and call the others to thank them for their efforts. You don't have to accept the lowest bid, but it probably makes sense to do so since you have already honed the list to builders you trust. Inform this builder of your intentions to finalize a contract.

Cost-Plus-Fee Contracts

Under a cost-plus-fee contract, you agree to pay the builder for the costs of labor and materials, as verified by receipts, plus a fee that represents the builder's overhead and profit. This arrangement is sometimes referred to as "time and materials." The fee can range between 15 and 30 percent of the incurred costs. Because you ultimately pick up the tab—whatever the costs—the contractor is never at risk, as he is with a lump-sum contract. You won't know the final total cost of a cost-plus-fee contract until the project is built and paid for. If you can live with that uncertainty, there are offsetting advantages. First, this form allows you to accommodate unknown conditions much more easily than does a lump-sum contract. And rather than being tied down by the project documents, you will be free to make changes at any point along the way. This can be a trap, though. Watching the project take shape will spark the desire to add something or do something differently. Each change costs more, and the accumulation can easily exceed your budget. Because of the uncertainty of the final tab and the built-in advantage to the contractor, you should think twice before entering into this form of contract.

Contract Content

The conditions of your agreement should be spelled out thoroughly in writing and signed by both parties, whatever contractual arrangement you make with your builder. Your contract should include provisions for the following:

- The names and addresses of the owner and builder.
- A description of the work to be included ("As described in the plans and specifications dated . . .").
- The date that the work will be completed if time is of the essence.
- The contract price for lump-sum contracts and the builder's allowed profit and overhead costs for changes.
- The builder's fee for cost-plus-fee contracts and the method of accounting and requesting payment.
- The criteria for progress payments (monthly, by project milestones) and the conditions of final payment.
- A list of each drawing and specification section that is to be included as part of the contract.
- Requirements for guarantees. (One year is the standard period for which contractors guarantee the entire project, but you may require specific guarantees on

When submitting bids, all of the builders should base their estimates on the same specifications. Once the work begins, communicate with your builder to keep the work proceeding smoothly.

Inspect your newly built home, if possible, before the builder closes it up and finishes it.

certain parts of the project, such as a 20-year guarantee on the roofing.)
- Provisions for insurance.
- A description of how changes in the work orders will be handled.

The builder may have a standard contract that you can tailor to the specifics of your project. These contain complete specific conditions with blanks that you can fill in to fit your project and a set of "general conditions" that cover a host of issues from insurance to termination provisions. It's always a good idea to have an attorney review the draft of your completed contract before signing it.

Working with Your Builder

The construction phase officially begins when you have a signed copy of the contract and copies of any insurance required from the builder. It's not unheard of for a builder to request an initial payment of 10 to 20 percent of the total cost to cover mobilization costs, those costs associated with obtaining permits and getting set up to begin the actual construction. If you agree to this, keep a careful eye on the progress of the work to ensure that the total paid out at any one time doesn't get too far out of sync with the actual work completed.

What about changes? From here on, it's up to you and your builder to proceed in good faith and to keep the channels of communication open. Even so, changes of one sort or another beset every project, and they usually add to its cost.

Light at the End of the Tunnel.

The builder's request for a final inspection marks the end of the construction phase—almost. At the final inspection meeting, you and the builder will inspect the work, noting any defects or incomplete items on a "punch list." When the builder tidies up the punch list items, you should reinspect. Sometimes, builders go on to another job and take forever to clean up the last few details, so only after all items on the list have been completed satisfactorily should you release the final payment, which often accounts for the builder's profit.

Some Final Words

Having a positive attitude is important when undertaking a project as large as building a home. A positive attitude can help you ride out the rigors and stress of the construction process.

Stay Flexible. Expect problems, because they certainly will occur. Weather can upset the schedule you have established for subcontractors. A supplier may get behind on deliveries, which also affects the schedule. An unexpected pipe may surprise you during excavation. Just as certain, every problem that comes along has a solution if you are open to it.

Be Patient. The extra days it may take to resolve a construction problem will be forgotten once the project is completed.

Express Yourself. If what you see isn't exactly what you thought you were getting, don't be afraid to look into changing it. Or you may spot an unforeseen opportunity for an improvement. Changes usually cost more money, though, so don't make frivolous decisions.

Finally, watching your home go up is exciting, so stay upbeat. Get away from your project from time to time. Dine out. Take time to relax. A positive attitude will make for smoother relations with your builder. An optimistic outlook will yield better-quality work if you are doing your own construction. And though the project might seem endless while it is under way, keep in mind that all the planning and construction will fade to a faint memory at some time in the future, and you will be getting a lifetime of pleasure from a home that is just right for you.

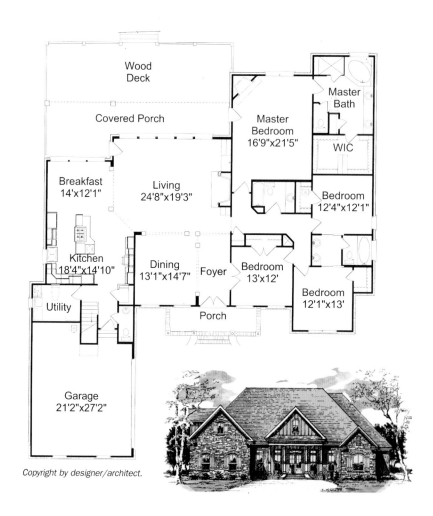

Images provided by designer/architect. Living Room

Plan #111004

Dimensions: 76' W x 85' D
Levels: 1
Square Footage: 2,698
Bedrooms: 4
Full Bathrooms: 3½
Foundation: Slab
Materials List Available: No
Price Category: F

If you've been looking for a home that includes a special master suite, this one could be the answer to your dreams.

Features:

- Living Room: Make a sitting area around the fireplace here so that the whole family can enjoy the warmth on chilly days and winter evenings. A door from this room leads to the rear covered porch, making this room the heart of your home.

- Kitchen: An island with a cooktop makes cooking a pleasure in this well-designed kitchen, and the breakfast bar invites visitors at all times of day.

- Utility Room: A sink and a built-in ironing board make this room totally practical.

- Master Suite: A private fireplace in the corner sets a romantic tone for this bedroom, and the door to the covered porch allows you to sit outside on warm summer nights. The bath has two vanities, a divided walk-in closet, a standing shower, and a deluxe corner bathtub.

Wood Deck

Covered Porch

Breakfast
14'x12'1"

Living
24'8"x19'3"

Master
Bedroom
16'9"x21'5"

Master
Bath

WIC

Kitchen
18'4"x14'10"

Dining
13'1"x14'7"

Foyer

Bedroom
13'x12'

Bedroom
12'4"x12'1"

Bedroom
12'1"x13'

Utility

Porch

Garage
21'2"x27'2"

Copyright by designer/architect.

Kitchen

Dining Room

Master Bath

Master Bath

SMARTtip

How to Quit Smoking — Lighting Your Fireplace

Before attempting to light a wood fire, make certain that the damper is open all the way. This allows a good draft (flow of air up the chimney) to prevent smoke from blowing back into the room. To ensure a good draft—particularly if your home is well insulated —open a window a bit when lighting a fire.

The opposite of draft is downdraft, which occurs when cold air flows down the chimney and into the room. If the fireplace is properly designed and maintained, the smoke shelf will prevent backpuffing from downdraft most of the time by redirecting cold air currents back up the chimney. The open damper also helps prevent backpuffing.

Also, build a fire slowly to let the chimney liner heat up, which will create a good draft and minimize the chances of downdraft.

Don't wait until fall to inspect the chimney. Do this job, or call a chimney sweep, when the weather is mild. Because some repairs take a while to make, it's best to have them done when the fireplace is not normally in use. If you do the inspection yourself, wear old clothes, eye goggles, and a mask.

Plan #151171

Dimensions: 63'10" W x 72'2" D

Levels: 1

Square Footage: 2,131

Bedrooms: 3

Bathrooms: 2½

Foundation: Crawl space, slab (basement or daylight basement option for fee)

Materials List Available: Yes

Price Category: D

Images provided by designer/architect.

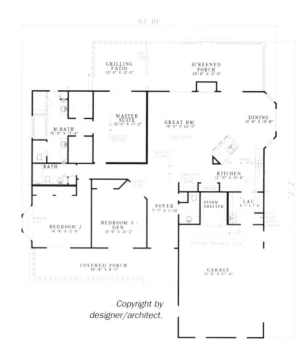

Copyright by designer/architect.

Plan #151169

Dimensions: 51'6" W x 49'10" D

Levels: 1

Square Footage: 1,525

Bedrooms: 3

Bathrooms: 2

Foundation: Basement, daylight basement, crawl space, or slab

Materials List Available: Yes

Price Category: C

Images provided by designer/architect.

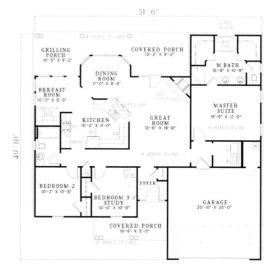

Copyright by designer/architect.

Rear Elevation

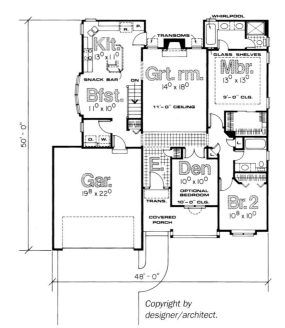

Images provided by designer/architect.

Copyright by designer/architect.

Optional Third Bedroom Floor Plan

Plan #121056

Dimensions: 48' W x 50' D
Levels: 1
Square Footage: 1,479
Bedrooms: 2
Bathrooms: 2
Foundation: Basement
Materials List Available: Yes
Price Category: B

Images provided by designer/architect.

Copyright by designer/architect.

Optional Upper Level Floor Plan

Plan #151083

Dimensions: 63'4" W x 58'6" D
Levels: 1
Square Footage: 2,034
Bedrooms: 4
Bathrooms: 2
Foundation: Crawl space, slab (basement option for fee)
Materials List Available: Yes
Price Category: D

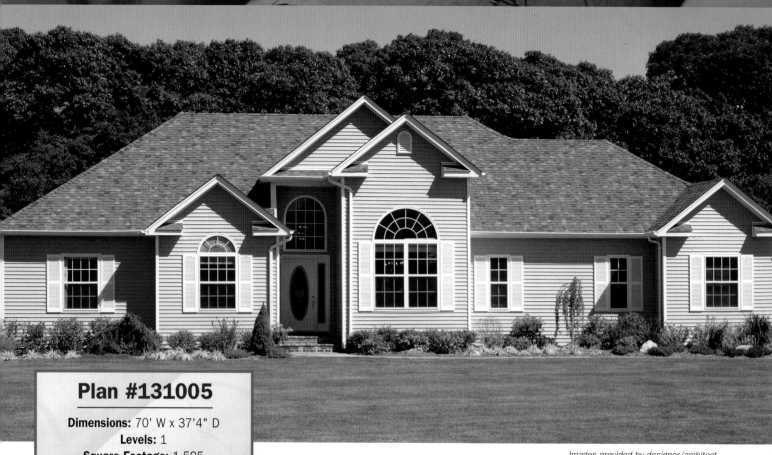

Plan #131005

Dimensions: 70' W x 37'4" D
Levels: 1
Square Footage: 1,595
Bedrooms: 3
Bathrooms: 2
Foundation: Basement, crawl space, or slab
Materials List Available: Yes
Price Category: D

SMARTtip

Create a Courtyard

Create a private walled-garden retreat with fences covered by climbing vines. Add height with trellises, and divide spaces with clipped boxwood hedges. Include an (almost) instant patio by digging away an area of sod and then covering it with a layer of sand and landscaping mesh to discourage weeds. Then cover it with pea gravel, and add a garden bench, statuary, and perhaps an antique or two. The result? European ambiance for even the most nondescript suburban yard.

Images provided by designer/architect.

With the finest features of an open design in the main living areas, this home gives privacy where you need it. Best of all, it's wheelchair accessible.

Features:

• Foyer: A high ceiling gives this area real presence and serves to blend it seamlessly with the great room and the dining room.

• Great Room: The open design allows you to use this room as an extension of the dining room or, if you wish, furnish it to create a private reading nook or visually separate media center.

• Breakfast Room: Both this room and the adjacent well-appointed kitchen flow into the rest of the living area. However, access to the rear porch, where you can sit out and enjoy the weather while you eat, distinguishes this room.

• Master Suite: Located in the same wing as the other bedrooms, this suite has a separate entrance and features a vaulted ceiling, three closets, and a compartmented bath.

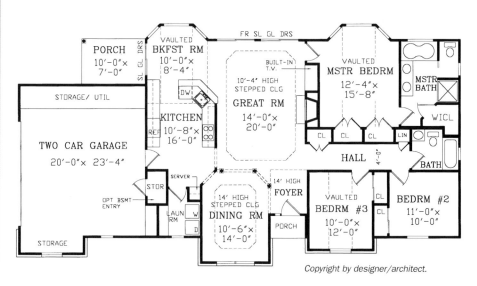

Copyright by designer/architect.

Foyer

Dining Room

Living Room

Great Room

SMARTtip

Natural Trellis

Create a natural rustic trellis that might even, if growing conditions are right, produce its own pretty blooms. Cut and place saplings in the ground as uprights. Then weave old grapevines with smaller saplings for the lattice.

Plan #161013

Dimensions: 59'4" W x 46'4" D

Levels: 1

Square Footage: 1,509

Bedrooms: 3

Bathrooms: 2

Foundation: Slab

Materials List Available: Yes

Price Category: C

Images provided by designer/architect.

Copyright by designer/architect.

Rear Elevation

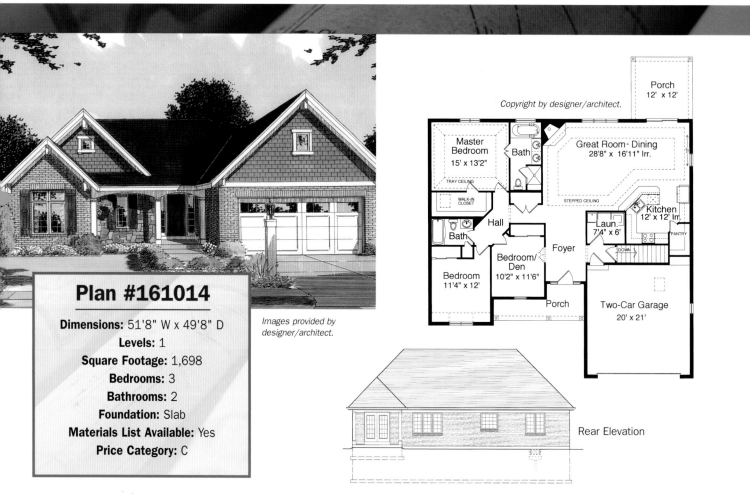

Plan #161014

Dimensions: 51'8" W x 49'8" D

Levels: 1

Square Footage: 1,698

Bedrooms: 3

Bathrooms: 2

Foundation: Slab

Materials List Available: Yes

Price Category: C

Images provided by designer/architect.

Copyright by designer/architect.

Rear Elevation

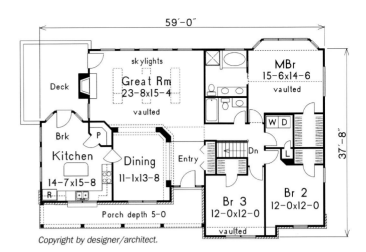

Copyright by designer/architect.

Plan #321010

Dimensions: 59' W x 37'8" D
Levels: 1
Square Footage: 1,787
Bedrooms: 3
Bathrooms: 2
Foundation: Basement
Materials List Available: Yes
Price Category: C

Images provided by designer/architect.

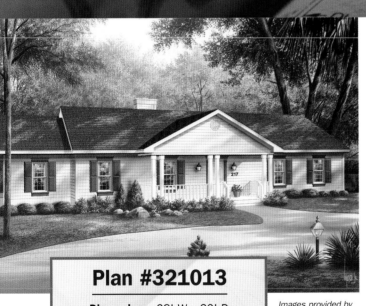

Copyright by designer/architect.

Plan #321013

Dimensions: 68' W x 30' D
Levels: 1
Square Footage: 1,360
Bedrooms: 3
Bathrooms: 2
Foundation: Basement
Materials List Available: Yes
Price Category: B

Images provided by designer/architect.

Plan #221002

Dimensions: 52' W x 46' D

Levels: 1

Square Footage: 1,508

Bedrooms: 3

Bathrooms: 2

Foundation: Basement

Materials List Available: No

Price Category: C

The classic brick-and-siding exterior of this ranch allows you to choose landscaping plants of any size, shape, or color.

Features:

- Ceiling Height: 8 ft.

- Entry: A vaulted ceiling announces the distinction of this design.

- Living Room: Also with a vaulted ceiling for a feeling of spaciousness, this living room features well-positioned windows that look out to the backyard.

- Dining Room: Sliding glass doors in this room open to the outside.

- Kitchen: This thoughtfully designed kitchen will please even the most discerning cook. For serving ease, the bright and cheery room is open to the dining room.

- Master Bedroom: You can look out to the backyard from the windows in this private retreat or relax in the charming, fully equipped bath.

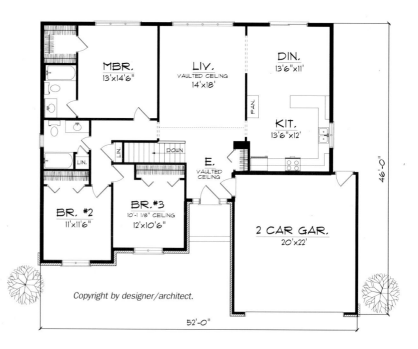

Rear Elevation

MBR.
13'x14'6"

LIV.
VAULTED CEILING
14'x18'

DIN.
13'6"x11'

KIT.
13'6"x12'

PAN.

DOWN

LIN.

LIN.

E.
VAULTED CEILING

BR. #2
11'x11'6"

BR. #3
12'x10'6"
10'-1 1/8" CEILING

2 CAR GAR.
20'x22'

46'-0"

52'-0"

Copyright by designer/architect.

Plan #101002

Dimensions: 46' W x 42' D
Levels: 1
Square Footage: 1,296
Bedrooms: 3
Bathrooms: 2
Foundation: Crawl space, slab, basement
Materials List Available: No
Price Category: B

This affordable compact home is also strikingly attractive.

Features:

- Ceiling Height: 8 ft.

- Foyer: Beveled glass front provides a luxurious entry.

- Family Room: This spacious 16-ft. x 20-ft. room has a vaulted ceiling.

- Laundry Room: Here is ample space to fold clothes—and a convenient sink.

- Master Bedroom Suite: Split from other bedrooms, this suite has many his and her features.

- Kitchen: This galley kitchen offers open traffic patterns with a breakfast bar.

- Breakfast Eating Area: A growing family will find additional seating space that leads to a covered porch providing a pleasant retreat

Images provided by designer/architect.

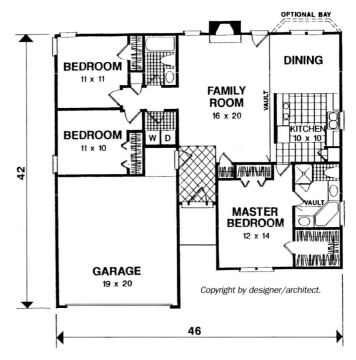

Copyright by designer/architect.

SMARTtip

Preparing Walls for Paint

Poor surface preparation is the number-one cause of paint failure. Preparing surfaces properly—including removing loose paint and thoroughly sanding—may be tedious, but it's important for a good-looking and long-lasting finish.

Plan #101022

Dimensions: 66'2" W x 62' D

Levels: 1

Square Footage: 1,992

Bedrooms: 3

Bathrooms: 3

Foundation: Basement, crawl space, or slab

Materials List Available: Yes

Price Category: D

Images provided by designer/architect.

The exterior of this lovely home is traditional, but the unusually shaped rooms and amenities are contemporary.

Features:

- Foyer: This two-story foyer is open to the family room, but columns divide it from the dining room.

- Family Room: A gas fireplace and TV niche, flanked by doors to the covered porch, sit at the rear of this seven-sided, spacious room.

- Breakfast Room: Set off from the family room by columns, this area shares a snack bar with the kitchen and has windows looking over the porch.

- Bedroom 3: Use this room as a living room if you wish, and transform the guestroom to a media room or a family bedroom.

- Master Suite: The bedroom features a tray ceiling, has his and her dressing areas, and opens to the porch. The bath has a large corner tub, separate shower, linen closet, and two vanities.

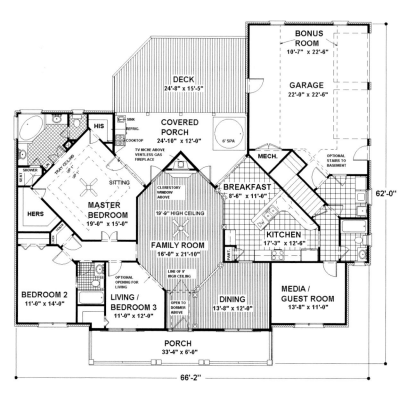

Copyright by designer/architect.

Plan #301002

Dimensions: 57'2" W x 54'10" D

Levels: 1

Square Footage: 1,845

Bedrooms: 3

Bathrooms: 2½

Foundation: Crawl space, slab

Materials List Available: Yes

Price Category: D

Images provided by designer/architect.

Although compact, this home is filled with surprisingly luxurious features.

Features:

- Ceiling Height: 8 ft. unless otherwise noted.

- Front Porch: Guests will be sheltered from the rain by this lovely little porch.

- Foyer: This elegant foyer features a 10-ft. ceiling and is open to the dining room and the rear great room.

- Dining Room: The 10-ft. ceiling from the foyer continues into this spacious dining room.

- Family Room: This family room features a vaulted ceiling and a fireplace with built-in bookcases.

- Kitchen: This kitchen boasts a pantry and plenty of storage and counter space.

- Master Bedroom: This master bedroom includes a cathedral ceiling and two walk-in closets. The master bath has two vanities, a corner spa, and a walk-in closet.

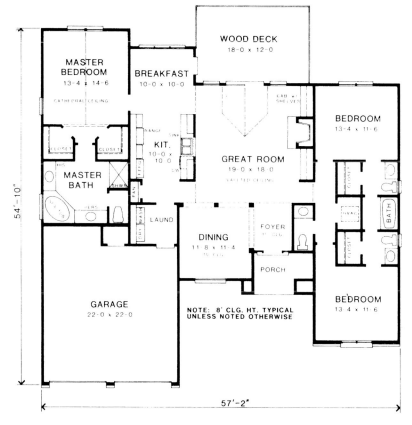

Copyright by designer/architect.

Plan #161002

Dimensions: 64'2" W x 44'2" D
Levels: 1
Square Footage: 1,860
Bedrooms: 3
Bathrooms: 2
Foundation: Basement
Materials List Available: Yes
Price Category: D

Images provided by designer/architect.

The brick, stone, and cedar shake facade provides color and texture to the exterior, while the unique nooks and angles inside this delightful one-level home give it character.

Features:

• Great Room/Dining Room: This spacious great room is furnished with a wood-burning fireplace, a high ceiling, and French doors. Wide entrances to the breakfast room and dining room expand its space to comfortably hold large gatherings.

• Kitchen: The breakfast bar offers additional seating. The covered porch lets you enjoy a view of the landscape and is conveniently located for outdoor meals off this kitchen and breakfast area.

• Master Bedroom: The master bedroom is a private retreat. An alcove creates a comfortable sitting area, and an angled entry leads to the bath with whirlpool and a double-bowl vanity.

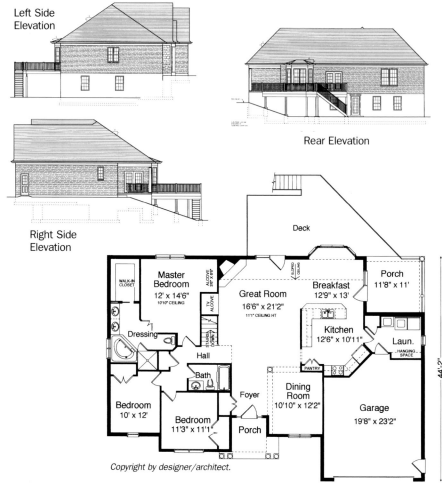

Left Side Elevation

Right Side Elevation

Rear Elevation

Copyright by designer/architect.

Dining Room

Living Room / Dining Room

Great Room/Breakfast Area

Great Room

SMARTtip

Installing Rods and Poles

The way to install a rod or pole depends on the type it is, the brackets that will hold it, the weight of the window treatment, and the surface to which it is being fastened. Given below are some general guidelines, but for specific installation procedures, refer to the instructions that accompany the rod or pole.

- Use a stepladder to reach high places.

- Use the proper tools.

- Take accurate measurements.

- Work with a helper.

- If attaching a bracket to wood, first drill small pilot holes to avoid splitting the wood.

- Consider using wall anchors, particularly for the heavier window treatments.

- Use a level as needed to help you position the brackets for the pole or rod.

- Take care not to drill or hammer into any pipes or electrical wiring.

Because they're designed to stand out, decorative poles and their finials require more room for installation than conventional drapery rods. Finials add inches to the ends of a window treatment, so make sure you have enough wall room to display your hardware to its full advantage. And because decorative rods are often heavy, be certain your window frames and walls can support the weight.

Plan #241001

Dimensions: 65' W x 56'3" D
Levels: 1
Square Footage: 2,350
Bedrooms: 3
Bathrooms: 2½
Foundation: Slab
Materials List Available: No
Price Category: E

Classic, traditional rooflines combine with arched windows to draw immediate attention to this lovely three-bedroom home.

Features:

- Great Room: The foyer introduces you to this impressive great room, with its grand 10-ft. ceiling and handsome fireplace.

- Kitchen: Certain to become the hub of such a family-oriented home, this spacious kitchen, which adjoins the breakfast area and a delightful sunroom, features an abundance of counter space, a pantry, and a convenient eating bar.

- Master Suite: You will enjoy the privacy and comfort of this master suite, which features a whirlpool tub, split vanities, and a separate shower.

- Study: Adjourn to the front of the house, and enjoy the quiet confines of this private study with built-in bookshelves to work, read, or just relax.

Images provided by designer/architect.

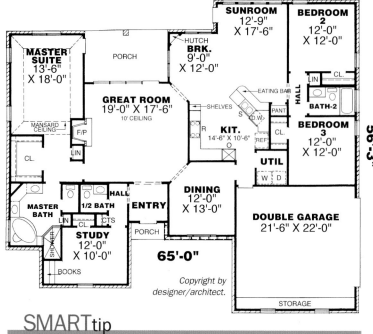

Copyright by designer/architect.

SMARTtip

Kitchen Counters

Make use of counter inserts to help with the cooking chores. For example, ceramic tiles inlaid in a laminate counter create a heat-proof landing zone near the range. A marble or granite insert is tailor-made for pastry chefs. And a butcher-block inlay is a great addition to the food prep area.

Plan #181015

Dimensions: 58' W x 28'4" D
Levels: 1
Square Footage: 1,776
Bedrooms: 3
Bathrooms: 1
Foundation: Basement
Materials List Available: Yes
Price Category: B

A pillared front porch and beautifully arched windows enhance the stucco exterior.

Features:

- Ceiling Height: 8 ft.

- Kitchen: Cooking will be a pleasure in this bright and spacious kitchen. There is ample counter space for food preparation, in addition to a center island. The kitchen is flooded with light from sliding glass doors that provide access to the outdoors.

- Family Room: Nothing warms you on a cold winter day quite like the radiant heat from the cozy wood-burning fireplace/stove you will find in this family gathering room.

- Front Porch: Step directly out of the living room onto this spacious front porch. Relax in a porch rocker, and enjoy a summer breeze with your favorite book or just rock and watch the sun set.

- Bedrooms: Three family bedrooms share a full bathroom complete with dual vanities and laundry facilities.

15'-0" X 26'-4"
4,50 X 7,90

15'-0" X 12'-0"
4,60 X 3,60

15'-0" X 12'-0"
4,60 X 3,60

9'-0" X 12'-4"
2,70 X 3,70

12'-0" X 10'-4"
3,60 X 3,10

12'-0" X 12'-4"
3,60 X 3,70

28'-0"
8,4 m

58'-0"
17,4 m

SMARTtip

Electrical Safety in the Kitchen

Sometimes the special needs of the disabled may seem to conflict with those of the very young. A case in point is accessible switch placement, which is lower on a wall. The NKBA recommends locating outlets and switches inside the front of an adult-accessible tilt-down drawer to conceal them from children. Alternatively, an outlet strip can be kept out of a child's reach and at a convenient adult location while lessening the reach to outlets and switches installed in the backsplash.

Plan #221001

Dimensions: 87' W x 60' D
Levels: 1
Square Footage: 2,600
Bedrooms: 2
Bathrooms: 2½
Foundation: Basement
Materials List Available: No
Price Category: F

Images provided by designer/architect.

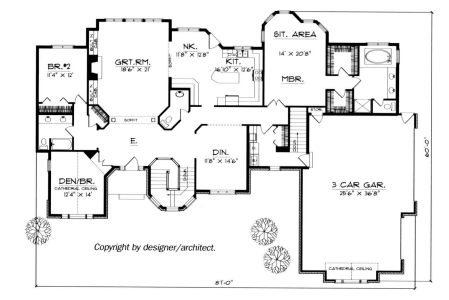

Copyright by designer/architect.

You'll love this traditional ranch for its unusual spaciousness and many comfortable amenities.

Features:

- **Great Room:** As you enter the home, you'll have a clear view all the way to the backyard through the many windows in this huge room. Built-ins here provide a practical touch, and the fireplace makes this room cozy when the weather's cool.

- **Kitchen:** This large kitchen has been thoughtfully designed to make cooking a pleasure. It flows into a lovely dining nook, so it's also a great place to entertain.

- **Master Suite:** Relaxing will come naturally in this lovely suite, with its two walk-in closets, private sitting area, and large, sumptuous bathroom that features a Jacuzzi tub.

- **Additional Bedrooms:** Located on the opposite side of the house from the master

suite, these bedrooms are both convenient to a full bath. You can use one room as a den if you wish.

Rear Elevation

Kitchen

Images provided by designer/architect.

Plan #251005

Dimensions: 48' W x 44' D
Levels: 1
Square Footage: 1,631
Bedrooms: 3
Bathrooms: 2
Foundation: Basement
Materials List Available: Yes
Price Category: C

This elegant home features hip roof lines that will add appeal in any neighborhood.

Features:

- Ceiling Height: 9 ft.

- Front Porch: The porch stretches across the entire front of the home, offering plenty of space to sit and enjoy evening breezes.

- Family Room: This family room features a handsome fireplace and has plenty of room for all kinds of family activities.

- Dining Room: This dining room has plenty of room for dinner parties. After dinner, guests can step through French doors onto the rear deck.

- Kitchen: This kitchen is a pleasure in which to work. It features an angled snack bar with plenty of room for informal family meals.

- Master Bedroom: You'll enjoy retiring at day's end to this master bedroom, with its large walk-in closet.

- Master Bath. This master bath features a double vanity, a deluxe tub, and a walk-in shower.

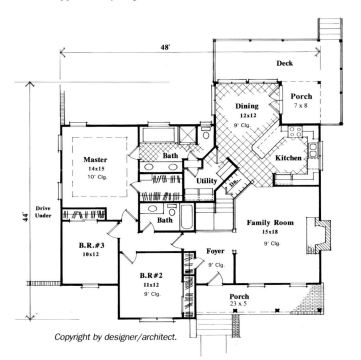

Copyright by designer/architect.

SMARTtip

Victorian Style

Victorian, today, is a very romantic look. To underscore this, add the scent of lavender or some other dried flower to the room or use potpourri, which you can keep in a bowl on the vanity. Hang a fragrant pomander on a hook, display lavender soaps on a wall shelf, or tuck sachets between towels on a shelf. For an authentic touch, display a Victorian favorite, the spider plant.

Plan #321001

Dimensions: 83' W x 42' D

Levels: 1

Square Footage: 1,721

Bedrooms: 3

Bathrooms: 2

Foundation: Basement, crawl space, or slab

Materials List Available: Yes

Price Category: C

Images provided by designer/architect.

Rear View

You'll love the atrium that creates a warm, naturally lit space inside this gracious home, as well as the roof dormers that give it wonderful curb appeal from the outside.

Features:

- **Great Room:** Bathed in light from the atrium window wall, this room, with its vaulted ceiling, will be the hub of your family life.

- **Dining Room:** This room also has a vaulted ceiling and is lit by the atrium, but you can draw drapes at night to create a cozy, warm feeling.

- **Kitchen:** Designed for functionality, this step-saving kitchen is easy to organize and makes cooking a pleasure.

- **Breakfast Room:** For convenience, this room is located between the kitchen and the rear covered porch.

- **Master Suite:** Retire with pleasure to this lovely retreat, with its luxurious bath.

Copyright by designer/architect.

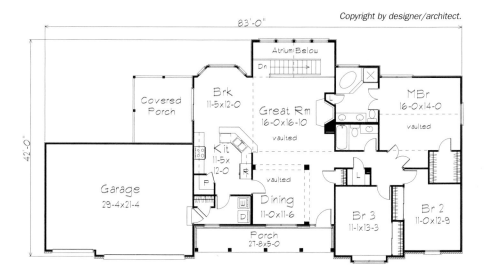

Plan #131009

Dimensions: 64'10" W x 57'8" D
Levels: 1
Square Footage: 2,018
Bedrooms: 3
Bathrooms: 2
Foundation: Basement, crawl space, or slab
Materials List Available: Yes
Price Category: D

Images provided by designer/architect.

The pavilion-styled great room at the heart of this H-shaped ranch gives it an unusual elegance that you're sure to enjoy.

Features:

- **Great Room:** The tray ceiling sets off this room, and a fireplace warms it on chilly nights and cool days. Two sets of sliding glass doors leading to the backyard terrace let in natural light and create an efficient traffic flow.

- **Kitchen:** Designed for a gourmet cook, this kitchen features a snack bar that everyone will enjoy and easy access to the breakfast room.

- **Breakfast Room:** Open to the columned rear porch, this breakfast room is an ideal spot for company or family brunches.

- **Master Suite:** A sitting area and access to the porch make the bedroom luxurious, while the private bath featuring a whirlpool tub creates a spa atmosphere.

Floor plan labels:
VAULTED BEDRM #2 14'-8" x 11'-0" · CL · CL · BEDRM #3 11'-0" x 13'-0" · BATH #2 · STOR · UTIL · LOCATION OF OPT. BSMT STAIR · TWO CAR GARAGE 20'-0" x 21'-0" · ALT. FRONT ENTRY GARAGE · BUILT-IN · TERRACE · 11'-6" HIGH STEPPED CLG GREAT RM 21'-0" x 16'-0" · TV · CL · HIGH CEIL GALLERY · COV. PORCH · COV. PORCH 24'-8" x 10'-2" · 9'-6" HIGH CEILING BKFST RM 13'-0" x 20'-2" · KITCHEN · REF · PANT · DW · 9'-6" HIGH STEPPED CLG DINING RM 12'-0" x 14'-0" · SITTING · CL. DR BUILT-IN · 11'-6" HIGH STEPPED CLG MSTR BEDRM 13'-0" x 18'-0" · DRSG · WICL · LIN · WICL · MSTR BATH · STEAM SHOWER · SEAT

Copyright by designer/architect.

Great Room

Plan #131006

Dimensions: 61' W x 53'6" D
Levels: 1
Square Footage: 2,193
Bedrooms: 3
Bathrooms: 2
Foundation: Basement, crawl space, or slab
Materials List Available: Yes
Price Category: E

Images provided by designer/architect.

This compact home is perfect for a small lot, but even so, has all the features of a much larger home, thanks to its space-saving interior design that lets one area flow into the next.

Features:

• Great Room: This wonderful room is sure to be the heart of your home. Visually, it flows from the foyer and dining room to the rear of the house, giving you enough space to create a private nook or two in it or treat it as a single, large room.

• Dining Room: Emphasize the formality of this room by decorating with subdued colors and sumptuous fabrics.

• Kitchen: Designed for efficiency, this kitchen features ample counter space and cabinets in a layout guaranteed to please you.

• Master Suite: You'll love the amenities in this private master suite, with its lovely bedroom and a bath filled with contemporary fixtures.

Rear View

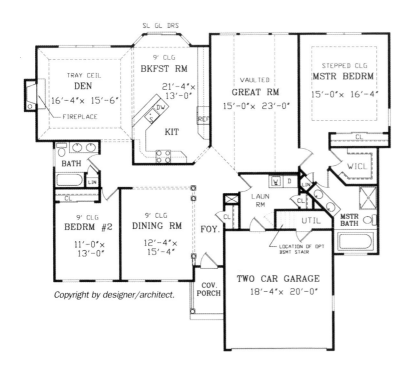

DEN
TRAY CEIL
16'-4"x 15'-6"

— FIREPLACE

SL GL DRS

BKFST RM
9' CLG
21'-4"x
13'-0"

KIT

DW

REF

GREAT RM
VAULTED
15'-0"x 23'-0"

MSTR BEDRM
STEPPED CLG
15'-0"x 16'-4"

CL

WICL

BATH

LIN

CL

BEDRM #2
9' CLG
11'-0"x
13'-0"

DINING RM
9' CLG
12'-4"x
15'-4"

FOY.

CL

W D

LIN
CL

LAUN
RM

UTIL

MSTR
BATH

LOCATION OF OPT
BSMT STAIR

COV.
PORCH

TWO CAR GARAGE
18'-4"x 20'-0"

Copyright by designer/architect.

BEDRM #3
9' CLG
16'-4"x
13'-4"

REF

BKFST RM
9' CLG
21'-4"x
13'-0"

KIT

DW

BUILT-IN

FIREPLACE

GREAT RM
VAULTED
15'-0"x 23'-0"

CL

BATH

LIN

CL

Foyer / Dining Room

Kitchen

Great Room

Plan #141004

Dimensions: 48' W x 29' D

Levels: 1

Square Footage: 1,514

Bedrooms: 3

Bathrooms: 2

Foundation: Slab, basement

Materials List Available: No

Price Category: C

Designed for the narrow lot, this cottage-style home features Craftsman-style exterior columns.

Features:

- Ceiling Height: 8 ft. unless otherwise noted.

- Entry: There's no defined foyer, so you enter immediately into the living area, with its vaulted ceiling that flattens over the dining area at a soaring 14 ft.

- Living/Dining Areas: The see-through fireplace flanked by bookcases is a main focal point of the home. It serves as the divider between the living room and dining room.

- Kitchen: This kitchen shares the vaulted ceiling with the dining room and living room. A plant shelf over the cabinets facing the dining room defines the space without obstructing the view of the fireplace.

- Master Suite: This private retreat has its own entrance away from the other bedrooms and boasts a cathedral ceiling over both bedroom and bath.

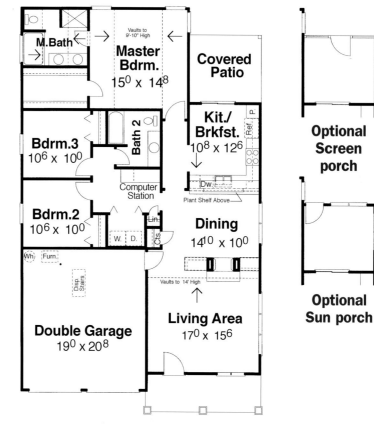

M.Bath

Vaults to 9'-10" High

Master Bdrm.
15^0 x 14^8

Covered Patio

Bdrm.3
10^6 x 10^0

Bath 2

Kit./ Brkfst.
10^8 x 12^6

Computer Station

Plant Shelf Above

Bdrm.2
10^6 x 10^0

Lin

W. D. Cts

Dining
14^{10} x 10^0

Wh Furn.

Disp Stairs

Double Garage
19^0 x 20^8

Vaults to 14' High

Living Area
17^0 x 15^6

Optional Screen porch

Optional Sun porch

Plan #311002

Dimensions: 56'6" W x 82' D
Levels: 1
Square Footage: 2,402
Bedrooms: 4
Bathrooms: 2½
Foundation: Crawl space, slab
Materials List Available: Yes
Price Category: E

Images provided by designer/architect.

This lovely home has an open floor plan in the main living area but privacy in the bedrooms.

Features:

- **Foyer:** With an 11-ft. ceiling, this foyer opens to both the great room and the dining room.

- **Great Room:** A 10-ft. ceiling and handsome fireplace highlight this spacious room, which is open to both the kitchen and breakfast room.

- **Dining Room:** A butler's pantry and built-in china closet spell convenience in this lovely room.

- **Breakfast Room:** Bask in the sunshine flowing through the bay windows in this room, which opens to the rear porch.

- **Kitchen:** Designed for efficiency, this kitchen will charm all the cooks in the family.

- **Master Suite:** It's easy to feel pampered by the huge closet and bath with corner tub and two vanities.

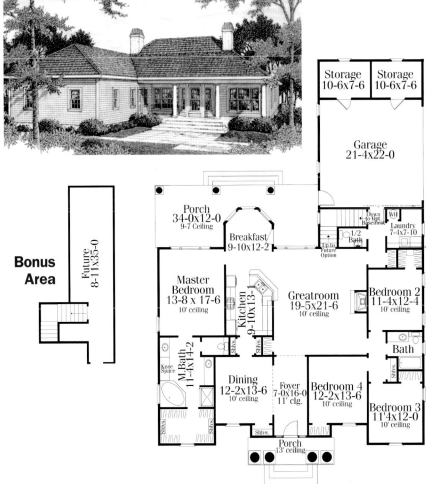

Bonus Area — Future 8-11x35-0

Porch 34-0x12-0 9-7 Ceiling
Breakfast 9-10x12-2
Master Bedroom 13-8 x 17-6 10' ceiling
Kitchen 9-10x13-1
Greatroom 19-5x21-6 10' ceiling
Bedroom 2 11-4x12-4 10' ceiling
M.Bath 11-4x14-2
Knee Space
Dining 12-2x13-6 10' ceiling
Foyer 7-0x16-0 11' clg.
Bedroom 4 12-2x13-6 10' ceiling
Bath
Bedroom 3 11'4x12-0 10' ceiling
Porch 13' ceiling
Storage 10-6x7-6
Storage 10-6x7-6
Garage 21-4x22-0
Down to Opt. Basement
Laundry 7-4x7-10
1/2 Bath
Up to Future Option

Plan #151037

Dimensions: 50' W x 56' D
Levels: 1
Square Footage: 1,538
Bedrooms: 3
Bathrooms: 2
Foundation: Crawl space, slab, or basement
Materials List Available: Yes
Price Category: C

You'll love this traditional-looking home, with its covered porch and interesting front windows.

Features:

- Ceiling Height: 8 ft.

- Great Room: This large room has a boxed window that emphasizes its dimensions and a fireplace where everyone will gather on chilly evenings. A door opens to the backyard.

- Dining Room: A bay window overlooking the front porch makes this room easy to decorate.

- Kitchen: This well-planned kitchen features ample counter space, a full pantry, and an eating bar that it shares with the dining room.

- Master Suite: A pan ceiling in this lovely room gives an elegant touch. The huge private bath includes two walk-in closets, a whirlpool tub, a dual-sink vanity, and a skylight in the ceiling.

- Additional Bedrooms: On the opposite side of the house, these bedrooms share a large bath, and both feature excellent closet space.

Copyright by designer/architect.

Plan #161003

Dimensions: 60' W x 47' D

Levels: 1

Square Footage: 1,508

Bedrooms: 3

Bathrooms: 2

Foundation: Basement

Materials List Available: Yes

Price Category: C

Multiple gables and a cozy front porch invite you to this enchanting one-story home.

Features:

- Great Room: This bright and cheery room features a sloped ceiling and fireplace. The great room is designed for convenience, with easy access to the foyer and dining area, creating the look and feel of a home much larger than its actual size.

- Dining Area: Adjacent to the great room, this dining area has multiple windows and angles that add light and dimension.

- Kitchen: This spacious kitchen is designed for easy work patterns with an abundance of counter and cabinet space. It also features a snack bar.

- Master Bedroom: Designed for step-saving convenience, this master bedroom includes a compartmented bath, double-bowl vanity, and large walk-in closet.

Rear Elevation

Plan #291002

Dimensions: 63' W x 37' D
Levels: 1
Square Footage: 1,550
Bedrooms: 3
Bathrooms: 2
Foundation: Basement
Materials List Available: No
Price Category: C

This comfortable Southwestern-style ranch house will fit perfectly into any setting.

Features:

• Ceiling Height: 8 ft. unless otherwise noted.

• Front Porch: This scalloped front porch offers plenty of room for enjoying a cool summer breeze.

• Foyer: Upon entering this impressive foyer you'll be greeted by a soaring space encompassing the living room and dining room.

• Living/Dining Area: This combined living room and dining room has a handsome fireplace as its focal point. When dinner is served, guests will flow casually into the dining area.

• Kitchen: Take your cooking up a notch in this terrific kitchen. It features a 42-in.-high counter that will do double-duty as a snack bar for family meals and a wet bar for entertaining.

• Master Suite: This master retreat is separated from the other bedrooms and features an elegant vaulted ceiling. The dressing area has a compartmentalized bath and a walk-in closet.

Images provided by designer/architect.

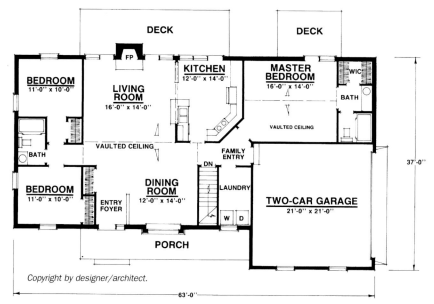

Rear View

Copyright by designer/architect.

Plan #171013

Dimensions: 74' W x 72' D

Levels: 1

Square Footage: 3,084

Bedrooms: 4

Bathrooms: 3½

Foundation: Slab, crawl space

Materials List Available: Yes

Price Category: G

Images provided by designer/architect.

Impressive porch columns add to the country charm of this amenity-filled family home.

Features:

- Ceiling Height: 10 ft.

- Foyer: The sense of style continues from the front porch into this foyer, which opens to the formal dining room and the living room.

- Dining Room: Two handsome support columns accentuate the elegance of this dining room.

- Living Room: This living room features a cozy corner fireplace and plenty of room for the entire family to gather and relax.

- Kitchen: You'll be inspired to new culinary heights in this kitchen, which offers plenty of counter space, a snack bar, a built-in pantry, and a china closet.

- Master Suite: The bedroom of this master suite has a fireplace and overlooks a rear courtyard. The bath has two vanities a large walk-in closet, a deluxe tub, a walk-in shower, and a skylight.

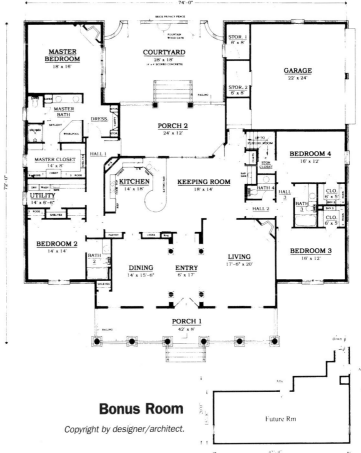

Bonus Room

Copyright by designer/architect.

Plan #211003

Dimensions: 62' W x 64'8" D
Levels: 1
Square Footage: 1,865
Bedrooms: 3
Bathrooms: 2
Foundation: Slab
Materials List Available: Yes
Price Category: D

SMARTtip

Fire Extinguishers

The word PASS is an easy way to remember the proper way to use a fire extinguisher.

Pull the pin at the top of the extinguisher that keeps the handle from being accidentally pressed.

Aim the nozzle of the extinguisher toward the base of the fire.

Squeeze the handle to discharge the extinguisher. Stand approximately 8 feet away from the fire.

Sweep the nozzle back and forth at the base of the fire. After the fire appears to be out, watch it carefully because it may reignite!

The traditional style of this home is blended with all the amenities required for today's lifestyle.

Features:

• Ceiling Height: 8 ft. unless otherwise noted.

• Front Porch: Guests will feel welcome arriving at the front door under this sheltering front porch.

• Dining Room: This large room will accommodate dinner parties of all sizes, from large formal gatherings to more intimate family get-togethers.

• Living Room: Guests and family alike will feel right at home in this inviting room. Sunlight streaming through the skylights in the 12-ft. ceiling, combined with the handsome fireplace, makes the space both airy and warm.

• Back Patio: When warm weather comes around, step out the sliding glass doors in the living room to enjoy entertaining or just relaxing on this patio.

• Kitchen: A cathedral ceiling soars over this efficient modern kitchen. It includes an eating area that is perfect for informal family meals.

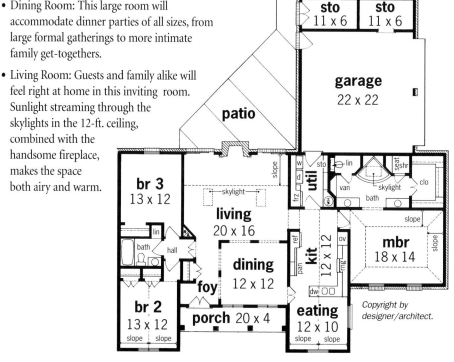

Copyright by designer/architect.

Plan #111006

Dimensions: 56' W x 67' D

Levels: 1

Square Footage: 2,241

Bedrooms: 4

Bathrooms: 2½

Foundation: Slab

Materials List Available: No

Price Category: E

You'll love this plan if you're looking for a home with fantastic curb appeal on the outside and comfortable amenities on the inside.

Features:

- **Foyer:** This lovely foyer opens to both the living and dining rooms.

- **Dining Room:** Three columns in this room accentuate both its large dimensions and its slightly formal air.

- **Living Room:** This room gives an airy feeling, and the fireplace here makes it especially inviting when the weather's cool.

- **Kitchen:** This G-shaped kitchen is designed to save steps while you're working, and the ample counter area adds even more to its convenience. The breakfast bar is a great gathering area.

- **Master Suite:** Two walk-in closets provide storage space, and the bath includes separate vanities, a standing shower, and a deluxe corner bathtub.

Front Elevation

Copyright by designer/architect.

Plan #281011

Dimensions: 50' W x 54' D
Levels: 1
Square Footage: 1,314
Bedrooms: 3
Bathrooms: 2
Foundation: Basement
Materials List Available: Yes
Price Category: B

Images provided by designer/architect.

This attractive ranch home takes advantage of views at both the front and rear.

Features:

• Ceiling Height: 8 ft.

• Porch: This large, inviting porch welcomes your guests and provides shade for the big living-room window on hot summer days.

• Living Room: This large main living area has plenty of room for entertaining and family activities.

• Dining Room: This room can accommodate large dinner parties. It's located near the living room and the kitchen for convenient entertaining.

• Deck: Family and friends will enjoy stepping out on this large covered sun deck that is accessible from the living room, dining room, and kitchen.

• Master Suite: You'll enjoy retiring at the end of the day to this luxurious master suite, which features its own walk-in closet and bathroom.

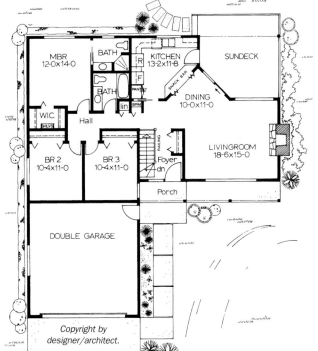

Copyright by designer/architect.

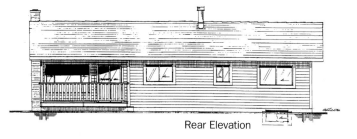

Rear Elevation

SMARTtip

Rag-Rolling Off

Paint Tip: Work with a partner. One person can roll on the glaze while the other lifts it off with the rag in a rhythmic pattern of even, steady strokes.

Plan #221003

Dimensions: 69' W x 51'4" D

Levels: 1

Square Footage: 1,802

Bedrooms: 3

Bathrooms: 2

Foundation: Basement

Materials List Available: No

Price Category: D

Images provided by designer/architect.

Rear Elevation

If you'd love to enjoy the evening breeze from a rocker on your own front porch, this stylish ranch design could be the home of your dreams.

Features:

- Ceiling Height: 8 ft.

- Great Room: A cathedral ceiling in this room gives it grandeur as well as a spacious feeling. Large windows that look out to the backyard flank the classic fireplace here.

- Kitchen: This step-saving layout will delight the cooks in the family. Everyone will gather in the dining nook here, and when there's a party, you'll appreciate the open design between the kitchen/nook area and the great room.

- Master Suite: You'll love the storage space in the bedroom's walk-in closet and revel in the luxury of the fully equipped private bath.

- Garage: You can park two cars in this garage and still have room to store a mower, tools and equipment, and even off-season clothing.

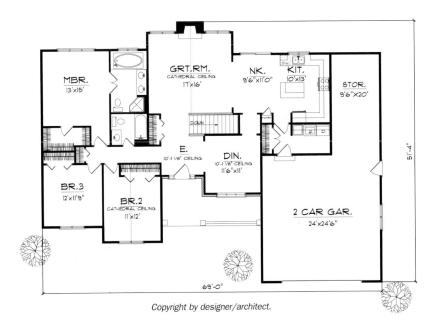

Copyright by designer/architect.

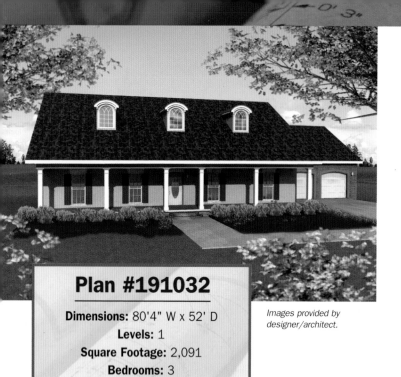

Plan #191032

Dimensions: 80'4" W x 52' D

Levels: 1

Square Footage: 2,091

Bedrooms: 3

Bathrooms: 2

Foundation: Slab

Materials List Available: No

Price Category: D

Images provided by designer/architect.

Copyright by designer/architect.

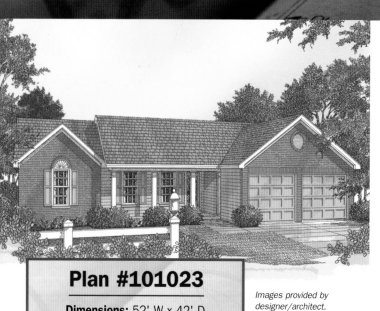

Copyright by designer/architect.

Images provided by designer/architect.

Plan #101023

Dimensions: 52' W x 42' D

Levels: 1

Square Footage: 1,197

Bedrooms: 3

Bathrooms: 2

Foundation: Crawl space, slab

Materials List Available: No

Price Category: B

Plan #191033

Dimensions: 68'4" W x 80' D
Levels: 1
Square Footage: 2,214
Bedrooms: 3
Bathrooms: 2
Foundation: Crawl space, slab
Materials List Available: No
Price Category: E

Images provided by designer/architect.

The classic good looks of this lovely home's exterior perfectly suit the interior, which is designed for the comfort of your family.

Features:

- Great Room: A fireplace and a door to the rear covered porch make this room a natural gathering spot for the whole family.

- Dining Room: Situated between the foyer and kitchen/breakfast area, this room is ideal for entertaining or serving family meals.

- Kitchen: You'll love the convenient center island with a cooktop and snack bar. An adjacent walk-in pantry, large laundry room, and mudroom add practical touches.

- Breakfast Area: Set a table between the windows to bask in sunny morning light.

- Owner's Suite: This suite features a walk-in closet and a private bath with a large tub, separate shower, and dual vanity.

Copyright by designer/architect.

Rear Elevation

Plan #121001

Dimensions: 56' W x 58' D

Levels: 1

Square Footage: 1,911

Bedrooms: 3

Bathrooms: 2

Foundation: Basement

Materials List Available: Yes

Price Category: D

Images provided by designer/architect.

Detailed, soaring ceilings and top-notch amenities set this distinctive home apart.

Features:

- Ceiling Height: 8 ft. except as noted.

- Great Room: A soaring ceiling and six tall transom-topped windows make this a light and airy spot for entertaining.

- Formal Dining Room: The entry enjoys a pleasing view of this dining room's detailed 12-ft. ceiling and picture window.

- Great Room: At the back of the home, a see-through fireplace in this great room is joined by a built-in entertainment center.

- Hearth Room: This bayed room shares the see-through fireplace with the great room.

- Master Suite: Enjoy the stars and the sun in the private bath's whirlpool and separate shower. The bath features the same decorative ceiling as the dining room.

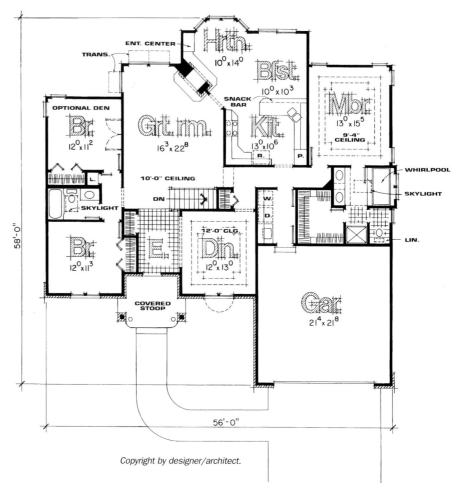

Copyright by designer/architect.

Plan #131003

Dimensions: 60' W x 39'10" D
Levels: 1
Square Footage: 1,466
Bedrooms: 3
Bathrooms: 2
Foundation: Basement, crawl space, or slab
Materials List Available: Yes
Price Category: B

Victorian styling adds elegance to this compact and easy-to-maintain ranch design.

Features:

- Ceiling Height: 8 ft.

- Foyer: Bridging between the front door and the great room, this foyer is a surprise feature.

- Great Room: A 10-ft. ceiling adds to the spacious feeling of this room, while the corner fireplace gives it an intimate feeling. Sliding glass doors at the rear of the room open to the backyard.

- Dining Room: This formal room adjoins the great room, allowing guests and family to flow between the rooms.

- Breakfast Room: Turrets add a Victorian feeling to this room that's just off the kitchen and overlooks the front porch.

- Master Suite: Privacy is assured in this suite, which is separated from the main part of the house. A compartmented bath and large walk-in closet add convenience to its beauty.

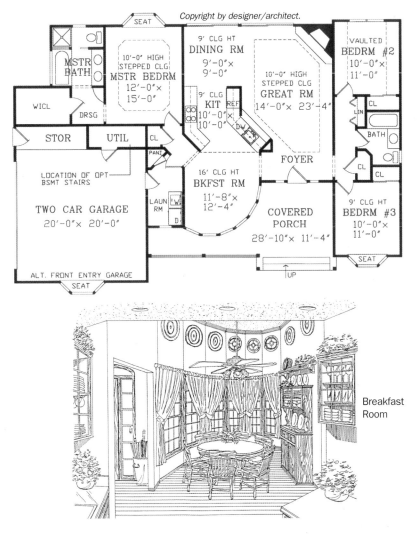

Breakfast Room

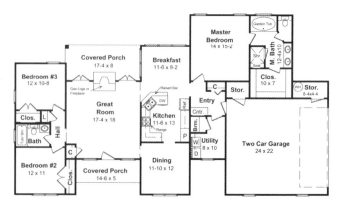

Stair Location for Basement Option

Plan #351006

Dimensions: 72'10" W x 41' D

Levels: 1

Square Footage: 1,638

Bedrooms: 3

Bathrooms: 2

Foundation: Basement, crawl space, or slab

Materials List Available: Yes

Price Category: C

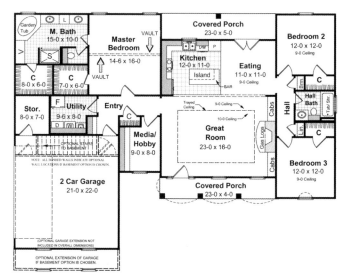

Plan #351003

Dimensions: 64' W x 45'10" D

Levels: 1

Square Footage: 1,751

Bedrooms: 3

Bathrooms: 2

Foundation: Basement, crawl space, or slab

Materials List Available: Yes

Price Category: C

Plan #181018

Dimensions: 39' W x 45' D
Levels: 1
Square Footage: 1,231
Bedrooms: 2
Bathrooms: 1
Foundation: Basement
Materials List Available: Yes
Price Category: B

Images provided by designer/architect.

The dramatic double-glass-door arched entry sets the tone for this elegant European beauty.

Features:

- Ceiling Height: 8 ft.

- Family Room: Family and friends will be drawn to the warmth and grace of this room, which is filled with natural light streaming from the spectacular full wall of windows. Warm yourself by the fireplace.

- Kitchen: This kitchen shares the fireplace with the adjoining family room. Cooking will be a pleasure, thanks to plenty of counter space and a double pantry.

- Breakfast Area: This eat-in area off the kitchen offers plenty of room for the whole family to enjoy informal meals.

- Bedrooms: The flexible floor plan offers either one large master suite with a walk-in closet or two nicely sized bedrooms, each with its own closets. Both options include a luxurious full bathroom with a relaxing whirlpool tub.

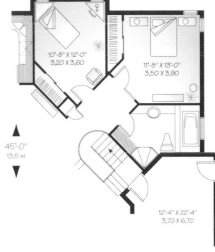

**Alternate
Floor Plan**

*Copyright by
designer/architect.*

Plan #321002

Dimensions: 72' W x 28' D
Levels: 1
Square Footage: 1,400
Bedrooms: 3
Bathrooms: 2
Foundation: Basement, crawl space
Materials List Available: Yes
Price Category: B

If you're looking for a well-designed compact home with contemporary amenities, this could be the home of your dreams.

Features:

- Porch: Just the right size for some rockers and a swing, this porch could become your outdoor living area when the weather is fine.

- Living Room: A vaulted ceiling adds to the spacious feeling in this room, where friends and family are sure to gather.

- Kitchen: This space-saving design, in combination with the ample counter and cabinet space, makes cooking a pleasure.

- Utility Room: This large room is fitted with cabinets for extra storage space. You'll find storage space in the large garage, too.

- Master Bedroom: This room is somewhat secluded for privacy, making it an ideal place for some quiet time at the end of the day.

Images provided by designer/architect.

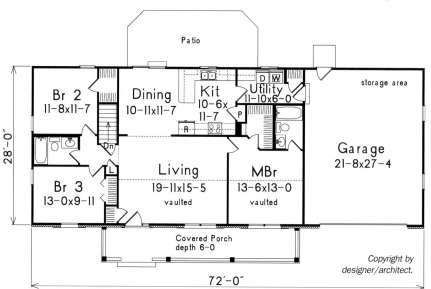

Copyright by designer/architect.

SMARTtip

Fabric Draping Ability

Test a fabric's draping ability by looking at a large piece in a fabric store. Gather at least two to three yards of material, holding one end in your hand. Check how it drapes. Does it fall into folds easily? Also look at the pattern when it is gathered. Does the design become lost in the folds? Ask a salesclerk or a friend to hold the fabric, and look at it from a few feet away.

Plan #131010

Dimensions: 70' W x 34'4" D
Levels: 1
Square Footage: 1,667
Bedrooms: 3
Bathrooms: 2
Foundation: Basement, crawl space, or slab
Materials List Available: Yes
Price Category: D

Images provided by designer/architect.

You'll love this affordable ranch house, with its open floor plan that gives so much usable space, and its graceful layout.

Features:

- **Living Room:** Adjacent to the dining room, this living room features a pass-through fireplace that is open to the family room beyond.

- **Family Room:** A vaulted ceiling with a sky light gives character to this room, where everyone will gather on weekend afternoons and in the evening, to relax.

- **Kitchen:** Also lit from above by a skylight, this kitchen features an island work space.

- **Breakfast Room:** Just off the kitchen, this breakfast room is sure to be a popular spot at any time of day.

- **Master Bedroom:** Get away from it all in this lovely room, with space to spread out and relax in private.

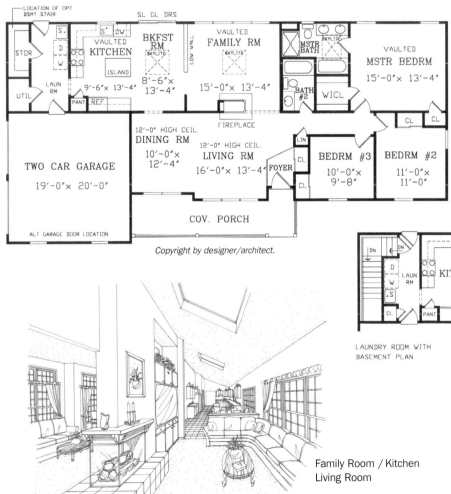

Copyright by designer/architect.

Family Room / Kitchen
Living Room

LAUNDRY ROOM WITH
BASEMENT PLAN

Plan #161026

Dimensions: 67'6" W x 63'6" D
Levels: 1
Square Footage: 2,041
Bedrooms: 3
Bathrooms: 2
Foundation: Basement
Materials List Available: No
Price Category: D

You'll love the special features of this home, which has been designed for efficiency and comfort.

Images provided by designer/architect.

Features:

- Foyer: This raised foyer offers a view through the great room and beyond it to the covered deck.

- Great Room: Elegant windows allow versatility — decorate casually or more formally.

- Kitchen: You'll find ample counter space and cabinets in this spacious room, which adjoins the dining room and opens onto the rear yard.

- Library: Curl up on the window seat that wraps around the tower in this quiet spot.

- Laundry Room: A tub makes this large room practical for crafts as well as laundry.

- Master Suite: A vaulted ceiling gives grace to the sitting area, and the garden bath with a walk-in closet and whirlpool tub adds luxury.

Rear Elevation

Main Level Floor Plan

Basement Level Floor Plan

Copyright by designer/architect.

Left Side Elevation

Right Side Elevation

Front View

Living Room

Plan #311001

Dimensions: 65'11" W x 67'9" D

Levels: 1

Square Footage: 2,085

Bedrooms: 3

Bathrooms: 2½

Foundation: Crawl space, slab

Materials List Available: No

Price Category: D

Images provided by designer/architect.

Rear View

Copyright by designer/architect.

Optional Bonus Area

Plan #311004

Dimensions: 68'2" W x 57'4" D

Levels: 1

Square Footage: 2,046

Bedrooms: 3

Bathrooms: 2½

Foundation: Basement, crawl space, or slab

Materials List Available: Yes

Price Category: D

Images provided by designer/architect.

Copyright by designer/architect.

Rear View

Plan #151040

Dimensions: 70' W x 51'10" D
Levels: 1
Square Footage: 2,444
Bedrooms: 4
Bathrooms: 2½
Foundation: Crawl space, slab
(basement option for fee)
Materials List Available: Yes
Price Category: E

Images provided by designer/architect.

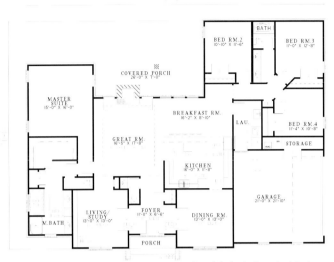

Copyright by designer/architect.

Plan #171008

Dimensions: 72' W x 40' D
Levels: 1
Square Footage: 1,652
Bedrooms: 3
Bathrooms: 2
Foundation: Slab, crawl space
Materials List Available: Yes
Price Category: C

Images provided by designer/architect.

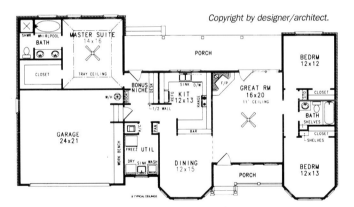

Copyright by designer/architect.

SMARTtip

Lighting for Decorative Shadows

Use lighting to create decorative shadows. For interesting, undefined shadows, set lights at ground level aiming upward in front of a shrub or tree that is close to a wall. For silhouetting, place lights directly behind a plant or garden statue that is near a wall. In both cases, using a wide beam will increase the effect.

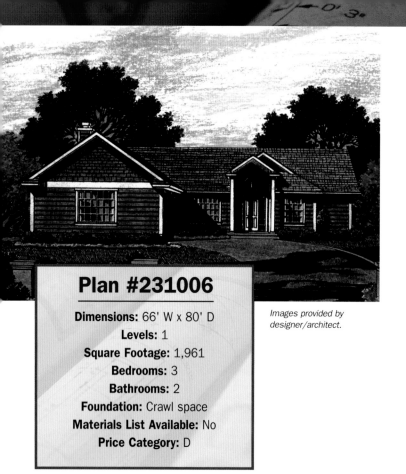

Plan #231006

Dimensions: 66' W x 80' D
Levels: 1
Square Footage: 1,961
Bedrooms: 3
Bathrooms: 2
Foundation: Crawl space
Materials List Available: No
Price Category: D

Images provided by designer/architect.

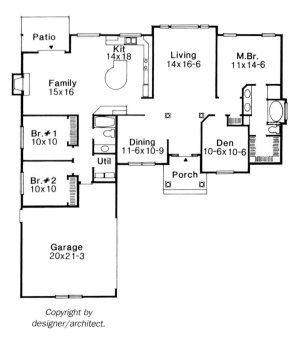

Copyright by designer/architect.

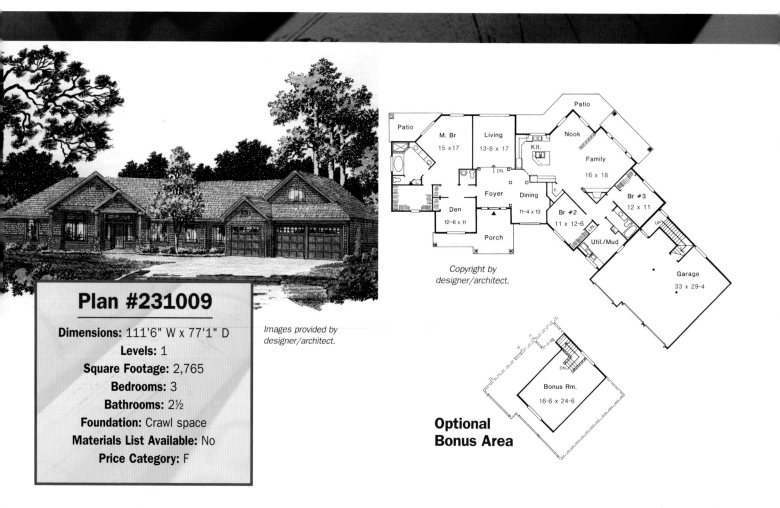

Plan #231009

Dimensions: 111'6" W x 77'1" D
Levels: 1
Square Footage: 2,765
Bedrooms: 3
Bathrooms: 2½
Foundation: Crawl space
Materials List Available: No
Price Category: F

Images provided by designer/architect.

Copyright by designer/architect.

Optional Bonus Area

Plan #341036

Dimensions: 51'6" W x 34' D

Levels: 1

Square Footage: 1,134

Bedrooms: 3

Bathrooms: 2

Foundation: Crawl space, slab (basement option for fee)

Materials List Available: Yes

Price Category: B

Images provided by designer/architect.

Copyright by designer/architect.

PATIO

BEDROOM 1
12'-0" X 13'-2"

BATH 1

KITCHEN
8'-3" X 9'-9"

SINK DW
RANGE
REF

DINING AREA
10'-9" X 13'-7"

GARAGE
13'-7" X 23'-3"

CLOSET

WASH DRY COATS

BATH 2

LINENS CLOSET

BEDROOM 3
10'-0" X 10'-0"

FAMILY ROOM
12'-9" X 13'-8"

BEDROOM 2
10'-9" X 10'-0"

CLOSET

PORCH

34'-0"

51'-6"

Plan #341035

Dimensions: 60' W x 28' D

Levels: 1

Square Footage: 1,680

Bedrooms: 4

Bathrooms: 2

Foundation: Crawl space, slab (basement option for fee)

Materials List Available: Yes

Price Category: C

Images provided by designer/architect.

Copyright by designer/architect.

DECK
12'-0" X 10'-0"

GARDEN TUB

BATH 1

CLOSET

KITCHEN
13'-1" X 13'-5"

SINK DW
RANGE
REF
ISLAND

DRY WASH

BEDROOM 2
10'-6" X 13'-5"

BATH 2

BEDROOM 3
10'-6" X 10'-11"

SHWR

PANTRY CLOSET

CLOSET

LINENS

CLOSET

BEDROOM 1
13'-11" X 13'-5"

DINING ROOM
12'-4" X 13'-5"

PREFAB VENTLESS GAS LOG FIREPLACE

LIVING ROOM
18'-10" X 13'-5"

COAT

BEDROOM 4
10'-6" X 10'-11"

SHELVES

PORCH

28'-0"

60'-0"

Plan #141005

Dimensions: 38' W x 66' D

Levels: 1

Square Footage: 1,532

Bedrooms: 3

Bathrooms: 2

Foundation: Slab, basement

Materials List Available: No

Price Category: C

Board and batten combine with shake siding to give this cottage an appealing Tudor style.

Features:

- Ceiling Height: 8 ft. unless otherwise noted.

- Entry: This front entry is highlighted by a dormer that opens to the cathedral ceiling of the spacious open great room.

- Open Floor Plan: The living room, dining areas, and kitchen all flow together to create the feeling of a much larger home.

- Kitchen: This kitchen is defined by a curved bar, which can house a bench seat to service a small cafe-style table.

- Master Suite: This private suite is separated from the rest of the bedrooms. It features a volume ceiling and separate sitting area.

- Basement Option: The house is designed primarily for a slab on a narrow lot but can also be built over a basement.

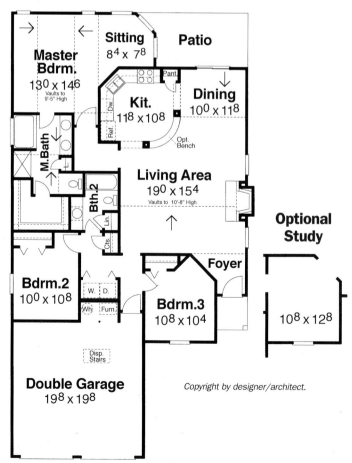

Plan #151050

Dimensions: 69'2" W x 74'10" D
Levels: 1
Square Footage: 2,096
Bedrooms: 3
Bathrooms: 2½
Foundation: Crawl space, slab, or basement
Materials List Available: Yes
Price Category: D

Images provided by designer/architect.

You'll love this spacious home for both its elegance and its convenient design.

Features:

- Ceiling Height: 8 ft.

- Great Room: A 9-ft. boxed ceiling complements this large room, which sits just beyond the front gallery. A fireplace and door to the rear porch make it a natural gathering spot.

- Kitchen: This well-designed kitchen includes a central work island and shares an angled eating bar with the adjacent breakfast room.

- Breakfast Room: This room's bay window is gorgeous, and the door to the garage is practical.

- Master Suite: You'll love the 9-ft. boxed ceiling in the bedroom and the vaulted ceiling in the bath, which also includes two walk-in closets, a corner whirlpool tub, split vanities, a shower, and a compartmentalized toilet.

- Workshop: A huge workshop with half-bath is ideal for anyone who loves to build or repair.

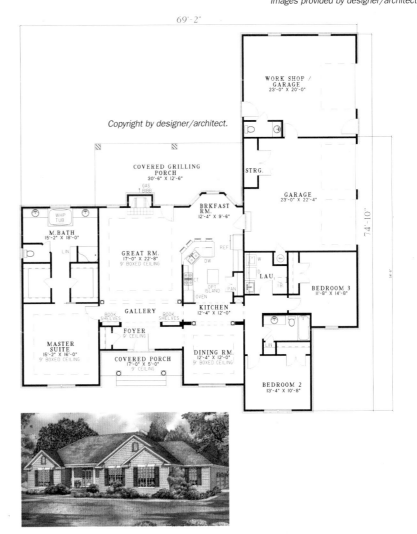

Copyright by designer/architect.

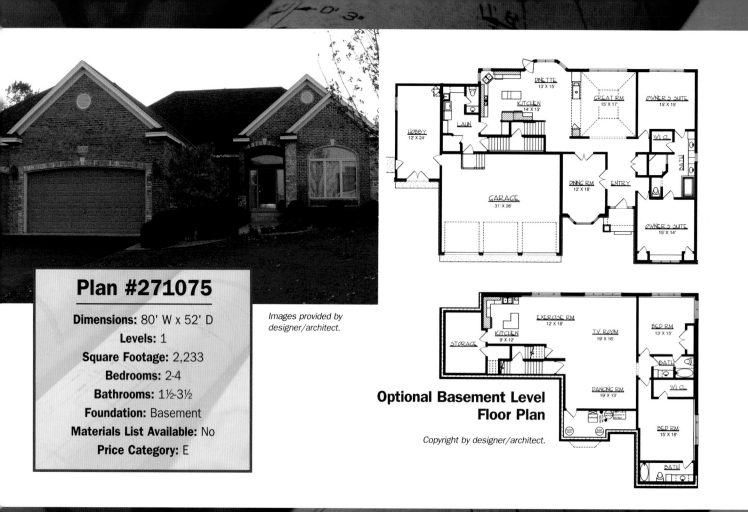

Plan #271075

Dimensions: 80' W x 52' D

Levels: 1

Square Footage: 2,233

Bedrooms: 2-4

Bathrooms: 1½-3½

Foundation: Basement

Materials List Available: No

Price Category: E

Images provided by designer/architect.

Optional Basement Level Floor Plan

Copyright by designer/architect.

Plan #271076

Dimensions: 69' W x 57' D

Levels: 1

Square Footage: 2,188

Bedrooms: 2-4

Bathrooms: 1½-2½

Foundation: Daylight basement

Materials List Available: No

Price Category: D

Images provided by designer/architect.

Optional Basement Level Floor Plan

Copyright by designer/architect.

Plan #271077

Dimensions: 70' W x 53' D

Levels: 1

Square Footage: 1,786

Bedrooms: 1-4

Bathrooms: 1½-2½

Foundation: Daylight basement

Materials List Available: No

Price Category: C

Images provided by designer/architect.

Optional Basement Level Floor Plan

Copyright by designer/architect.

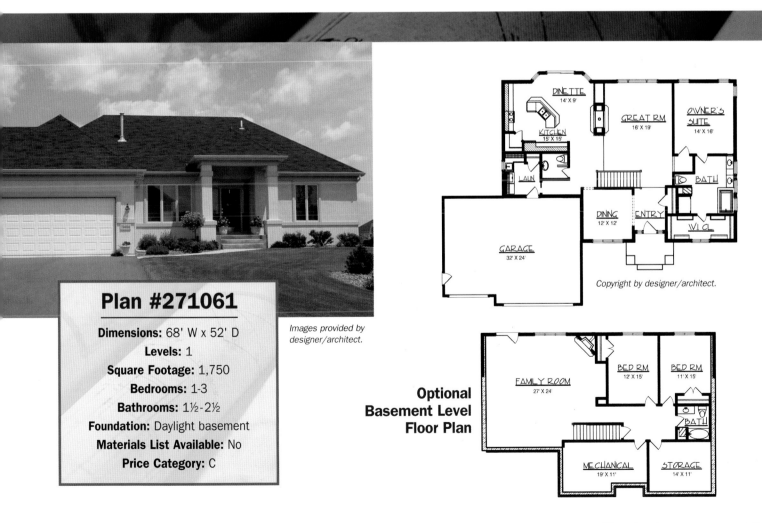

Plan #271061

Dimensions: 68' W x 52' D

Levels: 1

Square Footage: 1,750

Bedrooms: 1-3

Bathrooms: 1½-2½

Foundation: Daylight basement

Materials List Available: No

Price Category: C

Images provided by designer/architect.

Copyright by designer/architect.

Optional Basement Level Floor Plan

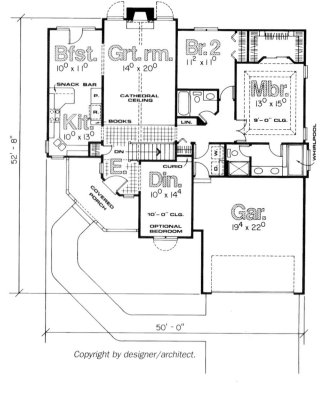

Plan #121058

Dimensions: 50' W x 52'8" D

Levels: 1

Square Footage: 1,554

Bedrooms: 2

Bathrooms: 2

Foundation: Basement

Materials List Available: Yes

Price Category: C

Images provided by designer/architect.

Copyright by designer/architect.

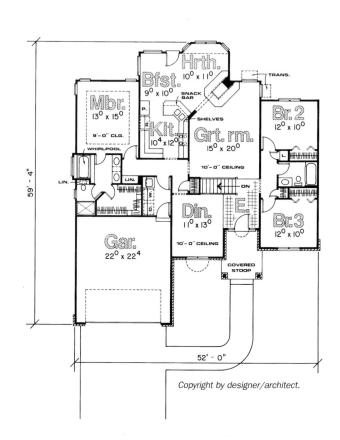

Plan #121059

Dimensions: 52' W x 59'4" D

Levels: 1

Square Footage: 1,782

Bedrooms: 3

Bathrooms: 2

Foundation: Basement

Materials List Available: Yes

Price Category: C

Images provided by designer/architect.

Copyright by designer/architect.

Plan #321024

Dimensions: 47' W x 32' D

Levels: 1

Square Footage: 1,403

Bedrooms: 3

Bathrooms: 1-2

Foundation: Daylight basement

Materials List Available: Yes

Price Category: B

Images provided by designer/architect.

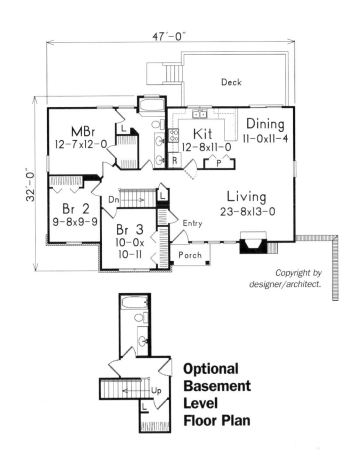

Copyright by designer/architect.

Optional Basement Level Floor Plan

Plan #291003

Dimensions: 42'4" W x 73'4" D

Levels: 1

Square Footage: 1,890

Bedrooms: 3

Bathrooms: 2

Foundation: Crawl space

Materials List Available: No

Price Category: D

Images provided by designer/architect.

Copyright by designer/architect.

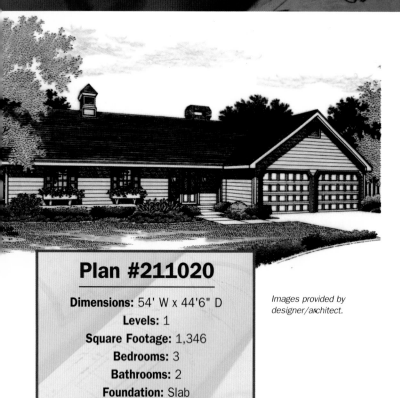

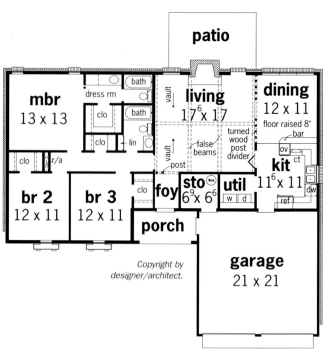

patio

| mbr 13 x 13 | dress rm | living 17⁶ x 17 | dining 12 x 11 floor raised 8" |

living 17⁶ x 17

dining 12 x 11 floor raised 8"

bar

clo / bath / bath / clo / lin

vault

false beams

turned wood post divider

ov / ct

kit 11⁶ x 11

dw

clo / w/a

br 2 12 x 11

br 3 12 x 11

clo

foy

post

sto 6⁹ x 6⁶

util w d

ref

porch

Copyright by designer/architect.

garage 21 x 21

Plan #211020

Dimensions: 54' W x 44'6" D

Levels: 1

Square Footage: 1,346

Bedrooms: 3

Bathrooms: 2

Foundation: Slab

Materials List Available: Yes

Price Category: B

Images provided by designer/architect.

patio

mbr 15 x 14

dw

rng kit pan

ref

dining 13 x 10

d w

sto 9 x 10

util

clo / shvs

HEAT & A/C

living 20 x 15

beam

cathedral ceiling

carport 21 x 20

br 3 12 x 10

clo

br 2 13 x 11

clo

porch

Copyright by designer/architect.

Plan #211021

Dimensions: 61' W x 35' D

Levels: 1

Square Footage: 1,375

Bedrooms: 3

Bathrooms: 2

Foundation: Slab

Materials List Available: Yes

Price Category: B

Images provided by designer/architect.

SMARTtip

Creating Built-up Cornices

Combine various base, crown, and cove moldings to create an elaborate cornice that is both imaginative and tasteful. Use the pattern throughout your home to establish a unique architectural element having the appearance of being professionally designed.

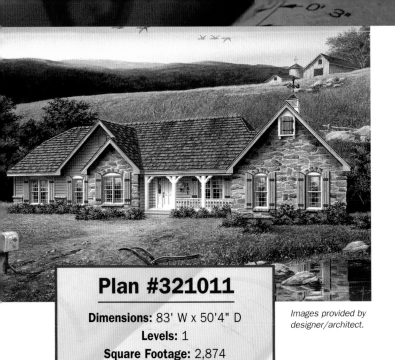

Images provided by
designer/architect.

Plan #321011

Dimensions: 83' W x 50'4" D

Levels: 1

Square Footage: 2,874

Bedrooms: 4

Bathrooms: 2½

Foundation: Basement

Materials List Available: Yes

Price Category: F

SMARTtip

Drilling for Kitchen Plumbing

Drill holes for plumbing and waste lines before installing the cabinets. It is easier to work when the cabinets are out in the middle of the floor, and there is no danger of knocking them out of alignment when creating the holes if they are not screwed to the wall studs or one another yet.

Plan #321012

Dimensions: 58'8" W x 51'2" D

Levels: 1

Square Footage: 1,882

Bedrooms: 3

Bathrooms: 2

Foundation: Basement

Materials List Available: Yes

Price Category: D

Images provided by
designer/architect.

Plan #221004

Dimensions: 67'8" W x 43' D

Levels: 1

Square Footage: 1,763

Bedrooms: 3

Bathrooms: 2

Foundation: Basement

Materials List Available: No

Price Category: C

Images provided by designer/architect.

You'll love the spacious feeling provided by the open design of this traditional ranch.

Features:

- Ceiling Height: 8 ft.

- Dining Room: This formal room is perfect for entertaining groups both large and small, and the open design makes it easy to serve.

- Living Room: The vaulted ceiling here and in the dining room adds to the elegance of these rooms. Use window treatments that emphasize these ceilings for a truly sumptuous look.

- Kitchen: Designed for practicality and efficiency, this kitchen will thrill all the cooks in the family. An attached dining nook makes a natural gathering place for friends and family.

- Master Suite: The private bath in this suite features a double vanity and whirlpool tub. You'll find a walk-in closet in the bedroom.

- Garage: You'll love the extra storage space in this two-car garage.

Rear Elevation

Copyright by designer/architect.

Plan #101004

Dimensions: 55'8" W x 56'6" D
Levels: 1
Square Footage: 1,787
Bedrooms: 3
Bathrooms: 2
Foundation: Slab, crawl space, or basement
Materials List Available: No
Price Category: C

This carefully designed ranch provides the feel and features of a much larger home.

Features:

- Ceiling Height: 9 ft. unless otherwise noted.

- Foyer: Guests will step up onto the inviting front porch and into this foyer, with its impressive 11-ft. ceiling.

- Dining Room: Open to the entry and to its left is this elegant dining room, perfect for entertaining or informal family gatherings.

- Family Room: This family gathering place features an 11-ft. ceiling to enhance its sense of spaciousness.

- Kitchen: This intelligently designed kitchen has an open plan. A breakfast bar and a serving bar are features that add to its convenience.

- Master Suite: This suite is loaded with amenities, including a double-step tray ceiling, direct access to the screened porch, a sitting room, deluxe bath, and his and her walk-in closets.

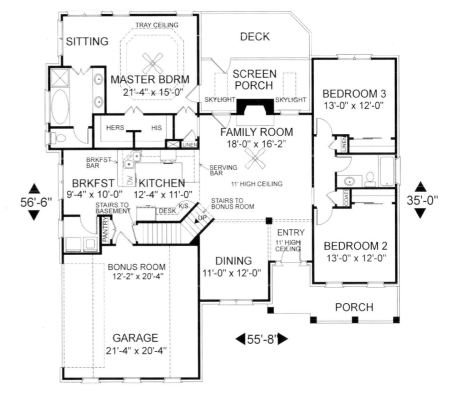

Copyright by designer/architect.

Plan #211033

Dimensions: 46' W x 66' D
Levels: 1
Square Footage: 1,732
Bedrooms: 3
Bathrooms: 2
Foundation: Slab
Materials List Available: Yes
Price Category: C

You'll love the good taste with which this home was designed, as well as the versatility its mixture of formal and informal areas affords.

Features:

- Ceiling Height: 9-ft. ceilings.

- Living Room: The dimensions of this room make it easy to decorate for either formal or informal occasions and entertaining.

- Dining Room: Close to the kitchen for convenience, this dining room is also versatile enough to be appropriate for any sort of entertaining.

- Kitchen: The practical design here allows you to work without needlessly wasting precious time or energy, and the location of this kitchen means that serving and clearing-up chores are eased.

- Master Suite: Retreat to this area after a long, stressful day so that you can recharge your batteries—either by resting or showering.

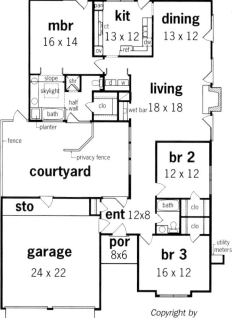

Copyright by designer/architect.

SMARTtip

Types of Paintbrush Bristles

Nylon Bristles. Bristles made of nylon are most suitable for latex paint, although they can also be used with solvent-based paint.

Natural Bristles. Also called "China bristle," natural bristle brushes are preferred for use with solvent-based paints and varnishes because they tend to hold more paint and generally brush out to a smoother looking finish. Natural bristle brushes should not be used with latex paint. The water in the paint will cause the bristles to expand and ruin the brush.

Choosing Brushes. When buying a brush, check for thick, resilient bristles that are firmly held in place. Be sure, also, to get the proper type brush for the job.

Plan #241003

Dimensions: 60' W x 58' D
Levels: 1
Square Footage: 2,080
Bedrooms: 3
Bathrooms: 2
Foundation: Slab
Materials List Available: No
Price Category: D

Striking rooflines combine with a stone-and-shingle exterior to give this lovely country home immediate appeal.

Features:

- Great Room: Certain to become a favorite gathering place for friends and family, this great room features a fireplace, bookshelves, and an entertainment center.

- Kitchen: This well-designed kitchen—with ample counter space and cabinets—features a pantry, island, and large breakfast area. It also includes a convenient computer nook, well suited for managing today's complexities.

- Master Suite: Separated for privacy, this master suite features his and her vanities, a corner tub, a separate shower, a large walk-in closet, and a delightful window seat for your relaxing pleasure.

- Garage: Use the extra space in this garage for storage.

Images provided by designer/architect.

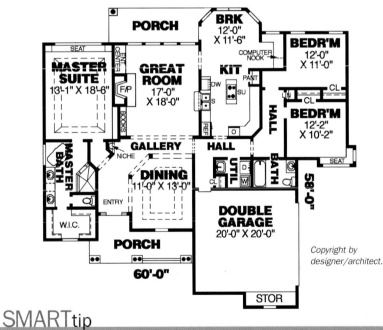

Copyright by designer/architect.

SMARTtip

Color Basics for Kids' Rooms

Use color effectively to enhance the perception of the space itself. Make a large room feel cozy with warm colors, which tend to advance. Conversely, open up a small room with cool colors or neutrals, which tend to recede. The less-intense version of a color will generally reduce its tendency to advance or recede, as well. Other tricks: Sharp contrasts often have the same impact as a dark color, reducing perceived space. Monochromatic schemes enlarge space. Neutrals of similar value make walls appear to retreat.

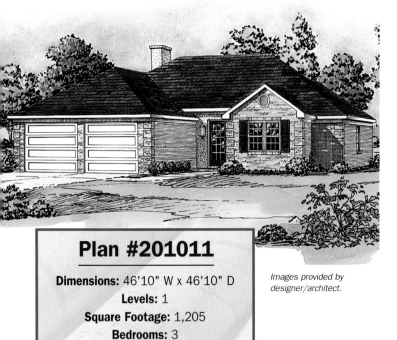

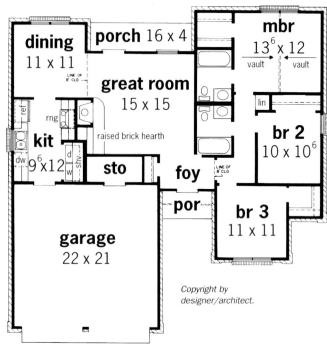

Plan #201011

Dimensions: 46'10" W x 46'10" D

Levels: 1

Square Footage: 1,205

Bedrooms: 3

Bathrooms: 2

Foundation: Crawl space, slab

Materials List Available: Yes

Price Category: B

Images provided by designer/architect.

Copyright by designer/architect.

Floor plan labels: dining 11 x 11 • porch 16 x 4 • mbr 13⁶ x 12 vault vault • great room 15 x 15 • kit 9⁶ x 12 • raised brick hearth • sto • foy • br 2 10 x 10⁶ • por • br 3 11 x 11 • garage 22 x 21 • ref • rng • dw • d/w • shv. • LINE OF 8' CLG

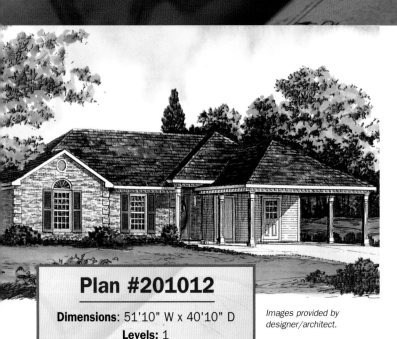

Plan #201012

Dimensions: 51'10" W x 40'10" D

Levels: 1

Square Footage: 1,221

Bedrooms: 3

Bathrooms: 2

Foundation: Crawl space, slab

Materials List Available: Yes

Price Category: B

Images provided by designer/architect.

SMARTtip

Kitchen Cabinet Styles

You may not need to purchase expensive kitchen cabinetry to get fine-furniture quality details. Try adding crown molding to the top of basic cabinets and replacing the hardware with reproduction polished-brass door and drawer pulls to achieve a traditional look.

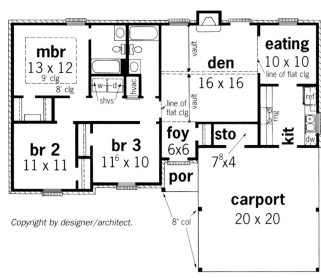

Floor plan labels: mbr 13 x 12 9' clg 8' clg • den 16 x 16 vault • eating 10 x 10 line of flat clg • br 2 11 x 11 • br 3 11⁶ x 10 • foy 6x6 • sto 7⁸x4 • kit • por • carport 20 x 20 • w/d • hvac • shvs • line of flat clg • ref • rng • dw • 8" col

Copyright by designer/architect.

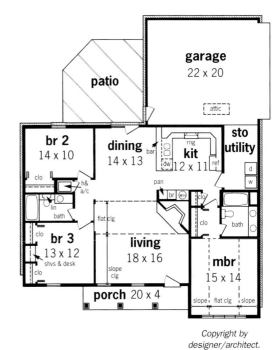

Copyright by
designer/architect.

Plan #211022

Dimensions: 46' W x 56' D

Levels: 1

Square Footage: 1,380

Bedrooms: 3

Bathrooms: 2

Foundation: Slab

Materials List Available: Yes

Price Category: B

*Images provided by
designer/architect.*

Floor plan labels: garage 22 x 20, patio, attic, sto, utility, br 2 14 x 10, dining 14 x 13, bar, kit 12 x 11, rng, ref, dw, clo, h& a/c, br, w/h, pan, clo, d, w, lin, bath, flat clg, living 18 x 16, clo, bath, br 3 13 x 12, shvs & desk, clo, clo, slope clg, mbr 15 x 14, porch 20 x 4, slope, flat clg, slope

Plan #361004

Dimensions: 77' W x 81' D

Levels: 1

Square Footage: 2, 191

Bedrooms: 3

Bathrooms: 2

Foundation: Crawl space

Materials List Available: No

Price Category: D

*Images provided by
designer/architect.*

Copyright by
designer/architect.

Floor plan labels: Deck, Deck, Deck, Great Room 35' x 24', Dining, Living, Kitchen, Bedroom 11'4" x 12', Bedroom 14' x 12', Entry, Utility, Sitting, Covered Porch, Master Suite 21' x 18'6", Garage 21'4" x 30'8"

Creating a Stylish Kitchen

Style meets state of the art in the kitchen. If you need inspiration when the time comes to make decorating decisions about your new kitchen, think about some of today's popular decorating styles: country, contemporary, cottage, French country, Shaker, and Arts and Crafts. Which one says the most about you and your lifestyle? You might try starting with the cabinets, which will have the most impact on how your kitchen will look because they will be the largest element in the space. The key is to build a room around a theme while incorporating your personality into it. A favorite color is one way to do this; another way is a repeated pattern or theme.

For inspiration, visit showrooms and read magazines. Is there someone you know who has a kitchen that you've particularly admired? Was it a painted finish on the cabinetry? The color or pattern of the wallpaper or window treatment? A handsome wood floor? A pretty collection displayed in a hutch or on a wall? How did the room make you feel? Cheerful? Relaxed? Animated? Nostalgic? This is the kind of thinking that will help you to zero in on a design that will have staying power.

In addition, look for clues in the details you are planning for the rest your house. What is the intended architectural style?

Will there be elaborate trimwork, or will the walls, doors, and windows be streamlined and spare? Even if the rest of the house will be plain, you can introduce a period flavor in the kitchen with reproduction cabinets and fixtures, window treatments, wallpaper, and accessories.

Do you like antiques or modern art? Are you a collector or someone who prefers pared-down space? You can build on these

Today's traditional styles, below, are updated with fresh finishes and details.

Moldings and raised-panel doors, opposite, dress up any style of cabinetry.

preferences or depart from them entirely. If your kitchen will be open to other areas, such as the family room, link the two spaces with color or related materials.

Whatever you do, your approach to decorating the new kitchen should be deliberate. Let it evolve over time; don't rush your choices. Live with paint, tile, and wallpaper samples for a while.

You might start with some of the ideas that are discussed here. They are just suggestions, however. Let your own preferences be your ultimate guide. If you're not sure about something, don't do it right away or just keep your decorating simple until you're ready to add the details.

Traditional Style

Today's traditional style incorporates elements of English and American eighteenth- and early nineteenth-century design. Marked by symmetry and balance and enhanced by the look of fine-crafted details, it is dignified, rich, and formal.

Choose wood cabinetry finished with a cherry or mahogany stain or painted white, with details such as fluted panels, bull's-eye corner blocks, and dentil and crown molding. For the door style, a raised cathedral panel (top slightly arched) is typical. On the countertop, use marble or a laminate faux version, and install tiles on the back-

splash. Polished brass hardware and fittings add a refined touch.

Colors to consider include classic Wedgwood blue or deep rich tones. Windows and French doors with true divided lights or double-hung units with pop-in muntins have great traditional-style appeal. Dress them with formal curtain panels or swags. Botanical-inspired patterns, formal stripes, or tapestry fabrics are perfect for window treatments or for chair cushions and table linens.

Furnish the kitchen with an antique or reproduction hutch, where you can display formal china, and a table and chairs in traditional Windsor or Queen Anne style.

Contemporary Style

What's referred to as "contemporary" style evokes images of clean architectural lines; an absence of decoration and color; and materials such as stainless steel, chrome, glass, and stone. Indeed, its roots are at the turn of the last century, when architects and designers flatly rejected the exaggerated artificial embellishments of the Victorians by turning to natural products and pared-down forms. Various modern movements, evolving over the course of the industrialized twentieth century, gradually incorporated new man-made materials into their streamlined forms. Hence the high-tech look popularized in the 1970s and 1980s.

Today, contemporary style is taking a softer turn, even in the kitchen, a place where hard edges, cool reflective surfaces, and cutting-edge technology abound. It's not unusual to see updated versions of tra-

Color finishes on cabinets, below, can be combined with artful wall treatments.

Furniture-like pieces, right, make a kitchen less utilitarian looking.

Reproduction light fixtures, opposite, capture a mood or period style.

ditional fixtures and fittings or new uses for natural materials in a contemporary kitchen, especially as improved finishes make these products more durable and easier to maintain.

Although a contemporary room is often monochromatic or neutral, don't be afraid to use color or to mix several materials. Combinations of wood and various metals—stainless steel, chrome, copper, brass, and pewter on surfaces like cabinet doors, countertops, and floors—make strong statements, as do stone and glass.

Country Style

Country cabinets are typically made of wood with framed or raised-panel doors. Beadboard cabinets are a typical American country choice. Or leave the doors off, allowing colorful dishes and canned and boxed goods to create a fun display. For the countertop, install butcher block or hand-painted or silk-screened tiles. Another option is a colorful or patterned countertop fabricated from inlaid solid-surfacing material. A working fireplace will

definitely add charm to your country kitchen, but a simple potted herb garden on the windowsill will, too.

Wood floors are a natural choice in this setting. For a custom touch, add a stenciled backsplash or wall border. Or try a faux finish like sponging, ragging, or combing. These techniques are fun and easy, and they add texture to your walls.

Install double-hung windows. (Standard casement windows look too contemporary in this setting.) Finish them with full trim, and dress them with simple curtains.

The Cottage Look

This vintage look, inspired by quaint English-country style, is appealing in the kitchen because it's cozy, casual, and warm. Framed wood cabinets with an unfitted or unmatched appearance provide a good starting point for building on this theme, especially in a finish such as a honey maple paired with a color stain that looks properly distressed but not shabby. Muntin-glass doors, plate or pot racks, and open shelves should be part of the cabinetry's design. Milk- or clear-glass knobs and pulls complement cottage cabinets. But you could also mix a couple of different styles for mismatched chic.

Beadboard on the walls or ceiling always looks at home in this style kitchen, as does brick. Use brick as a backsplash or as a surround at the cooker. An English import, the AGA cooker, is a great way to bring the old-time European look of a cast-iron stove into the room while providing all the modern-day conveniences. Install an exposed-apron (farmhouse-style) sink with a reproduction chrome-and-porcelain faucet set to add more charm. On the floor, use wide wood planks or stone with a colorful hand-painted floorcloth on top. Bring more color into the room with blue-green surfaces accented in varying shades of rose and cream.

A double-hung window lends a traditional note, but if you can make the style work with the exterior of your house, a Gothic-inspired architectural design would tie it all together. Accent with lighting fixtures that resemble old-fashioned Victorian gas lamps.

For furniture, include a good-size farmhouse table in your plan, as well as a Welsh dresser and plate rack for displaying a pretty collection of transferware.

French Country Style

To create the rustic charm of a French-country farmhouse, whitewash the walls or apply a subtle glaze finish in an earth tone, such as rose ocher or sienna. Install wood ceiling beams with an aged or distressed look. Use limestone tile or clay pavers, which also have a warm, earthy appeal, on the floor. For the appearance of a hearth, design a cooking alcove to house the range or cooktop. Accent it with colorful tiles or brick. Create a focal point at the cooking area with a handsome copper range hood. Hang a rack for copper pots and pans. Pair an exposed apron sink with a high-arc spout.

Use unfitted cabinetry, open shelves, or a baker's rack for storage. Decorate with provincial mini-prints in mustard yellow, clay red, and deep blue. Dress windows with lace café curtains, and stencil a pretty fleur de lis border around the trim.

Add details such as flavored oils and vinegars displayed in pretty glass bottles, fresh herbs growing from racks in sunny windows, and blue and white tiles.

An exposed-apron sink, left, comes in many finishes and colors.

A stone look, below left, can be reproduced in solid-surfacing material.

A high-arc faucet, below, captures nostalgic styles and practicality.

Cabinet Door Style Choices

Shaker Style

The Shakers' plain, practical designs featured dovetailed joints and hand-planed tops, plain panels on doors, and legs tapered almost to a pencil point. The finishes on original Shaker cabinets were always dyes and oils, never varnishes, to enhance the wood.

Accent woodwork in colors inspired by natural dyes—terra cotta, yellow ochre, olive green, green-blue, and denim. Ceramic tile installed in a quiltlike pattern on the countertop or backsplash or as a mural above the cooktop can add more color accents and a reasonable amount of decoration, unless you're a purist at heart. The fixtures could be white, bisque, or black, with plain fittings in a brushed chrome or pewter finish. Trim kits, available from appliance and cabinet manufacturers, can camouflage modern-day appliances that the Shakers eschewed.

A traditional double-hung window, with or without muntins, fits in fine with the Shaker theme. Install plain wood shutters and panel-style curtains with simple cotton tab tops.

Shaker-inspired furniture is widely available today. Tall ladder-back chairs with tape-woven seats look at home around a simple trestle table. A pegged chair rail is a Shaker classic. Installed high on the wall, it can be a display for a collection of hand-woven baskets, dried flowers, tapered candles, or even small wooden chairs.

Many period looks include wood floors, which can be impractical in a kitchen. A laminate look-alike is a good substitute.

Arts & Crafts Style

Styles that are related to or part of the Arts and Crafts movement include Mission, Craftsman, and Prairie, the signature style of the architect Frank Lloyd Wright. Start with plain oak cabinets with a handcrafted appearance. Several manufacturers make reproduction wood cabinets, metal hardware, and period wallpaper and lighting fixtures today.

Decorate with colors that reflect natural hues, such as brown, green, blue, and orange. Accessorize with organically shaped pottery in these colors, too. Pull it all together by incorporating Native American textiles, such as a rug, into this room. Design a custom-tiled backsplash with matte or "art pottery" glazed tiles.

Plain windows should be curtained very simply—if at all—in an Arts and Crafts-style room, using natural fabrics such as linen or muslin with an embroidered border. Typical motifs include ginkgo leaves and poppy seeds. Instead of traditional treatments, use stained-glass or art-glass windows. To complete the look, furnish the kitchen in period style with a Mission table and chairs and a hutch, if there is room for one.

Plan #131007

Dimensions: 59'10" W x 47'8" D
Levels: 1
Square Footage: 1,595
Bedrooms: 3
Bathrooms: 2
Foundation: Crawl space, slab, basement, or walkout
Materials List Available: Yes
Price Category: D

Images provided by designer/architect.

Imagine living in this home, with its traditional country comfort and individual brand of charm.

Features:

- **Exterior elements:** The mixture of a front porch with a cameo front door, decorative posts, bay windows, and dormers will delight you.

- **Great Room:** A tray ceiling gives distinction to this large room, and a wet bar eases entertaining.

- **Screened Porch:** At dusk and dawn, this porch is sure to be your favorite outdoor spot.

- **Kitchen:** Eat any meal in this large kitchen for a touch of homey charm.

- **Dining Room:** Perfect for hosting a formal dinner, this bayed dining room can increase your enjoyment of simple family meals.

- **Master Bedroom:** For the sake of privacy, this room is somewhat secluded. Decorate to emphasize the elegant tray ceiling.

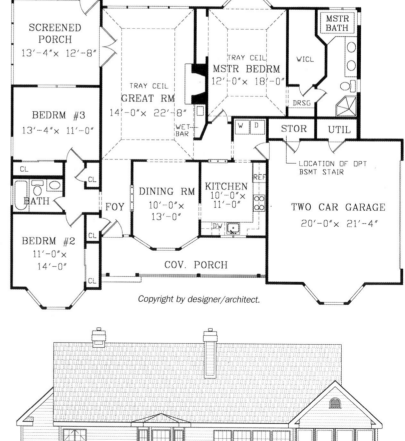

Copyright by designer/architect.

Rear Elevation

Alternate Front View

Foyer / Dining Room

Great Room

Add the Extras

Simple or plain, it's the little conveniences and miscellaneous touches that push the dining experience to perfection. Here are some extra things to think about.

- You can never have too many serving trays when you entertain outside. For carrying food or drinks from the kitchen or the grill, trays are indispensable.

- A serving cart on wheels makes a perfect movable outdoor bar and provides an additional serving surface. Look for one at yard sales or buy one new.

- Chances are you won't have a sideboard, but a few small tables to hold excess items are great substitutes for one. They're also easier to position in the different places where you need them.

- For cooler weather or even a summer's evening with a bit of nip in the air, nothing beats an outdoor fireplace for comfort. You could build one into the house, but various types of stand-alone units are sold in home centers. To add a Southwest ambiance, consider a chiminea, a clay fireplace. Try burning some piñon pine, and you'll feel as if you're in Santa Fe. Be sure to follow manufacturers' instructions when using these fireplaces. You might also have to store them during the winter.

- Pots of fragrant plants—lavender, scented geraniums, flowering tobacco, or jasmine—provide a sensual aroma. Flowers such as roses climbing up an arbor or trellis are beautiful, evoke a romantic feeling, and lend a delicate scent to the atmosphere as well.

Nothing adds romance and intrigue to an evening soiree as candlelight does. Include just a few candles for an intimate dinner. Use more for a larger gathering, placing one or more on each table. Scatter luminaries around the yard. As the beautiful evening dusk begins, light candles, a few at a time, so your eyes can adjust to the dimming light. Not only do the candles illuminate the night in a magical way but they can also keep bugs at bay.

Plan #321003

Dimensions: 67'4" W x 48' D
Levels: 1
Square Footage: 1,791
Bedrooms: 4
Bathrooms: 2
Foundation: Basement
Materials List Available: Yes
Price Category: C

The traditional good looks of the exterior of this home are complemented by the stunning contemporary design of the interior.

Features:

- Great Room: With a vaulted ceiling to highlight its spacious dimensions, this room is certain to be the central gathering spot for friends and family.

- Dining Room: Also with a vaulted ceiling, this room has an octagonal shape for added interest. Windows here and in the great room look out to the covered patio.

- Kitchen: A center island gives a convenient work space in this well-designed kitchen, which features a pass-through to the dining room for easy serving, and large, walk-in pantry for storage.

- Breakfast Room: A bay window lets sunshine pour in to start your morning with a smile.

- Master Bedroom: A vaulted ceiling and a sitting area make you feel truly pampered in this room.

Images provided by designer/architect.

Great Rm
22–8x16–10
vaulted clg

MBr
15–8x13–9
vaulted clg

Covered Patio

Dining
12–0x12–0

Stor
8–0x
7–7

Laundry

Br 2
10–0x
9–0

48'–0"

Kit/
Brkfst
17–4x14–2

Foyer

Dn

Br 3
10–0x
10–0

Garage
19–4x21–0

Study/
Br 4
11–4x12–7
vaulted clg

Porch depth
5–10

67'–4"

Copyright by designer/architect.

SMARTtip

Bay & Bow Windows

Occasionally too little room exists between the window frame (if there is one) and the ceiling. In this situation you might be able to use ceiling-mounted hardware. Alternatively, a cornice across the top and a rod mounted inside the cornice will give you the dual benefit of visually lowering the top of the window and concealing the hardware.

Plan #131011

Dimensions: 75'2" W x 60'9" D
Levels: 1
Square Footage: 1,897
Bedrooms: 4
Bathrooms: 2
Foundation: Basement, crawl space, or slab
Materials List Available: Yes
Price Category: E

You'll love this home if you're looking for a plan for a sloping lot or flat one or if you want to orient the rear porch to face into or away from the sun.

Features:

- Ceiling Height: 8 ft.

- Living Area: The whole family will find it easy to congregate in this lovely room.

- Kitchen: The angle of this home makes the kitchen especially convenient while also giving it an unusual amount of character.

- Study: Located near the front door, this room can serve as a home office or fourth bedroom as easily as it does a private study.

- Master Suite: Located at the opposite end of the home from the other two bedrooms, this master suite offers privacy and quiet.

- Additional Bedrooms: These two bedrooms share a distinctive hall bathroom.

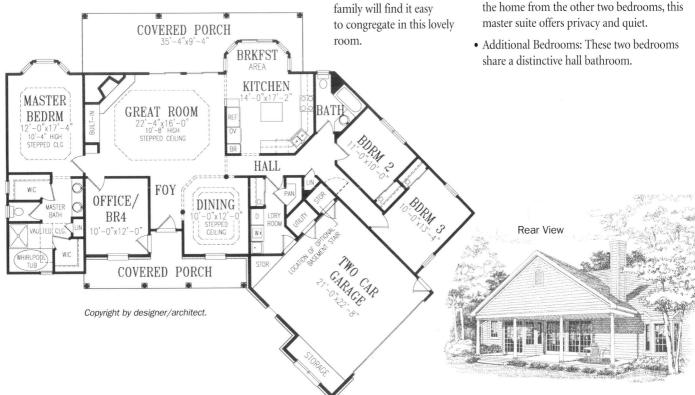

Copyright by designer/architect.

Rear View

Plan #141006

Dimensions: 64' W x 52' D

Levels: 1

Square Footage: 1,787

Bedrooms: 3

Bathrooms: 2½

Foundation: Basement

Materials List Available: No

Price Category: C

This stately and traditional ranch has a well-designed floor plan that makes it seem larger.

Features:

- Ceiling Height: 9 ft. unless otherwise noted:

- Tall Main Ceilings: The main part of the house has an elegant look, with 12-ft. ceilings in the foyer, living area, and dining room. The taller windows allow room for transom windows that fill the rooms with sunlight.

- Fireplace: The handsome fireplace is designed to vent directly to the outside. Without the need for a chimney, a television niche can be installed above the fireplace, maximizing the use of space in the room.

- Kitchen: This kitchen gains light from the breakfast room and the living area. The sink is angled to allow the cook to participate in living-area conversation.

- Master Suite: This elegant private suite has its own access off the rear entry hall.

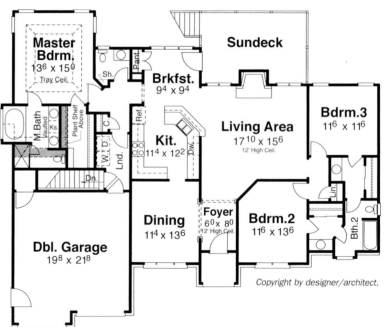

SMARTtip

Arts and Crafts Style in Your Kitchen

The heart of this style lies in its earthy connection. The more you can bring nature into it, the more authentic it will appear. An easy way to do this is with plants. Open the space up to nature with glass doors that provide a view to a green garden.

Plan #161004

Dimensions: 50' W x 54'8" D
Levels: 1
Square Footage: 1,315
Bedrooms: 3
Bathrooms: 2
Foundation: Slab
Materials List Available: Yes
Price Category: B

This multi-featured ranch has a covered porch, a ceiling that slopes to an 11-ft. height, an optional library, and a full basement to enhance your living enjoyment.

Features:

- **Great Room:** Experience the expansive entertainment area created by this open great room and the dining area. Enjoy the lovely fireplace, with full glass on both sides.

- **Kitchen:** This kitchen is designed for total convenience and easy work patterns with immediate access to the first-floor laundry area.

- **Master Bedroom:** This master bedroom, split from the other bedrooms, offers privacy and features tray ceiling design.

- **Basement:** Designed with the future in mind, this full basement has open stairs leading to it and can be updated to expand your living space.

Images provided by designer/architect.

Copyright by designer/architect.

Deck

Master Bedroom
12'-4" x 13'-0"

Great Room
18'-8" x 17'-4"

Bedroom
11'-4" x 10'-8"

Bath

Dining

Bath

Kitchen
13'-4" x 9'-11"

Foyer

Bedroom
12'-4" x 10'-10"

Laun.

Porch

54'-8"

Garage
20'-0" x 26'-2"

50'-0"

Optional Library

Bath

Rear Elevation

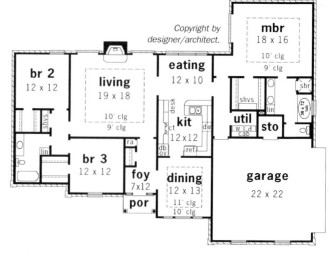

Floor plan labels: br 2 12 x 12, living 19 x 18 10' clg 9' clg, eating 12 x 10, mbr 18 x 16 10' clg 9' clg, shvs, kit 12x12, util, sto, br 3 12 x 12, foy 7x12, dining 12 x 13 11' clg 10' clg, garage 22 x 22, por

Plan #201053

Dimensions: 65'10" W x 51'10" D
Levels: 1
Square Footage: 1,959
Bedrooms: 3
Bathrooms: 2
Foundation: Crawl space, slab
Materials List Available: Yes
Price Category: D

Images provided by designer/architect.

SMARTtip
Choosing Awning Colors

When choosing a color for your awning, instead of blending with the landscape or house, you can pick one that contrasts its surroundings. This will draw attention to a handsome deck.

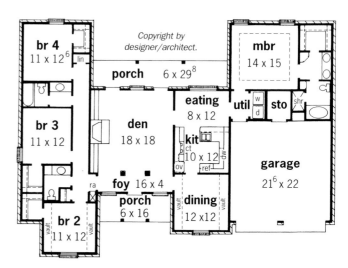

Floor plan labels: br 4 11 x 12⁶, porch 6 x 29⁸, mbr 14 x 15, br 3 11 x 12, den 18 x 18, eating 8 x 12, util, sto, kit 10 x 12, garage 21⁶ x 22, foy 16 x 4, br 2 11 x 12, porch 6 x 16, dining 12 x 12

Plan #201054

Dimensions: 67'10" W x 49'10" D
Levels: 1
Square Footage: 1,987
Bedrooms: 4
Bathrooms: 2½
Foundation: Crawl space, slab
Materials List Available: Yes
Price Category: D

Images provided by designer/architect.

SMARTtip
Reed Porch Furniture

Reed furniture comes in wicker, rattan, or bamboo. Favored for its decorative appeal and comfort, reed furniture needs some protection from the elements if it is to last. For easy care, check out synthetic look-alikes.

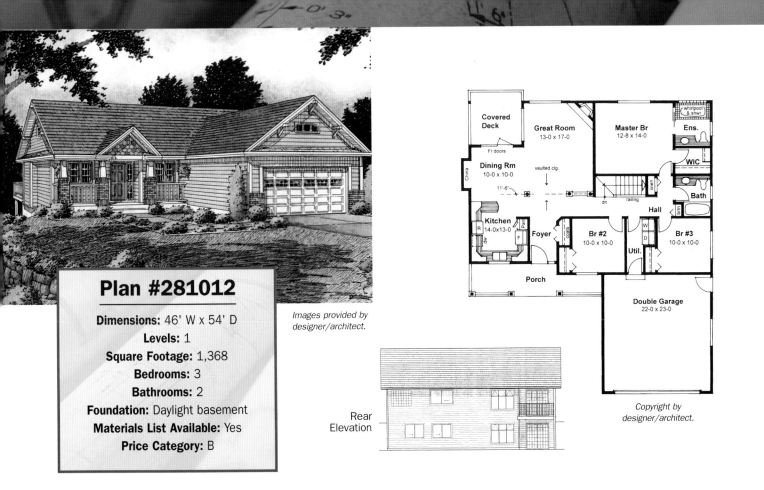

Plan #281012

Dimensions: 46' W x 54' D

Levels: 1

Square Footage: 1,368

Bedrooms: 3

Bathrooms: 2

Foundation: Daylight basement

Materials List Available: Yes

Price Category: B

Images provided by designer/architect.

Rear Elevation

Copyright by designer/architect.

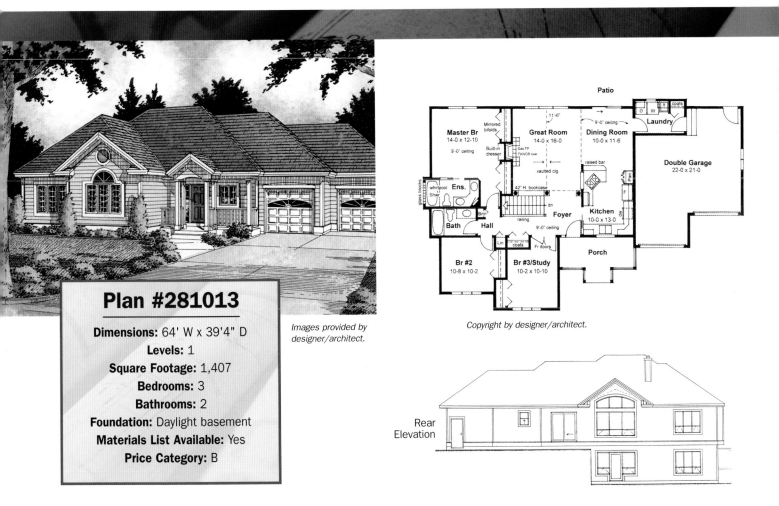

Plan #281013

Dimensions: 64' W x 39'4" D

Levels: 1

Square Footage: 1,407

Bedrooms: 3

Bathrooms: 2

Foundation: Daylight basement

Materials List Available: Yes

Price Category: B

Images provided by designer/architect.

Copyright by designer/architect.

Rear Elevation

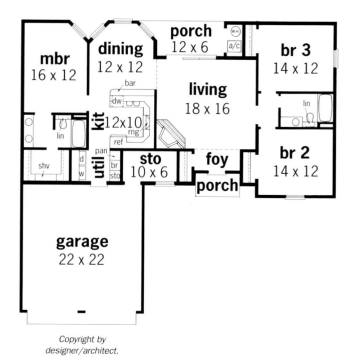

Images provided by designer/architect.

Copyright by designer/architect.

Plan #211026

Dimensions: 56' W x 50' D
Levels: 1
Square Footage: 1,415
Bedrooms: 3
Bathrooms: 2
Foundation: Slab
Materials List Available: Yes
Price Category: B

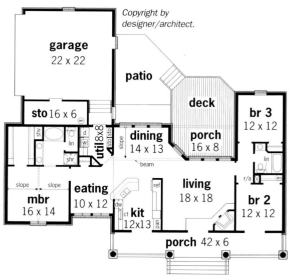

Copyright by designer/architect.

Plan #211029

Dimensions: 68' W x 60' D
Levels: 1
Square Footage: 1,672
Bedrooms: 3
Bathrooms: 2
Foundation: Crawl space
Materials List Available: Yes
Price Category: C

Images provided by designer/architect.

SMARTtip

Ponds

If a pond or small body of water already exists on your property, arrange your garden elements to take advantage of it. Build a bridge over it to connect it to other areas of the garden. If there's a dock already in place, make use of it for an instant midday picnic for one.

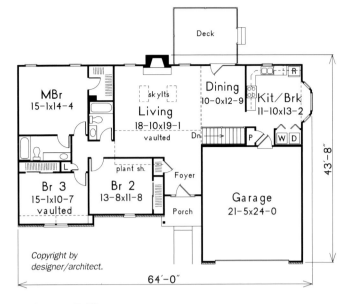

Copyright by designer/architect.

Plan #321014

Dimensions: 64' W x 43'8" D
Levels: 1
Square Footage: 1,676
Bedrooms: 3
Bathrooms: 2
Foundation: Basement
Materials List Available: Yes
Price Category: C

Images provided by designer/architect.

SMARTtip

Blending Architecture

An easy way to blend the new deck with the architecture of a house is with railings. Precut railings and caps come in many styles and sizes.

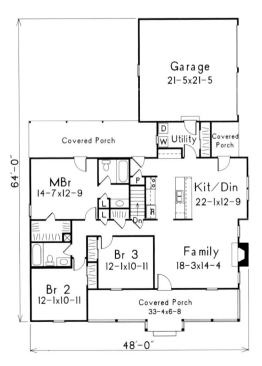

Plan #321015

Dimensions: 48' W x 64' D
Levels: 1
Square Footage: 1,501
Bedrooms: 3
Bathrooms: 2
Foundation: Basement
Materials List Available: Yes
Price Category: C

Images provided by designer/architect.

Copyright by designer/architect.

Plan #221007

Dimensions: 48' W x 55' D

Levels: 1

Square Footage: 1,472

Bedrooms: 3

Bathrooms: 2

Foundation: Basement

Materials List Available: No

Price Category: B

Illustration provided by designer/architect.

Rear Elevation

If you're looking for a compact home with a floor plan that makes every square inch count, you'll love this design.

Features:

- Ceiling Height: 8 ft.

- Great Room: A cathedral ceiling gives stature to this room and the corner fireplace creates a cozy nook where everyone will gather.

- Dining Room: A cathedral ceiling adds an elegant touch, and the door to the screened-in porch makes outdoor entertaining easy.

- Kitchen: This well-planned kitchen is adjacent to the dining room for serving ease and includes a breakfast bar for casual snacking.

- Master Suite: A huge walk-in closet gives a practical touch to this luxurious area, which includes a door to the screened-in porch. The bath includes a whirlpool tub and standing shower.

- Secondary Bedrooms: Both rooms feature large closets and share a full bath.

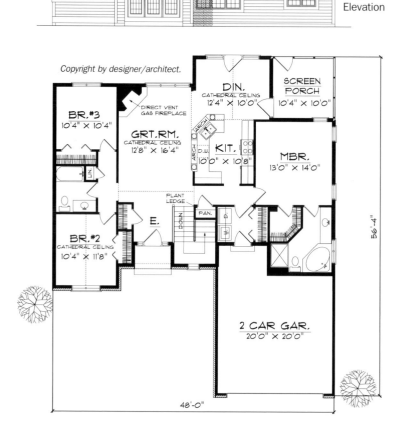

Copyright by designer/architect.

Plan #101005

Dimensions: 63' W x 57'2" D

Levels: 1

Square Footage: 1,992

Bedrooms: 3

Bathrooms: 2½

Foundation: Slab, crawl space, or basement

Materials List Available: Yes

Price Category: D

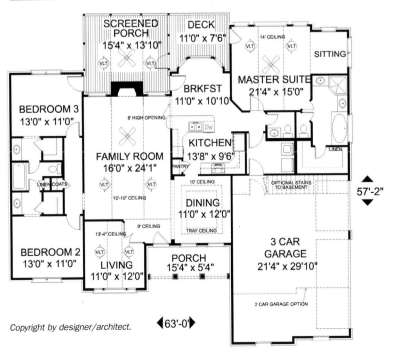

Rear View

This midsized ranch is accented with Palladian windows and inviting front porch.

Features:

• Ceiling Height: 9 ft. unless otherwise noted.

• Special Ceilings: Tray or vaulted ceilings adorn the living room, family room, dining room, and master suite.

• Kitchen: This bright and airy kitchen is designed to be a pleasure in which to work. It shares a big bay window with the contiguous breakfast room.

• Breakfast Room: The light streaming in from the bay window makes this the perfect place to linger with coffee and the Sunday paper.

• Master Suite: This exceptional suite has a sitting area and direct access to the deck, as well as a sitting area, full-featured bath, and spacious walk-in closet.

• Secondary Bedrooms: The other bedrooms each measure about 13 ft. x 11 ft. They have walk-in closets and share a "Jack-and-Jill" bath.

SCREENED PORCH 15'4" x 13'10"

DECK 11'0" x 7'6"

14' CEILING

SITTING

BRKFST 11'0" x 10'10"

MASTER SUITE 21'4" x 15'0"

BEDROOM 3 13'0" x 11'0"

8' HIGH OPENING

KITCHEN 13'8" x 9'6"

LINEN

FAMILY ROOM 16'0" x 24'1"

PANTRY

10' CEILING

OPTIONAL STAIRS TO BASEMENT

LINEN COATS

13'-10" CEILING

DINING 11'0" x 12'0"

57'-2"

9' CEILING

TRAY CEILING

13'-4" CEILING

3 CAR GARAGE 21'4" x 29'10"

BEDROOM 2 13'0" x 11'0"

LIVING 11'0" x 12'0"

PORCH 15'4" x 5'4"

2 CAR GARAGE OPTION

Copyright by designer/architect.

◄ 63'-0' ►

Plan #211038

Dimensions: 72' W x 42' D
Levels: 1
Square Footage: 1,898
Bedrooms: 3
Bathrooms: 2
Foundation: Slab
Materials List Available: Yes
Price Category: D

Images provided by designer/architect.

A railed front porch, a charming cupola, and stylish shutters add classic flair to this home.

Features:

- Ceiling Height: 8 ft. unless otherwise noted.

- Family Room: The welcoming entry flows into this attractive family gathering area. The room features a handsome fireplace and a 14-ft. vaulted ceiling with exposed beams. French doors lead to a backyard patio.

- Formal Dining Room: This elegant room adjoins the living room. You'll usher your guests through a half-wall with decorative spindles.

- Kitchen: Food preparation will be a pleasure working at the wraparound counter.

- Eating Nook: Modern life includes lots of quick, informal meals, and this is the spot to enjoy them. The nook includes a laundry closet, so you can change loads while cooking.

- Master Suite: This private retreat boasts a private bath with a separate dressing area and a roomy walk-in closet.

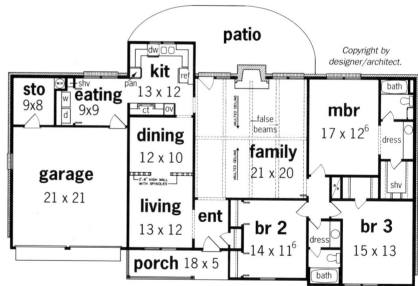

Copyright by designer/architect.

SMARTtip

Efficient Kitchen Appliances

Appliances that carry the **Energy Star** label—a program of the Department of Energy—are significantly more energy efficient than most other appliances. Dishwashers, for example, must be 25 percent more energy efficient than models that meet minimum federal energy requirements. Energy Star refrigerators must be 10 percent more efficient than the newest standards.

Plan #241005

Dimensions: 53' W x 55'9" D
Levels: 1
Square Footage: 1,670
Bedrooms: 3
Bathrooms: 2
Foundation: Slab
Materials List Available: No
Price Category: C

This charming starter home, in split-bedroom format, combines big-house features in a compact design.

Features:

- Great Room: With easy access to the formal dining room, kitchen, and breakfast area, this great room features a cozy fireplace.

- Kitchen: This big kitchen, with easy access to a walk-in pantry, features an island for added work space and a lovely plant shelf that separates it from the great room.

- Master Suite: Separated for privacy, this master suite offers a roomy bath with whirlpool tub, dual vanities, a separate shower, and a large walk-in closet.

- Additional Rooms: Additional rooms include a laundry/utility room—with space for a washer, dryer, and freezer—a large area above the garage, well-suited for a media or game room, and two secondary bedrooms.

Images provided by designer/architect.

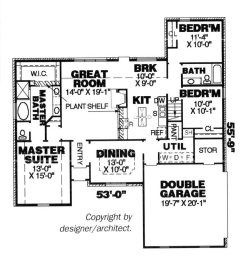

Copyright by designer/architect.

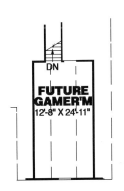

SMARTtip

Window Scarf

The best way to wrap a window scarf around a pole is as follows:

- Lay out the material on a large, clean surface. Gather the fabric at the top of each jabot, and use elastic to hold it together.

- Swing one jabot into place over the pole and, starting from there, wind the swag portion as many times as you need around the pole until you reach the elastic at the second jabot, which should have landed at the opposite pole end.

- Readjust wraps along the pole. Generally, wrapped swags just touch or slightly overlap.

- For a dramatic effect, stuff the wrapped swags with tissue paper or thin foam, depending on the translucence and weight of fabric.

- Release elastics at tops of jabots.

Plan #321004

Dimensions: 91'8" W x 62'4" D
Levels: 1
Square Footage: 2,808
Bedrooms: 3
Bathrooms: 2½
Foundation: Basement
Materials List Available: Yes
Price Category: F

Images provided by designer/architect.

You'll love the sophistication of this design, with its three porches and elegance at every turn.

Features:

- Entry: This impressive space welcomes guests into the living room on one side and the dining room on the other.

- Living Room: This spacious room will be a family favorite, especially in warm weather when you can use the adjoining porch as an outdoor extension of this area.

- Dining Room: Decorate this room to highlight its slightly formal feeling or to create a more casual ambiance for large family dinners.

- Kitchen: The family cooks will appreciate the thought that went into designing the convenient counter space and generous storage areas here.

- Master Suite: A vaulted ceiling, bath with a corner tub, double vanities, walk-in closet, and secluded screened porch make this area a joy.

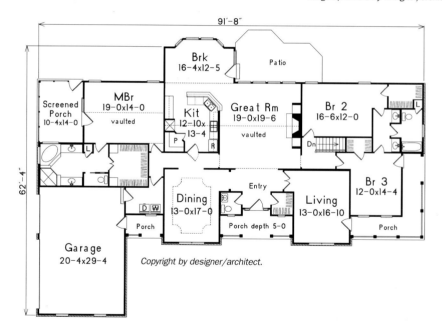

Copyright by designer/architect.

SMARTtip

Ornaments in a Garden

Placement is everything with ornaments in a garden. Some elements are best sitting by themselves. Others are better when they are part of a cohesive whole, perhaps placed in the greenery at a corner or flanking a structure.

Plan #131012

Dimensions: 71'4" W x 35'10" D
Levels: 1
Square Footage: 1,366
Bedrooms: 3
Bathrooms: 2
Foundation: Basement, crawl space, or slab
Materials List Available: Yes
Price Category: C

You're sure to love this home, with its covered front porch and gabled roofline.

Features:

- Entry: The 11-ft. ceiling height makes an impressive entryway.

- Living Room: A pair of French doors frames the fireplace in this room, and a central sky light provides natural lighting during the day and drama at night.

- Dining Room: Open to the living room, this area also features an 11-ft.-high ceiling.

- Kitchen: A laundry closet, ample counter space, and dinette opening to the expansive backyard terrace add up to convenience in this room.

- Master Suite: Enjoy the dressing area, two closets, and bath with whirlpool tub and shower.

- Additional Bedrooms: An arched window and 11-ft. ceiling mark the larger of these two rooms.

Images provided by designer/architect.

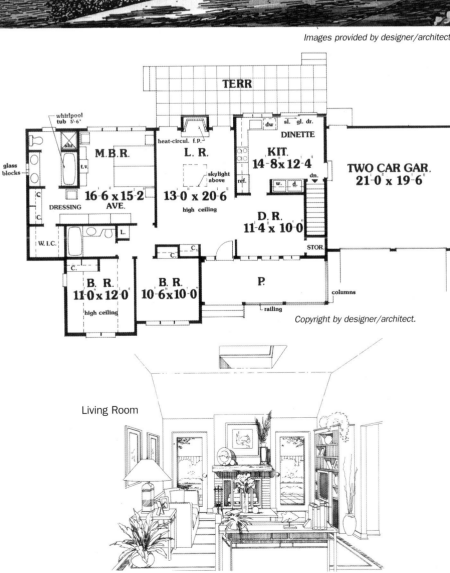

Copyright by designer/architect.

Living Room

Plan #141007

Dimensions: 65' W x 56'5" D
Levels: 1
Square Footage: 1,854
Bedrooms: 3
Bathrooms: 2½
Foundation: Basement
Materials List Available: No
Price Category: D

Images provided by designer/architect.

This home offers a spacious layout, all on one level for convenient modern living.

Features:

- Ceiling Height: 8 ft. unless otherwise noted.

- Dining Room: The 12-ft. ceiling makes this the perfect dining room for the most elegant of dinner parties.

- Living Room: The elegant 12-ft. ceiling continues into this living room. Its handsome fireplace will make it the focal point for all gatherings.

- Kitchen: This well-designed kitchen will make cooking a pleasure. It features a pantry and an island for food preparation.

- Breakfast Area: The breakfast area is just off the kitchen. Measuring 11 ft. x 11 ft., it offers plenty of room for the whole family to enjoy informal meals.

- Master Suite: Located away from the other bedrooms, this luxurious retreat has a tray ceiling. The master bath has separate vanities, a jet tub, and a separate shower.

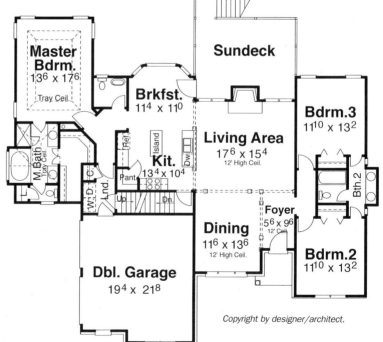

Copyright by designer/architect.

SMARTtip

Painting Walls

Paint won't hide imperfections. Rather, it will make them stand out. So shine a bright light at a low angle across the surface to spot problem areas before painting.

Plan #161005

Dimensions: 60' W x 48'10" D

Levels: 1

Square Footage: 1,593

Bedrooms: 3

Bathrooms: 2

Foundation: Basement

Materials List Available: Yes

Price Category: C

This delightful ranch home includes many thoughtful conveniences and a full basement to expand your living enjoyment.

Features:

- Great Room: Take pleasure in welcoming guests through a spacious foyer into the warm and friendly confines of this great room with corner fireplace, sloped ceiling, and view to the rear yard.

- Kitchen: Experience the convenience of enjoying meals while seated at the large island that separates the dining area from this well-designed kitchen. Also included is an over-sized pantry with an abundance of storage.

- Master Suite: This master suite features a compartmented bath, large walk-in closet, and master bedroom that has a tray ceiling with 9-ft. center height.

- Porch: Retreat to this delightful rear porch to enjoy a relaxing evening.

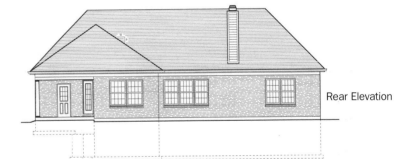

Rear Elevation

Copyright by designer/architect.

Plan #311005

Dimensions: 87' W x 57'3" D

Levels: 1

Square Footage: 2,497

Bedrooms: 3

Bathrooms: 3½

Foundation: Crawl space, slab

Materials List Available: Yes

Price Category: E

Images provided by designer/architect.

You'll love this home, which mixes practical features with a gracious appearance.

Features:

- Great Room: A handsome fireplace and flanking windows that give a view of the back patio are the highlights of this gracious room.

- Kitchen: A curved bar defines the perimeter of this well-planned kitchen.

- Breakfast Room: Open to both the great room and the kitchen, this sunny spot leads to the rear porch, which in turn, leads to the patio beyond.

- Master Suite: Vaulted ceilings, a huge walk-in closet, and deluxe bath create luxury here.

- Bonus Room: Finish this 966-sq.-ft. area as a huge game room, or divide it into a game room, study, and sewing or craft room.

- Additional Bedrooms: Each bedroom has a private bath and good closet space.

Main Level Floor Plan

Copyright by designer/architect.

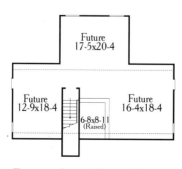

Bonus Area Floor Plan

SMARTtip

Front Porch

A front porch proclaims you to the outside world, so furnish it in a way that expresses what you want the world to know about you. Use the walls of your porch to hang interesting items such as sundials or old shutters. Set a mirror into an old window to reflect a portion of the garden.

Plan #271001

Dimensions: 55' W x 36' D
Levels: 1
Square Footage: 1,400
Bedrooms: 3
Bathrooms: 2
Foundation: Basement
Materials List Available: Yes
Price Category: B

Images provided by designer/architect.

Master Br
15-4x11

Great
Room
16-8x19

Dining

Kitchen/
Brkfst
13-8x12-8

Deck

Bar

dn

Garage
19-4x19-4

Den/Br 3
11-4x12-4

Br 2
11x10

35'-4"

52'-8"

Copyright by designer/architect.

This contemporary design builds on the basics, creating a comfortable home that offers possibilities for entertaining or quiet downtime.

Features:

- Great room: The heart of the home, this massive gathering room features a handsome fireplace and a handy wet bar, and flows into the dining space. Sliding glass doors between the two spaces lead to a deck.

- Kitchen/Breakfast: This combination space uses available space efficiently and comfortably.

- Master Suite: The inviting master bedroom includes a private bath.

SMARTtip

Candid Camera for Your Landscaping

To see your home and yard as others see them, take some camera shots. Seeing your house and landscaping on film will create an opportunity for objectivity. Problems will become more obvious, and you will then be better able to prioritize your home improvements, as well as your landscaping plan.

Plan #221008

Dimensions: 60'4" W x 46' D

Levels: 1

Square Footage: 1,540

Bedrooms: 3

Bathrooms: 2

Foundation: Basement

Materials List Available: Yes

Price Category: C

You'll love the well-designed interior of this traditional-looking ranch.

Features:

• Ceiling Height: 9 ft.

• Entry: This vaulted entry leads to the living room and includes a coat closet for convenience.

• Living Room: The highlights of this spacious room are the direct-vent gas fireplace in the corner and the large windows looking out to the backyard.

• Dining Room: Adjacent to the kitchen, this lovely room opens to a large screened porch where you'll love to entertain.

• Kitchen: A corner sink gives this well-designed kitchen a nice touch, and the breakfast bar it shares with the dining room adds convenience.

• Master Suite: A large walk-in closet and windows looking into the backyard give practicality to the bedroom, and the full private bath adds a note of luxury.

Images provided by designer/architect.

Rear Elevation

Copyright by designer/architect.

Plan #101006

Dimensions: 63' W x 58' D
Levels: 1
Square Footage: 1,982
Bedrooms: 3
Bathrooms: 2½
Foundation: Slab, crawl space, or basement
Materials List Available: Yes
Price Category: D

Radius-top windows and siding accented with wood shingles give this home a distinctive look.

Features:

- Ceiling Height: 9 ft. unless otherwise noted.

- Family Room: This room is perfect for all kinds of informal family activities. A vaulted ceiling adds to its sense of spaciousness.

- Dining Room: This room, with its tray ceiling, is designed for elegant dining.

- Porch: When the weather gets warm, you'll enjoy stepping out onto this large screened porch to catch a breeze.

- Master Suite: You'll love ending your day and getting up in the morning to this exquisite master suite, with its vaulted ceiling, sitting area, and large walk-in closet.

- Bonus Room: Just off the kitchen are stairs leading to this enormous bonus room, offering more than 330 sq. ft. of future expansion space.

Images provided by designer/architect.

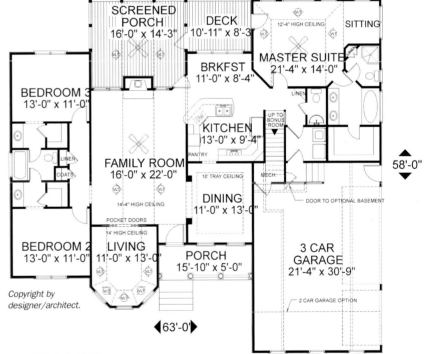

Copyright by designer/architect.

SMARTtip

Art in Pools

The tiled walls and floor of a pool make great canvases for art, so incorporate a serious or whimsical design. Also, make the stairs wide and shallow to form a wading area for kids.

Plan #211044

Dimensions: 70' W x 48' D

Levels: 1

Square Footage: 1,997

Bedrooms: 4

Bathrooms: 2½

Foundation: Slab

Materials List Available: Yes

Price Category: D

Images provided by designer/architect.

Interior angles add a touch of architectural excitement to this traditional home.

Features:

• Ceiling Height: 8 ft. unless otherwise noted.

• Wood-and-Stone Facade: This pleasantly charming exterior combines wood siding with stone to give the home a solid, comfortable look that fits into any neighborhood.

• Foyer: This entry is flanked by a formal living room and formal dining room.

• Dining Room: This formal room is designed to accommodate dinner parties of all sizes.

• Family Room: Accessible from the entry, this large living room will become the focal point of all informal gatherings. The 19-ft. vaulted ceiling adds plenty of drama, while the handsome fireplace and built-in bookshelves ensure that the room is still warm and cozy.

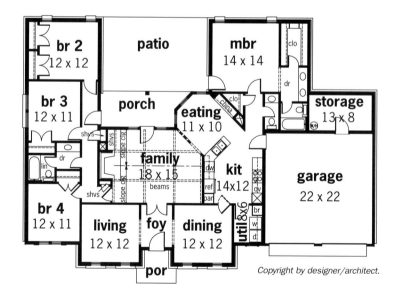

Copyright by designer/architect.

SMARTtip

Lubricating Window Tracks and Hinges

No one appreciates windows and doors that stick, especially in the winter, when energy losses from a window that won't shut properly can become expensive quickly. Use a lubricant on all hinges and window tracks to keep them operating smoothly and efficiently all year long.

Plan #241006

Dimensions: 51' W x 53' D

Levels: 1

Square Footage: 1,744

Bedrooms: 3

Bathrooms: 2

Foundation: Slab

Materials List Available: No

Price Category: C

The striking rooflines and arched window of this split-bedroom home will captivate onlookers and guests.

Features:

- Great Room: A spacious foyer introduces this great room, which features a cozy corner fireplace. Guests will enjoy a natural flow through a columned entry to the formal dining room or through a French door to the rear yard.

- Kitchen: Designed for total convenience, this kitchen features ample counter space, an eating bar, a pantry, and a roomy breakfast area. A 42-in.-high wall separating it from the dining room maximizes the openness of the kitchen.

- Master Suite: You will enjoy the comfort and privacy of this master suite, which features a whirlpool tub, dual vanities, a corner glass shower, and a large walk-in closet.

- Additional Bedrooms: Two secondary bedrooms share a common bath.

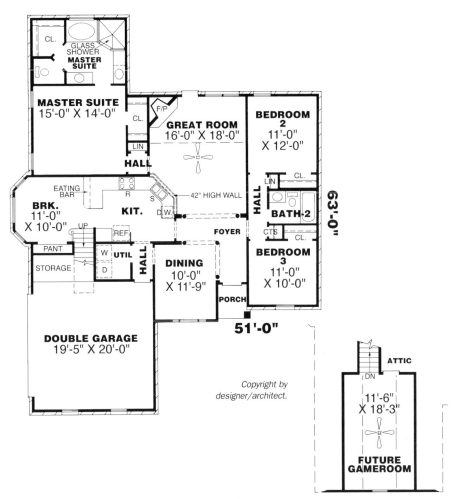

Plan #321005

Dimensions: 69' W x 53'8" D
Levels: 1
Square Footage: 2,483
Bedrooms: 4
Bathrooms: 2
Foundation: Basement
Materials List Available: Yes
Price Category: E

You'll love the grand feeling of this home, which combines with the very practical features that make living in it a pleasure.

Features:

- **Porch:** The open brick arches and Palladian door set the tone for this magnificent home.

- **Great Room:** An alcove for the entertainment center and vaulted ceiling show the care that went into designing this room.

- **Dining Room:** A tray ceiling sets off the formality of this large room.

- **Kitchen:** The layout in this room is designed to make your work patterns more efficient and to save you steps and time.

- **Study:** This quiet room can be a wonderful refuge, or you can use it for a fourth bedroom if you wish.

- **Master Suite:** Made for relaxing at the end of the day, this suite will pamper you with luxuries.

Images provided by designer/architect.

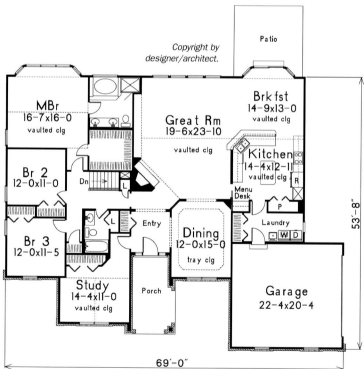

Copyright by designer/architect.

SMARTtip

Art in Pools

The tiled walls and floor of a pool make great canvases for art, so incorporate a serious or whimsical design. Also, make the stairs wide and shallow to form a wading area for kids.

Plan #131014

Dimensions: 48' W x 43'4" D
Levels: 1
Square Footage: 1,380
Bedrooms: 3
Bathrooms: 2
Foundation: Basement, crawl space, or slab
Materials List Available: Yes
Price Category: C

The exterior of this home looks formal, thanks to its twin dormers, gables, and the bay windows that flank the columned porch, but the inside is contemporary in both design and features.

Features:

- Great Room: Centrally located, this great room has a 10-ft. ceiling. A fireplace, built-in cabinets, and windows that overlook the rear covered porch make it as practical as it is attractive.

- Dining Room: A bay window adds to the charm of this versatile room.

- Kitchen: This U-shaped room is designed to make cooking and cleaning jobs efficient.

- Master Suite: With a bay window, a walk-in closet, and a private bath with an oval tub, the master suite may be your favorite area.

- Additional Bedrooms: Located on the opposite side of the house from the master suite, these rooms share a full bath in the hall.

Images provided by designer/architect.

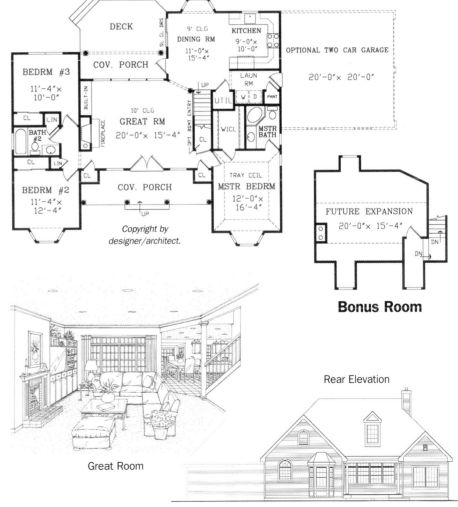

Copyright by designer/architect.

Bonus Room

Rear Elevation

Great Room

Plan #141011

Dimensions: 54' W x 60'6" D

Levels: 1

Square Footage: 1,869

Bedrooms: 3

Bathrooms: 2

Foundation: Basement, crawl space, or slab

Materials List Available: Yes

Price Category: D

The blending of brick and stone on this plan gives the home an old-world appeal.

Features:

- Ceiling Height: 8 ft. unless otherwise noted.

- Tall Ceilings: The main living areas feature dramatic 12-ft. ceilings.

- Open Plan: This home's open floor plan maximizes the use of space and makes it flexible. This main living area has plenty of room for large gatherings.

- Kitchen: The kitchen is integrated into the main living area. It features a breakfast room that is ideal for informal family meals.

- Master Suite: You'll enjoy unwinding at the end of the day in this luxurious space. It's located away from the rest of the house for maximum privacy.

- Secondary Bedrooms: You have the option of adding extra style to the secondary bedrooms by including volume ceilings.

Images provided by designer/architect.

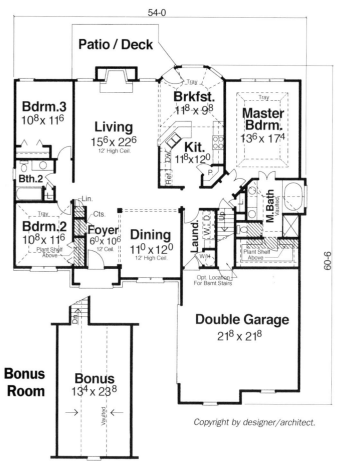

Copyright by designer/architect.

Plan #161006

Dimensions: 78'6" W x 47'7" D
Levels: 1
Square Footage: 1,755
Bedrooms: 3
Bathrooms: 2
Foundation: Basement
Materials List Available: Yes
Price Category: C

This enchanting, family-friendly home combines a solid brick exterior with an arched window, front porch, and three-car garage.

Features:

- **Great Room:** The 10-ft. ceiling complements the grand first impression created by the warm and friendly fireplace, which is flanked by matching French doors.

- **Kitchen:** In this functional kitchen, you can enjoy sitting at the bar or in the spacious dining area, with its angled bay and view of a delightful rear porch.

- **Master Bedroom:** Whether beginning your day or relaxing at its end, enjoy the comfort and luxury of the lavishly equipped bath and large walk-in closet.

- **Additional Bedrooms:** A full bath is easily accessible from both rooms which feature ample closet space.

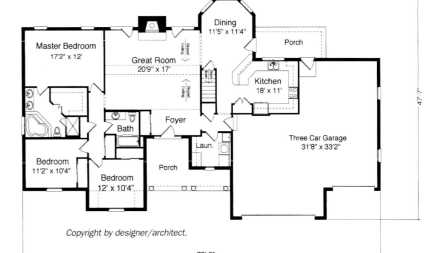

Copyright by designer/architect.

Rear Elevation

Plan #151005

Dimensions: 58' W x 54'10" D
Levels: 1
Square Footage: 1,940
Bedrooms: 4
Bathrooms: 2
Foundation: Basement, crawl space, or slab
Materials List Available: Yes
Price Category: D

Images provided by designer/architect.

A covered front porch with stately 10-in. round columns and a classically-styled foyer invite family and guests into this well-designed, traditional 4-bedroom home.

Features:

- Great Room: The 9-ft. boxed-ceiling, radiant fireplace, and built-in shelving add up to create a cozy and practical room where friends and family will love to gather.

- Dining Room: Open access from this dining room to the kitchen, and from there to the breakfast room, makes this room an ideal place for entertaining.

- Master Suite: This luxuriously appointed suite, with a 9-ft. pan ceiling in the bedroom, is located just of the breakfast room. The spectacular bath is fitted with a whirlpool tub, separate shower, and double vanities.

- Bedrooms 2 and 3: Large walk-in closets make these rooms easy to organize and keep tidy.

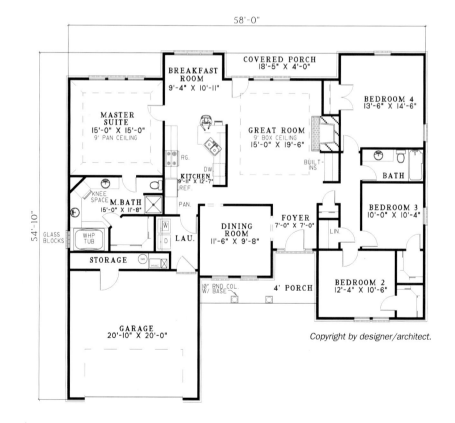

Copyright by designer/architect.

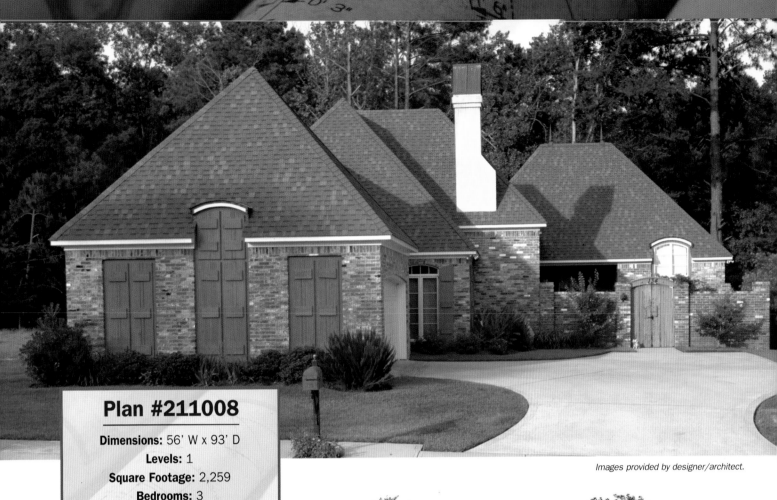

Plan #211008

Dimensions: 56' W x 93' D

Levels: 1

Square Footage: 2,259

Bedrooms: 3

Bathrooms: 2½

Foundation: Slab

Materials List Available: Yes

Price Category: E

Images provided by designer/architect.

If you're looking for a design that suits a narrow building lot, you'll love this home, with its exterior that resembles an old European cottage.

Features:

- Ceiling Height: 10-ft. except as noted.

- Courtyards: Use formal gardens full of easy-care plants to make the most of the lovely courtyards.

- Living Room: The massive glass wall in this room with 16-ft. ceilings looks out to the entry courtyard. In cool weather you'll love the fireplace, which is flanked by lovely built-ins that can hold everything from books to collectables.

- Kitchen: With a contemporary layout and up-to-date conveniences, this kitchen is as convenient as it is attractive.

- Master Suite: Relax beside the bedroom fireplace, or luxuriate in the bath, with its two walk-in closets, soaking tub, shower, two vanities, linen closet, and private room for toilet and bidet.

Copyright by designer/architect.

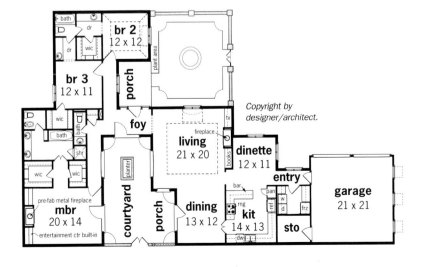

Plan #221009

Dimensions: 68' W x 59' D

Levels: 1

Square Footage: 1,795

Bedrooms: 3

Bathrooms: 2

Foundation: Basement

Materials List Available: No

Price Category: C

Images provided by designer/architect.

Rear Elevation

If your family likes the spaciousness and convenience of an open floor plan, they'll love this ranch-style home.

Features:

- **Ceiling Height:** 9 ft.

- **Entry:** From this lovely entryway, with its convenient coat closet, openings into both the great room and the dining room give you a glimpse of the home's open design.

- **Living Room:** A fireplace in this living room is flanked by windows that look out to the back.

- **Dining Room:** The highlight of this area is the door to the screened-in porch, where you'll love to serve meals in fine weather.

- **Kitchen:** Merging with the dining room, this well-designed kitchen is a delight for any cook. An island provides extra counter space, and you'll have the corner pantry for a generous storage area.

- **Master Suite:** Enjoy the walk-in closet and the bath with whirlpool tub and double sinks.

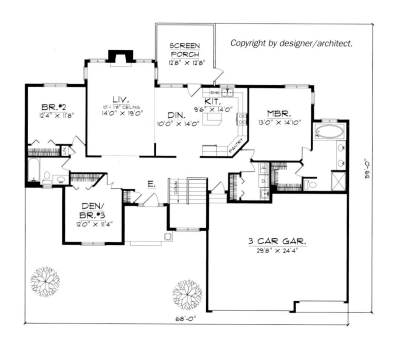

Copyright by designer/architect.

Plan #101008

Dimensions: 67'8" W x 52'6" D
Levels: 1
Square Footage: 2,088
Bedrooms: 3
Bathrooms: 2 ½
Foundation: Slab, crawl space, or basement
Materials List Available: Yes
Price Category: D

This ranch sports an attractive brick-and-stucco exterior accented with quoins and layered trim.

Features:

- Ceiling Height: 11 ft. unless otherwise noted.

- Kitchen: You'll love cooking in this bright, airy kitchen, which is lit by an abundance of windows.

- Breakfast room: Off the kitchen is this breakfast room, the perfect spot for informal family meals.

- Master Suite: You'll look forward to retiring at the end of the day to this truly exceptional master suite, with its grand bath, spacious walk-in closet, and direct access to the porch.

- Morning Porch: Greet the day with your first cup of coffee on this porch, which is accessible from the master suite.

- Secondary Bedrooms: These bedrooms measure a generous 11 ft. x 14 ft. They share a compartmented bath.

Images provided by designer/architect.

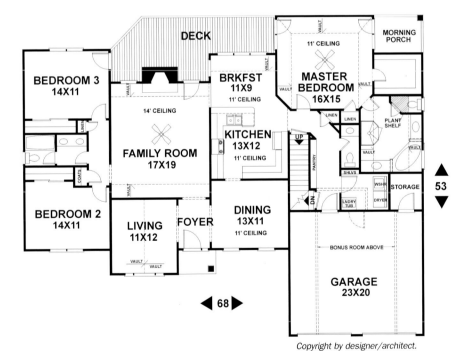

Copyright by designer/architect.

SMARTtip

Accentuating Your Bathroom with Details

No matter how big or small the room, details will pull the style together. Some of the best details that you can include are the smallest—drawer pulls from an antique store or shells in a glass jar or just left on the countertop. Add period flavor with crown molding, or dress up contemporary fixtures with polished stone fittings.

Plan #211054

Dimensions: 80' W x 62' D
Levels: 1
Square Footage: 2,358
Bedrooms: 3
Bathrooms: 2½
Foundation: Slab
Materials List Available: Yes
Price Category: E

Images provided by designer/architect.

This ranch has a low-maintenance exterior of brick combined with board-and-batten siding.

Features:

• Ceiling Height: 8 ft. unless otherwise noted.

• Foyer: Guests will be greeted by a view of the living room when they step into this inviting entry area.

• Living Room: There's plenty of room for all kinds of entertaining in this generously sized living room. The room seems even more spacious, thanks to the vaulted and beamed ceiling and the built-ins, which maximize the use of floor space. When you entertain, you can gather around the handsome brick fireplace and fix your guests a drink from the small wet bar that is tucked behind the bi-fold doors.

• Game Room: The kids will love this super-sized game room located just behind the living room. It features a volume ceiling and lots of built-ins.

• Garage: In addition to parking for two cars, you will find lots of extra storage space in this attached garage.

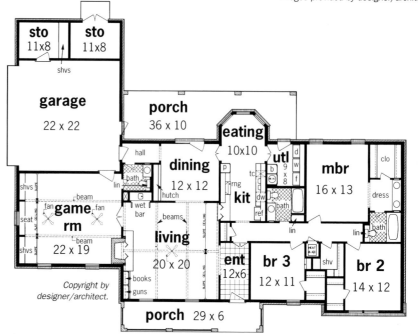

Copyright by designer/architect.

SMARTtip

Dressing Up a Simple Fireplace

Painting a wood surround with a faux marble or faux bois (wood) is inexpensive. Adding a simple, prefabricated wooden shelf mantel can add lots of architectural character.

Plan #241008

Dimensions: 65' W x 56'8" D
Levels: 1
Square Footage: 2,526
Bedrooms: 4
Bathrooms: 3
Foundation: Slab
Materials List Available: No
Price Category: E

A covered back porch—with access from the master suite and the breakfast area—makes this traditional home ideal for siting near a golf course or with a backyard pool.

Features:

- Great Room: From the foyer, guests enter this spacious and comfortable great room, which features a handsome fireplace.

- Kitchen: This kitchen—the hub of this family-oriented home—is a joy in which to work, thanks to abundant counter space, a pantry, a convenient eating bar, and an adjoining breakfast area and sunroom.

- Master Suite: Enjoy the quiet comfort of this coffered-ceiling master suite, which features dual vanities and separate walk-in closets.

- Additional Bedrooms: Two secondary bedrooms, which share a full bath, are located at the opposite end of the house from the master suite. Bedroom 4—in front of the house—can be converted into a study.

Images provided by designer/architect.

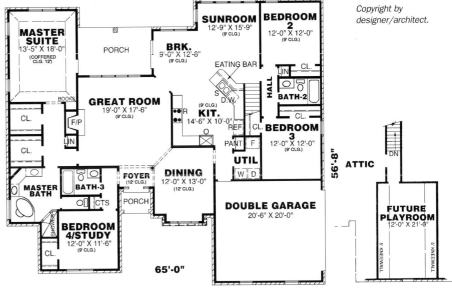

Copyright by designer/architect.

SMARTtip

Traditional-Style Kitchen Cabinetry

You can modify stock kitchen cabinetry to enjoy fine furniture-quality details. Prefabricated trims may be purchased at local lumber mills and home centers. For example, crown molding, applied to the top of stock cabinetry and stained or painted to match the door style, may be all you need. Likewise, you can replace hardware with reproduction polished-brass door and drawer knobs or pulls for a finishing touch.

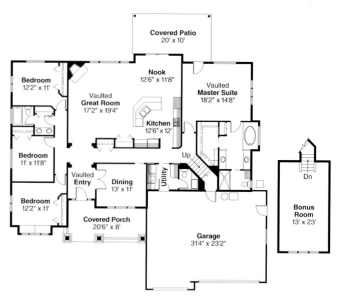

Plan #361005

Dimensions: 68' W x 71' D

Levels: 1

Square Footage: 2,759

Bedrooms: 4

Bathrooms: 2½

Foundation: Crawl space

Materials List Available: No

Price Category: F

Images provided by designer/architect.

Copyright by designer/architect.

Covered Patio 20' x 10'

Bedroom 12'2" x 11'

Nook 12'6" x 11'8"

Vaulted Master Suite 18'2" x 14'8"

Vaulted Great Room 17'2" x 19'4"

Kitchen 12'6" x 12'

Bedroom 11' x 11'8"

Up

Dn

Vaulted Entry

Dining 13' x 11'

Utility

Bonus Room 13' x 23'

Bedroom 12'2" x 11'

Covered Porch 20'6" x 8'

Garage 31'4" x 23'2"

Plan #361006

Dimensions: 70' W x 62' D

Levels: 1

Square Footage: 2,274

Bedrooms: 3

Bathrooms: 2½

Foundation: Crawl space, basement

Materials List Available: No

Price Category: E

Images provided by designer/architect.

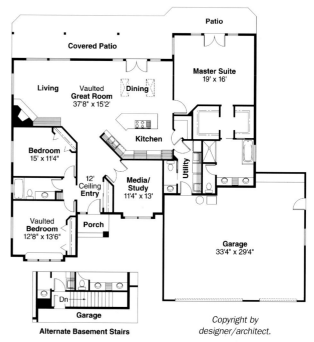

Patio

Covered Patio

Living

Vaulted Great Room 37'8" x 15'2"

Dining

Master Suite 19' x 16'

Kitchen

Bedroom 15' x 11'4"

12' Ceiling Entry

Media/ Study 11'4" x 13'

Utility

Vaulted Bedroom 12'8" x 13'6"

Porch

Garage 33'4" x 29'4"

Dn

Garage

Alternate Basement Stairs

Copyright by designer/architect.

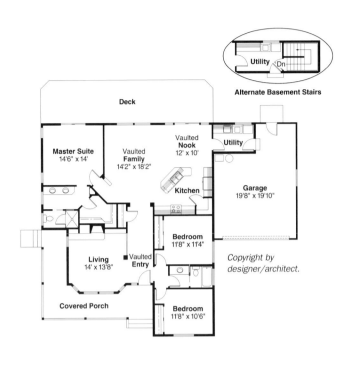

Deck

Utility | Dn

Alternate Basement Stairs

Master Suite
14'6" x 14'

Vaulted
Family
14'2" x 18'2"

Vaulted
Nook
12' x 10'

Utility

Garage
19'8" x 19'10"

Kitchen

Living
14' x 13'8"

Vaulted
Entry

Bedroom
11'8" x 11'4"

Covered Porch

Bedroom
11'8" x 10'6"

Copyright by designer/architect.

Plan #361002

Dimensions: 62' W x 50' D

Levels: 1

Square Footage: 1,794

Bedrooms: 3

Bathrooms: 2

Foundation: Crawl space, basement

Materials List Available: No

Price Category: C

Images provided by designer/architect.

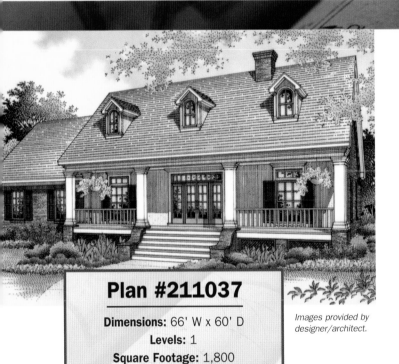

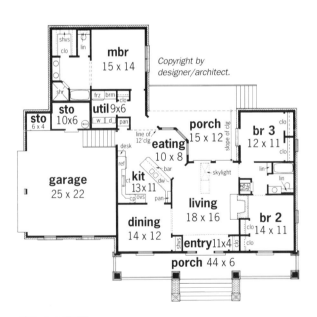

Copyright by designer/architect.

mbr
15 x 14

sto
10x6

sto
6 x 4

util 9x6

garage
25 x 22

porch
15 x 12

eating
10 x 8

kit
13 x 11

dining
14 x 12

living
18 x 16

skylight

br 3
12 x 11

br 2
14 x 11

entry 11x4

porch 44 x 6

Plan #211037

Dimensions: 66' W x 60' D

Levels: 1

Square Footage: 1,800

Bedrooms: 3

Bathrooms: 2

Foundation: Crawl space

Materials List Available: Yes

Price Category: D

Images provided by designer/architect.

SMARTtip

Reflected Light in the Bathroom

The addition of a large mirror can bring reflected light into a small bathroom, adding the illusion of space without the expense of renovation.

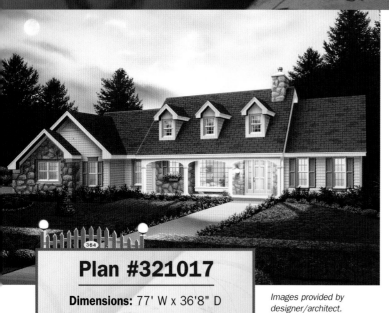

Rear View

Plan #321017

Dimensions: 77' W x 36'8" D

Levels: 1

Square Footage: 2,531

Bedrooms: 1-4

Bathrooms: 1-2½

Foundation: Daylight basement

Materials List Available: Yes

Price Category: E

Images provided by designer/architect.

Optional Basement Level Floor Plan

Copyright by designer/architect.

Plan #321018

Dimensions: 88'4" W x 48'4" D

Levels: 1

Square Footage: 2,523

Bedrooms: 3

Bathrooms: 2

Foundation: Basement

Materials List Available: Yes

Price Category: E

Images provided by designer/architect.

Copyright by designer/architect.

SMARTtip

Tiebacks

You don't have to limit yourself to tiebacks made from matching or contrasting fabric. Achieve creative custom looks by making tiebacks from unexpected items. Some materials to consider are old cotton bandannas or silk scarves, strings of beads, lengths of leather, or old belts and chains.

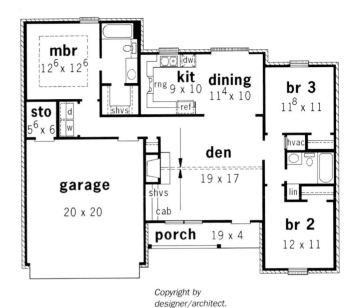

Plan #201016

Dimensions: 51'10" W x 40'4" D

Levels: 1

Square Footage: 1,293

Bedrooms: 3

Bathrooms: 2

Foundation: Crawl space, slab, or basement

Materials List Available: Yes

Price Category: B

mbr
12^6 x 12^6

sto
5^6 x 6

d
w

kit
9 x 10

dining
11^4 x 10

br 3
11^8 x 11

garage
20 x 20

den
19 x 17

shvs
cab

hvac

lin

porch   19 x 4

br 2
12 x 11

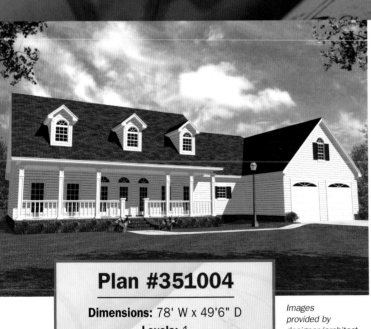

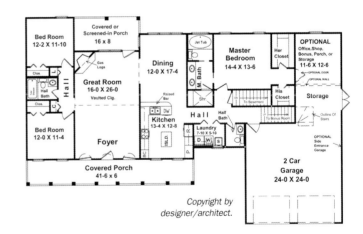

Bed Room
12-2 X 11-10

Covered or Screened-in Porch
16 x 8

Dining
12-0 X 17-4

Master Bedroom
14-4 X 13-6

Her Closet

OPTIONAL
Office, Shop, Bonus, Porch, or Storage
11-6 X 12-6

Great Room
16-0 X 26-0
Vaulted Clg.

Bed Room
12-0 X 11-4

Foyer

Kitchen
13-4 X 12-8

Hall

Laundry
7-10 X 5-10

His Closet

Storage

2 Car Garage
24-0 X 24-0

Covered Porch
41-6 X 6

Plan #351004

Dimensions: 78' W x 49'6" D

Levels: 1

Square Footage: 1,852

Bedrooms: 3

Bathrooms: 2½

Foundation: Crawl space, slab, or basement

Materials List Available: Yes

Price Category: D

Rear Elevation

Bonus Room

FUTURE HALF BATH

FUTURE BONUS ROOM
14-8 x 24

Plan #321006

Dimensions: 76' W x 45' D

Levels: 1, optional lower

Square Footage: 1,977

Optional Basement Level Sq. Ft.: 1,416

Bedrooms: 4

Bathrooms: 2½

Foundation: Basement

Materials List Available: Yes

Price Category: D

Images provided by designer/architect.

This design is ideal if you're looking for a home with space to finish as your family and your budget grow.

Features:

- Great Room: A vaulted ceiling in this room sets an elegant tone that the gorgeous atrium windows pick up and amplify.

- Atrium: Elegance marks the staircase here that leads to the optional lower level.

- Kitchen: Both experienced cooks and beginners will appreciate the care that went into the design of this step-saving kitchen, with its ample counter space and generous cabinets.

- Master Suite: Enjoy the luxuries you'll find in this suite, and revel in the quiet that the bedroom can provide.

- Lower Level: Finish the 1,416 sq. ft. here to create a family room, two bedrooms, two bathrooms, and a study.

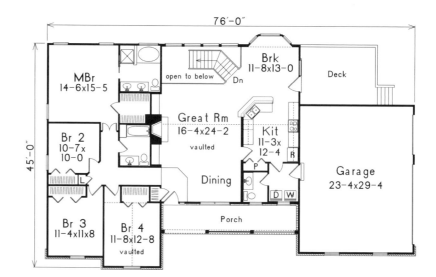

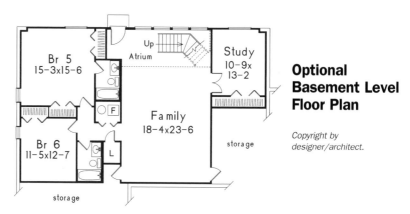

Optional Basement Level Floor Plan

Copyright by designer/architect.

Plan #131018

Dimensions: 66'4" W x 30'4" D
Levels: 1
Square Footage: 1,243
Bedrooms: 3
Bathrooms: 2
Foundation: Basement, crawl space, or slab
Materials List Available: Yes
Price Category: C

Images provided by designer/architect.

If you're looking for an easy-care home that makes your family and your guests feel welcome, this charming ranch will delight you.

Features:

- **Living Room:** Everyone will gravitate to this central area, not only because of its location but also because it forms the hub of this home.

- **Dining Room:** Flowing from the living room, this dining room is large enough for a crowd but cozy enough for intimate dinners.

- **Kitchen:** This well-designed kitchen is a pleasure in which to work, thanks to the ample counter area and good-sized cabinets. It's also large enough that so you can use it as a second eating area.

- **Laundry Room:** Having a separate space for laundry simplifies this chore.

- **Patio:** Enjoy the large backyard patio at any time of year, but make it a special place to entertain during the warm months.

Copyright by designer/architect.

SMARTtip

Fabric for Outdoor Use

For outdoor furnishings, pick a fabric that contains a fade-resistant coating, particularly if you are using dark colors. Sunlight also weakens fibers, so look for sun-resistant coatings as well. But don't be surprised if outdoor fabrics wear faster than those indoors.

Plan #121002

Dimensions: 42' W x 54' D

Levels: 1

Square Footage: 1,347

Bedrooms: 3

Bathrooms: 2

Foundation: Basement

Materials List Available: Yes

Price Category: B

Images provided by designer/architect.

This home's convenient single level and luxury amenities are a recipe for gracious living.

Features:

- Ceiling Height: 8 ft. except as noted.

- Great Room: The entry enjoys a long view into this great room where a pair of transom-topped windows flanks the fireplace and a 10-ft. ceiling visually expands the space.

- Snack Bar: This special feature adjoins the great room, making it a real plus for informal entertaining, as well as the perfect spot for family get-togethers.

- Kitchen: An island is the centerpiece of this well-designed convenient kitchen that features an island, a door to the backyard, a pantry, and convenient access to the laundry room.

- Master Suite: Located at the back of the home for extra privacy, the master suite feels like its own world. It features a tiered ceiling and sunlit corner whirlpool.

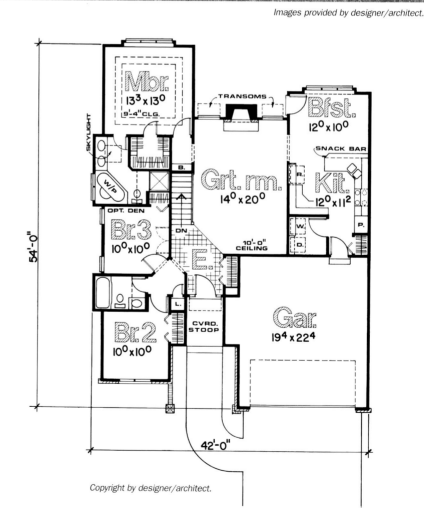

Copyright by designer/architect.

Plan #271002

Dimensions: 45' W x 51' D
Levels: 1
Square Footage: 1,252
Bedrooms: 3
Bathrooms: 2
Foundation: Basement
Materials List Available: Yes
Price Category: B

This traditional home combines a modest square footage with stylish extras.

Features:

- Living Room: Spacious and inviting, this gathering spot is brightened by a Palladian window arrangement, warmed by a fireplace, and topped by a vaulted ceiling.

- Dining Room: The vaulted ceiling also crowns this room, which shares the living room's fireplace. Sliding doors lead to a backyard deck.

- Kitchen: Smart design ensures a place for everything.

- Master Suite: The master bedroom boasts a vaulted ceiling, cheery windows, and a private bath.

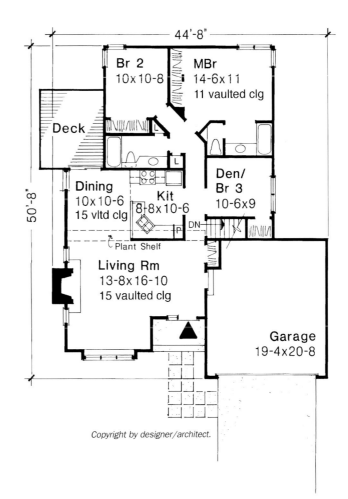

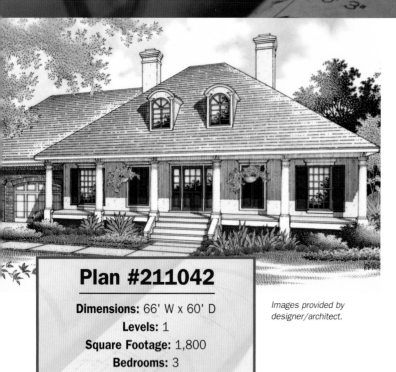

Plan #211042

Dimensions: 66' W x 60' D

Levels: 1

Square Footage: 1,800

Bedrooms: 3

Bathrooms: 2

Foundation: Crawl space

Materials List Available: Yes

Price Category: D

Images provided by designer/architect.

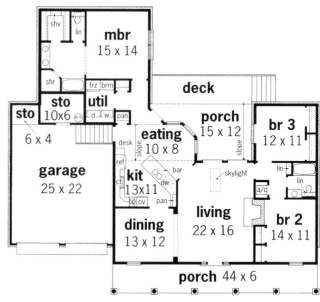

Copyright by designer/architect.

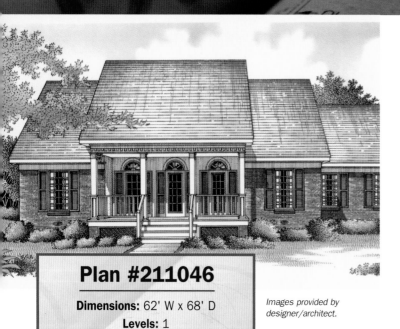

Plan #211046

Dimensions: 62' W x 68' D

Levels: 1

Square Footage: 1,936

Bedrooms: 3

Bathrooms: 2

Foundation: Crawl space

Materials List Available: Yes

Price Category: D

Images provided by designer/architect.

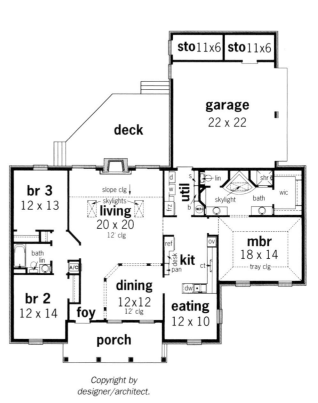

Copyright by designer/architect.

Images provided by designer/architect.

Plan #321020

Dimensions: 58' W x 47'6" D

Levels: 1

Square Footage: 1,882

Bedrooms: 4

Bathrooms: 2

Foundation: Basement

Materials List Available: Yes

Price Category: D

Copyright by designer/architect.

Plan #321021

Dimensions: 80' W x 42' D

Levels: 1

Square Footage: 1,708

Bedrooms: 3

Bathrooms: 2

Foundation: Basement

Materials List Available: Yes

Price Category: C

Images provided by designer/architect.

SMARTtip

Planning a Safe Children's Room

Keep safety in mind when planning a child's room. Make sure that there are covers on electrical outlets, guard rails on high windows, sturdy screens in front of radiators, and gates blocking any steps. Other suggestions include safety hinges for chests and nonskid backing for rugs.

Copyright by designer/architect.

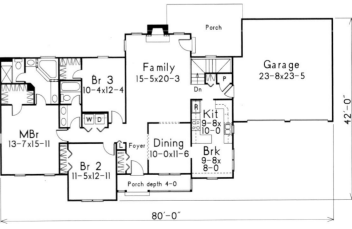

Images provided by designer/architect.

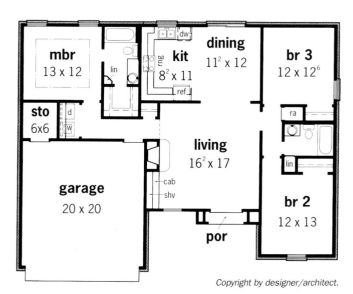

Copyright by designer/architect.

Plan #201023

Dimensions: 67'4" W x 32'10" D
Levels: 1
Square Footage: 1,390
Bedrooms: 3
Bathrooms: 2
Foundation: Crawl space, slab
Materials List Available: Yes
Price Category: B

Images provided by designer/architect.

Plan #201024

Dimensions: 50'10" W x 38'10" D
Levels: 1
Square Footage: 1,324
Bedrooms: 3
Bathrooms: 2
Foundation: Crawl space, slab
Materials List Available: Yes
Price Category: B

Copyright by designer/architect.

Plan #211047

Dimensions: 74'6" W x 50' D

Levels: 1

Square Footage: 2,009

Bedrooms: 3

Bathrooms: 2

Foundation: Slab

Materials List Available: Yes

Price Category: D

Images provided by designer/architect.

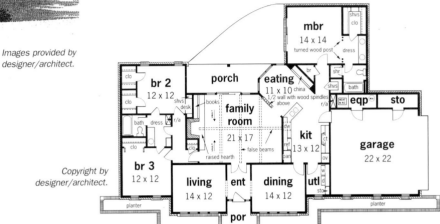

SMARTtip

Saw Setup

If you're using a new saw, it's tempting to plug it in and start cutting. But you should take the time to read the owner's manual, including the safety precautions.

Plan #211051

Dimensions: 58' W x 71' D

Levels: 1

Square Footage: 2,123

Bedrooms: 3

Bathrooms: 2½

Foundation: Crawl space

Materials List Available: Yes

Price Category: D

Images provided by designer/architect.

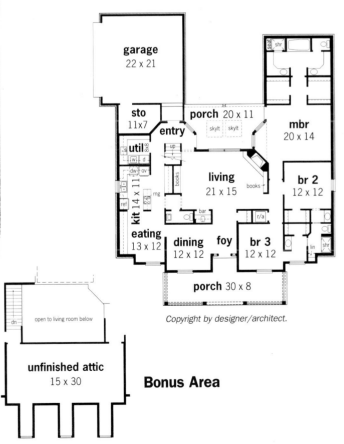

unfinished attic
15 x 30

open to living room below

Bonus Area

Plan #161007

Dimensions: 66'4" W x 43'10" D
Levels: 1
Square Footage: 1,611
Bedrooms: 3
Bathrooms: 2
Foundation: Basement
Materials List Available: Yes
Price Category: C

Images provided by designer/architect.

A lovely front porch and an entry with side-lights invite you to experience the impressive amenities offered in this exceptional ranch home.

Features:

- Great Room: Grand openings, featuring columns from the foyer to this great room and continuing to the bayed dining area, convey an open, spacious feel. The fireplace and matching windows on the rear wall of the great room enhance this effect.

- Kitchen: This well-designed kitchen offers convenient access to the laundry and garage. It also features an angled counter with ample space and an abundance of cabinets.

- Master Suite: This deluxe master suite contains many exciting amenities, including a lavishly appointed dressing room and a large walk-in closet.

- Porch: Sliding doors lead to this delightful screened porch for relaxing summer interludes.

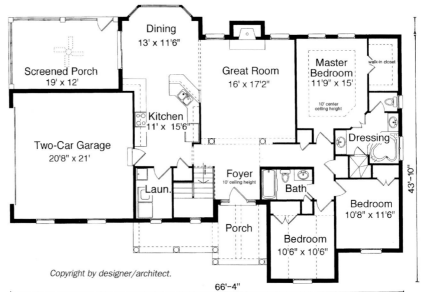

Copyright by designer/architect.

Rear Elevation

Plan #221010

Dimensions: 73' W x 58'8" D

Levels: 1

Square Footage: 2,196

Bedrooms: 3

Bathrooms: 2½

Foundation: Basement

Materials List Available: Yes

Price Category: D

If you've been looking for a plan that combines traditional good looks with contemporary comforts, you'll love this home.

Features:

- Ceiling Height: 8 ft.

- Great Room: A vaulted ceiling speaks elegance, and the handsome fireplace with flanking windows adds warmth and light.

- Dining Room: Near the kitchen, this room is ideal for family meals or formal dining.

- Kitchen: Ample counter and cabinet space will steal the family chef's heart, and the large nook with a door to the huge screened porch will be everybody's favorite gathering spot.

- Master Suite: You'll love the walk-in closet and the luxurious private bath with its whirlpool tub.

- Garage: This three-car garage has plenty of extra space for storage.

- Laundry Room: You'll find everything you'll need in this work space.

Rear Elevation

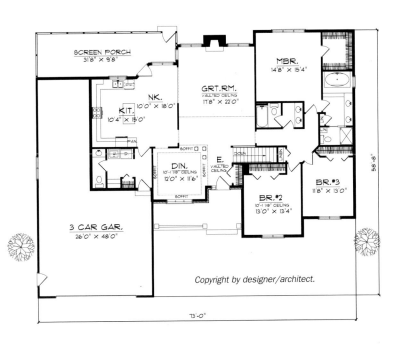

Plan #101009

Dimensions: 70'2" W x 59' D

Levels: 1

Square Footage: 2,097

Bedrooms: 3

Bathrooms: 3

Foundation: Slab

Materials List Available: No

Price Category: D

Round columns enhance this country porch design, which will nestle into any neighborhood.

Features:

• Ceiling Height: 9 ft. unless otherwise noted.

• Family Room: This large family room seems even more spacious, thanks to the vaulted ceiling. It's the perfect spot for all kinds of family activities.

• Dining Room: This elegant dining room is adorned with a decorative round column and a tray ceiling.

• Kitchen: You'll love the convenience of this enormous 14-ft.-3-in. x 22-ft.-6-in. country kitchen, which is open to the living room.

• Screened Porch: A French door leads to this breezy porch, with its vaulted ceiling.

• Master Suite: This sumptuous suite includes a double tray ceiling, a sitting area, a large walk-in closet, and a luxurious bath.

• Patio or Deck: This area is accessible from both the screened porch and master bedroom.

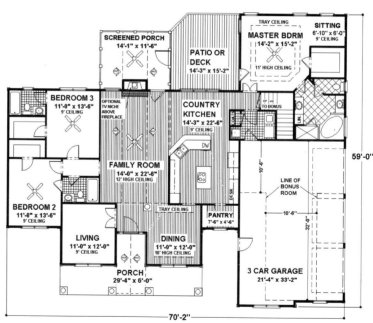

Copyright by designer/architect.

SMARTtip

Single-Level Decks

A single-level deck can use a strong vertical element, such as a pergola or a gazebo, to make it interesting. A simple and less-expensive option is a potted conical shrub or a clematis growing on a trellis.

Plan #211055

Dimensions: 88' W x 64' D

Levels: 1

Square Footage: 2,394

Bedrooms: 3

Bathrooms: 2

Foundation: Crawl space

Materials List Available: Yes

Price Category: E

Images provided by designer/architect.

Except for the porch areas, this traditional design is finished with a no-maintenance brick veneer.

Features:

- Ceiling Height: 8 ft.

- Living Room: There is plenty of space for entertaining and family activities in this well-designed open living room.

- Formal Parlor: This traditional parlor is open to the living area, or alternately, it can be used as a bedroom by relocating the door to the hall.

- Kitchen: This smartly designed kitchen is set at an angle to take advantage of the rear views. It's open to the bay eating area and the living room, so the cook won't be isolated from the festivities.

- Eating Area: This eating area is perfect for entertaining and family meals.

- Master Suite: Featuring private access to the rear porch, this luxurious retreat has its own sitting area and a plush bath with twin giant walk-in closets and a quarter-circle whirlpool.

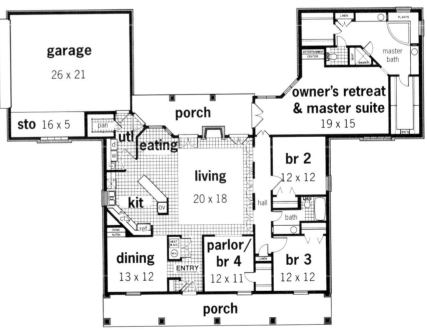

Copyright by designer/architect.

Plan #321007

Dimensions: 76' W x 55'2" D
Levels: 1
Square Footage: 2,695
Bedrooms: 3
Bathrooms: 2½
Foundation: Basement
Materials List Available: Yes
Price Category: F

You'll love the way this spacious ranch reminds you of a French country home.

Features:

- Foyer: Come into this lovely home's foyer, and be greeted with a view of the gracious staircase and the great room just beyond.

- Great Room: Settle down by the cozy fireplace in cool weather, and reach for a book on the built-in shelves that surround it.

- Kitchen: Designed for efficient work patterns, this large kitchen is open to the great room.

- Breakfast Room: Just off the kitchen, this sunny room will be a family favorite all through the day.

- Master Suite: A bay window, walk-in closet, and shower built for two are highlights of this area.

- Additional Bedrooms: These large bedrooms both have walk-in closets and share a Jack-and-Jill bath for total convenience.

Images provided by designer/architect.

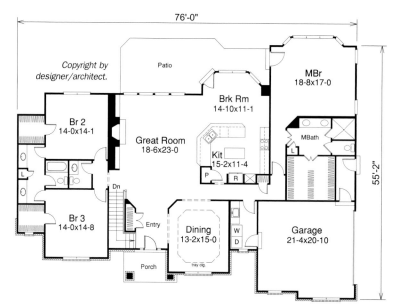

SMARTtip

Decorative Poles

Drapery poles are supported by the brackets fastened to the window frame or wall. The brackets that are provided with the poles generally coordinate and blend in with the pole finish. Brackets can be simple but also decorative. If you opt for a spectacular, attention-grabbing bracket, consider choosing less showy finials for the ends of the pole.

Plan #131019

Dimensions: 83'6" W x 53'4" D
Levels: 1
Square Footage: 2,243
Bedrooms: 3
Bathrooms: 2½
Foundation: Basement, crawl space, or slab
Materials List Available: Yes
Price Category: F

Images provided by designer/architect.

Drama marks this contemporary, angled ranch-style home which can be placed to suit any site, even the most difficult.

Features:

- Great Room: Imagine having an octagonal great room! The shape alone makes it spectacular, but the view to the backyard from its four exterior sides adds to the impression it creates, and you'll love its 16-ft. tray ceiling, fireplace, and wall designed to fit a large entertainment center.

- Kitchen: This room is adjacent to and visually connected to the great room but has excellent features of its own that make it an easy place to cook or clean.

- Master Suite: Separated from the other bedrooms, this suite is planned for privacy. You'll love the bath here and look forward to the quiet you can find at the end of the day.

- Additional Bedrooms: In a wing of their own, the other two bedrooms share a bath.

Rear Elevation

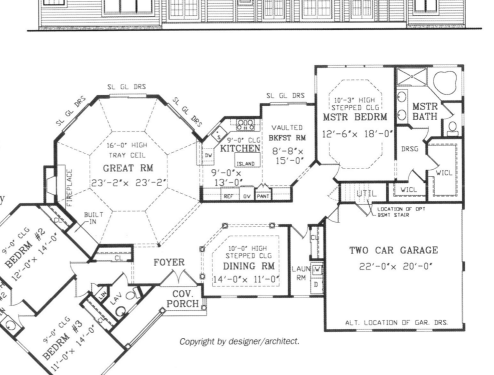

Copyright by designer/architect.

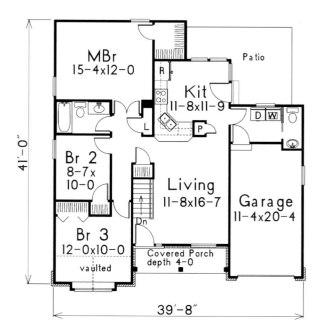

Plan #321022

Dimensions: 44' W x 27' D
Levels: 1
Square Footage: 1,140
Bedrooms: 3
Bathrooms: 2
Foundation: Basement
Materials List Available: Yes
Price Category: B

Images provided by designer/architect.

Copyright by designer/architect.

44'-0"

27'-0"

MBr
13-4x10-8

Kit
11-0x9-6

Din
10-4x
11-0

Deck

Dn

Br 2
10-0x8-9

Br 3
9-1x10-0

Living
19-0x13-4

Porch depth 5-0

SMARTtip

Basement Moldings

Keep moldings simple in a basement with lower ceilings. Elaborate moldings around the ceiling or floor can shorten the height of the room.

Plan #321023

Dimensions: 39'8" W x 41' D
Levels: 1
Square Footage: 1,092
Bedrooms: 3
Bathrooms: 1½
Foundation: Basement
Materials List Available: Yes
Price Category: B

Images provided by designer/architect.

MBr
15-4x12-0

Patio

Kit
11-8x11-9

41'-0"

Br 2
8-7x
10-0

Living
11-8x16-7

Garage
11-4x20-4

Dn

Br 3
12-0x10-0
vaulted

Covered Porch
depth 4-0

39'-8"

Copyright by designer/architect.

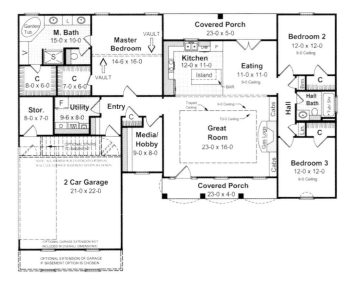

Plan #351002

Dimensions: 64' W x 45'10" D

Levels: 1

Square Footage: 1,751

Bedrooms: 3

Bathrooms: 2

Foundation: Basement, crawl space, or slab

Materials List Available: Yes

Price Category: C

Plan #351007

Dimensions: 73'8" W x 53'2" D

Levels: 1

Square Footage: 2,251

Bedrooms: 3

Bathrooms: 2½

Foundation: Basement, crawl space, or slab

Materials List Available: Yes

Price Category: E

Bonus Room

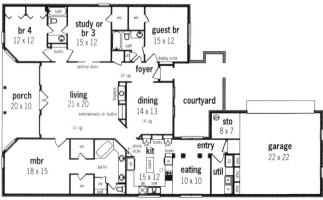

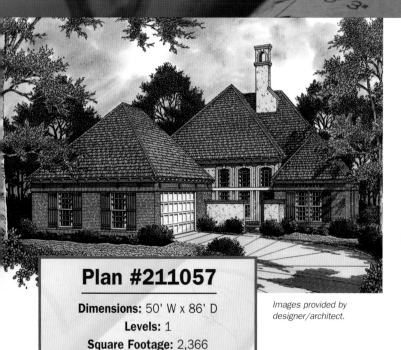

Plan #211057

Dimensions: 50' W x 86' D

Levels: 1

Square Footage: 2,366

Bedrooms: 4

Bathrooms: 3

Foundation: Slab

Materials List Available: No

Price Category: E

Images provided by designer/architect.

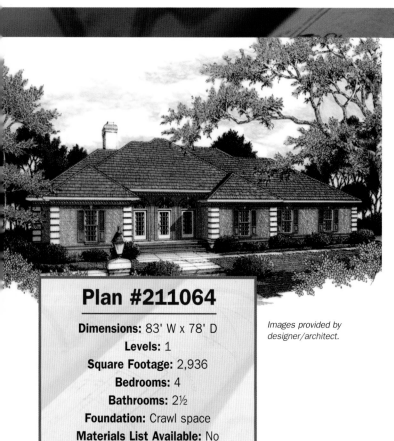

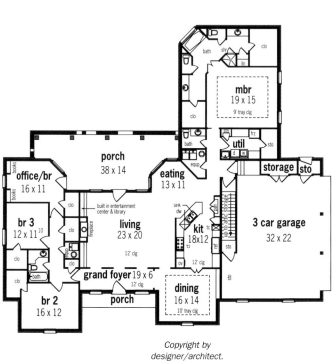

Plan #211064

Dimensions: 83' W x 78' D

Levels: 1

Square Footage: 2,936

Bedrooms: 4

Bathrooms: 2½

Foundation: Crawl space

Materials List Available: No

Price Category: F

Images provided by designer/architect.

Copyright by designer/architect.

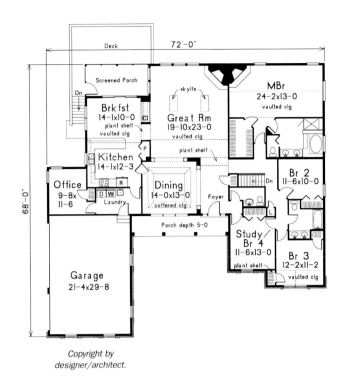

Plan #321027

Dimensions: 72' W x 68' D

Levels: 1

Square Footage: 2,758

Bedrooms: 4

Bathrooms: 2½

Foundation: Basement

Materials List Available: Yes

Price Category: F

Images provided by designer/architect.

Copyright by designer/architect.

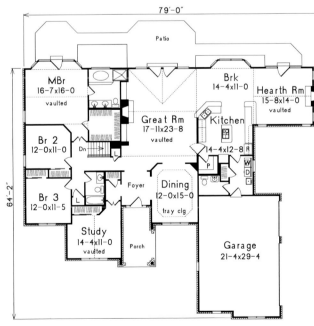

Plan #321028

Dimensions: 79' W x 64'2" D

Levels: 1

Square Footage: 2,723

Bedrooms: 3

Bathrooms: 2½

Foundation: Basement

Materials List Available: Yes

Price Category: F

Images provided by designer/architect.

Copyright by designer/architect.

Plan #161008

Dimensions: 64'2" W x 46'6" D
Levels: 1
Square Footage: 1,860
Bedrooms: 3
Bathrooms: 2
Foundation: Slab
Materials List Available: No
Price Category: D

Images provided by designer/architect.

If you enjoy casual living and formal entertaining, this delightful floor plan will attract your eye.

Features:

- Great Room: A sloped ceiling and corner fireplace combine to provide this great room with an open and cozy atmosphere, perfect for relaxing evenings.

- Kitchen: This kitchen offers ample counter and cabinet space. A convenient snack bar provides a view to the breakfast area and great room

- Master Suite: Enjoy the elegance and style of this master suite, with its deluxe bath, large walk-in closet, and secluded alcove.

- Laundry Room: You will appreciate the ample counter space in this large laundry room with utility closet.

- Porch: From the breakfast area, enjoy a relaxed meal on this rear covered porch in warm weather.

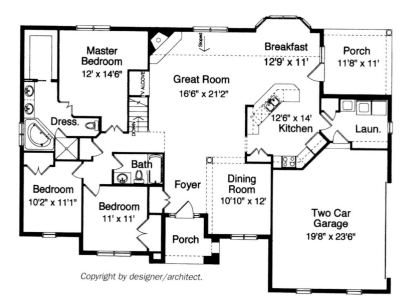

Copyright by designer/architect.

SMARTtip
Espaliered Fruit Trees

Try a technique used by the royal gardeners at Versailles—espalier. They trained the fruit trees to grow flat against the walls, creating patterns. It's not difficult, especially if you go to a reputable nursery and purchase an apple or pear tree that has already been espaliered. Plant it against a flat surface that's in a sunny spot.

Plan #221011

Dimensions: 59' W x 58' D
Levels: 1
Square Footage: 1,756
Bedrooms: 3
Bathrooms: 2
Foundation: Basement
Materials List Available: No
Price Category: C

Images provided by designer/architect.

You'll love this design if you've been looking for a compact design with a spacious, open feeling.

Features:

- Ceiling Height: 8 ft.

- Entry: A vaulted ceiling here sets a luxurious tone for the whole house.

- Family Room: Also with a vaulted ceiling, this room features a handsome fireplace that's flanked on either side by windows looking out to the backyard.

- Dining Room: Open to the family room, this large room has large, well-placed windows that flood the room with natural light.

- Kitchen: The eating bar that divides this room from the dining room gives family members a great place to perch while they chat with the cook or do their homework.

- Master Suite: Located just off the kitchen for privacy, this suite includes a walk-in closet and a full bath with its own linen closet.

Rear Elevation

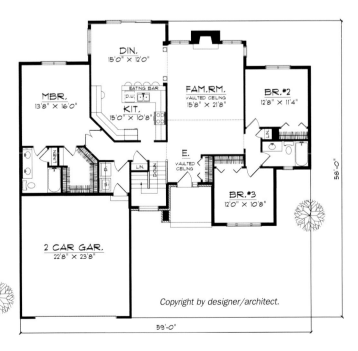

Copyright by designer/architect.

Plan #151009

Dimensions: 44' W x 86'2" D
Levels: 1
Square Footage: 1,601
Bedrooms: 3
Bathrooms: 2
Foundation: Crawl, slab
Materials List Available: Yes
Price Category: C

Images provided by designer/architect.

This can be the perfect home for a site with views you can enjoy in all seasons and at all times.

Features:

- Porches: Enjoy the front porch with its 10-ft. ceiling and the more private back porch where you can set up a grill or just get away from it all.

- Foyer: With a 10-ft. ceiling, this foyer opens to the great room for a warm welcome.

- Great Room: Your family will love the media center and the easy access to the rear porch.

- Kitchen: This well-designed kitchen is open to the dining room and the breakfast nook, which also opens to the rear porch.

- Master Suite: The bedroom has a 10-ft. boxed ceiling and a door to the rear. The bath includes a corner whirlpool tub with glass block windows.

- Bedrooms: Bedroom 2 has a vaulted ceiling, while bedroom 3 features a built-in desk.

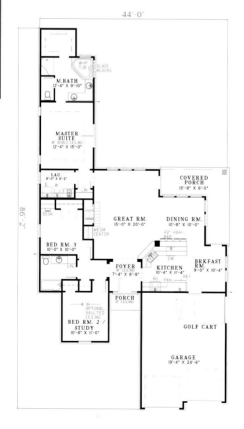

Copyright by designer/architect.

SMARTtip
Fertilizing Your Grass

Fertilizers contain nutrients balanced for different kinds of growth. The ratio of nutrients is indicated on the package by three numbers (for example, 10-10-10). The first specifies nitrogen content; the second, phosphorus; and the third, potash.

Nitrogen helps grass blades to grow and improves the quality and thickness of the turf. Fertilizers contain up to 30 percent nitrogen.

Phosphorus helps grass to develop a healthy root system. It also speeds up the maturation process of the plant.

Potash helps grass stay healthy by providing amino acids and proteins to the plants.

Plan #121005

Dimensions: 48' W x 52' D
Levels: 1
Square Footage: 1,496
Bedrooms: 3
Bathrooms: 2
Foundation: Basement
Materials List Available: Yes
Price Category: B

Images provided by designer/architect.

A beautiful starter or retirement home with all the amenities you'd expect in a much bigger house.

Features:

• Ceiling Height: 8 ft.

• Great Room: A cathedral ceiling visually expands the great room making it the perfect place for family gatherings or formal entertaining.

• Formal Dining Room: This elegant room is ideal for entertaining dinner guests. It conveniently shares a wet bar and service counter with a bayed breakfast area next door.

• Breakfast Area: In addition to the service area shared with the dining room, this cozy area features a snack bar, pantry, and desk that's perfect for household paperwork.

• Master Suite: The master bedroom features special ceiling details. It's joined by a private bath with a whirlpool, shower, and spacious walk-in closet.

• Garage: The two-bay garage offers plenty of storage space.

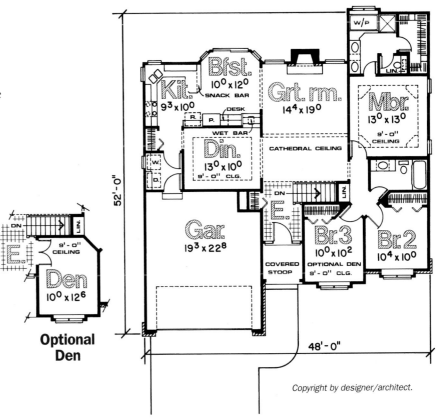

Optional Den

Copyright by designer/architect.

Flooring

Selecting a flooring material is one of the most important decisions you will make when decorating a room. The right material can enhance the color scheme and the overall look of the room, and flooring provides a unique tactile component to the design.

If you are are acting as your own designer, one of the first things you should do is learn about the various types of flooring—from wood to stone to vinyl—on today's market. The choices are myriad and innovations in technology have widened the range of finishes.

Choices in Wood

In bygone eras, a wood floor was simply one that was created by laying wide wood planks side by side. Later, as the milling of lumber improved, homeowners were able to choose narrower planks that look more refined than rustic. Parquet floors were created by woodcrafters with a flair for the dramatic and an appreciation of the artistic richness of wood grains set in nonlinear patterns.

Today's manufacturers have made it possible to have it all. The wood floor, factory- or custom-stained to suit a particular style or mood in a room, is still a traditional favorite. It's readily available in strips of 1 to 2¼ inches wide, or in country-style planks of 3 to 8 inches wide. The formal, sophisticated look of a parquet floor is unparalleled for richness of visual texture.

Types of Wood Flooring

Wood varieties available as a surface material are vast, and cost varies widely, depending on the type and grade of wood and on the choice of design.

Softwoods, like pine and fir, are often used to make simple tongue-and-groove floorboards. These floors are less expensive than hardwoods but also less durable. The hardwoods—maple, birch, oak, ash—are far less likely to mar with normal use. A hardwood floor is not indestructible; however, it will stand up to demanding use.

Both hardwoods and softwoods are graded according to their color, grain, and imperfections. The top of the line is known as clear, followed by select, No. 1 common, and No. 2 common. In addition to budget considerations, the decision whether to pay top dollar for clear wood or to economize with a lesser grade depends on use factors and on the design objectives. For example, if you plan to install a wood floor in a small room and then cover most of it with an area rug, the No. 2 common grade may be a good choice; lesser grades are also fine for informal rooms where a few defects just enhance a lived-in look. If your design calls for larger areas of rich wood grain that will be exposed, with scatter rugs used for color accents, a clear or select grade will make an attractive choice.

Finishing Options

Color stains—reds, blues, and greens—may work in settings where a casual or rustic feeling is desired. This, however, is a departure from the traditional use of

Wood flooring, below, fits well in both formal and informal spaces.

Laminate flooring, opposite, can mimic the look of real wood or natural stone.

Laminate Flooring

Laminate flooring is the great pretender among flooring materials. When your creative side tells you to install wood but your practical side knows it just won't hold up in the traffic-heavy location for which you're considering it, a wood floor look-alike might be just the thing. Faux wood and faux stone laminate floors provide you with the look you want, tempered with physical wear and care properties that you and your family can live with. Laminate is particularly suited to rooms where floors are likely to see heavy duty—kitchens, family rooms, hallways, and children's bedrooms and playrooms—anywhere stain and scratch resistance and easy cleanup count. Prolonged exposure to moisture will damage some laminate products, but many can now be used in wet areas. Manufacturers of laminate offer warranties against staining, scratching, cracking, and peeling for up to 25 years.

Laminate is made from paper impregnated with melamine, an organic resin, and bonded to a core of particleboard, fiberboard, or other wood byproducts. It can be laid over virtually any subflooring surface, including wood and concrete. It can also be applied on top of an existing wood, ceramic, or vinyl tile, as well as vinyl or other sheet flooring. You can even install it over certain types of carpeting, but check the manufacturer's guidelines before doing so.

Installation and Care

The installation of laminate flooring is a reasonably quick and relatively easy do-it-yourself project. It requires sheets of a special foam underlayment followed by the careful placement, cutting, and gluing of the laminate.

Laminate is available in sheets that are ideal when your design calls for a uniform look, such as monotone stone, or a linear design that mimics strip or plank wood flooring. Laminate planks, squares, and blocks offer added design flexibility: with them, you can design your own tile patterns, lay strips of wood-look planks with alternating "stain" finishes, or border your floor with a contrasting color.

---

wood. Wood is not typically used to deliver color impact; instead it blends with and subtly enhances its surroundings. Natural wood stains range from light ash tones to deep, coffee-like colors. Generally, lighter stains make a room feel less formal, and darker, richer stains suggest a stately atmosphere. As with lighter colors, lighter stains create a feeling of openness; darker stains foster a more intimate feeling and can reduce the visual vastness of a large space.

Installation

If the design plan calls for the laying of unfinished wood strips, factor the cost of hiring a skilled professional into your budget. Many manufacturers offer products with installation kits that make wood flooring a do-it-yourself option for those whose skills are good but don't necessarily approach a professional carpenter's level. Some make strips or planks already finished and sealed. Most parquet tiles come finished and sealed as well.

Vinyl Sheet & Tile Flooring

Like laminate, resilient flooring is also available in design-friendly sheet or tile form. Resilient floors can be made from a variety of materials, including linoleum, asphalt, cork, or rubber. However, the most commonly used material in manufacturing today's resilient floors for homes is vinyl.

Price, durability, and easy maintenance make resilient flooring an attractive and popular choice. Do-it-yourself installation, an option even for those who are not particularly skilled, can mean further savings.

Sheet versus Tiles

Resilient flooring comes in an enormous array of colors and patterns, plus many of the flooring styles have a textured surface. With the tiles, you can combine color and pattern in limitless ways. Even the sheet form of resilient flooring can be customized with inlay strips.

Cushioned sheet vinyl offers the most resilience. It provides excellent stain resistance; it's comfortable and quiet underfoot and easy to maintain, with no-wax and never-wax finishes often available. These features make the floor especially attractive for areas with lots of kid traffic. Beware though: only the more expensive grades show an acceptable degree of resistance to nicking and denting. In rooms where furniture is often moved around, this could be a problem. Although the range of colors, patterns, and surface textures is wide, sheet floor-

Vinyl sheet flooring, left, is a good choice for high-traffic areas, such as kitchens, family rooms, and playrooms. Most products have a no-wax finish that is easy to maintain.

Vinyl flooring, above, comes in a variety of styles and colors. Tiles and sheet flooring can look like ceramic tiles and natural stone.

Ceramic tile, opposite, offers a number of possibilities—from simple patterns to more elaborate designs that feature borders and inlays.

ing is not as flexible as vinyl tile when it comes to customizing your look.

Regular sheet vinyl is less expensive than the cushioned types, but it carries the same disadvantages and is slightly less resilient. Except for the availability of no-wax finishes, a vinyl tile floor is as stain resistant and as easy to maintain as the sheet-vinyl products. Increased design possibilities are the trade-off.

Here, as with other flooring materials, one possible way out of the choice maze is to take the unconventional step of mixing flooring materials. For example, use a durable cushioned sheet vinyl in more trafficked areas, but frame it with a pretty vinyl tile or laminate border.

Ceramic Choices

Ceramic tile—actually fired clay—is an excellent choice for areas subject to a lot of traffic and in rooms where resistance to moisture and stains is needed. These features, combined with easy cleanup, have made ceramic tile a centuries-old tradition for flooring, walls, and ceilings in bathrooms and kitchens. Color, texture, and pattern choices available today make ceramic tile the most versatile flooring option in terms of design possibilities.

Tile Options

Some handcrafted ceramic tiles are very costly, but manufacturers have created a market full of design and style options.

Tiles come in a variety of sizes, beginning with 1-inch-square mosaic tiles up to large 16 x 16-inch squares. Other shapes, such as triangles, diamonds, and rectangles, are also available. Tile textures range from shiny to matte-finished and from glass-smooth to ripple-surfaced. Tiles are available either glazed or unglazed. Glazed tiles have a hard, often colored, surface that is applied during the firing process; the resulting finish can range from glossy to matte. Unglazed tiles, such as terra-cotta or quarry tiles, have a matte finish, are porous, and need to be sealed to prevent staining.

Consider using accent borders to create unique designs, such as a faux area rug, that visually separate sections of a room or separate one room from another. When added in a random pattern, embossed accent tiles add interest, variety, and elegance to an expanse of single-colored tiles.

Alas, no surfacing material is perfect. Ceramic tile offers long-lasting beauty, design versatility, and simplicity of maintenance, but it also has some hard-to-live-with features. Tile is cold underfoot, noisy when someone walks across it in hard-soled shoes, and not at all resilient—always expect the worst when something breakable falls on a tile floor. If you have infants and toddlers around, it may be best to wait a few years for your tiled floor.

Natural Stone

Like ceramic tile, stone and marble are classified as "non-resilients." Like tile, these materials offer richness of color, durability, moisture and stain resistance, and ease of maintenance. They also share with tile the drawbacks of being cold to the touch, noisy to walk on, and unforgivingly hard.

Stone and marble floors are clearly, unmistakably natural. As remarkably good as some faux surfaces look, no product manufactured today actually matches the rustic irregularity and random color variation of natural stone.

Picking a Flooring Material

Now that you've got the facts about each floor surface option, picking the right one for your design will be much less confusing. The following steps can make it downright simple.

Step 1: Make a "Use/Abuse" Analysis. Begin by asking yourself the most important question: How will this room used? Your answer should tell you just what kind of traffic the future floor surface will endure. With a relatively expensive investment like a floor, it's best not to guess. Instead, use this system to arrive at an accurate use/abuse analysis.

On a piece of paper, make columns headed "Who" and "Activities," and then list who in the family will use the room and what activities will occur there. Will the kids play with toys on the floor? Will they do arts and crafts projects with paint, glue, and glitter? Will the family gather on Saturday afternoons and snack while watching a football game on television? Is it a formal living room where you will entertain your friends and business clients? Is it a busy kitchen? Does the hallway extend from your front entrance or from a busier back door where the kids will drop off their hockey skates?

The answers to these questions will help you to determine how durable and resilient a flooring surface needs to be, whether warmth and softness are requirements, and how much maintenance will be necessary to keep the surface clean.

Step 2: Determine Your Design Objectives. Your choices are limited by the other elements in the room. Your color choices can enhance the color palette you are planning. Because you will be starting from scratch—including walls, furniture, and accessories—you have more flexibility, although your job is a bit more complex and involves more decisions.

Once you've determined your design objectives, compare your use/abuse analysis

High-traffic areas, below left, require flooring that can stand up to abuse.

Laminate flooring, below right, is a good choice for a variety of rooms.

to the types of flooring that meet both your style and use needs. From the list of options that are left, you can narrow down your choices even more.

Step 3: Draw and Use a Floor Plan.

After you have completed the use/abuse analysis and the list of design objectives, draw up a floor plan—a separate one for experimenting with your flooring ideas. Follow these guidelines: measure the length and width of the room, and plot it on graph paper, using a scale of 1 inch to 1 foot. If your room is larger than 8 x 10 feet, you can tape two pieces of 8½- x 11-inch graph paper together. Measure and mark the locations of entryways and any permanent features in the room, such as cabinets, fixtures, or appliances.

Make several photocopies of your floor plan. Reserve one copy as a template. Use the other copies for previewing pattern ideas for flooring that comes in tiles (ceramic, vinyl, or carpeting tiles). Buy multicolored pencils, and fill in your grid. You'll be able to determine not only how the pattern will look but also how many tiles of various colors you'll need to buy to complete the project. Don't forget to include such items as borders and inlays.

Step 4: Convert Your Overall Budget to Cost per Square Foot.

After you've completed the use/abuse analysis, determined your design objectives, and created a floor plan, the next step is determining cost.

Most flooring is priced in terms of square feet. To determine how many square feet are in your room, round the measurements up to the next foot. Then simply multiply the length by the width. For example, for a room measuring 10 feet 4 inches x 12 feet 6 inches, round the figures to 11 x 13 feet. Multiply 11 x 13 feet (that's 143 square feet). You will end up with extra flooring, but it is better to have more than less.

Some flooring—like carpeting—is priced in terms of square yards. To determine the number of square yards in your room, divide the number of square feet by nine. In our example, there are just under 16 square yards in 143 square feet.

Let's say you have a budget of $850 to purchase tile for your 10-foot-4-inch x 12-foot-6-inch room. For the sake of the illustration, let's assume your subflooring is adequate, you have the tools, and the cost of adhesive and grout for your room is about $75. That leaves you with $775. To determine how much you can spend per tile, divide the remainder by the number of square feet in the room. In our example, $775 divided by 143 square feet equals about $5.40 per square foot of tile.

Light colors, below left, make a room feel more open than darker colors.

Consider the rest of the room, below, when selecting flooring.

Plan #271073

Dimensions: 69' W x 56' D

Levels: 1

Square Footage: 1,920

Bedrooms: 3

Bathrooms: 2

Foundation: Daylight basement

Materials List Available: No

Price Category: B

Images provided by designer/architect.

A great floor plan and plenty of space make this home perfect for people who welcome family members back home to visit.

Features:

- Great Room: This vaulted space shares a see-through fireplace with a cozy hearth room.

- Kitchen: An angled island and a step-in pantry are the highlights of this room.

- Study: Double doors introduce this versatile space, which shows off a nice bay window.

- Master Suite: Double doors lead to the bedroom. The private bath hosts a whirlpool tub and a separate shower.

- Basement: This level contains more bedrooms and family spaces for visiting relatives.

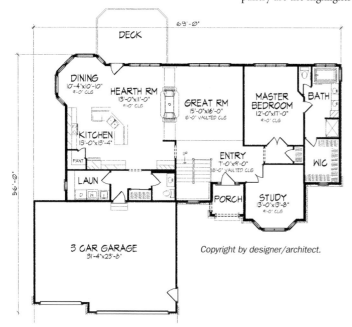

Copyright by designer/architect.

Basement Level Floor Plan

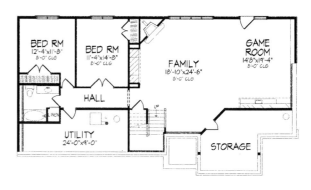

Plan #151034

Dimensions: 58'6" W x 64'6" D

Levels: 1

Square Footage: 2,133

Bedrooms: 3

Bathrooms: 2

Foundation: Crawl space, slab, or basement

Materials List Available: Yes

Price Category: D

Images provided by designer/architect.

You'll love the high ceilings, open floor plan, and contemporary design features in this home.

Features:

- **Great Room:** A pass-through tiled fireplace between this lovely large room and the adjacent hearth room allows you to notice the mirror effect created by the 10-ft. boxed ceilings in both rooms.

- **Dining Room:** An 11-ft. ceiling and 8-in. boxed column give formality to this lovely room, where you're certain to entertain.

- **Kitchen:** If you're a cook, this room may become your favorite spot in the house, thanks to its great design, which includes plenty of work and storage space, and a very practical layout.

- **Master Suite:** A 10-ft. boxed ceiling gives elegance to this room. A pocket door opens to the private bath, with its huge walk-in closet, glass-blocked whirlpool tub, separate glass shower, and private toilet room.

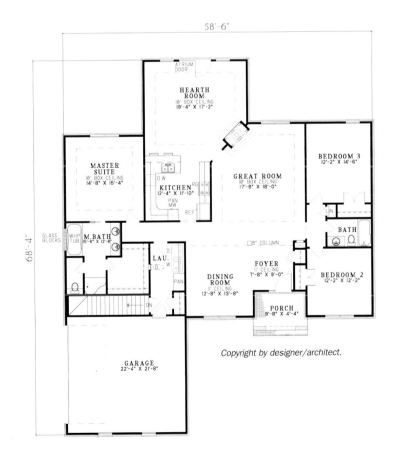

Copyright by designer/architect.

Plan #101011

Dimensions: 71'2" W x 58'1" D

Levels: 1

Square Footage: 2,184

Bedrooms: 3

Bathrooms: 3

Foundation: Slab, crawl space, or basement

Materials List Available: No

Price Category: D

A classic design and spacious interior add up to a flexible design suitable to any modern lifestyle.

Features:

• Ceiling Height: 9 ft. unless otherwise noted.

• Formal Dining room: A decorative square column and a tray ceiling adorn this elegant dining room.

• Screened Porch: Enjoy summer breezes in style by stepping out of the French doors into this vaulted screened porch.

• Kitchen: Does everyone want to hang out in the kitchen while you are cooking? No problem. True to the home's country style, this huge 14-ft.-3-in. x 22-ft.-6-in. has plenty of room for helpers.

• The kitchen is open to the vaulted family room.

• Patio or Deck: This pleasant outdoor area is accessible from both the screened porch and the master bedroom.

• Master Suite: This luxurious suite includes a double tray ceiling, a sitting area, two walk-in closets, and an exquisite bath.

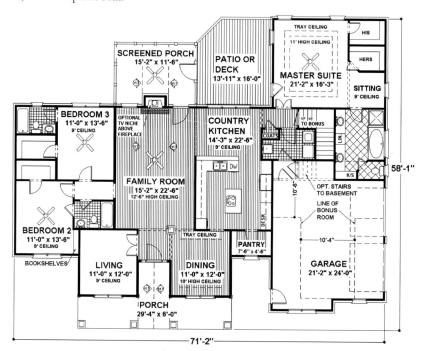

Copyright by designer/architect.

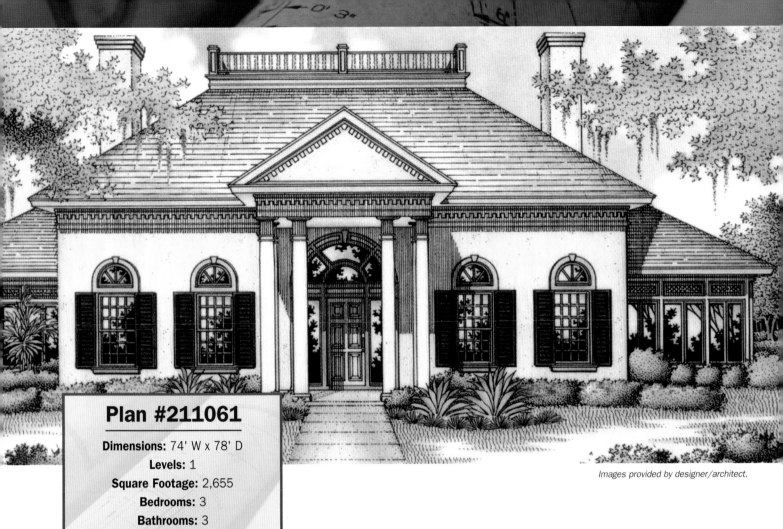

Plan #211061

Dimensions: 74' W x 78' D

Levels: 1

Square Footage: 2,655

Bedrooms: 3

Bathrooms: 3

Foundation: Slab, crawl space, or basement

Materials List Available: Yes

Price Category: F

Images provided by designer/architect.

The exterior of this home is a replica of an Antebellum home located in Natchez, Mississippi.

Features:

- Ceiling Height: 9 ft. unless otherwise noted.

- Open Plan: The interior living spaces of this home are open and flowing. This makes it the ideal home for entertaining and allows lots of flexibility in the use of space.

- Wet Bar: This triangular wet bar is neatly tucked between the living room and the sunroom. It's also convenient to the kitchen and the eating areas.

- Sunroom: There's nothing quite like enjoying the warmth of the sun streaming into this beautiful sunroom on a cold winter day.

- Living Room: This large living room seems even more spacious, thanks to its 14-ft. ceiling.

- Master Bath: This luxurious master bath features a his-and-her arrangement and a wraparound mirrored dressing table.

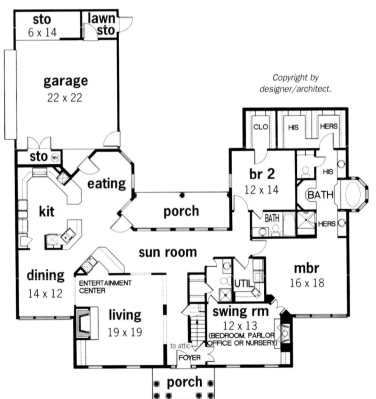

Copyright by designer/architect.

Plan #271078

Dimensions: 83' W x 52' D

Levels: 1

Square Footage: 1,855

Bedrooms: 1-2

Bathrooms: 1½-2½

Foundation: Daylight basement

Materials List Available: No

Price Category: D

Images provided by designer/architect.

Optional Basement Level Floor Plan

Copyright by designer/architect.

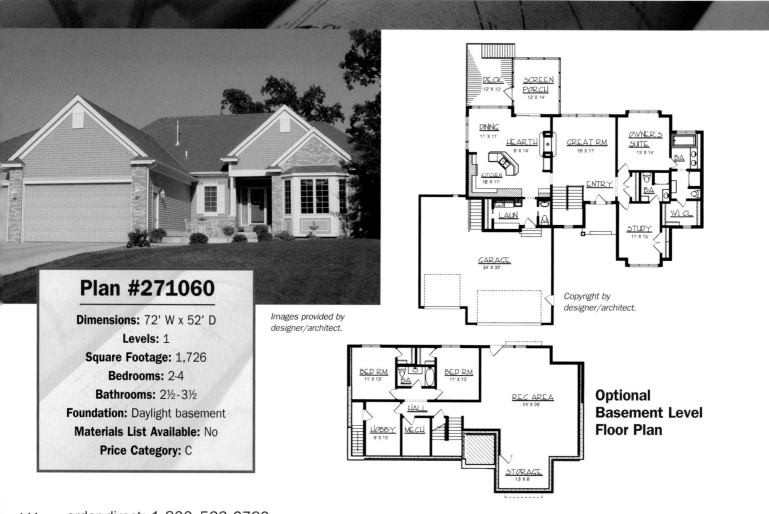

Plan #271060

Dimensions: 72' W x 52' D

Levels: 1

Square Footage: 1,726

Bedrooms: 2-4

Bathrooms: 2½-3½

Foundation: Daylight basement

Materials List Available: No

Price Category: C

Images provided by designer/architect.

Copyright by designer/architect.

Optional Basement Level Floor Plan

Copyright by designer/architect.

Plan #271059

Dimensions: 67' W x 57' D

Levels: 1

Square Footage: 1,790

Bedrooms: 1-3

Bathrooms: 1½-2½

Foundation: Daylight basement

Materials List Available: No

Price Category: C

Images provided by designer/architect.

Optional Basement Level Floor Plan

Plan #111018

Dimensions: 67' W x 79' D

Levels: 1

Square Footage: 2,745

Bedrooms: 4

Bathrooms: 3½

Foundation: Basement

Materials List Available: No

Price Category: F

Images provided by designer/architect.

Copyright by designer/architect.

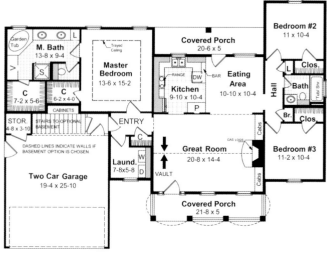

Plan #351005

Dimensions: 61' W x 47'4" D

Levels: 1

Square Footage: 1,501

Bedrooms: 3

Bathrooms: 2

Foundation: Basement, crawl space, or slab

Materials List Available: Yes

Price Category: C

Images provided by designer/architect.

Copyright by designer/architect.

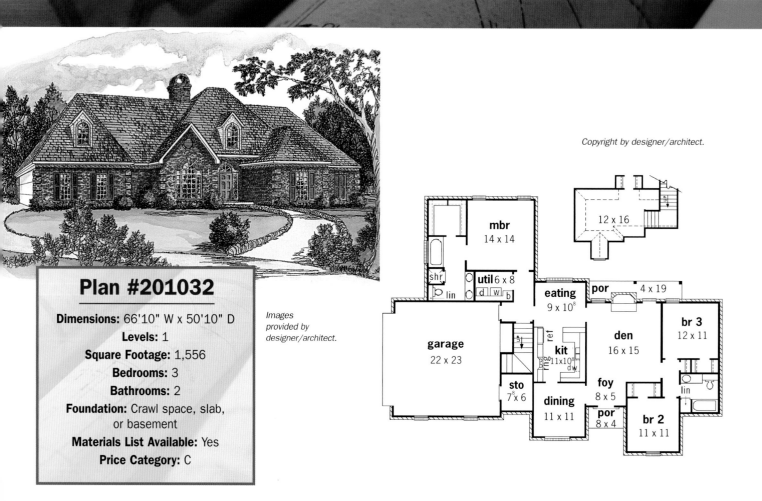

Copyright by designer/architect.

Plan #201032

Dimensions: 66'10" W x 50'10" D

Levels: 1

Square Footage: 1,556

Bedrooms: 3

Bathrooms: 2

Foundation: Crawl space, slab, or basement

Materials List Available: Yes

Price Category: C

Images provided by designer/architect.

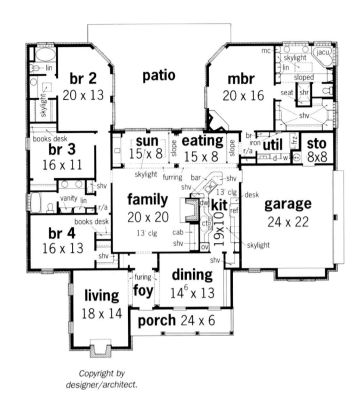

Images provided by
designer/architect.

Plan #211065

Dimensions: 72' W x 70' D

Levels: 1

Square Footage: 3,158

Bedrooms: 4

Bathrooms: 3

Foundation: Crawl space

Materials List Available: Yes

Price Category: G

Copyright by
designer/architect.

Floor plan labels (Plan #211065): br 2 20 x 13, patio, mbr 20 x 16, mc, skylight, jacu, lin, sloped, seat, shr, shv, books desk, skylight, sun 15 x 8, slope, eating 15 x 8, slope, br iron r/a, util, frz, sto 8x8, d w, br 3 16 x 11, skylight, furring, bar, shv, desk, garage 24 x 22, shv, vanity lin, family 20 x 20, 13' clg, kit 19x10, ref, shv, r/a, books desk, cab, ov, skylight, br 4 16 x 13, shv, dw, 13' clg, shv, furing, dining 14⁶ x 13, living 18 x 14, foy, porch 24 x 6

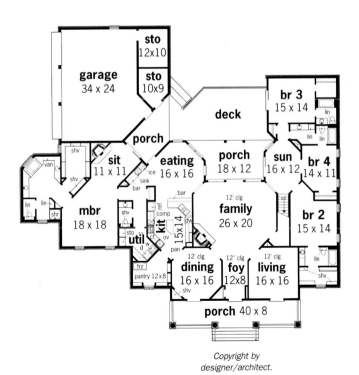

Images provided by
designer/architect.

Plan #211067

Dimensions: 96' W x 90' D

Levels: 1

Square Footage: 4,038

Bedrooms: 4

Bathrooms: 4½

Foundation: Crawl space

Materials List Available: Yes

Price Category: I

Copyright by
designer/architect.

Floor plan labels (Plan #211067): garage 34 x 24, sto 12x10, sto 10x9, deck, br 3 15 x 14, lin, porch, sit 11 x 11, eating 16 x 16, porch 18 x 12, sun 16 x 12, br 4 14 x 11, ice, sink, bar, van, shv, mbr 18 x 18, util, kit 15x14, comp, ref, dw, ov, family 26 x 20, 12' clg, up, br 2 15 x 14, frz, d, pan, bar, 12' clg, 12' clg, 12' clg, pantry 12 x 8, dining 16 x 16, foy 12x8, living 16 x 16, shv, lin, porch 40 x 8

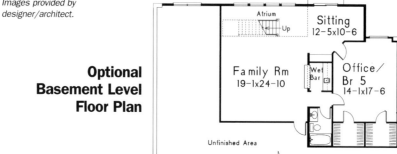

Copyright by designer/architect.

Plan #321034

Dimensions: 75'8" W x 50'6" D

Levels: 1

Square Footage: 3,508

Bedrooms: 4

Bathrooms: 3

Foundation: Daylight basement

Materials List Available: Yes

Price Category: H

Images provided by designer/architect.

Optional Basement Level Floor Plan

Plan #321029

Dimensions: 50' W x 56' D

Levels: 1

Square Footage: 2,334

Bedrooms: 3

Bathrooms: 2

Foundation: Daylight basement

Materials List Available: Yes

Price Category: E

Images provided by designer/architect.

Rear View

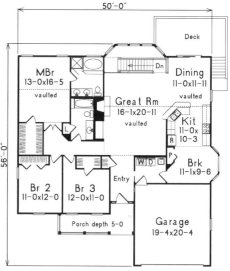

Optional Basement Level Floor Plan

Copyright by designer/architect.

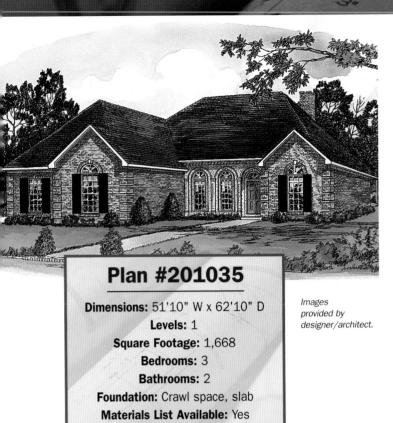

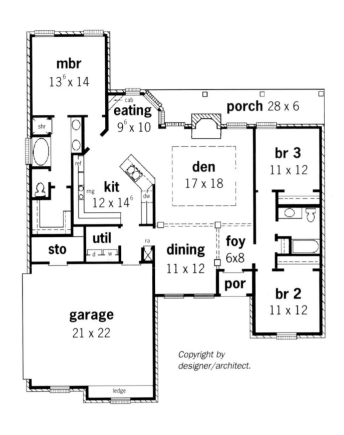

Plan #201035

Dimensions: 51'10" W x 62'10" D
Levels: 1
Square Footage: 1,668
Bedrooms: 3
Bathrooms: 2
Foundation: Crawl space, slab
Materials List Available: Yes
Price Category: C

Images provided by designer/architect.

Copyright by designer/architect.

Floor plan labels:
- mbr 13⁶ x 14
- eating 9⁶ x 10
- porch 28 x 6
- den 17 x 18
- br 3 11 x 12
- kit 12 x 14⁶
- sto
- util
- dining 11 x 12
- foy 6x8
- por
- br 2 11 x 12
- garage 21 x 22
- ledge
- cab, shr, ref, rng, dw, d, w, ra

Plan #201036

Dimensions: 67'10" W x 44'10" D
Levels: 1
Square Footage: 1,671
Bedrooms: 3
Bathrooms: 2
Foundation: Crawl space, slab
Materials List Available: Yes
Price Category: C

Images provided by designer/architect.

SMARTtip

Bathroom Style Without Fallbacks

Retrofit an antique chest for bathroom storage, but make sure that you seal the wood against moisture. Even smarter—buy a new cabinet that's made to look like an antique and won't fall prey to the assaults of humidity and water. Leave chest open to display linens, soaps, and pretty bottled toiletries to create a focal point.

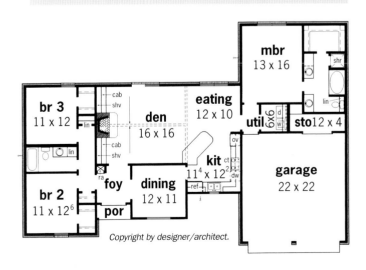

Floor plan labels:
- br 3 11 x 12
- mbr 13 x 16
- eating 12 x 10
- den 16 x 16
- util 6x6
- sto 12 x 4
- kit 11⁴ x 12²
- foy
- dining 12 x 11
- br 2 11 x 12⁶
- por
- garage 22 x 22
- cab, shv, lin, ra, ref, ov, ct, d, w, i

Copyright by designer/architect.

Plan #321008

Dimensions: 57' W x 52'2" D

Levels: 1

Square Footage: 1,761

Bedrooms: 4

Bathrooms: 2

Foundation: Basement

Materials List Available: Yes

Price Category: C

One look at the roof dormers and planter boxes that grace the outside of this ranch, and you'll know that the interior is planned for comfortable family living.

Features:

- **Great Room:** A vaulted ceiling in this room points up its generous dimensions. Put a grouping of chairs near the fireplace to take advantage of the cozy spot it creates in chilly weather.

- **Kitchen:** Open to the great room, this kitchen has been planned for convenience. It features a pass-through to the dining area for easy serving when you've got a crowd to feed.

- **Master Bedroom:** A vaulted ceiling here makes you feel especially pampered, and the walk-in closet and amenity-filled bath add to that feeling.

- **Additional Bedrooms:** Great closet space characterizes all the rooms in this home, making it easy for children of any age to keep it organized and tidy.

Copyright by designer/architect.

Patio

MBr 14-6x13-0 vaulted clg

Great Rm 16-0x17-10 vaulted clg

Brkfst 11-8x10-8

Kit 11-5x 12-9

Br 2 11-0x10-0

Dn

L

Dining 12-4x10-0

P

W D

R

Br 3 11-0x10-0

Covered Porch

Br 4 12-0x10-0 vaulted clg

Garage 20-4x20-10

52'-2"

57'-0"

SMARTtip

Hanging Wallpaper

Use liner paper to smooth out a damaged wall and to provide uniform support for expensive paper.

Plan #131020

Dimensions: 67'2" W x 48'10" D
Levels: 1
Square Footage: 1,735
Bedrooms: 3
Bathrooms: 2
Foundation: Basement, crawl space, or slab
Materials List Available: Yes
Price Category: C

This gorgeous ranch is designed for entertaining but is also comfortable for family living.

Features:

- **Living Room:** A 9-ft. stepped ceiling highlights the spaciousness of this room, which gives a view of one of the two covered porches.

- **Dining Room:** Also with a 9-ft. stepped ceiling and a view of the porch, this room features a bay window.

- **Family Room:** An 11-ft. vaulted ceiling and gliding French doors to the porch define this central gathering area.

- **Kitchen:** Enjoy the skylight, a fireplace that's shared with the family room, a central island cooktop, and a snack bar in this room.

- **Master Suite:** The tray ceiling is 9 ft. 9 in. high, and this area includes a sitting area and a bath with a whirlpool tub and dual-sink vanity.

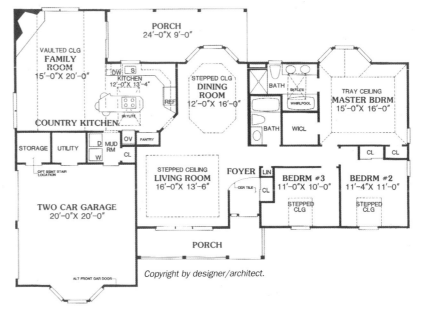

Copyright by designer/architect.

Kitchen

Foyer/Dining Room

Plan #161009

Dimensions: 60'9" W x 49' D

Levels: 1

Square Footage: 1,651

Bedrooms: 3

Bathrooms: 2

Foundation: Slab

Materials List Available: Yes

Price Category: C

The warm, textured exterior combines with the elegance of double-entry doors to preview both the casual lifestyle and formal entertaining capabilities of this versatile home.

Features:

• **Great Room:** Experience the openness provided by the sloped ceiling topping both this great room and the formal dining area. Enjoy the warmth and light supplied by the gas fireplace and dual sliding doors.

• **Kitchen:** This kitchen, convenient to the living space, is designed for easy work patterns and features an open bar that separates the work area from the more richly decorated gathering rooms.

• **Master Bedroom:** Separated for privacy, this master bedroom includes a tray ceiling and lavishly equipped bath.

• **Basement:** This full basement allows you to expand your living space to meet your needs.

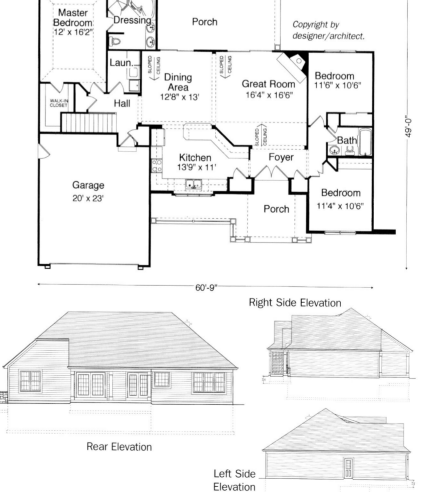

Images provided by designer/architect.

Copyright by designer/architect.

Rear Elevation

Right Side Elevation

Left Side Elevation

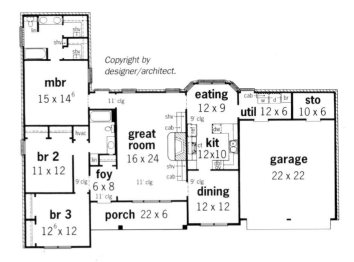

mbr
15 x 14⁶

11' clg

br 2
11 x 12

9' clg

foy
6 x 8
11' clg

br 3
12⁶ x 12

porch 22 x 6

great room
16 x 24
11' clg

eating
12 x 9
9' clg

kit
12 x 10

dining
12 x 12

util 12 x 6

sto
10 x 6

garage
22 x 22

Plan #201038

Dimensions: 71'10" W x 51'5" D
Levels: 1
Square Footage: 1,789
Bedrooms: 3
Bathrooms: 2
Foundation: Crawl space, slab
Materials List Available: Yes
Price Category: C

Images provided by designer/architect.

SMARTtip

Assembling Wall Frames

It's important to square up the pieces to start with. Then, even a tick mark across the joint will serve as an accurate registration mark for the plate joiner.

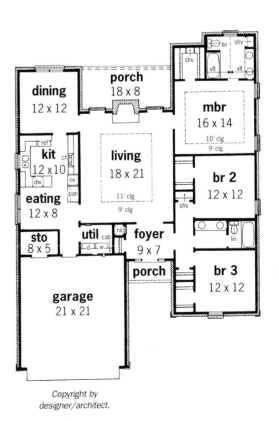

dining
12 x 12

porch
18 x 8

mbr
16 x 14
10' clg
9' clg

kit
12 x 10

living
18 x 21
11' clg
9' clg

br 2
12 x 12

eating
12 x 8

sto
8 x 5

util
9 x 7

foyer
9 x 7

porch

br 3
12 x 12

garage
21 x 21

Plan #201039

Dimensions: 46'10" W x 62'5" D
Levels: 1
Square Footage: 1,775
Bedrooms: 3
Bathrooms: 2
Foundation: Crawl space, slab
Materials List Available: Yes
Price Category: C

Images provided by designer/architect.

Images provided by designer/architect.

Plan #121013

Dimensions: 40' W x 55'8" D
Levels: 1
Square Footage: 1,375
Bedrooms: 1
Bathrooms: 2
Foundation: Basement
Materials List Available: Yes
Price Category: B

This convenient open plan is well-suited to retirement or as a starter home.

Features:

- Ceiling Height: 8 ft., unless otherwise noted.

- Den: To the left of the entry, French doors lead to a den that can convert to a second bedroom.

- Kitchen: A center island doubles as a snack bar while the breakfast area includes a pantry and a desk for compiling shopping lists and menus.

- Open Plan: The sense of spaciousness is enhanced by the large open area that includes the family room, kitchen, and breakfast area.

- Family Room: A handsome fireplace invites family and friends to gather in this area.

- Porch: Step through the breakfast area to enjoy the fresh air on this secluded porch.

- Master Bedroom: This distinctive bedroom features a boxed ceiling. It's served by a private bath with a walk-in closet.

SMARTtip

Paint Color Choices for Your Home

Earth tones are easy to decorate with because they are neutral colors. Use neutral or muted tones, such as light grays, browns, or greens with either lighter or darker shades for accenting.

Use bright colors sparingly, to catch the eye. Painting the front door a bright color creates a cheerful entryway.

Investigate home shows, magazines, and houses in your area for color ideas. Paint suppliers can also give you valuable tips on appropriate color schemes.

Colors that look just right on a color card may need to be toned down for painting large areas. If in doubt, buy a quart of paint and test it.

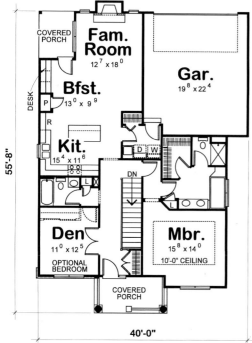

Copyright by designer/architect.

Plan #271080

Dimensions: 71' W x 83' D

Levels: 1

Square Footage: 2,581

Bedrooms: 3

Bathrooms: 3

Foundation: Basement

Materials List Available: Yes

Price Category: E

Images provided by designer/architect.

An open floor plan and beautiful adornments promise comfortable living within this appealing one-story home.

Features:

- Living Room: Beyond the sidelighted entry, this spacious living room is bordered on two sides by striking arched openings.

- Kitchen: This island kitchen flows into a bayed eating nook, which shares a two-sided fireplace with the living room.

- Master Suite: A bright sitting room is a nice feature in this luxurious suite, which is secluded to the rear of the home. The private bath boasts a corner tub, a separate shower, two vanities, and a walk-in closet.

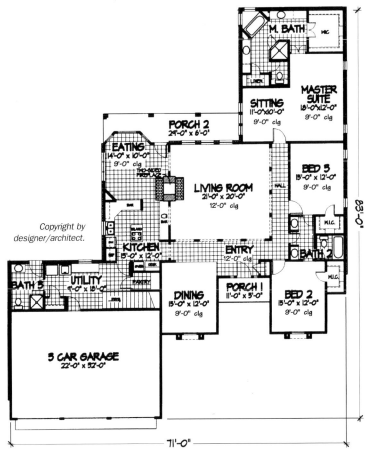

Copyright by designer/architect.

Plan #221012

Dimensions: 71' W x 51' D

Levels: 1

Square Footage: 1,802

Bedrooms: 3

Bathrooms: 2½

Foundation: Basement

Materials List Available: No

Price Category: D

Images provided by designer/architect.

Rear Elevation

The interesting roofline and covered porch on this one-story beauty give it great curb appeal.

Features:

- Ceiling Height: 8 ft.

- Great Room: Highlighted by a fireplace flanked by large windows on both sides, this large room also boasts a tall cathedral ceiling.

- Dining Room: This room opens from the entry for the convenience of your guests. Thanks to the nook by the kitchen, you can save this space for formal family dining and hosting dinner parties.

- Kitchen: This well-planned kitchen with ample counter and cabinet space also has an island and opens to the family room. Use the large, adjacent nook for casual meals, and take advantage of the sliding glass doors that open to the backyard.

- Master Suite: Relax in this suite's bedroom, where you'll find a large walk-in closet. The bath features both a soaking tub and a standing shower for the ultimate in versatility.

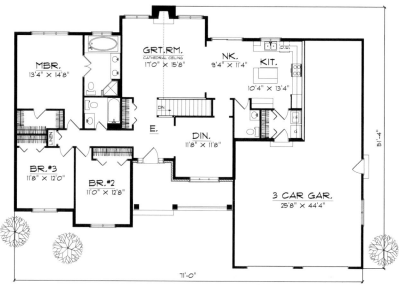

Copyright by designer/architect.

Plan #101012

Dimensions: 69'4" W x 62'9" D

Levels: 1

Square Footage: 2,288

Bedrooms: 3

Bathrooms: 2½

Foundation: Slab, crawl space, or basement

Materials List Available: No

Price Category: E

Images provided by designer/architect.

This classic brick ranch boasts traditional styling and an exciting up-to-date floor plan.

Features:

- Ceiling Height: 9 ft. unless otherwise noted.

- Front Porch: Guests will be welcome by this inviting front porch, which features a 12-ft. ceiling.

- Family Room: This warm and inviting room measures 16 ft. x 19 ft. It features a 14-ft. ceiling and a rear wall of windows. French doors lead to an enormous deck.

- Kitchen: This unique angled kitchen is open to the hearth room and eating areas, all of which enjoy vaulted ceilings and are surrounded by windows. The hearth room has a TV niche.

- Master Suite: This 16-ft. x 15-ft. master suite is truly sumptuous, with its 12-ft. ceiling, sitting area, two walk-in closets, and full-featured bath.

- Bonus Room: Here is plenty of storage or room for future expansion. Just beyond the entry are stairs leading to a bonus room measuring approximately 12 ft. x 21 ft.

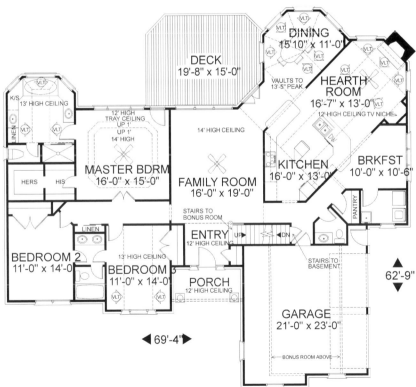

Copyright by designer/architect.

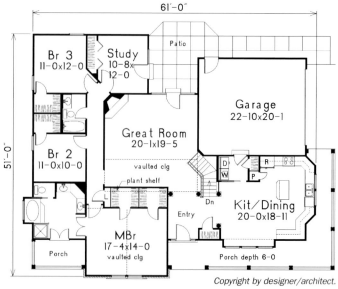

Copyright by designer/architect.

Plan #321030

Dimensions: 61' W x 51' D
Levels: 1
Square Footage: 2,029
Bedrooms: 4
Bathrooms: 2
Foundation: Basement
Materials List Available: Yes
Price Category: D

Images provided by designer/architect.

SMARTtip

Measuring Angles

A sure-fire way to accurately measure the wall-frame acute angle is to cut a piece of scrap lumber to emulate the angle, and then measure it.

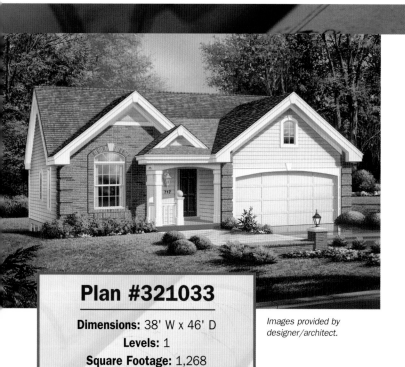

Plan #321033

Dimensions: 38' W x 46' D
Levels: 1
Square Footage: 1,268
Bedrooms: 3
Bathrooms: 2
Foundation: Basement
Materials List Available: Yes
Price Category: B

Images provided by designer/architect.

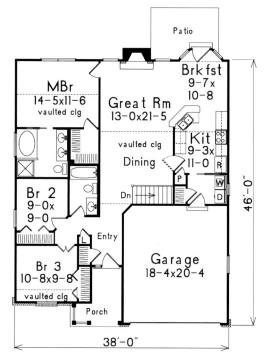

Copyright by designer/architect.

Plan #201042

Dimensions: 67'10" W x 49'10" D
Levels: 1
Square Footage: 1,880
Bedrooms: 3
Bathrooms: 2
Foundation: Crawl space, slab
Materials List Available: Yes
Price Category: D

Images provided by designer/architect.

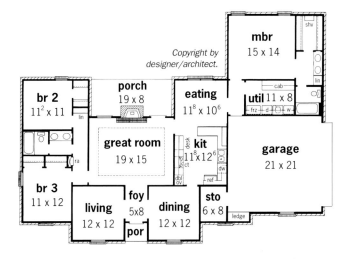

Copyright by designer/architect.

- mbr 15 x 14
- shv
- br 2 11² x 11
- porch 19 x 8
- eating 11⁸ x 10⁶
- cab
- util 11 x 8
- lin
- great room 19 x 15
- desk
- kit 11⁸ x 12⁶
- ct
- garage 21 x 21
- frz
- d
- w
- dbl ov
- ref
- dw
- br 3 11 x 12
- foy 5x8
- living 12 x 12
- por
- dining 12 x 12
- sto 6 x 8
- ledge

SMARTtip
Two Dishwashers

Sometimes two is better than one. If you have the need (yours is a large household, you do a lot of cooking and baking, or you entertain often), two dishwashers make sense. That way, when one is full, you won't have to pile the sink with dirty dishes, pots, and pans. If you don't have space for a second full-size model, consider a dishwasher drawer.

Plan #201045

Dimensions: 63'10" W x 54'5" D
Levels: 1
Square Footage: 1,866
Bedrooms: 3
Bathrooms: 2
Foundation: Crawl space, slab
Materials List Available: Yes
Price Category: D

Images provided by designer/architect.

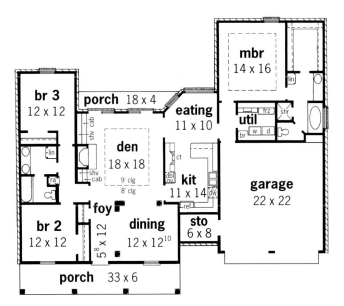

- mbr 14 x 16
- lin
- br 3 12 x 12
- porch 18 x 4
- eating 11 x 10
- frz
- shr
- util
- shv cab
- den 18 x 18
- 9' clg
- 8' clg
- ct
- kit 11 x 14
- br
- w
- d
- garage 22 x 22
- shv cab
- dbl ov
- dw
- ref
- foy 5⁸ x 12
- br 2 12 x 12
- dining 12 x 12¹⁰
- sto 6 x 8
- porch 33 x 6

Copyright by designer/architect.

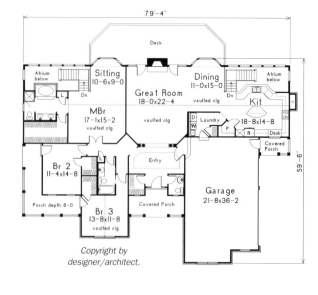

Deck

Atrium below

Sitting
10-6x9-0

Dining
11-0x15-0

Atrium below

Great Room
18-0x22-4
vaulted clg

MBr
17-1x15-2
vaulted clg

Kit
18-8x14-8

vaulted clg

Laundry

Covered Porch

Br 2
11-4x14-8

Entry

Garage
21-8x36-2

Porch depth 6-0

Br 3
13-8x11-8
vaulted clg

Covered Porch

Copyright by designer/architect.

Images provided by designer/architect.

Plan #321031

Dimensions: 79'4" W x 59'6' D

Levels: 1

Square Footage: 3,200

Bedrooms: 3

Bathrooms: 2½

Foundation: Daylight basement

Materials List Available: Yes

Price Category: G

Optional Basement Level Floor Plan

Up

Study
16-7x21-4

Unfinished Basement

Family Room
18-4x19-4

Up

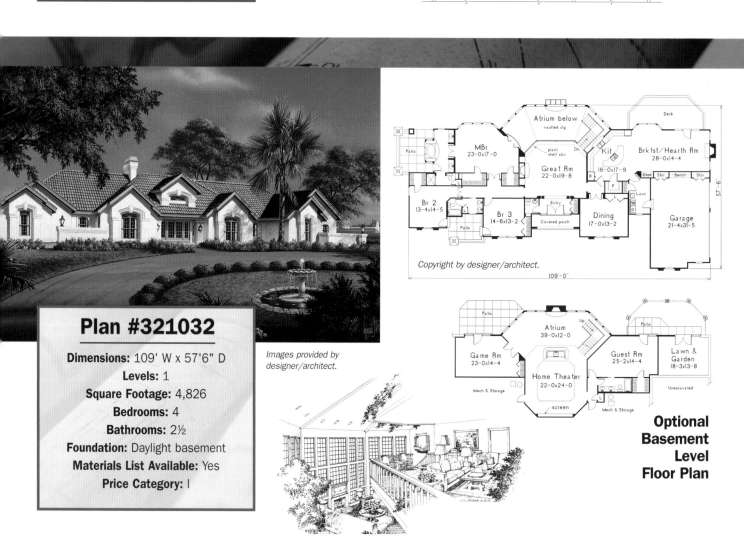

Atrium below
vaulted clg

MBr
23-0x17-0

plant shell abv

Kit
16-0x17-9

Brkfst/Hearth Rm
28-0x14-4

Patio

Great Rm
22-0x19-8

Stor   Bench   Stor

Br 2
13-4x14-5

Br 3
14-6x13-2

Entry

Covered porch

Dining
17-0x13-2

Lawn

Garage
21-4x31-5

Patio

Copyright by designer/architect.

109'-0"

Plan #321032

Dimensions: 109' W x 57'6" D

Levels: 1

Square Footage: 4,826

Bedrooms: 4

Bathrooms: 2½

Foundation: Daylight basement

Materials List Available: Yes

Price Category: I

Images provided by designer/architect.

Patio

Atrium
39-0x12-0

Up

Patio

Game Rm
23-0x14-4

Home Theater
22-0x24-0

Guest Rm
25-2x14-4

Lawn & Garden
18-3x13-8

Mech & Storage

screen

Mech & Storage

Unexcavated

Optional Basement Level Floor Plan

Plan #201046

Dimensions: 58'10" W x 59'10" D

Levels: 1

Square Footage: 1,871

Bedrooms: 3

Bathrooms: 2

Foundation: Crawl space, slab

Materials List Available: Yes

Price Category: D

Images provided by designer/architect.

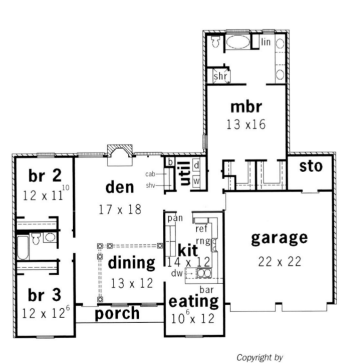

Copyright by designer/architect.

mbr 14 x 15

porch 31 x 8

eating 13 x 9⁶

den 18 x 18

br 2 12 x 11⁶

kit 13 x 12

util

sto

dining 14 x 12

foy 10x5⁶

br 3 11⁴ x 12

garage 22 x 22

por

Plan #201048

Dimensions: 64'10" W x 58'11" D

Levels: 1

Square Footage: 1,888

Bedrooms: 3

Bathrooms: 2

Foundation: Crawl space, slab

Materials List Available: Yes

Price Category: D

Images provided by designer/architect.

mbr 13 x16

sto

br 2 12 x 11¹⁰

den 17 x 18

util

garage 22 x 22

br 3 12 x 12⁶

dining 13 x 12

kit 14 x 12

porch

eating 10⁶ x 12

Copyright by designer/architect.

Plan #221013

Dimensions: 48' W x 58'8" D

Levels: 1

Square Footage: 1,495

Bedrooms: 3

Bathrooms: 2

Foundation: Basement

Materials List Available: No

Price Category: B

Images provided by designer/architect.

Rear Elevation

If you love rooms with unusual shapes, angled features, and interesting ceilings, this could be the home of your dreams.

Features:

- Ceiling Height: 8 ft.

- Great Room: A cathedral ceiling complements this huge room, and the fireplace and flanking windows make a lovely focal point.

- Dining Room: You'll love the cathedral ceiling that gives elegance to this open dining room, as well as its doors, which lead to both the backyard and the screened-in porch.

- Kitchen: Arched openings let you look into the dining room and the great room, and the angled counter area gives distinction to this room, with its step-saving floor plan.

- Master Suite: Enjoy the tray ceiling, walk-in closet, plant ledge, and luxurious bath.

- Additional Bedrooms: Bedroom #2 has a cathedral ceiling, and shares a bath with bedroom #3.

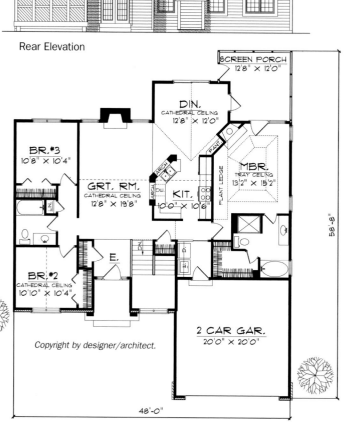

Copyright by designer/architect.

Plan #101013

Dimensions: 71'4" W x 65'3" D
Levels: 1
Square Footage: 2,564
Bedrooms: 3
Bathrooms: 2½
Foundation: Slab, crawl space, basement
Materials List Available: No
Price Category: E

Images provided by designer/architect.

This exciting design combines a striking classic exterior with a highly functional floor plan.

Features:

- Ceiling Height: 9 ft. unless otherwise noted.

- Family Room: This warm and inviting room measures 18 ft. x 22 ft. It features a 14-ft. ceiling and a rear wall of windows. French doors lead to an enormous deck.

- Kitchen: This unique angled kitchen is open to the hearth room and eating areas, all of which enjoy vaulted ceilings and are surrounded by windows. The hearth room has a TV niche.

- Master Suite: This 19-ft. x 18-ft. master suite is truly sumptuous, with its 12-ft. ceiling, sitting area, two walk-in closets, and full-featured bath.

- Secondary Bedrooms: Each of the secondary bedrooms measures 11 ft. x 14 ft. and has direct access to a shared bath.

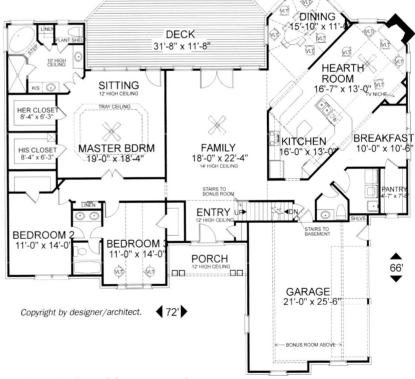

Copyright by designer/architect.

- Bonus Room: Just beyond the entry are stairs leading to this bonus room, which measures approximately 12 ft. x 21 ft.—plenty of room for storage or future expansion.

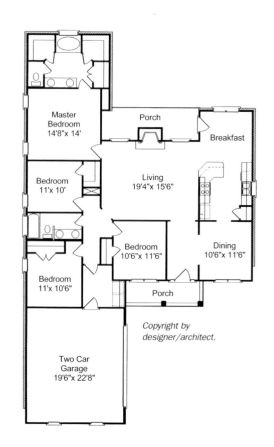

Plan #111014

Dimensions: 78' W x 47' D

Levels: 1

Square Footage: 1,865

Bedrooms: 4

Bathrooms: 2

Foundation: Crawl space

Materials List Available: No

Price Category: D

Images provided by designer/architect.

Copyright by designer/architect.

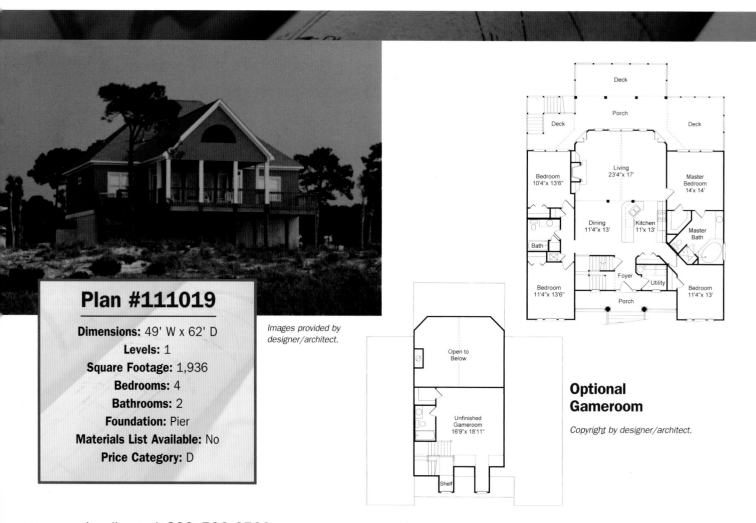

Plan #111019

Dimensions: 49' W x 62' D

Levels: 1

Square Footage: 1,936

Bedrooms: 4

Bathrooms: 2

Foundation: Pier

Materials List Available: No

Price Category: D

Images provided by designer/architect.

Optional Gameroom

Copyright by designer/architect.

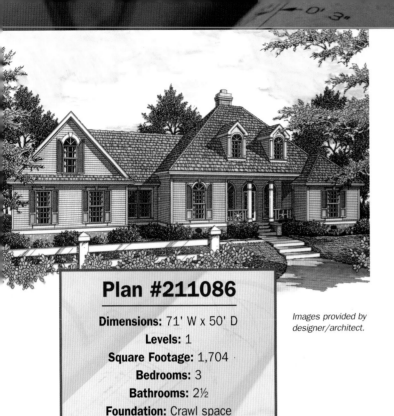

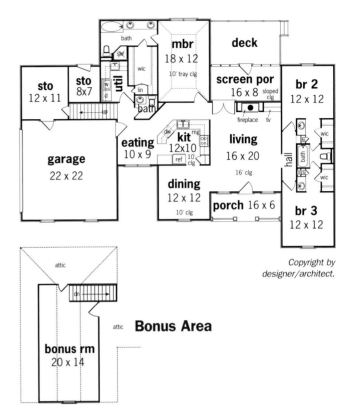

Images provided by designer/architect.

Copyright by designer/architect.

Bonus Area

Plan #211086

Dimensions: 71' W x 50' D

Levels: 1

Square Footage: 1,704

Bedrooms: 3

Bathrooms: 2½

Foundation: Crawl space

Materials List Available: Yes

Price Category: C

Images provided by designer/architect.

Plan #251006

Dimensions: 65'5" W x 59'11" D

Levels: 1

Square Footage: 1,849

Bedrooms: 3

Bathrooms: 2

Foundation: Crawl space

Materials List Available: Yes

Price Category: D

Copyright by designer/architect.

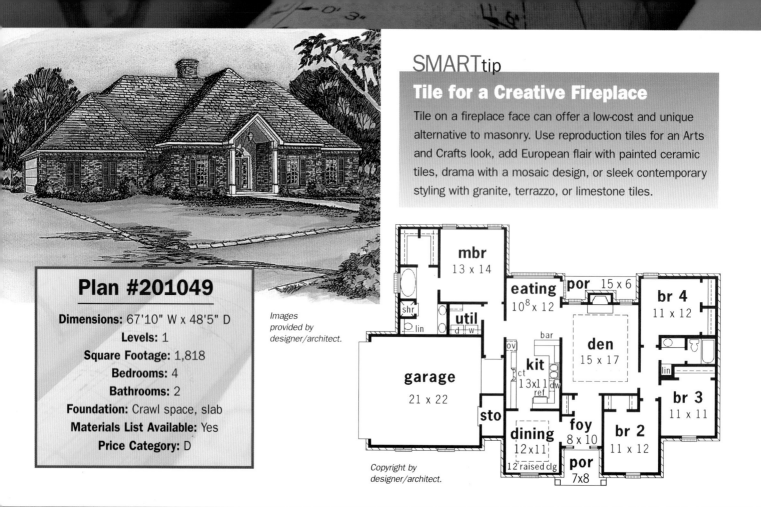

Tile for a Creative Fireplace

Tile on a fireplace face can offer a low-cost and unique alternative to masonry. Use reproduction tiles for an Arts and Crafts look, add European flair with painted ceramic tiles, drama with a mosaic design, or sleek contemporary styling with granite, terrazzo, or limestone tiles.

Plan #201049

Dimensions: 67'10" W x 48'5" D
Levels: 1
Square Footage: 1,818
Bedrooms: 4
Bathrooms: 2
Foundation: Crawl space, slab
Materials List Available: Yes
Price Category: D

Images provided by designer/architect.

Copyright by designer/architect.

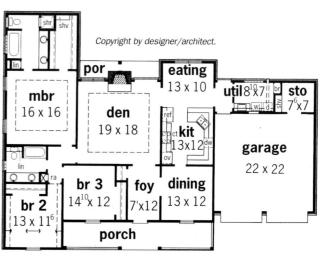

Copyright by designer/architect.

Plan #201056

Dimensions: 70'10" W x 50'10" D
Levels: 1
Square Footage: 1,956
Bedrooms: 3
Bathrooms: 2
Foundation: Crawl space, slab
Materials List Available: Yes
Price Category: D

Images provided by designer/architect.

Plan #201061

Dimensions: 64'10" W x 54'10" D

Levels: 1

Square Footage: 2,387

Bedrooms: 4

Bathrooms: 2½

Foundation: Crawl space, slab

Materials List Available: Yes

Price Category: E

Images provided by designer/architect.

mbr
15 x 14

porch
19 x 8

garage
21 x 22

br 4
12 x 11

den
19 x 20

sto

util

shr
shv
cab
shv
cab
lin
ra

ref

kit
15 x 14

br 2
11⁶ x 12⁶

foy
9x12

dining
14 x 12⁶

ov
ct

br 3
12 x 12⁴

eating
10 x 15

w d

dw

Copyright by designer/architect.

Plan #201063

Dimensions: 74'10" W x 70'10" D

Levels: 1

Square Footage: 2,697

Bedrooms: 4

Bathrooms: 3

Foundation: Crawl space, slab

Materials List Available: Yes

Price Category: F

Images provided by designer/architect.

por 33⁸x5

eating
14 x 10

den
20⁶ x 18

br 4
12 x 14

mbr
19⁸ x 16

kit
14 x 14

dw
pan
ct
ov
ref
lin

dining
14' x 16

foy
8 x 14

br 2
12 x 12

br 3
12 x 16

ra
ra

sto
7 x 8

util 8x8

por

frz
w h
d
br
ra
lin

garage
22 x 22

Copyright by designer/architect.

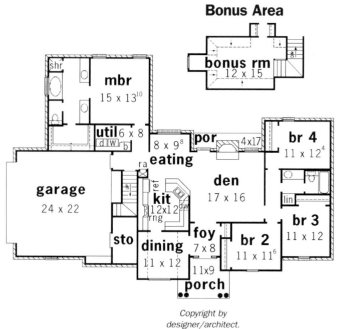

Bonus Area

bonus rm
12 x 15

shr

mbr
15 x 13¹⁰

util 6 x 8
8 x 9⁸
por 4 x 17

br 4
11 x 12⁴

garage
24 x 22

eating
kit
12 x 12
den
17 x 16

br 3
11 x 12

sto
foy
7 x 8

dining
11 x 12
br 2
11 x 11⁶

11 x 9
porch

Images provided by designer/architect.

Copyright by designer/architect.

Plan #201089

Dimensions: 72'10" W x 54'5" D

Levels: 1

Square Footage: 1,873

Bedrooms: 4

Bathrooms: 2

Foundation: Crawl space, slab

Materials List Available: Yes

Price Category: D

garage
22 x 23⁶

porch 30 x 8

br 4
11¹⁰ x 12²

sto
7 x 8⁴
util 9²x 8⁴

eating
12 x 11

den
18 x 22

br 3
11¹⁰ x 12

mbr
20²x 16²

kit
13¹⁰ x 11

dining
13⁸ x 12
foy
8¹⁰ x 8

porch

br 2
12 x 14

Images provided by designer/architect.

Plan #201064

Dimensions: 68'10" W x 67'4" D

Levels: 1

Square Footage: 2,682

Bedrooms: 4

Bathrooms: 3

Foundation: Crawl space, slab

Materials List Available: Yes

Price Category: F

Copyright by designer/architect.

Plan #211090

Dimensions: 66' W x 72' D
Levels: 1
Square Footage: 1,932
Bedrooms: 3
Bathrooms: 2
Foundation: Crawl space
Materials List Available: No
Price Category: D

This home has a magnificent raised-cottage exterior that makes it seem much larger than it actually is.

Features:

- Ceiling Height: 8 ft.

- Living Room: There is plenty of room for entertaining and family activities in this living room. Pairs of French doors lead from here to the rear covered deck and porch.

- Kitchen: The smart, modern design of this kitchen makes cooking a pleasure. The room is angled to provide a commanding view to the outside through the parallel angles of the adjacent eating area. This kitchen includes a built-in pantry and a desk for menu planning and compiling shopping lists.

- Master Suite: This luxurious master suite includes a bath with a large walk-in closet, twin lavatories, a dressing area, linen storage, a soaking tub, and a separate shower.

- Room to Expand: A conveniently located stairwell leads to an abundance of space waiting for future expansion.

Images provided by designer/architect.

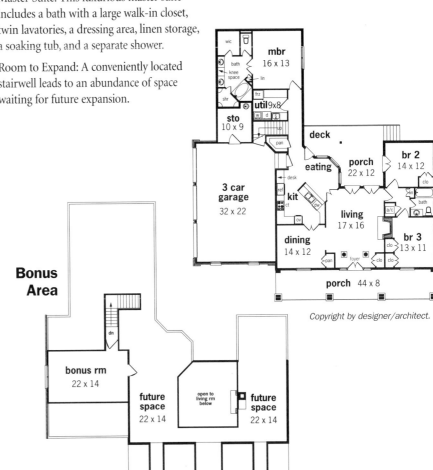

Copyright by designer/architect.

Plan #131044

Dimensions: 57'6" W x 42'4" D
Levels: 1
Square Footage: 1,994
Bedrooms: 3
Bathrooms: 2
Foundation: Basement, crawl space, or slab
Materials List Available: Yes
Price Category: E

Under a covered porch, Victorian-detailed bay windows grace each side of the brick-faced facade at the center of this ranch-style home, giving it a formal air.

Features:

• Ceiling Height: 10-ft. ceilings grace the central living area and the master bedroom of this home.

• Entry: Round top windows make this area and the flanking rooms bright and cheery.

• Great Room: A fireplace and built-ins that are visible from anywhere in this large room make it a natural gathering place for friends and family.

• Optional Office: Use the room just off the central hall as a home office, fourth bedroom, or study.

• Master Suite: You'll love the bay window, tray ceiling, two walk-in closets, and private bath.

• Bonus Space: Finish this large area in the attic for extra living space, or use it for storage.

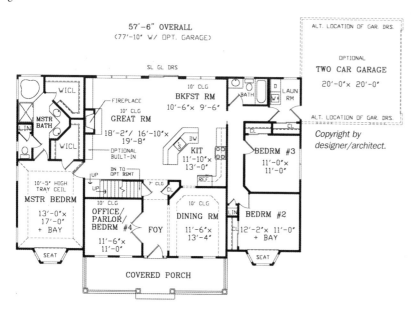

Rear Elevation

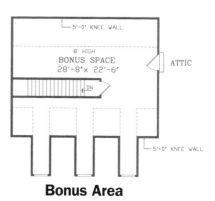

Bonus Area

Images provided by designer/architect.

Plan #161010

Dimensions: 50'8" W x 44'2" D
Levels: 1
Square Footage: 1,544
Bedrooms: 3
Bathrooms: 2
Foundation: Basement
Materials List Available: Yes
Price Category: C

This one-story home's many distinctive and elegant features—including arched openings and sloped ceilings—will surprise and excite you at every turn.

Features:

- Great Room: Decorative columns frame the entrance from the foyer to this great room and are repeated at the opening to the formal dining area.

- Kitchen: Designed for quick meals or to accommodate an oversized crowd, this kitchen features a curved countertop with seating that functions as a delightful bar.

- Master Bedroom: This master bedroom is split to afford you more privacy and features a compartmented bath that forms a separate vanity area.

- Additional Bedrooms: Take advantage of the double doors off the foyer to allow one bedroom to function as a library.

Right Side Elevation

Left Side Elevation

Rear Elevation

Copyright by designer/architect.

Plan #221014

Dimensions: 72' W x 44'8" D

Levels: 1

Square Footage: 1,906

Bedrooms: 3

Bathrooms: 2½

Foundation: Basement

Materials List Available: No

Price Category: D

Images provided by designer/architect.

If elegance is your cup of tea but you also have a practical streak, you'll love everything about this home.

Features:

- Ceiling Height: 8 ft.

- Living Room: The tall vaulted ceiling gives stature to this spacious room. Decorate to highlight the cozy fireplace, and let your guests flow into the adjacent dining room.

- Dining Room: A bayed area with a central doorway to the backyard highlights this room, which is open to the kitchen.

- Kitchen: The family chefs will love the central island and ample counter and cabinet space in this well-planned kitchen, which opens to a fully equipped laundry room and half-bath.

- Master Suite: A tray ceiling and large bay window are the elegant features in this suite's bedroom. The bath includes a whirlpool tub, standing shower, and two-sink vanity. The adjacent walk-in closet gives a practical touch.

Rear Elevation

Copyright by designer/architect.

Plan #131045

Dimensions: 81'4" W x 68'3" D
Levels: 1
Square Footage: 2,347
Bedrooms: 4
Bathrooms: 2½
Foundation: Basement, crawl space, or slab
Materials List Available: Yes
Price Category: E

You'll love the character and flexibility in siting that the angled design gives to this contemporary ranch-style home.

Features:

- Porch: A wraparound rear porch adds distinction to this lovely home.

- Great Room: Facing the rear of the house, this great room has a high, stepped ceiling, fireplace, and ample space for built-ins.

- Kitchen: This large room sits at an angle to the great room and is adjacent to both a laundry room and extra powder room.

- Office: Use the 4th bedroom as a home office, study, or living room, depending on your needs.

- Master Suite: This area is separated from the other bedrooms in the house to give it privacy. The beautiful bay window at the rear, two large walk-in closets, and luxurious bath make it an ideal retreat after a hectic day.

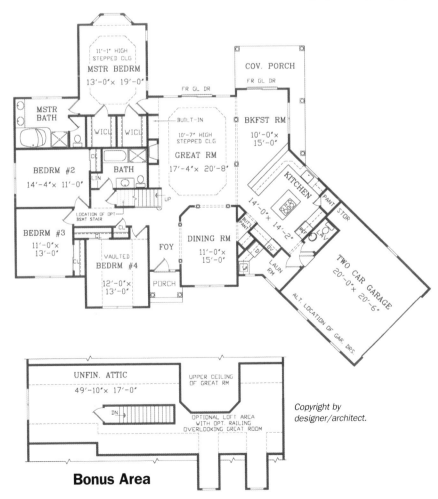

Bonus Area

Plan #151131

Dimensions: 28' W x 77' D
Levels: 1
Square Footage: 1,446
Bedrooms: 3
Bathrooms: 2
Foundation: Crawl space, slab
Materials List Available: Yes
Price Category: B

The 10-in. columns on the lovely front porch make this traditional and gracious home seem a part of the old South.

Features:

- **Great Room:** A 10-ft. boxed ceiling gives presence to this spacious room, and an angled corner fireplace lets you create a cozy nook where everyone will gather in chilly weather.

- **Kitchen:** The snack bar and large adjoining breakfast room encourage friends and family to gather here at all times of day. All the household cooks will appreciate the thoughtful layout that makes cooking a delight.

- **Master Suite:** A 10-ft. ceiling emphasizes the luxury you'll find in both the bedroom and private bath, with its two vanities, spacious walk-in closets, and whirlpool tub.

- **Additional Bedrooms:** A deluxe full bath separates bedrooms 2 and 3, and both rooms feature generous closet space.

Copyright by designer/architect.

SMARTtip

Creating Depth with Wall Frames

Wall frames create an illusion of depth and density because 1) they are three-dimensional and 2) they divide the wall area into smaller, denser segments. The three-dimensional quality of wall frames is fundamentally different from that of the alternative treatment: raised panels. Despite the name, raised panels actually produce a concave-like, or receding, effect whereas wall frames are more convex, protruding outward. In terms of sculpture, concave units create negative space while convex units create positive space. Raised panels, therefore, deliver a uniform sense of volume, mass, and density, while wall frames create a higher level of tension and dramatic interest.

Plan #121034

Dimensions: 92'8" W x 59'4" D

Levels: 1

Square Footage: 2,223

Bedrooms: 2

Bathrooms: 2

Foundation: Basement

Materials List Available: Yes

Price Category: E

Images provided by designer/architect.

This home features a flowing, open floor plan coupled with an abundance of amenities.

Features:

- Ceiling Height: 8 ft. unless otherwise noted.
- Foyer: This elegant entry features a curved staircase and a view of the formal dining room.
- Formal Dining Room: Magnificent arched openings lead from the foyer into this dining room. The boxed ceiling adds to the architectural interest.
- Great Room: A wall of windows, a see-through fireplace, and built-in entertainment center make this the perfect gathering place.
- Covered Deck: The view of this deck, through the wall of windows in the great room, will lure guests out to this large deck.
- Hearth Room: This room share a panoramic view with the eating area.
- Kitchen: This kitchen features a corner pantry, a built-in desk, and a curved island.

Main Level Floor Plan

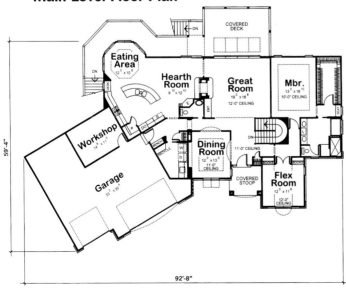

Optional Basement Level Floor Plan

Copyright by designer/architect.

Plan #201067

Dimensions: 68'10" W x 67'4" D

Levels: 1

Square Footage: 2,735

Bedrooms: 4

Bathrooms: 3

Foundation: Crawl space, slab

Materials List Available: Yes

Price Category: F

Images provided by designer/architect.

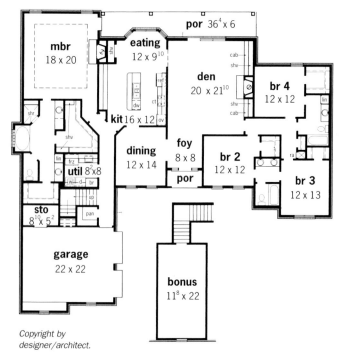

mbr
15 x 21^4
raised clg

porch
8 x 30^8

br 4
14 x 12

sto
8^6 x 8

util 8^6 x 9^2

eating
13 x 11

den
18 x 24

raised clg

br 3
14 x 12

garage
21 x 22

kit
12^8 x 13

foy
8 x 9^6

dining
14 x 12

porch

br 2
14^2 x 12

ledge

Copyright by designer/architect.

Plan #201068

Dimensions: 74'10" W x 73'10" D

Levels: 1

Square Footage: 2,780

Bedrooms: 4

Bathrooms: 3

Foundation: Crawl space, slab

Materials List Available: Yes

Price Category: F

Images provided by designer/architect.

mbr
18 x 20

eating
12 x 9^{10}

por 36^4 x 6

den
20 x 21^{10}

br 4
12 x 12

kit 16 x 12

dining
12 x 14

foy
8 x 8

br 2
12 x 12

br 3
12 x 13

util 8^{2}x8

por

sto
8^{10} x 5^2

pan

garage
22 x 22

bonus
11^8 x 22

Copyright by designer/architect.

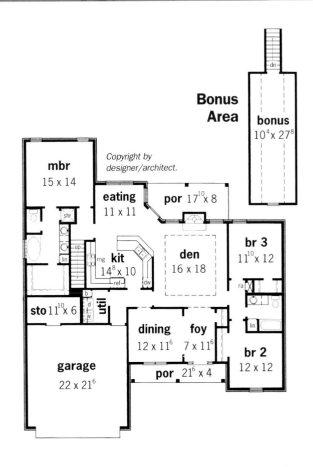

Plan #201079

Dimensions: 56'4" W x 60'10" D

Levels: 1

Square Footage: 1,856

Bedrooms: 3

Bathrooms: 2

Foundation: Crawl space, slab

Materials List Available: Yes

Price Category: D

Bonus Area

bonus
10^4 x 27^8

*Copyright by
designer/architect.*

mbr
15 x 14

eating
11 x 11

por 17^{10} x 8

br 3
11^{10} x 12

den
16 x 18

kit
14^8 x 10

sto 11^{10} x 6

util

dining
12 x 11^6

foy
7 x 11^6

br 2
12 x 12

garage
22 x 21^6

por 21^6 x 4

Plan #201074

Dimensions: 56' W x 59' D

Levels: 1

Square Footage: 1,692

Bedrooms: 3

Bathrooms: 2

Foundation: Crawl space, slab

Materials List Available: Yes

Price Category: C

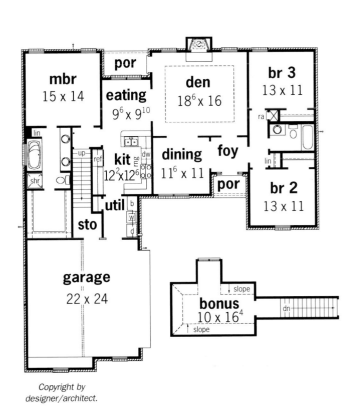

mbr
15 x 14

por

eating
9^6 x 9^{10}

den
18^6 x 16

br 3
13 x 11

kit
12^2x12^6

dining
11^6 x 11

foy

br 2
13 x 11

util

sto

por

garage
22 x 24

bonus
10 x 16^4

slope

slope

*Copyright by
designer/architect.*

Plan #161011

Dimensions: 66' W x 69' D

Levels: 1

Square Footage: 1,788

Bedrooms: 3

Bathrooms: 2

Foundation: Basement

Materials List Available: Yes

Price Category: C

A beautiful facade, an exciting interior, and step-saving convenience combine to make this lovely home appealing to a variety of discriminating tastes.

Features:

- Great Room: This great room provides easy access to the formal dining area and breakfast area. You will enjoy the openness of the sloped ceiling and the warmth of the corner fireplace.

- Kitchen: This well-designed, spacious kitchen offers the convenience of island seating, the charm of a boxed window at the sink, and the luxury of a large breakfast area that opens to a spectacular screened porch.

- Master Suite: Pamper yourself and relax at the end of the day in the luxurious bath that this master suite provides.

- Laundry Room: You will appreciate the convenience of a separate area to simplify the chore of wash days.

Images provided by designer/architect.

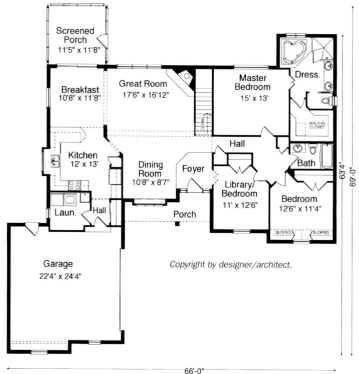

Copyright by designer/architect.

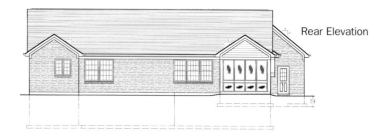

Rear Elevation

Plan #221015

Dimensions: 69'8" W x 46' D

Levels: 1

Square Footage: 1,926

Bedrooms: 3

Bathrooms: 2½

Foundation: Basement; optional walk-out basement available for extra fee

Materials List Available: No

Price Category: D

Images provided by designer/architect.

You'll love the open plan in this lovely ranch and admire its many features, which are usually reserved for much larger homes.

Features:

- Ceiling Height: 8 ft.

- Great Room: A vaulted ceiling and tall windows surrounding the centrally located fireplace give distinction to this handsome room.

- Dining Room: Positioned just off the entry, this formal room makes a lovely spot for quiet dinner parties.

- Dining Nook: This nook sits between the kitchen and the great room. Central doors in the bayed area open to the backyard.

- Kitchen: An island will invite visitors while you cook in this well-planned kitchen, with its corner pantry and ample counter space.

- Master Suite: A tray ceiling, bay window, walk-in closet, and bath with whirlpool tub, dual-sink vanity, and standing shower pamper you here.

Rear Elevation

Copyright by designer/architect.

Plan #271081

Dimensions: 86' W x 54' D
Levels: 1
Square Footage: 2,539
Bedrooms: 4
Bathrooms: 2
Foundation: Slab
Materials List Available: No
Price Category: E

Images provided by designer/architect.

This traditional home is sure to impress your guests and even your neighbors.

Features:

• Living Room: This quiet space off the foyer is perfect for pleasant conversation.

• Family Room: A perfect gathering spot, this room is nicely enhanced by a fireplace.

• Kitchen: This room easily serves the bayed morning room and the formal dining room.

• Master Suite: The master bedroom overlooks a side patio, and boasts a private bath with a skylight and a whirlpool tub.

• Library: This cozy room is perfect for curling up with a good novel. It would also make a great extra bedroom.

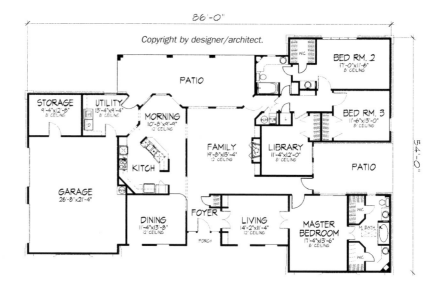

Copyright by designer/architect.

SMARTtip

Determining Curtain Length

Follow length guidelines for foolproof results, but remember that they're not rules. Go ahead and play with curtain and drapery lengths. Instead of shortening long panels at the hem, for instance, take up excess material by blousing them over tiebacks for a pleasing effect.

Plan #121060

Dimensions: 50' W x 46' D

Levels: 1

Square Footage: 1,339

Bedrooms: 3

Full Bathrooms: 2

Foundation: Basement

Materials List Available: Yes

Price Category: B

Images provided by designer/architect.

You'll love this compact design if you're looking for either a starter home or a luxurious place to spend your retirement years.

Features:

- **Foyer:** A covered stoop and arched entry open to this gracious foyer, where you'll love to greet guests.

- **Great Room:** From the foyer, you'll walk into this large area with its 10-ft. ceilings. A fireplace gives you a cozy spot on chilly days and cool evenings.

- **Kitchen:** This kitchen is truly step-saving and convenient. In addition to plenty of counter and storage space, it features a snack bar and an adjoining breakfast area.

- **Master Suite:** A 9-ft. ceiling gives a touch of elegance to the bedroom, and the walk-in closet adds practicality. In the bath, you'll find two vanities and a whirlpool tub.

- **Garage:** There's room for storage, a work bench, and three cars in this huge garage.

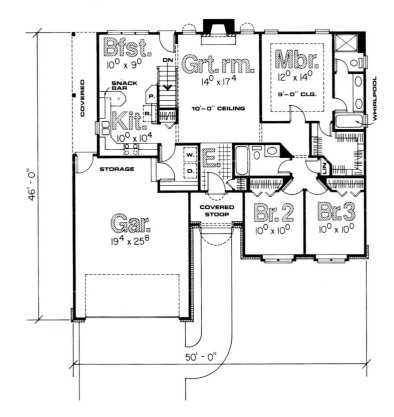

Copyright by designer/architect.

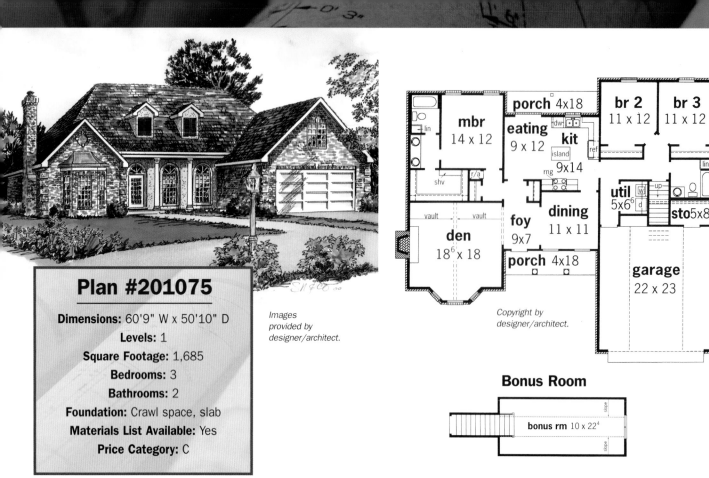

Plan #201075

Dimensions: 60'9" W x 50'10" D

Levels: 1

Square Footage: 1,685

Bedrooms: 3

Bathrooms: 2

Foundation: Crawl space, slab

Materials List Available: Yes

Price Category: C

Images provided by designer/architect.

Copyright by designer/architect.

Bonus Room

bonus rm 10 x 22⁴

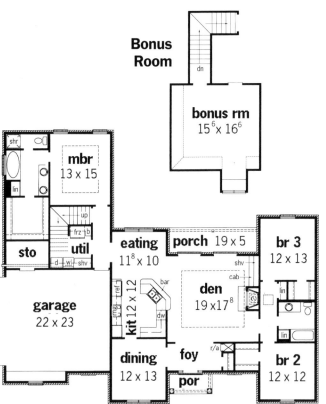

Plan #201081

Dimensions: 65'10" W x 55'10" D

Levels: 1

Square Footage: 1,940

Bedrooms: 3

Bathrooms: 2

Foundation: Crawl space, slab

Materials List Available: Yes

Price Category: D

Images provided by designer/architect.

Bonus Room

bonus rm 15⁶x 16⁶

Copyright by designer/architect.

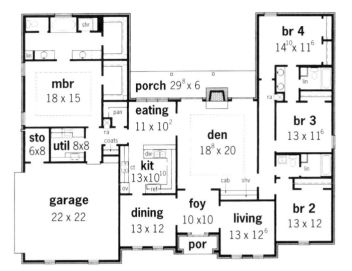

Plan #201083

Dimensions: 71'10" W x 54'10" D

Levels: 1

Square Footage: 2,733

Bedrooms: 4

Bathrooms: 3

Foundation: Crawl space, slab

Materials List Available: Yes

Price Category: F

Images provided by designer/architect.

Copyright by designer/architect.

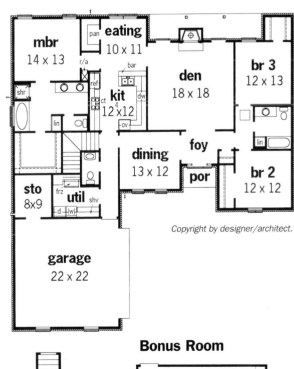

Plan #201085

Dimensions: 58'10" W x 63'4" D

Levels: 1

Square Footage: 2,015

Bedrooms: 3

Bathrooms: 2

Foundation: Crawl space, slab

Materials List Available: Yes

Price Category: D

Images provided by designer/architect.

Copyright by designer/architect.

Bonus Room

Plan #161012

Dimensions: 69' W x 50'10" D
Levels: 1
Square Footage: 1,648
Bedrooms: 3
Bathrooms: 2
Foundation: Basement
Materials List Available: Yes
Price Category: C

Images provided by designer/architect.

This delightful brick home, with multiple gables and an inviting front porch, offers an exciting interior with varied ceiling heights and an open floor plan.

Features:

- **Great Room:** This great room showcases an 11-ft. ceiling and a gas fireplace. Enjoy a beverage seated at the convenient bar, and move freely through a generous opening to the relaxed dining area.

- **Kitchen:** This galley kitchen is expanded by easy access to the garage and laundry room.

- **Master Bedroom:** You will appreciate the openness of this large master bedroom, which features an 11-ft. ceiling. You can also retreat to the privacy of an adjoining covered porch.

- **Library:** Thoughtful design allows you to exercise the option of converting the bedroom off the foyer into a library.

Right Side Elevation

Left Side Elevation

Rear Elevation

Covered Porch 14' X 12'

Dining 13'6" x 11'

Master Bedroom 16' x 15'8"

Great Room 17'8" x 16'2"

Two-Car Garage 22'6" x 22'

Kitchen

Bath

Laun.

Foyer

Library/ Bedroom 10' x 11'6"

Bath

Bedroom 10' x 11'6"

Porch

Copyright by designer/architect.

50'-10"

69'-0"

Plan #221016

Dimensions: 56' W x 42' D

Levels: 1

Square Footage: 1,461

Bedrooms: 3

Bathrooms: 2

Foundation: Basement

Materials List Available: No

Price Category: B

Images provided by designer/architect.

Rear Elevation

The interesting roofline and classic siding give this traditional ranch home an instant appeal.

Features:

- Ceiling Height: 8 ft.

- Great Room: From the entry, you'll look into this great room, where a handsome fireplace with large flanking windows makes you feel at home.

- Dining Room: Open to the great room, this room features access to the rear deck. An eating island shared with the kitchen allows the whole living area to flow together.

- Kitchen: The step-saving layout and ample counter space will delight the family chef.

- Master Suite: With a large walk-in closet and deluxe bath with a whirlpool tub, separate shower, and two-sink vanity, this private area will become a real retreat at the end of the day.

- Additional Bedrooms: Add the optional door from the entry to transform bedroom #2 into a quiet den, or use it as a bedroom.

Copyright by designer/architect.

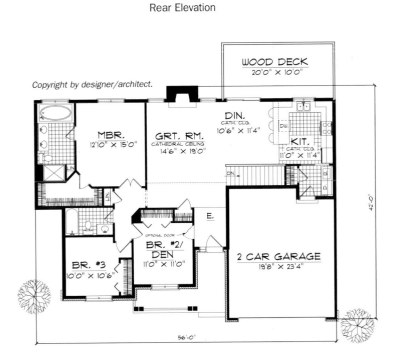

Plan #221017

Dimensions: 65' W x 56' D

Levels: 1

Square Footage: 2,229

Bedrooms: 3

Bathrooms: 2

Foundation: Basement

Materials List Available: No

Price Category: E

Images provided by designer/architect.

You'll love both the traditional appearance and practical layout of this gracious home.

Features:

- Ceiling Height: 9 ft.

- Great Room: A cathedral ceiling highlights the spaciousness of this room. Large rear windows and a handsome fireplace give it a comfortable atmosphere.

- Dining Room: Featuring a high tray ceiling, this dining room has an arched entryway to the great room and opens to the kitchen for convenience.

- Kitchen: This large room has a center cooktop island with space for an eating area, a corner pantry, and an arched doorway to the dining nook with easy access to the backyard.

- Master Suite: A cathedral ceiling and large windows looking out to the backyard give a graceful feeling to the bedroom. Two walk-in closets, plus a bath with a whirlpool tub, standing shower, and dual-sink vanity, add a practical and luxurious touch.

Rear Elevation

Copyright by designer/architect.

Images provided by
designer/architect.

Plan #111001

Dimensions: 66'8" W x 76'11" D

Levels: 1

Square Footage: 2,832

Bedrooms: 4

Bathrooms: 2½

Foundation: Slab

Materials List Available: No

Price Category: F

Copyright by
designer/architect.

Images provided by
designer/architect.

Plan #111013

Dimensions: 33' W x 59' D

Levels: 1

Square Footage: 1,606

Bedrooms: 3

Bathrooms: 2

Foundation: Slab

Materials List Available: No

Price Category: C

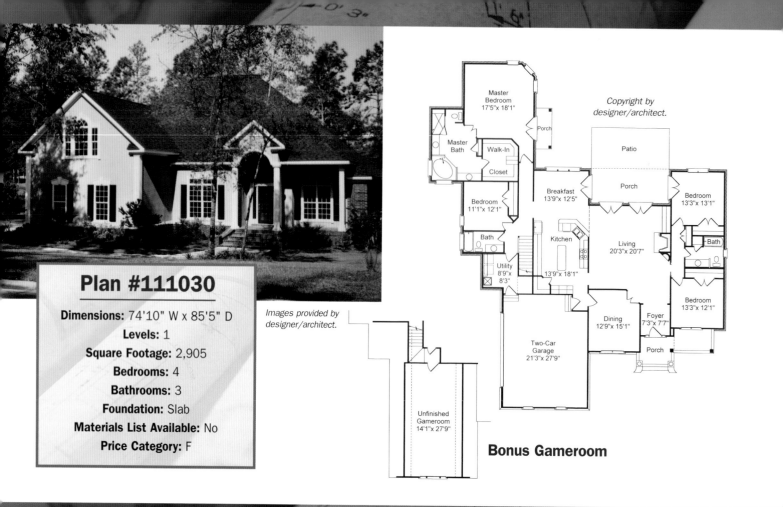

Plan #111030

Dimensions: 74'10" W x 85'5" D

Levels: 1

Square Footage: 2,905

Bedrooms: 4

Bathrooms: 3

Foundation: Slab

Materials List Available: No

Price Category: F

Images provided by designer/architect.

Bonus Gameroom

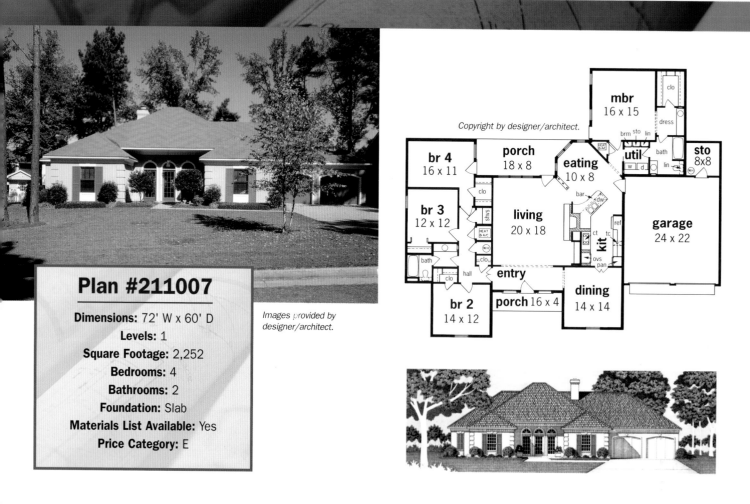

Plan #211007

Dimensions: 72' W x 60' D

Levels: 1

Square Footage: 2,252

Bedrooms: 4

Bathrooms: 2

Foundation: Slab

Materials List Available: Yes

Price Category: E

Images provided by designer/architect.

Bonus Room

bonus 10 x 22⁴

Plan #201086

Dimensions: 68'6" W x 46' D

Levels: 1

Square Footage: 1,573

Bedrooms: 3

Bathrooms: 2

Foundation: Crawl space, slab

Materials List Available: Yes

Price Category: C

Images provided by designer/architect.

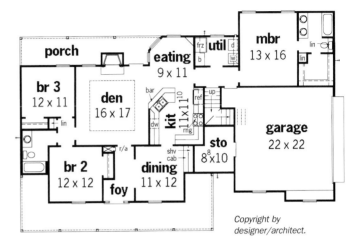

porch

br 3
12 x 11

den
16 x 17

bar

kit
11 x 11¹⁰

eating
9 x 11

util

mbr
13 x 16

up

br 2
12 x 12

foy

dining
11 x 12

sto
8⁸ x 10

garage
22 x 22

Copyright by designer/architect.

Plan #201087

Dimensions: 69'10" W x 51'5" D

Levels: 1

Square Footage: 1,672

Bedrooms: 3

Bathrooms: 2

Foundation: Crawl space, slab

Materials List Available: Yes

Price Category: C

Images provided by designer/architect.

Bonus Room

bonus rm
15⁸ x 12

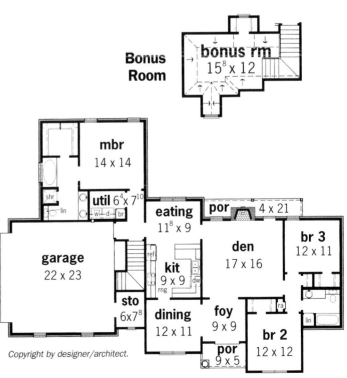

mbr
14 x 14

util 6⁴ x 7¹⁰

eating
11⁸ x 9

por
4 x 21

garage
22 x 23

kit
9 x 9

den
17 x 16

br 3
12 x 11

sto
6 x 7⁸

dining
12 x 11

foy
9 x 9

br 2
12 x 12

por
9 x 5

Copyright by designer/architect.

Plan #201069

Dimensions: 70'10" W x 64'10" D

Levels: 1

Square Footage: 2,735

Bedrooms: 4

Bathrooms: 3½

Foundation: Crawl space, slab

Materials List Available: Yes

Price Category: F

Images provided by designer/architect.

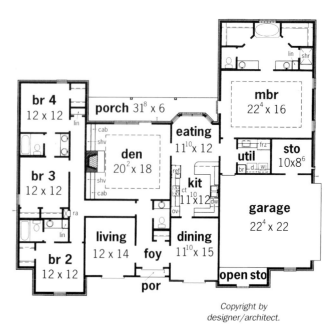

br 4
12 x 12

porch 31^8 x 6

mbr
22^4 x 16

br 3
12 x 12

den
20^2 x 18

eating
11^{10} x 12

util

sto
10x8^6

kit
11^{10}x12

living
12 x 14

dining
11^{10}x 15

foy

garage
22^4 x 22

br 2
12 x 12

por

open sto

Copyright by designer/architect.

Plan #321039

Dimensions: 31'8" W x 45' D

Levels: 1

Square Footage: 1,231

Bedrooms: 2

Bathrooms: 2

Foundation: Basement

Materials List Available: Yes

Price Category: B

Images provided by designer/architect.

31'-8"

balcony

Kit
10-6x
10-7

Din
9-4x13-0

Dn

Living
17-0x18-2

45'-0"

Br 2
10-0x
11-0

Entry

Porch

MBr
13-8x14-5
vaulted

Copyright by designer/architect.

Optional Basement Level Floor Plan

Dn

Garage
14-9x22-10

Family
15-0x17-6

storage

Plan #221018

Dimensions: 67' W x 53' D

Levels: 1

Square Footage: 2,007

Bedrooms: 3

Bathrooms: 2

Foundation: Basement

Materials List Available: No

Price Category: D

Images provided by designer/architect.

You'll love this ranch design, with its traditional stucco facade and interesting roofline.

Features:

• Ceiling Height: 9 ft.

• Great Room: A cathedral ceiling points up the large dimensions of this room, and the handsome fireplace with tall flanking windows lets you decorate for a formal or a casual feeling.

• Dining Room: A tray ceiling imparts elegance to this room, and a butler's pantry just across from the kitchen area lets you serve in style.

• Kitchen: You'll love the extensive counter space in this well-designed kitchen. The adjoining nook is large enough for a full-size dining set and features a door to the outside deck, where you can set up a third dining area.

• Master Suite: Located away from the other bedrooms for privacy, this suite includes a huge walk-in closet, windows overlooking the backyard, and a large bath with a whirlpool tub, standing shower, and dual-sink vanity.

Rear Elevation

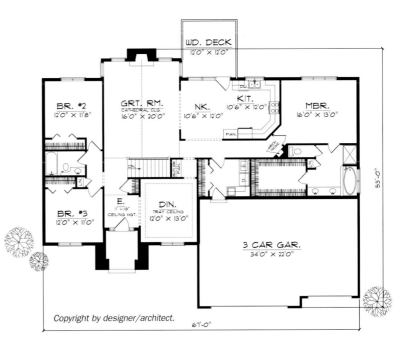

Copyright by designer/architect.

Plan #221019

Dimensions: 64'8" W x 57' D

Levels: 1

Square Footage: 1,591

Bedrooms: 3

Bathrooms: 2

Foundation: Basement

Materials List Available: No

Price Category: C

Images provided by designer/architect.

You'll be delighted with the many luxurious elements included in this compact home.

Features:

- Ceiling Height: 9 ft.

- Great Room: A vaulted ceiling sets the elegant tone you'll find reflected in the rest of this gracious home. The fireplace, flanked by windows, and the open entry to the dining room make everyone feel comfortable.

- Dining Room: A tray ceiling distinguishes this formal room. You'll find a door to the large screened porch from this room, so it's easy to serve meals here when the weather's fine or relax with a beverage at the end of the day.

- Kitchen: The ample counter and cabinet space make this kitchen a delight, and the eating bar encourages lots of little visitors.

- Master Suite: With a tray ceiling and huge walk-in closet, this suite's bedroom makes you feel elegant. The large bathroom, with its whirlpool tub, standing shower, and dual-sink vanity, confirms the feeling.

Rear Elevation

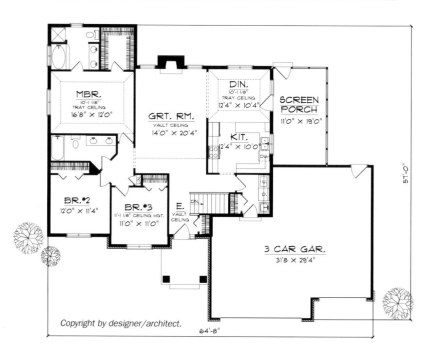
Copyright by designer/architect.

Plan #221020

Dimensions: 69'8" W x 43' D

Levels: 1

Square Footage: 1,859

Bedrooms: 3

Bathrooms: 2½

Foundation: Basement

Materials List Available: No

Price Category: D

Images provided by designer/architect.

You'll love this design if you're looking for a compact home with amenities usually found in much larger designs.

Features:

- Ceiling Height: 8 ft.

- Living Room: A vaulted ceiling gives an elegant feeling, and a bank of windows lets natural light pour in during the daytime.

- Dining Room: Located just off the entry for the convenience of your guests, this room is ideal for intimate family meals or formal dinner parties.

- Kitchen: Just across from the dining room, this kitchen is distinguished by its ample counter space. The adjacent nook is large enough to use as a casual dining area, and it features access to the backyard.

- Master Suite: The large bay window lends interest to this room, and you'll love the walk-in closet and private bath, with its whirlpool tub, standing shower, and dual-sink vanity.

Rear Elevation

Copyright by designer/architect.

Plan #271082

Dimensions: 71' W x 62' D
Levels: 1
Square Footage: 2,074
Bedrooms: 4
Bathrooms: 2
Foundation: Crawl space or slab
Materials List Available: No
Price Category: D

Magnificent pillars and a huge transom window add stature to the impressive entry of this traditional home.

Features:

- Living Room: A corner fireplace warms this spacious room, which shares a 12-ft. ceiling with the dining room and the kitchen.

- Backyard: A French door provides direct access to a covered porch, which in turn flows into a wide deck and a sunny patio.

- Master Suite: A cathedral ceiling enhances the master bedroom, which offers a large walk-in closet. The private bath is certainly luxurious, with its whirlpool tub and two vanities

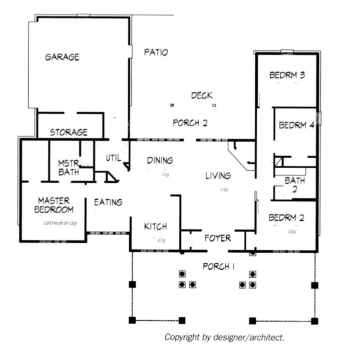

SMARTtip

Making a Cornice

Any new cornice or cornice shelf includes mounting hardware and directions for its installation. But you'll probably need to purchase mounting brackets to install older or homemade cornices. If you're not comfortable with the idea of working on a ladder, especially while handling the cornice and various tools, call a pro. A professional installer will charge a flat rate for coming to your house plus an additional fee for each treatment. Prices vary, but your location, the size of the treatment (measured by the foot), and the difficulty of the job will determine its price.

Plan #211009

Dimensions: 72' W x 60' D
Levels: 1
Square Footage: 2,396
Bedrooms: 4
Bathrooms: 2
Foundation: Slab
Materials List Available: Yes
Price Category: E

Images provided by designer/architect.

Beautiful arched windows lend a luxurious feeling to the exterior of this one-story home.

Features:

• Ceiling Height: 9 ft. unless otherwise noted.

• Entry: Guests will be greeted by a dramatic 12-ft. ceiling in this elegant foyer.

• Living Room: The 12-ft. ceiling continues through the foyer into this inviting living room. Everyone will feel welcomed by the crackling fire in the handsome fireplace.

• Covered Porch: When the weather is warm, invite guests to step out of the living room directly into this covered porch.

• Kitchen: This bright and cheery kitchen is designed for the way we live today. It includes a pantry and an angled eating bar that will see plenty of impromptu family meals.

• Energy-Efficient Walls: All the outside walls are framed with 2x6 lumber instead of 2x4. The extra thickness makes room for more insulation to lower your heating and cooling bills.

Copyright by designer/architect.

SMARTtip

Ornaments in a Garden

Placement is everything with ornaments in a garden. Some elements are best sitting by themselves. Others are better when they are part of a cohesive whole, perhaps placed in the greenery at a corner or flanking a structure.

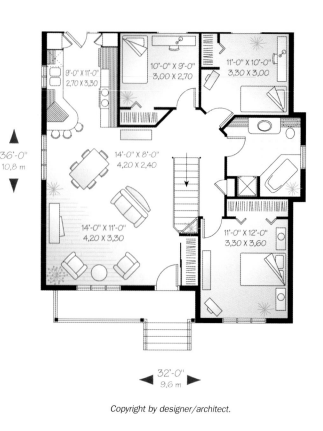

36'-0"
10,8 m

9'-0" X 11'-0"
2,70 X 3,30

10'-0" X 9'-0"
3,00 X 2,70

11'-0" X 10'-0"
3,30 X 3,00

14'-0" X 8'-0"
4,20 X 2,40

14'-0" X 11'-0"
4,20 X 3,30

11'-0" X 12'-0"
3,30 X 3,60

32'-0"
9,6 m

Copyright by designer/architect.

Plan #181007

Dimensions: : 32' W x 36' D

Levels: 1

Square Footage: 1,090

Bedrooms: 3

Bathrooms: 1

Foundation: Full basement

Materials List Available: Yes

Price Category: B

Images provided by designer/architect.

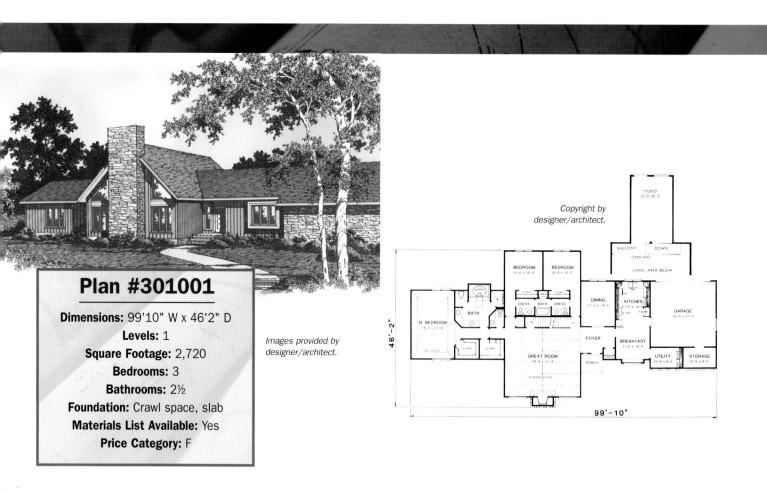

Plan #301001

Dimensions: 99'10" W x 46'2" D

Levels: 1

Square Footage: 2,720

Bedrooms: 3

Bathrooms: 2½

Foundation: Crawl space, slab

Materials List Available: Yes

Price Category: F

Images provided by designer/architect.

Copyright by designer/architect.

STUDIO
13-0 x 20-0

BALCONY   DOWN
OPEN RAIL
LIVING AREA BELOW

BEDROOM
12-0 x 12-0

BEDROOM
12-0 x 12-0

DINING
11-0 x 14-0

KITCHEN
11-0 x 14-0

GARAGE
22-0 x 21-0

M. BEDROOM
14-0 x 21-4

BATH

DRESS   BATH   DRESS

FOYER

BREAKFAST
11-0 x 10-4

46'-2"

GREAT ROOM
24-4 x 21-4
CATHEDRAL CEILING

PORCH

UTILITY
10-6 x 6-0

STORAGE
10-6 x 6-0

99'-10"

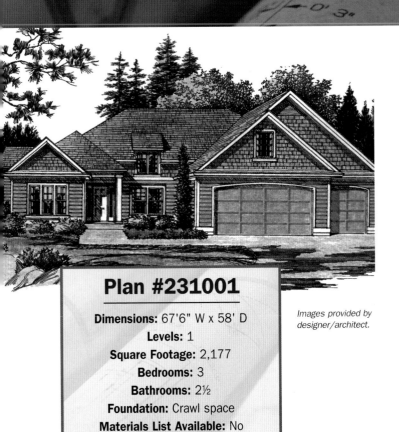

Plan #231001

Dimensions: 67'6" W x 58' D

Levels: 1

Square Footage: 2,177

Bedrooms: 3

Bathrooms: 2½

Foundation: Crawl space

Materials List Available: No

Price Category: D

Images provided by designer/architect.

Copyright by designer/architect.

Plan #231004

Dimensions: 44' W x 37'6" D

Levels: 1

Square Footage: 1,463

Bedrooms: 2

Bathrooms: 2

Foundation: Crawl space

Materials List Available: No

Price Category: A

Images provided by designer/architect.

Copyright by designer/architect.

Plan #211049

Dimensions: 73' W x 66' D
Levels: 1
Square Footage: 2,000
Bedrooms: 3
Bathrooms: 2
Foundation: Slab
Materials List Available: Yes
Price Category: D

Images provided by designer/architect.

This European-style home features an open floor plan that maximizes use and flexibility of space.

Features:

- Ceiling Height: 8 ft. unless otherwise noted.
- Living/Dining Area: This combined living-and-dining area features high ceilings, which make the large area seem even more spacious. Corner windows will fill the room with light. The wet bar and cozy fireplace make this the perfect place for entertaining.
- Backyard Porch: This huge covered backyard

porch is accessible from the living/dining area, so the entire party can step outdoors on a warm summer night.

- Kitchen: More than just efficient, this modern kitchen is actually an exciting place to cook. It features a dramatic high ceiling and plenty of work space.
- Utility Area: Located off the kitchen, this area has extra freezer space, a walk-in pantry, and access to the garage.
- Eating Nook: Informal family meals will be a true delight in this nook that adjoins the kitchen and faces a lovely private courtyard.

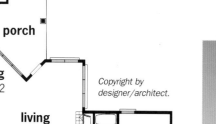

Copyright by designer/architect.

SMARTtip

Outdoor Lighting Safety

Lighting is necessary for walkways, paths, stairways, and transition areas (from the deck to the yard, hot tub, or pool) to prevent accidents. Choose from low-voltage rail, path, and post lighting for these areas. The corners of planters or built-in seating should also be delineated with lighting. Consider installing floodlights near doorways or large open spaces for security reasons.

Plan #321036

Dimensions: 78'4" W x 68'6" D

Levels: 1, optional lower

Square Footage: 2,900

**Optional Basement Level
Sq. Ft.:** 1,018

Bedrooms: 4

Bathrooms: 2½

Foundation: Basement

Materials List Available: Yes

Price Category: F

Images provided by designer/architect.

This classic contemporary is wrapped in brick.

Features:

- Great Room: This grand-scale room offers a vaulted ceiling and Palladian windows flanking an 8-ft.-wide brick fireplace.

- Kitchen: This built-in-a-bay room features a picture window above the sink, a huge pantry, and a cooktop island. It opens to the large morning room.

- Breakfast Area: Open to the kitchen, this area features 12 ft. of cabinetry.

- Master Bedroom: This room features a coffered ceiling, and a walk-in closet gives you good storage space in this luxurious bedroom.

- Garage: This area can fit three cars with plenty of room to spare.

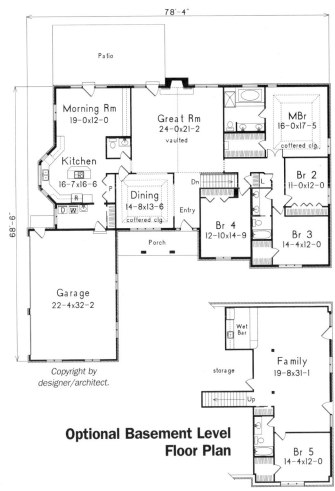

Copyright by designer/architect.

**Optional Basement Level
Floor Plan**

Plan #121009

Dimensions: 50' W x 58' D
Levels: 1
Square Footage: 1,422
Bedrooms: 3
Bathrooms: 2
Foundation: Basement
Materials List Available: Yes
Price Category: B

Images provided by designer/architect.

This amenity-filled home is perfect for the growing family or as a retirement retreat.

Features:

- Ceiling Height: 8 ft. unless otherwise noted.

- Great Room: This inviting space is the perfect place for gatherings of all sizes. It shares 12-ft. ceilings with the dining room and kitchen.

- Dining Room: In addition to the 12-ft. ceiling, arched openings, and built-in book cases make this an elegant place to dine.

- Private Porch: After dinner, step through a door in the dining room to enjoy a summer breeze in this inviting porch.

- Master Suite: The boxed ceiling lends drama to this suite and a walk-in closet adds convenience. Luxury comes from the whirlpool bath.

- Garage: You won't be short of parking and storage space in this two-bay garage. As a bonus there is space for a workbench.

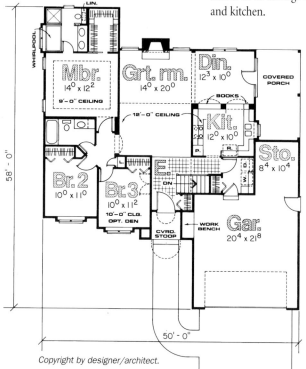

Copyright by designer/architect.

SMARTtip
Window Cornices

You can transform plain rooms by making jogs in cornice molding that will hold shades, blinds, and other window treatments. You can create individual pockets over each window or continue the molding past narrow wall sections between windows to form a more expansive detail. Housings below the cornice can be painted or papered.

Plan #121011

Dimensions: 50' W x 50' D
Levels: 1
Square Footage: 1,724
Bedrooms: 3
Bathrooms: 2
Foundation: Basement
Materials List Available: Yes
Price Category: C

Images provided by designer/architect.

This one-level home is perfect for retirement or for convenient living for the growing family.

Features:

- Ceiling Height: 8 ft.
- Master Suite: For privacy and quiet, the master suite is segregated from the other bedrooms.
- Family Room: Sit by the fire and read as light streams through the windows flanking the fireplace. Or enjoy the built-in entertainment center.
- Breakfast Area: Located just off the family room, the sunny breakfast area will lure you to linger over impromptu family meals. Here you will find a built-in desk for compiling shopping lists and menus.
- Private Porch: Step out of the breakfast area to enjoy a breeze on this porch.
- Kitchen: Efficient and attractive, this kitchen offers an angled pantry and an island that doubles as a snack bar.

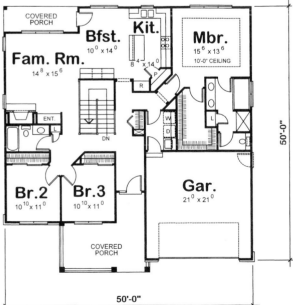

Copyright by designer/architect.

SMARTtip

Measuring for Kitchen Countertops

Custom cabinetmakers will sometimes come to your house to measure for a countertop, but home centers and kitchen stores may require that you come to them with the dimensions already in hand. Be sure to double-check measurements carefully. Being off by only ½ in. can be quite upsetting.

To ensure accuracy, sketch out the countertop on a sheet of graph paper. Include all the essential dimensions. To be on the safe side, have someone else double-check your numbers.

Decks

Many people are reluctant to make design decisions because they don't think of themselves as designers. But if you take the time to think things through carefully, you may be surprised at the ideas you generate. Start with memories of places you have enjoyed. Of course, dreams can rarely be re-created in the real world. But by letting your imagination run loose and tapping into those images, you can develop a font of design concepts that will help you come up with a deck design.

Beginning Your Design

Begin by imagining your ideal deck, and ask family members to do the same. Think about its design, accessories, and any special elements you would like your deck to contain. Keep track of your ideas by drawing a series of rough sketches as you proceed. Expect to fill a wastebasket or two with these. Don't think of them as actual designs so much as focal points for conversations—it's easier to point to a drawing than to walk around the house.

Feel free to steal ideas from other people. (The best architects do not hesitate to do so.) When you see a deck you like, take photos and jot down some notes. Talk to the owners about how their deck works for them. Most people will be flattered that you like their deck and will be more than glad to talk to you about it. You will not only learn about pleasing designs and materials, but you can avoid the mistakes they made.

Screened porches, left, are popular deck amenities.

Eating areas, above, require ample room for tables and chairs.

Multilevel decks, opposite, provide room for separate activity areas.

Uses for Your New Deck

Call a family meeting to discuss your deck plans. Find out everyone's vision of the deck. What would they like it to look like? Where would they like it to be? The backyard is the logical choice, but an enlarged front porch may better suit your needs. Or it may make more sense to design a deck that wraps around two sides of your house. How large a deck do you want? If a large deck would cut into your yard area, making it tough to play croquet, or if it would throw shade on the flower bed, you may want to scale back your plans. But if you rarely use your yard or hate maintaining the lawn, a larger deck will make gardening chores easier. Most importantly at this point, consider the activities that will take place on the deck.

Cooking and Entertaining

Entertainment is high on many people's list. Plan for a cooking area as well as a place for a good-sized table for seating smaller groups or for buffet settings if you have large parties. For nighttime entertaining, think about installing lighting.

Locate the grill area as far as possible from other use areas so that you don't have to worry about kids bumping into a hot barbecue. Leave ample room for cooking "assistants" so that friends can gather around and talk as you turn the steaks.

Make the deck easy to get to. The more entrances, the better. Large doorways and oversized windows tend to entice people outside. If you plan on eating on the deck often, make sure it is close to the kitchen. Ideally, try to plan for a direct connection between the deck and kitchen.

A Place to Relax

Consider what your future deck will be like during all the seasons when you are likely to use it.

Decide how much sun and how much shade you want, and take this into account when siting your deck. If you live in the northern hemisphere, a north-facing space will be in shade most of the day. This can be an advantage if you live in a very hot climate and a disadvantage for most everyone else. An eastern exposure gives the deck morning sun and afternoon shade; this is often the best choice in warm climates. In cold climates, a southwest exposure usually provides full and late afternoon sun.

Shade structures, left, offer protection from late afternoon sun.

Built-in seating, below, makes a deck inviting and contributes to its design.

Separate activity areas, opposite, help define the uses of the new deck.

Lighting. If you tend to eat and entertain after dark, consider your deck's lighting. A motion-sensing floodlight provides security and lights your way as you bring in groceries, but it makes for an unappealing dining ambiance. Subtle, low-voltage fixtures set into steps or posts provide a better solution for dining and entertaining on the deck. Most lighting plans call for a combination of both types of lighting.

In addition to placing low-voltage lights in steps and posts, consider lining a path that leads up to the deck with small lights. When choosing these fixtures, be sure to select fixtures that are attractive during the day as well as at night.

You may also want to consider using lights for decorative effect. For example, you can install low-voltage lights in the garden to highlight plantings that are visible from the deck. In-ground fixtures cast their light upward, creating interesting areas of shadow and light on trees and shrubs. Many fixtures have lenses that let you aim the light beam.

Avoid installing too many lights. With low-voltage layouts, a few well-placed lights is more dramatic than the glare produced by too many lights.

Private Spaces

Decks are often raised off the ground, which might mean you and your family will be on display for all the neighborhood to see. Existing fences may be too low to shield you from view. Sometimes the problem can be solved by stepping the deck down in stages. In most settings, decks work best when built low to the ground. If your entry door occupies a high position, you'll find it best to build a landing and stairs or a series of tiers leading down to a low-built main deck.

Privacy Options. You may have to take direct action to achieve privacy. You don't have to build an unfriendly, solid wall to avoid the feeling you are being watched. If you feel overexposed, a well-placed trellis provides the base for some nice climbing plants to look at and creates a pleasant enclosure. Another solution is to plant border trees and shrubs.

Fences are another option. There are many styles and materials from which to choose. High solid fences provide the most privacy, but an imposing design isn't very friendly, and it can make your yard seem closed in and smaller than it really is. Soften fences by using them as a backdrop for plantings.

Family members need some privacy among themselves as well. By building with different levels, including a conversation pit, or even by just letting the deck ramble a bit, you can create areas that are separate but not walled off. Careful placement of activity areas can also help create private sections. For example, if you are installing a spa or a cooking center—areas that tend to draw a crowd—place private areas on the other side of the deck.

Open or Cozy. Think about whether you want your deck to feel airy and open to the world or cozy and secluded. These effects can be achieved in many ways. A small deck will feel cozier than a large deck. Low benches and railings designed with large open spaces in them give an open feeling. A deck that hugs the house will have a more sequestered feel than one that juts out into the yard.

Images provided by designer/architect.

Plan #271005

Dimensions: 48' W x 50' D
Levels: 1
Square Footage: 1,368
Bedrooms: 3
Bathrooms: 2
Foundation: Basement
Materials List Available: Yes
Price Category: B

This traditional home boasts an open floor plan that is further expanded by soaring vaulted ceilings.

Features:

- Great Room: Front and center, this large multipurpose room features a gorgeous corner fireplace, an eye-catching boxed out window, and dedicated space for casual dining—all beneath a vaulted ceiling.

- Kitchen: A vaulted ceiling crowns this galley kitchen and its adjoining breakfast nook.

- Master Suite: This spacious master bedroom, brightened by a boxed-out window, features a vaulted ceiling in the sleeping chamber and the private bath.

Copyright by designer/architect.

SMARTtip

Design with Computers

Consider using a computer-aided design (CAD) program to plan your deck. Some programs let you see three-dimensional views of your design complete with railings, stairs, planters, hot tubs, and the surrounding landscaping.

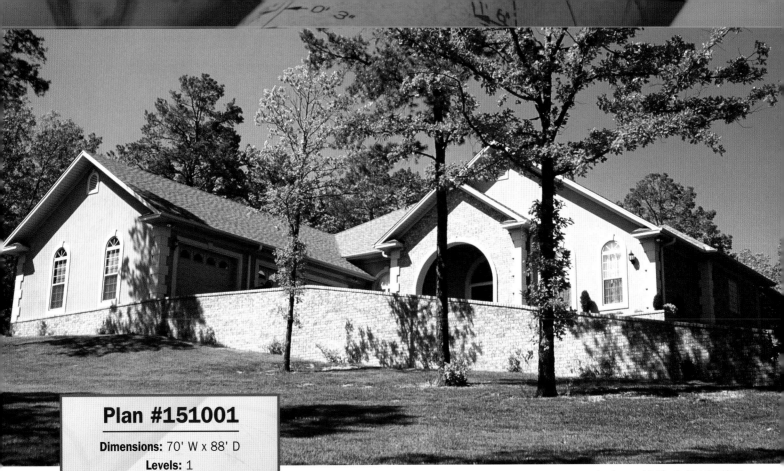

Plan #151001

Dimensions: 70' W x 88' D
Levels: 1
Square Footage: 3,124
Bedrooms: 4
Bathrooms: 3½
Foundation: Crawl space, slab
Materials List Available: Yes
Price Category: G

From the double front doors to sleek arches, columns, and a gallery with arched openings to the bedrooms, you'll love this elegant home.

Features:

• Grand Room: With a 13-ft. pan ceiling and column entry, this room opens to the rear covered porch as well as through French doors to the bay-windowed morning room that, in turn, leads to the gathering room.

• Gathering Room: A majestic fireplace, built-in entertainment center, and book shelves give comfort and ease.

• Kitchen: A double oven, built-in desk, and a work island add up to a design for efficiency.

• Master Suite: Enjoy the practicality of walk-in closets, the comfort of a private sitting area, and the convenience of an adjacent study or nursery. The bath features a step-up whirlpool tub and separate shower.

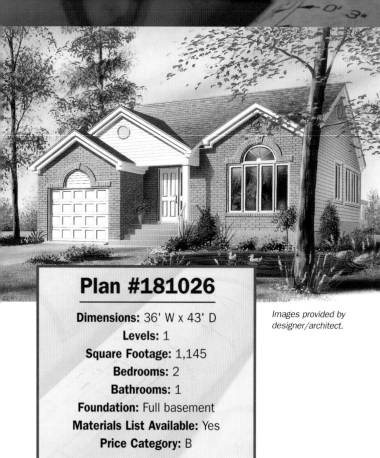

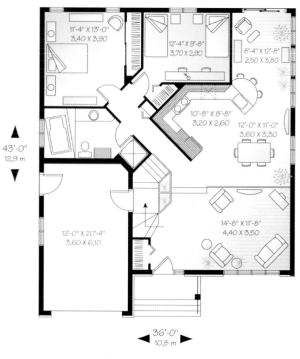

Plan #181026

Dimensions: 36' W x 43' D

Levels: 1

Square Footage: 1,145

Bedrooms: 2

Bathrooms: 1

Foundation: Full basement

Materials List Available: Yes

Price Category: B

Images provided by designer/architect.

43'-0"
12,9 m

36'-0"
10,8 m

Copyright by designer/architect.

Plan #181027

Dimensions: 30'8" W x 48' D

Levels: 1

Square Footage: 1,103

Bedrooms: 2

Bathrooms: 1

Foundation: Full basement

Materials List Available: Yes

Price Category: B

Images provided by designer/architect.

48'-0"
14,4 m

30'-8"
9,2 m

Copyright by designer/architect.

Plan #181023

Dimensions: 50' W x 36' D
Levels: 1
Square Footage: 1,191
Bedrooms: 2
Bathrooms: 1
Foundation: Full basement
Materials List Available: Yes
Price Category: B

Images provided by designer/architect.

Copyright by designer/architect.

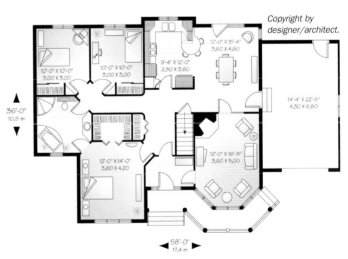

Copyright by designer/architect.

Plan #181024

Dimensions: 58' W x 36' D
Levels: 1
Square Footage: 1,370
Bedrooms: 3
Bathrooms: 1
Foundation: Full basement
Materials List Available: Yes
Price Category: B

Images provided by designer/architect.

SMARTtip

Neoclassical Style

Instead of expensive hand-crafted plasterwork, look into the many prefabricated moldings, ceiling medallions, pillars, cornices, and the like that are made of lightweight molded plastic. They can be faux painted to resemble marble or stone and are fairly easy to install yourself.

Plan #131040

Dimensions: 50' W x 37' D
Levels: 1
Square Footage: 1,630
Bedrooms: 3
Bathrooms: 2
Foundation: Basement, crawl space, or slab
Materials List Available: Yes
Price Category: D

Images provided by designer/architect.

The raised main level of this home makes this plan ideal for any site that has an expansive view, and you can finish the lower level as an office, library, or space for the kids to play.

Features:

• Living Room: This sunken living room with a prow-shaped front is sure to be a focal point where both guests and family gather in this lovely ranch home. A see-through fireplace separates this room from the dining room.

• Dining Room: A dramatic vaulted ceiling covers both this room and the adjacent living room, creating a spacious feeling.

• Kitchen: Designed for efficiency, you'll love the features and location of this convenient kitchen.

• Master Suite: Luxuriate in the privacy this suite affords and enjoy the two large closets, sumptuous private bath, and sliding glass doors that can open to the optional rear deck.

Rear Elevation

Main Level Floor Plan

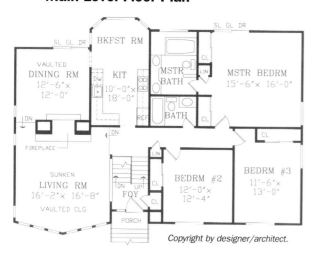

Copyright by designer/architect.

Lower Level Floor Plan

Images provided by
designer/architect.

Plan #321019

Dimensions: 70'8" W x 70' D

Levels: 1

Square Footage: 2,452

Bedrooms: 4

Bathrooms: 2½

Foundation: Basement

Materials List Available: Yes

Price Category: E

Copyright by
designer/architect.

Plan #231008

Dimensions: 60' W x 62' D

Levels: 1

Square Footage: 1,941

Bedrooms: 3

Bathrooms: 2½

Foundation: Crawl space

Materials List Available: No

Price Category: D

Images provided by
designer/architect.

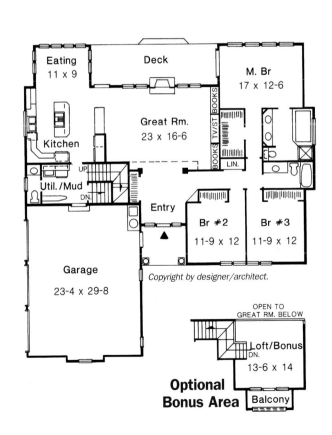

Copyright by designer/architect.

Plan #121006

Dimensions: 46' W x 58' D

Levels: 1

Square Footage: 1,762

Bedrooms: 3

Bathrooms: 2

Foundation: Slab, crawl space, or basement

Materials List Available: Yes

Price Category: C

Images provided by designer/architect.

The entry has a trio of arched openings that leads you to other areas of this amenity-packed home.

Features:

- Ceiling Height: 8 ft. except as noted.

- Eating Bar: Conveniently located between the kitchen and family room, this is sure to be a favorite spot for informal entertaining and family gatherings.

- Family room: A wall of windows, a fireplace, and a vaulted ceiling stretching to 11 ft. work together to make this a bright and warm room.

- Kitchen: There's no shortage of counter space in this well-planned kitchen that features a center island in addition to the eating bar.

- Master Suite: Luxuriate at the end of the day in this large bedroom with its decorative tray ceiling and walk-in closet. Enjoy the pampering bath with its sunlit corner whirlpool flanked by vanities.

- Garage: Two bays provide room for cars and plenty of storage as well.

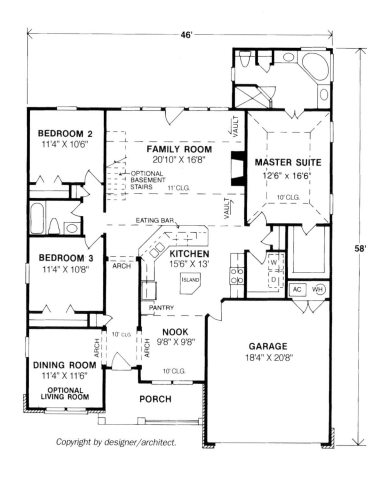

Copyright by designer/architect.

Plan #131001

Dimensions: 72'4" W x 32'4" D
Levels: 1
Square Footage: 1,615
Bedrooms: 3
Bathrooms: 2
Foundation: Basement, crawl space, or slab
Materials List Available: Yes
Price Category: D

Images provided by designer/architect.

Cathedral ceilings and illuminating skylights add drama and beauty to this practical ranch house.

Features:

Ceiling Height: 8 ft.

- Front Porch: Watch the rain in comfort from the covered front porch.

- Foyer: The stone-tiled foyer flows into the living areas.

- Living Room: Oriented towards the front of the house, the living room opens to the dining room and shares a lovely three-sided fireplace with the family room.

- Family Room: Conveniently located to share the fireplace with the living room, this room is bright and cheery thanks to its skylights as well as the sliding glass doors that open onto the rear patio.

- Kitchen: An island makes this sunny room both efficient and attractive.

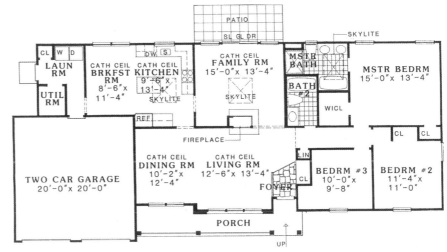

Copyright by designer/architect.

- Breakfast Nook: Located just off the kitchen, this area can serve double-duty as a spot for kitchen visitors to sit.

- Dining Room: The open design between the dining and living rooms adds to the spacious feeling that the cathedral ceiling creates in this area.

- Laundry Room: This area opens from the kitchen for convenience.

- Master Suite: A walk-in closet makes this room practical, but the master bathroom with a skylight, dual-sink vanity, soaking tub, and separate shower makes it luxurious.

- Bedrooms: The two additional bedrooms share a bathroom.

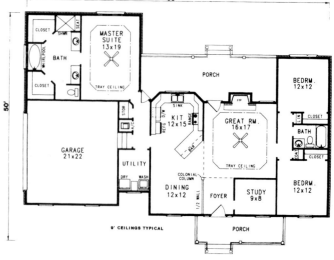

Plan #171009

Dimensions: 68' W x 50' D
Levels: 1
Square Footage: 1,771
Bedrooms: 3
Bathrooms: 2
Foundation: Slab, crawl space
Materials List Available: Yes
Price Category: C

Images provided by designer/architect.

SMARTtip

Deck Awnings

Awnings come in bright colors. As light filters through, it will cast a hue to anything under the deck. Warm colors, such as red or pink, will create a rosy glow; cool colors, such blues or greens, will enhance the shade.

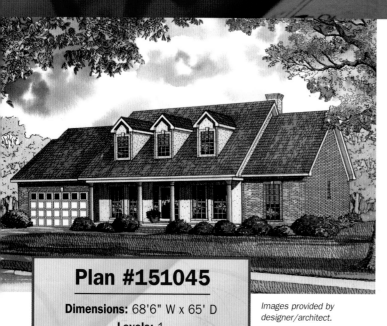

Plan #151045

Dimensions: 68'6" W x 65' D
Levels: 1
Square Footage: 2,250
Bedrooms: 4
Bathrooms: 2
Foundation: Crawl space, slab (basement option for fee)
Materials List Available: Yes
Price Category: E

Images provided by designer/architect.

Copyright by designer/architect.

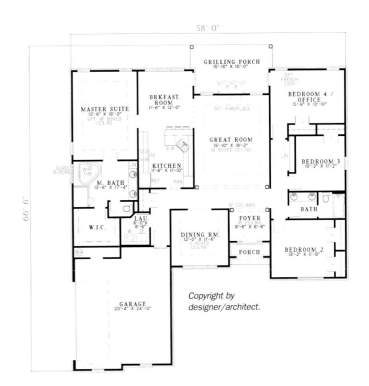

Images provided by designer/architect.

Plan #151076

Dimensions: 58' W x 66'6" D

Levels: 1

Square Footage: 2,187

Bedrooms: 4

Bathrooms: 2

Foundations: crawl space, slab with basement option for fee

Materials List Available: Yes

Price Category: D

Copyright by designer/architect.

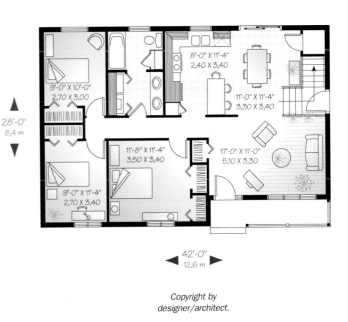

Images provided by designer/architect.

Plan #181008

Dimensions: 42' W x 28' D

Levels: 1

Square Footage: 1,106

Bedrooms: 3

Bathrooms: 1

Foundation: Full basement

Materials List Available: Yes

Price Category: B

Copyright by designer/architect.

Planning Your Landscape

Landscapes change over the years. As plants grow, the overall look evolves from sparse to lush. Trees cast cool shade where the sun used to shine. Shrubs and hedges grow tall and dense enough to provide privacy. Perennials and ground covers spread to form colorful patches of foliage and flowers. Meanwhile, paths, arbors, fences, and other structures gain the comfortable patina of age.

Constant change over the years—sometimes rapid and dramatic, sometimes slow and subtle—is one of the joys of landscaping. It is also one of the challenges. Anticipating how fast plants will grow and how big they will eventually get is difficult, even for professional designers, and was a major concern in formulating the designs for this book.

As Your Landscape Grows

To illustrate the kinds of changes to expect in a planting, these pages show one of the designs at three different "ages." Even though a new planting may look sparse at first, it will soon fill in. And because of careful spacing, the planting will look as good in 10 to 15 years as it does after 3 to 5. It will, of course, look different, but that's part of the fun.

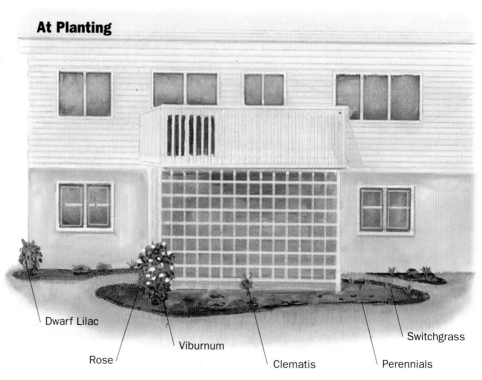

At Planting

Dwarf Lilac

Rose

Viburnum

Clematis

Switchgrass

Perennials

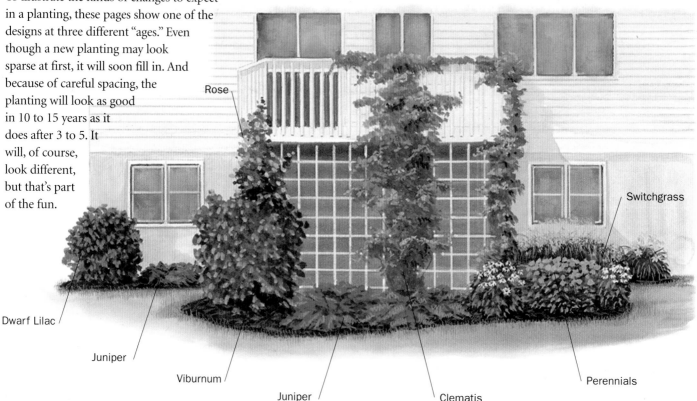

Three to Five Years

Rose

Switchgrass

Dwarf Lilac

Juniper

Viburnum

Juniper

Clematis

Perennials

At Planting—Here's how a raised-deck planting might appear in late spring immediately after planting. The rose and clematis haven't begun to climb the new lattice trellis. The viburnum and lilac, usually sold in 2- to 5-gal. cans, start blooming as young plants and may have flowers when you buy them, but there will be enough space that you may want to plant some short annuals around them for the first few growing seasons. You can put short annuals between the new little junipers, too. The switchgrass and perennials, transplanted from quart- or gallon-size containers, are just low tufts of foliage now, but they grow fast enough to produce a few flowers the first summer.

Three to Five Years—As shown here in midsummer, the rose and clematis now reach most of the way up the supports. Although they aren't mature yet, the lilac, viburnum, and junipers look nice and bushy, and they're big enough that you don't need to fill around them with annuals. So far, the vines and shrubs have needed only minimal pruning. Most grasses and perennials reach full size about three to five years after planting; after that, they need to be divided and replanted in freshly amended soil to keep them healthy and vigorous.

Ten to Fifteen Years—Shown again in summer, the rose and clematis now cover their supports, and the lilac and viburnum are as tall as they'll get. To maintain all of these plants, you'll need to start pruning out some of the older stems every year in early spring. The junipers have spread sideways to form a solid mass; prune them as needed along the edge of the lawn and pathways. When the junipers crowd them out, move the daylilies to another part of your property, or move them to the front of the bed to replace the other perennials, as shown here.

Ten to Fifteen Years

Rose

Clematis

Dwarf Lilac

Juniper

Viburnum

Juniper

Daylily

Switchgrass

A Step Up

Plant a Foundation Garden

Homes on raised foundations usually have foundation plantings. These simple skirtings of greenery hide unattractive concrete-block underpinnings and help overcome the impression that the house is hovering a few feet above the ground. Useful as these plantings are, they are too often just monochromatic expanses of clipped junipers, dull as dishwater. But, as this design shows, a durable, low-maintenance foundation planting can be more varied, more colorful, and more fun.

Because a foundation planting should look good year-round, the design is anchored by a row of cherry laurels, broad-leaved evergreens covered each spring by heavily scented flowers. A small garden of shrubs, perennials, and a graceful arching grass will catch the eye of visitors approaching the front door. Colorful perennials bloom from spring to fall along the edge of the bed. At the far end is a tidy viburnum, whose spicy-scented flowers will encourage springtime strolls around that corner of the house.

'Morning Light' D
Japanese silver grass

'Autumn Joy' sedum E

'Crimson Pygmy' C
Japanese barberry

Lamb's ears I

Plants & Projects

From spring to fall, something is always blooming here, but foliage texture and color play an even greater role than flowers in this design. From the slender, shimmering leaves of Japanese silver grass rising behind mounded barberries, to furry lamb's ears, feathery coreopsis, and fleshy sedum, textures abound, colored in a variety of reds, greens, and silvers. Winter offers glossy green cherry laurels, the tawny leaves and striking seed heads of silver grass, and the rich russets of the sedum. Other than an annual cutback in spring and a little pruning to shape the viburnum, the planting requires little maintenance.

A **Korean spice viburnum** (use 1 plant)
At the corner of the house, this deciduous shrub produces spicy-scented flowers in spring (preceded by pretty pink buds) and dense green foliage in summer and fall. Shape by annual pruning.

B **'Otto Luyken' cherry laurel** (use 4)
The glossy dark leaves and spreading habit of these evergreen shrubs will clothe the foundation year-round. As a bonus, spring produces a profusion of fragrant white flowers in spikes.

C **'Crimson Pygmy' Japanese barberry** (use 3)
A compact deciduous shrub with small, teardrop-shaped maroon leaves that turn crimson in fall, when they are joined by bright red berries.

D **'Morning Light' Japanese silver grass** (use 1)
A rustling sentinel by the door, this grass is silvery all summer, then turns tawny after frost. Its fluffy seed heads last through the winter.

E **'Autumn Joy' sedum** (use 3)
Flat-topped flower clusters emerge in late summer above clumps of fleshy gray-green leaves, turning from white through shades of ever deeper pink to rust-colored seed heads that can stand through the winter.

F **'East Friesland' salvia** (use 4)
Shown against the green backdrop, reddish purple flower spikes cover these perennials from May through fall.

G **'Longwood Blue' bluebeard** (use 1)
A small deciduous shrub with silvery gray foliage and fringed blue flowers from late summer to frost.

H **'Moonbeam' coreopsis** (use 4)
A perennial with fine foliage and tiny pale yellow flowers from July into September.

I **Lamb's ears** (use 3)
A perennial with fuzzy silver-white leaves. Use the large-leaved, wide-spreading cultivar 'Helene von Stein' (sometimes called 'Big Ears').

J **'Big Blue' lilyturf** (use 4)
This grasslike evergreen perennial under the viburnum has dark blue flowers in summer.

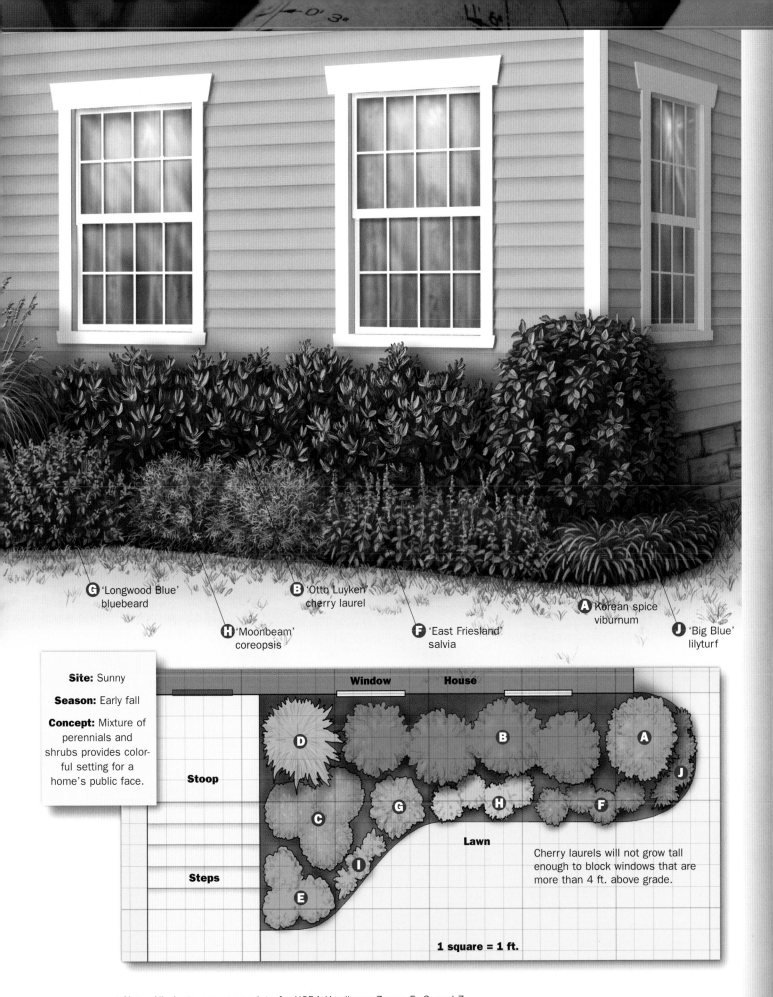

G 'Longwood Blue' bluebeard

B 'Otto Luyken' cherry laurel

A Korean spice viburnum

H 'Moonbeam' coreopsis

F 'East Friesland' salvia

J 'Big Blue' lilyturf

Site: Sunny

Season: Early fall

Concept: Mixture of perennials and shrubs provides colorful setting for a home's public face.

Window   House

Stoop

Steps

Lawn

Cherry laurels will not grow tall enough to block windows that are more than 4 ft. above grade.

1 square = 1 ft.

Note: All plants are appropriate for USDA Hardiness Zones 5, 6, and 7.

Plan #211048

Dimensions: 66' W x 60'8" D
Levels: 1
Square Footage: 2,002
Bedrooms: 3
Bathrooms: 2
Foundation: Crawl space, slab
Materials List Available: Yes
Price Category: D

This southern-style home is filled with inviting spaces and will fit into any neighborhood.

Features:

- Ceiling Height: 8 ft.

- Front Porch: Enjoy summer breezes on this porch, which features accented shutters that are both functional and stylish.

- Living Room: From the porch, French doors lead into the side-lit entry and this gracious living room.

- Sundeck: You can bask in the summer sun on this private rear deck, or if you prefer, enjoy a cool breeze under the shade of the rear porch. Each is accessible through its own set of French doors.

- Master Suite: This suite is secluded from the rest of the house for privacy, making it the perfect retreat at the end of a busy day. From the bedroom, open double doors to gain access to the luxurious bath, with a dual-sink vanity and his and her walk-in closets.

SMARTtip

Eye Appeal

Not everything in a landscaping plan needs to be in the ground. You might want to consider hanging flowering plants on a front porch or placing hardy potted plants on outdoor steps and decks or strategically along a paved walkway. Even a window box, viewed from outside, becomes a part of the landscaping.

Plan #201084

Dimensions: 66'10" W x 54'5" D

Levels: 1

Square Footage: 2,056

Bedrooms: 3

Bathrooms: 2

Foundation: Crawl space, slab

Materials List Available: Yes

Price Category: D

This classic family home features beautiful country styling with lots of curb appeal.

Features:

• Ceiling Height: 8 ft.

• Open Plan: When guests arrive, they'll enter a foyer that is open to the dining room and den. This open area makes the home seem especially spacious and offers the flexibility for all kinds of entertaining and family activities.

• Kitchen: You'll love preparing meals in this large, well-designed kitchen. There's plenty of counter space, and the breakfast bar is perfect impromptu family meals.

• Master Suite: This spacious and elegant master suite is separated from the other bedroom for maximum privacy.

• Bonus Room: This unfinished bonus room awaits the time to add another bedroom or a home office.

• Garage: This attached garage offers parking for two cars, plus plenty of storage space.

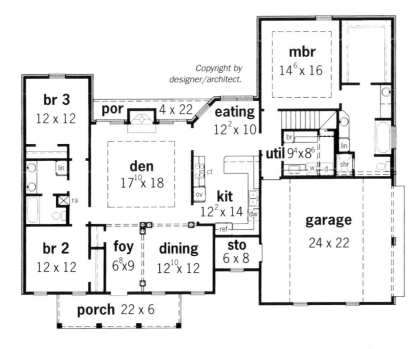

Copyright by designer/architect.

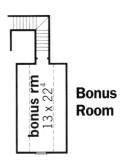

Bonus Room

Images provided by designer/architect.

Plan #211024

Dimensions: 61' W x 44' D

Levels: 1

Square Footage: 1,418

Bedrooms: 3

Bathrooms: 2

Foundation: Slab

Materials List Available: Yes

Price Category: B

Copyright by designer/architect.

Floor plan labels: br 3 12 x 11; living 18 x 18; patio; mbr 16 x 14; lin; bath; clo; sto; br 2 12 x 12; foy; dining 12 x 11; kit 12x9; ref; w; d; porch 39 x 6; garage 22 x 22; bath; lin

---

Plan #211030

Dimensions: 75' W x 37' D

Levels: 1

Square Footage: 1,600

Bedrooms: 3

Bathrooms: 2

Foundation: Slab

Materials List Available: Yes

Price Category: C

Images provided by designer/architect.

SMARTtip

Brackets in Window Treatments

Although it is rarely noticed, a bracket plays an important role in supporting rods and poles. If a treatment rubs against a window frame, an extension bracket solves the problem. It projects from the wall at an adjustable length, providing enough clearance. A hold-down bracket anchors a cellular shade or a blind to the bottom of a door, preventing the treatment from moving when the door is opened or closed.

Copyright by designer/architect.

Floor plan labels: br 2 12 x 12; living 18 x 18; mbr 14 x 12; sitting; sto 11 x 9; br 3 12 x 12; entry; dining 12 x 11; kit 12x10; sew; util 9x8; garage 22 x 22; porch 42 x 7; work bench; sto

Plan #241007

Dimensions: 58'10" W x 59'1" D
Levels: 1
Square Footage: 2,036
Bedrooms: 3
Bathrooms: 2
Foundation: Slab
Materials List Available: No
Price Category: D

Images provided by designer/architect.

Enjoy summer breezes while relaxing on the large front porch of this charming country cottage.

Features:

- Great Room: Whether you enter from the front door or from the kitchen, you will feel welcome in this comfortable great room, which features a corner fireplace.

- Kitchen: This well-designed kitchen with extensive counter space offers a delightful eating bar, perfect for quick or informal meals.

- Master Suite: This luxurious master suite, located on the first floor for privacy, features his and her walk-in closets, separate vanities, a deluxe corner tub, a linen closet, and a walk-in shower.

- Additional Bedrooms: Two secondary bedrooms and an optional, large game room —well suited for a growing family— are located on the second floor.

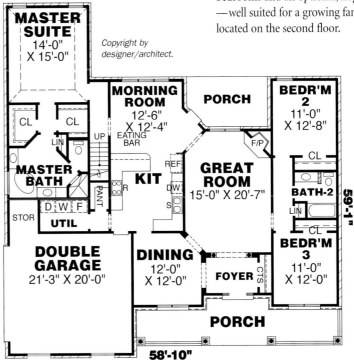

Copyright by designer/architect.

Plan #181021

Dimensions: 37' W x 44' D

Levels: 1

Square Footage: 1,124

Bedrooms: 2

Bathrooms: 1

Foundation: Basement

Materials List Available: Yes

Price Category: B

This cozy country cottage is enhanced by lattice trim details over the porch and garage.

Features:

• Ceiling Height: 8 ft.

• Living Room: This living room gets extra architectural interest from a sunken floor. The room, located directly to the left of the entry hall, has plenty of space for entertaining.

• Dining Room: This dining room is located in center of the home. It's adjacent to the kitchen to make it easy to serve meals.

• Kitchen: This bright and efficient kitchen is a real pleasure in which to work. It includes a pantry and double sinks. There's a breakfast bar that will see plenty of informal meals for families on the go.

• Covered Porch: This is the perfect place to which to retire after dinner on a warm summer evening.

• Bedrooms: Each of the two bedrooms has its own closet. They share a full bathroom.

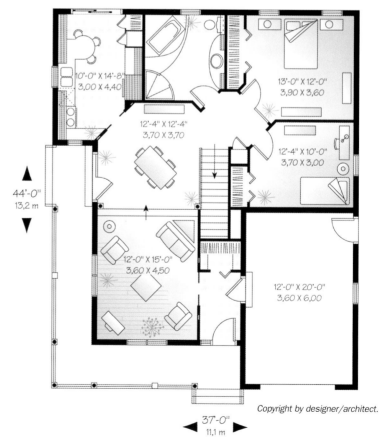

10'-0" X 14'-8"
3,00 X 4,40

13'-0" X 12'-0"
3,90 X 3,60

12'-4" X 12'-4"
3,70 X 3,70

12'-4" X 10'-0"
3,70 X 3,00

12'-0" X 15'-0"
3,60 X 4,50

12'-0" X 20'-0"
3,60 X 6,00

44'-0"
13,2 m

37'-0"
11,1 m

Plan #251001

Dimensions: 61'3" W x 40'6" D
Levels: 1
Square Footage: 1,253
Bedrooms: 3
Bathrooms: 2
Foundation: Crawl space, basement
Materials List Available: Yes
Price Category: B

Images provided by designer/architect.

- Master Bedroom: This master bedroom features a large walk-in closet. It has its own master bath with a single vanity, a tub, and a walk-in shower.

- Garage: This attached garage provides plenty of extra storage space, as well as parking for two cars.

This charming country home has a classic full front porch for enjoying summertime breezes.

Features:

- Ceiling Height: 8 ft.

- Foyer: Guests will walk through the front porch into this foyer, which opens to the family room.

- Screened Porch: A second porch is screened and is located at the rear of the home off the dining room, so your guests can step out for a bit of fresh air after dinner.

- Family Room: Family and friends will be drawn to this large open space, with its handsome fireplace and sloped ceiling.

- Kitchen: This open and airy kitchen is a pleasure in which to work. It has ample counter space and a pantry.

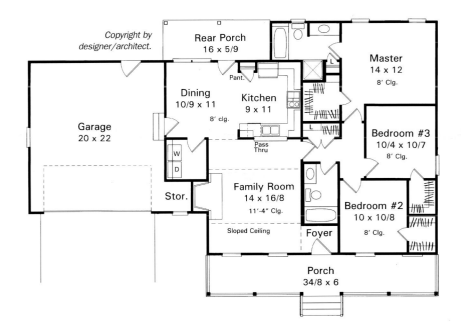

Copyright by designer/architect.

www.ultimateplans.com   225

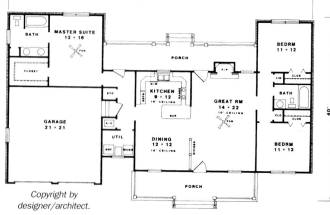

Copyright by designer/architect.

Images provided by designer/architect.

Plan #171002

Dimensions: 44' W x 41' D
Levels: 1
Square Footage: 1,458
Bedrooms: 3
Bathrooms: 2
Foundation: Slab, crawl space
Materials List Available: Yes
Price Category: B

SMARTtip

Accent Landscape Lighting

Accent highlights elements in your landscape. It creates ambiance and helps integrate the garden with the deck. Conventional low-voltage floodlights are excellent for creating effects such as wall grazing, silhouetting, and uplighting.

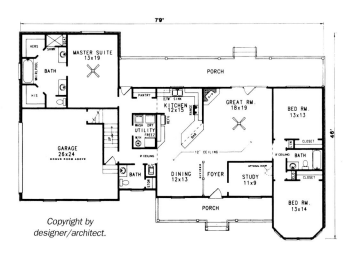

Copyright by designer/architect.

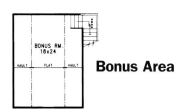

Bonus Area

Plan #171015

Dimensions: 79' W x 52' D
Levels: 1
Square Footage: 2,089
Bedrooms: 3
Bathrooms: 2½
Foundation: Slab, crawl space
Materials List Available: Yes
Price Category: D

Images provided by designer/architect.

Plan #201071

Dimensions: 48'10" W x 29'10" D

Levels: 1

Square Footage: 984

Bedrooms: 2

Bathrooms: 1

Foundation: Crawl space, slab

Materials List Available: Yes

Price Category: A

Images provided by designer/architect.

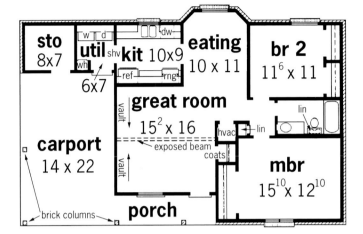

sto 8x7

util

shv

kit 10x9

eating 10 x 11

br 2 11^6 x 11

w d

dw

wh

6x7

ref

rng

lin

great room 15^2 x 16

vault

exposed beam

hvac

lin

coats

carport 14 x 22

vault

mbr 15^{10} x 12^{10}

brick columns

porch

Copyright by designer/architect.

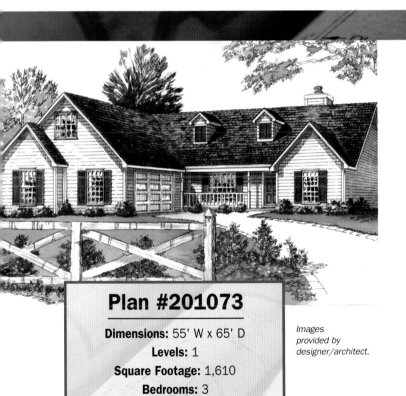

Plan #201073

Dimensions: 55' W x 65' D

Levels: 1

Square Footage: 1,610

Bedrooms: 3

Bathrooms: 2

Foundation: Crawl space, slab

Materials List Available: Yes

Price Category: C

Images provided by designer/architect.

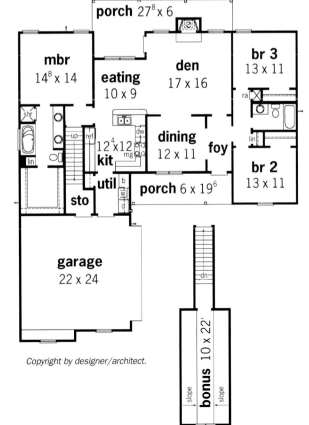

porch 27^8 x 6

mbr 14^8 x 14

eating 10 x 9

den 17 x 16

br 3 13 x 11

up

ref

shr

kit 12^4 x12

rng

dw

dining 12 x 11

foy

lin

br 2 13 x 11

util

sto

porch 6 x 19^6

garage 22 x 24

dn

bonus 10 x 22'

slope

slope

Copyright by designer/architect.

Plan #251002

Dimensions: 55'6" W x 64'3" D
Levels: 1
Square Footage: 1,333
Bedrooms: 3
Bathrooms: 2
Foundation: Crawl space, slab
Materials List Available: Yes
Price Category: B

Images provided by designer/architect.

Although compact, this farmhouse has all the amenities for comfortable modern living.

Features:

- Ceiling Height: 8 ft. unless otherwise noted.

- Foyer: This gracious and welcoming foyer opens to the family room.

- Family Room: This inviting family room is designed to accommodate all kinds of family activities. It features a 9-ft. ceiling and a handsome, warming fireplace.

- Kitchen: Cooking in this kitchen is a real pleasure. It includes a center island, so you'll never run out of counter space for food preparation.

- Master Bedroom: This master bedroom features a large walk-in closet and an elegant 9-ft. recessed ceiling.

- Master Bath: This master bath offers a double vanity, a tub, and a walk-in shower.

- Garage: This attached garage provides plenty of extra storage space, as well as parking for two cars.

SMARTtip

Arts and Crafts Style

The heart of this style rests in its earthy connection. The more you can bring nature into it, the more authentic it will be. An easy way to do this is with plants. A bonus is that plants naturally thrive in the bathroom, where they enjoy the humid environment.

Copyright by designer/architect.

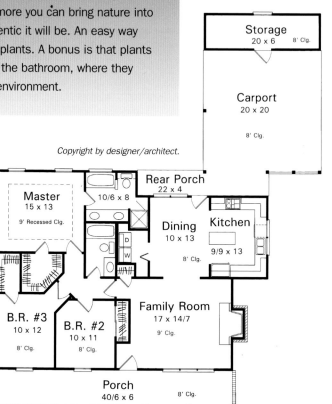

Plan #131013

Dimensions: 50' W x 41'8" D
Levels: 1
Square Footage: 1,489
Bedrooms: 3
Bathrooms: 2
Foundation: Basement, crawl space, or slab
Materials List Available: Yes
Price Category: C

Images provided by designer/architect.

You'll love the Victorian details on the exterior of this charming ranch-style home.

Features:

- **Front Porch:** This porch is large enough so that you can sit out on warm summer nights to catch a breeze or create a garden of potted ornamentals.

- **Great Room:** Running from the front of the house to the rear, this great room is bathed in natural light from both directions. The volume ceiling adds a luxurious feeling to it, and the fireplace creates a cozy place on chilly afternoons.

- **Kitchen:** Cooking will be a pleasure in this kitchen, thanks to the thoughtful layout and well-designed work areas.

- **Master Suite:** Enjoy the quiet in this room, where it will be easy to relax and unwind, no matter what the time of day. The walk-in closet gives you plenty of storage space, and you're sure to appreciate both the privacy and large size of the master bath.

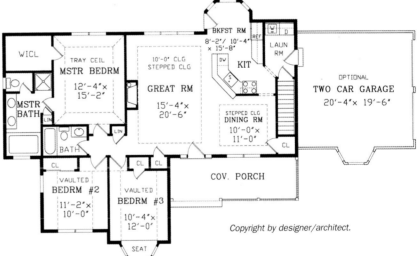

Copyright by designer/architect.

Rear Elevation

Plan #141001

Dimensions: 48' W x 29' D
Levels: 1
Square Footage: 1,208
Bedrooms: 3
Bathrooms: 2
Foundation: Basement
Materials List Available: Yes
Price Category: B

Images provided by designer/architect.

The spacious feel of this raised ranch belies its compact floor plan.

Features:

- Ceiling Height: 8 ft. unless otherwise noted.

- Porch: This country-style porch lends character and lots of curb appeal.

- Drive-Under Garage: The garage is tucked below for a more attractive facade but can also be built with a front entry if lot restrictions dictate.

- Living Room: The cathedral ceiling in the living room creates a dramatic fireplace wall.

- Kitchen: You'll love cooking in this super-efficient U-shaped kitchen, with its generous counter space and storage.

- Laundry: The laundry closet is conveniently located in the hall bath.

- Master Suite: A cathedral ceiling makes this bedroom seem spacious. The oversize tub has a showerhead so that you can enjoy an oversize shower as well.

Copyright by designer/architect.

SMARTtip

Hydro-seeding

An alternative to traditional seeding is hydro-seeding. In this process, a slurry of grass seed, wood fibers, and fertilizer is spray-applied in one step. Hydro-seeding is relatively inexpensive. Compared with seeding by hand, hydro-seeding is also very fast.

Plan #251004

Dimensions: 50'9" W x 42'1" D

Levels: 1

Square Footage: 1,500

Bedrooms: 3

Bathrooms: 2

Foundation: Crawl space, slab

Materials List Available: Yes

Price Category: C

Combine the old-fashioned appeal of a country farmhouse with all the comforts of modern living.

Features:

- Ceiling Height: 9 ft.

- Foyer: When guests enter this inviting foyer, they will be greeted by a view of the lovely family room.

- Family Room: Usher family and friends into this welcoming family room, where they can warm up in front of the fireplace. The room's 12-ft. ceiling enhances its sense of spaciousness.

- Kitchen: Gather around and keep the cook company at the snack bar in this roomy kitchen. There's still plenty of counter space for food preparation, thanks to the kitchen island.

- Master Bedroom: This elegant master bedroom features a large walk-in closet and a 9-ft. recessed ceiling.

- Master Bath. This master bath includes a double vanity, a tub, and a walk-in shower.

- Garage: This attached garage provides plenty of extra storage space, as well as parking for two cars.

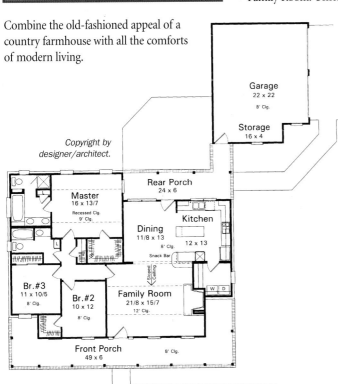

Copyright by designer/architect.

SMARTtip

Shaker Style in Your Bathroom

This warm, likable style fits in perfectly with a country home because of its old-fashioned values. But it blends in well with contemporary interiors, too, because of its clean lines and plain geometric shapes. In fact, adding a few Shaker elements can warm up the sometimes cold look of a thoroughly modern room.

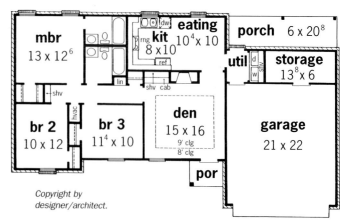

Copyright by
designer/architect.

Plan #201004

Dimensions: 60'10" W x 34'10" D
Levels: 1
Square Footage: 1,121
Bedrooms: 3
Bathrooms: 2
Foundation: Crawl space, slab,
or basement
Materials List Available: Yes
Price Category: B

*Images provided by
designer/architect.*

SMARTtip

Color Basics

Use color effectively to enhance the perception of the space itself. Make a large room feel cozy with warm colors, which tend to advance. Conversely, open up a small room with cool colors or neutrals, which tend to recede.

*Images provided by
designer/architect.*

Plan #151168

Dimensions: 66' W x 65'2" D
Levels: 1
Square Footage: 2,261
Bedrooms: 4
Bathrooms: 2½
Foundation: Basement, daylight basement, crawl space, or slab
Materials List Available: Yes
Price Category: E

Copyright by designer/architect.

Bonus Room

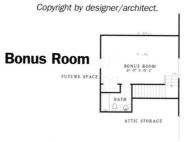

Plan #201006

Dimensions: 69'10" W x 25'10" D

Levels: 1

Square Footage: 1,172

Bedrooms: 3

Bathrooms: 2

Foundation: Crawl space, slab

Materials List Available: Yes

Price Category: B

Images provided by designer/architect.

SMARTtip

Bathroom Fans

Especially in large bathrooms, more than one fan is recommended for efficient venting. Of course, first check with your local building department about codes that may stipulate where to install bathrooms fans. If possible, include a fan in the toilet area, one near the shower, and one over the bathtub.

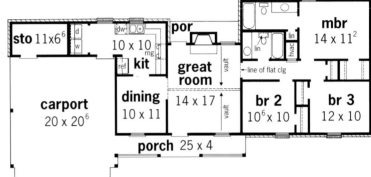

sto 11x6⁶

d / w

dw

10 x 10 / rng

ref

kit

por

great room 14 x 17

vault

vault

line of flat clg

mbr 14 x 11²

lin / lin

tvac

lin

carport 20 x 20⁶

dining 10 x 11

br 2 10⁶ x 10

br 3 12 x 10

porch 25 x 4

Plan #201007

Dimensions: 56'10" W x 34'10" D

Levels: 1

Square Footage: 1,239

Bedrooms: 3

Bathrooms: 2

Foundation: Crawl space, slab

Materials List Available: Yes

Price Category: B

Images provided by designer/architect.

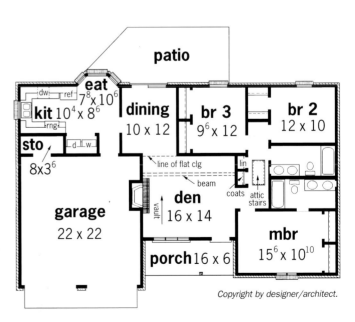

patio

dw / ref

eat 7⁸ x 10⁶

kit 10⁴ x 8⁶

rng

sto 8x3⁶

d / w

dining 10 x 12

br 3 9⁶ x 12

br 2 12 x 10

line of flat clg

beam

lin

coats

attic stairs

garage 22 x 22

vault

den 16 x 14

porch 16 x 6

mbr 15⁶ x 10¹⁰

Images provided by designer/architect.

Plan #131016

Dimensions: 75' W x 45' D
Levels: 1
Square Footage: 1,902
Bedrooms: 3
Bathrooms: 2
Foundation: Basement, crawl space, or slab
Materials List Available: Yes
Price Category: E

If traditional country looks appeal to you, you'll be delighted by the wraparound covered porch that forms the entryway to this comfortable home.

Features:

- **Great Room:** Sit by the fireplace in this room with feature walls so large that they'll suit a home theater or large media center.

- **Kitchen:** Overlooking the great room, this well-designed kitchen has great cabinets and ample counter space to make all your cooking and cleaning a pleasure.

- **Master Suite:** A large bay window makes the bedroom in this private suite sophisticated, and two walk-in closets make it practical. You'll love to relax in the master bath, whether in the whirlpool tub or the separate shower. A dual-sink vanity completes the amenities in this room.

- **Garage:** Find extra storage space in this two-bayed, attached garage.

Copyright by designer/architect.

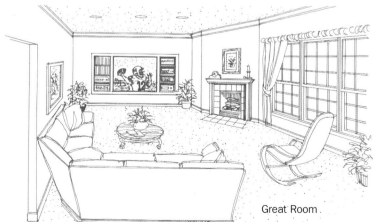

Great Room

Plan #171006

Dimensions: 68' W x 50' D
Levels: 1
Square Footage: 2,296
Bedrooms: 3
Bathrooms: 2½
Foundation: Slab, crawl space
Materials List Available: Yes
Price Category: E

This classic country farmhouse features a large, open rocking-chair front porch.

Features:

- Ceiling Height: 9 ft. unless otherwise noted.
- Great Room: This spacious great room is perfect for all types of entertaining.

SMARTtip

Window Shades

While decorative hems add interest to roller shades, they also increase the cost. If you're handy with a glue gun, choose one of the trims available at fabric and craft stores, and consider attaching it yourself. Give your shades fancy pulls for an inexpensive dash of pizzazz.

Images provided by designer/architect.

- Dining Room: This dining room is designed to accommodate formal dinner parties as well as less-formal family occasions. After dinner, step from the dining room onto the covered rear porch.
- Family Room: On cool evenings, enjoy the handsome fireplace in this family room. There's plenty of room for all kinds of family activities.

- Kitchen: This is truly a cook's kitchen with its cooktop range and U-shaped open traffic pattern. The snack bar will see lots of use for quick family meals.
- Master Suite: This master suite is separated from the other bedrooms for additional privacy. The large bedroom has a paddle fan and a roomy walk-in closet. The bathroom features his and her vanities, a deluxe bath, and a walk-in shower.

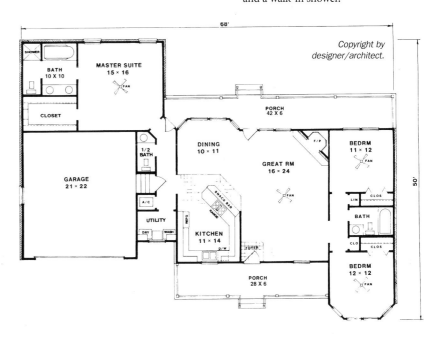

Copyright by designer/architect.

Plan #271074

Dimensions: 68' W x 86' D

Levels: 1

Square Footage: 2,400

Bedrooms: 4

Bathrooms: 3

Foundation: Crawl space or slab

Materials List Available: No

Price Category: E

Perfect for families with aging relatives or boomerang children, this home includes a completely separate suite at the rear.

Features:

- **Living Room:** A corner fireplace casts a friendly glow over this gathering space.

- **Kitchen:** This efficient space offers a serving bar that extends toward the eating nook

and the formal dining room.

- **Master Suite:** A cathedral ceiling presides over this deluxe suite, which boasts a whirlpool tub, dual-sink vanity, and walk-in closet.

- **In-law Suite:** This separate wing has its own vaulted living room, plus a kitchen, a dining room, and a bedroom suite.

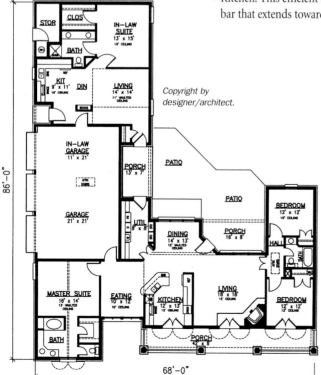

Copyright by designer/architect.

SMARTtip

Adding Professional Flair to Window Treatments

You can give your window treatment designs a professional look by using decorator tricks to customize readymades or dress your own home-sewn designs. These could include contrast linings, tassels, cording, ribbons, or couture trimmings such as buttons, coins, or bows applied to edges. Another trick is to sew a fine wire into the hem of curtains or valances to create a pliable edge that you can shape yourself. Small weights that you can sew into the hem of drapery panels or jabots will make them hang better. For more inspiration look at fashion magazines and visit showrooms.

Plan #131004

Dimensions: 59'4" W x 35'8" D
Levels: 1
Square Footage: 1,097
Bedrooms: 3
Bathrooms: 2
Foundation: Basement, crawl space, or slab
Materials List Available: Yes
Price Category: B

Images provided by designer/architect.

You'll love the extra features you'll find in this charming but easy-to-build ranch home.

Features:

- Porch: This full-width porch is graced with impressive round columns, decorative railings, and ornamental moldings.

- Living Room: Just beyond the front door, the living room entrance has a railing that creates the illusion of a hallway. The 10-ft. tray ceiling makes this room feel spacious.

- Dining Room: Flowing from the living room, this room has a 9-ft.-high stepped ceiling and leads to sliding glass doors that open to the large rear patio.

- Kitchen: This kitchen is adjacent to the dining room for convenience and has a large island for efficient work patterns.

- Master Suite: Enjoy the privacy in this bedroom with its private bathroom.

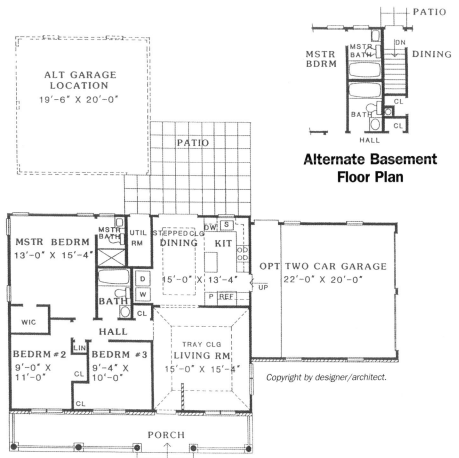

Alternate Basement Floor Plan

Copyright by designer/architect.

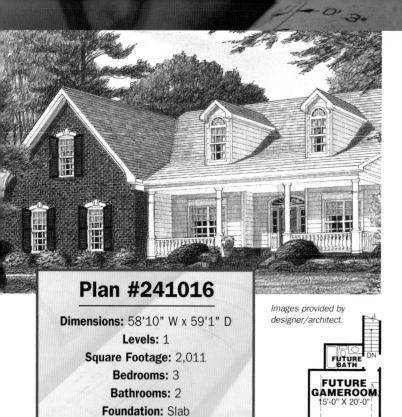

Plan #241016

Dimensions: 58'10" W x 59'1" D

Levels: 1

Square Footage: 2,011

Bedrooms: 3

Bathrooms: 2

Foundation: Slab

Materials List Available: No

Price Category: D

Images provided by designer/architect.

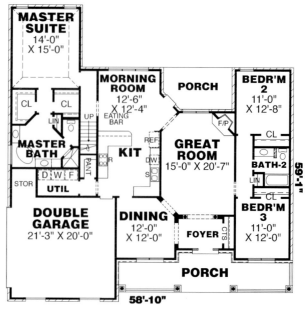

Copyright by designer/architect.

FUTURE BATH

FUTURE GAMEROOM 15'-0" X 20'-0"

MASTER SUITE 14'-0" X 15'-0"

MORNING ROOM 12'-6" X 12'-4"

PORCH

BEDR'M 2 11'-0" X 12'-8"

MASTER BATH

KIT

GREAT ROOM 15'-0" X 20'-7"

BATH-2

UTIL

STOR

DOUBLE GARAGE 21'-3" X 20'-0"

DINING 12'-0" X 12'-0"

FOYER

BEDR'M 3 11'-0" X 12'-0"

PORCH

58'-10"

59'-1"

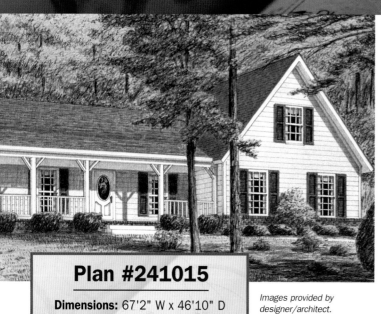

Plan #241015

Dimensions: 67'2" W x 46'10" D

Levels: 1

Square Footage: 1,609

Bedrooms: 3

Bathrooms: 2

Foundation: Slab

Materials List Available: No

Price Category: C

Images provided by designer/architect.

Copyright by designer/architect.

MASTER BATH

PATIO AREA

MASTER SUITE 13'-3" X 16'-0"

BATH-2

GREAT ROOM 16'-6" X 16'-0"

STOR

STOR

KIT

DOUBLE GARAGE 20'-0" X 21'-3"

BEDR'M 2 12'-6" X 11'-3"

BEDR'M 3 12'-8" X 11'-3"

HALL

FOYER

DINING 12'-0" X 11'-4"

PORCH

67'-2"

46'-10"

Plan #351010

Dimensions: 61'8" W x 45'8" D
Levels: 1
Square Footage: 1,502
Bedrooms: 3
Bathrooms: 2
Foundation: Basement, crawl space, or slab
Materials List Available: Yes
Price Category: C

Images provided by designer/architect.

Copyright by designer/architect.

Plan #201025

Dimensions: 62' W x 46' D
Levels: 1
Square Footage: 1,379
Bedrooms: 3
Bathrooms: 2
Foundation: Crawl space, slab
Materials List Available: Yes
Price Category: B

Images provided by designer/architect.

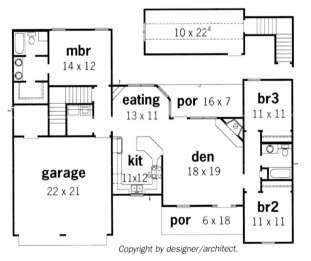

Copyright by designer/architect.

SMARTtip

Arrangement of Mantle Objects

On a fireplace mantle, group objects of different heights for visual interest—a straight line can be boring. Raise one or two pieces with a small pedestal or stand, and stagger the pieces from back to front. If you have three or more objects, make a triangle or overlapping triangles.

Plan #291001

Dimensions: 63' W x 37' D
Levels: 1
Square Footage: 1,550
Bedrooms: 3
Bathrooms: 2
Foundation: Basement
Materials List Available: No
Price Category: C

Images provided by designer/architect.

A handsome porch with Greek Revival details greets visitors to this Early-American style home.

Features:

- Ceiling Height: 8 ft. unless otherwise noted.

- Foyer: Upon entering this foyer you'll be struck by the space provided by the vaulted ceiling in the dining room, living room, and kitchen.

- Dining Room: This dining room is perfectly suited for formal dinner parties as well as less formal family meals.

- Decks: Two rear decks are conveniently accessible from the master bedroom, kitchen, and living room.

- Kitchen: You'll enjoy cooking in this well-designed kitchen, which features an eating area that is perfect for informal family meals.

- Master Bedroom: This master retreat is separated from the other bedrooms for additional privacy. It features an elegant vaulted ceiling and is graced with a dressing area, private bath, and walk-in closet.

Rear View

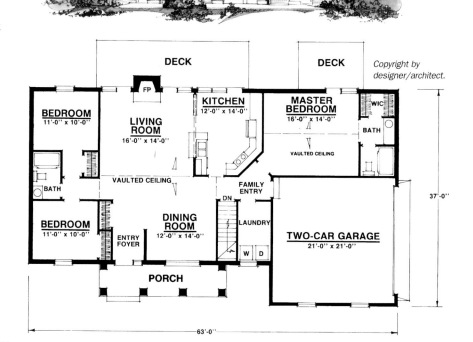

Copyright by designer/architect.

Plan #171011

Dimensions: 70' W x 58' D
Levels: 1
Square Footage: 2,069
Bedrooms: 3
Bathrooms: 2½
Foundation: Slab, crawl space
Materials List Available: Yes
Price Category: D

Images provided by designer/architect.

This home combines the charm of a country cottage with all the modern amenities.

Features:

- Ceiling Height: 9 ft. unless otherwise noted.
- Front Porch: Watch the sun set, read a book, or just relax on this spacious front porch.

- Foyer: This gracious foyer has two closets and opens to the formal dining room and the study.
- Dining Room: This big dining room works just as well for family Sunday dinner as it does for entertaining guests on Saturday night.
- Family Room: This inviting family room features an 11-ft. ceiling, a paddle fan, and a corner fireplace.
- Kitchen: This smart kitchen includes lots of counter space, a built-in desk, and a breakfast bar.
- Master Bedroom: This master bedroom is separate from the other bedrooms for added privacy. It includes a paddle fan.
- Master Bath: This master bath has two vanities, walk-in closets, a deluxe tub, and a walk-in shower.

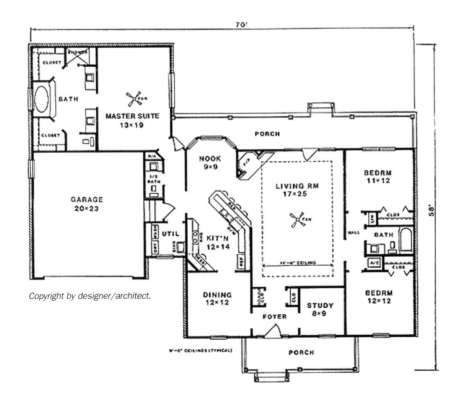

Copyright by designer/architect.

Plan #281022

Dimensions: 48' W x 58' D

Levels: 1

Square Footage: 1,506

Bedrooms: 3

Bathrooms: 2

Foundation: Basement

Materials List Available: Yes

Price Category: C

Images provided by designer/architect.

Rear Elevation

Copyright by designer/architect.

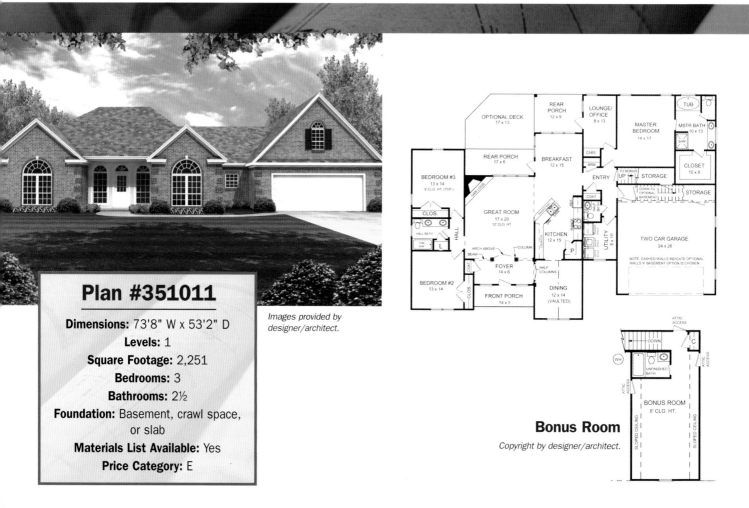

Plan #351011

Dimensions: 73'8" W x 53'2" D

Levels: 1

Square Footage: 2,251

Bedrooms: 3

Bathrooms: 2½

Foundation: Basement, crawl space, or slab

Materials List Available: Yes

Price Category: E

Images provided by designer/architect.

Bonus Room

Copyright by designer/architect.

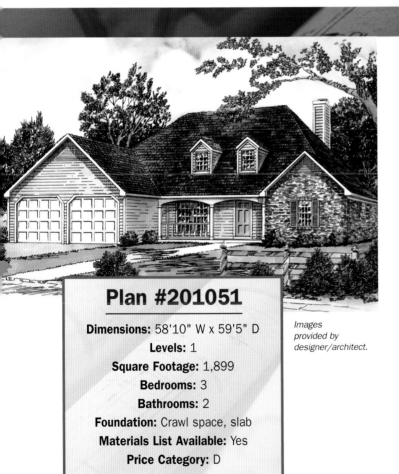

Plan #201034

Dimensions: 66'10" W x 46'10" D
Levels: 1
Square Footage: 1,660
Bedrooms: 3
Bathrooms: 2
Foundation: Crawl space, slab
Materials List Available: Yes
Price Category: C

Images provided by designer/architect.

SMARTtip

Wall Frame Widths

Trim Tip: Depending on the room, widths of wall frames usually vary from wall to wall. This is okay as long as you keep variations as small as possible while trying to maintain dimensions close to the ideal 1:0.635 ratio of the Golden Rectangle. Doors and windows will dictate exceptions to the rule.

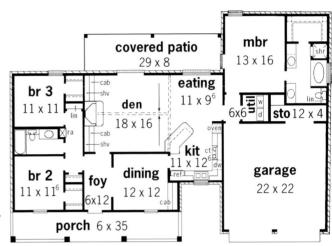

covered patio 29 x 8

mbr 13 x 16

shr

br 3 11 x 11

cab
shv
lin

den 18 x 16

eating 11 x 9^6

util 6x6

w
d

sto 12 x 4

lin

oven

kit 11 x 12^6

ct

dw

garage 22 x 22

br 2 11 x 11^6

foy 6x12

dining 12 x 12

ref

cab

porch 6 x 35

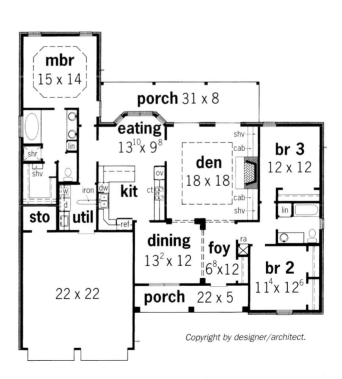

mbr 15 x 14

porch 31 x 8

shr
shv

lin

eating 13^{10} x 9^8

shv
cab

den 18 x 18

br 3 12 x 12

iron

dw

kit

ov

ct

cab
shv

lin

sto

util

w
d

ref

dining 13^2 x 12

foy 6^{8}x12

ra

br 2 11^4 x 12^6

22 x 22

porch 22 x 5

Plan #201051

Dimensions: 58'10" W x 59'5" D
Levels: 1
Square Footage: 1,899
Bedrooms: 3
Bathrooms: 2
Foundation: Crawl space, slab
Materials List Available: Yes
Price Category: D

Images provided by designer/architect.

Plan #141002

Dimensions: 48' W x 29' D
Levels: 1
Square Footage: 1,365
Bedrooms: 3
Bathrooms: 2
Foundation: Slab, basement
Materials List Available: No
Price Category: B

This warm country cottage-style house is perfect for the growing family.

Features:

- Ceiling Height: 8 ft. unless otherwise noted.

- Foyer: Guests will be greeted by a full vaulted ceiling that soars to a height of 11 ft. 8 in.

- Dining Area: This dining area flows from the foyer but is defined by a plant shelf over a column.

- Kitchen: This kitchen is open and spacious, with large windows facing the front of the house so that the cook can keep an eye on the kids playing in the front yard. It includes a pass-through over the sink.

- Master Bedroom: This bedroom is separated from the others to create more privacy. Its distinctive look comes from a ceiling that slopes to flat at 9 ft. 6 in.

- Laundry: For maximum efficiency, the washer and dryer are closeted in the hall of the secondary bedrooms.

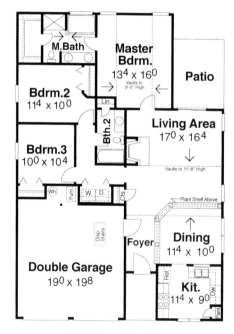

Copyright by designer/architect.

SMARTtip

Contemporary Style in Your Bathroom

Incorporate elements of Arts and Crafts, Art Deco, or other designs associated with the modern movement of the twentieth century (International Style, Bauhaus, Memphis, and the influence of Scandinavian design). Their clean geometric lines are quite compatible with this environment. This eclectic approach can be very sophisticated. Look for framed art prints, a vintage-inspired wallpaper, or reproduction hardware, faucets, or light fixtures to underscore your theme. Fortunately, manufacturers are reproducing art tiles from original molds or designs that can be used as accents.

Plan #131017

Dimensions: 69'8" W x 39'4" D
Levels: 1
Square Footage: 1,480
Bedrooms: 3
Bathrooms: 2
Foundation: Basement, crawl space, or slab
Materials List Available: Yes
Price Category: C

Images provided by designer/architect.

This fully accessible home is designed for wheelchair access to every area, giving everyone true enjoyment and freedom of movement.

Features:

- Great Room: Facing towards the rear, this great room features a volume ceiling that adds to the spacious feeling of the room.

- Kitchen: Designed for total convenience and easy work patterns, this kitchen also offers a view out to the covered front porch.

- Master Bedroom: Enjoy the quiet in this room which is sure to become your favorite place to relax at the end of the day.

- Additional Bedrooms: Both rooms have easy access to a full bath and feature nicely sized closet spaces.

- Garage: Use the extra space in this attached garage for storage..

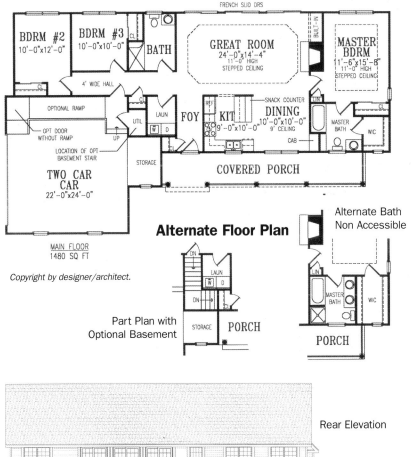

Copyright by designer/architect.

Plan #131002

Dimensions: 70'1" W x 60'7" D
Levels: 1
Square Footage: 1,709
Bedrooms: 3
Bathrooms: 2½
Foundation: Basement, crawl space, or slab
Materials List Available: Yes
Price Category: D

Images provided by designer/architect.

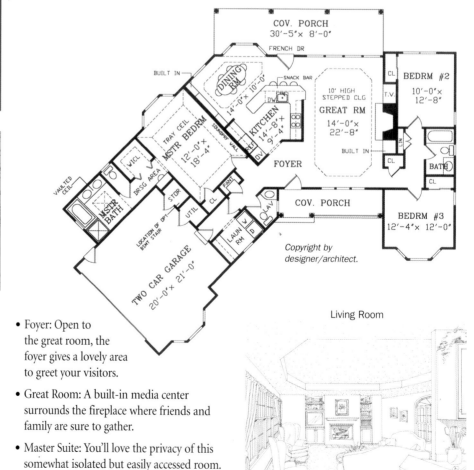

Copyright by designer/architect.

Living Room

Rear View

You'll love the way this angled ranch brings out the best in a corner lot or on a slope.

Features:

Ceiling Height: 8 ft.

- **Front Porch:** Hang baskets of plants from the roof of this porch, which is just the right size for a couple of rockers and a side table.

- **Dining Room:** Well-placed windows flood this room with sunlight during the day and a built-in cabinet gives ample storage space for all your china, linens, and collectables.

- **Foyer:** Open to the great room, the foyer gives a lovely area to greet your visitors.

- **Great Room:** A built-in media center surrounds the fireplace where friends and family are sure to gather.

- **Master Suite:** You'll love the privacy of this somewhat isolated but easily accessed room. Decorate to show off the large bay window and tray ceiling, and enjoy the luxury of a compartmented bathroom.

Plan #121012

Dimensions: 40' W x 48'8" D
Levels: 1
Square Footage: 1,195
Bedrooms: 3
Bathrooms: 2
Foundation: Basement
Materials List Available: Yes
Price Category: B

This compact one-level home uses an open plan to make the most of its square footage.

Features:

• Ceiling Height: 8 ft.

• Covered Porch: This delightful area, located off the kitchen, provides a private spot to enjoy some fresh air.

• Open Plan: The family room, dining area and kitchen share a big open space to provide a sense of spaciousness. Moving so easily between these interrelated areas provides the convenience demanded by a busy lifestyle.

• Master Suite: An open plan is convenient, but it is still important for everyone to have their private space. The master suite enjoys its own bath and walk-in closet. The secondary bedrooms share a nearby bath.

• Garage: Here you will find parking for two cars and plenty of extra storage space as well.

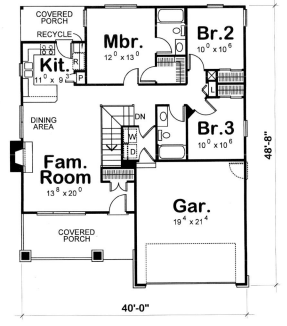

SMARTtip

Painting Doors

To protect the door finish while working, cover the sawhorses with towels or carpet scraps. Be sure to allow sufficient time for the door to dry before flipping it over.

To paint both sides of the door at one time, drive a pair of 16d nails into the top and bottom edges of the door, and then rest the door on the sawhorses, as shown below. After painting one side, simply flip the door over to paint the other side. (Note: This method may not work quite as well with very heavy wood or steel doors.)

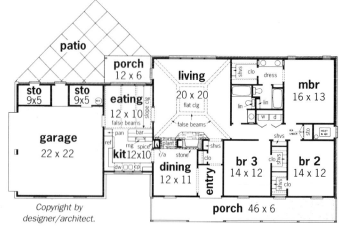

Images provided by designer/architect.

Plan #211036

Dimensions: 80' W x 40' D
Levels: 1
Square Footage: 1,800
Bedrooms: 3
Bathrooms: 2
Foundation: Slab
Materials List Available: Yes
Price Category: D

Floor plan labels: patio, porch 12 x 6, sto 9x5, sto 9x5, eating 12 x 10, false beams, pan, ref, bar, rng, spice, kit 12x10, dw, living 20 x 20 flat clg, false beams, plant, stone, r/a, dining 12 x 11, entry, garage 22 x 22, shvs, clo, dress, lin, lin, w d, mbr 16 x 13, sto, HEAT & AC, br 3 14 x 12, br 2 14 x 12, shvs, clo, shvs, porch 46 x 6

SMARTtip

Dimmer Switches

You can dim lights just slightly to extend lamp life and save energy, and there will be very little perceptible change in light level. For instance, dimming the light to 50 percent will be perceived as though the light were only dimmed to 70 percent. Therefore, there is no dramatic dilation or constriction of the eye due to light level change.

Plan #251003

Dimensions: 42' W x 42' D
Levels: 1
Square Footage: 1,393
Bedrooms: 3
Bathrooms: 2
Foundation: Crawl space, slab
Materials List Available: Yes
Price Category: B

Images provided by designer/architect.

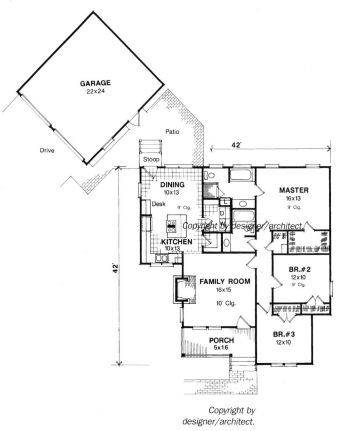

Floor plan labels: GARAGE 22x24, Drive, Patio, Stoop, 42', DINING 10x13, Desk, 9' Clg., KITCHEN 10x13, MASTER 16x13 9' Clg., BR.#2 12x10 9' Clg., FAMILY ROOM 16x15 10' Clg., BR.#3 12x10, PORCH 5x16, 42'

Plan #351008

Dimensions: 64'6" W x 61'4" D

Levels: 1

Square Footage: 2,002

Bedrooms: 3

Bathrooms: 2

Foundation: Basement, crawl space

Materials List Available: Yes

Price Category: D

Images provided by designer/architect.

Copyright by designer/architect.

COVERED PORCH OR PATIO
23 x 10

M. BATH
15 x 10

JET TUB

MAKE UP

3 x 4 SHWR

CLOS.
7 x 8

CLOS.
8 x 6

M. BEDROOM
(RAISED CLG.)
14-6 x 16

9' CLG. HT.

10' CLG. HT.

BREAKFAST
11-6 x 7

RAISED BAR

KITCHEN
11-6 x 11

ISLAND

PANTRY

9' CLG. HT.

10' CLG. HT.

DINING ROOM
(RAISED CLG.)
11-6 x 16

CEILING BEAM

COLUMNS

BED #2
12-6 x 12

HALL

BATH

C

C

UTIL.
9-6 x 8

STOR.
7 x 10

D   W

OPTIONAL HALF BATH

ENTRY

OFFICE/ NURSERY
8-6 x 12

ATTIC ACCESS

VAULTED CEILING

GREAT ROOM
23 x 16

GAS LOGS

VAULTED CEILING

CABS

CABS

BED #3
12-6 x 12

COVERED PORCH
23 x 6

RAILING

2 or 3 CAR GARAGE
21 x 22 (TWO CAR)
21 x 32 (THREE CAR)

THIRD CAR GARAGE or STORAGE

NOTE: OVERALL DIMENSIONS DO NOT INCLUDE OPTIONAL THIRD CAR GARAGE

Plan #351009

Dimensions: 54' W x 47' D

Levels: 1

Square Footage: 1,400

Bedrooms: 3

Bathrooms: 2

Foundation: Crawl space, slab
(basement option for fee)

Materials List Available: Yes

Price Category: B

Images provided by designer/architect.

PATIO
19-8 x 11-6

Garden Tub

V

Bath

Bath

Master Bedroom
15-8 x 14-8
8-0 Ceiling

Clos.

Stor.

Utility

Entry

Kitchen
9-10 x 12-0

Dining
9-10 x 12-0
8-0 Ceiling

Great Room
19-8 x 15-6
8-0 Ceiling

Bedroom 2
12-2 x 11-0
8-0 Ceiling

Clos.

Hall

Hall

Bath

Clos.

Bedroom 3
12-2 x 11-0
8-0 Ceiling

Covered Porch
19-8 x 5

Two Car Garage
22-2 x 25-0

OPTIONAL GARAGE EXTENSION NOT INCLUDED IN OVERALL DIMENSIONS

OPTIONAL EXTENSION OF GARAGE IF BASEMENT OPTION IS CHOSEN

Optional Basement Floor Plan

Copyright by designer/architect.

PATIO
19-8 x 11-6

Garden Tub

V

Bath

BATH

Master Bedroom
15-8 x 14-8

Clos.

Stor.

S W D

Utility

Entry

Kitchen
9-10 x 12-0

Dining
9-10 x 12-0

Great Room
19-8 x 15-6

Bedroom #2
12-2 x 11-0

Clos.

Hall

Hall Bath

Bedroom #3
12-2 x 11-0

Covered Porch
19-8 x 5

Two Car Garage
22-2 x 25-0

Plan #131035

Dimensions: 65'4" W x 45'10" D
Levels: 1
Square Footage: 1,892
Bedrooms: 3
Bathrooms: 2½
Foundation: Basement, crawl space, or slab
Materials List Available: Yes
Price Category: D

Images provided by designer/architect.

Families who love a mixture of traditional — a big front porch, simple roofline, and bay windows—and contemporary—an open floor plan—will love this charming home.

Features:

- **Great Room:** Central to this home, the open living and entertaining areas allow the family to gather effortlessly and create the perfect spot for entertaining.

- **Dining Room:** Volume ceilings both here and in the great room further enhance the spaciousness the open floor plan creates.

- **Master Suite:** Positioned on the opposite end of the other two bedrooms in the split-bedroom plan, this master suite gives an unusual amount of privacy and quiet in a home of this size.

- **Bonus Room:** Located over the attached garage, this bonus room gives you a place to finish for a study or a separate game room.

Rear Elevation

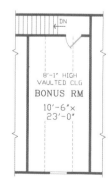

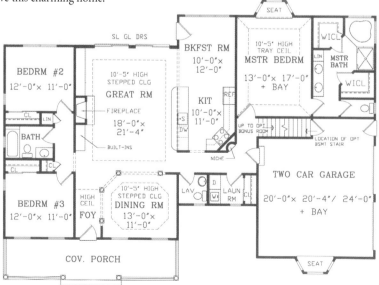

Copyright by designer/architect.

Bonus Area

Plan #131047

Dimensions: 69'10" W x 51'8" D
Levels: 1
Square Footage: 1,793
Bedrooms: 3
Bathrooms: 2
Foundation: Basement, crawl space, or slab
Materials List Available: Yes
Price Category: E

Images provided by designer/architect.

The country charm of this well-designed home is mixed with the convenience and luxury normally reserved for more contemporary plans.

Features:

- Great Room: The spaciousness of this great room is enhanced by the 11-ft. stepped ceiling. A fireplace makes it cozy on cool evenings or on chilly winter days, and two sets of French sliding glass doors open to the back porch.

- Kitchen: In addition to the convenient layout of this design, you'll also love its bright, airy position. It includes an old-fashioned pantry,

a sink under a window, and a sunny breakfast area that opens to the wraparound porch.

- Master Suite: You'll find 11-ft. ceilings in both the master bedroom and the bayed sitting area that the suite includes. In the bath, the circular spa tub is surrounded by a glass-block wall.

- Bonus Space: A permanent staircase leads to an unfinished bonus space on the upper level.

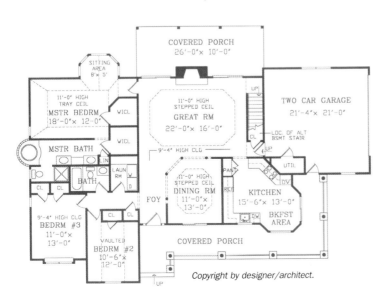

Copyright by designer/architect.

Rear View

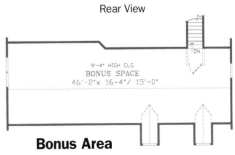

Bonus Area

Plan #131048

Dimensions: 67'6" W x 53'2" D
Levels: 1
Square Footage: 1,579
Bedrooms: 3
Bathrooms: 2
Foundation: Basement, crawl space, or slab
Materials List Available: Yes
Price Category: D

Images provided by designer/architect.

You'll love the country appearance of this expandable ranch, with its covered porch and shuttered windows.

Features:

- Foyer: This foyer flows into the great room but gives you a gracious space to welcome guests.

- Great Room: Enjoy the 9-ft. ceiling, fireplace, and tall windows in this room, which gives you a view of the front porch.

- Dining Room: Adjoining the great room, this dining room opens through French doors to the backyard terrace, making this area ideal

for hosting a party or grilling a family meal.

- Kitchen: The dinette in this kitchen area opens to the terrace, and an angled pass-through to the dining room makes entertaining a pleasure.

- Mudroom: With access to the garage and terrace, this mudroom also includes laundry facilities.

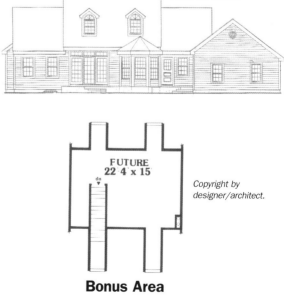

Rear Elevation

Copyright by designer/architect.

Bonus Area

Plan #301005

Dimensions: 71' W x 42' D
Levels: 1
Square Footage: 1,930
Bedrooms: 3
Bathrooms: 2
Foundation: Crawl space, slab
Materials List Available: Yes
Price Category: D

Images provided by designer/architect.

This home features an old-fashioned rocking-chair porch that enhances the streetscape.

Features:

- Ceiling Height: 8 ft.

- Dining Room: When the weather is warm, guests can step through French doors from this elegant dining room and enjoy a breeze on the rear screened porch.

- Family Room: This family room is a warm and inviting place to gather, with its handsome fireplace and built-in bookcases.

- Kitchen: This kitchen offers plenty of counter space for preparing your favorite recipes. Its U-shape creates a convenient open traffic pattern.

- Master Suite: You'll look forward to retiring at the end of the day in this truly luxurious master suite. The bedroom has a fireplace and opens through French doors to a private rear deck. The bath features a corner spa tub, a walk-in shower, double vanities, and a linen closet.

Copyright by designer/architect.

SMARTtip

Light With Shutters

For the maximum the amount of light coming through shutters, use the largest panel possible on the window. Make sure the shutters have the same number of louvers per panel so that all of the windows in the room look unified. However, don't choose a panel that is over 48 inches high, because the shutter becomes unwieldy. Also, any window that is wider than 96 inches requires extra framing to support the shutters.

Plan #121010

Dimensions: 50' W x 62' D
Levels: 1
Square Footage: 1,902
Bedrooms: 2
Bathrooms: 2
Foundation: Basement
Materials List Available: Yes
Price Category: D

Images provided by designer/architect.

This home is replete with architectural details that provide a convenient and gracious lifestyle.

Features:

- Ceiling Height: 8 ft.

- Great Room: The entry enjoys a long view into this room. Family and friends will be drawn to the warmth of its handsome fireplace flanked by windows.

- Breakfast Area: You'll pass through cased openings from the great room into the cozy breakfast area that will lure the whole family to linger over informal meals.

- Kitchen: Another cased opening leads from the breakfast area into the well-designed kitchen with its convenient island.

- Master Bedroom: To the right of the great room special ceiling details highlight the master bedroom where a cased opening and columns lead to a private sitting area.

- Den/Library: Whether you are listening to music or relaxing with a book, this special room will always enhance your lifestyle.

SMARTtip

Accentuating Your Fireplace with Faux Effects

Experiment with faux effects to add an aged look or a specific style to a fireplace mantel and surround. Craft stores sell inexpensive kits with directions for adding the appearance of antiqued or paneled wood or plaster, rusticated stone, marble, terra cotta, and other effects that make any style achievable.

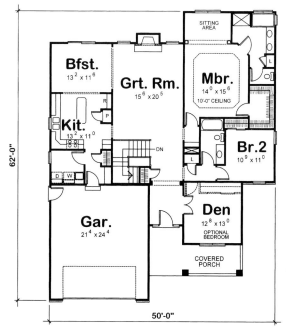

Copyright by designer/architect.

Plan #241017

Dimensions: 74'4" W x 55'4" D

Levels: 1

Square Footage: 2,431

Bedrooms: 4

Bathrooms: 2½

Foundation: Slab

Materials List Available: No

Price Category: E

Images provided by designer/architect.

The turret, arched window details, and wraparound porch hint at the interesting interior design of this lovely home.

Features:

- Great Room: This room features a 12-ft. ceiling, angled walls, a corner fireplace, and sliding doors leading to the rear porch.

- Dining Room: Located in the turret, the highlights of this room are the deep bay and 10-ft. ceiling.

- Morning Room: The angled walls and windows over the rear porch echo those in the great room.

- Kitchen: With an angled snack bar accessible from the great room and morning room, this well-designed kitchen is ideal for the family cooks.

- Master Suite: Situated for privacy, the master suite has an angled wall in the bedroom and a door onto the rear porch. The bath has two walk-in closets, two vanities, a garden tub, and a separate shower stall.

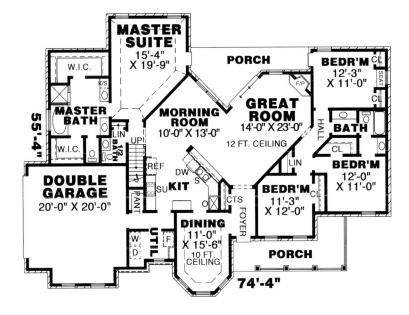

Copyright by designer/architect.

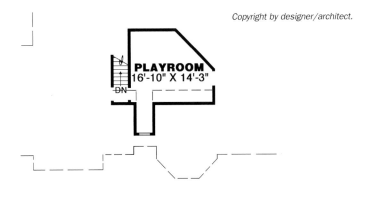

Plan #151010

Dimensions: 38'4" W x 68'6" D
Levels: 1
Square Footage: 1,379
Bedrooms: 3
Bathrooms: 2
Foundation: Crawl, slab
Materials List Available: Yes
Price Category: B

Images provided by designer/architect.

This French Country home has a spacious great room for friends and family to gather, but you can sneak away to the covered rear porch or patio off the master suite for cozy tête-à-têtes.

Features:

- Entry: Take advantage of the marvelous 10-ft. ceilings to hang groups of potted flowering plants.

- Great Room: This spacious room, with an optional 10-ft. boxed ceiling, is the place to curl up by the gas fireplace on a cold winter night.

- Kitchen: The kitchen includes a bar for casual meals, and is open to the breakfast room.

- Rear Porch: Enjoy leisurely meals on the covered rear porch that you can access from both the master suite and the breakfast room.

- Master Suite: The 10-ft. boxed ceiling in the bedroom and the master bath with a whirlpool tub and separate shower make this suite a luxurious place to end a long day.

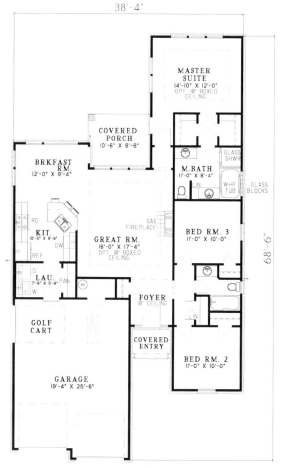

Copyright by designer/architect.

Plan #111007

Dimensions: 72' W x 91' D
Levels: 1
Square Footage: 3,668
Bedrooms: 4
Bathrooms: 3½
Foundation: Crawl space
Materials List Available: No
Price Category: H

This Mediterranean-inspired, traditional manor home offers an enormous amount of space and every amenity you can imagine, but to do it justice, site it on a large lot with wonderful views.

Features:

- **Living Room:** With a fireplace and built-in media center, this room has the potential to become a gathering place for guests as well as family members.

- **Kitchen:** Enjoy this well-designed kitchen which will surely have you whistling as you work.

- **Breakfast Area:** Unusually large for a breakfast room, this space invites a crowd at any time of day. French doors at the back of the room open to the gracious rear porch.

- **Master Suite:** Privacy is guaranteed by the location of this spacious suite. The separate walk-in closets give plenty of storage space, and the master bath features separate vanities as well as a large corner whirlpool tub.

Bedroom 15'7"x 13'
WIC
Bath Dressing
Porch
Breakfast 14'1"x 14'8"
Master Bedroom 17'11"x 17'6"
Bedroom 11'7"x 12'1"
WIC WIC
Bath TV
Living 22'1"x 23'11"
Kitchen 14'1"x 15'
Master Bath
Dress
WIC
Hunting Room 11'7"x 7'3"
Bedroom 13'1"x 16'3"
Foyer 6'9"x14'
Dining 14'1"x 14'1"
1/2 Bath
Utility 9'11"x 9'9"
Workshop 11'11"x 11'7"
Porch
Two-Car Garage 23'3"x 24'8"
Extra Storage 12'3"x 7'9"

Copyright by designer/architect.

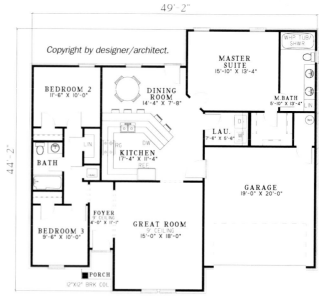

Copyright by designer/architect.

Images provided by
designer/architect.

Plan #151061

Dimensions: 49'2" W x 44'2" D

Levels: 1

Square Footage: 1,466

Bedrooms: 3

Bathrooms: 2

Foundation: Crawl space, slab
(basement option for fee)

Materials List Available: Yes

Price Category: B

SMARTtip

Using a Miter Trimmer

Most pros who use this type of tool hold the molding by hand close to the fence. But watch those fingertips; the blade is extremely sharp.

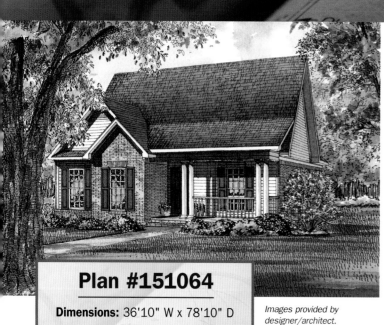

Images provided by
designer/architect.

Copyright by
designer/architect.

Plan #151064

Dimensions: 36'10" W x 78'10" D

Levels: 1

Square Footage: 1,935

Bedrooms: 3

Bathrooms: 2

Foundation: Crawl space, slab

Materials List Available: Yes

Price Category: D

Plan #151065

Dimensions: 51' W x 71'4" D

Levels: 1

Square Footage: 1,881

Bedrooms: 3

Bathrooms: 2

Foundation: Crawl space, slab

Materials List Available: Yes

Price Category: D

Images provided by designer/architect.

Copyright by designer/architect.

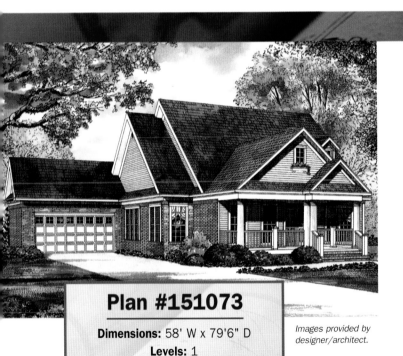

Plan #151073

Dimensions: 58' W x 79'6" D

Levels: 1

Square Footage: 2,026

Bedrooms: 3

Bathrooms: 2

Foundation: Crawl space, slab (basement option for fee)

Materials List Available: Yes

Price Category: D

Images provided by designer/architect.

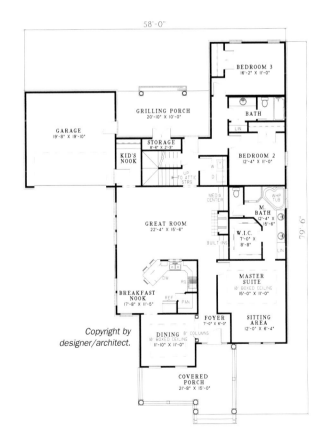

Copyright by designer/architect.

Plan #151049

Dimensions: 41'6" W x 57'8" D
Levels: 1
Square Footage: 1,355
Bedrooms: 3
Bathrooms: 2
Foundation: Crawl space, slab (basement option for fee)
Materials List Available: Yes
Price Category: B

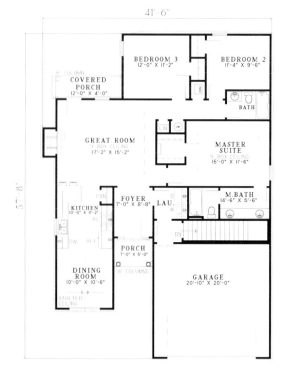

Images provided by designer/architect.

Copyright by designer/architect.

Plan #151052

Dimensions: 33'10" W x 69'6" D
Levels: 1
Square Footage: 1,660
Bedrooms: 3
Bathrooms: 2
Foundation: Crawl space, slab
Materials List Available: Yes
Price Category: C

Images provided by designer/architect.

Copyright by designer/architect.

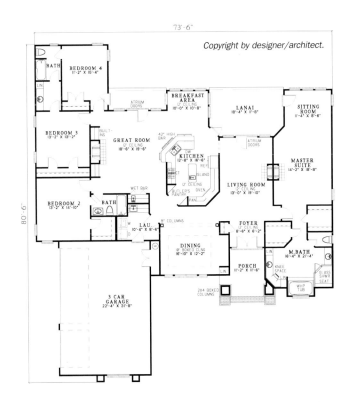

Plan #151054

Dimensions: 71'2" W x 54'10" D
Levels: 1
Square Footage: 1,746
Bedrooms: 3
Bathrooms: 2
Foundation: Crawl space, slab, with basement option for fee
Materials List Available: Yes
Price Category: C

Images provided by designer/architect.

SMARTtip

Mixing and Matching Windows

Windows, both fixed and operable, are made in various styles and shapes. While mixing styles should be carefully avoided, a variety of interesting window sizes and shapes may nevertheless be combined to achieve symmetry, harmony, and rhythm on the exterior of a home.

Plan #151057

Dimensions: 73'6" W x 80'6" D
Levels: 1
Square Footage: 2,951
Bedrooms: 4
Bathrooms: 3
Foundation: Crawl space, slab, or basement
Materials List Available: Yes
Price Category: F

Images provided by designer/architect.

Plan #151170

Dimensions: 57' W x 64'4" D
Levels: 1
Square Footage: 1,965
Bedrooms: 4
Bathrooms: 2
Foundation: Crawl space, slab
(basement or daylight basement
option for fee)
Materials List Available: Yes
Price Category: D

Images provided by designer/architect.

The clean lines of the open floor plan and high ceilings match the classic good looks of this home's exterior.

Features:

- **Foyer:** The 10-ft. ceiling here sets the stage for the open, airy feeling of this lovely home.

- **Dining Room:** Set off by columns from the foyer and great room, this area is ideal for entertaining.

- **Great Room:** Open to the breakfast room beyond, this great room features a masonry fireplace and a door to the rear grilling porch.

- **Breakfast Room:** A deep bay overlooking the porch is the focal point here.

- **Kitchen:** Planned for efficiency, the kitchen has an angled island with storage and snack bar.

- **Master Suite:** A boxed ceiling adds elegance to the bedroom, and the bath features a whirlpool tub, double vanity, and separate shower.

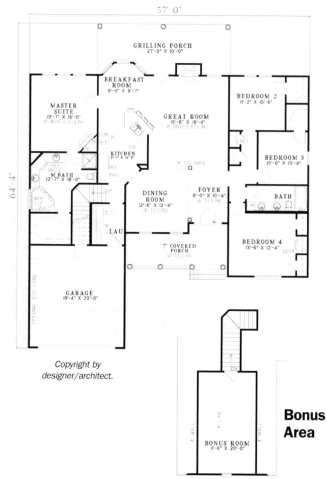

Copyright by designer/architect.

Bonus Area

Plan #121050

Dimensions: 64' W x 50' D
Levels: 1
Square Footage: 1,996
Bedrooms: 2
Bathrooms: 2
Foundation: Basement
Materials List Available: Yes
Price Category: D

Images provided by designer/architect.

This compact design includes features usually reserved for larger homes and has styling that is typical of more-exclusive home designs.

Features:

- **Entry:** As you enter this home, you'll see the formal living and dining rooms—both with special ceiling detailing—on either side.

- **Great Room:** Located in the rear of the home for convenience, this great room is likely to be your favorite spot. The fireplace is framed by transom-topped windows, so you'll love curling up here, no matter what the weather or time of day.

- **Kitchen:** Ample counter and cabinet space make this kitchen a dream in which to work.

- **Master Suite:** A tray ceiling and lovely corner windows create an elegant feeling in the bedroom, and two walk-in closets make it easy to keep this space tidy and organized. The private bath has a skylight, corner whirlpool tub, and two separate vanities.

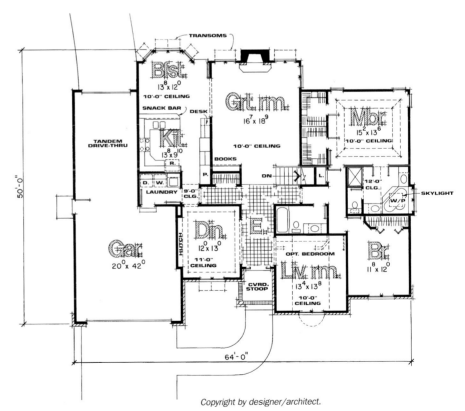

Copyright by designer/architect.

Images provided by designer/architect.

Copyright by designer/architect.

Plan #151070

Dimensions: 54'2" W x 57'4" D
Levels: 1
Square Footage: 1,786
Bedrooms: 3
Bathrooms: 2
Foundation: Crawl space, slab (basement option for fee)
Materials List Available: Yes
Price Category: C

SMARTtip

Using Wall Anchors

Where a pilaster doesn't fall over a stud, use a combination of construction adhesive and an anchor-type fastener.

Plan #151072

Dimensions: 27'2" W x 72'10" D
Levels: 1
Square Footage: 1,263
Bedrooms: 3
Bathrooms: 2
Foundation: Crawl space, slab
Materials List Available: Yes
Price Category: B

Images provided by designer/architect.

Copyright by designer/architect.

Images provided by designer/architect.

Copyright by designer/architect.

Plan #201043

Dimensions: 57'10" W x 54'5" D

Levels: 1

Square Footage: 1,887

Bedrooms: 3

Bathrooms: 2

Foundation: Crawl space, slab, or basement

Materials List Available: Yes

Price Category: D

Plan #201044

Dimensions: 74'10" W x 44'4" D

Levels: 1

Square Footage: 1,869

Bedrooms: 3

Bathrooms: 2

Foundation: Crawl space, slab, or basement

Materials List Available: Yes

Price Category: D

Images provided by designer/architect.

SMARTtip

Resin Outdoor Furniture

Resin furniture is made of molded plastic. Most resin pieces are quite affordable, but lacquered resin with brass fittings is a high-end item. Resin doesn't corrode and cleans easily, but a scratched finish cannot be repaired. Lacquered resin can be touched up, however.

Copyright by designer/architect.

Images provided by designer/architect.

Copyright by designer/architect.

Plan #171003

Dimensions: 69' W x 64' D
Levels: 1
Square Footage: 2,098
Bedrooms: 4
Bathrooms: 3
Foundation: Slab, crawl space
Materials List Available: Yes
Price Category: D

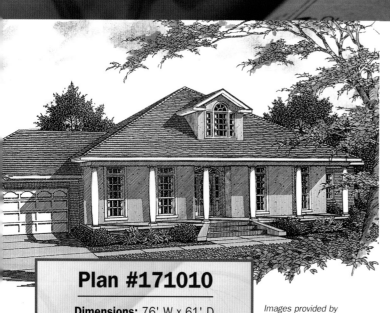

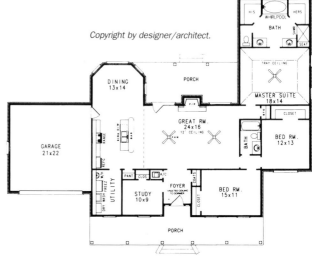

Copyright by designer/architect.

Images provided by designer/architect.

Plan #171010

Dimensions: 76' W x 61' D
Levels: 1
Square Footage: 1,972
Bedrooms: 3
Bathrooms: 2
Foundation: Slab, crawl space
Materials List Available: Yes
Price Category: D

SMARTtip

Testing Grill Hoses for Leaks

Hoses on gas grills can develop leaks. To check the hose on your gas grill, brush soapy water over it. If you see any bubbles, turn off the gas valve and disconnect the tank. Then replace the hose.

Copyright by designer/architect.

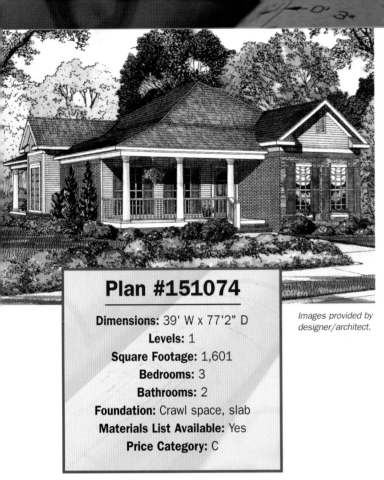

Plan #151074

Dimensions: 39' W x 77'2" D

Levels: 1

Square Footage: 1,601

Bedrooms: 3

Bathrooms: 2

Foundation: Crawl space, slab

Materials List Available: Yes

Price Category: C

Images provided by designer/architect.

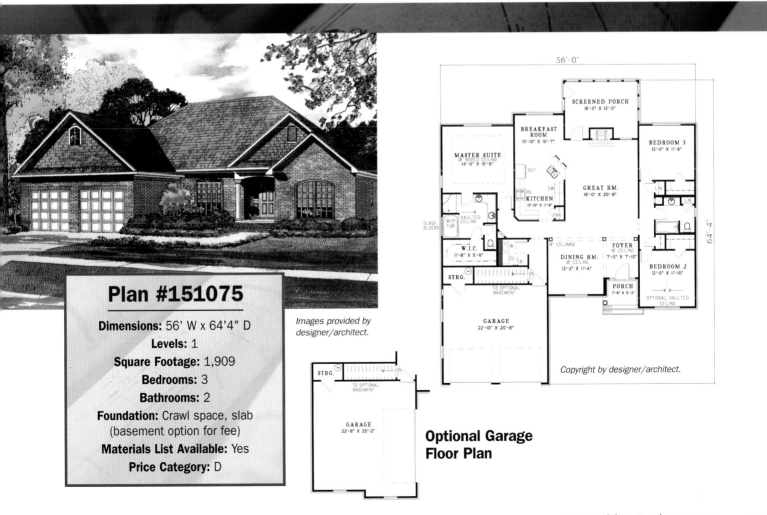

Plan #151075

Dimensions: 56' W x 64'4" D

Levels: 1

Square Footage: 1,909

Bedrooms: 3

Bathrooms: 2

Foundation: Crawl space, slab (basement option for fee)

Materials List Available: Yes

Price Category: D

Images provided by designer/architect.

Optional Garage Floor Plan

Copyright by designer/architect.

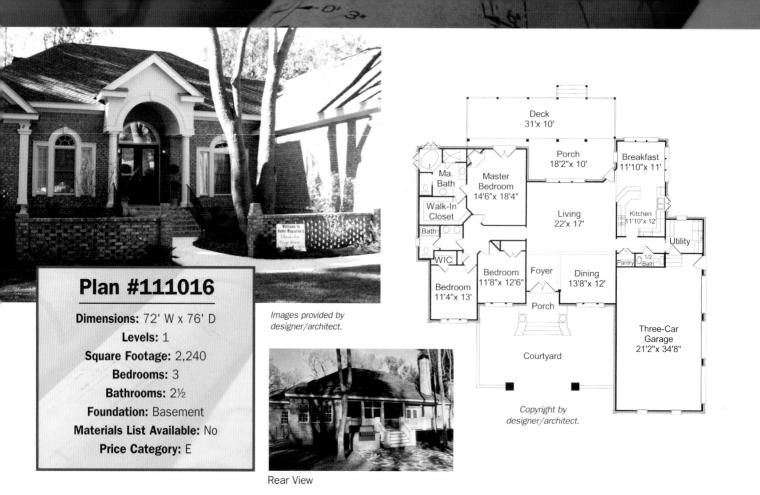

Plan #111016

Dimensions: 72' W x 76' D

Levels: 1

Square Footage: 2,240

Bedrooms: 3

Bathrooms: 2½

Foundation: Basement

Materials List Available: No

Price Category: E

Images provided by designer/architect.

Rear View

Deck 31'x 10'

Porch 18'2"x 10'

Breakfast 11'10"x 11'

Ma. Bath

Master Bedroom 14'6"x 18'4"

Living 22'x 17'

Kitchen 11'10"x 12'

Utility

Walk-In Closet

Bath

WIC

Bedroom 11'8"x 12'6"

Foyer

Dining 13'8"x 12'

Pantry

1/2 Bath

Bedroom 11'4"x 13'

Porch

Three-Car Garage 21'2"x 34'8"

Courtyard

Copyright by designer/architect.

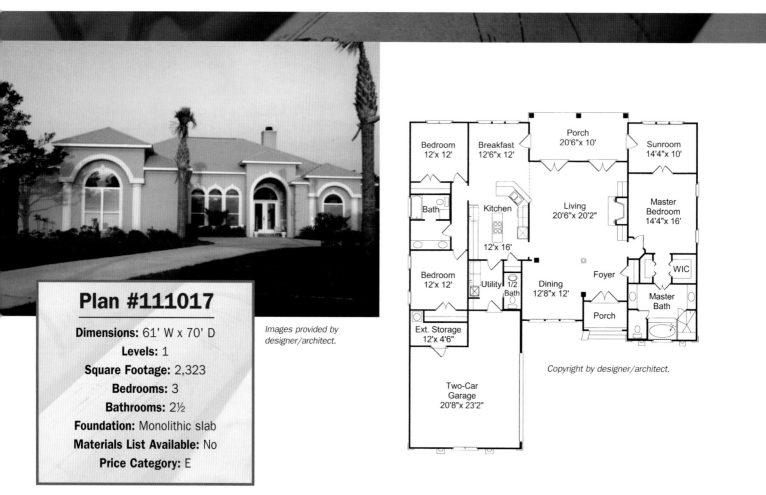

Plan #111017

Dimensions: 61' W x 70' D

Levels: 1

Square Footage: 2,323

Bedrooms: 3

Bathrooms: 2½

Foundation: Monolithic slab

Materials List Available: No

Price Category: E

Images provided by designer/architect.

Bedroom 12'x 12'

Breakfast 12'6"x 12'

Porch 20'6"x 10'

Sunroom 14'4"x 10'

Bath

Kitchen 12'x 16'

Living 20'6"x 20'2"

Master Bedroom 14'4"x 16'

Bedroom 12'x 12'

Utility

1/2 Bath

Dining 12'8"x 12'

Foyer

WIC

Ext. Storage 12'x 4'6"

Porch

Master Bath

Two-Car Garage 20'8"x 23'2"

Copyright by designer/architect.

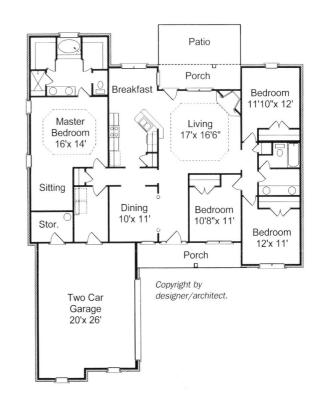

Images provided by designer/architect.

Copyright by designer/architect.

Plan #111015

Dimensions: 64' W x 58' D

Levels: 1

Square Footage: 2,208

Bedrooms: 4

Bathrooms: 2

Foundation: Crawl space

Materials List Available: No

Price Category: E

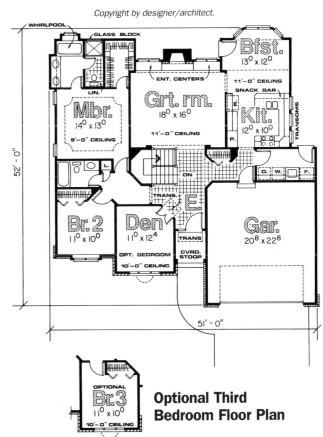

Images provided by designer/architect.

**Optional Third
Bedroom Floor Plan**

Plan #121055

Dimensions: 51' W x 52' D

Levels: 1

Square Footage: 1,622

Bedrooms: 3

Bathrooms: 2

Foundation: Basement

Materials List Available: Yes

Price Category: C

Color

No other decorating component has more power and greater effect at such little cost than color. It can fill a space and make furnishings look fresh and new. Color can also show off fine architectural details or downplay a room's structural flaws. A particular color can make a cold room cozy, while another hue can cool down a sunny cooker. And color comes cheap, giving a tremendous impact for your decorating dollar: elbow grease, supplies, prep work, and paint will all cost pretty much the same if you choose a gorgeous hue over plain white.

But finding the color—the right color—isn't easy. Where do you begin to look? Like the economy, color has leading indicators. You have a market basket full of choices, and there are lots of signposts to direct you where to go.

The Lay of the Land

For the past 200 years, white has been the most popular choice for American home exteriors. And it still is, followed by tan, brown, and beige. You can play it safe and follow the leader. But you should also think about the architecture of your house and where you live when you're considering exterior color. For example, traditional Colonials have a color-combination range of about two that look appropriate: white with black or green shutters and gray with white trim. Mediterranean-style houses typically pick up the colors of terra-cotta and the tile that are indigenous to the regions that developed the architecture—France, Italy, and Spain. A ranch-style house shouldn't be overdone—it is, after all, usually a modest structure. On the other hand, a cottage can be fanciful. Whimsical colors also look charming on Victorian houses in San Francisco, but they would be out of place in conservative Scarsdale, New York, where you must

check with the local building board even when you want to change the exterior color of your house.

How's the Weather?

Like exteriors, interiors often take their color cues from their environs and local traditions. In the rainy and often chilly Pacific Northwest, cozy blanket plaids in strong reds and black abound. In the hot-and-arid climate of the West, indigo or brown ticking-stripes and faded denim look appropriately casual and cool. Subtle grays and neutrals, reflecting steel, limestone, and concrete, look apropos for sophisticated city life. In extremely warm southern climates, the brilliant sun tends to overpower lighter colors. That explains the popularity of strong hues in tropical, sun-drenched locales.

Natural Light. That's the one you don't pay for. Its direction and intensity greatly affects color. A room with a window that faces trees will look markedly different in summer, when warm white sunlight is filtered through the leaves, than in winter, when the trees are bare and the color of natural light takes on a cool blue cast. Time of day affects color, too. Yellow walls that are pleasant and cheerful in the early morning can be stifling and blinding in the afternoon. That's because afternoon

The yellow-colored wall, above, complements the antique painted dresser.

Warm neutral-color walls, opposite, and touches of red make this bedroom cozy.

sun is stronger than morning sun.

When you're choosing a color for an interior, always view it at different times of day, but especially during the hours in which you will inhabit the room.

Artificial Light. Because artificial light affects color rendition as much as natural light, don't judge a color in the typically chilly fluorescence of a hardware store. The very same color chip will look completely different when you bring it home, which is why it's so important to test out a paint color in your own home. Most fluorescent light is bluish and distorts colors. It depresses red and exaggerates green, for example. A romantic faded rose on your dining room walls will just wash out in the kitchen if your use a fluorescent light there. Incandescent light, the type produced by the standard bulbs you probably use in your chandelier and in most of your home's light fixtures, is warm but slightly yellow. Halogen light, which comes from another newer type of incandescent bulb, is white and the closest to natural sunlight. Of all three types of bulbs, halogen is truest in rendering color.

 # red

RED is powerful, dramatic, motivating. Red is also hospitable, and it stimulates the appetite, which makes it a favorite choice for dining rooms. Some studies have indicated that a red room actually makes people feel warmer.

yellow

YELLOW illuminates the colors it surrounds. It warms rooms that receive northern light but can be too bright in a sunny room. It's best for daytime rooms, not bedrooms. It has a short range, which means as white is added to yellow, it disappears. Yellow highlights and calls attention to features—think of bright taxicabs.

green

GREEN is tranquil, nurturing, rejuvenating. It is a psychological primary, and because it is mixed from yellow and blue, it can appear both warm and cool. Time seems to pass more quickly in green rooms. Perhaps that's why waiting rooms off-stage are called "green rooms."

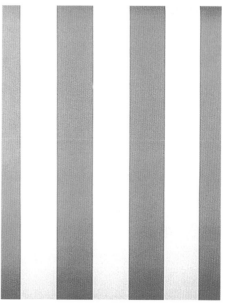

 **neutrals**

GRAY goes with all colors—it is a good neighbor. Various tones of gray range from dark charcoal to pale oyster.

BLACK (technically the absence of color) enhances and brightens other colors, making for livelier decorating schemes when used as an accent.

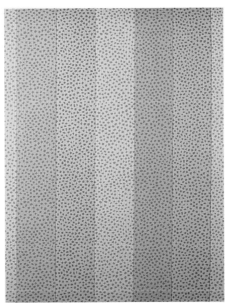

 # pink

PINK is perceived as outgoing and active. It's also a color that flatters skin tones. Hot shades are invigorating, while soft, toned-down versions can be relaxed and charming.

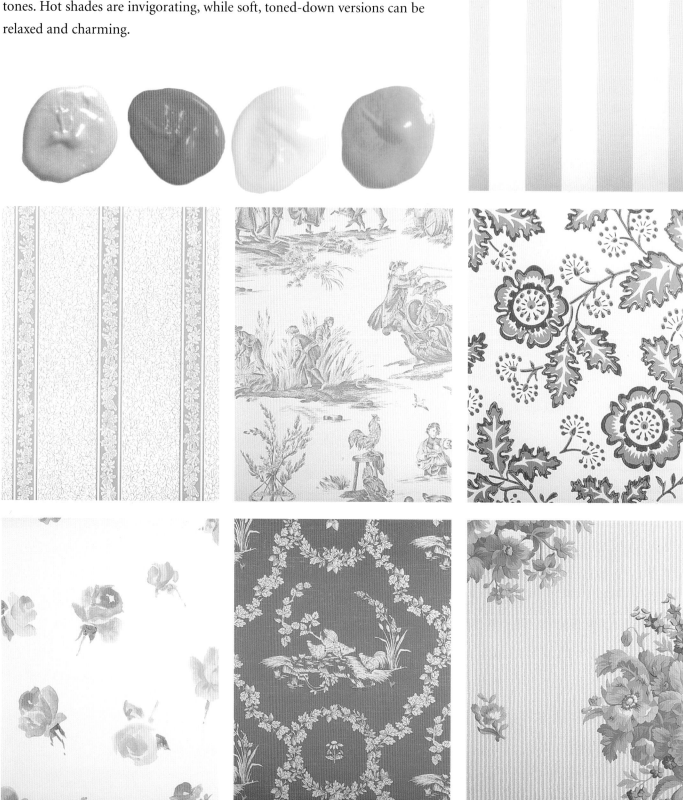

order direct: 1-800-523-6789

 # blue

BLUE, with its associations of sea and sky, offers serenity, which is why it is a favorite in bedrooms. Studies have shown that people think better in blue rooms. Perhaps that explains the popularity of the navy blue suit. Cooler blues show this color's melancholy side, however.

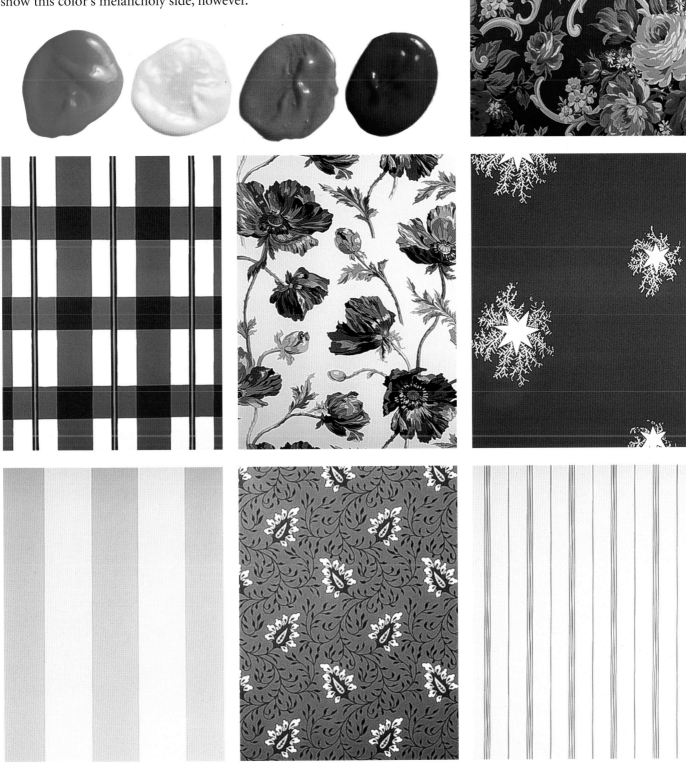

Plan #211002

Dimensions: 68' W x 62' D
Levels: 1
Square Footage: 1,792
Bedrooms: 3
Bathrooms: 2
Foundation: Crawl space
Materials List Available: Yes
Price Category: C

Arched windows on the front of this home give it a European style that you're sure to love.

SMARTtip

Water Features

Water features create the ambiance of a soothing oasis on a deck. A water-filled urn becomes a mirror that reflects the sky— making a small deck look larger. Fish flashing in an ornamental pool add color and act as a focal point for a deck with no view.

A water fountain introduces a pleasant rhythmical sound that helps drown out the background noises of traffic and nearby neighbors.

Features:

- Living Room: The 12-ft. ceiling in this large, open room enhances its spacious feeling. A fireplace adds warmth on chilly days and cool evenings.

- Dining Room: Decorate to accentuate the 12-ft. ceiling and formal feeling of this room.

- Kitchen: Designed for comfort and efficiency, this room also has a 12-ft. ceiling. The cozy breakfast bar is a natural gathering spot for friends and family.

- Master Suite: A split design guarantees privacy here. A sloped cathedral ceiling adds elegance, and a walk-in closet makes it practical. The bath has two vanities, a tub, and a walk-in shower.

- Garage: Park two cars here, and use the balance of this 520 sq. ft. area as a handy storage area.

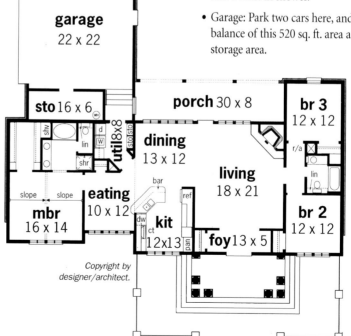

Plan #131015

Dimensions: 57'4" W x 56'10" D
Levels: 1
Square Footage: 1,860
Bedrooms: 3
Bathrooms: 2
Foundation: Basement, crawl space, or slab
Materials List Available: Yes
Price Category: D

Images provided by designer/architect.

The mixture of country charm and formal elegance is sure to thrill any family looking for a distinctive and comfortable home.

Features:

• Great Room: Separated from the dining room by a columned arch, this spacious room has a stepped ceiling, a built-in media center, and a fireplace. French doors within a rear bay lead to the large backyard patio at the rear of the house.

• Dining Room: Graced by a bay window, this formal room has an impressive 11-ft. 6-in.-high stepped ceiling.

• Breakfast Room: With a 12-ft. sloped ceiling, this room shares an eating bar with the kitchen.

• Master Bedroom: The 10-ft. tray ceiling and bay window contribute elegance, and the walk-in closet and bath with a bayed nook, whirlpool tub, and separate shower make it practical.

Copyright by designer/architect.

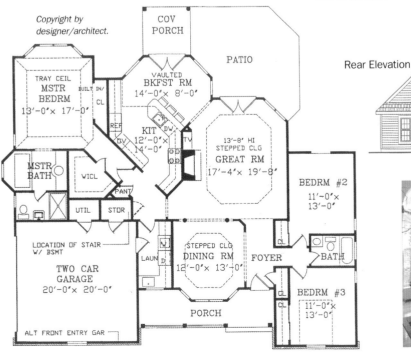

Rear Elevation

Great Room

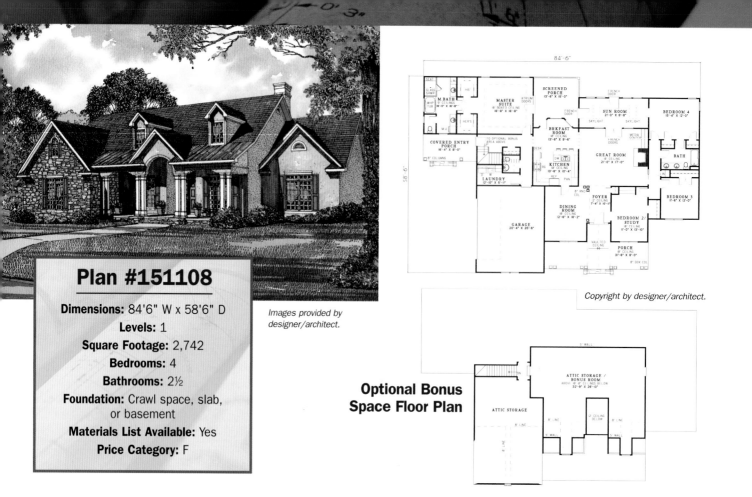

Plan #151108

Dimensions: 84'6" W x 58'6" D
Levels: 1
Square Footage: 2,742
Bedrooms: 4
Bathrooms: 2½
Foundation: Crawl space, slab, or basement
Materials List Available: Yes
Price Category: F

Images provided by designer/architect.

Copyright by designer/architect.

Optional Bonus Space Floor Plan

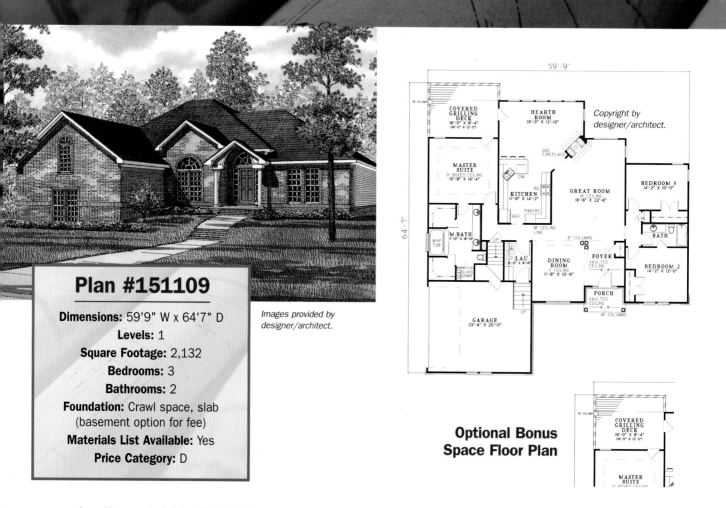

Plan #151109

Dimensions: 59'9" W x 64'7" D
Levels: 1
Square Footage: 2,132
Bedrooms: 3
Bathrooms: 2
Foundation: Crawl space, slab (basement option for fee)
Materials List Available: Yes
Price Category: D

Images provided by designer/architect.

Copyright by designer/architect.

Optional Bonus Space Floor Plan

Rear Elevation

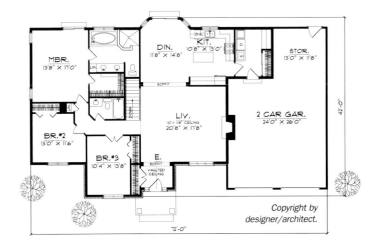

Plan #221005

Dimensions: 72' W x 42' D

Levels: 1

Square Footage: 1,868

Bedrooms: 3

Bathrooms: 2

Foundation: Basement

Materials List Available: No

Price Category: D

Images provided by designer/architect.

Copyright by designer/architect.

Rear Elevation

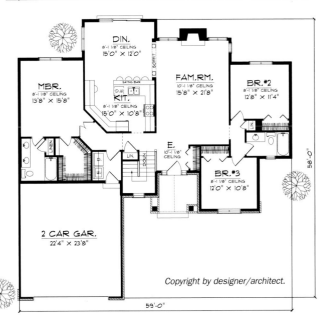

Plan #221006

Dimensions: 59' W x 58' D

Levels: 1

Square Footage: 1,756

Bedrooms: 3

Bathrooms: 2

Foundation: Basement

Materials List Available: No

Price Category: C

Images provided by designer/architect.

Copyright by designer/architect.

Plan #151058

Dimensions: 58'8" W x 58'6" D

Levels: 1

Square Footage: 1,854

Bedrooms: 4

Bathrooms: 2

Foundation: Crawl space, slab
(basement option for fee)

Materials List Available: Yes

Price Category: D

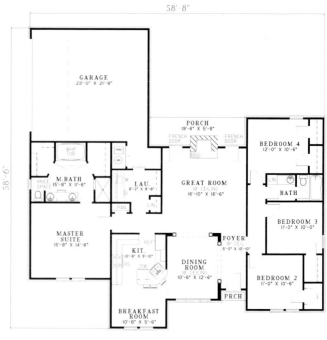

*Images provided by
designer/architect.*

*Copyright by
designer/architect.*

Plan #151056

Dimensions: 56'8" W x 58'4" D

Levels: 1

Square Footage: 1,950

Bedrooms: 3

Bathrooms: 2

Foundation: Crawl space, slab,
or basement

Materials List Available: Yes

Price Category: D

*Images provided by
designer/architect.*

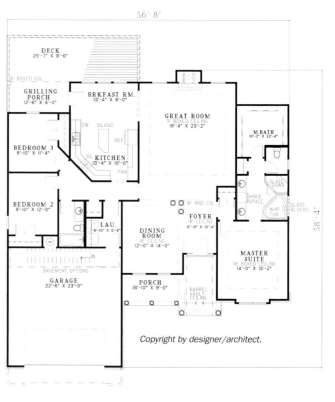

Copyright by designer/architect.

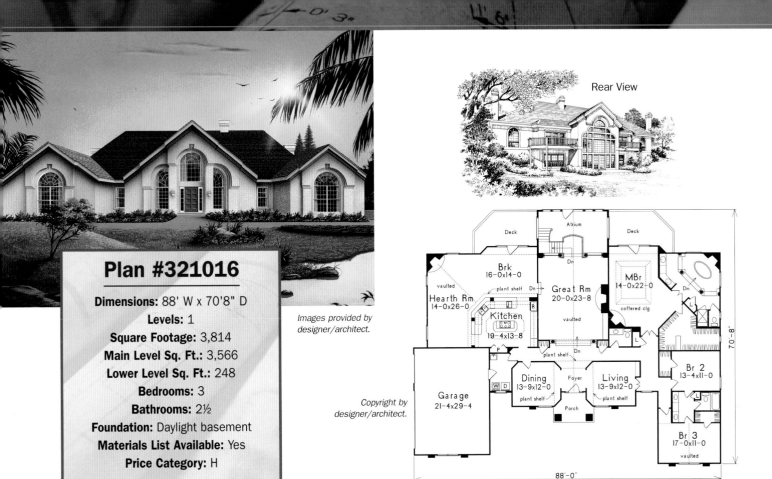

Rear View

Images provided by designer/architect.

Copyright by designer/architect.

Plan #321016

Dimensions: 88' W x 70'8" D

Levels: 1

Square Footage: 3,814

Main Level Sq. Ft.: 3,566

Lower Level Sq. Ft.: 248

Bedrooms: 3

Bathrooms: 2½

Foundation: Daylight basement

Materials List Available: Yes

Price Category: H

Plan #321026

Dimensions: 67' W x 42'4" D

Levels: 1

Square Footage: 1,712

Bedrooms: 3

Bathrooms: 2½

Foundation: Crawl space

Materials List Available: Yes

Price Category: C

Images provided by designer/architect.

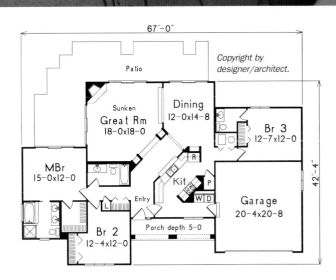

Copyright by designer/architect.

SMARTtip

Deck Design with Computers

Consider using a computer-aided design (CAD) program to plan your deck. Some programs let you see three-dimensional views of your design complete with railings, stairs, planters, hot tubs, and the surrounding landscaping.

Plan #351001

Dimensions: 78'8" W x 51' D
Levels: 1
Square Footage: 1,855
Bedrooms: 3
Bathrooms: 2½
Foundation: Basement, crawl space, or slab
Materials List Available: Yes
Price Category: D

From the lovely arched windows on the front to the front and back covered porches, this home is as comfortable as it is beautiful.

Features:

- **Great Room:** Come into this room with 12-ft. ceilings, and you're sure to admire the corner gas stove and three windows overlooking the porch.

- **Dining Room:** Set off from the open design, this room is designed to be used formally or not.

- **Kitchen:** You'll love the practical walk-in pantry, broom closet, and angled snack bar here.

- **Breakfast Room:** Brightly lit and leading to the covered porch, this room will be a favorite spot.

- **Bonus Room:** Develop a playroom or study in this area.

- **Master Suite:** The large bedroom is complemented by the private bath with garden tub, separate shower, double vanity, and spacious walk-in closet.

Images provided by designer/architect.

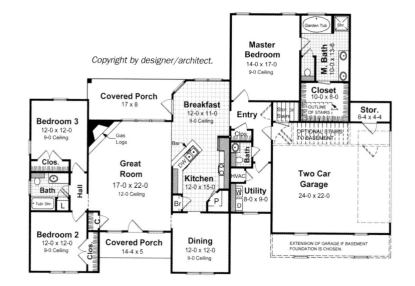

Copyright by designer/architect.

Kitchen/Great Room

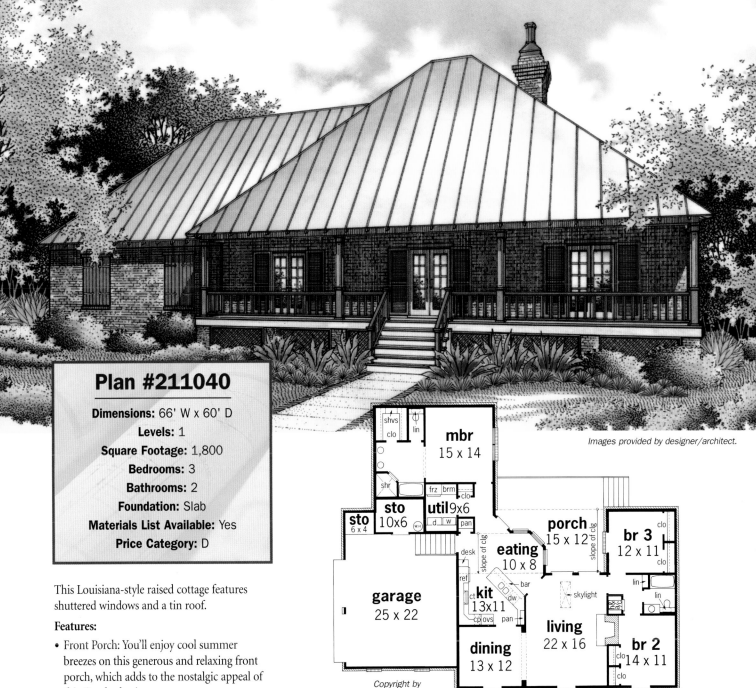

Plan #211040

Dimensions: 66' W x 60' D
Levels: 1
Square Footage: 1,800
Bedrooms: 3
Bathrooms: 2
Foundation: Slab
Materials List Available: Yes
Price Category: D

This Louisiana-style raised cottage features shuttered windows and a tin roof.

Features:

- Front Porch: You'll enjoy cool summer breezes on this generous and relaxing front porch, which adds to the nostalgic appeal of this Creole classic.

- French Doors: These elegant doors lead from the front porch to the formal living areas and the front bedroom.

- Master Bedroom Suite: You'll enjoy the open space, walk-in closet, and master bath amenities.

Images provided by designer/architect.

Copyright by designer/architect.

SMARTtip

Folding and Draping Swags

Plaids and stripes are a traditional choice for swags and jabots. But how they are folded and draped has a significant effect on the resulting overall pattern. For example, the lines can be positioned to be vertical and horizontal, or they can be draped as a diagonal. In addition, installing the darker-value stripes as the outer part of the pleat will create a totally different look from the one produced by setting the lighter value there. Try folding the fabric in different ways and pleat depths before you finally decide on the look that you prefer.

Plan #161001

Dimensions: 67'2" W x 47' D

Levels: 1

Square Footage: 1,782

Bedrooms: 3

Bathrooms: 2

Foundation: Basement

Materials List Available: Yes

Price Category: C

An all-brick exterior displays the solid strength that characterizes this gracious home.

Features:

• Gathering Area: A feeling of spaciousness permeates this gathering area, created by the foyer, great room, and dining room. Multiple windows provide natural light that dances along a sloped ceiling, spilling onto decorative columns and a fireplace.

• Breakfast Area: A continuation of the sloped ceiling leads to this breakfast area, where French doors open to a screened porch.

• Kitchen: An abundance of cabinets and counter space are the hallmarks of this large kitchen, with its easy access to a spacious laundry room and storage area.

• Master Suite: A tray ceiling and spacious walk-in closet in the master bedroom, along with a whirlpool tub and double-bowl vanity in the bathroom, enable you to pamper yourself.

Images provided by designer/architect.

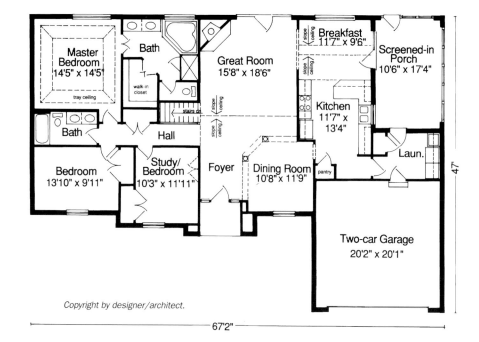

Copyright by designer/architect.

Rear Elevation

Left Side Elevation

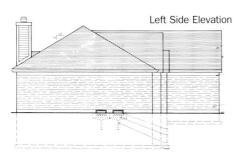

Right Side Elevation

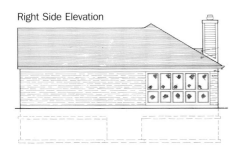

Front View

Great Room / Foyer

Plan #151004

Dimensions: 64'8" W x 62'1" D
Levels: 1
Square Footage: 2,158
Bedrooms: 4
Bathrooms: 2½
Foundation: Basement, slab, crawl space
Materials List Available: Yes
Price Category: D

Images provided by designer/architect.

You'll love the spacious feeling in this comfortable home designed for a family.

Features:

- Foyer: A 10-ft. ceiling greets you in this home.

- Great Room: A 10-ft. ceiling complements this large room, with its fireplace, built-in cabinets, and easy access to the rear covered porch.

- Dining Room: The 9-ft. boxed ceiling in this large room helps to create a beautiful formal feeling.

- Kitchen: The island in this kitchen is open to the breakfast room for true convenience.

- Breakfast Room: Morning light will stream through the bay window here.

- Master Suite: A 9-ft. pan ceiling adds a distinctive note to this room with access to the rear porch. In the bath, you'll find a whirlpool tub, separate shower, double vanities, and two walk-in closets.

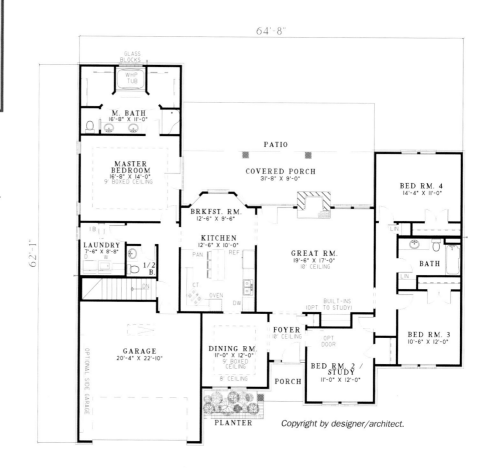

Copyright by designer/architect.

Plan #121004

Dimensions: 55'4" W x 48' D
Levels: 1
Square Footage: 1,666
Bedrooms: 3
Bathrooms: 2
Foundation: Basement
Materials List Available: Yes
Price Category: C

Images provided by designer/architect.

An efficient floor plan and plenty of amenities create a luxurious lifestyle.

Features:

- Ceiling Height: 8 ft. except as noted.

- Entry: Enjoy summer breezes on the porch; then step inside the entry where sidelights and an arched transom create a bright, cheery welcome.

- Great Room: The 10-ft. ceiling and the transom-topped windows flooding the room with light provide a sense of spaciousness. The fireplace adds warmth and style.

- Dining Room: You'll usher your guests into this room located just off the great room.

- Breakfast Area: Also located off the great room, the breakfast area offers another dining option.

- Master Suite: The master bedroom is highlighted by a tray ceiling and a large walk-in closet. Luxuriate in the private bath with its sunlit whirlpool, separate shower, and double vanity.

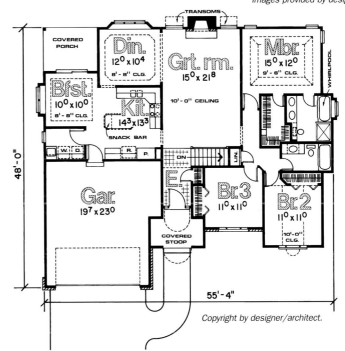

Copyright by designer/architect.

SMARTtip

Carpeting

Install the best underlayment padding available, as well as the highest grade of carpeting you can afford. This will guarantee a feeling of softness beneath your feet and protect your investment for years to come by reducing wear and tear on the carpet.

Plan #211004

Dimensions: 64' W x 62' D
Levels: 1
Square Footage: 1,828
Bedrooms: 4
Bathrooms: 2
Foundation: Slab, crawl space, basement
Materials List Available: Yes
Price Category: D

This super-energy-efficient home has the curb appeal of a much larger house.

Features:

- Ceiling Height: 9 ft.

- Kitchen: You will love cooking in this bright, airy, and efficient kitchen. It features an angled layout that allows a great view to the outside through a window wall in the breakfast area.

- Breakfast Area: With morning sunlight streaming through the wall of windows in

this area, you won't be able to resist lingering over a cup of coffee.

- Rear Porch: This breezy rear porch is designed to accommodate the pleasure of old-fashioned rockers or swings.

- Master Bedroom: Retreat at the end of a long day to this bedroom, which is isolated for privacy yet conveniently located a few steps from the kitchen and utility area.

- Attic Storage: No need to fuss with creaky pull-down stairs. This attic has a permanent stairwell to provide easy access to its abundant storage.

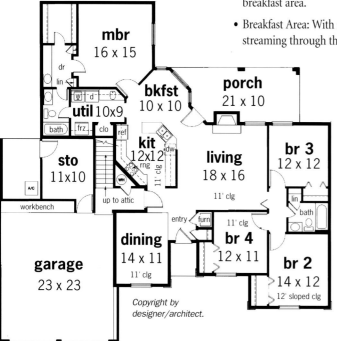

Copyright by designer/architect.

SMARTtip

Resin Furniture

Resin furniture is made of molded plastic. Most resin pieces are quite affordable, but lacquered resin with brass fittings is a high-end item. Resin doesn't corrode and cleans easily, but a scratched finish cannot be repaired. However, lacquered resin can be touched up.

Plan #271063

Dimensions: 62' W x 70' D
Levels: 1
Square Footage: 2,572
Bedrooms: 3
Bathrooms: 2
Foundation: Daylight basement
Materials List Available: No
Price Category: E

European detailing gives this home a unique flair and elegant curb appeal.

Features:

- Entry Rotunda: This welcoming area opens to a quiet den with a cozy fireplace.
- Living Room: This open space leads back to a wall of windows overlooking a backyard deck.
- Country Kitchen: A central island and dramatic overhead glass make for a great spot for meal preparation and eating. A four-season porch is nearby.
- Master Suite: Double doors and a coffered ceiling enhance this secluded suite. The private bath has everything you can imagine, including a whirlpool tub.

Copyright by designer/architect.

Basement Level Floor Plan

Plan #111051

Dimensions: 72' W x 91' D
Levels: 1
Square Footage: 3,668
Bedrooms: 4
Bathrooms: 2½
Foundation: Crawl space
Materials List Available: No
Price Category: H

You'll find everything you want in this traditional cottage-style home, and it's all on one floor!

Features:

• Living Room: Both this room and the dining room are just off the foyer for convenience. A corner fireplace and windows overlooking the backyard give character to the room.

• Kitchen: The kitchen island contains a sink and dishwasher as well as a bar. A nearby hall way leads to a half-bath, the utility room, and the two-car garage.

• Breakfast Area: Adjacent to the kitchen, the large breakfast area leads to the back porch.

• Master Suite: Featuring a walk-in closet and bath with a garden tub, standing shower, and private toilet area, this room opens to the back porch.

• Additional Bedrooms: Walk-in closets in two bedrooms and a wide closet with a double door in the third provide good storage space.

Kitchen/Breakfast Area

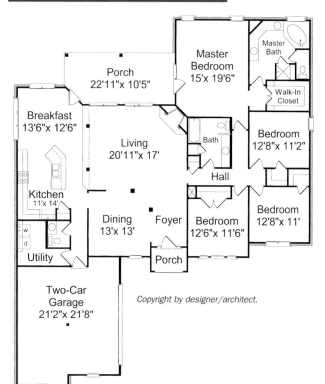

Plan #211006

Dimensions: 61' W x 77' D
Levels: 1
Square Footage: 2,177
Bedrooms: 3
Bathrooms: 2
Foundation: Slab, optional basement
Materials List Available: Yes
Price Category: D

This traditional home with a stucco exterior is distinguished by its 9-ft. ceilings throughout and its sleek, contemporary interior.

Features:

- **Living Room:** A series of arched openings that surround this room adds strong visual interest. Settle down by the fireplace on cold winter nights.

- **Dining Room:** Step up to enter this room with a raised floor that sets it apart from other areas.

- **Kitchen:** Ideal for cooking as well as casual socializing, this kitchen has a stovetop island and a breakfast bar.

- **Master Suite:** The sitting area in this suite is so big that you might want to watch TV here or make it a study. In the bath, you'll find a skylight above the angled tub with a mirror surround and well-placed plant ledge.

- **Rear Porch:** This 200-sq.-ft. covered porch gives you plenty of space for entertaining.

SMARTtip

DECK Furniture Style

Mix-and-match tabletops, frames, and legs are stylish. Combine materials such as glass, metal, wood, and mosaic tiles.

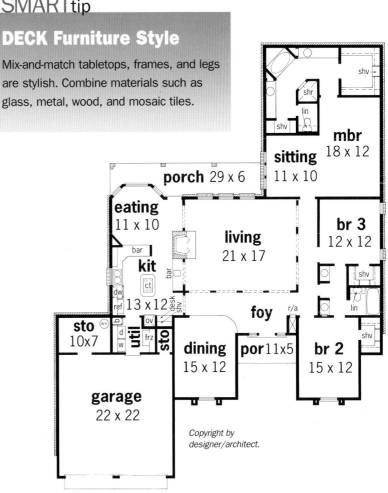

Copyright by designer/architect.

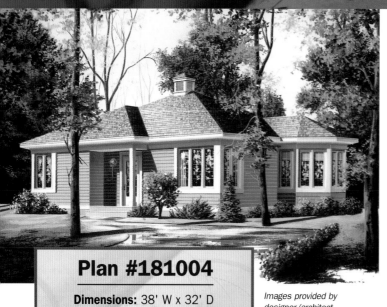

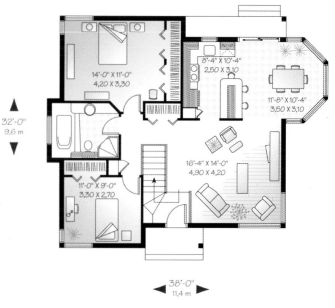

Images provided by designer/architect.

32'-0"
9,6 m

38'-0"
11,4 m

14'-0" X 11'-0"
4,20 X 3,30

8'-4" X 10'-4"
2,50 X 3,10

11'-8" X 10'-4"
3,50 X 3,10

16'-4" X 14'-0"
4,90 X 4,20

11'-0" X 9'-0"
3,30 X 2,70

Copyright by designer/architect.

Plan #181004

Dimensions: 38' W x 32' D

Levels: 1

Square Footage: 994

Bedrooms: 2

Bathrooms: 1

Foundation: Full basement

Materials List Available: Yes

Price Category: A

Plan #151048

Dimensions: 60'6" W x 69'2" D

Levels: 1

Square Footage: 2,238

Bedrooms: 4

Bathrooms: 2

Foundation: Crawl space, slab (basement option for fee)

Materials List Available: Yes

Price Category: E

Images provided by designer/architect.

GRILLING PORCH
19'-8" X 8'-0"

BEDROOM 4
11'-8" X 11'-0"

HEARTH ROOM
19'-4" X 12'-10"

BEDROOM 3
11'-0" X 11'-6"

MASTER SUITE
14'-10" X 15'-4"

GREAT RM.
17'-0" X 21'-8"

KITCHEN
12'-4" X 11'-8"

BATH

M. BATH
14'-2" X 18'-8"

FOYER

LAU./ HOBBY
10'-4" X 8'-6"

BEDROOM 2
11'-8" X 12'-0"

DINING RM.
11'-0" X 13'-2"

ENTRY PORCH
10'-8" X 7'-0"

GARAGE
22'-4" X 23'-2"

Copyright by designer/architect.

Plan #151046

Dimensions: 63'4" W x 59'10" D

Levels: 1

Square Footage: 2,525

Bedrooms: 3

Bathrooms: 2½

Foundation: Crawl space, slab, or basement

Materials List Available: Yes

Price Category: E

Images provided by designer/architect.

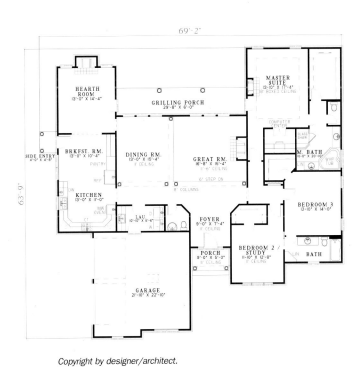

Copyright by designer/architect.

Plan #151047

Dimensions: 69'2" W x 63'9" D

Levels: 1

Square Footage: 2,422

Bedrooms: 3

Bathrooms: 2½

Foundation: Crawl space, slab (basement option for fee)

Materials List Available: Yes

Price Category: E

Images provided by designer/architect.

Copyright by designer/architect.

Plan #121003

Dimensions: 76' W x 55'4" D
Levels: 1
Square Footage: 2,498
Bedrooms: 4
Bathrooms: 3
Foundation: Basement
Materials List Available: Yes
Price Category: E

Images provided by designer/architect.

Repeated arches bring style and distinction to the interior and exterior of this spacious home.

Features:

- Ceiling Height: 8 ft. except as noted.

- Den: A decorative volume ceiling helps make this spacious retreat the perfect place to relax after a long day.

- Formal Living Room: The decorative volume ceiling carries through to the living room that invites large formal gatherings.

- Formal Dining Room: There's plenty of room for all the guests to move into this gracious formal space that also features a decorative volume ceiling.

- Master Suite: Retire to this suite with its glamorous bayed whirlpool, his and her vanities, and a walk-in closet.

- Optional Sitting Room: With the addition of French doors, one of the bedrooms can be converted into a sitting room for the master suite.

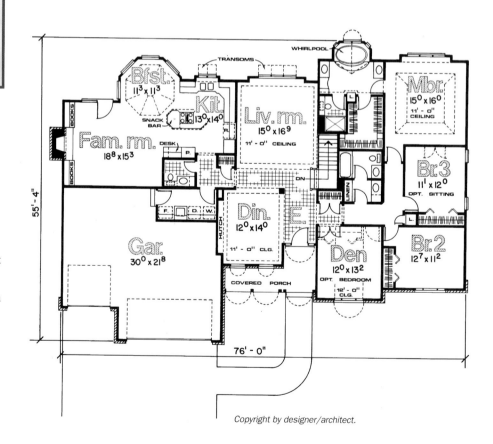

Copyright by designer/architect.

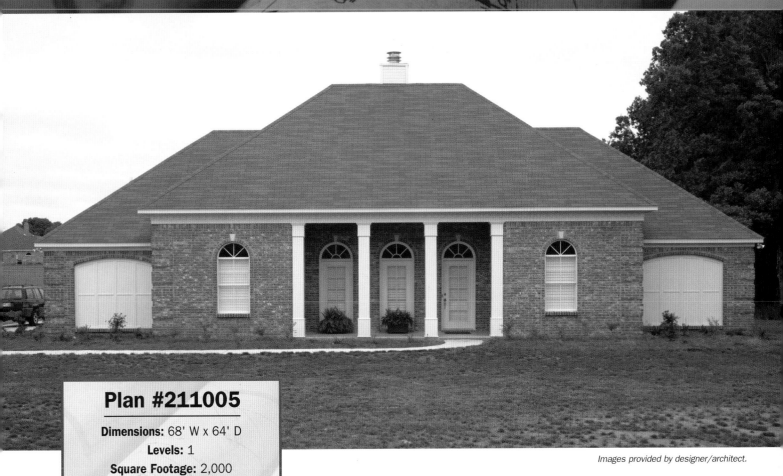

Plan #211005

Dimensions: 68' W x 64' D
Levels: 1
Square Footage: 2,000
Bedrooms: 3
Bathrooms: 2
Foundation: Slab
Materials List Available: Yes
Price Category: D

Images provided by designer/architect.

A brick veneer exterior complements the columned porch to make this a striking home.

SMARTtip

Do-It-Yourself Ponds

To avoid disturbing utility lines, contact your utility companies before doing any digging. Locate a freestanding container pond on your deck near an existing (GFCI) outlet. For an in-ground pond, have an electrician run a buried line and install a GFCI outlet near the pond so you can plug in a pump or fountain.

Features:

- Ceiling Height: 9 ft. unless otherwise noted.

- Living Room: From the front porch, the foyer unfolds into this expansive living room. Family and friends will be drawn to the warmth of the living room's cozy fireplace.

- Formal Dining Room: This elegant room is designed for dinner parties of any size.

- Kitchen: Located between the formal dining room and the dinette, the kitchen can serve formal meals as easily as quick family repasts.

- Master Suite: There's plenty of room to unwind at the end of a long day in the huge master bedroom. Luxuriate in the private bath, with its spa tub, separate shower, dual sinks, and two walk-in closets.

- Home Office: The home office, accessible from the master bedroom, is the perfect quiet spot to work, study, or pay the bills.

Copyright by designer/architect.

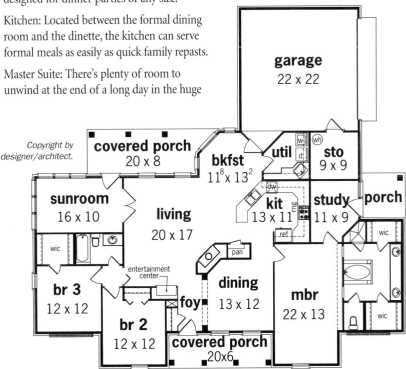

Plan #211041

Dimensions: 49' W x 64' D
Levels: 1
Square Footage: 1,891
Bedrooms: 3
Bathrooms: 2
Foundation: Slab
Materials List Available: Yes
Price Category: D

Images provided by designer/architect.

Privacy is possible in an urban setting, thanks to an entry courtyard and covered rear porch.

Features:

- Ceiling Height: 9 ft. unless otherwise noted.

- Kitchen: The innovative interior design of this home centers on this unique kitchen, which directs traffic away from the working areas while still serving the entire home.

- Family Room: Family and friends will be drawn to this casual sunken family room with its soaring 14-ft. vaulted ceiling and its handsome, warming fireplace.

- Formal Living Room: This room is designed and placed in such a way that it can easily become a third bedroom, den, office or study room, depending on your family's needs and lifestyle.

- Master Suite: This is the perfect retreat at the end of the busy day. The bedroom offers a large walk-in closet. The sumptuous master bath features an oversize shower and a whirlpool tub.

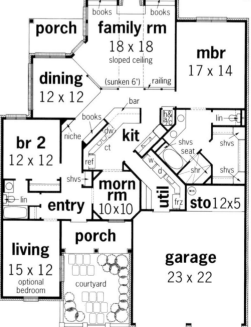

Copyright by designer/architect.

SMARTtip

Window Treatment Trims

If conventional trims and braids don't excite you, look for untraditional or unusual elements for decorating your window treatments. Attach single beads, small shells, or crystal drops at regular intervals along the edge. Either glue them in place or, if they have holes, sew them on. A series of stars, leaves, or some other appropriate shape made of stiffened fabric and then glued or stitched on is another idea. Consider old or new buttons, jewelry, or metal chains. If your embroidery skills are good, use them to embellish the window treatment.

Plan #121051

Dimensions: 64' W x 44' D
Levels: 1
Square Footage: 1,808
Bedrooms: 3
Bathrooms: 2½
Foundation: Basement
Materials List Available: Yes
Price Category: D

Images provided by designer/architect.

You'll love the way that natural light pours into this home from the gorgeous windows you'll find in room after room.

Features:

- Great Room: You'll notice the bayed, transom-topped window in the great room as soon as you step into this lovely home. A wet-bar makes this great room a natural place for entertaining, and the see-through fireplace makes it cozy on chilly days and winter evenings.

- Kitchen: This well-designed kitchen will be a delight for everyone who cooks here, not only because of the ample counter and cabinet space but also because of its location in the home.

- Master Suite: Angled ceilings in both the bedroom and the bathroom of this suite make it feel luxurious, and the picturesque window in the bedroom gives it character. The bath includes a corner whirlpool tub where you'll love to relax at the end of the day.

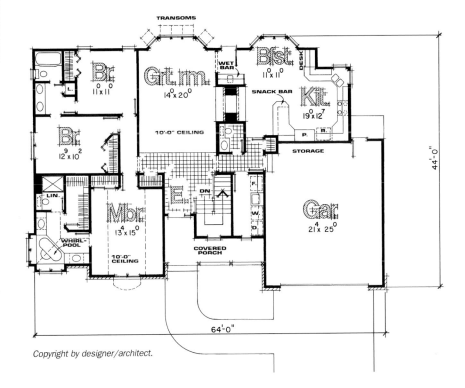

Copyright by designer/architect.

Plan #211052

Dimensions: 49' W x 74' D
Levels: 1
Square Footage: 2,111
Bedrooms: 3
Bathrooms: 2
Foundation: Slab, crawl space
Materials List Available: No
Price Category: D

This Florida-style home offers convenient gracious living on one level.

Features:

• Ceiling Height: 9 ft. unless otherwise noted.

• Kitchen: You'll love cooking in this kitchen, thanks to its efficient, innovative layout. Its unusual shape makes the kitchen the heart of this design.

• Family Room: This comfortable, informal room features a 6-in. sunken floor complemented by a sloped ceiling with exposed beams. The massive fireplace is flanked by built-in bookshelves, so you can curl up by the fire with a good book.

• Master Suite: This large bedroom provides plenty of room to relax at the end of a hectic day, and the luxurious bathroom features his and her walk-in closets.

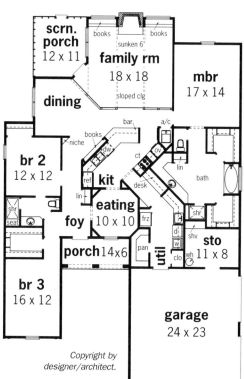

Copyright by designer/architect.

SMARTtip

General and Task Lighting Outdoors

General lighting also known as ambient lighting, provides overall diffused illumination. Ceiling lights and wall sconces are good examples of the types of fixtures that can typically provide general lighting. Post-and-rail lighting on a deck may also satisfy this function, but space the fixtures evenly around the deck for the best advantage.

Task lighting illuminates a specific area or activity. In an "outdoor room" like a screened deck, for example, you'll want to use the space during summer evenings as well as on sunny days. That means you'll need good task lighting for an outdoor food-preparation and cooking area. Keep task lights on a switch that you can control separately from other types of outdoor light sources. Flood mounts or cylinder lights, which are typically used for general lighting, can accommodate task-lighting needs because they help to focus and direct light beams.

Plan #121052

Dimensions: 56' W x 70' D
Levels: 1
Square Footage: 2,093
Bedrooms: 4
Bathrooms: 2
Foundation: Basement
Materials List Available: Yes
Price Category: D

Images provided by designer/architect.

You'll love this one story home with all the amenities that usually go with a larger home with more levels.

Features:

- Entry: As you enter this home, you'll have a long view into the great room, letting you feel welcome right away.

- Great Room: Enjoy the fireplace in this large room during cool evenings, and during the day, bask in the sunlight streaming through the arched windows that flank the fireplace.

- Den: French doors from the great room open into this room that features a spider-beamed ceiling.

- Kitchen: An island, pantry, and built-in desk make this kitchen a versatile work space. It includes a lovely breakfast area, too, that opens into the backyard.

- Master Suite: This secluded suite features an angled ceiling in the private bathroom.

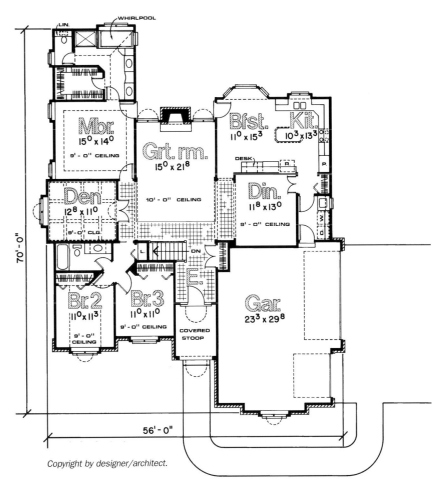

Copyright by designer/architect.

Plan #101010

Dimensions: 70' W x 47' D

Levels: 1

Square Footage: 2,187

Bedrooms: 4

Bathrooms: 2½

Foundation: Slab, crawl space, or basement

Materials List Available: Yes

Price Category: D

Images provided by designer/architect.

This stately ranch features a brick-and-stucco exterior, layered trim, and copper roofing returns.

Features:

- Ceiling Height: 11 ft. unless otherwise noted.

- Special Ceilings: Vaulted and raised ceilings adorn the living room, family room, dining room, foyer, kitchen, breakfast room, and master suite.

- Kitchen: This roomy kitchen is brightened by an abundance of windows.

- Breakfast Room: Located off the kitchen, this breakfast room is the perfect spot for informal family meals.

- Master Suite: This truly exceptional master suite features a bath, and a spacious walk in closet.

- Morning Porch: Step out of the master bedroom, and greet the day on this lovely porch.

- Additional Bedrooms: The three additional bedrooms each measure approximately 11 ft. x 12 ft. Two of them have walk-in closets.

Copyright by designer/architect.

SMARTtip

Using Slipcovers in Your Dining Area

Change the look of your dining room by slipcovering chairs. Short-skirted slipcovers give a more informal appearance; fabrics in graphic patterns, such as checks or floral prints, complement this style of slipcover best. Long-skirted covers are elegant additions to a formal dining room, particularly in solid color or tone-on-tone fabrics. Ties, buttons, or trim can add personality.

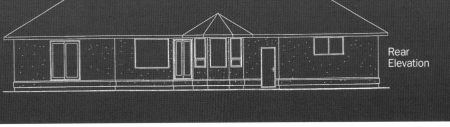

Rear
Elevation

Plan #281008

Dimensions: 74' W x 45' D

Levels: 1

Square Footage: 1,731

Bedrooms: 3

Bathrooms: 2½

Foundation: Basement, crawl space

Materials List Available: Yes

Price Category: C

Here is a cheery ranch home characterized by lots of windows and an open, airy plan.

Features:

• Ceiling Height: 8 ft.

• Foyer: This home was originally designed to sit on the edge of a golf course with panoramic vistas in every direction, hence the open design. As you step into the spacious foyer, your eye travels across the great room out the view at the rear.

• Great Room: This room seems even larger than it is, thanks to the open plan and the great views that seem to bring the outdoors in.

• Kitchen: This open, airy kitchen is a pleasure in which to work. It features an unusual octagonal breakfast nook that's the perfect place to enjoy informal meals with the family or pause with a morning cup of coffee.

• Laundry: This laundry facility is located on the main floor, so you won't have to carry clothing up and down stairs to the basement.

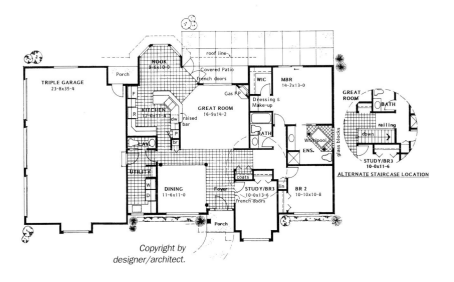

SMARTtip

The Provençal Style in Your Kitchen

No French country kitchen would be complete without a massive harvest table. If you can't find an affordable antique, create your own. Buy a long, unfinished pine table, and stain it a rich walnut color. Because pine is a softwood, you won't have to add "authentic" distress marks because normal wear and tear will do that for you. Pair the table with an assortment of unmatched chairs to add casual ambiance.

Plan #151003

Dimensions: 51'6" W x 52'4" D
Levels: 1
Square Footage: 1,680
Bedrooms: 3
Bathrooms: 2
Foundation: Basement, slab, or daylight basement.
Materials List Available: Yes
Price Category: C

Images provided by designer/architect.

A lovely front porch, bay windows, and dormers add sparkle to this country-style home.

Features:

- Great Room: Perfect for entertaining, this room features a tray ceiling, wet bar, and a quiet screened porch nearby.

- Dining Room: This bayed dining room facing the front porch is cozy yet roomy enough for family parties during the holidays.

- Kitchen: This eat-in kitchen also faces the front and is ideal for preparing meals for any occasion.

- Master Suite: The tray ceiling here gives an added feeling of space, while the distance from the other bedrooms allows for all the privacy you'll need.

Copyright by designer/architect.

Plan #211010

Dimensions: 81' W x 84' D
Levels: 1
Square Footage: 2,503
Bedrooms: 3
Bathrooms: 2½
Foundation: Slab
Materials List Available: Yes
Price Category: E

A well-designed floor plan makes maximum use of space and creates convenience and comfort.

Features:

- Ceiling Height: 10 ft. unless otherwise noted.

- Living Room: A stepped ceiling gives this living room special architectural interest. There's a full-service wet bar designed to handle parties of any size. When the weather gets warm, step out of the living room into a lovely screened rear porch.

- Master Bedroom: You'll love unwinding at the end of a busy day in this master suite. It's located away from the other bedrooms for more privacy.

- Study: This charming study adjoins the master bedroom. It's the perfect quiet spot to get some work done, surf the internet, or pay the bills.

SMARTtip

Deck Railings

Install caps and post finials to your railings. A rail cap protects the cut ends of the posts from the weather. Finials add another decorative layer to your design, and the styles are endless—ball, chamfered, grooved, and top hat are a few.

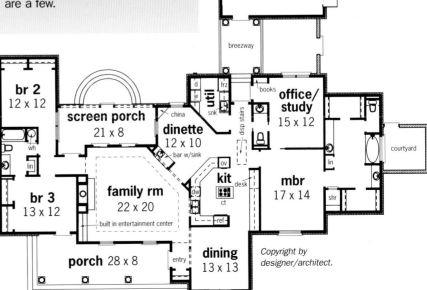

Plan #151008

Dimensions: 42' W x 67'10" D

Square Footage: 1,892

Bedrooms: 3

Bathrooms: 2

Foundation: Crawl space, slab, basement, or daylight basement

Materials List Available: Yes

Price Category: D

This cozy home features a foyer with 8-in. columns and a wide-open welcoming great room and kitchen.

Features:

- **Great Room/Kitchen:** Enjoy the fireplace in the great room while seated at the kitchen island or in the breakfast room. Access to the rear patio and covered porch makes this room a natural spot for family as well as for entertaining.

- **Dining Room:** For a formal evening, entertain in this dining room, with its grand entrance through elegant 8-in. columns.

- **Master Suite:** Luxuriate in the privacy of this master suite, with its 10-ft. ceiling and private access to the covered porch. The master bath pampers you with a whirlpool tub, separate vanities, a shower, and a walk-in closet.

- **Bedrooms:** A bedroom with walk-in closet and private access to full bath is a cozy retreat, while the other bedroom makes room for one more!

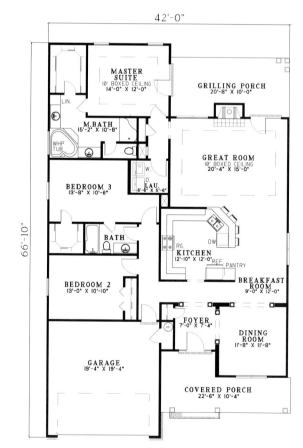

Copyright by designer/architect.

Plan #121007

Dimensions: 74' W x 67'8" D
Levels: 1
Square Footage: 2,512
Bedrooms: 3
Bathrooms: 2½
Foundation: Basement
Materials List Available: Yes
Price Category: E

Images provided by designer/architect.

A series of arches brings grace to this home's interior and exterior.

Features:

- Ceiling Height: 8 ft.

- Formal Dining Room: Tapered columns give this dining room a classical look that lends elegance to any dinner party.

- Great Room: Just beyond the dining room is this light-filled room, with its wall of arched windows and see-through fireplace.

- Hearth Room: On the other side of the fire place you will find this cozy area, with its corner entertainment center.

- Dinette: A gazebo-shaped dinette is the architectural surprise of the house layout.

- Kitchen: This well-conceived working kitchen features a generous center island.

- Garage: With three garage bays you'll never be short of parking space or storage.

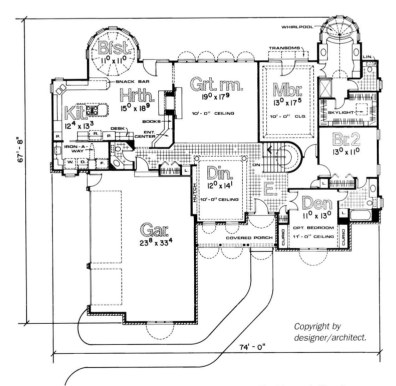

Copyright by designer/architect.

Optional Bedroom

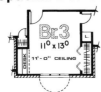

Plan #131052

Dimensions: 67' W x 63'10" D
Levels: 1
Square Footage: 2,171
Bedrooms: 2
Bathrooms: 2
Foundation: Basement, crawl space, or slab (walk-out option for fee)
Materials List Available: Yes
Price Category: D

The front and back turrets, in combination with the vaulted ceilings and unusually shaped rooms, make this house a treasure.

Features:

- **Covered Porch:** The circular covered front porch is an endlessly versatile area.

- **Dining Room:** The shape of this room echoes that of the front porch. Windows let in plenty of light; the ceiling is vaulted; and columns separate the room from the Great Room.

- **Great Room:** A fireplace, door to the patio, and vaulted ceiling highlight this spacious room.

- **Library:** Use this room, with its deep bay, as a third bedroom, or turn it into a den or media room.

- **Kitchen:** The center island and U-shaped counter make this a convenient work space.

- **Master Suite:** You'll love the turreted sitting room, tray ceiling, two walk-in closets, whirlpool tub, separate shower, and two vanities here.

Rear Elevation

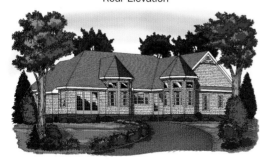

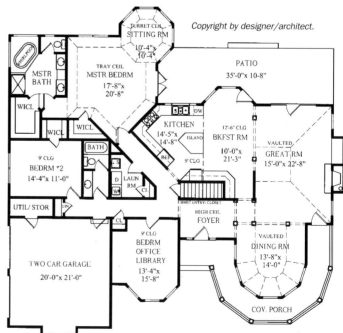

Plan #121053

Dimensions: 66' W x 68' D
Levels: 1
Square Footage: 2,456
Bedrooms: 3
Bathrooms: 2½
Foundation: Basement
Materials List Available: Yes
Price Category: E

If you're looking for a home that gives comfort at every turn, this could be the one.

Features:

- Entry: Airy and open, this entry imparts a welcoming feeling.

- Great Room: You'll love the style built into this centrally located room. A row of transom-topped windows adds natural light, and a fireplace gives it character.

- Dining Room: Just off the entry for convenience, this formal room has a boxed ceiling that accentuates its interesting angled shape.

- Gathering Room: This lovely room features an angled ceiling, snack bar, built-in entertainment center, built-in desk, and abundance of windows. A door leads to the large, covered rear porch with skylights.

- Master Suite: Relax in comfort after a long day, or sit on the adjoining, covered rear porch to enjoy the evening breezes.

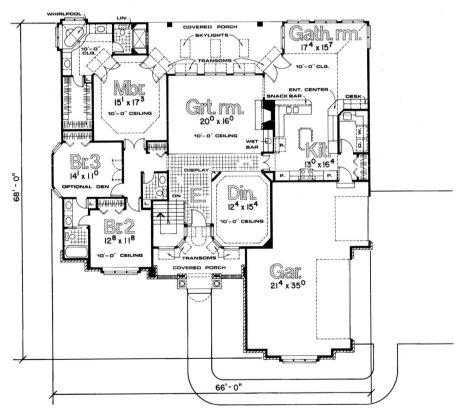

Images provided by designer/architect.

Plan #211050

Dimensions: 68' W x 64' D
Levels: 1
Square Footage: 2,000
Bedrooms: 3
Bathrooms: 2
Foundation: Slab, crawl space, or basement
Materials List Available: Yes
Price Category: D

SMARTtip

Lighting

For lighting in hard-to-reach areas, use a lamp (bulb) with a long life so that you don't have to replace it often.

Stucco siding creates a distinctive counterpoint to the columned front porch.

Features:

• Ceiling Height: 9 ft. unless otherwise noted.

• Living Room: This truly massive living room will accommodate parties of any size, from large formal affairs to more intimate family gatherings.

• Kitchen: This U-shaped kitchen offers generous counter space to make food preparation a pleasure.

• Dinette: Open to the living room, this dinette is the perfect spot for informal family dining.

• Sunroom: There's nothing more pleasant than basking indoors in the warmth of the sun on a cold winter day. When the winter sun is bright, just throw open the double doors between the living room and this delightful sunroom.

• Master Bedroom: This lush retreat boasts a large bedroom and an adjoining study or home office. The master bath has a spa tub, separate shower, dual sinks, and two walk-in closets.

garage
22 x 22

covered porch
20 x 8

eating

util

sto
9 x 9

sun rm
16 x 10

living
20 x 17
12' clg

kit rng
13x11

study
11 x 9

porch

entertainment ctr

pan

ref

shr

wic

br 3
12 x 12

dining
13 x 12
12' clg

mbr
22 x 13

br 2
12 x 12

foy

wic

porch 20 x 6

Copyright by designer/architect.

Plan #211056

Dimensions: 63' W x 74' D

Levels: 1

Square Footage: 2,349

Bedrooms: 3

Bathrooms: 2

Foundation: Crawl space

Materials List Available: No

Price Category: E

This distinctive Florida-style home offers convenient modern living on one level.

Features:

- Ceiling Height: 9 ft. unless otherwise noted.
- Family Room: This inviting and spacious sunken room is the perfect place for casual entertainment or just to relax with the family. It features a handsome fireplace flanked by bookshelves.

- Screened Porch. Located near the family room, this screened porch is the perfect place to catch a breeze on a warm summer evening.
- Kitchen: This well-planned kitchen features a built-in menu desk and an eating nook. Put a round table in this octagonal nook, and you'll have the ideal spot for informal family meals.
- Master Suite: Unwind at the end of a busy day in this luxurious master suite.
- Private Study: Conveniently located next to the master suite, this study is the spot to work at the computer or pay the bills.

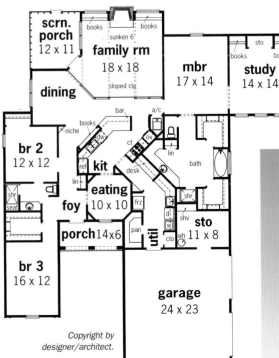

Copyright by designer/architect.

SMARTtip

Porch Maintenance

Because most porches are made of wood, they do require upkeep. From time to time and particularly if your porch is old, check it for dry rot and insect damage. Unfortunately, termites love porches almost as much as people do and, very often, older ones need extensive repairs. Once your porch is stable, finish it with paint or stain. This is one of the best ways you can preserve it. Your choice of colors will add to the ambiance, and most paint companies now provide "period palettes" to help you make the best selection for your home.

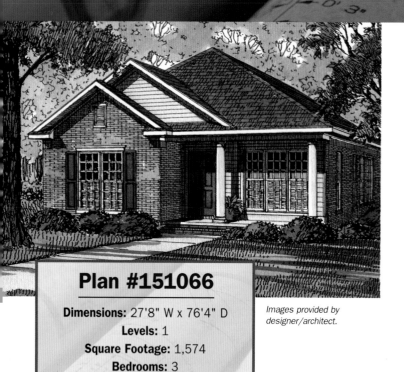

Plan #151066

Dimensions: 27'8" W x 76'4" D

Levels: 1

Square Footage: 1,574

Bedrooms: 3

Bathrooms: 2

Foundation: Crawl space, slab

Materials List Available: Yes

Price Category: C

Images provided by designer/architect.

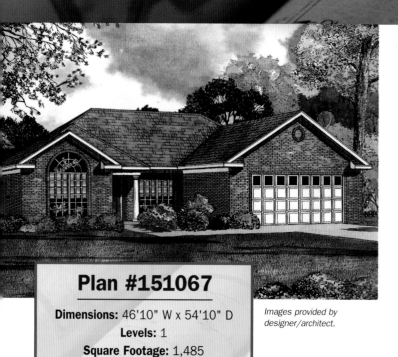

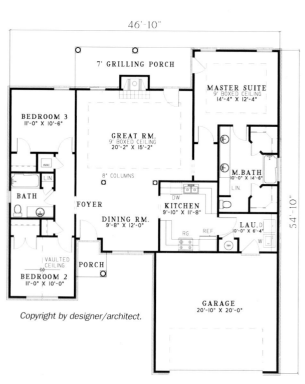

Plan #151067

Dimensions: 46'10" W x 54'10" D

Levels: 1

Square Footage: 1,485

Bedrooms: 3

Bathrooms: 2

Foundation: Crawl space, slab (basement option for fee)

Materials List Available: Yes

Price Category: B

Images provided by designer/architect.

Plan #151043

Dimensions: 53' W x 64' D

Levels: 1

Square Footage: 1,636

Bedrooms: 3

Bathrooms: 2

Foundation: Crawl space, slab (basement option for fee)

Materials List Available: Yes

Price Category: C

Images provided by designer/architect.

Copyright by designer/architect.

Plan #151044

Dimensions: 40' W x 84'4" D

Levels: 1

Square Footage: 2,140

Bedrooms: 3

Bathrooms: 2

Foundation: Crawl space, slab (basement option for fee)

Materials List Available: Yes

Price Category: D

Images provided by designer/architect.

Copyright by designer/architect.

Plan #211058

Dimensions: 74'6" W x 68' D
Levels: 1
Square Footage: 2,564
Bedrooms: 4
Bathrooms: 4
Foundation: Slab
Materials List Available: No
Price Category: E

The style of this spacious home is traditional but the amenities are attuned to modern life.

SMARTtip

Outdoor Furniture

Too much of the same is too much! Avoid matched sets of outdoor furniture. Instead, pair a cast-iron table with wooden chairs, for example. Another trick is to choose all the same chairs from one collection, but buy them in several different finishes. Finally, when it comes time for chair cushions, select fabrics that feel and look good together but don't necessarily match each other or that of the umbrella.

Images provided by designer/architect.

Features:

- Ceiling Height: 8 ft.

- Family Room: This is a great room for family gatherings and relaxation. Everyone will want to gather around the handsome fireplace. A built-in television niche makes maximum use of floor space.

- Home Office: Whether you work full-time at home or just need a spot for the home computer and bill-paying, you'll appreciate this generous office. It even has its own full bath, so all you need is a sofa bed for double-duty as a guest room.

- Porch: Step through sliding glass doors in the family room onto this generous porch, which is also accessible to the bedroom hallway and the garage.

- Courtyard: This private courtyard off the porch adds offers another spot for relaxation.

- Garage: The garage offers parking for three cars, along with plenty of extra storage.

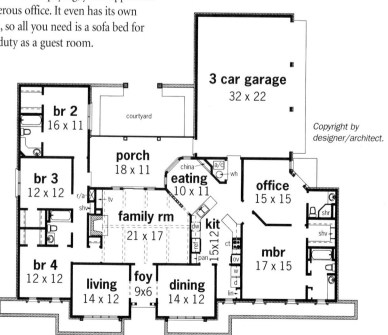

Copyright by designer/architect.

Plan #171004

Dimensions: 72' W x 52' D
Levels: 1
Square Footage: 2,256
Bedrooms: 3
Bathrooms: 2
Foundation: Slab, crawl space
Materials List Available: Yes
Price Category: E

This home greets you with a front porch featuring a high roofline and stucco columns.

Images provided by designer/architect.

Features:

- Ceiling Height: 9 ft. unless otherwise noted.
- Foyer: Step through the front porch into this impressive foyer, which opens to the formal dining room and the study.
- Dining Room: This dining room's 12-ft. ceiling enhances its sense of spaciousness, with plenty of room for large dinner parties.
- Family Room: With plenty of room for all kinds of family activities, this room also has a 12-ft. ceiling, a fireplace, and two paddle fans.

- Kitchen: This kitchen has all the counter space you'll need to prepare your favorite recipes. There's a pantry, desk, and angled snack bar.
- Master Bedroom: This master retreat is separate from the other bedrooms for added privacy. It has an elegant, high step-up ceiling and a paddle fan.
- Master Bath: This master bath features a large walk-in closet, deluxe corner bath, walk-in shower, and his and her vanities.

Copyright by designer/architect.

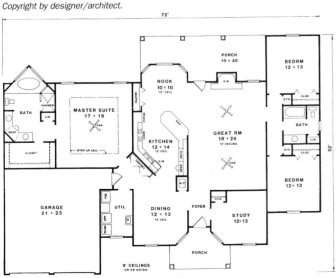

SMARTtip

Windows – Privacy

You can easily stencil a work of art onto a windowpane, perhaps only as a border around the edge. Choose or create a design that gives you as little or as much privacy and light control as you need. Use a ready-made stencil or a piece of openwork fabric such as lace, or mask a design onto the glass using tape and a razor knife. Then apply glass paint or frosted glass spray, referring to the instructions and guidelines that come with the product.

Plan #151173

Dimensions: 58' W x 53'6" D
Levels: 1
Square Footage: 1,722
Bedrooms: 3
Bathrooms: 2
Foundation: Basement, crawl space,
slab, or daylight basement
Materials List Available: Yes
Price Category: C

Images provided by designer/architect.

Copyright by designer/architect.

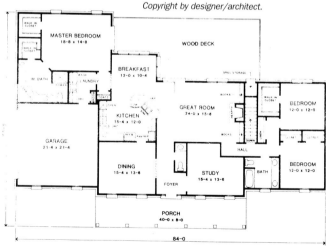

Plan #301003

Dimensions: 84' W x 55'8" D
Levels: 1
Square Footage: 2,485
Bedrooms: 3
Bathrooms: 2½
Foundation: Crawl space, basement
Materials List Available: Yes
Price Category: E

Images provided by designer/architect.

SMARTtip

Making Mitered Returns

Cut the small return piece from a substantial board that you can hold safely and securely against the saw fence.

Plan #211011

Dimensions: 84' W x 54' D
Levels: 1
Square Footage: 2,791
Bedrooms: 3 or 4
Bathrooms: 2
Foundation: Slab or crawl space
Materials List Available: Yes
Price Category: F

Images provided by designer/architect.

SMARTtip

Types of Decks

Ground-level decks resemble a low platform and are best for flat locations. They can be the most economical type to build because they don't require stairs.

Raised decks can rise just a few steps up or meet the second story of a house. Lifted high on post supports, they adapt well to uneven or sloped locations.

Multilevel decks feature two or more stories and are connected by stairways or ramps. They can follow the contours of a sloped lot, unifying the deck with the outdoors.

Plenty of room plus an open, flexible floor plan make this a home that will adapt to your needs.

Features:

• Ceiling Height: 8 ft. unless otherwise noted.

• Living Room: This distinctive room features a 12-ft. ceiling and is designed so that it can also serve as a master suite with a sitting room.

• Family Room: The whole family will want to gather in this large, inviting family room.

• Morning Room: The family room blends into this sunny spot, which is perfect for informal family meals.

• Kitchen: This spacious kitchen offers a smart layout. It is also contiguous to the family room.

• Master Suite: You'll look forward to the end of the day when you can enjoy this master suite. It includes a huge, luxurious master bath with two large walk-in closets and two vanity sinks.

• Optional Bedroom: This optional fourth bedroom is located so that it can easily serve as a library, den, office, or music room.

Copyright by designer/architect.

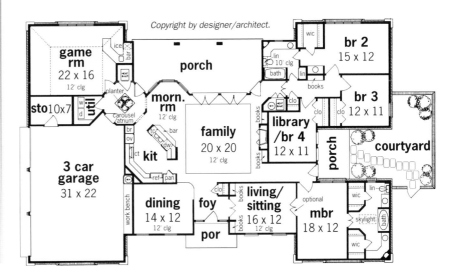

Plan #151007

Dimensions: 54'2" W x 56'2" D
Levels: 1
Square Footage: 1,787
Bedrooms: 3
Bathrooms: 2
Foundation: Basement, crawl space, or slab
Materials List Available: Yes
Price Category: C

Images provided by designer/architect.

This compact, well-designed home is graced with amenities usually reserved for larger houses.

Features:

- Foyer: A 10-ft. ceiling creates unity between the foyer and the dining room just beyond it.

- Dining Room: 8-in. boxed columns welcome you to this dining room, with its 10-ft. ceilings.

- Great Room: The 9-ft. boxed ceiling suits the spacious design. Enjoy the fireplace in the winter and the rear-grilling porch in the summer.

- Breakfast Room: This bright room is a lovely spot for any time of day.

- Master Suite: Double vanities and a large walk-in closet add practicality to this quiet room with a 9-ft. pan ceiling. The master bath includes whirlpool tub with glass block and a separate shower.

- Bedrooms: Bedroom 2 features a bay window, and both rooms are convenient to the bathroom.

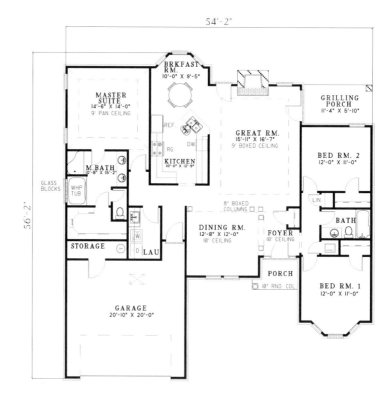

Copyright by designer/architect.

Plan #121008

Dimensions: 62' W x 56' D
Levels: 1
Square Footage: 1,651
Bedrooms: 2
Bathrooms: 2
Foundation: Basement
Materials List Available: Yes
Price Category: C

This elegant home is packed with amenities that belie its compact size.

Features:

- Ceiling Height: 8 ft.

- Dining Room: The foyer opens into a view of the dining room, with its distinctive boxed ceiling.

- Great Room: The whole family will want to gather around the fireplace and enjoy the views and sunlight streaming through the transom-topped window.

- Breakfast Area: Next to the great room and sharing the transom-topped windows, this cozy area invites you to linger over morning coffee.

- Covered Porch: When the weather is nice, take your coffee through the door in the breakfast area and enjoy this large covered porch.

- Master Suite: French doors lead to this comfortable suite featuring a walk-in. Enjoy long, luxurious soaks in the corner whirlpool accented with boxed windows.

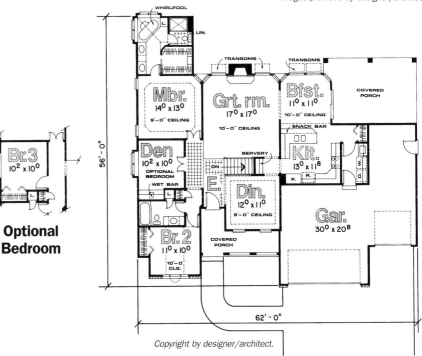

Optional Bedroom

SMARTtip
Finishing Your Fireplace with Tile

An excellent finishing material for a fireplace is tile. Luckily, there are reproductions of art tiles today. Most showrooms carry examples of Arts and Crafts, Art Nouveau, California, Delft, and other European tiles. Granite, limestone, and marble tiles are affordable alternatives to custom stone slabs.

Images provided by designer/architect.

Plan #211059

Dimensions: 68' W x 84' D
Levels: 1
Square Footage: 2,299
Bedrooms: 3
Bathrooms: 2
Foundation: Slab, basement
Materials List Available: No
Price Category: E

This well designed home features plenty of space and all the amenities you seek.

Features:

- Ceiling Height: 9 ft.

- Living Room: This living room is the center of the home's activity. It boasts an attractive, unique angled fireplace and a built-in entertainment room.

- Sunroom: This glass room fills the living room with light. In fact, if you open its interior door on a sunny winter day, it can bring solar heat into the home. The sunroom also has direct access to the porch.

- Master Suite: This suite is located opposite the other bedrooms for maximum privacy. This is truly a master retreat. The private bath features two convenient entries, his and her walk-in closets, dual-sink vanity, luxurious tub, and separate shower.

- Bonus Room: Located over the garage, this room offers 352 ft. of additional space.

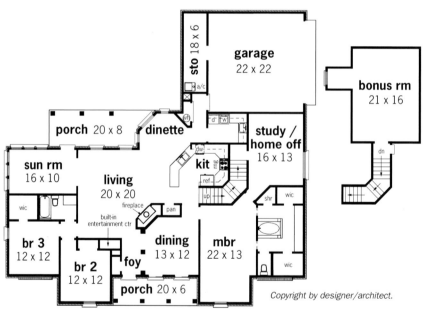

Copyright by designer/architect.

SMARTtip

Outdoor Decorating

Arrange outdoor spaces as you would an interior room. Choose a dominant element around which everything else flows. It can be a pool, a fire pit, or the garden. One major furniture piece, such as a dining table, can anchor an area.

Plan #211028

Dimensions: 68' W x 41' D
Levels: 1
Square Footage: 1,507
Bedrooms: 3
Bathrooms: 2
Foundation: Slab
Materials List Available: Yes
Price Category: C

Images provided by designer/architect.

Surprise yourself with this ranch-style home, which features every amenity you'll ever need.

Features:

- **Living Room:** A 12-ft. ceiling here adds dimension to the room, and the angled wall blends perfectly with the bay window in the adjoining eating nook. Both rooms overlook the rear covered porch.

- **Dining Room:** The formality of this room complements the stately entry it adjoins.

- **Kitchen:** Shaped and positioned as a hub of the home, this kitchen is also designed for efficient work patterns while you cook.

- **Master Suite:** With a skylight over the dressing room, a walk-in closet, and a private bath, this suite affords privacy and luxury.

- **Additional Bedrooms:** Each has a walk-in closet, and the larger one has an 11-ft.-high ceiling to accommodate its transom windows.

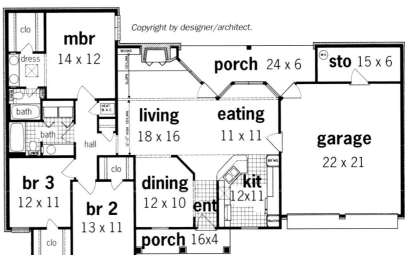

Copyright by designer/architect.

SMARTtip

Nailing Asphalt Roof Shingles

Shingles are typically fastened with four nails—one at each end of the shingle, and one above each tab slot. In windy areas use six nails to affix the shingles, placing one on each side of the tab slots. Position the nails just beneath the adhesive patch but above the tab slots. Roofing nails should be long enough to penetrate sheathing by ¾ inch, whether shingling over or replacing existing roofing.

Plan #151002

Dimensions: 67' W x 66' D

Levels: 1

Square Footage: 2,444

Bedrooms: 3

Bathrooms: 2½

Foundation: Basement, crawl space, or slab

Materials List Available: Yes

Price Category: E

This gracious, traditional home is designed for practicality and convenience.

Features:

- Ceiling Height: 9 ft. except as noted below.

- Great Room: This room is ideal for entertaining, thanks to its lovely fireplace and French doors that open to the covered rear porch. Built-in cabinets give convenient storage space.

- Family Room: With access to the kitchen as well as the rear porch, this room will become your family's "headquarters."

- Study: Enjoy the quiet in this room with its 12-ft. ceiling and doorway to a private patio on the side of the house.

- Dining Room: Take advantage of the 8-in. wood columns and 12-ft. ceilings to create a formal dining area.

- Kitchen: An eat-in bar is a great place to snack, and the handy computer nook allows the kids to do their homework while you cook.

Images provided by designer/architect.

Copyright by designer/architect.

- Breakfast Room: Opening from the kitchen, this area gives added space for the family to gather any time.

- Master Suite: Featuring a 10-ft. boxed ceiling, the master bedroom also has a door way that opens onto the covered rear porch. The master bathroom has a step-up whirlpool tub, separate shower, and twin vanities with a makeup area.

Plan #211039

Dimensions: 62' W x 64' D
Levels: 1
Square Footage: 1,868
Bedrooms: 3
Bathrooms: 2
Foundation: Slab
Materials List Available: Yes
Price Category: D

This home exudes traditional charm, but its layout and amenities are thoroughly modern.

Features:

- **Formal Dining Room:** This elegant room is perfect for dinner parties of any size.
- **Kitchen:** If you love to cook, you will love this kitchen. It's U-shaped for maximum efficiency, and it boasts a built-in desk for making menus and shopping lists, as well as a handy pantry closet. The kitchen has access to the carport, so groceries make a short trip to the counter.
- **Eating Area:** Just off the kitchen you'll find this informal eating area designed for quick meals on the go.
- **Master Suite:** Here is the perfect place to unwind after a long day. This generous bedroom hosts a lavish master bath with a spa tub, separate shower, and his and hers dressing areas.
- **Secondary Bedrooms:** Located across the home from the master suite, the two secondary bedrooms share another full bath.

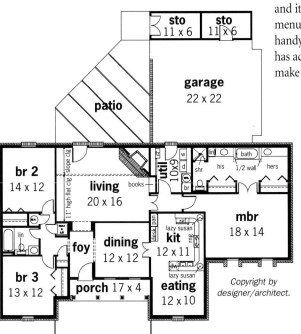

SMARTtip

Kitchen Wallpapering

For wrapping outside corners, measure from the last piece to the corner, and add ½ inch to the measurement. Cut the paper to size, and place it in position, but before wrapping it around the corner, make small slits in the waste portions of the paper near the ceiling and the baseboard. The cuts will allow you to turn the corner without wrinkling or tearing the paper. Hang the other part of the cut sheet so that it overlaps the first portion.

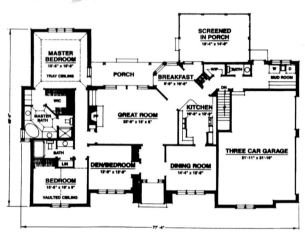

Rear View

Plan #291004

Dimensions: 77'4" W x 54'4" D

Levels: 1

Square Footage: 2,529

Bedrooms: 3

Bathrooms: 2½

Foundation: Basement

Materials List Available: No

Price Category: E

Illustration provided by designer/architect.

Copyright by designer/architect.

Copyright by designer/architect.

Plan #171016

Dimensions: 68' W x 70' D

Levels: 1

Square Footage: 2,482

Bedrooms: 4

Bathrooms: 3

Foundation: Slab, crawl space

Materials List Available: Yes

Price Category: E

Illustration provided by designer/architect.

Bonus Area

Images provided by designer/architect.

Plan #151059

Dimensions: 41'10" W x 53' D

Levels: 1

Square Footage: 1,382

Bedrooms: 3

Bathrooms: 2

Foundation: Crawl space, slab, with basement option for fee

Materials List Available: Yes

Price Category: B

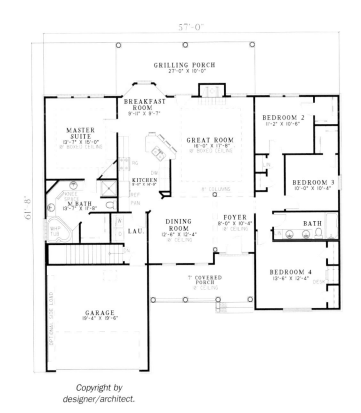

Images provided by designer/architect.

Plan #151068

Dimensions: 57' W x 61'8" D

Levels: 1

Square Footage: 1,880

Bedrooms: 4

Bathrooms: 2

Foundation: Crawl space, slab, or basement

Materials List Available: Yes

Price Category: D

Illustration provided by designer/architect.

Plan #151039

Dimensions: 48'2" W x 50'4" D
Levels: 1
Square Footage: 1,353
Bedrooms: 3
Bathrooms: 2
Foundation: Crawl space, slab
Materials List Available: Yes
Price Category: B

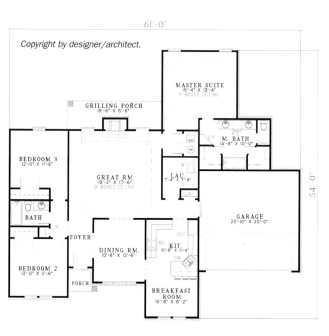

Illustration provided by designer/architect.

Plan #151041

Dimensions: 61' W x 54' D
Levels: 1
Square Footage: 1,734
Bedrooms: 3
Bathrooms: 2
Foundation: Crawl space, slab
Materials List Available: Yes
Price Category: C

Plan #231003

Dimensions: 74' W x 69' D

Levels: 1

Square Footage: 2,254

Bedrooms: 2

Bathrooms: 3

Foundation: Crawl space

Materials List Available: No

Price Category: A

Illustration provided by designer/architect.

Copyright by designer/architect.

Plan #221021

Dimensions: 57' W x 66' D

Levels: 1

Square Footage: 1,642

Bedrooms: 3

Bathrooms: 2½

Foundation: Basement

Materials List Available: No

Price Category: C

Illustration provided by designer/architect.

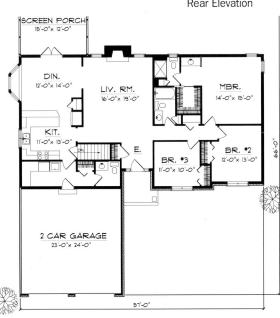

Rear Elevation

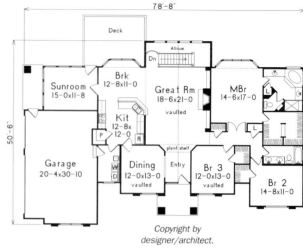

78'-8"

Deck

Atrium
Dn

Sunroom
15-0x11-8

Brk
12-8x11-0

Great Rm
18-6x21-0
vaulted

MBr
14-6x17-0

Kit
12-8x
12-0

50'-6"

Garage
20-4x30-10

Dining
12-0x13-0
vaulted

Entry

Br 3
12-0x13-0
vaulted

Br 2
14-8x11-0

plant shelf

Copyright by
designer/architect.

Images provided by
designer/architect.

Plan #321037

Dimensions: 78'8" W x 50'6" D

Levels: 1

Square Footage: 2,397

Bedrooms: 3

Bathrooms: 2

Foundation: Basement

Materials List Available: Yes

Price Category: E

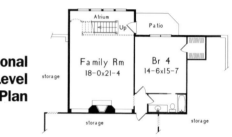

Atrium

Up

Patio

Family Rm
18-0x21-4

Br 4
14-6x15-7

storage

storage

storage

**Optional
Basement Level
Floor Plan**

BAR
11' X 11'

BED RM
10' X 16'

FAMILY RM
21' X 16'

BILLARDS
22' X 18'

STORAGE
8' X 24'

BED RM
13' X 14'

BATH

EXERCISE
13' X 11'

MECH
11' X 11'

Optional Basement Level Floor Plan

Plan #271079

Dimensions: 104' W x 55' D

Levels: 1

Square Footage: 2,228

Bedrooms: 1-3

Bathrooms: 1½

Foundation: Daylight basement

Materials List Available: No

Price Category: E

Images provided by
designer/architect.

Copyright by
designer/architect.

DINETTE
11' X 7'

SCREEN
PORCH
18' X 12'

SCREEN
PORCH
8' X 9'

OWNER'S
SUITE
15' X 19'

GREAT RM
18' X 18'

KITCHEN
19' X 17'

LAUN

WIC

BATH

STUDY
13' X 13'

ENTRY

PIANO
14' X 12'

GARAGE
34' X 26'

Copyright by
designer/architect.

Plan #241004

Dimensions: 74'9" W x 70'8" D
Levels: 1
Square Footage: 2,771
Bedrooms: 3
Bathrooms: 2½
Foundation: Slab
Materials List Available: No
Price Category: F

Images provided by
designer/architect.

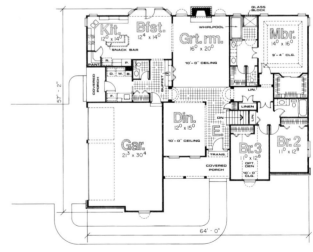

Copyright by designer/architect.

Plan #121057

Dimensions: 64' W x 57'2" D
Levels: 1
Square Footage: 2,311
Bedrooms: 3
Bathrooms: 2½
Foundation: Basement
Materials List Available: Yes
Price Category: E

Images provided by
designer/architect.

SMARTtip

Installing Crown Molding

Test for the direction and location of ceiling joists with a stud sensor, by tapping with a hammer to hear the sound of hollow or solid areas or by tapping in test finishing nails.

Plan #211062

Dimensions: 74'6" W x 75' D
Levels: 1
Square Footage: 2,682
Bedrooms: 4
Bathrooms: 3½
Foundation: Slab, optional crawl space
Materials List Available: Yes
Price Category: F

Images provided by designer/architect.

If you're looking for a beautiful home that combines luxurious amenities with a separate, professional office space, this could be the one.

Features:

- Living Room: Enjoy an 11-ft. ceiling, brick fireplace, and built-in shelving in this room.

- Dining Room: A 2-story ceiling gives presence to this room.

- Kitchen: A breakfast bar here is open to the breakfast room beyond for ease of serving.

- Breakfast Room: A built-in corner china closet adds to the practicality you'll find here.

- Office: A separate entrance makes it possible to run a professional business from this home.

- Master Suite: Separated for privacy, this suite includes two vanities and a walk-in closet.

- Porch: The rear screened porch opens to a courtyard where you'll love to entertain.

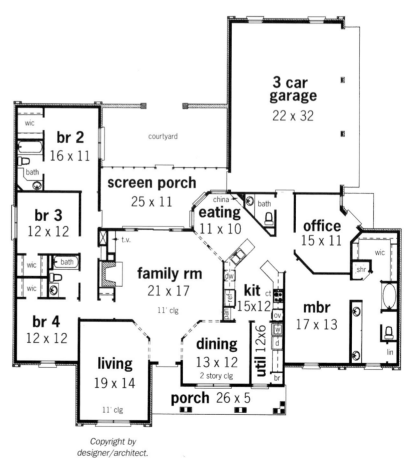

Copyright by
designer/architect.

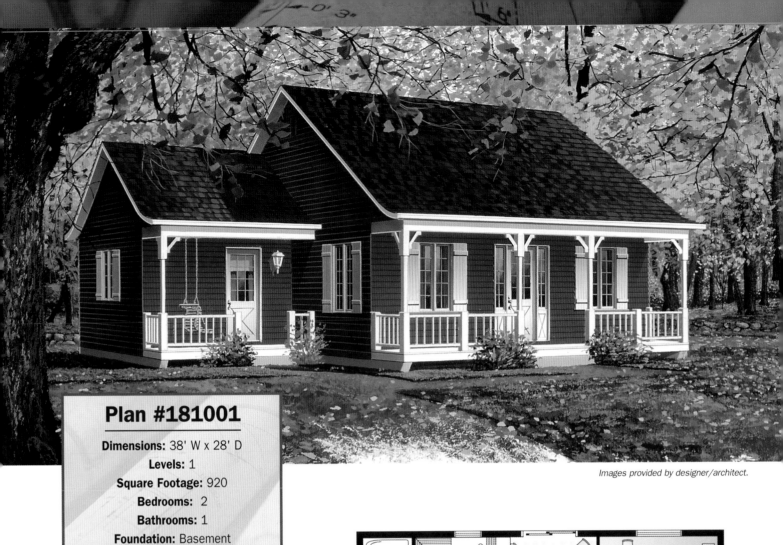

Plan #181001

Dimensions: 38' W x 28' D

Levels: 1

Square Footage: 920

Bedrooms: 2

Bathrooms: 1

Foundation: Basement

Materials List Available: Yes

Price Category: A

Images provided by designer/architect.

This cozy and charming one-story cottage offers many amenities in its well-designed layout.

Features:

- Ceiling Height: 8 ft.

- Porch: Enjoy summer evenings relaxing on the front porch.

- Kitchen: This kitchen has ample work and storage space as well as a breakfast bar and enough room for the family to dine together.

- Family Room: Natural light streaming through the windows makes this an appealing place for family activities.

- Bedrooms: There's a generous master bedroom and one secondary bedroom. Each has its own closet.

- Laundry Room: A fully equipped laundry room is conveniently located adjacent to the kitchen.

- Full Basement: Here is plenty of storage room as well as the opportunity for expanded living space.

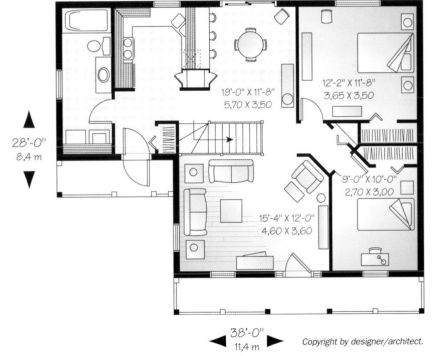

28'-0"
8,4 m

19'-0" X 11'-8"
5,70 X 3,50

12'-2" X 11'-8"
3,65 X 3,50

9'-0" X 10'-0"
2,70 X 3,00

15'-4" X 12'-0"
4,60 X 3,60

38'-0"
11,4 m

Copyright by designer/architect.

Plan #181005

Dimensions: 30' W x 30' D

Levels: 1

Square Footage: 869

Bedrooms: 2

Bathrooms: 1

Foundation: Full basement

Materials List Available: Yes

Price Category: A

Images provided by designer/architect.

30'-0"
9,0 m

30'-0"
9,0 m

7'-4" X 11'-0"
2,20 X 3,30

11'-0" X 8'-8"
3,30 X 2,60

10'-0" X 11'-4"
3,00 X 3,40

13'-0" X 15'-0"
3,90 X 4,50

12'-0" X 10'-0"
3,60 X 3,00

Copyright by designer/architect.

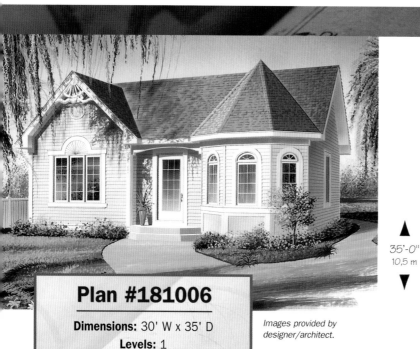

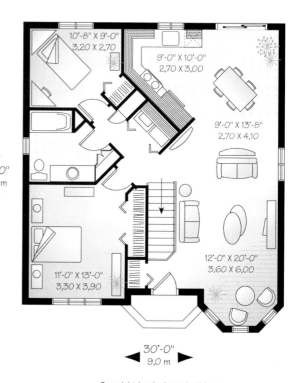

Plan #181006

Dimensions: 30' W x 35' D

Levels: 1

Square Footage: 972

Bedrooms: 2

Bathrooms: 1

Foundation: Full basement

Materials List Available: Yes

Price Category: A

Images provided by designer/architect.

35'-0"
10,5 m

30'-0"
9,0 m

10'-8" X 9'-0"
3,20 X 2,70

9'-0" X 10'-0"
2,70 X 3,00

9'-0" X 13'-8"
2,70 X 4,10

11'-0" X 13'-0"
3,30 X 3,90

12'-0" X 20'-0"
3,60 X 6,00

Copyright by designer/architect.

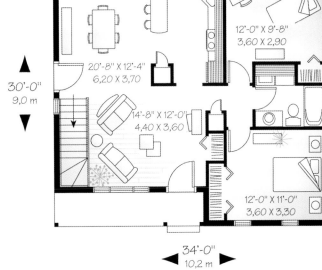

Plan #181010

Dimensions: 34' W x 30' D

Levels: 1

Square Footage: 947

Bedrooms: 2

Bathrooms: 1

Foundation: Full basement

Materials List Available: Yes

Price Category: A

Images provided by designer/architect.

30'-0"
9,0 m

20'-8" X 12'-4"
6,20 X 3,70

12'-0" X 9'-8"
3,60 X 2,90

14'-8" X 12'-0"
4,40 X 3,60

12'-0" X 11'-0"
3,60 X 3,30

34'-0"
10,2 m

Copyright by designer/architect.

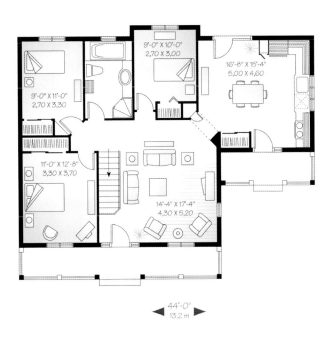

Plan #181013

Dimensions: 44' W x 30' D

Levels: 1

Square Footage: 1,147

Bedrooms: 3

Bathrooms: 1

Foundation: Full basement

Materials List Available: Yes

Price Category: B

Images provided by designer/architect.

9'-0" X 11'-0"
2,70 X 3,30

9'-0" X 10'-0"
2,70 X 3,00

16'-8" X 15'-4"
5,00 X 4,60

11'-0" X 12'-8"
3,30 X 3,70

14'-4" X 17'-4"
4,30 X 5,20

44'-0"
13,2 m

Copyright by designer/architect.

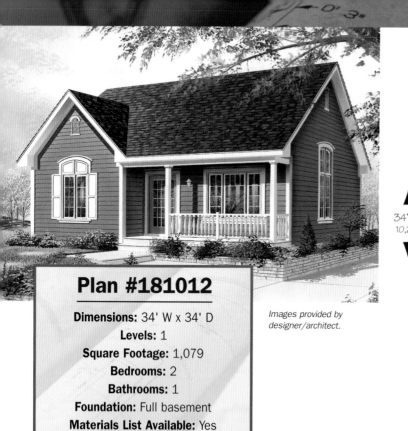

Plan #181012

Dimensions: 34' W x 34' D

Levels: 1

Square Footage: 1,079

Bedrooms: 2

Bathrooms: 1

Foundation: Full basement

Materials List Available: Yes

Price Category: B

Images provided by designer/architect.

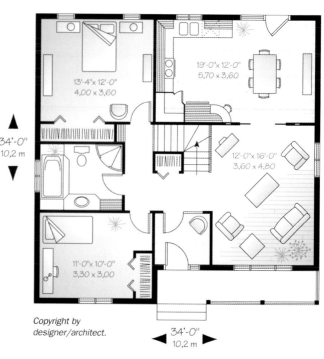

34'-0"
10,2 m

13'-4"x 12'-0"
4,00 x 3,60

19'-0"x 12'-0"
5,70 x 3,60

12'-0"x 16'-0"
3,60 x 4,80

11'-0"x 10'-0"
3,30 x 3,00

Copyright by designer/architect.

34'-0"
10,2 m

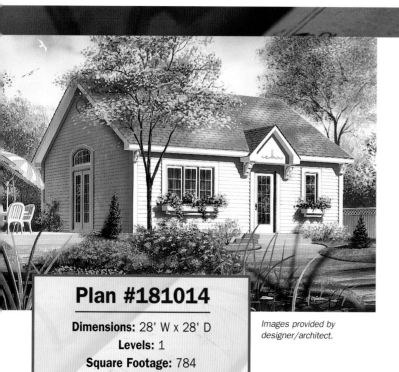

Plan #181014

Dimensions: 28' W x 28' D

Levels: 1

Square Footage: 784

Bedrooms: 1

Bathrooms: 1

Foundation: Monolithic slab

Materials List Available: Yes

Price Category: A

Images provided by designer/architect.

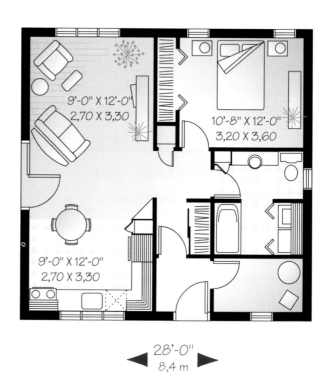

9'-0" X 12'-0"
2,70 X 3,30

10'-8" X 12'-0"
3,20 X 3,60

9'-0" X 12'-0"
2,70 X 3,30

28'-0"
8,4 m

Copyright by designer/architect.

Plan #181025

Dimensions: 32' W x 36'8" D
Levels: 1
Square Footage: 975
Bedrooms: 2
Bathrooms: 1
Foundation: Full basement
Materials List Available: Yes
Price Category: A

Images provided by designer/architect.

36'-8"
11,0 m

32'-0"
9,6 m

9'-0" X 12'-0"
2,70 X 3,60

10'-4" X 14'-0"
3,10 X 4,20

12'-0" X 17'-4"
3,60 X 5,20

11'-0" X 9'-0"
3,30 X 2,70

11'-0" X 11'-0"
3,30 X 3,30

Copyright by designer/architect.

Plan #181017

Dimensions: 62' W x 43' D
Levels: 1
Square Footage: 1,736
Bedrooms: 3
Bathrooms: 2
Foundation: Full basement
Materials List Available: Yes
Price Category: C

Images provided by designer/architect.

43'-0"
12,9 m

62'-0"
18,6 m

15'-0" X 12'-0"
4,50 X 3,60

16'-4" X 15'-0"
4,90 X 4,50

11'-0" X 11'-0"
3,30 X 3,30

19'-4" X 20'-8"
5,80 X 6,20

13'-0" X 14'-0"
3,90 X 4,20

11'-0" X 11'-0"
3,30 X 3,30

12'-0" X 11'-0"
3,60 X 3,30

Copyright by designer/architect.

SMARTtip

Simplify Your Deck Design

If your railing is an elaborate Chinese-Chippendale style, you may want to keep the design of benches, planters, and decking basic to prevent visual competition between the elements.

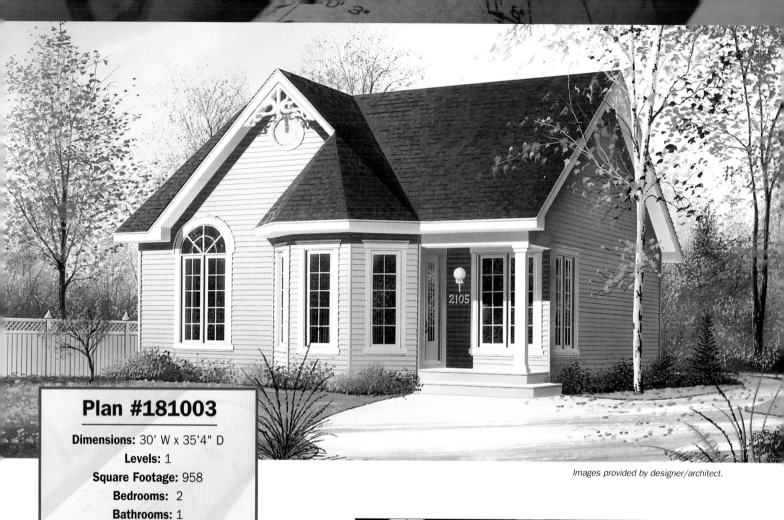

Plan #181003

Dimensions: 30' W x 35'4" D

Levels: 1

Square Footage: 958

Bedrooms: 2

Bathrooms: 1

Foundation: Basement

Materials List Available: Yes

Price Category: A

A front bay and an arched window prove that a house needn't be big to be beautiful.

Features:

- Ceiling Height: 8 ft.

- Porch: This charming covered entry porch invites you to enjoy summer breezes in an old-fashioned rocker or porch swing.

- Family Room: This large family gathering area enjoys plenty of sunlight from the multi-pane corner windows.

- Dining Room: Located adjacent to the family room for convenient entertaining, this dining room has a sliding glass door for access to the backyard.

- Kitchen: This convenient and pleasant kitchen features a single large sink overlooked by double windows.

- Bedroom: Each of the two bedrooms has its own closet. They share a luxurious full bathroom equipped with both a shower and a tub.

- Basement: The full basement provides plenty of storage and room for future expansion.

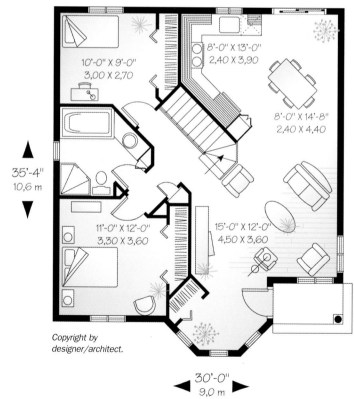

10'-0" X 9'-0"
3,00 X 2,70

8'-0" X 13'-0"
2,40 X 3,90

8'-0" X 14'-8"
2,40 X 4,40

35'-4"
10,6 m

11'-0" X 12'-0"
3,30 X 3,60

15'-0" X 12'-0"
4,50 X 3,60

Copyright by
designer/architect.

30'-0"
9,0 m

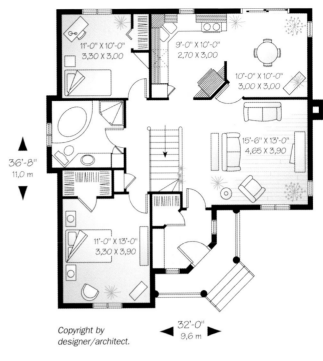

Plan #181009

Dimensions: 32' W x 36'8" D

Levels: 1

Square Footage: 1,006

Bedrooms: 2

Bathrooms: 1

Foundation: Full basement

Materials List Available: Yes

Price Category: B

Images provided by designer/architect.

Copyright by designer/architect.

36'-8"
11,0 m

32'-0"
9,6 m

11'-0" X 10'-0"
3,30 X 3,00

9'-0" X 10'-0"
2,70 X 3,00

10'-0" X 10'-0"
3,00 X 3,00

15'-6" X 13'-0"
4,65 X 3,90

11'-0" X 13'-0"
3,30 X 3,90

Plan #181011

Dimensions: 41'4" W x 42' D

Levels: 1

Square Footage: 1,347

Bedrooms: 3

Bathrooms: 1

Foundation: Full basement

Materials List Available: Yes

Price Category: B

Images provided by designer/architect.

Copyright by designer/architect.

42'-0"
12,6 m

41'-4"
12,4 m

8'-8" X 12'-0"
2,60 X 3,60

10'-8" X 14'-0"
3,20 X 4,20

10'-0" X 9'-0"
3,00 X 2,70

10'-8" X 9'-0"
3,20 X 2,70

17'-4" X 12'-0"
5,20 X 3,60

14'-0" X 11'-0"
4,20 X 3,30

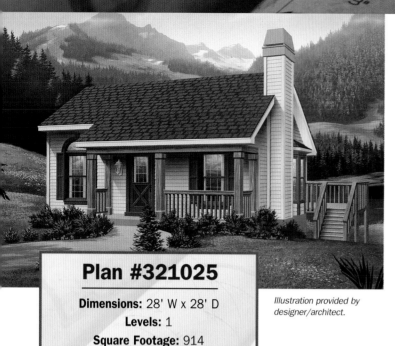

Plan #321025

Dimensions: 28' W x 28' D

Levels: 1

Square Footage: 914

Bedrooms: 2

Bathrooms: 1

Foundation: Daylight basement

Materials List Available: Yes

Price Category: A

Illustration provided by designer/architect.

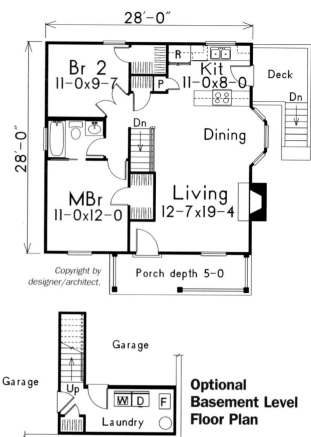

28'-0"

28'-0"

Br 2
11-0x9-7

Kit
11-0x8-0

Deck

Dn

Dining

Dn

MBr
11-0x12-0

Living
12-7x19-4

Copyright by designer/architect.

Porch depth 5-0

Garage

Garage

Up

W D F

Laundry

Optional Basement Level Floor Plan

Plan #321035

Dimensions: 55'8" W x 46' D

Levels: 1

Square Footage: 1,384

Bedrooms: 2

Bathrooms: 2

Foundation: Basement

Materials List Available: Yes

Price Category: B

Illustration provided by designer/architect.

Rear View

55'-8"

46'-0"

Atrium below

Dn

Dining Area

Kit
10-2x11-9

Garage
22-0x11-9

Great Rm
18-0x21-8
vaulted

Laundry

D W

R

Cover porch depth 6-0

Copyright by designer/architect.

Br 2
11-4x12-6

MBr
12-8x15-0

Up

Patio

Optional Basement Level Floor Plan

Family Rm
25-0x21-4

Unexcavated

Unfinished Basement

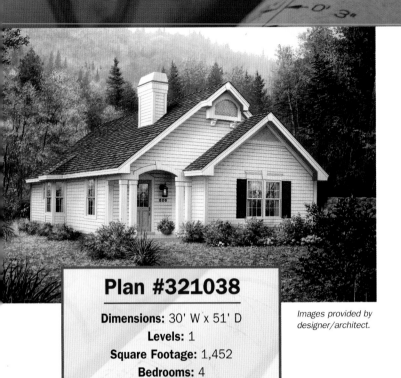

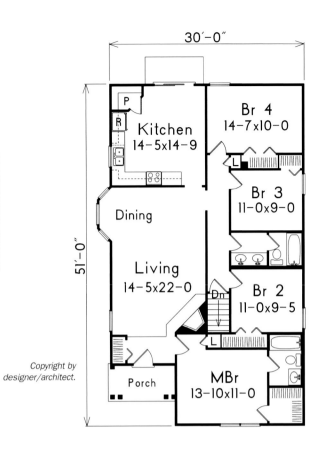

Plan #321038

Dimensions: 30' W x 51' D

Levels: 1

Square Footage: 1,452

Bedrooms: 4

Bathrooms: 2

Foundation: Basement

Materials List Available: Yes

Price Category: B

Images provided by designer/architect.

Copyright by designer/architect.

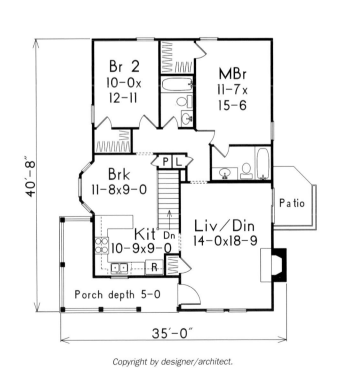

Plan #321040

Dimensions: 35' W x 40'8" D

Levels: 1

Square Footage: 1,084

Bedrooms: 2

Bathrooms: 2

Foundation: Basement

Materials List Available: Yes

Price Category: B

Images provided by designer/architect.

Copyright by designer/architect.

Plan #321009

Dimensions: 55'8" W x 46'4" D

Levels: 1

Square Footage: 2,295

Bedrooms: 3

Bathrooms: 2

Foundation: Basement

Materials List Available: Yes

Price Category: E

Images provided by designer/architect.

If you've got a site with great views, you'll love this home, which is designed to make the most of them.

Features:

- **Porch:** This wraparound porch is an ideal spot to watch the sun come up or go down. Add potted plants to create a lush atmosphere or grow some culinary herbs.

- **Great Room:** You couldn't ask for more luxury than this room provides, with its vaulted ceiling, large bay window, fireplace, dining balcony, and atrium window wall.

- **Kitchen:** No matter whether you're an avid cook or not, you'll relish the thoughtful design of this room.

- **Master Suite:** This suite is truly a retreat you'll treasure. It has two large walk-in closets for good storage space, and sliding doors that open to an exterior balcony where you can sit out to enjoy the stars. The amenity-filled bath adds to your enjoyment of this suite.

Rear View

Optional Basement Level Floor Plan

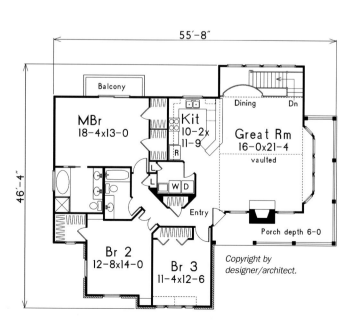

Copyright by designer/architect.

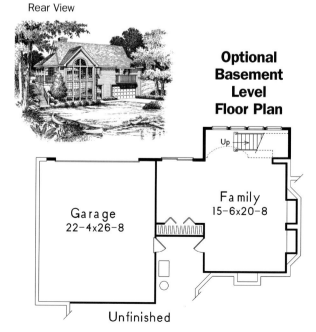

Plan #131008

Dimensions: 45'4" W x 36'4" D
Levels: 1
Square Footage: 1,299
Bedrooms: 3
Bathrooms: 2
Foundation: Crawl space, basement
Materials List Available: Yes
Price Category: C

Images provided by designer/architect.

Build this home in a vacation spot or any other location where you'll treasure the convenience of having three different outdoor entrances.

Features:

- Ceiling Height: 8 ft.

- Living Room: Sliding glass doors open onto the large deck area and serve to let bright, natural light stream into the home during the day. Add drapes to keep the house cozy at night and on cloudy winter days.

- Kitchen: Shaped like a galley, this kitchen is so well designed that you'll love working in it. Counter space and cabinets add to its practicality, and a windowed nook makes it charming.

- Master Suite: Enjoy the private bath attached to the bedroom in this quiet area.

- Additional Bedrooms: These nicely sized rooms share another full bathroom.

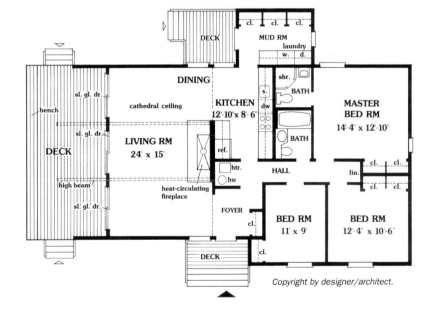

Copyright by designer/architect.

Rear View

Plan #281010

Dimensions: 34' W x 31' D

Levels: 1

Square Footage: 884

Bedrooms: 2

Bathrooms: 1

Foundation: Crawl space

Materials List Available: Yes

Price Category: A

This cute vacation or retirement home is modest in size yet contains all the necessary amenities.

Features:

- Ceiling Height: 8 ft.

- Open Plan: The living room, dining room, and kitchen are all contained in one open space. This makes the space versatile and allows plenty of room for entertaining despite the home's small size.

- Covered Deck: Step outdoors and enjoy warm breezes on this covered deck, which is accessible from the open main living area.

- Master Bedroom: This master bedroom is separated from the other bedroom to allow maximum privacy.

- Second Bedroom: This bedroom is perfect for when friends and family come to spend the night.

- Cedar Siding: This vertical cedar siding weathers to a beautiful silver gray when left unstained.

Illustration provided by designer/architect.

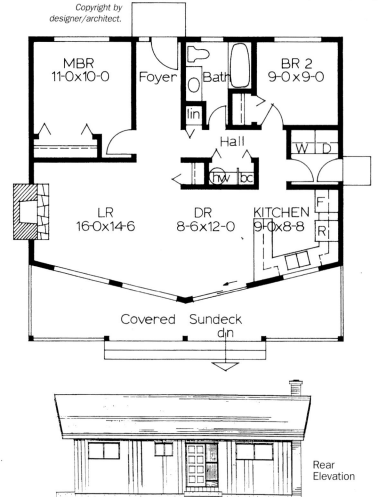

Rear Elevation

Plan #321061

Dimensions: 55' W x 49'4" D
Levels: 2
Square Footage: 3,169
Main Level Sq. Ft.: 1,679
Upper Level Sq. Ft.: 1,490
Bedrooms: 4
Bathrooms: 2½
Foundation: Basement
Materials List Available: Yes
Price Category: G

Images provided by designer/architect.

Features:

- **Entryway:** This large area features a hand crafted stairway to the upper floor, French doors leading to the living room, and an adjacent powder room.

- **Living Room:** This lovely room is ideal for quiet times or lively entertaining.

- **Family Room:** You'll enjoy all the amenities in this large room, with its lovely bay window, handsome fireplace, and walk-in wet bar.

- **Dining Area:** This area is open to the living room but is visually set apart by a gracious tray ceiling.

- **Study:** Adjacent to the front bedroom on the main floor, this study provides a place for quiet times.

- **Master Suite:** Located on the second floor for privacy, this area is luxurious in every respect.

This spacious home combines a truly elegant appearance with family-oriented, comfortable design elements.

Main Level Floor Plan

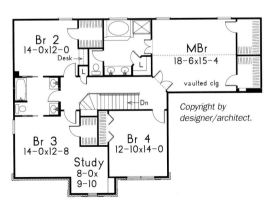

Copyright by designer/architect.

Upper Level Floor Plan

Plan #321042

Dimensions: 71' W x 54'7" D
Levels: 2
Square Footage: 3,368
Main Level Sq. Ft.: 2,150
Upper Level Sq. Ft.: 1,218
Bedrooms: 4
Bathrooms: 3 full, 2 half
Foundation: Basement
Materials List Available: Yes
Price Category: G

Images provided by designer/architect.

If your family loves contemporary interiors and spacious rooms, this could be their dream home.

Features:

- **Great Room:** A cathedral ceiling with wooden beams adds height and interest to this sunken room. Skylights add to the ambiance, and the masonry fireplace is beautiful in any season.

- **Dining Room:** Entertain in this lovely room, or use it for quiet family dinners.

- **Kitchen:** This thoughtfully designed kitchen will thrill any cook, thanks to the ample work and storage space it features.

- **Breakfast Room:** Octagon-shaped, this room features a domed ceiling with prominent beams, large windows, and a door to the rear patio.

- **Master Suite:** Located in a separate wing for privacy, this suite is filled with amenities such as the dressing area adjacent to the bedroom and a luxurious bathroom with adequate space for two.

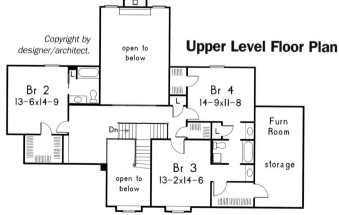

Plan #321048

Dimensions: 77'6" W x 30' D
Levels: 2
Square Footage: 3,216
Main Level Sq. Ft.: 1,834
Upper Level Sq. Ft.: 1,382
Bedrooms: 4
Bathrooms: 4½
Foundation: Basement
Materials List Available: Yes
Price Category: G

Images provided by designer/architect.

You'll love the columns and well-proportioned dormers that grace the exterior of this home, which is as spacious as it is comfortable.

Features:

- **Family Room:** This large room, featuring a graceful bay window and a wet bar, is sure to be the heart of your home. On chilly evenings, the whole family will gather around the fireplace.

- **Dining Room:** Whether you're serving a family dinner or hosting a formal dinner party, everyone will feel at home in this lovely room.

- **Kitchen:** The family cooks will appreciate the thought that went into designing this kitchen, which includes ample work and storage space. A breakfast room adjoins the kitchen.

- **Hearth Room:** This room also adjoins the kitchen, creating a large area for informal entertaining.

- **Bedrooms:** Each bedroom is really a suite, because it includes a private, full bath.

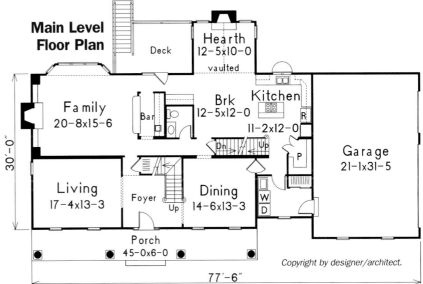

Main Level Floor Plan

Deck
Hearth 12-5x10-0 vaulted
Family 20-8x15-6
Bar
Brk 12-5x12-0
Kitchen 11-2x12-0
R
Garage 21-1x31-5
Dn / Up
P
Living 17-4x13-3
Foyer
Up
Dining 14-6x13-3
W D
30'-0"
Porch 45-0x6-0
77'-6"

Copyright by designer/architect.

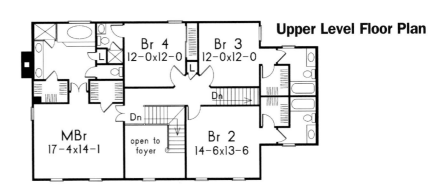

Upper Level Floor Plan

Br 4 12-0x12-0
Br 3 12-0x12-0
L
L
Dn
MBr 17-4x14-1
open to foyer
Dn
Br 2 14-6x13-6

Plan #331002

Dimensions: 62'2" W x 66'8" D

Levels: 2

Square Footage: 2,299

Main Level Sq. Ft.: 1,517

Upper Level Sq. Ft.: 782

Bedrooms: 3

Bathrooms: 2½

Foundation: Basement, crawl space, or slab

Materials List Available: No

Price Category: E

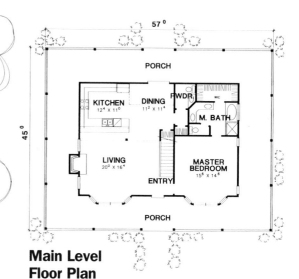

Images provided by designer/architect.

Main Level Floor Plan

Upper Level Floor Plan

Copyright by designer/architect.

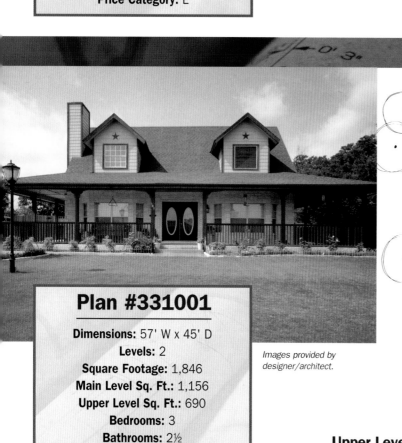

Plan #331001

Dimensions: 57' W x 45' D

Levels: 2

Square Footage: 1,846

Main Level Sq. Ft.: 1,156

Upper Level Sq. Ft.: 690

Bedrooms: 3

Bathrooms: 2½

Foundation: Basement, crawl space, or slab

Materials List Available: No

Price Category: D

Images provided by designer/architect.

Main Level Floor Plan

Upper Level Floor Plan

Copyright by designer/architect.

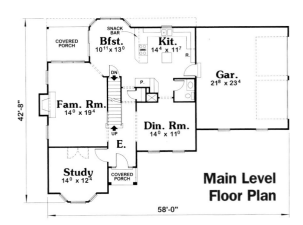

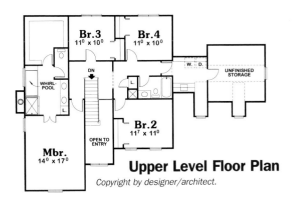

Main Level Floor Plan

Covered Porch
Snack Bar
Bfst. 10¹¹ x 13⁰
Kit. 14⁴ x 11⁷
Gar. 21⁸ x 23⁴
DN
P.
Fam. Rm. 14⁰ x 19⁴
Din. Rm. 14⁰ x 11⁰
UP
E.
Study 14⁰ x 12⁴
Covered Porch
42'-8"
58'-0"

Images provided by designer/architect.

Plan #121097

Dimensions: 58' W x 42'8" D
Levels: 2
Square Footage: 2,417
Main Level Sq. Ft.: 1,162
Upper Level Sq. Ft.: 1,255
Bedrooms: 4
Bathrooms: 2½
Foundation: Basement
Materials List Available: Yes
Price Category: E

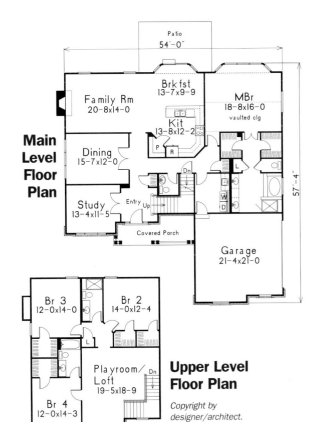

Upper Level Floor Plan

Br.3 11⁰ x 10⁰
Br.4 11⁰ x 10⁰
W. D.
UNFINISHED STORAGE
DN
WHIRL-POOL
L
Br.2 11⁷ x 11⁰
Mbr. 14⁰ x 17⁰
OPEN TO ENTRY

Plan #321062

Dimensions: 54' W x 57'4" D
Levels: 2
Square Footage: 3,138
Main Level Sq. Ft.: 1,958
Upper Level Sq. Ft.: 1,180
Bedrooms: 4
Bathrooms: 3½
Foundation: Basement
Materials List Available: Yes
Price Category: G

Images provided by designer/architect.

Main Level Floor Plan

Patio 54'-0"
Brkfst 13-7x9-9
Family Rm 20-8x14-0
MBr 18-8x16-0 vaulted clg
Kit 13-8x12-2
P R
Dining 15-7x12-0
Dn
L
W D
Study 13-4x11-5
Entry Up
Covered Porch
Garage 21-4x21-0
57'-4"

Upper Level Floor Plan

Br 3 12-0x14-0
Br 2 14-0x12-4
L
Playroom/ Loft 19-5x18-9
Dn
Br 4 12-0x14-3

Plan #121091

Dimensions: 56' W x 50' D
Levels: 2
Square Footage: 2,689
Main Level Sq. Ft.: 1,415
Upper Level Sq. Ft.: 1,214
Bedrooms: 4
Bathrooms: 2½
Foundation: Basement
Materials List Available: Yes
Price Category: F

Photo provided by designer/architect.

You'll love the unusual details that make this home as elegant as it is comfortable.

Features:

- **Entry:** This two-story entry is filled with natural light that streams in through the sidelights and transom window.

- **Den:** To the right of the entry, French doors open to this room, with its 11-ft. high, spider-beamed ceiling. A triple-wide,

transom-topped window brightens this room during the daytime.

- **Family Room:** A fireplace and built-in entertainment center add comfort to this room, and the cased opening to the kitchen area makes it convenient.

- **Kitchen:** With an adjoining breakfast area, this kitchen is another natural gathering spot.

Main Level Floor Plan

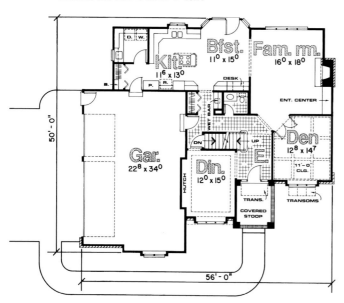

Upper Level Floor Plan

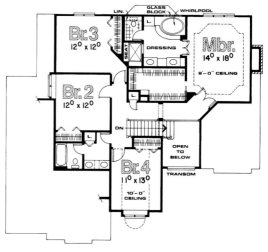

Copyright by designer/architect.

Plan #121093

Dimensions: 62' W x 60'8" D
Levels: 2
Square Footage: 2,603
Main Level Sq. Ft.: 1,800
Upper Level Sq. Ft.: 803
Bedrooms: 4
Bathrooms: 3½
Foundation: Basement
Materials List Available: Yes
Price Category: F

If you love family life but also treasure your privacy, you'll appreciate the layout of this home.

Features:

• Entry: This two-story, open area features plant shelves to display a group of lovely specimens.

• Dining Room: Open to the entry, this room features 12-ft. ceilings and corner hutches.

• Den: French doors lead to this quiet room, with its bowed window and spider-beamed ceiling.

• Gathering Room: A three-sided fireplace, shared with both the kitchen and the breakfast area, is the highlight of this room.

• Master Suite: Secluded for privacy, this suite also has a private covered deck where you can sit and recharge at any time of day. A walk-in closet is practical, and a whirlpool tub is pure comfort.

Main Level Floor Plan

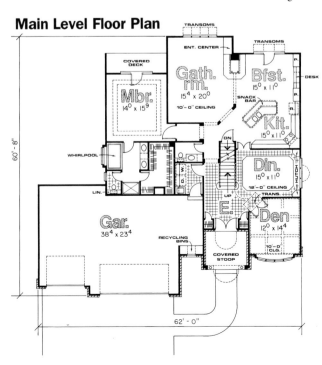

Upper Level Floor Plan

Main Level
Floor Plan

Upper Level
Floor Plan

Illustration provided by designer/architect.

Copyright by designer/architect.

Plan #151100

Dimensions: 69'6" W x 31' D
Levels: 2
Square Footage: 2,247
Main Level Sq. Ft.: 1,154
Upper Level Sq. Ft.: 1,093
Bedrooms: 3
Bathrooms: 2½
Foundation: Crawl space, slab, or basement
Materials List Available: Yes
Price Category: E

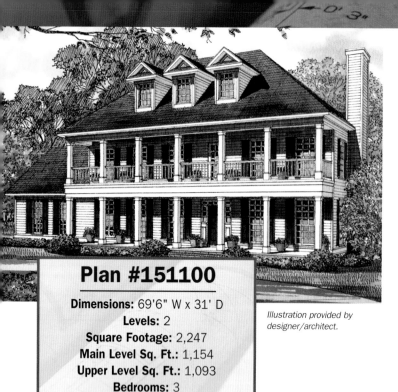

Upper Level
Floor Plan

Main Level
Floor Plan

Illustration provided by designer/architect.

Copyright by designer/architect.

Plan #151118

Dimensions: 54'2" W x 73'6" D
Levels: 2
Square Footage: 2,784
Main Level Sq. Ft.: 1,895
Upper Level Sq. Ft.: 889
Bedrooms: 4
Bathrooms: 2½
Foundation: Crawl space, slab, or basement
Materials List Available: Yes
Price Category: F

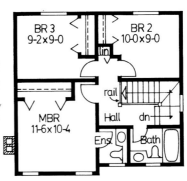

Main Level Floor Plan

DR
11-6x9-0

Nook

KITCHEN
12-2x9-0

dw

F   R

up

rail

dn

GARAGE
13-6x20-6

LIVINGROOM
11-6x17-8

BRM

Foyer

Lav

Porch

**Main Level
Floor Plan**

*Illustration provided by
designer/architect.*

Plan #281007

Dimensions: 37' W x 31' D
Levels: 2
Square Footage: 1,206
Main Level Sq. Ft.: 670
Upper Level Sq. Ft.: 536
Bedrooms: 3
Bathrooms: 1 full, 2 half
Foundation: Full basement
Materials List Available: Yes
Price Category: B

**Upper Level
Floor Plan**

*Copyright by
designer/architect.*

BR 3
9-2x9-0

BR 2
10-0x9-0

lin

rail

dn

MBR
11-6x10-4

Hall

Ens

Bath

Main Level Floor Plan

68'-0"

PATIO

PATIO

MASTER BEDROOM
15'-8" x 12'-9"

MR. BATH

PR

GREAT ROOM
21'-3" x 9'-2"

BOOKS

FP

GARAGE
20'-6"x22'-0"

BOOKS

32'-0"

KIT.
8'-6"

W LDY

DINING ROOM
12'-10"x11'-2"

ENTRY

MORNING RM
8'-6"x7'-8"

MORNING
PATIO

FIRST FLOOR PLAN

Copyright by designer/architect.

Plan #291011

Dimensions: 68'6" W x 33' D
Levels: 2
Square Footage: 1,898
Main Level Sq. Ft.: 1,182
Upper Level Sq. Ft.: 716
Bedrooms: 4
Bathrooms: 2½
Foundation: Basement
Materials List Available: No
Price Category: D

*Illustrations provided by
designer/architect.*

Upper Level Floor Plan

BATH#2

BEDROOM#4
11'-6" x 10'-2"

BEDROOM#2
13'-4" x 14'-4"

BEDROOM#3
11'-0" x 14'-11"

Photo provided by designer/architect.

Plan #121078

Dimensions: 50' W x 48' D
Levels: 2
Square Footage: 2,248
Main Level Sq. Ft.: 1,568
Upper Level Sq. Ft.: 680
Bedrooms: 4
Bathrooms: 2½
Foundation: Slab
Materials List Available: Yes
Price Category: E

This design is wonderful for any family but has features that make it ideal for one with teens.

Features:

- **Family Room:** A vaulted ceiling gives a touch of elegance here and a corner fireplace makes it comfortable, especially when the weather's cool.

- **Living Room:** Both this room and the dining room have a formal feeling, but don't let that stop you from making them a family gathering spot.

- **Kitchen:** A built-in desk, butler's pantry, and a walk-in pantry make this kitchen easy to organize. The breakfast nook shares an angled eating bar with the family room.

- **Master Suite:** A walk-in closet and corner whirlpool tub and shower make this suite feel luxurious.

Main Level Floor Plan

Copyright by designer/architect.

Upper Level Floor Plan

Plan #121079

Dimensions: 50' W x 60' D
Levels: 2
Square Footage: 2,688
Main Level Sq. Ft.: 1,650
Upper Level Sq. Ft.: 1,038
Bedrooms: 4
Bathrooms: 3½
Foundation: Slab
Materials List Available: Yes
Price Category: F

Photo provided by designer/architect.

You'll love this open design if you're looking for a home that gives a spacious feeling while also providing private areas.

Features:

- Entry: The cased openings and corner columns here give an attractive view into the dining room.

- Living Room: Another cased opening defines the entry to this living room but lets traffic flow into it.

- Kitchen: This well-designed kitchen is built around a center island that gives you extra work space. A snack bar makes an easy, open transition between the sunny dining nook and the kitchen.

- Master Suite: An 11-ft. ceiling sets the tone for this private space. With a walk-in closet and adjoining full bath, it will delight you.

Main Level Floor Plan

50'

60'

NOOK 12'4" X 11'8"
EATING BAR
KITCHEN ISLAND 13" X 12'
PANTRY
D W
UP
LIVING ROOM 16' X 19'6" 9' CLG.
OPTIONAL BASEMENT STAIRS
MASTER SUITE 16'2" X 13'6" 11' CLG.
AC
3 CAR GARAGE 20'4" X 28'6"
9' CLG.
DINING ROOM 10'8" X 15'
OPTIONAL STUDY
FOYER 9' CLG.
PORCH

Upper Level Floor Plan

WINDOW SEAT
SLOPE   SLOPE
PLAY ROOM 16' X 16'
AC
ATTIC
DN
BEDROOM 4 12'6" X 11'4"
BEDROOM 2 11'6" X 13'6"
LIN
BEDROOM 3 10'8" X 15'
SLOPE

Copyright by designer/architect.

**Main Level
Floor Plan**

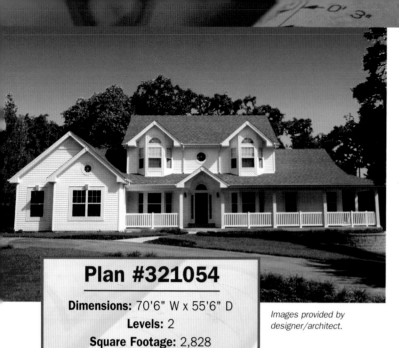

Plan #321054

Dimensions: 70'6" W x 55'6" D

Levels: 2

Square Footage: 2,828

Main Level Sq. Ft.: 2,006

Upper Level Sq. Ft.: 822

Bedrooms: 5

Bathrooms: 3½

Foundation: Basement

Materials List Available: Yes

Price Category: F

*Images provided by
designer/architect.*

**Upper Level
Floor Plan**

*Copyright by
designer/architect.*

**Main
Level
Floor
Plan**

Plan #321044

Dimensions: 61' W x 49'4" D

Levels: 2

Square Footage: 2,618

Main Level Sq. Ft.: 1,804

Upper Level Sq. Ft.: 814

Bedrooms: 4

Bathrooms: 2½

Foundation: Basement

Materials List Available: Yes

Price Category: F

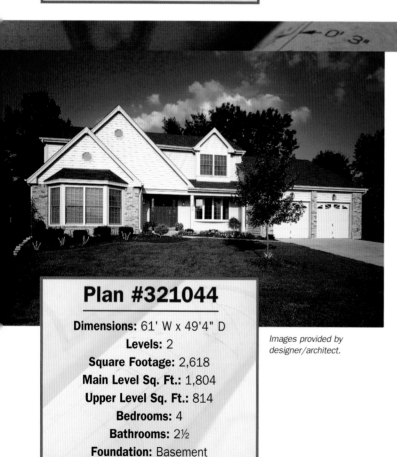

*Images provided by
designer/architect.*

**Upper Level
Floor Plan**

*Copyright by
designer/architect.*

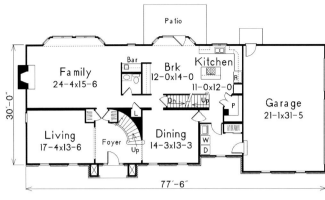

Main Level Floor Plan

Family 24-4x15-6
Living 17-4x13-6
Foyer
Dining 14-3x13-3
Brk 12-0x14-0
Kitchen 11-0x12-0
Garage 21-1x31-5
Patio
Bar
30'-0"
77'-6"

Images provided by designer/architect.

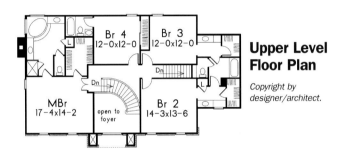

Upper Level Floor Plan

Br 4 12-0x12-0
Br 3 12-0x12-0
MBr 17-4x14-2
open to foyer
Br 2 14-3x13-6

Copyright by designer/architect.

Plan #321049

Dimensions: 77'6" W x 30' D
Levels: 2
Square Footage: 3,144
Main Level Sq. Ft.: 1,724
Upper Level Sq. Ft.: 1,420
Bedrooms: 4
Bathrooms: 4½
Foundation: Basement
Materials List Available: Yes
Price Category: G

Plan #321046

Dimensions: 66' W x 40' D
Levels: 2
Square Footage: 2,411
Main Level Sq. Ft.: 1,293
Upper Level Sq. Ft.: 1,118
Bedrooms: 4
Bathrooms: 2½
Foundation: Basement
Materials List Available: Yes
Price Category: E

Images provided by designer/architect.

Deck
66'-0"
Family 16-1x15-5
Brk 12-7x9-4
Kit 11-1x11-1
Bar
Living 13-8x13-4
Foyer
Dining 13-6x13-4
Garage 22-8x21-5
Porch
40'-0"

Main Level Floor Plan

Upper Level Floor Plan

Study 11-5x11-8
Br 3 11-11x10-0
MBr 13-8x15-4
open to below
vaulted
Br 2 13-8x11-0

Copyright by designer/architect.

Plan #341015

Dimensions: 57' W x 36'4" D

Levels: 2

Square Footage: 2,418

Main Level Sq. Ft.: 1,083

Upper Level Sq. Ft.: 1,335

Bedrooms: 4

Bathrooms: 2½

Foundation: Crawl space, slab, or basement

Materials List Available: Yes

Price Category: E

Images provided by designer/architect.

You'll be charmed by the surprising amenities in this comfortable home, with its old-fashioned country farmhouse appearance.

Features:

• Front Porch: Put out a couple of rockers and a swing, hang baskets of fragrant flowering plants, and watch the world go by from this cozy porch.

• Living Room: Use this room for entertaining or as a place for quiet talks and reading in the evening.

• Family Room: Everyone will gather in this room, with its handsome fireplace and French doors leading to the yard.

• Kitchen: This well-planned room features corner dual sinks, a large pantry, lots of work space, and a breakfast bar where everyone will perch.

• Master Suite: Retreat to this luxurious suite at the end of the day. You'll love the large walk-in closet here, as well as the bath, with its deluxe tub, dual vanities, and walk-in shower.

Main Level Floor Plan

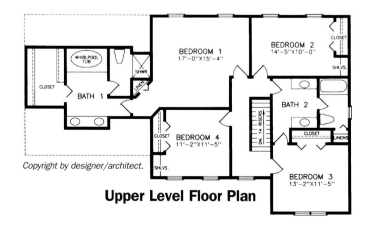

Copyright by designer/architect.

Upper Level Floor Plan

Plan #341014

Dimensions: 57'9" W x 40' D

Levels: 2

Square Footage: 2,128

Main Level Sq. Ft.: 1,064

Upper Level Sq. Ft.: 1,064

Bedrooms: 3

Bathrooms: 2½

Foundation: Crawl space, slab, or basement

Materials List Available: Yes

Price Category: E

Images provided by designer/architect.

You'll love the serene appearance of this traditionally styled home, with its romantic front porch and practical backyard deck.

Features:

- Foyer: Look onto this two-story foyer from the sunlit upper floor balcony.

- Dining Room: A tray ceiling sets the formal tone for this lovely room.

- Living Room: A fireplace, built-in cabinets or shelves, and generous windows make this room as practical as it is welcoming.

- Kitchen: A pantry and a work island make this an ideal kitchen for all the cooks in the family.

- Master Suite: A walk-in closet and private bath with double vanities, garden tub, and separate shower make this suite a pleasure.

- Bonus Room: Use this room however you wish — as a study, media room, or play space.

Main Level Floor Plan

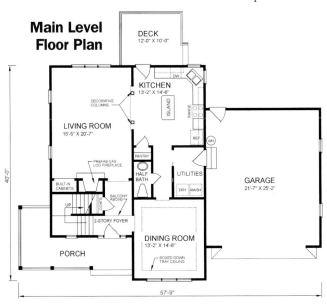

Upper Level Floor Plan

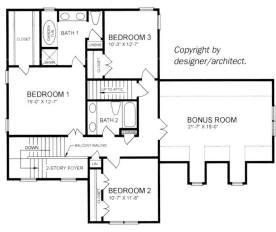

Copyright by designer/architect.

Photo provided by designer/architect.

Plan #121080

Dimensions: 56' W x 49' D
Levels: 2
Square Footage: 2,384
Main Level Sq. Ft.: 1,616
Upper Level Sq. Ft.: 768
Bedrooms: 4
Bathrooms: 2½
Foundation: Slab
Materials List Available: Yes
Price Category: E

This design is ideal if you want a generously sized home now and room to expand later.

Features:

• Living Room: Your eyes will be drawn towards the ceiling as soon as you enter this lovely room. The ceiling is vaulted, giving a sense of grandeur, and a graceful balcony from the second floor adds extra interest to this room.

• Kitchen: Designed with lots of counter space to make your work convenient, this kitchen also shares an eating bar with the breakfast nook.

• Breakfast Nook: Eat here or go out to the adjoining private porch where you can enjoy your meal in the morning sunshine.

• Master Suite: The bayed area in the bedroom makes a picturesque sitting area. French doors in the bedroom open to a private bath that's fitted with a whirlpool tub, separate shower, two vanities, and a walk-in closet.

Main Level Floor Plan

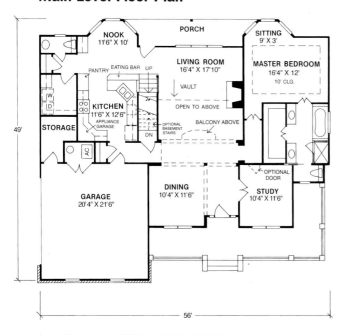

Upper Level Floor Plan

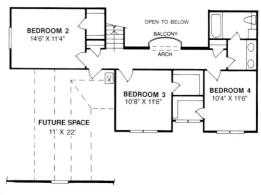

Copyright by designer/architect.

Plan #121090

Dimensions: 60' W x 58' D
Levels: 2
Square Footage: 2,645
Main Level Sq. Ft.: 1,972
Upper Level Sq. Ft.: 673
Bedrooms: 4
Bathrooms: 2½
Foundation: Basement
Materials List Available: Yes
Price Category: F

Photo provided by designer/architect.

You'll be amazed at the amenities that have been designed into this lovely home.

Features:

- **Den:** French doors just off the entry lead to this lovely room, with its bowed window and spider-beamed ceiling.
- **Great Room:** A trio of graceful arched windows highlights the volume ceiling in this room. You might want to curl up to read next to the see-through fireplace into the hearth room.
- **Kitchen:** Enjoy the good design in this room.
- **Hearth Room:** The shared fireplace with the great room makes this a cozy spot in cool weather.
- **Master Suite:** French doors lead to this well-lit area, with its roomy walk-in closet, sunlit whirlpool tub, separate shower, and two vanities.

Main Level Floor Plan

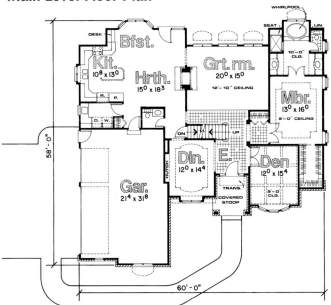

Upper Level Floor Plan

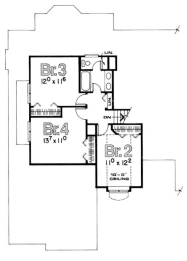

Copyright by designer/architect.

Plan #181064

Dimensions: 91'4" W x 40'8" D

Levels: 2

Square Footage: 2,802

Main Level Sq. Ft.: 2,219

Upper Level Sq. Ft.: 583

Bedrooms: 4

Bathrooms: 2½

Foundation: Crawl space

Materials List Available: Yes

Price Category: F

Illustration provided by designer/architect.

Upper Level Floor Plan

Copyright by designer/architect.

Main Level Floor Plan

Plan #181065

Dimensions: 26' W x 26' D

Levels: 2

Square Footage: 1,352

Main Level Sq. Ft.: 676

Upper Level Sq. Ft.: 676

Bedrooms: 3

Bathrooms: 2

Foundation: Full basement

Materials List Available: Yes

Price Category: B

Illustration provided by designer/architect.

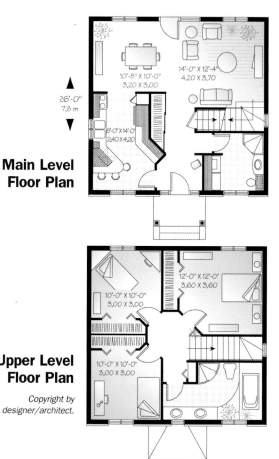

Main Level Floor Plan

Upper Level Floor Plan

Copyright by designer/architect.

Main Level Floor Plan

Upper Level Floor Plan

Illustration provided by designer/architect.

Copyright by designer/architect.

Plan #181137

Dimensions: 68' W x 34' D
Levels: 2
Square Footage: 2,353
Main Level Sq. Ft.: 1,281
Upper Level Sq. Ft.: 1,072
Bedrooms: 3
Bathrooms: 2½
Foundation: Full basement
Materials List Available: Yes
Price Category: E

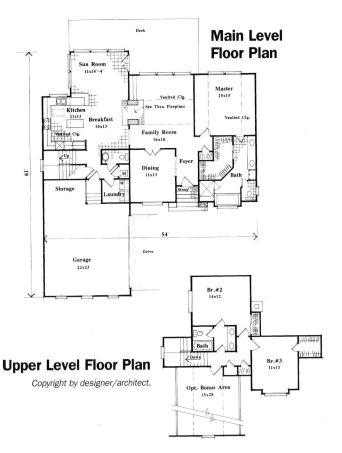

Main Level Floor Plan

Upper Level Floor Plan

Copyright by designer/architect.

Illustration provided by designer/architect.

Plan #251014

Dimensions: 53'8" W x 61' D
Levels: 2
Square Footage: 2,210
Main Level Sq. Ft.: 1,670
Upper Level Sq. Ft.: 540
Bedrooms: 3
Bathrooms: 2½
Foundation: Crawl space, basement
Materials List Available: Yes
Price Category: E

Plan #341008

Dimensions: 55'6" W x 61'7" D

Levels: 2

Square Footage: 2,508

Main Level Sq. Ft.: 1,500

Upper Level Sq. Ft.: 1,008

Bedrooms: 4

Bathrooms: 4½

Foundation: Crawl space, slab, or basement

Materials List Available: Yes

Price Category: E

Features:

- **Family Room:** Enjoy the fireplace in cool weather, and walk through the French doors to the screened porch when it's warm.

- **Dining Room:** Two tall windows give extra stature to this formal room, which is ideal for entertaining.

- **Kitchen:** A pantry and ample work area make this room a cook's dream come true.

- **Breakfast Room:** You'll use this convenient room all through the day, not just at breakfast.

- **Bonus Room:** Use the extra room and full bath over the garage as an office, media room, or play space for the children.

- **Bedroom Suites:** Suites on both the main and upper floors feature a private bath filled with amenities that make you feel pampered.

This traditional-looking home is filled with contemporary amenities that the family will love.

Main Level Floor Plan

Upper Level Floor Plan

Copyright by designer/architect.

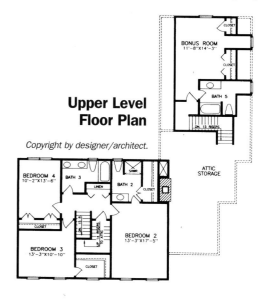

Plan #341002

Dimensions: 62' W x 37'6" D

Levels: 2

Square Footage: 2,528

Main Level Sq. Ft.: 1,193

Upper Level Sq. Ft.: 1,335

Bedrooms: 4

Bathrooms: 2½

Foundation: Crawl space, slab, or basement

Materials List Available: Yes

Price Category: E

Images provided by designer/architect.

You'll love the amenities and versatility found in this comfortable family home.

Features:

- **Front Porch:** Enjoy the view from this porch, which opens into the elegant entryway of the home.

- **Ceilings:** The 9-foot ceilings add dimension to this home's already spacious rooms.

- **Dining Room:** This formal room features a large bayed area, which is a treat to decorate.

- **Family Room:** This room is large enough for a crowd and cozy enough for the family.

- **Kitchen:** Planned for convenience, this kitchen features an elevated bar and good storage area.

- **Deck:** Use this space as an outdoor dining room, a grilling porch, or a sunning area.

- **Master Suite:** Enjoy the walk-in closet and bath with double vanity, shower, and garden tub.

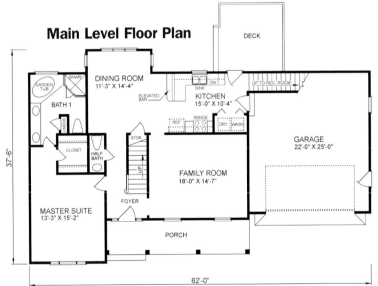

Main Level Floor Plan

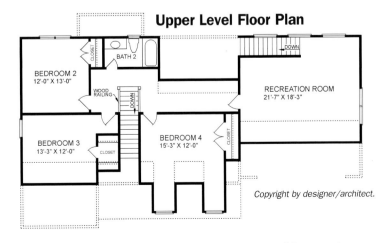

Upper Level Floor Plan

Copyright by designer/architect.

Plan #121064

Dimensions: 44' W x 40' D
Levels: 2
Square Footage: 1,846
Main Level Sq. Ft.: 919
Upper Level Sq. Ft.: 927
Bedrooms: 4
Bathrooms: 2½
Foundation: Basement
Materials List Available: Yes
Price Category: D

Photo provided by designer/architect.

You'll love the features and design in this compact but amenity-filled home.

Features:

- Entry: A balcony overlooks this two-story entry, where a plant shelf tops the coat closet.

- Great Room: A trio of tall windows points up the large dimensions of this room, which is sure to be the hub of your home. Arrange the

furniture to create a cozy space around the fireplace, or leave it open to the room.

- Kitchen: You'll love to work in this well-designed kitchen area.

- Master Suite: On the second floor, this master suite features a tiered ceiling and two walk-in closets. In the bath, you'll find a double vanity, whirlpool tub, and separate shower.

Main Level Floor Plan

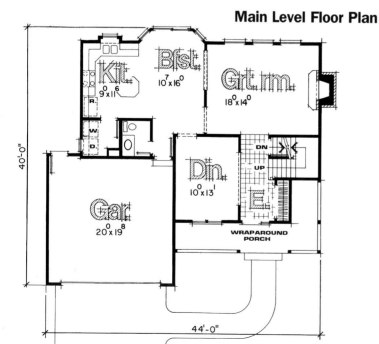

Upper Level Floor Plan

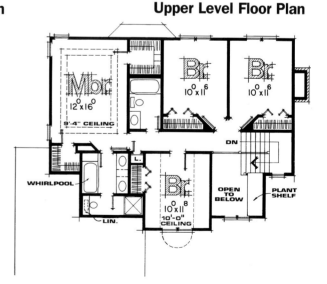

Copyright by designer/architect.

Plan #121066

Dimensions: 46' W x 41'5" D
Levels: 2
Square Footage: 2,078
Main Level Sq. Ft.: 1,113
Upper Level Sq. Ft.: 965
Bedrooms: 4
Bathrooms: 2½
Foundation: Basement
Materials List Available: Yes
Price Category: D

Photo provided by designer/architect.

This lovely home has an unusual dignity, perhaps because its rooms are so well-proportioned and thoughtfully laid out.

Features:

• Family Room: This room is sunken, giving it an unusually cozy, comfortable feeling. Its abundance of windows let natural light stream in during the day, and the fireplace warms it when the weather's chilly.

• Dining Room: This dining room links to the parlor beyond through a cased opening.

• Parlor: A tall, angled ceiling highlights a large, arched window that's the focal point of this room.

• Breakfast Area: A wooden rail visually links this bayed breakfast area to the family room.

• Master Suite: A roomy walk-in closet adds a practical touch to this luxurious suite. The bath features a skylight, whirlpool tub, and separate shower.

Main Level Floor Plan

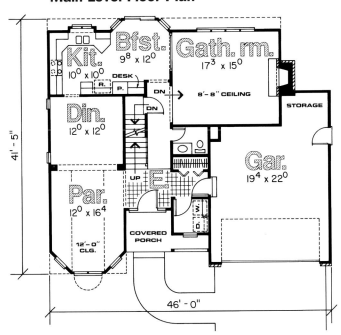

Upper Level Floor Plan

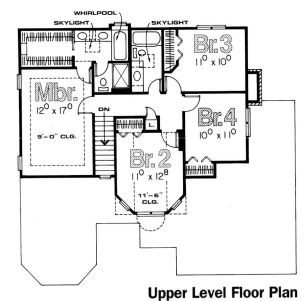

Copyright by designer/architect.

Plan #121074

Dimensions: 68'8" W x 47'8" D
Levels: 2
Square Footage: 2,486
Main Level Sq. Ft.: 1,829
Upper Level Sq. Ft.: 657
Bedrooms: 4
Bathrooms: 2½
Foundation: Basement
Materials List Available: Yes
Price Category: E

Enjoy the natural light that streams through the many lovely windows in this well-designed home.

Features:

- Living Room: This room is sure to be your family's headquarters, thanks to the lovely 15-ft. ceiling, stacked windows, central location, and cozy fireplace.

- Dining Room: A boxed ceiling adds formality to this well-positioned room.

- Kitchen: The island cooktop in this kitchen is so large that it includes a snack bar area. A pantry gives ample storage space, and a built-in desk—where you can set up a computer station or a record-keeping area—adds efficiency.

- Master Suite: For the sake of privacy, this master suite is located on the opposite side of the home from the other living areas. You'll love the roomy bedroom and luxuriate in the private bath with its many amenities.

Main Level Floor Plan

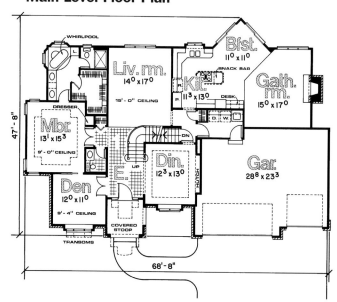

Upper Level Floor Plan

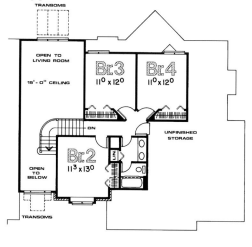

Copyright by designer/architect.

Plan #271093

Dimensions: 74' W x 52' D
Levels: 2
Square Footage: 2,813
Main Level Sq. Ft.: 1,828
Upper Level Sq. Ft.: 985
Bedrooms: 3
Bathrooms: 3
Foundation: Full basement
Materials List Available: No
Price Category: F

Images provided by designer/architect.

Main Level Floor Plan

Upper Level Floor Plan

Copyright by designer/architect.

Plan #271056

Dimensions: 73' W x 52' D
Levels: 2
Square Footage: 2,850
Main Level Sq. Ft.: 1,596
Upper Level Sq. Ft.: 1,254
Bedrooms: 3
Bathrooms: 2½
Foundation: Daylight basement
Materials List Available: No
Price Category: F

Images provided by designer/architect.

Main Level Floor Plan

Upper Level Floor Plan

Copyright by designer/architect.

Plan #211070

Dimensions: 46' W x 68' D

Levels: 2

Square Footage: 1,700

Main Level Sq. Ft.: 1,160

Upper Level Sq. Ft.: 540

Bedrooms: 3

Bathrooms: 2½

Foundation: Crawl space, optional slab, or basement

Materials List Available: Yes

Price Category: C

Photo provided by designer/architect.

You'll be charmed by the three roof dormers and the full-width covered porch on this traditional home.

Features:

• Living Room: With 9-ft. ceilings throughout the living room, dining room, and kitchen merge to maximize usable space and create a spacious, airy feeling in this home. You'll find a fireplace here and three pairs of French doors.

• Dining Room: Walk through this room to the rear covered porch beyond that connects the house to the garage.

• Kitchen: Designed for convenience, this kitchen features a wet bar that is centrally located so that it can easily serve both the living and dining rooms.

• Master Suite: A sloped ceiling with a skylight and French doors leading to the front porch make this area luxurious. The bath includes a raised marble tub, dual-sink vanity, and walk-in closet.

Main Level Floor Plan

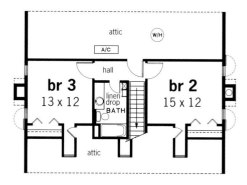

Upper Level Floor Plan

Copyright by designer/architect.

Plan #121094

Dimensions: 40'8" W x 46' D
Levels: 2
Square Footage: 1,768
Main Level Sq. Ft.: 905
Upper Level Sq. Ft.: 863
Bedrooms: 3
Bathrooms: 2½
Foundation: Basement
Materials List Available: Yes
Price Category: C

You'll love this design if you're looking for a home to complement a site with a lovely rear view.

Features:

- **Great Room:** A trio of lovely windows looks out to the front entry of this home. The French doors in this room open to the breakfast area for everyone's convenience.

- **Kitchen:** Designed to suit a gourmet cook, this kitchen includes a roomy pantry and an island with a snack bar.

- **Breakfast Area:** The boxed window here is perfect for houseplants or a collection of culinary herbs. A door leads to the rear porch, where you'll love to dine in good weather.

- **Master Suite:** On the upper level, the bedroom features a cathedral ceiling, two walk-in closets, and a window seat. The bath also has a cathedral ceiling and includes dual lavatories, a large dressing area, and a sunlit whirlpool tub.

Main Level Floor Plan

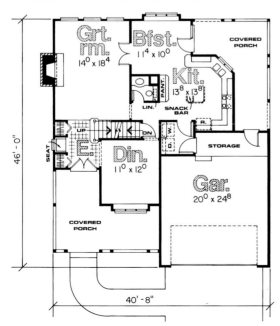

Upper Level Floor Plan

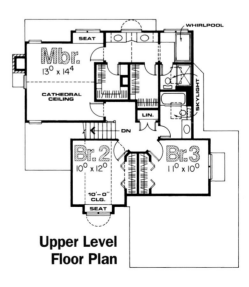

Photos provided by designer/architect.

Plan #131028

Dimensions: 69'2" W x 50'2" D
Levels: 2
Square Footage: 2,696
Main Level Sq. Ft.: 1,960
Upper Level Sq. Ft.: 736
Bedrooms: 4
Bathrooms: 3
Foundation: Crawl space, slab, or basement
Materials List Available: Yes
Price Category: G

Imagine owning a home with Victorian styling and a dramatic, contemporary interior design.

Features:

• Foyer: Enter from the curved covered porch into this foyer with its 17-ft. ceiling.

• Great Room: A vaulted ceiling sets the tone for this large room, where friends and family are sure to congregate.

• Dining Room: A 14-ft. ceiling here accentuates the rounded shape of this room.

• Kitchen: From the angled corner sink to the angled island with a snack bar, this room has character. A pantry adds convenience.

• Master Suite: A 13-ft. tray ceiling exudes elegance, and the bath features a spa tub and designer shower.

• Upper Level: The balcony hall leads to a turreted recreation room, two bedrooms, and a full bath.

Main Level Floor Plan

Upper Level Floor Plan

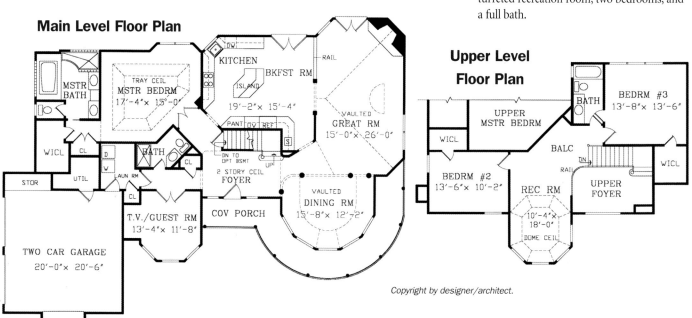

Copyright by designer/architect.

Rear View

Entry

Dining Room

Kitchen View to Great Room   Great Room

Main Level Floor Plan

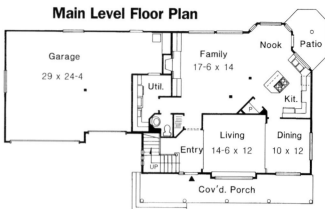

Garage
29 x 24-4

Family
17-6 x 14

Nook

Patio

Util.

Kit.

Living
14-6 x 12

Dining
10 x 12

Entry

UP

Cov'd. Porch

Illustration provided by designer/architect.

Playroom
13 x 19

DESK

Br #4
10 x 10

DESK

M. Br
15 x 14

LINEN

Br #3
11 x 10

DN.

BALCONY

Br #2
11 x 12

Upper Level Floor Plan

Copyright by designer/architect.

Plan #231013

Dimensions: 71'6" W x 40' D
Levels: 2
Square Footage: 2,780
Main Level Sq. Ft.: 1,200
Upper Level Sq. Ft.: 1,580
Bedrooms: 4
Bathrooms: 3½
Foundation: Crawl space
Materials List Available: No
Price Category: F

Nook

Patio

Kit.

Dining
10 x 12-6

DN.

PANT

Family
15 x 14-2

Garage
21-4 x 35-4

Living
12 x 15-8

Util.

Foyer

DN.

UP

P.

Porch

Main Level Floor Plan

Illustration provided by designer/architect.

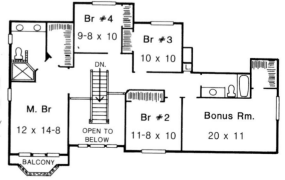

Br #4
9-8 x 10

Br #3
10 x 10

DN.

M. Br
12 x 14-8

OPEN TO BELOW

Br #2
11-8 x 10

Bonus Rm.
20 x 11

BALCONY

Upper Level Floor Plan

Copyright by designer/architect.

Plan #231015

Dimensions: 63' W x 42' D
Levels: 2
Square Footage: 2,360
Main Level Sq. Ft.: 1,054
Upper Level Sq. Ft.: 1,306
Bedrooms: 4
Bathrooms: 2½
Foundation: Crawl space
Materials List Available: No
Price Category: E

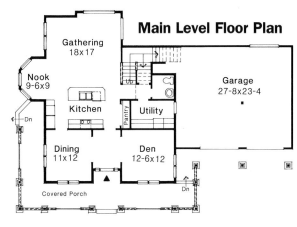

Main Level Floor Plan

Gathering
18x17

Nook
9-6x9

Kitchen

Pantry

Utility

Garage
27-8x23-4

Dining
11x12

Den
12-6x12

Dn

Covered Porch

Dn

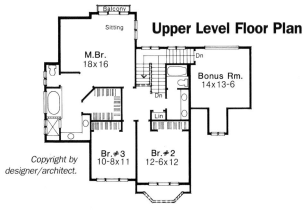

Upper Level Floor Plan

Balcony

Sitting

M.Br.
18x16

Dn

Bonus Rm.
14x13-6

Dn

Lin

Br.#3
10-8x11

Br.#2
12-6x12

Illustration provided by designer/architect.

Copyright by designer/architect.

Plan #231025

Dimensions: 66' W x 46' D

Levels: 2

Square Footage: 2,501

Main Level Sq. Ft.: 1,170

Upper Level Sq. Ft.: 1,331

Bedrooms: 3

Bathrooms: 2½

Foundation: Crawl space

Materials List Available: No

Price Category: E

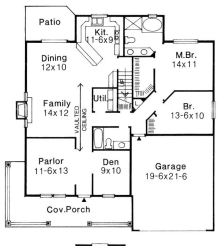

Patio

Kit.
11-6x9

Dining
12x10

M.Br.
14x11

Family
14x12

VAULTED CEILING

Util.

Br.
13-6x10

Parlor
11-6x13

Den
9x10

Garage
19-6x21-6

Cov.Porch

Main Level Floor Plan

Illustration provided by designer/architect.

Upper Level Floor Plan

OPEN TO BELOW

DN

Loft

Br.
11x12-4

Copyright by designer/architect.

Plan #231035

Dimensions: 50' W x 50' D

Levels: 2

Square Footage: 1,954

Main Level Sq. Ft.: 1,508

Upper Level Sq. Ft.: 446

Bedrooms: 3

Bathrooms: 3

Foundation: Crawl space, slab

Materials List Available: No

Price Category: D

Plan #121027

Dimensions: 46' W x 48' D

Levels: 2

Square Footage: 1,660

Main Level Sq. Ft.: 1,265

Upper Level Sq. Ft.: 395

Bedrooms: 3

Bathrooms: 2½

Foundation: Basement

Materials List Available: Yes

Price Category: C

This elegant home is designed for architectural interest and gracious living.

Features:

- Ceiling Height: 8 ft. unless otherwise noted.

- Great Room: Family and guests will be drawn to this inviting, sun-filled room with its 13-ft. ceiling and raised-hearth fireplace.

- Formal Dining Room: An angled ceiling lends architectural interest to this elegant room. Alternately, this room can be used as a parlor.

- Master Bedroom: Corner windows are designed to ease window placement.

- Master Bath: The master bedroom is served by a private bath. The sunlit whirlpool bath invites you to take time to luxuriate and rejuvenate. There's a double vanity, separate shower, and a walk-in closet.

- Garage: This two bay garage offers plenty of space for storage in addition to parking.

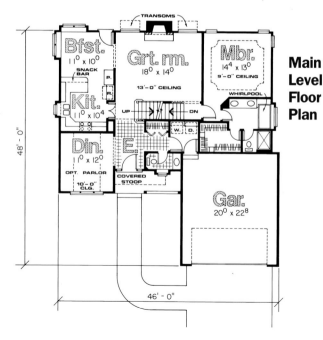

Main Level Floor Plan

Upper Level Floor Plan

Copyright by designer/architect.

Plan #121032

Dimensions: 54'8" W x 45'4" D
Levels: 2
Square Footage: 2,339
Main Level Sq. Ft.: 1,665
Upper Level Sq. Ft.: 674
Bedrooms: 4
Bathrooms: 2½
Foundation: Basement
Materials List Available: Yes
Price Category: E

Images provided by designer/architect.

This home is designed for gracious living and is distinguished by many architectural details.

Features:

- Ceiling Height: 8 ft. unless otherwise noted.

- Foyer: This is truly a grand foyer with a dramatic ceiling that soars to 18 ft.

- Great Room: The foyer's 18-ft. ceiling extends into the great room where an open staircase adds architectural windows. Warm yourself by the fireplace that is framed by windows.

- Kitchen: An island is the centerpiece of this handsome and efficient kitchen that features a breakfast area for informal family meals. The room also includes a handy desk.

- Private Wing: The master suite and study are in a private wing of the house.

- Room to Expand: In addition to the three bedrooms, the second level has an unfinished storage space that can become another bedroom or office.

Main Level Floor Plan

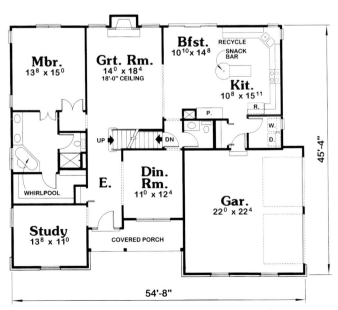

Upper Level Floor Plan

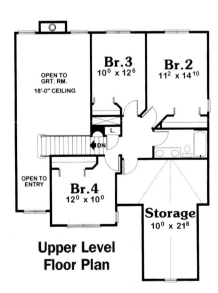

Copyright by designer/architect.

Plan #271067

Dimensions: 72'2" W x 46'5" D
Levels: 2
Square Footage: 3,015
Main Level Sq. Ft.: 1,367
Upper Level Sq. Ft.: 1,648
Bedrooms: 3
Bathrooms: 2½
Foundation: Basement or crawl space
Materials List Available: No
Price Category: G

Images provided by designer/architect.

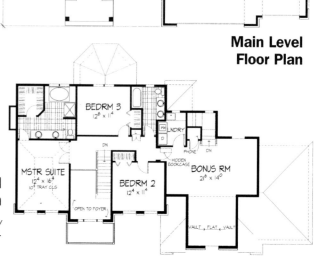

Main Level Floor Plan

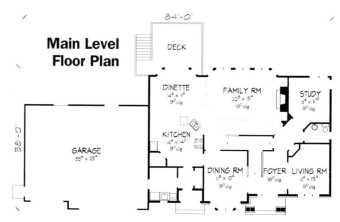

Upper Level Floor Plan

Copyright by designer/architect.

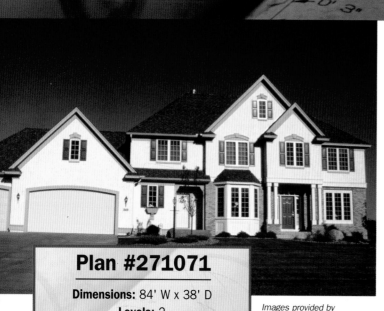

Plan #271071

Dimensions: 84' W x 38' D
Levels: 2
Square Footage: 3,194
Main Level Sq. Ft.: 1,709
Upper Level Sq. Ft.: 1,485
Bedrooms: 4
Bathrooms: 2½
Foundation: Basement or crawl space
Materials List Available: No
Price Category: G

Images provided by designer/architect.

Main Level Floor Plan

Upper Level Floor Plan

Copyright by designer/architect.

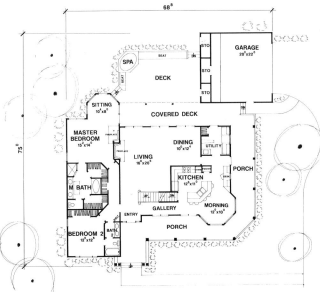

Main Level Floor Plan

Photo provided by designer/architect.

Plan #331003

Dimensions: 68'8" W x 75' D
Levels: 2
Square Footage: 2,661
Main Level Sq. Ft.: 2,000
Upper Level Sq. Ft.: 660
Bedrooms: 4
Bathrooms: 3
Foundation: Basement, crawl space, or slab
Materials List Available: No
Price Category: F

Upper Level Floor Plan
Copyright by designer/architect.

Plan #331004

Dimensions: 81' W x 49'10" D
Levels: 2
Square Footage: 3,125
Main Level Sq. Ft.: 2,147
Upper Level Sq. Ft.: 978
Bedrooms: 4
Bathrooms: 3½
Foundation: Basement, crawl space, or slab
Materials List Available: No
Price Category: G

Photo provided by designer/architect.

Main Level Floor Plan

Upper Level Floor Plan
Copyright by designer/architect.

Main Level Floor Plan

Upper Level Floor Plan

Illustration provided by designer/architect.

Copyright by designer/architect.

Plan #241009

Dimensions: 62'9" W x 38'6" D

Levels: 2

Square Footage: 1,974

Main Level Sq. Ft.: 1,480

Upper Level Sq. Ft.: 494

Bedrooms: 3

Bathrooms: 2½

Foundation: Slab

Materials List Available: No

Price Category: D

Main Level Floor Plan

Upper Level Floor Plan

Illustration provided by designer/architect.

Copyright by designer/architect.

Plan #241013

Dimensions: 68' W x 46' D

Levels: 2

Square Footage: 2,779

Main Level Sq. Ft.: 1,918

Upper Level Sq. Ft.: 861

Bedrooms: 4

Bathrooms: 3½

Foundation: Slab

Materials List Available: No

Price Category: F

Plan #261004

Dimensions: 82' W x 48'8" D
Levels: 2
Square Footage: 2,707
Main Level Sq. Ft.: 1,484
Upper Level Sq. Ft.: 1,223
Bedrooms: 3
Bathrooms: 2½
Foundation: Basement
Materials List Available: No
Price Category: F

Inside the classic Victorian exterior is a spacious home filled with contemporary amenities that the whole family is sure to love.

Features:

- Porch: This wraparound porch provides space for entertaining or sitting out to enjoy the evening.

- Foyer: Two stories high, the foyer opens to the formal dining room and front parlor.

- Family Room: French doors open from the parlor into this room, with its cozy fireplace.

- Sunroom: A cathedral ceiling adds drama to this versatile room.

- Kitchen: A pantry and a work island make this well-planned kitchen even more convenient.

- Master Suite: A tray ceiling and French doors to the bath give the bedroom elegance, while the sumptuous bath features a deluxe tub, walk-in shower, and split vanities.

Main Level Floor Plan

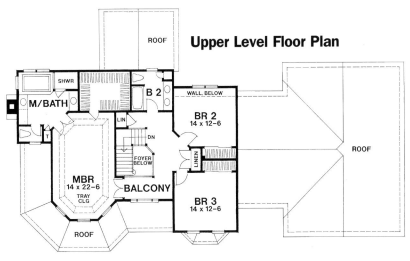

Upper Level Floor Plan

Plan #121070

Dimensions: 50' W x 58' D
Levels: 2
Square Footage: 2,139
Main Level Sq. Ft.: 1,506
Upper Level Sq. Ft.: 633
Bedrooms: 4
Bathrooms: 2½
Foundation: Basement
Materials List Available: Yes
Price Category: D

You'll love this design if you're looking for a bright, airy home where you can easily entertain.

Features:

- **Entry:** A volume ceiling sets the tone for this home when you first walk in.

- **Great Room:** With a volume ceiling extending from the entry, this great room has an open feeling. Transom-topped windows contribute

natural light during the day.

- **Dining Room:** Because it is joined to the great room through a cased opening, this dining room can serve as an extension of the great room.

- **Kitchen:** An island with a snack bar, desk, and pantry make this kitchen a treat, and a door from the breakfast area leads to a private covered patio where dining will be a pleasure.

Main Level Floor Plan

Upper Level Floor Plan

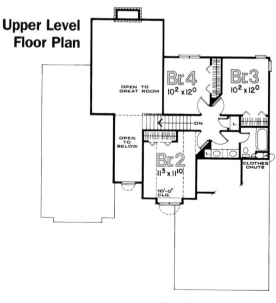

Plan #121088

Dimensions: 56' W x 48' D
Levels: 2
Square Footage: 2,340
Main Level Sq. Ft.: 1,701
Upper Level Sq. Ft.: 639
Bedrooms: 4
Bathrooms: 2½
Foundation: Basement
Materials List Available: Yes
Price Category: E

Photo provided by designer/architect.

You'll love this cheerful home, with its many large windows that let in natural light and cozy spaces that encourage family gatherings.

Features:

- Entry: Use the built-in curio cabinet here to display your best collector's pieces.

- Den: French doors from the entry lead to this room, with its built-in bookcase and triple-wide, transom-topped window.

- Great Room: The 14-ft. ceiling in this room accentuates the floor-to-ceiling windows that frame the raised-hearth fireplace.

- Kitchen: Both the layout and the work space make this room a delight for any cook.

- Master Suite: The bedroom has a tray ceiling for built-in elegance. A skylight helps to light the master bath, and an oval whirlpool tub, separate shower, and double vanity provide a luxurious touch.

Main Level Floor Plan

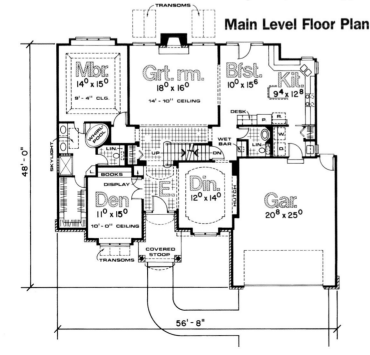

Upper Level Floor Plan

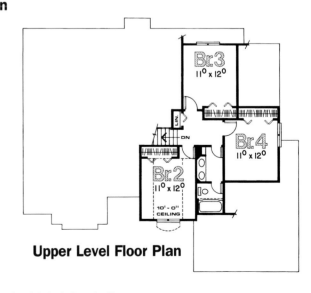

Copyright by designer/architect.

Plan #261007

Dimensions: 58' W x 44' D

Levels: 2

Square Footage: 2,635

Main Level Sq. Ft.: 1,435

Upper Level Sq. Ft.: 1,200

Bedrooms: 4

Bathrooms: 2½

Foundation: Basement

Materials List Available: No

Price Category: F

You'll love the dramatic roofline of this gracious home, which is as carefully designed inside as it is on the exterior.

Features:

- Foyer: This 2-story area opens to the formal dining and living rooms.

- Living Room: A pocket door between this room and the family room allows for plenty of space for large gatherings.

- Dining Room: Convenient to the kitchen, this room can be used for family meals as well as formal parties.

- Family Room: Enjoy the fireplace in this comfortable room.

- Den: You'll love the quiet and privacy here.

- Master Suite: This luxurious suite features a large walk-in closet and bath with two vanities, a corner whirlpool tub, and a separate shower.

Images provided by designer/architect.

Main Level Floor Plan

Copyright by designer/architect.

Upper Level Floor Plan

Plan #261005

Dimensions: 64' W x 31' D

Levels: 2

Square Footage: 2,419

Main Level Sq. Ft.: 1,228

Upper Level Sq. Ft.: 1,191

Bedrooms: 4

Bathrooms: 2½

Foundation: Basement

Materials List Available: No

Price Category: E

You'll love the spacious rooms and convenient layout of this lovely Colonial-style home.

Features:

- **Ceilings:** Ceilings are 9 ft. tall or higher, adding to the airy feeling inside this home.

- **Foyer:** This two-story foyer gives a warm welcome.

- **Family Room:** Everyone will gather in this well-positioned room, with its handsome fireplace and generous dimensions.

- **Living Room:** Both this room and the dining room are ideal for formal entertaining.

- **Kitchen:** A cook's dream, this kitchen has ample counter space, a large island, and a pantry.

- **Master Suite:** Enjoy the luxury of the walk-in closet, dual vanities, whirlpool tub, and shower here.

- **Additional Bedrooms:** Extensive closet space makes it easy to live in each of the bedrooms.

Main Level Floor Plan

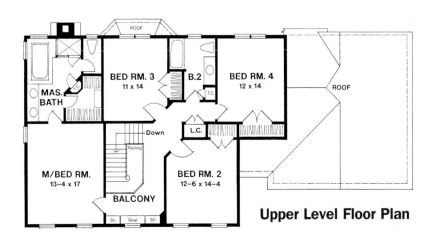

Upper Level Floor Plan

Plan #201096

Dimensions: 46' W x 70' D
Levels: 2
Square Footage: 2,125
Main Level Sq. Ft.: 1,555
Upper Level Sq. Ft.: 570
Bedrooms: 3
Bathrooms: 2½
Foundation: Crawl space, slab, and basement
Materials List Available: Yes
Price Category: D

Images provided by designer/architect.

Main Level Floor Plan

garage 22 x 22

sto

patio

breezeway

util

eating 13 x 10

den 20 x 18

study 12 x 9

kit 14 x 10

mbr 16 x 16

dining 14 x 14

foy 10 x 9

porch

Upper Level Floor Plan

br 2 16 x 12²

br 3 11 x 13

Copyright by designer/architect.

Plan #301006

Dimensions: 60' W x 32' D
Levels: 2
Square Footage: 2,162
Main Level Sq. Ft.: 1,098
Upper Level Sq. Ft.: 1,064
Bedrooms: 3
Bathrooms: 2½
Foundation: Crawl space, slab
Materials List Available: Yes
Price Category: D

Images provided by designer/architect.

Main Level Floor Plan

WOOD DECK

BREAKFAST 9-8 x 9-8

KITCHEN 12-0 x 13-6

LAUNDRY

GARAGE 22-0 x 22-0

GREAT ROOM 13-6 x 22-4

DINING 13-6 x 13-6

FOYER

PORCH

60-0

Copyright by designer/architect.

Optional Third Level

BATH

BEDROOM 4 11-0 x 12-0

HALL

BEDROOM 5 11-0 x 12-0

ATTIC STORAGE

Upper Level Floor Plan

BATH

WALK-IN CLOSET

BEDROOM 2 13-6 x 12-0

WALK IN CLOSET

BATH

M. BEDROOM 13-6 x 16-0

HALL

BEDROOM 3 13-6 x 12-0

Plan #251010

Dimensions: 53' W x 52' D

Levels: 2

Square Footage: 1,854

Main Level Sq. Ft.: 1,317

Upper Level Sq. Ft.: 537

Bedrooms: 3

Bathrooms: 2½

Foundation: Basement

Materials List Available: Yes

Price Category: D

Illustration provided by designer/architect.

Main Level Floor Plan

Upper Level Floor Plan

Copyright by designer/architect.

Plan #251011

Dimensions: 49' W x 47' D

Levels: 2

Square Footage: 2,008

Main Level Sq. Ft.: 1,318

Upper Level Sq. Ft.: 690

Bedrooms: 4

Bathrooms: 2½

Foundation: Basement

Materials List Available: Yes

Price Category: D

Illustration provided by designer/architect.

Upper Level Floor Plan

Main Level Floor Plan

Copyright by designer/architect.

Plan #291009

Dimensions: 74'8" W x 41'4" D
Levels: 2
Square Footage: 1,655
Main Level Sq. Ft.: 1,277
Upper Level Sq. Ft.: 378
Bedrooms: 3
Bathrooms: 2
Foundation: Basement
Materials List Available: No
Price Category: C

If your family loves a northern European look, they'll appreciate the curved eaves and arched window that give this lovely home its character.

Features:

- **Entryway:** The front door welcomes both friends and family into a lovely open design on the first floor of this home.

- **Living Room:** The enormous arched window floods this room with natural light in the daytime. At night, draw drapes across it to create a warm, intimate feeling.

- **Dining Room:** Windows are the highlight of this room, too, but here, the angled bay window area opens to the rear deck.

- **Kitchen:** The family cook will be delighted with this well-planned kitchen, which is a snap to organize.

- **Master Suite:** Located on the first floor, this suite includes a private bath for total convenience.

Images provided by designer/architect.

Main Level Floor Plan

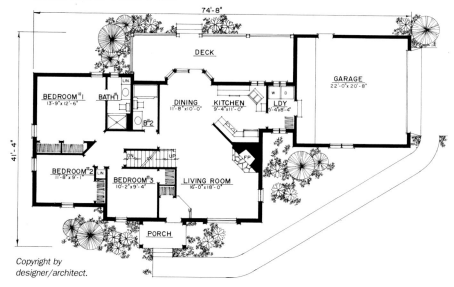

Copyright by designer/architect.

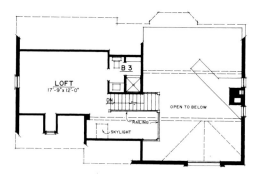

Upper Level Floor Plan

Plan #141010

Dimensions: 43'4" W x 37' D

Levels: 2

Square Footage: 1,765

Main Level Sq. Ft.: 1,210

Upper Level Sq. Ft.: 555

Bedrooms: 3

Bathrooms: 3

Foundation: Basement

Materials List Available: No

Price Category: C

A Palladian window in a stone gable adds a new twist to a classical cottage design.

Features:

- Ceiling Height: 8 ft. unless otherwise noted.

- Living Area: Dormers open into this handsome living area, which is designed to accommodate gatherings of any size.

- Master Suite: This beautiful master bedroom opens off the foyer. It features a modified cathedral ceiling that makes the front Palladian window a focal point inside as well as out. The master bath offers a dramatic cathedral ceiling over the tub and vanity.

- Balcony: U-shaped stairs lead to this elegant balcony, which overlooks the foyer while providing access to two additional bedrooms.

- Garage: This garage is tucked under the house to improve the appearance from the street. It offers two bays for plenty of parking and storage space.

Images provided by designer/architect.

Main Level Floor Plan

Upper Level Floor Plan

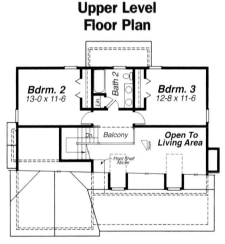

Copyright by designer/architect.

Basement Floor Plan

SMARTtip

Stone Tables

Marble- and stone-topped tables with plants are perfect for use in light-filled rooms. Warmed by the sun during the day, the tabletops catch leaf droppings and can stand up to the splatters of watering cans and plant sprayers.

Photo provided by designer/architect.

Plan #121075

Dimensions: 57'4" W x 30' D
Levels: 2
Square Footage: 2,345
Main Level Sq. Ft.: 1,000
Upper Level Sq. Ft.: 1,345
Bedrooms: 4
Bathrooms: 3½
Foundation: Basement
Materials List Available: Yes
Price Category: E

Imagine owning a home with a Colonial-styled exterior and a practical, amenity-filled interior with both formal and informal areas.

Features:

- **Family Room:** This room will be the heart of your home. A bay window lets you create a special nook for reading or quiet conversation, and a fireplace begs for a circle of comfortable chairs or soft cushions around it.
- **Living Room:** Connected to the family room by a set of French doors, you can use this

room for formal entertaining or informal family fun.

- **Kitchen:** This kitchen has been designed for efficient work patterns. However, the snack bar that links it to the breakfast area beyond also invites company while the cook is working.
- **Master Suite:** Located on the second level, this suite features an entertainment center, a separate sitting area, built-in dressers, two walk-in closets, and a whirlpool tub.

Main Level Floor Plan

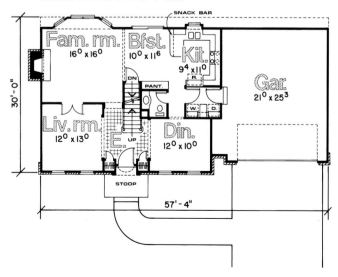

Upper Level Floor Plan

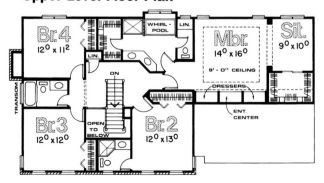

Copyright by designer/architect.

Plan #161019

Dimensions: 54'6" D x 41'10" W

Levels: 2

Square Footage: 2,428

Main Level Sq. Ft.: 1,309

Upper Level Sq. Ft.: 1,119

Bedrooms: 4

Bathrooms: 2½

Foundation: Slab

Materials List Available: No

Price Category: E

Elegant and designed for comfortable family living, this home is full of amenities.

Features:

- Foyer: The elegant staircase and arched opening to the living room are visible from this foyer, and a balcony on the upper level lets you look into it.

- Family Room: Let the family relax and play here so that you can save the formal living room for entertaining and quiet activities.

- Kitchen: The central location of this kitchen makes it the heart of this home. It's visually open to the family room and breakfast area and naturally lit by a bank of rear windows.

- Master Suite: Relax in this quiet area, or enjoy the luxury of the master bath, with its whirl-pool tub, separate shower, and dual vanities.

- Upper Level: 3 bedrooms and a bath with a skylight and double-bowl vanity make this area comfortable for guests or family.

Images provided by designer/architect.

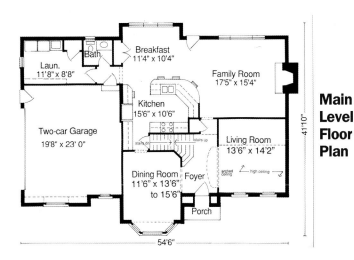

Main Level Floor Plan

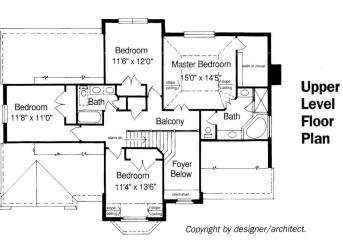

Upper Level Floor Plan

Copyright by designer/architect.

Plan #121019

Dimensions: 70' W x 60' D
Levels: 2
Square Footage: 3,775
Main Level Sq. Ft.: 1,923
Upper Level Sq. Ft.: 1,852
Bedrooms: 4
Bathrooms: 3
Foundation: Basement
Materials List Available: Yes
Price Category: H

Photo provided by designer/architect.

The grand exterior presence is carried inside, beginning with the dramatic curved staircase.

Features:

- Ceiling Height: 8 ft.

- Den: French doors lead to the sophisticated den, with its bayed windows and wall of bookcases.

- Living Room: A curved wall and a series of arched windows highlight this large space.

- Formal Dining Room: The living room shares the curved wall and arched windows found in the living room.

- Screened Porch: This huge space features skylights and is accessible by another French door from the dining room.

- Family Room: Family and guests alike will be drawn to this room, with its trio of arched windows and fireplace flanked by bookcases.

- Kitchen: An island adds convenience and distinction to this large, functional kitchen.

- Garage: This spacious three-bay garage provides plenty of space for cars and storage.

Main Level Floor Plan

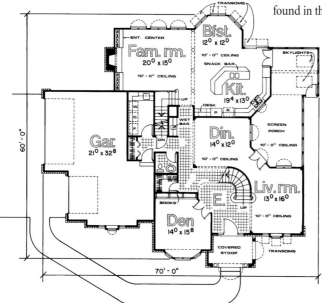

Upper Level Floor Plan

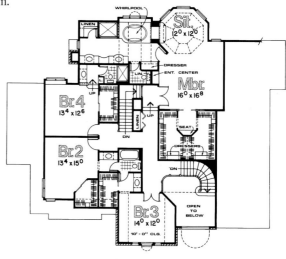

Copyright by designer/architect.

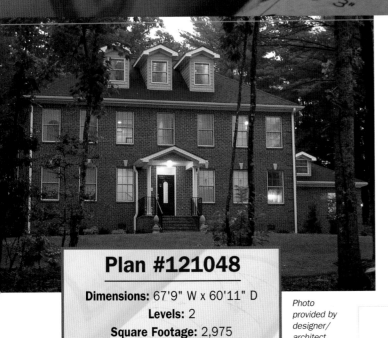

Main Level Floor Plan

Plan #121048

Dimensions: 67'9" W x 60'11" D

Levels: 2

Square Footage: 2,975

Main Level Sq. Ft.: 1,548

Upper Level Sq. Ft.: 1,427

Bedrooms: 4

Bathrooms: 3½

Foundation: Slab

Materials List Available: Yes

Price Category: F

Photo provided by designer/ architect.

Upper Level Floor Plan

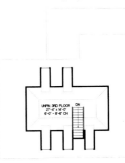

Bonus Area

Copyright by designer/architect.

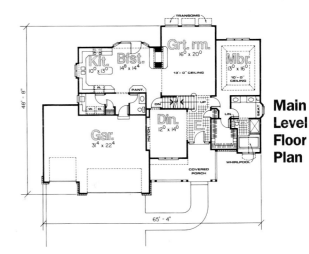

Main Level Floor Plan

Plan #121095

Dimensions: 65'4" W x 48'8" D

Levels: 2

Square Footage: 2,282

Main Level Sq. Ft.: 1,597

Upper Level Sq. Ft.: 685

Bedrooms: 4

Bathrooms: 2½

Foundation: Basement

Materials List Available: Yes

Price Category: E

Photo provided by designer/architect.

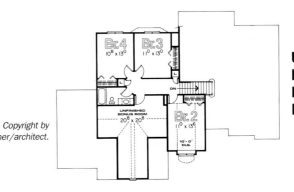

Upper Level Floor Plan

Copyright by designer/architect.

Photo provided by designer/architect.

Plan #121068

Dimensions: 54' W x 49'10" D
Levels: 2
Square Footage: 2,391
Main Level Sq. Ft.: 1,697
Upper Level Sq. Ft.: 694
Bedrooms: 4
Bathrooms: 2½
Foundation: Basement
Materials List Available: Yes
Price Category: E

This home allows you a great deal of latitude in the way you choose to finish it, so you can truly make it "your own."

Features:

• **Living Room:** Located just off the entryway, this living room is easy to convert to a stylish den. Add French doors for privacy, and relish the style that the 12-ft. angled ceiling and picturesque arched window provide.

• **Great Room:** The highlight of this room is the two-sided fireplace that easily adds as much design interest as warmth to this area. The three transom-topped windows here fill the room with light.

• **Kitchen:** A center island, walk-in pantry, and built-in desk combine to create this wonderful kitchen, and the attached gazebo breakfast area adds the finishing touch.

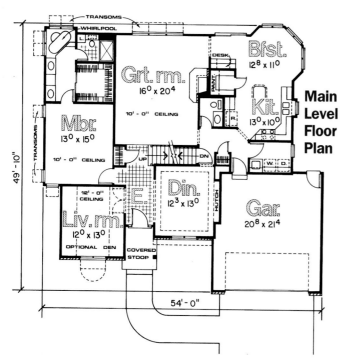

Main Level Floor Plan

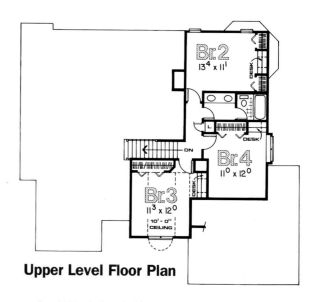

Upper Level Floor Plan

Copyright by designer/architect.

Plan #121071

Dimensions: 72'8" W x 51'4" D
Levels: 2
Square Footage: 2,957
Main Level Sq. Ft.: 2,063
Upper Level Sq. Ft.: 894
Bedrooms: 4
Bathrooms: 4½
Foundation: Basement
Materials List Available: Yes
Price Category: F

You'll appreciate the mix of open public areas and private quarters that the layout of this home guarantees.

Features:

- Entry: From this entry, the formal living and dining rooms, as well as the great room, are all visible.
- Great Room: A soaring cathedral ceiling sets an elegant tone for this room, and the fireplace that's flanked with lovely transom-topped windows adds to it.
- Den: French doors from the great room lead to this den, where you'll find a generous bay window, a wet bar, and a decorative ceiling.
- Master Suite: On the main floor to give it needed privacy, this master suite will make you feel at home the first time you walk into it. The private bath has an angled ceiling and a whirlpool tub.

Main Level Floor Plan

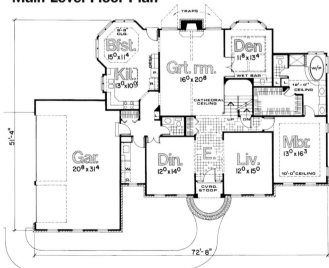

Upper Level Floor Plan

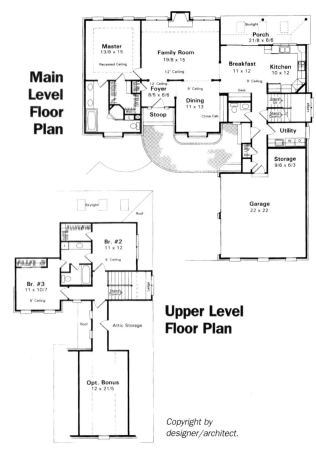

Main Level Floor Plan

Illustration provided by designer/architect.

Upper Level Floor Plan

Copyright by designer/architect.

Plan #251012

Dimensions: 57'9" W x 62'10" D

Levels: 2

Square Footage: 2,009

Main Level Sq. Ft.: 1,520

Upper Level Sq. Ft.: 489

Bedrooms: 3

Bathrooms: 2½

Foundation: Basement

Materials List Available: Yes

Price Category: D

Illustration provided by designer/architect.

Main Level Floor Plan

Upper Level Floor Plan

Copyright by designer/architect.

Plan #251013

Dimensions: 58' W x 44' D

Levels: 2

Square Footage: 2,073

Main Level Sq. Ft.: 1,441

Upper Level Sq. Ft.: 632

Bedrooms: 4

Bathrooms: 2½

Foundation: Basement

Materials List Available: Yes

Price Category: D

Main Level Floor Plan

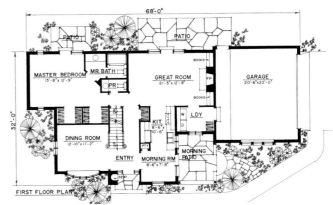

68'-0"

PATIO | PATIO

MASTER BEDROOM
15'-8"x12'-9"

MR. BATH

PR.

GREAT ROOM
21'-3"x12'-9"

BOOKS
FP
BOOKS

GARAGE
20'-6"x22'-0"

32'-0"

DINING ROOM
12'-10"x11'-2"

KIT.
8'-6"x10'-6"

W | LDY
D

MORNING
PATIO

ENTRY

MORNING RM
8'-6"x7'-8"

SEAT

FIRST FLOOR PLAN

Copyright by designer/architect.

Illustrations provided by designer/architect.

Upper Level Floor Plan

BATH #2

OPEN TO VAULTED CEILING

BEDROOM #2
13'-4"x14'-4"

RAILING

BEDROOM #3
11'-0"x14'-11"

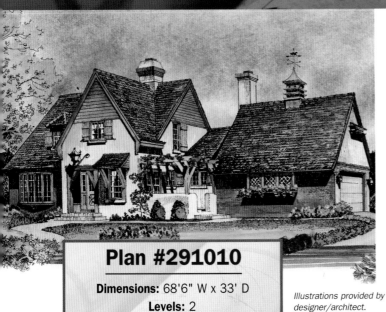

Plan #291010

Dimensions: 68'6" W x 33' D

Levels: 2

Square Footage: 1,776

Main Level Sq. Ft.: 1,182

Upper Level Sq. Ft.: 594

Bedrooms: 3

Bathrooms: 2½

Foundation: Basement

Materials List Available: No

Price Category: C

Copyright by designer/architect.

35'-0"

PORCH

FAMILY ROOM
18'-0"x19'-6"

VAULTED CEILING

FAMILY ENTRY

FP

KITCHEN

MORNING ROOM
8'-0"x11'-6"

10'-0"x11'-6"

DN

DN

PANTRY

LAV.

LAUNDRY
W D

DINING ROOM
13'-9"x14'-4"

LIVING ROOM
13'-9"x18'-6"

44'-0"

TWO-CAR GARAGE
23'-4"x23'-2"

ENTRY FOYER

UP

PORCH

Main Level Floor Plan

58'-0"

Illustrations provided by designer/architect.

Upper Level Floor Plan

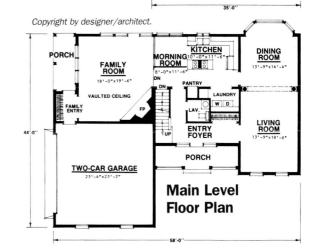

BEDROOM
13'-0"x8'-10"

WIC

BEDROOM
12'-8"x11'-0"

LIN

DN

UPPER HALL

BATH

MASTER BATH

BEDROOM
12'-0"x11'-0"

WIC

MASTER BEDROOM
13'-9"x14'-2"

32'-0"

35'-0"

Plan #291012

Dimensions: 68'6" W x 33' D

Levels: 2

Square Footage: 1,898

Main Level Sq. Ft.: 1,182

Upper Level Sq. Ft.: 716

Bedrooms: 4

Bathrooms: 2½

Foundation: Basement

Materials List Available: No

Price Category: D

Photo provided by designer/architect.

Plan #121084

Dimensions: 40' W x 42' D
Levels: 2
Square Footage: 1,728
Main Level Sq. Ft.: 845
Upper Level Sq. Ft.: 883
Bedrooms: 4
Bathrooms: 2½
Foundation: Basement
Materials List Available: Yes
Price Category: C

If you're looking for a home where the whole family will be comfortable, you'll love this design.

Features:

- Great Room: The heart of the home, this great room has a fireplace with a raised hearth, a sloped ceiling, and transom-topped windows.

- Dining Room: A cased opening lets you flow from the great room into this formal

dining room. A built-in display hutch is the highlight here.

- Kitchen: What could be nicer than this wraparound kitchen with peninsula snack bar? The sunny, attached breakfast area has a pantry and built-in desk.

- Master Suite: A double vanity, whirlpool tub, shower, and walk-in closet exude luxury in this upper-floor master suite.

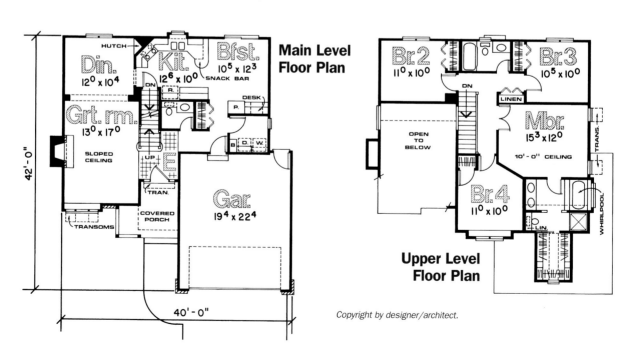

Copyright by designer/architect.

Plan #121085

Dimensions: 42' W x 54' D
Levels: 2
Square Footage: 1,948
Main Level Sq. Ft.: 1,517
Upper Level Sq. Ft.: 431
Bedrooms: 4
Bathrooms: 3
Foundation: Basement
Materials List Available: Yes
Price Category: D

Photo provided by designer/architect.

You'll love the spacious feeling in this home, with its generous rooms and excellent design.

Features:

- Great Room: This room is lofty and open, thanks in part to the transom-topped windows that flank the fireplace. However, you can furnish to create a cozy nook for reading or a private spot to watch TV or enjoy some quiet music.

- Kitchen: Wrapping counters add an unusual touch to this kitchen, and a pantry gives extra storage area. A snack bar links the kitchen with a separate breakfast area.

- Master Suite: A tiered ceiling adds elegance to this area, and a walk-in closet adds practicality. The private bath features a sunlit whirlpool tub, separate shower, and double vanity.

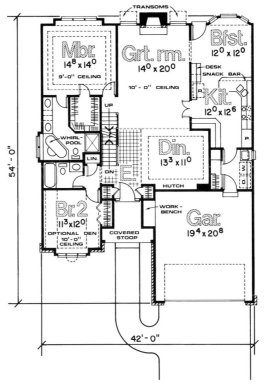

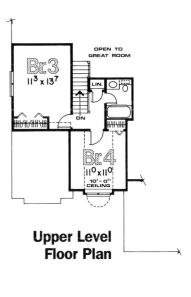

Main Level Floor Plan

Upper Level Floor Plan

Copyright by designer/architect.

- Upper-Level Bedrooms: The upper-level placement is just right for these bedrooms, which share an amenity-filled full bathroom.

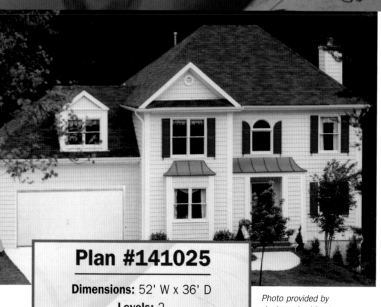

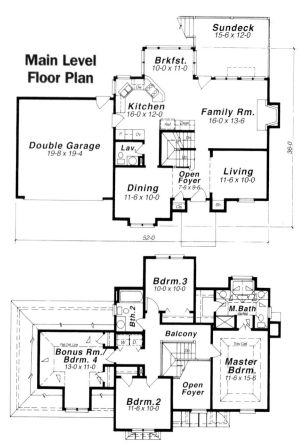

Main Level Floor Plan

Sundeck
15-6 x 12-0

Brkfst.
10-0 x 11-0

Kitchen
16-0 x 12-0

Family Rm.
16-0 x 13-6

Double Garage
19-8 x 19-4

Lav.

Dining
11-6 x 10-0

Open Foyer
7-6 x 9-6

Living
11-6 x 10-0

36-0

52-0

Photo provided by designer/architect.

Plan #141025

Dimensions: 52' W x 36' D

Levels: 2

Square Footage: 1,721

Main Level Sq. Ft.: 902

Upper Level Sq. Ft.: 819

Bedrooms: 4

Bathrooms: 2½

Foundation: Basement

Materials List Available: Yes

Price Category: C

Upper Level Floor Plan

Copyright by designer/architect.

Bdrm.3
10-0 x 10-0

Bth.2

M.Bath

Balcony

Bonus Rm./
Bdrm. 4
13-0 x 11-0

Master
Bdrm.
11-6 x 15-6

Open
Foyer

Bdrm.2
11-6 x 10-0

Plan #141027

Dimensions: 46' W x 38' D

Levels: 2

Square Footage: 2,088

Main Level Sq. Ft.: 1,048

Upper Level Sq. Ft.: 1,040

Bedrooms: 3

Bathrooms: 2½

Foundation: Basement

Materials List Available: Yes

Price Category: D

Photo provided by designer/architect.

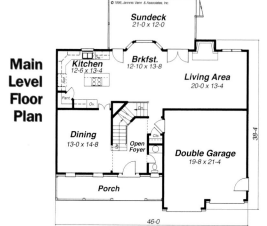

Main Level Floor Plan

© 1996 Jannine Vann & Associates, Inc.

Sundeck
21-0 x 12-0

Kitchen
12-6 x 13-4

Brkfst.
12-10 x 13-8

Living Area
20-0 x 13-4

Dining
13-0 x 14-8

Open Foyer

Double Garage
19-8 x 21-4

Porch

46-0

38-4

Upper Level Floor Plan

Copyright by designer/architect.

M.Bath

Bdrm.3
13-0 x 10-10

Master
Bdrm.
13-0 x 18-6

Open
To
Foyer

Bdrm.2
13-0 x 10-0

Main Level Floor Plan

Patio / Sundeck

Bdrm.4
11⁰ x 12⁰

Two Story Living
16⁴ x 14⁶

Brkfst.
10⁰ x 13⁴

Kitchen
9⁸ x 13⁴

Bath 3

Open Foyer
7² x 11¹⁰

Dining
10⁸ x 12¹⁰

Double Garage
19⁴ x 21⁸

Pantry | Ref.

Dn. | Up

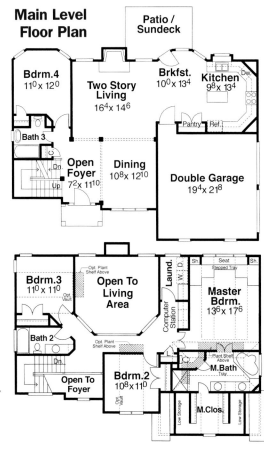

Bdrm.3
11⁰ x 11⁰

Opt. Plant Shelf Above
Opt. Vault

Open To Living Area

Laund. | W.D.

Sh. | Seat Stepped Tray | Sh.

Master Bdrm.
13⁶ x 17⁶

Computer Station

Bath 2

Opt. Plant Shelf Above

M.Bath Tray

Plant Shelf Above

Upper Level Floor Plan

Copyright by designer/architect.

Dn.

Open To Foyer

Bdrm.2
10⁸ x 11⁰

Opt. Vault

M.Clos.

Low Storage | M.Clos. | Low Storage

Photo provided by designer/architect.

Plan #141028

Dimensions: 48' W x 36'4" D

Levels: 2

Square Footage: 2,215

Main Level Sq. Ft.: 1,075

Upper Level Sq. Ft.: 1,140

Bedrooms: 4

Bathrooms: 3

Foundation: Basement

Materials List Available: Yes

Price Category: E

Plan #141029

Dimensions: 55' W x 42' D

Levels: 2

Square Footage: 2,289

Main Level Sq. Ft.: 1,382

Upper Level Sq. Ft.: 907

Bedrooms: 4

Bathrooms: 2½

Foundation: Basement

Materials List Available: Yes

Price Category: E

Photo provided by designer/architect.

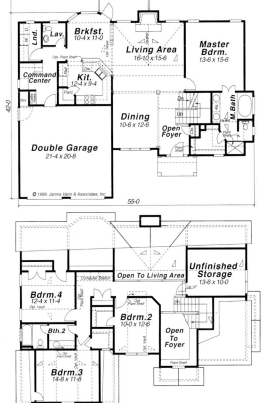

Main Level Floor Plan

8-0

Sundeck
12-0 x 11-0

Lnd. | Lav.

Brkfst.
10-4 x 11-0

Living Area
16-10 x 15-6

Master Bdrm.
13-6 x 15-6

Command Center

Kit.
12-4 x 9-4

Pant.

Dining
10-6 x 12-6

Open Foyer

M.Bath

42-0

Double Garage
21-4 x 20-8

© 1999, Jannis Vann & Associates, Inc

55-0

Upper Level Floor Plan

Copyright by designer/architect.

Computer Station

Open To Living Area

Unfinished Storage
13-6 x 10-0

Bdrm.4
12-4 x 11-4
Opt. Vault

Bth.2

Bdrm.2
10-0 x 12-6

Open To Foyer

Bdrm.3
14-8 x 11-8

Plant Shelf

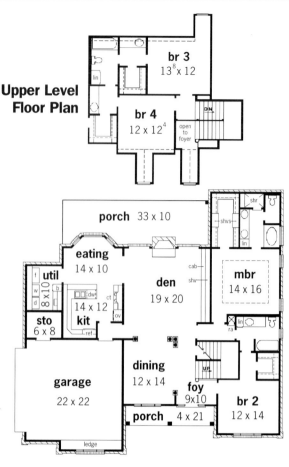

Upper Level Floor Plan

br 3
13⁸ x 12

br 4
12 x 12⁴

open to foyer

Main Level Floor Plan

porch 33 x 10

eating
14 x 10

den
19 x 20

mbr
14 x 16

util
8 x 10

kit
14 x 12

sto
6 x 8

garage
22 x 22

dining
12 x 14

foy
9x10

br 2
12 x 14

porch 4 x 21

ledge

Copyright by designer/architect.

Plan #201103

Dimensions: 57'10" W x 56'10" D

Levels: 2

Square Footage: 2,490

Main Level Sq. Ft.: 1,911

Upper Level Sq. Ft.: 579

Bedrooms: 4

Bathrooms: 3

Foundation: Crawl space, slab, or basement

Materials List Available: Yes

Price Category: E

Illustration provided by designer/architect.

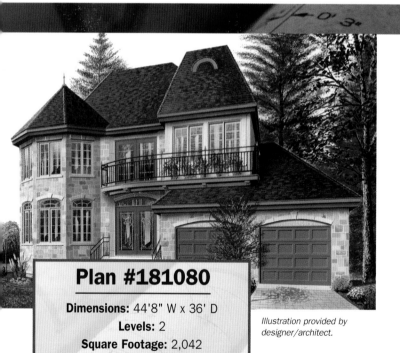

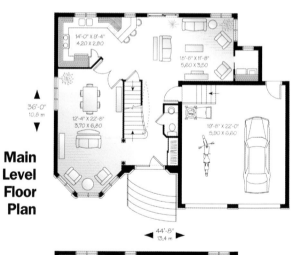

Main Level Floor Plan

14'-0" X 9'-4"
4,20 x 2,80

18'-8" X 11'-8"
5,60 x 3,50

12'-4" X 22'-8"
3,70 x 6,80

19'-8" X 22'-0"
5,90 x 6,60

36'-0"
10,8 m

44'-8"
13,4 m

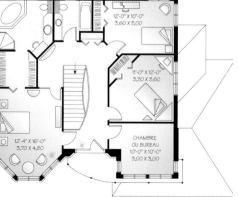

Upper Level Floor Plan

12'-0" X 10'-0"
3,60 x 3,00

11'-0" X 12'-0"
3,30 x 3,60

12'-4" X 16'-0"
3,70 x 4,80

CHAMBRE OU BUREAU
10'-0" X 10'-0"
3,00 x 3,00

Copyright by designer/architect.

Plan #181080

Dimensions: 44'8" W x 36' D

Levels: 2

Square Footage: 2,042

Main Level Sq. Ft.: 934

Upper Level Sq. Ft.: 1,108

Bedrooms: 3

Bathrooms: 2½

Foundation: Full basement

Materials List Available: Yes

Price Category: D

Illustration provided by designer/architect.

Plan #101017

Dimensions: 57' W x 51' D
Levels: 2
Square Footage: 2,253
Main Level Sq. Ft.: 1,719
Upper Level Sq. Ft.: 247
Bedrooms: 4
Bathrooms: 2½
Foundation: Basement
Materials List Available: No
Price Category: E

Illustration provided by designer/architect.

Main Level Floor Plan

LOWER LEVEL

3 CAR GARAGE OPTION

Upper Level Floor Plan

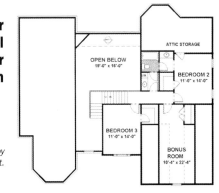

Copyright by designer/architect.

Plan #181102

Dimensions: 58' W x 58'4" D
Levels: 2
Square Footage: 2,265
Main Level Sq. Ft.: 1,371
Upper Level Sq. Ft.: 894
Bedrooms: 4
Bathrooms: 3½
Foundation: Full basement
Materials List Available: Yes
Price Category: E

Illustration provided by designer/architect.

Upper Level Floor Plan

Main Level Floor Plan

Copyright by designer/architect.

Images provided by designer/architect.

Plan #131026

Dimensions: 55'10" W x 41' D
Levels: 2
Square Footage: 2,796
Main Level Sq. Ft.: 1,481
Upper level Sq. Ft.: 1,315
Bedrooms: 4
Bathrooms: 2½
Foundation: Basement, crawl space, or slab
Materials List Available: Yes
Price Category: G

Handsome half rounds add to curb appeal.

Features:

• Ceiling Height: 8 ft.

• Library: This room features a 10-ft. ceiling with a bright bay window.

• Great Room: A 10-ft. ceiling adds to the spacious feeling of this room, while the corner fireplace gives it an intimate feeling. Sliding glass doors at the rear of the room open to the backyard.

• Dining Room: This formal room adjoins the great room, allowing guests and family to flow between the rooms, and it opens to the backyard through sliding glass doors.

• Breakfast Room: Turrets add a Victorian feeling to this room, which is just off the kitchen and overlooks the front porch.

• Master Suite: Privacy is assured in this suite, which is separated from the main part of the house. A compartmented bath and large walk-in closet add convenience to its beauty.

Master Bathroom

Family Room

Rear
Elevation

Upper Level Floor Plan

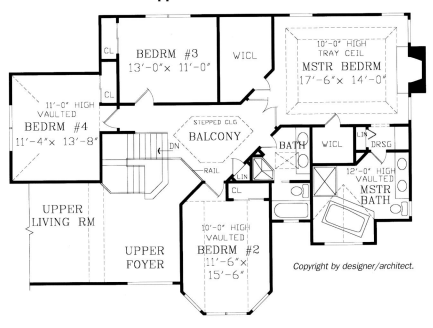

BEDRM #3
13'-0" x 11'-0"

CL

CL

WICL

10'-0" HIGH
TRAY CEIL
MSTR BEDRM
17'-6" x 14'-0"

11'-0" HIGH
VAULTED
BEDRM #4
11'-4" x 13'-8"

STEPPED CLG
BALCONY

DN

RAIL

BATH

WICL

LIN

LIN

DRSG

CL

12'-0" HIGH
VAULTED
MSTR
BATH

UPPER
LIVING RM

UPPER
FOYER

10'-0" HIGH
VAULTED
BEDRM #2
11'-6" x
15'-6"

Copyright by designer/architect.

Main Level Floor Plan

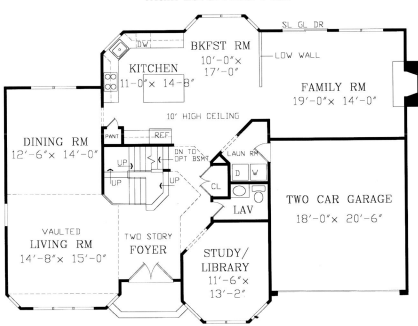

DW

BKFST RM
10'-0" x
17'-0"

SL GL DR

LOW WALL

KITCHEN
11'-0" x 14'-8"

FAMILY RM
19'-0" x 14'-0"

10' HIGH CEILING

DINING RM
12'-6" x 14'-0"

PANT

REF

UP

UP

UP

DN TO
OPT BSMT

LAUN RM

D

W

CL

LAV

TWO CAR GARAGE
18'-0" x 20'-6"

VAULTED
LIVING RM
14'-8" x 15'-0"

TWO STORY
FOYER

STUDY/
LIBRARY
11'-6" x
13'-2"

Illustration provided by designer/architect.

Plan #141015

Dimensions: 46' W x 36'8" D

Levels: 2

Square Footage: 2,350

Main Level Sq. Ft.: 1,155

Upper Level Sq. Ft.: 1,195

Bedrooms: 4

Bathrooms: 2½

Foundation: Basement

Materials List Available: Yes

Price Category: E

This home offers classic Victorian details combined with modern amenities.

Features:

• Ceiling Height: 9 ft. unless otherwise noted.

• Porch: Enjoy summer breezes on this large wraparound porch, with its classic turret corner.

• Family Room: This room has a fireplace and two sets of French doors. One set of doors leads to the porch; the other leads to a rear sun deck.

• Living Room: This large room at the front of the house is designed for formal entertaining.

• Kitchen: This convenient kitchen features an island and a writing desk.

• Master Bedroom: Enjoy the cozy sitting area in the turret corner. The bedroom offers access to a second story balcony.

• Laundry: The second-floor laundry means you won't have to haul clothing up and down stairs.

Main Level Floor Plan

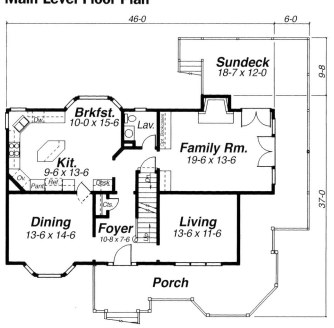

Upper Level Floor Plan

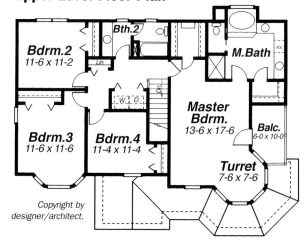

Copyright by designer/architect.

Plan #161038

Dimensions: 58'6" W x 49' D
Levels: 2
Square Footage: 2,209
Main Level Sq. Ft.: 1,542
Upper Level Sq. Ft.: 667
Bedrooms: 3
Bathrooms: 2½
Foundation: Slab
Materials List Available: No
Price Category: E

Images provided by designer/architect.

Brick trim, sidelights, and a transom window at the entry are a few of the many features that convey the elegance and style of this exciting home.

Features:

- **Great Room:** This great room is truly the centerpiece of this elegant home. The ceiling at the rear wall is 14 ft. and slopes forward to a second floor study loft that overlooks the magnificent fireplace and entertainment alcove. The high ceiling continues through the foyer, showcasing a deluxe staircase.

- **Kitchen:** This modern kitchen is designed for efficient work patterns and serves both the formal dining room and breakfast area.

- **Master Suite:** The highlight of this master suite is a wonderful whirlpool tub. Also included are two matching vanities and a large walk-in closet.

- **Bonus Room:** A bonus room above the garage completes this exciting home.

Rear Elevation

Main Level Floor Plan

Great Room 15'6" x 18'1"
high ceiling
Breakfast 11'7" x 12'0"
Laun.
hanging space
Bath
walk-in closet
Hall
walk-in pantry
Kitchen 11'9" x 11'
Master Bedroom 13' x 13'11"
Foyer
Dining Room 11' x 13'
Bath
Porch
Two-car Garage 20' x 21'
49'
58'6"

Copyright by designer/architect.

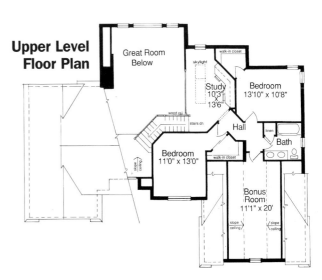

Upper Level Floor Plan

Great Room Below
skylight
walk-in closet
Study 10'3" x 13'6"
Bedroom 13'10" x 10'8"
wood rail
stairs dn
Hall
linen
Bath
Bedroom 11'0" x 13'0"
walk-in closet
slope ceiling
Bonus Room 11'1" x 20'
slope ceiling
slope ceiling

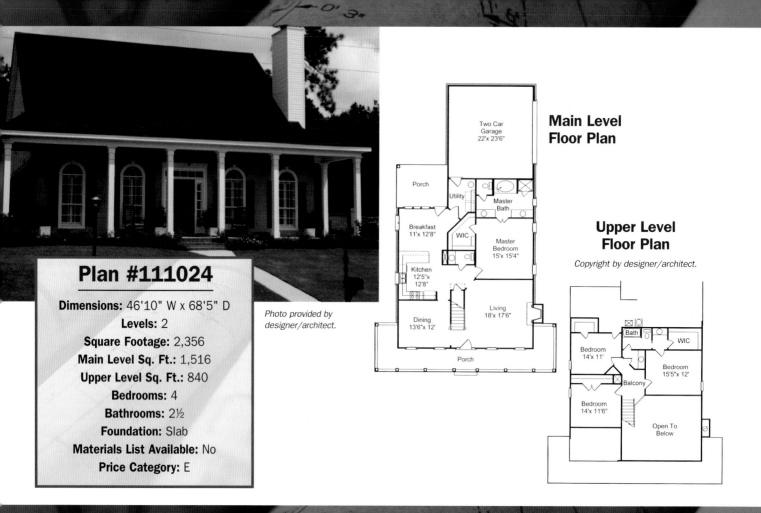

Plan #111024

Dimensions: 46'10" W x 68'5" D

Levels: 2

Square Footage: 2,356

Main Level Sq. Ft.: 1,516

Upper Level Sq. Ft.: 840

Bedrooms: 4

Bathrooms: 2½

Foundation: Slab

Materials List Available: No

Price Category: E

Photo provided by designer/architect.

Main Level Floor Plan

Upper Level Floor Plan

Copyright by designer/architect.

Two Car Garage 22'x 23'6"

Porch

Utility

Master Bath

Breakfast 11'x 12'8"

WIC

Master Bedroom 15'x 15'4"

Kitchen 12'5"x 12'8"

Living 18'x 17'6"

Dining 13'6"x 12'

Porch

Bedroom 14'x 11'

Bath

WIC

Bedroom 15'5"x 12'

Balcony

Bedroom 14'x 11'6"

Open To Below

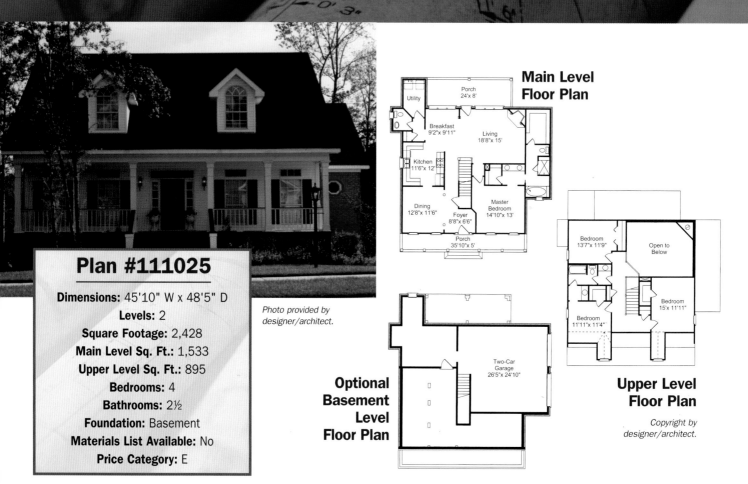

Plan #111025

Dimensions: 45'10" W x 48'5" D

Levels: 2

Square Footage: 2,428

Main Level Sq. Ft.: 1,533

Upper Level Sq. Ft.: 895

Bedrooms: 4

Bathrooms: 2½

Foundation: Basement

Materials List Available: No

Price Category: E

Photo provided by designer/architect.

Main Level Floor Plan

Utility

Porch 24'x 8'

Breakfast 9'2"x 9'11"

Living 18'8"x 15'

Kitchen 11'6"x 12'

Dining 12'8"x 11'6"

Foyer 8'8"x 6'6"

Master Bedroom 14'10"x 13'

Porch 35'10"x 5'

Optional Basement Level Floor Plan

Two-Car Garage 26'5"x 24'10"

Upper Level Floor Plan

Bedroom 13'7"x 11'9"

Open to Below

Bedroom 11'11"x 11'4"

Bedroom 15'x 11'11"

Copyright by designer/architect.

Main Level Floor Plan

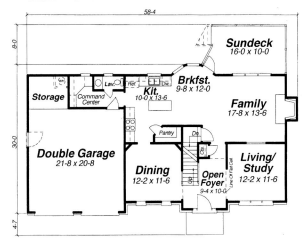

58-4

Sundeck
16-0 x 10-0

Storage

Command Center

Lav. Ref. Kit. Dw.

Brkfst.
9-8 x 12-0

Family
17-8 x 13-6

Double Garage
21-8 x 20-8

Pantry

Dining
12-2 x 11-6

Open Foyer
9-4 x 10-0

Living/ Study
12-2 x 11-6

30-0

8-0

4-7

Photo provided by designer/architect.

Upper Level Floor Plan

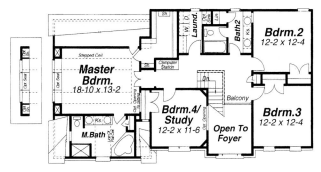

Stepped Ceil.

Master Bdrm.
18-10 x 13-2

Computer Station

W./D. Laund.

Bath2

Bdrm.2
12-2 x 12-4

M.Bath

Bdrm.4/ Study
12-2 x 11-6

Balcony

Open To Foyer

Bdrm.3
12-2 x 12-4

Copyright by designer/architect.

Plan #141031

Dimensions: 58'4" W x 30' D

Levels: 2

Square Footage: 2,367

Main Level Sq. Ft.: 1,025

Upper Level Sq. Ft.: 1,342

Bedrooms: 4

Bathrooms: 2½

Foundation: Basement

Materials List Available: No

Price Category: E

Main Level Floor Plan

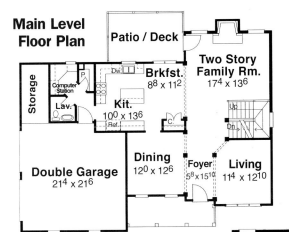

Patio / Deck

Storage

Computer Station

Lav.

Brkfst.
8^8 x 11^2

Two Story Family Rm.
17^4 x 13^6

Kit.
10^0 x 13^6

Ref.

Double Garage
21^4 x 21^6

Dining
12^0 x 12^6

Foyer
5^8 x 15^{10}

Living
11^4 x 12^{10}

Up

Dn

Photo provided by designer/architect.

Upper Level Floor Plan

M.Bath
Tray Ceil.

Bdrm.2
11^0 x 11^6
Opt. Vault W/ Plant Shelf

Bth.2

Two Story Family Rm.

Master Bdrm.
15^4 x 14^6
Tray Ceil.

Opt. Closet

Sitting
10^0 x 7^0

Bdrm.3
11^8 x 10^6
Opt. Vault W/ Plant Shelf

W./D. Laund.

Balcony

Opt. Vault W/ Plant Shelf

Open To Foyer

Bdrm.4
11^4 x 11^0

Copyright by designer/architect.

Plan #141032

Dimensions: 52' W x 44' D

Levels: 2

Square Footage: 2,476

Main Level Sq. Ft.: 1,160

Upper Level Sq. Ft.: 1,316

Bedrooms: 4

Bathrooms: 2½

Foundation: Basement

Materials List Available: Yes

Price Category: E

Photo provided by designer/architect.

Plan #121086

Dimensions: 55'4" W x 37'8" D

Levels: 2

Square Footage: 1,998

Main Level Sq. Ft.: 1,093

Upper Level Sq. Ft.: 905

Bedrooms: 3

Bathrooms: 2½

Foundation: Basement

Materials List Available: Yes

Price Category: D

You'll love the open design of this comfortable home if sunny, bright rooms make you happy.

Features:

• Entry: Walk into this two-story entry, and you're sure to admire the open staircase and balcony from the upper level.

• Dining Room: To the left of the entry, you'll see this dining room, with its special ceiling detail and built-in display cabinet.

• Living Room: Located immediately to the right, this living room features a charming bay window.

• Family Room: French doors from the living room open into this sunny space, where a handsome fireplace takes center stage.

• Kitchen: Combined with the breakfast area, this kitchen features an island cooktop, a large pantry, and a built-in desk.

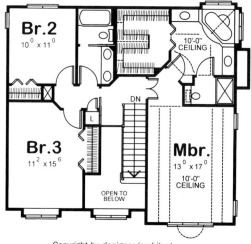

Main Level Floor Plan

RECYCLE

R

Eating Area
10⁰ x 11⁸

Family Room
13⁰ x 17⁰

D W P

SHELVES

O/M

CURIO

DN

Garage
19⁴ x 21⁰

Dining Room
11⁰ x 15⁰

UP

Living Room
13⁰ x 13⁸

COVERED PORCH

55'-4"

37'-8"

Upper Level Floor Plan

Br.2
10⁰ x 11⁰

10'-0" CEILING

DN

L

Br.3
11² x 15⁶

OPEN TO BELOW

Mbr.
13⁰ x 17⁰

10'-0" CEILING

Copyright by designer/architect.

Plan #121087

Dimensions: 50' W x 40' D
Levels: 2
Square Footage: 2,103
Main Level Sq. Ft.: 1,082
Upper Level Sq. Ft.: 1,021
Bedrooms: 4
Bathrooms: 2½
Foundation: Basement
Materials List Available: Yes
Price Category: D

You'll love the comfort and the unusual design details you'll find in this home.

Features:

- Entry: A T-shaped staircase frames this two-story entry, giving both visual interest and convenience.

- Family Room: Bookcases frame the lovely fireplace here, so you won't be amiss by decorating to create a special reading nook.

- Breakfast Area: Pass through the cased opening between the family room and this breakfast area, for convenience.

- Kitchen: Combined with the breakfast area, this kitchen features an island, pantry, and desk.

- Master Suite: On the upper floor, this suite has a walk-in closet and a bath with sunlit whirlpool tub, separate shower, and double vanity. A window seat makes the bedroom especially cozy, no matter what the outside weather.

Main Level Floor Plan

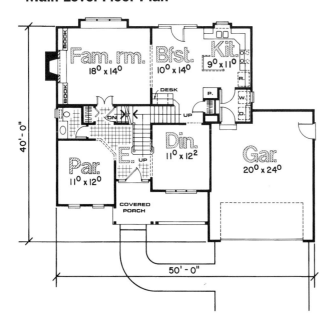

Upper Level Floor Plan

Plan #181072

Dimensions: 26' W x 28' D
Levels: 2
Square Footage: 1,456
Main Level Sq. Ft.: 728
Upper Level Sq. Ft.: 728
Bedrooms: 3
Bathrooms: 2
Foundation: Full basement
Materials List Available: Yes
Price Category: B

Illustration provided by designer/architect.

Main Level Floor Plan

Upper Level Floor Plan

Copyright by designer/architect.

Plan #181077

Dimensions: 38' W x 38' D
Levels: 2
Square Footage: 2,119
Main Level Sq. Ft.: 1,087
Upper Level Sq. Ft.: 1,032
Bedrooms: 4
Bathrooms: 2½
Foundation: Full basement
Materials List Available: Yes
Price Category: D

Illustration provided by designer/architect.

Main Level Floor Plan

Upper Level Floor Plan

Copyright by designer/architect.

Plan #151011

Dimensions: 59'6" W x 74'4" D
Levels: 2
Square Footage: 3,437
Main Level Sq. Ft.: 2,184
Upper Level Sq. Ft.: 1,253
Bedrooms: 5
Bathrooms: 4
Foundation: Crawl space, slab; optional basement or daylight basement
Price Category: G

Images provided by designer/architect.

Beauty, comfort, and convenience are yours in this luxurious, split-level home.

Main Level Features:

- Ceiling Height: 10 ft. unless otherwise noted.

- Master Suite: The 11-ft. pan ceiling sets the tone for this secluded area, with a lovely bay window that opens onto a rear porch, a pass-through fireplace to the great room, and a sitting room.

- Great Room: The pass-through fireplace makes this spacious room a cozy spot, while the French doors leading to a rear porch make it a perfect spot for entertaining.

- Dining Room: Gracious 8-in. columns set off the entrance to this room.

- Kitchen: An island bar provides an efficient work area that's fitted with a sink.

- Breakfast Room: Open to the kitchen, this room is defined by a bay window and a spiral staircase to the second floor.

- Laundry Room: Large enough to accommodate a folding table, this room can also be fitted with a swinging pet door.

Upper Level Features:

- Play Room: French doors in the children's playroom open onto a balcony where they can continue their games.

- Bedrooms: The 9-ft. ceilings on the second story make the rooms feel bright and airy.

Optional basement foundation or optional daylight basement foundation available for an additional $250.

Copyright by designer/architect.

**Main Level
Floor Plan**

**Upper Level
Floor Plan**

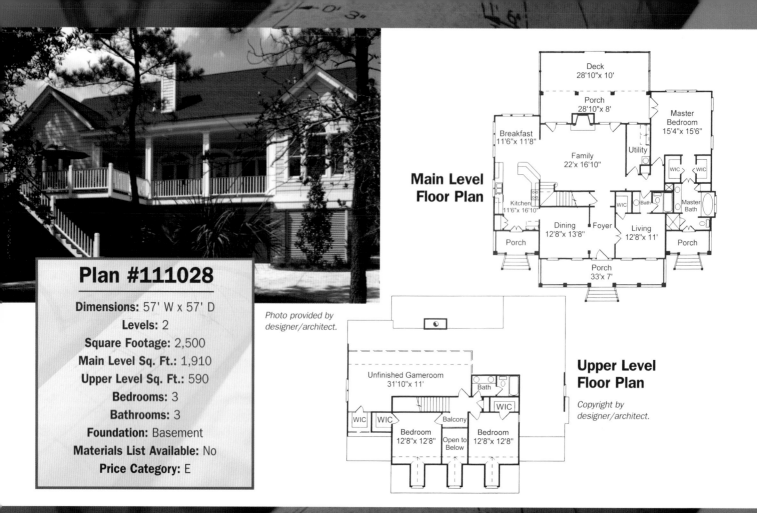

Plan #111028

Dimensions: 57' W x 57' D

Levels: 2

Square Footage: 2,500

Main Level Sq. Ft.: 1,910

Upper Level Sq. Ft.: 590

Bedrooms: 3

Bathrooms: 3

Foundation: Basement

Materials List Available: No

Price Category: E

Photo provided by designer/architect.

Main Level Floor Plan

Deck 28'10" x 10'
Porch 28'10" x 8'
Breakfast 11'6" x 11'8"
Family 22' x 16'10"
Master Bedroom 15'4" x 15'6"
Utility
WIC
WIC
Kitchen 11'6" x 16'10"
WIC
Bath
Master Bath
Dining 12'8" x 13'8"
Foyer
Living 12'8" x 11'
Porch
Porch
Porch 33' x 7'

Upper Level Floor Plan

Copyright by designer/architect.

Unfinished Gameroom 31'10" x 11'
Bath
WIC
WIC
WIC
Balcony
Bedroom 12'8" x 12'8"
Open to Below
Bedroom 12'8" x 12'8"

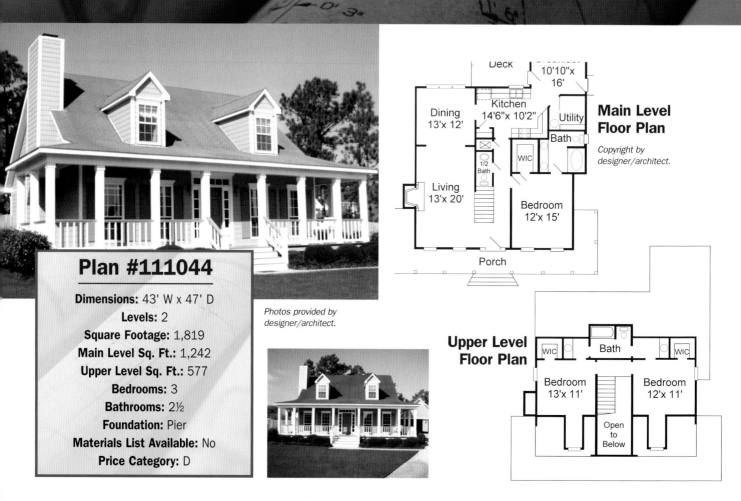

Plan #111044

Dimensions: 43' W x 47' D

Levels: 2

Square Footage: 1,819

Main Level Sq. Ft.: 1,242

Upper Level Sq. Ft.: 577

Bedrooms: 3

Bathrooms: 2½

Foundation: Pier

Materials List Available: No

Price Category: D

Photos provided by designer/architect.

Main Level Floor Plan

Copyright by designer/architect.

Deck
Breakfast 10'10" x 16'
Dining 13' x 12'
Kitchen 14'6" x 10'2"
Utility
Bath
WIC
1/2 Bath
Living 13' x 20'
Bedroom 12' x 15'
Porch

Upper Level Floor Plan

WIC
Bath
WIC
Bedroom 13' x 11'
Bedroom 12' x 11'
Open to Below

Plan #121082

Dimensions: 68'8" W x 60' D
Levels: 2
Square Footage: 2,932
Main Level Sq. Ft.: 2,084
Upper Level Sq. Ft.: 848
Bedrooms: 4
Bathrooms: 3½
Foundation: Basement
Materials List Available: Yes
Price Category: F

Photo provided by designer/architect.

Enjoy the spacious covered veranda that gives this house so much added charm.

Features:

- **Great Room:** A volume ceiling enhances the spacious feeling in this room, making it a natural gathering spot for friends and family. Transom-topped windows look onto the veranda, and French doors open to it.

- **Den:** French doors from the entry lead to this room, with its unusual ceiling detail, gracious fireplace, and transom-topped windows.

- **Hearth Room:** Three skylights punctuate the cathedral ceiling in this room, giving it an extra measure of light and warmth.

- **Kitchen:** This kitchen is a delight, thanks to its generous working and storage space.

Main Level Floor Plan

Upper Level Floor Plan

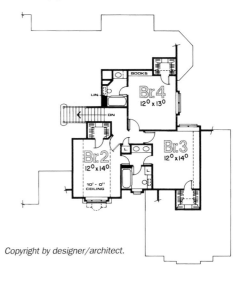

Copyright by designer/architect.

Plan #161017

Dimensions: 61' W x 37'6" D
Levels: 2
Square Footage: 2,653
Main Level Sq. Ft.: 1,365
Upper Level Sq. Ft.: 1,288
Bedrooms: 4
Bathrooms: 2½
Foundation: Slab
Materials List Available: No
Price Category: F

Images provided by designer/architect.

If a traditional look makes you feel comfortable, you'll love this spacious, family-friendly home.

Features:

• Family Room: Accessorize with cozy cushions to make the most of this sunken room. Windows flank the fireplace, adding warm, natural light. Doors leading to the rear deck make this room a family "headquarters."

• Living and Dining Rooms: These formal rooms open to each other, so you'll love hosting gatherings in this home.

• Kitchen: A handy pantry fits well with the traditional feeling of this home, and an island adds contemporary convenience.

• Master Suite: Relax in the whirlpool tub in your bath and enjoy the storage space in the two walk-in closets in the bedroom.

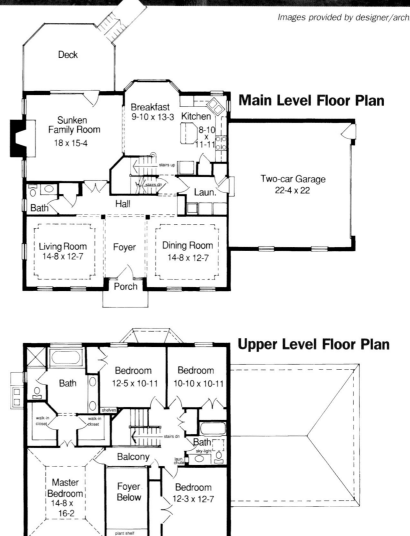

Main Level Floor Plan

Upper Level Floor Plan

Plan #271010

Dimensions: 47' W x 43' D
Levels: 2
Square Footage: 1,724
Main Level Sq. Ft.: 922
Upper Level Sq. Ft.: 802
Bedrooms: 3
Bathrooms: 2½
Foundation: Basement
Materials List Available: Yes
Price Category: C

Photo provided by designer/architect.

This traditional home features a wide assortment of windows that flood the interior with light and accentuate the open, airy atmosphere.

Features:

• Entry: A beautiful Palladian window enlivens this two-story-high space.

• Great Room: A second Palladian window brightens this primary gathering area, which is topped by a vaulted ceiling.

• Dining Room: Sliding glass doors connect this formal area to a large backyard deck.

• Kitchen: Centrally located, this kitchen includes a boxed-out window over the sink, providing a nice area for plants.

• Family/Breakfast Area: Smartly joined, this open space hosts a snack bar and a wet bar, in addition to a warming fireplace.

• Master Suite: Located on the upper floor, the master bedroom boasts corner windows, a large walk-in closet, and a split bath with a dual-sink vanity.

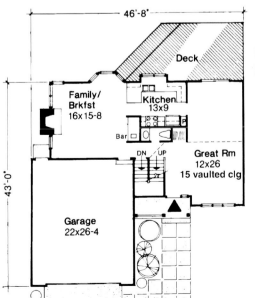

Main Level Floor Plan

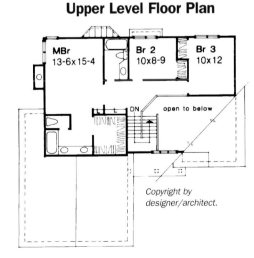

Upper Level Floor Plan

Copyright by designer/architect.

Upper Level Floor Plan

br 3 15 x 12

br 2 15 x 13

to attic

a/c

shv

br 4 13 x 12

open to lower level

balc

porch 34 x 6

garage 22 x 22

eating 10 x 10

living 20 x 19

util

sto 10 x 8

porch

mbr 20 x 12

kit 14x13

cab

shv

a/c

up

dining 13 x 12

sitting

foyer

porch 34 x 6

Main Level Floor Plan

Copyright by designer/architect.

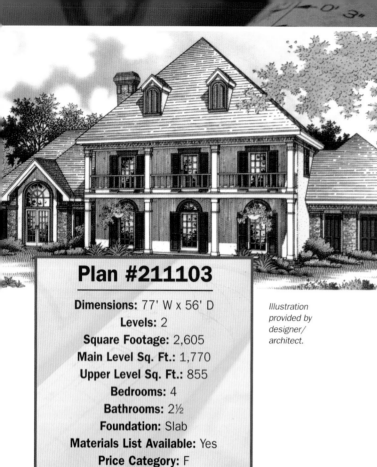

Plan #211103

Dimensions: 77' W x 56' D

Levels: 2

Square Footage: 2,605

Main Level Sq. Ft.: 1,770

Upper Level Sq. Ft.: 855

Bedrooms: 4

Bathrooms: 2½

Foundation: Slab

Materials List Available: Yes

Price Category: F

Illustration provided by designer/ architect.

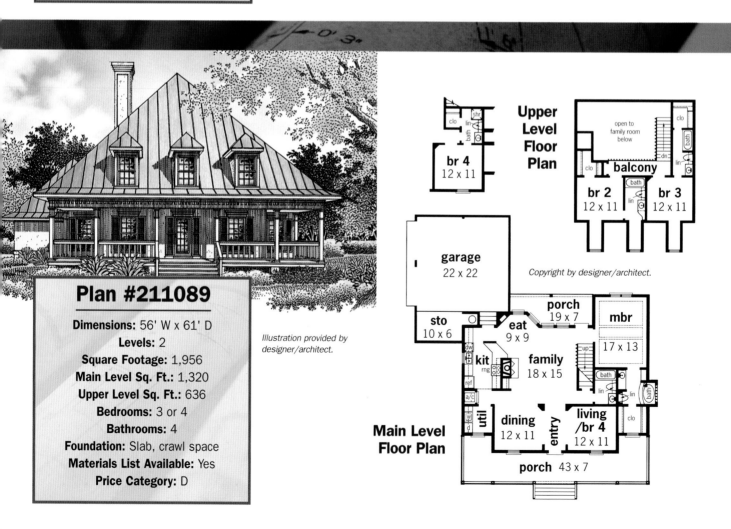

Upper Level Floor Plan

clo

bath

shr

lin

br 4 12 x 11

open to family room below

clo

clo

dn

bath

balcony

br 2 12 x 11

bath

lin

br 3 12 x 11

Copyright by designer/architect.

garage 22 x 22

sto 10 x 6

porch 19 x 7

mbr 17 x 13

eat 9 x 9

kit

family 18 x 15

up

bath

lin

dw

ref

a/c

util

w d

dining 12 x 11

entry

living /br 4 12 x 11

clo

porch 43 x 7

Main Level Floor Plan

Plan #211089

Dimensions: 56' W x 61' D

Levels: 2

Square Footage: 1,956

Main Level Sq. Ft.: 1,320

Upper Level Sq. Ft.: 636

Bedrooms: 3 or 4

Bathrooms: 4

Foundation: Slab, crawl space

Materials List Available: Yes

Price Category: D

Illustration provided by designer/architect.

Main Level Floor Plan

Laun.

Breakfast
11'-6" x 10'-1"

Great Room
16'-0" x 16'-4"

Garage
21'-0" x 21'-4"

Kitchen
10'1"x11'9"

Dining Room
13'-2" x 11'-0"

Foyer

Bath

Porch

50'-6"

38'-0"

Bath

Master Bedroom
12'-0" x 16'-8"

SKYLIGHT

WALK-IN CLOSET

Bonus Room
21'-0" x 14'-8"

Bedroom
11'-1" x 10'-2"

WALK-IN CLOSET

Hall

Bath

Bedroom
13'-2" x 10'-8"

COMPUTER

Upper Level Floor Plan

Copyright by designer/architect.

Plan #161043

Dimensions: 50'6" W x 38' D
Levels: 2
Square Footage: 1,856
Main Level Sq. Ft.: 980
Upper Level Sq. Ft.: 876
Bedrooms: 3
Bathrooms: 2½
Foundation: Slab
Materials List Available: Yes
Price Category: D

Images provided by designer/architect.

Rear Elevation

Rear Elevation

Patio

Great Room
15'2" x 18'2"

Breakfast
11'10" x 9'10"

Laun.

Dressing

Kitchen
11'10" x 11'11"

pantry

Bath

Master Bedroom
13' x 17'

Foyer

Dining Room
11' x 13'

Two Car Garage
20' x 21'

Porch

49'

Main Level Floor Plan

58'6"

Copyright by designer/architect.

Great Room Below

walk-in closet

Loft
10'4" x 13'8"

Bedroom
13'1" x 10'8"

Down

Bedroom
11' x 15'4"

walk in closet

Bath

Bonus
11'1" x 17'3"

Sloped Ceiling

Upper Level Floor Plan

Plan #161046

Dimensions: 58'6" W x 49' D
Levels: 2
Square Footage: 2,338
Main Level Sq. Ft.: 1,633
Upper Level Sq. Ft.: 705
Bedrooms: 4
Bathrooms: 2½
Foundation: Slab
Materials List Available: Yes
Price Category: E

Images provided by designer/architect.

Rear Elevation

Main Level Floor Plan

MBR.
TRAY CEILING
13'8" X 15'6"

DIN.
VAULTED
18'4" X 9'4"

KIT.
VAULTED

LIV.
VAULTED CEILING
18'4" X 15'8"

LAUNDRY CHUTE

BR. #2
10'4" X 10'0"

BR. #3
10'4" X 13'0"

E.

Images provided by designer/architect.

Plan #221024

Dimensions: 43' W x 40' D

Levels: 2

Square Footage: 1,732

Main Level Sq. Ft.: 1,289

Upper Level Sq. Ft.: 544

Bedrooms: 3

Bathrooms: 2½

Foundation: Basement

Materials List Available: No

Price Category: C

Upper Level Floor Plan

FAM.RM.
21'0" X 13'6"

UNFINISHED
18'0" X 29'8"

2 CAR GAR.
21'8" X 19'4"

FURN

Copyright by designer/architect.

43'-0"

40'-0"

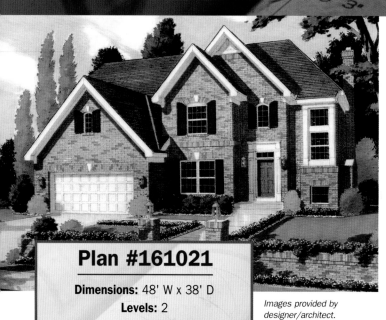

Plan #161021

Dimensions: 48' W x 38' D

Levels: 2

Square Footage: 1,897

Main Level Sq. Ft.: 1,036

Upper Level Sq. Ft.: 861

Bedrooms: 3

Bathrooms: 2½

Foundation: Slab

Materials List Available: No

Price Category: D

Images provided by designer/architect.

Main Level Floor Plan

Laun.
hanging space

Bath

Kitchen
10'6" x 13'6"

Breakfast
10'8" x 11'

Great Room
14'10" x 17'1"

high ceiling

pantry

Two-car Garage
20' x 21'

furniture alcove

Dining Room
11' x 13'7"

Foyer

wood rail
stairs up

stairs dn.

French doors w/ arched window above

48'

38'

Rear Elevation

walk-in closet

Master Bedroom
12' x 14'11"

Bedroom
10'6" x 11'2"

Great Room Below

Bath

Bath

computer desk

Balcony

Bedroom
11' x 12'

stairs dn.

window seat

Upper Level Floor Plan

Copyright by designer/architect.

Main Level Floor Plan

- Laun. 9'10" x 8'5"
- Bath
- Hall
- Kitchen
- Breakfast 19'7" x 12' 3"
- French Doors w/ arched window
- French Doors
- Great Room 15'8" x 16'5" – high ceiling
- Master Bedroom 13'8" x 14'8"
- slope ceiling
- Two-car Garage 19'10" x 21'4"
- Dining Room 11' x 15'9"
- butler's pantry
- Foyer
- Porch
- Hall
- Dressing
- Court Yard
- stairs up
- walk-in closet
- 61'
- 41'8"

Images provided by designer/architect.

Plan #161039

Dimensions: 61' W x 41'8" D

Levels: 2

Square Footage: 2,320

Main Level Sq. Ft.: 1,595

Upper Level Sq. Ft.: 725

Bedrooms: 4

Bathrooms: 2½

Foundation: Slab

Materials List Available: Yes

Price Category: E

Upper Level Floor Plan

Copyright by designer/architect.

- Bedroom 10'8" x 13'5"
- Bedroom 10'9" x 10'
- Great Room Below
- slope ceiling
- Hall
- linen / linen
- Bath
- Balcony
- Bedroom 11' x 11'2"
- Porch
- slope ceiling / slope ceiling

Plan #241010

Dimensions: 56' W x 44'5" D

Levels: 2

Square Footage: 2,044

Main Level Sq. Ft.: 1,203

Upper Level Sq. Ft.: 841

Bedrooms: 3

Bathrooms: 2½

Foundation: Slab

Materials List Available: No

Price Category: D

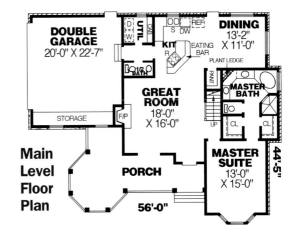

Main Level Floor Plan

- DOUBLE GARAGE 20'-0" X 22'-7"
- STORAGE
- UTIL
- DW / W / D
- REF
- KIT
- EATING BAR
- DINING 13'-2" X 11'-0"
- PLANT LEDGE
- BATH
- GREAT ROOM 18'-0" X 16'-0"
- F/P
- UP
- MASTER BATH
- CL / CL
- MASTER SUITE 13'-0" X 15'-0"
- PORCH
- 56'-0"
- 44'-5"

Images provided by designer/architect.

Upper Level Floor Plan

Copyright by designer/architect.

- CL
- BEDR'M-2 11'-9" X 10'-9"
- BATH
- CL
- BEDR'M-3 12'-0" X 12'-7"
- HALL
- DN
- PLAYROOM 18'-0" X 14'-0"
- CL

Plan #271012

Dimensions: 48' W x 30' D
Levels: 2
Square Footage: 1,359
Main Level Sq. Ft.: 668
Upper Level Sq. Ft.: 691
Bedrooms: 3
Bathrooms: 2½
Foundation: Basement
Materials List Available: Yes
Price Category: B

Photo provided by designer/architect.

This traditional home blends an updated exterior with a thoroughly modern interior.

Features:

- **Living Room:** This sunny, vaulted gathering room offers a handsome fireplace and open access to the adjoining dining room.

- **Dining Room:** Equally suited to intimate family gatherings and larger dinner parties, this space includes access to a spacious backyard deck.

- **Kitchen/Breakfast Nook:** Smartly joined, these two rooms are just perfect for speedy weekday mornings and lazy weekend breakfasts.

- **Master Suite:** A skylighted staircase leads to this upper-floor masterpiece, which includes a private bath, a walk-in closet, and bright, boxed-out window arrangement.

- **Secondary Bedrooms:** One of these is actually a loft/bedroom conversion, which makes it suitable for expansion space as your family grows.

Main Level Floor Plan

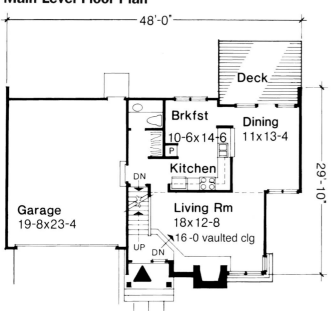

Upper Level Floor Plan

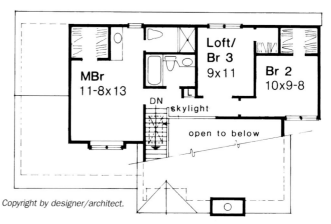

Copyright by designer/architect.

Photo provided by designer/architect.

Plan #271027

Dimensions: 61' W x 44' D
Levels: 2
Square Footage: 2,463
Main Level Sq. Ft.: 1,380
Upper Level Sq. Ft.: 1,083
Bedrooms: 4
Bathrooms: 2½
Foundation: Basement
Materials List Available: Yes
Price Category: D

This post-modern design uses half-round transom windows and a barrel-vaulted porch to lend elegance to its facade.

Features:

• Living Room: A vaulted ceiling and a striking fireplace enhance this formal gathering space.

• Dining Room: Introduced from the living room by square columns, this formal dining room is just steps from the kitchen.

• Kitchen: Thoroughly modern in its design, this walk-through kitchen includes an island cooktop and a large pantry. Nearby, a sunny, bayed breakfast area offers sliding-glass-door access to an angled backyard deck.

• Family Room: Columns provide an elegant preface to this fun gathering spot, which sports a vaulted ceiling and easy access to the deck.

• Master suite: A vaulted ceiling crowns this luxurious space, which includes a private bath and bright windows.

Main Level Floor Plan

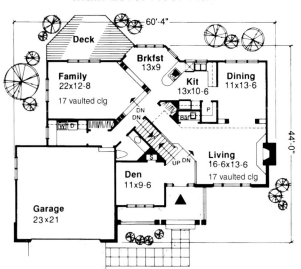

Upper Level Floor Plan

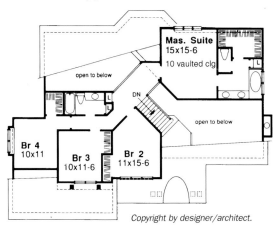

Copyright by designer/architect.

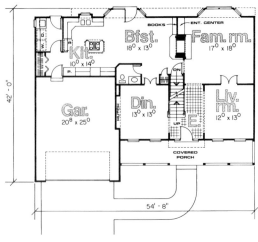

Main Level Floor Plan

Kit. 10⁰ x 14⁰

Bfst. 18⁰ x 13⁰

Fam. rm. 17⁰ x 18⁰

BOOKS

ENT. CENTER

Gar. 20⁸ x 25⁰

Din. 13⁰ x 13⁰

Liv. rm. 12⁰ x 13⁰

E

UP

HUTCH

42'-0"

54'-8"

COVERED PORCH

Photo provided by designer/architect.

Upper Level Floor Plan

Mbr. 14⁰ x 16⁰
10'-0" CLG.
9'-0" CEILING

WHIRLPOOL   SKYLIGHT

Br. 2 12⁰ x 13⁰

LINEN

DN

Br. 4 12⁰ x 12⁸

Br. 3 12⁰ x 13⁰

OPEN TO BELOW

PLANT SHELF

Copyright by designer/architect.

Plan #121028

Dimensions: 54'8" W x 42' D
Levels: 2
Square Footage: 2,644
Main Level Sq. Ft.: 1,366
Upper Level Sq. Ft.: 1,278
Bedrooms: 4
Bathrooms: 2½
Foundation: Basement
Materials List Available: Yes
Price Category: F

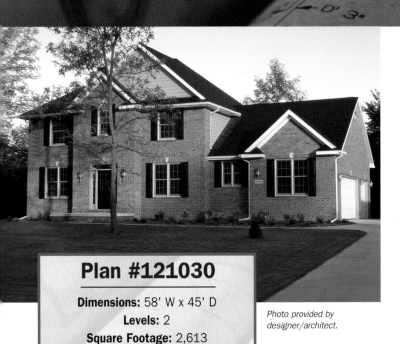

Bfst. 11⁰ x 11⁰

SNACK BAR

RECYCLE

Fam. Rm. 18⁰ x 15⁰

Kit. 11⁸ x 12⁰

DESK   P.

W. D.

R.

WET BAR

SEAT

DN

UP

OPTIONAL COMPUTER AREA

Liv. 14⁰ x 11⁰

E.

Din. 14⁰ x 11⁰

Gar. 21⁸ x 29⁴

45'-0"

STOOP

58'-0"

Main Level Floor Plan

Photo provided by designer/architect.

Upper Level Floor Plan

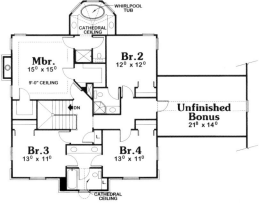

WHIRLPOOL TUB

CATHEDRAL CEILING

Mbr. 15⁰ x 15⁰
9'-0" CEILING

Br. 2 12⁰ x 12⁰

DN

Unfinished Bonus 21⁸ x 14⁰

Br. 3 13⁰ x 11⁰

Br. 4 13⁰ x 11⁰

L

CATHEDRAL CEILING

Copyright by designer/architect.

Plan #121030

Dimensions: 58' W x 45' D
Levels: 2
Square Footage: 2,613
Main Level Sq. Ft.: 1,333
Upper Level Sq. Ft.: 1,280
Bedrooms: 4
Bathrooms: 2½
Foundation: Basement
Materials List Available: Yes
Price Category: F

Plan #161016

Dimensions: 59'4" W x 58'8" D
Levels: 2
Square Footage: 2,101
Main Level Sq. Ft.: 1,626
Upper Level Sq. Ft.: 475
Bedrooms: 3
Bathrooms: 2½
Foundation: Basement
Materials List Available: Yes
Price Category: D

Features:

- **Great Room:** Made for relaxing and entertaining, the great room is sunken to set it off from the rest of the house. A balcony from the second floor looks down into this spacious area, making it easy to keep track of the kids while they are playing.

- **Kitchen:** Convenience marks this well laid-out kitchen where you'll love to cook for guests and for family.

- **Master Bedroom:** A vaulted ceiling complements the unusual octagonal shape

of the master bedroom. Located on the first floor, this room allows some privacy from the second floor bedrooms. It is also ideal for anyone who no longer wishes to climb stairs to reach a bedroom.

Rear Elevation

You'll love the exciting roofline that sets this elegant home apart from its neighbors as well as the embellished, solid look that declares how well-designed it is—from the inside to the exterior.

Main Level Floor Plan

Deck

Breakfast 9-2 x 16

Sunken Great Room 16-10 x 21

Kitchen 8 x 13-4

Bath

Walk-in closet

Dining Room 16 x 11-8

Foyer

Master Bedroom 14 x 17-4

Bath

Slope ceiling   Slope ceiling

Hall

Laundry

Two-car Garage 21 x 20-8

58'-8"

59'-4"

Copyright by designer/architect.

Upper Level Floor Plan

Bedroom 15x 10-8

Great Room Below

Bath

Bedroom 14x 10-6

Foyer Below

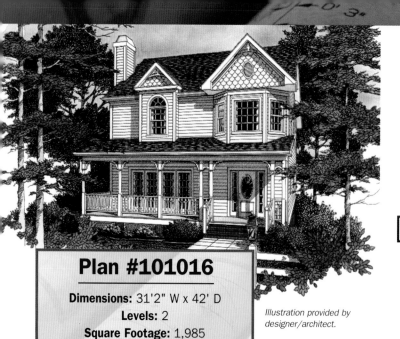

Plan #101016

Dimensions: 31'2" W x 42' D

Levels: 2

Square Footage: 1,985

Main Level Sq. Ft.: 1,009

Upper Level Sq. Ft.: 976

Bedrooms: 3

Bathrooms: 2½

Foundation: Slab, crawl space, or basement

Materials List Available: No

Price Category: D

Illustration provided by designer/architect.

Main Level Floor Plan

DECK
30'-6" x 11'-7"

BRKFST

DINING
14'-8" x 12'-8"

KITCHEN
15'-0" x 17'-0"

42'-0"

FAMILY
18'-8" x 16'-0"

ENTRY
7'-11" x 15'-6"

UP

PORCH
30'-6" x 7'-7"

◀ 31'-2" ▶

Upper Level Floor Plan

Copyright by designer/architect.

TRAY CEILING

MASTER BDRM
16'-4" x 15'-0"

D W

DN

BEDROOM 2
12'-0" x 12'-8"

BEDROOM 3
12'-8" x 12'-0"

WINDOW SEAT

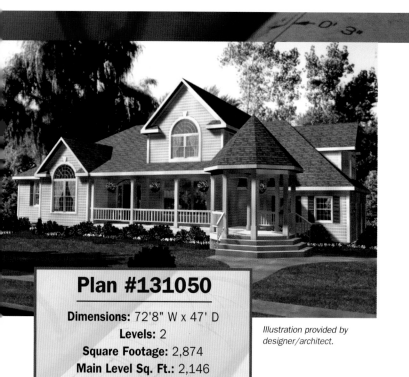

Plan #131050

Dimensions: 72'8" W x 47' D

Levels: 2

Square Footage: 2,874

Main Level Sq. Ft.: 2,146

Upper Level Sq. Ft.: 728

Bedrooms: 4

Bathrooms: 3

Foundation: Crawl space, slab, or basement

Materials List Available: Yes

Price Category: G

Illustration provided by designer/architect.

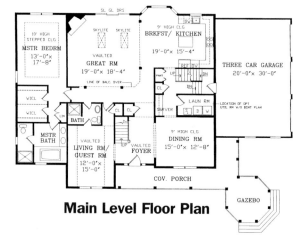

SL GL DRS

10' HIGH STEPPED CLG

MSTR BEDRM
13'-0" x 17'-8"

SKYLITE SKYLITE

VAULTED
GREAT RM
19'-0" x 18'-4"

9' HIGH CLG
BRKFST/ KITCHEN
19'-0" x 15'-4"

THREE CAR GARAGE
20'-0" x 30'-0"

WICL

WICL

LINE OF BALC. OVER

BATH

LIN

UP

DN

LAUN RM

LOCATION OF OPT. UTIL RM W/O BSMT PLAN

MSTR BATH

VAULTED
LIVING RM/
GUEST RM
12'-0" x 15'-0"

VAULTED
FOYER

9' HIGH CLG
DINING RM
15'-0" x 12'-8"

COV. PORCH

GAZEBO

Main Level Floor Plan

Upper Level Floor Plan

Copyright by designer/architect.

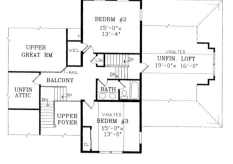

BEDRM #2
15'-0" x 13'-4"

UPPER GREAT RM

WICL

LIN

VAULTED
UNFIN. LOFT
19'-0" x 16'-0"

DN

BALCONY

RAIL

BATH

UNFIN ATTIC

DN

UPPER FOYER

VAULTED
BEDRM #3
15'-0" x 13'-0"

Main Level Floor Plan

Patio

Family
19-7x13-7

Brk
9-9x
13-7

Kit
13-6x13-7
vaulted

W
D

36'-0"

56'-0"

Living
13-4x13-6

Dn

Up

Dining
12-1x12-11

Garage
19-8x21-6

Porch

Images provided by designer/architect.

vaulted

Br 3
12-1x11-0

Upper Level Floor Plan

Copyright by designer/architect.

MBr
15-0x17-0

Dn

Br 2
12-1x10-4

Plan #321043

Dimensions: 56' W x 36' D

Levels: 2

Square Footage: 2,401

Main Level Sq. Ft.: 1,355

Upper Level Sq. Ft.: 1,046

Bedrooms: 3

Bathrooms: 2½

Foundation: Basement

Materials List Available: Yes

Price Category: E

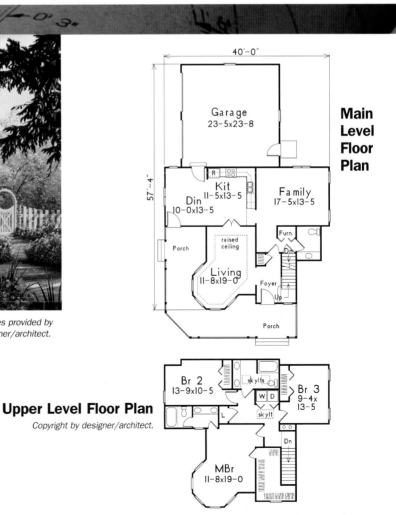

40'-0"

Garage
23-5x23-8

Main Level Floor Plan

57'-4"

Kit
11-5x13-5

Din
10-0x13-5

Family
17-5x13-5

R

Furn.

Porch

raised ceiling

Dn

Living
11-8x19-0

Foyer

Up

Porch

Images provided by designer/architect.

Br 2
13-9x10-5

skylts

W D

Br 3
9-4x
13-5

skylt

L

Upper Level Floor Plan

Copyright by designer/architect.

Dn

MBr
11-8x19-0

Plan #321056

Dimensions: 40' W x 57'4" D

Levels: 2

Square Footage: 2,050

Main Level Sq. Ft.: 1,028

Upper Level Sq. Ft.: 1,022

Bedrooms: 3

Bathrooms: 2½

Foundation: Basement

Materials List Available: Yes

Price Category: D

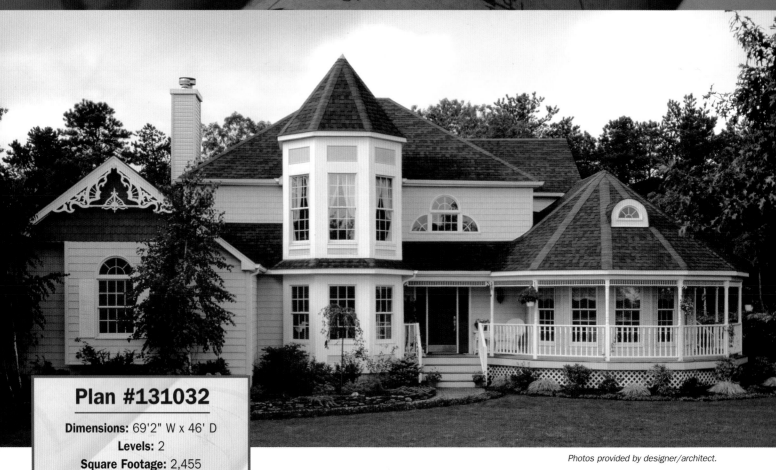

Plan #131032

Dimensions: 69'2" W x 46' D
Levels: 2
Square Footage: 2,455
Main Level Sq. Ft.: 1,499
Upper Level Sq. Ft.: 956
Bedrooms: 4
Bathrooms: 3
Foundation: Crawl space, slab, or basement
Materials List Available: Yes
Price Category: F

Photos provided by designer/architect.

If you love Victorian styling, you'll be charmed by the ornate, rounded front porch and the two-story bay that distinguish this home.

Features:

• Living Room: You'll love the 13-ft. ceiling in this room, as well as the panoramic view it gives of the front porch and yard.

• Kitchen: Sunlight streams into this room, where an angled island with a cooktop eases both prepping and cooking.

• Breakfast Room: This room shares an eating bar with the kitchen, making it easy for the family to congregate while the family chef is cooking.

• Guest Room: Use this lovely room on the first level as a home office or study if you wish.

• Master Suite: The dramatic bayed sitting area with a high ceiling has an octagonal shape that you'll adore, and the amenities in the private bath will soothe you at the end of a busy day.

Rear View

Upper Level Floor Plan

[Floor plan showing:]
- MSTR BATH
- WICL
- BEDRM #3 11'-0" x 11'-4"
- BATH
- BEDRM #2 10'-0" x 13'-6"
- LIN
- LIN
- CL
- CL
- BALC.
- DN
- MSTR BEDRM 20'-8" x 14'-6"
- UPPER FOYER
- PLANT LEDGE
- TRAY CLG. SITTING AREA 10'-4" x 8'-0"

Copyright by designer/architect.

Dining Room

Main Level Floor Plan

[Floor plan showing:]
- SUNKEN FAMILY RM 21'-4" x 15'-0"
- DN
- BKFST RM 9'-0" x 14'-0"
- KITCHEN 11'-0" x 14'-0"
- DW
- OV
- VAULTED DINING RM 13'-8" x 11'-0"
- DN TO OPT BSMT
- UP
- REF
- PANT
- BATH
- CL
- HIGH CEIL FOYER
- WET BAR
- UP
- VAULTED LIVING RM 15'-8" x 16'-4"
- W
- D
- UTIL
- LAUN RM
- STOR
- DEN/ GUEST RM 13'-4" x 11'-8"
- COV. PORCH
- TWO CAR GARAGE 20'-0" x 20'-6"
- COV. PORCH

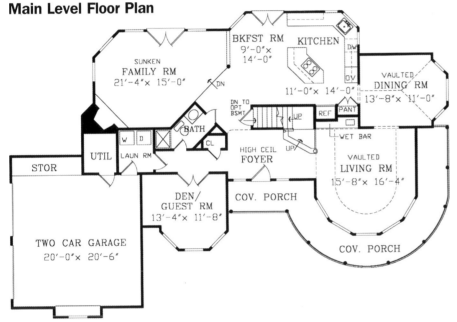

Living Room

Kitchen

Breakfast

Foyer

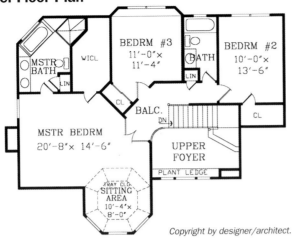

Plan #341011

Dimensions: 50' W x 58'4" D

Levels: 2

Square Footage: 2,560

Main Level Sq. Ft.: 1,387

Upper Level Sq. Ft.: 1,173

Bedrooms: 4

Bathrooms: 3½

Foundation: Crawl space, slab, or basement

Materials List Available: Yes

Price Category: E

Images provided by designer/architect.

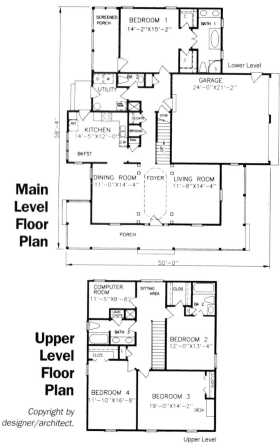

Main Level Floor Plan

Upper Level Floor Plan

Copyright by designer/architect.

Plan #341020

Dimensions: 62' W x 44'6" D

Levels: 2

Square Footage: 2,614

Main Level Sq. Ft.: 1,334

Upper Level Sq. Ft.: 1,280

Bedrooms: 3

Bathrooms: 2½

Foundation: Crawl space, slab, or basement

Materials List Available: Yes

Price Category: F

Images provided by designer/architect.

Main Level Floor Plan

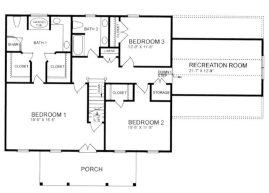

Upper Level Floor Plan

Copyright by designer/architect.

Plan #271083

Dimensions: 28' W x 54' D

Levels: 2

Square Footage: 1,690

Main Level Sq. Ft.: 810

Upper Level Sq. Ft.: 880

Bedrooms: 3

Bathrooms: 2½

Foundation: Daylight basement, crawl space

Materials List Available: Yes

Price Category: C

Images provided by designer/architect.

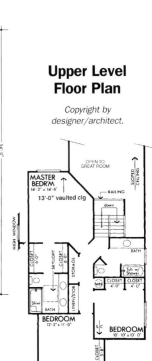

Upper Level Floor Plan

Copyright by designer/architect.

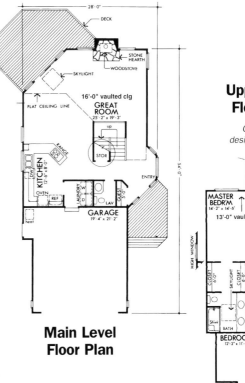

Main Level Floor Plan

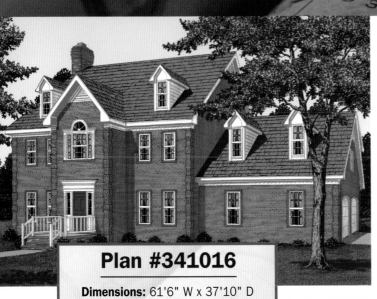

Plan #341016

Dimensions: 61'6" W x 37'10" D

Levels: 2

Square Footage: 2,630

Main Level Sq. Ft.: 1,124

Upper Level Sq. Ft.: 1,506

Bedrooms: 3

Bathrooms: 2½

Foundation: Crawl space, slab or basement

Materials List Available: Yes

Price Category: F

Images provided by designer/architect.

Main Level Floor Plan

Upper Level Floor Plan

Copyright by designer/architect.

**Main Level
Floor Plan**

72'-0"

36'-0"

GARAGE
31'-8"x21'-4"

KITCHEN
9'-6"x13'-4"

DINETTE
11'-0"x11'-4"
8' CEILING

FAMILY RM
16'-6"x13'-4"
9' CEILING

DINING
12'-4"x13'-4"
8' CEILING

FOYER

LIVING RM
13'-4"x11'-4"
8' CEILING

*Images provided by
designer/architect.*

**Upper Level
Floor Plan**

BEDRM 3
12'-4"x11'-0"
8' CEILING

BEDRM 4
11'-8"x9'-4"
8' CEILINGS

DN

BEDRM 2
9'-0"x10'-4"
8' CEILING

MSTR SUITE
16'-4"x12'-4"
9'-4' TRAY CLG

*Copyright by
designer/architect.*

Plan #271068

Dimensions: 72' W x 36' D

Levels: 2

Square Footage: 2,214

Main Level Sq. Ft.: 1,150

Upper Level Sq. Ft.: 1,064

Bedrooms: 4

Bathrooms: 2½

Foundation: Basement

Materials List Available: No

Price Category: E

37'-8"

38'-8"

DECK

MASTER BED.
14'-0" x 12'-4"

KIT
11'-0" x 9'-0"

DINING
10'-0" x 12'-4"
12'-0" clg

CLERESTORY
ABOVE

GARAGE
18'-4" x 18'-4"

UP

LIVING
13'-0" x 15'-8"
17'-0" vaulted clg

**Main
Level
Floor
Plan**

*Images provided by
designer/architect.*

LOFT/
BDRM 3
12'-0" x 12'-4"

BDRM 2
9'-8" x 12'-8"

DN

OPEN TO BELOW

**Upper Level
Floor Plan**

*Copyright by
designer/architect.*

Plan #271022

Dimensions: 37'8" W x 58'8" D

Levels: 2

Square Footage: 1,317

Main Level Sq. Ft.: 894

Upper Level Sq. Ft.: 423

Bedrooms: 2

Bathrooms: 2

Foundation: Basement

Materials List Available: Yes

Price Category: B

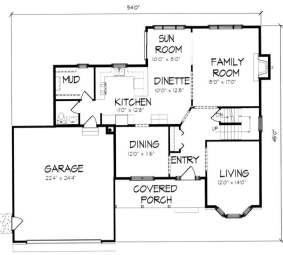

Plan #271062

Dimensions: 54' W x 45' D

Levels: 2

Square Footage: 2,356

Main Level Sq. Ft.: 1,222

Upper Level Sq. Ft.: 1,134

Bedrooms: 4

Bathrooms: 2½

Foundation: Daylight basement

Materials List Available: No

Price Category: E

Images provided by designer/architect.

Main Level Floor Plan

Upper Level Floor Plan

Copyright by designer/architect.

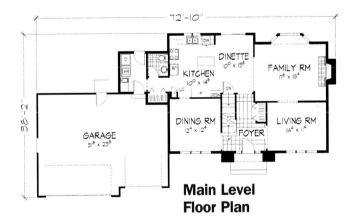

Plan #271066

Dimensions: 72'10" W x 38'2" D

Levels: 2

Square Footage: 2,249

Main Level Sq. Ft.: 1,209

Upper Level Sq. Ft.: 1,040

Bedrooms: 4

Bathrooms: 2½

Foundation: Basement or crawl space

Materials List Available: No

Price Category: E

Images provided by designer/architect.

Main Level Floor Plan

Upper Level Floor Plan

Copyright by designer/architect.

Plan #271030

Dimensions: 56' W x 45' D
Levels: 2
Square Footage: 1,926
Main Level Sq. Ft.: 1,490
Upper Level Sq. Ft.: 436
Bedrooms: 3
Bathrooms: 2½
Foundation: Basement
Materials List Available: Yes
Price Category: D

Photo provided by designer/architect.

This traditional home's main-floor master suite is hard to resist, with its inviting window seat and delightful bath.

Features:

- Master Suite: Just off from the entry foyer, this luxurious oasis is entered through double doors, and offers an airy vaulted ceiling, plus a private bath that includes a separate tub and shower, dual-sink vanity, and walk-in closet.

- Great Room: This space does it all in style, with a breathtaking wall of windows and a charming fireplace.

- Kitchen: A cooktop island makes dinnertime tasks a breeze. You'll also love the roomy pantry. The adjoining breakfast room, with its deck access and built-in desk, is sure to be a popular hangout for the teens.

- Secondary Bedrooms: Two additional bedrooms reside on the upper floor and allow the younger family members a measure of desired—and necessary—privacy.

Main Level Floor Plan

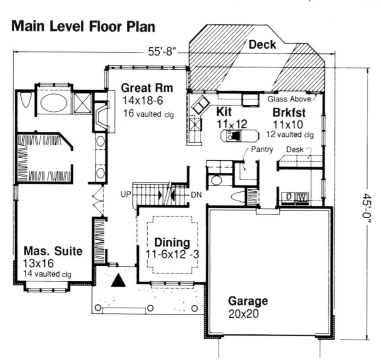

Upper Level Floor Plan

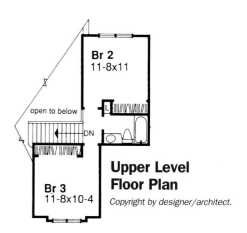

Copyright by designer/architect.

Plan #311003

Dimensions: 70'10" W x 65'4" D
Levels: 2
Square Footage: 2,428
Main Level Sq. Ft.: 2,348
Upper Level Sq. Ft.: 80
Bedrooms: 3
Bathrooms: 2½
Foundation: Crawl space, slab
Materials List Available: Yes
Price Category: E

Photo provided by designer/architect.

If you admire the gracious colonnaded porch, curved brick steps, and stunning front windows, you'll fall in love with the interior of this home.

Features:

- Great Room: Enjoy the vaulted ceiling, balcony from the upper level, and fireplace with flanking windows that let you look out to the patio.

- Dining Room: Columns define this formal room, which is adjacent to the breakfast room.

- Kitchen: A bayed sink area and extensive curved bar provide visual interest in this well-designed kitchen, which every cook will love.

- Breakfast Room: Huge windows let the sun shine into this room, which is open to the kitchen.

- Master Suite: The sitting area is open to the rear porch for a special touch in this gorgeous suite. Two walk-in closets and a vaulted ceiling and double vanity in the bath will make you feel completely pampered.

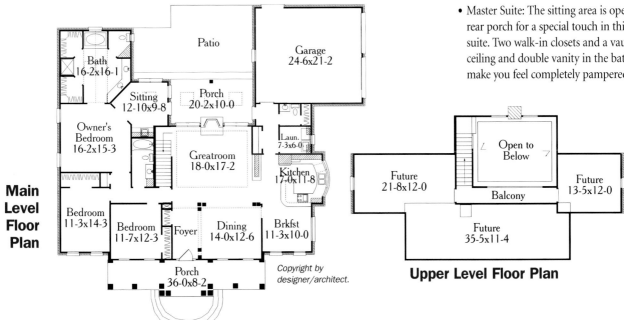

Main Level Floor Plan

Upper Level Floor Plan

Copyright by designer/architect.

Plan #141019

Dimensions: 57' W x 41' D
Levels: 2
Square Footage: 2,826
Main Level Sq. Ft.: 1,258
Second Level Sq. Ft.: 1,568
Bedrooms: 5
Bathrooms: 3
Foundation: Basement
Materials List Available: Yes
Price Category: F

Images provided by designer/architect.

Main Level Floor Plan

Patio / Deck
Office / Bdrm.5 11^0 x 11^4
Bth.3
Cubby Holes
Command Center
Living Area 15^0 x 19^2 11' Ceil. Boxed Tray
Brkfst. 13^4 x 10^0
Kit. 13^4 x 11^6
Double Garage 21^4 x 21^8
Two Story Foyer 7^0 x 5^{10}
Dining 13^4 x 11^6

Upper Level Floor Plan

Copyright by designer/architect.

Seat
Bdrm.2 11^0 x 13^4
Bth.2
Children's Den / Media Room 15^0 x 17^4
Master Bdrm. 13^6 x 17^4
Opt. Tray w/ Plant Shelf
Bdrm.3 12^8 x 11^8
Balcony
M.Bath
Opt. Tray w/ Plant Shelf
Linen
Two Story Foyer
Seat W/ Drawers
Bdrm.4 11^4 x 11^2

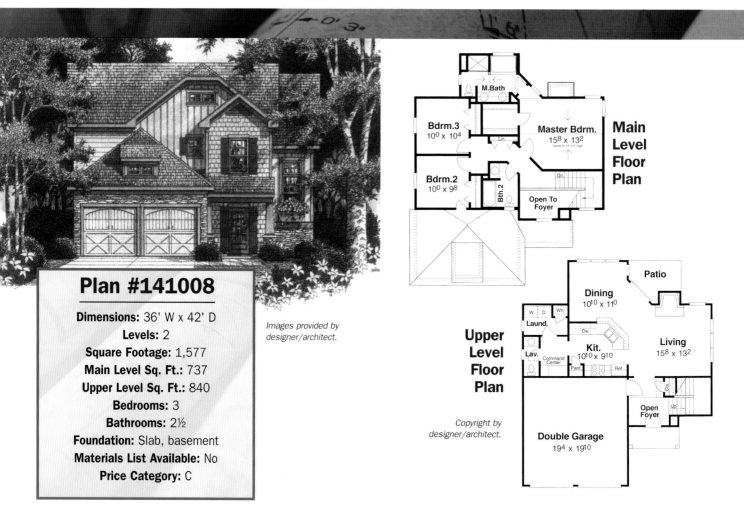

Plan #141008

Dimensions: 36' W x 42' D
Levels: 2
Square Footage: 1,577
Main Level Sq. Ft.: 737
Upper Level Sq. Ft.: 840
Bedrooms: 3
Bathrooms: 2½
Foundation: Slab, basement
Materials List Available: No
Price Category: C

Images provided by designer/architect.

Main Level Floor Plan

M.Bath
Bdrm.3 10^0 x 10^4
Master Bdrm. 15^8 x 13^2 Vaults to 10'-10" High
Bdrm.2 10^0 x 9^8
Bth.2
Open To Foyer

Upper Level Floor Plan

Copyright by designer/architect.

Patio
Dining 10^{10} x 11^0
Laund.
Lav.
Kit. 10^{10} x 9^{10}
Command Center
Living 15^8 x 13^2
Double Garage 19^4 x 19^{10}
Open Foyer

Plan #181081

Dimensions: 58' W x 33' D
Levels: 2
Square Footage: 2,350
Main Level Sq. Ft.: 1,107
Second Level Sq. Ft.: 1,243
Bedrooms: 3
Bathrooms: 2½
Foundation: Basement
Materials List Available: Yes
Price Category: E

Illustration provided by designer/architect.

This traditional country home features a wrap-around porch and a second-floor balcony.

Features:

- Ceiling Height: 8 ft. unless otherwise noted.
- Family Room: Double French doors and a fireplace in this inviting front room enhance the beauty and warmth of the home's open floor plan.
- Kitchen: You'll love working in this bright and convenient kitchen. The breakfast bar is the perfect place to gather for informal meals.

- Master Suite: You'll look forward to retiring to this elegant upstairs suite at the end of a busy day. The suite features a private bath with separate shower and tub, as well as dual vanities.
- Secondary Bedrooms: Two family bedrooms share a full bath with a third room that opens onto the balcony.
- Basement: An unfinished full basement provides plenty of storage and the potential to add additional finished living space.

Main Level Floor Plan

Copyright by designer/architect.

Upper Level Floor Plan

Plan #271069

Dimensions: 64' W x 52' D
Levels: 2
Square Footage: 2,376
Main Level Sq. Ft.: 1,248
Upper Level Sq. Ft.: 1,128
Bedrooms: 4
Bathrooms: 2½
Foundation: Basement, crawl space
Materials List Available: No
Price Category: E

This home's Federal-style facade has a simple elegance that is still popular among today's homeowners.

Features:

- **Living Room:** This formal space is perfect for serious conversation or thoughtful reflection. Optional double doors would open directly into the family room beyond.

- **Dining Room:** You won't find a more elegant room than this for hosting holiday feasts.

- **Kitchen:** This room has everything the cook could hope for—a central island, a handy pantry, and a menu desk. Sliding glass doors in the dinette let you step outside for some fresh air with your cup of coffee.

- **Family Room:** Here's the spot to spend a cold winter evening. Have hot chocolate in front of a crackling fire!

- **Master Suite:** With an optional vaulted ceiling, the sleeping chamber is bright and spacious. The private bath showcases a splashy whirlpool tub.

Main Level Floor Plan

Upper Level Floor Plan

Plan #161015

Dimensions: 55'4" W x 40'4" D

Levels: 2

Square Footage: 1,768

Main Level Sq. Ft.: 960

Upper Level Sq. Ft.: 808

Bedrooms: 3

Bathrooms: 2½

Foundation: Slab

Materials List Available: No

Price Category: C

One look at this dramatic exterior—a 12-ft. high entry with a transom and sidelights, multiple gables, and an impressive box window—you'll fall in love with this home.

Features:

- **Foyer:** This 2-story area announces the grace of this home to everyone who enters it.

- **Great Room:** A natural gathering spot, this room is sunken to set it off from the rest of the house. The 12-ft. ceiling adds a spacious feeling, and the access to the rear porch makes it ideal for friends and family.

- **Kitchen:** The kids will enjoy the snack bar and you'll love the adjoining breakfast room with its access to the rear porch.

- **Master Suite:** A whirlpool in the master bath and walk-in closets in the bedroom spell luxury.

- **Laundry Area:** Two large closets are so handy that you'll wonder how you ever did without them.

Images provided by designer/architect.

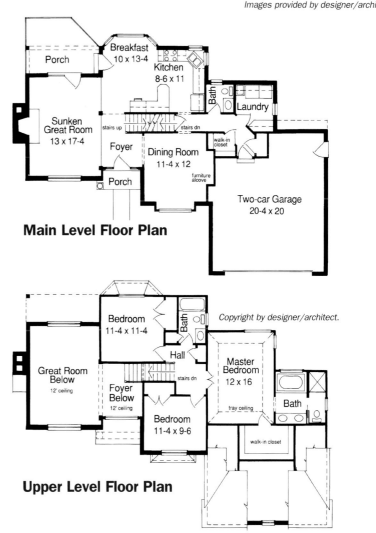

Main Level Floor Plan

Copyright by designer/architect.

Upper Level Floor Plan

Main Level Floor Plan

DINING
19' X 11'

GREAT RM
16' X 16'

KITCHEN
19' X 13'

GARAGE
32' X 24'

STUDY
11' X 11'

ENTRY

MUD RM

BATH

LAUN

Plan #271091

Dimensions: 68' W x 43' D

Levels: 2

Square Footage: 2,854

Main Level Sq. Ft.: 1,219

Upper Level Sq. Ft.: 1,635

Bedrooms: 3

Bathrooms: 2½

Foundation: Daylight basement

Materials List Available: No

Price Category: F

Images provided by designer/architect.

Upper Level Floor Plan

Copyright by designer/architect.

BATH

BED RM
11' X 13'

OWNER'S SUITE
15' X 15'

BONUS RM
28' X 14'

BATH

W.I.C.

BED RM
15' X 13'

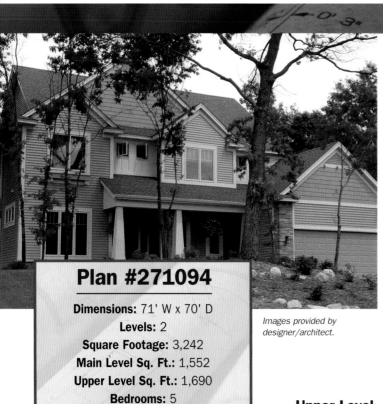

Main Level Floor Plan

GREAT RM
21' X 18'

DINING
21' X 10'

KITCHEN
15' X 14'

STUDY
11' X 13'

MUD RM

PORCH

GARAGE
40' X 24'

Plan #271094

Dimensions: 71' W x 70' D

Levels: 2

Square Footage: 3,242

Main Level Sq. Ft.: 1,552

Upper Level Sq. Ft.: 1,690

Bedrooms: 5

Bathrooms: 2½

Foundation: Full basement

Materials List Available: No

Price Category: G

Images provided by designer/architect.

Upper Level Floor Plan

Copyright by designer/architect.

BED RM
10' X 14'

BED RM
10' X 14'

BATH

OWNER'S SUITE
14' X 18'

LAUN

BATH

W.I.C.

BED RM
11' X 13'

BED RM
11' X 13'

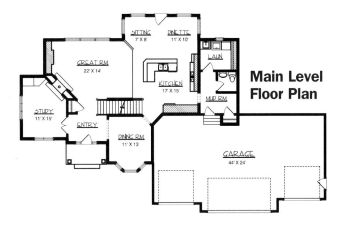

**Main Level
Floor Plan**

*Images provided by
designer/architect.*

Plan #271090

Dimensions: 78' W x 49' D

Levels: 2

Square Footage: 2,708

Main Level Sq. Ft.: 1,430

Upper Level Sq. Ft.: 1,278

Bedrooms: 3

Bathrooms: 2½

Foundation: Daylight basement

Materials List Available: No

Price Category: F

**Upper Level
Floor Plan**

*Copyright by
designer/architect.*

**Main Level
Floor Plan**

Plan #271089

Dimensions: 66' W x 51' D

Levels: 2

Square Footage: 2,476

Main Level Sq. Ft.: 1,266

Upper Level Sq. Ft.: 1,210

Bedrooms: 3

Bathrooms: 2½

Foundation: Daylight basement

Materials List Available: No

Price Category: E

*Images provided by
designer/architect.*

**Upper Level
Floor Plan**

*Copyright by
designer/architect.*

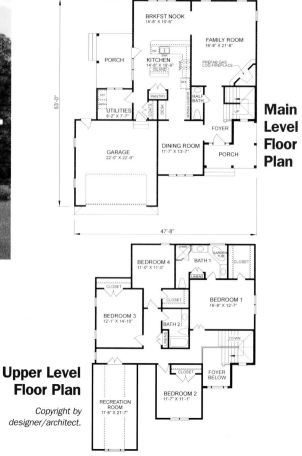

Plan #341001

Dimensions: 47'8" W x 53' D

Levels: 2

Square Footage: 2,867

Main Level Sq. Ft.: 1,306

Upper Level Sq. Ft.: 1,561

Bedrooms: 4

Bathrooms: 2½

Foundation: Crawl space, slab, or basement

Materials List Available: Yes

Price Category: F

Images provided by designer/architect.

Main Level Floor Plan

Upper Level Floor Plan

Copyright by designer/architect.

Upper Level Floor Plan

Copyright by designer/architect.

Plan #341006

Dimensions: 86'3" W x 35'4" D

Levels: 2

Square Footage: 2,588

Main Level Sq. Ft.: 1,660

Upper Level Sq. Ft.: 928

Bedrooms: 4

Bathrooms: 3½

Foundation: Crawl space, slab, or basement

Materials List Available: Yes

Price Category: E

Images provided by designer/architect.

Main Level Floor Plan

Main Level Floor Plan

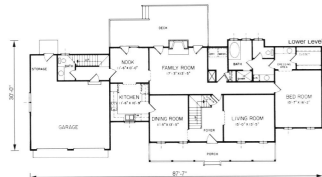

Images provided by designer/architect.

Upper Level Floor Plan

Copyright by designer/architect.

Plan #341007

Dimensions: 87'7" W x 30' D

Levels: 2

Square Footage: 4,068

Main Level Sq. Ft.: 3,218

Upper Level Sq. Ft.: 850

Bedrooms: 4

Bathrooms: 2½

Foundation: Crawl space, slab, or basement

Materials List Available: Yes

Price Category: I

Main Level Floor Plan

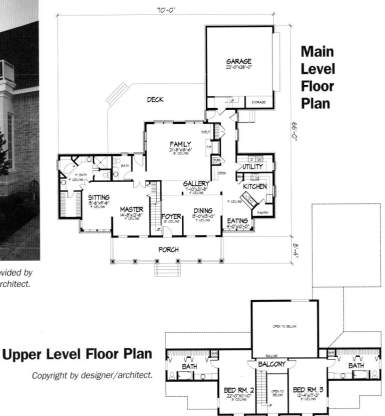

Images provided by designer/architect.

Upper Level Floor Plan

Copyright by designer/architect.

Plan #271095

Dimensions: 70' W x 75' D

Levels: 2

Square Footage: 3,220

Main Level Sq. Ft.: 2,040

Upper Level Sq. Ft.: 1,180

Bedrooms: 3

Bathrooms: 3½

Foundation: Crawl space, slab

Materials List Available: No

Price Category: G

Plan #161018

Dimensions: 74'4" W x 69'11" D
Levels: 2
Square Footage: 2,816
+ 325 Sq. Ft. bonus room
Main Level Sq. Ft.: 2,231
Upper Level Sq. Ft.: 624
Bedrooms: 3
Bathrooms: 3 full, 2 half
Foundation: Basement
Materials List Available: No
Price Category: F

Images provided by designer/architect.

If you love classic European designs, look closely at this home with its multiple gables and countless conveniences and luxuries.

Features:

- Foyer: Open to the great room, the 2-story foyer offers a view all the way to the rear windows.

- Great Room: A fireplace makes this room cozy in any kind of weather.

- Kitchen: This large room features an island with a sink, and an angled wall with French doors to the back yard.

- Dining Room: The furniture alcove and raised ceiling make this room both formal and practical.

- Master Suite: You'll love the quiet in the bedroom and the luxuries—a whirlpool tub, separate shower, and double vanities—in the bath.

- Basement: The door from the basement to the side yard adds convenience to outdoor work.

Rear View

Main Level Floor Plan

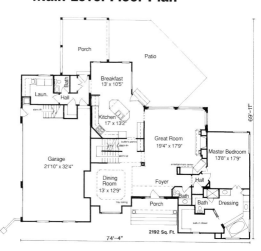

2192 Sq. Ft.
74'-4"

Upper Level Floor Plan

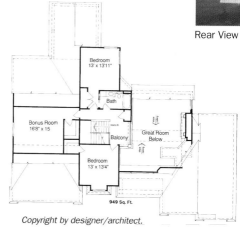

949 Sq. Ft.

Copyright by designer/architect.

Foyer/Dining Room

Plan #161022

Dimensions: 71'8" W x 38'10" D
Levels: 2
Square Footage: 1,898
Main Level Sq. Ft.: 1,065
Upper Level Sq. Ft.: 833
Bedrooms: 3
Bathrooms: 2½
Foundation: Slab
Materials List Available: No
Price Category: D

A covered porch and boxed window add to the charm of the stone exterior of this home.

Features:

- **Great Room:** This sunken room can be warmed by a fireplace on winter days and chilly evenings, and lit by natural light flowing through the bank of windows on the rear wall.

- **Kitchen:** You'll love the companionship that the snack bar in the kitchen naturally encourages. A large pantry in this area gives you ample storage space and helps to keep you organized.

- **Breakfast Room:** Quiet elegance marks this room with its sloped ceiling and arched windows that look out into the rear yard.

- **Master Suite:** Enjoy the vaulted ceiling and bath with a whirlpool tub.

- **Extra Spaces:** A loft on the second floor and a bonus room allow endless possibilities in this comfortable home.

Rear Elevation

Main Level Floor Plan

Upper Level Floor Plan

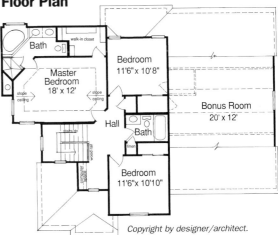

Copyright by designer/architect.

Upper Level Floor Plan

Copyright by designer/architect.

Main Level Floor Plan

Plan #161047

Dimensions: 60'2" W x 65'11" D

Levels: 2

Square Footage: 2,764

Main Level Sq. Ft.: 1,943

Upper Level Sq. Ft.: 821

Bedrooms: 4

Bathrooms: 2½

Foundation: Slab

Materials List Available: Yes

Price Category: F

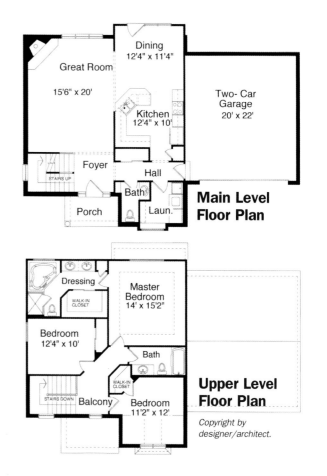

Main Level Floor Plan

Upper Level Floor Plan

Copyright by designer/architect.

Rear Elevation

Plan #161048

Dimensions: 50' W x 36'8" D

Levels: 2

Square Footage: 1,770

Main Level Sq. Ft.: 924

Upper Level Sq. Ft.: 846

Bedrooms: 3

Bathrooms: 2½

Foundation: Slab

Materials List Available: Yes

Price Category: C

Main Level Floor Plan

Deck

Master Bedroom
15'1" x 14'4"
9' CEILING HEIGHT

Great Room
19'2" x 16'1"
13' CEILING HEIGHT

Breakfast
11'3" x 10'
9' CEILING HEIGHT

Solarium
9' x 12'3"

Kitchen
11'3" x 12'

Laun.

Dressing

Bath

Foyer

Library
10'4" x 12'3"
9' CEILING HEIGHT

Dining Room
12'8" x 11'4"

WALK-IN CLOSET

Two-Car Garage
24'8" x 22'

Porch

53'-0"

69'-2"

Images provided by designer/architect.

Rear Elevation

Upper Level Floor Plan

Copyright by designer/architect.

Bedroom
12'2" x 14'

Bath

Rec Room
39'10" x 16'

Bath

Bedroom
11'8" x 14'4"

Basement

Unexcavated

Unexcavated

Unexcavated

Plan #161049

Dimensions: 69'2" W x 53' D
Levels: 2
Square Footage: 3,213
Main Level Sq. Ft.: 1,967
Finished Lower Level Sq. Ft.: 1,246
Bedrooms: 3
Bathrooms: 2 full, 2 half
Foundation: Slab
Materials List Available: Yes
Price Category: G

Upper Level Floor Plan

Copyright by designer/architect.

Bedroom
11'4" x 12'4"

Bath

Bedroom
13' x 12'

Hall

Bedroom
11'4" x 12'3"

Bath

Bonus Room
13' x 16'4"
9' CEILING

Main Level Floor Plan

Porch

Great Room
15' x 19'
11' CEILING

Master Bedroom
15' x 13'

Kitchen
10'3" x 12'1"

Breakfast
10'5" x 12'

Foyer
11' CEILING

Dressing

WALK-IN CLOSET

Dining Room
12'4" x 16'2"

Bath

Porch

Laun.

Hall

Two-Car Garage
21'8" x 21'

66'-4"

61'-8"

Plan #161050

Dimensions: 61'8" W x 66'4" D
Levels: 2
Square Footage: 3,213
Main Level Sq. Ft.: 1,967
Upper Level Sq. Ft.: 1,246
Bedrooms: 5
Bathrooms: 3½
Foundation: Slab
Materials List Available: Yes
Price Category: F

Images provided by designer/architect.

Rear Elevation

Plan #161024

Dimensions: 54'4" W x 26'8" D
Levels: 2
Square Footage: 1,698
Main Level Sq. Ft.: 868
Upper Level Sq. Ft.: 830
Bonus Space Sq. Ft.: 269
Bedrooms: 3
Bathrooms: 2½
Foundation: Slab
Materials List Available: No
Price Category: C

The covered porch, dormers, and center gable that grace the exterior let you know how comfortable your family will be in this home.

Features:

- Great Room: Walk from windows overlooking the front porch to a door into the rear yard in this spacious room, which runs the width of the house.

- Dining Room: Adjacent to the great room, the dining area gives your family space to spread out and makes it easy to entertain a large group.

- Kitchen: Designed for efficiency, the kitchen area includes a large pantry.

- Master Suite: Tucked away on the second floor, the master suite features a walk-in closet in the bedroom and a luxurious attached bathroom.

- Bonus Room: Finish the 269-sq.-ft. area over the 2-bay garage as a guest room, study, or getaway for the kids.

Images provided by designer/architect.

Main Level Floor Plan

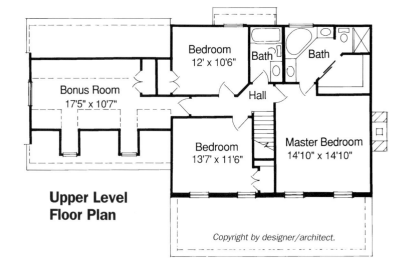

Upper Level Floor Plan

Copyright by designer/architect.

Plan #161025

Dimensions: 63'4" W x 48' D
Levels: 2
Square Footage: 2,738
Main Level Sq. Ft.: 1,915
Upper Level Sq. Ft.: 823
Bedrooms: 4
Bathrooms: 3½
Foundation: Slab
Materials List Available: No
Price Category: F

Images provided by designer/architect.

One look at the octagonal tower, boxed window, and wood-and-stone trim, and you'll know how much your family will love this home.

Features:

- Foyer: View the high windows across the rear wall, a fireplace, and open stairs as you come in.

- Great Room: Gather in this two-story-high area.

- Hearth Room: Open to the breakfast room, it's close to both the kitchen and dining room.

- Kitchen: A snack bar and an island make the kitchen ideal for family living.

- Master Suite: You'll love the 9-ft. ceiling in the bedroom and 11-ft. ceiling in the sitting area. The bath has a whirlpool tub, double-bowl vanity, and walk-in closet.

- Upper Level: A balcony leads to a bedroom with a private bath and 2 other rooms with private access to a shared bath.

Main Level Floor Plan

Upper Level Floor Plan

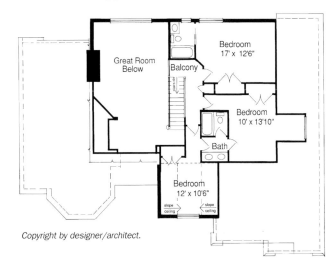

Copyright by designer/architect.

Main Level Floor Plan

Images provided by designer/architect.

Rear Elevation

Plan #161052

Dimensions: 57'10" W x 42'4" D

Levels: 2

Square Footage: 2,484

Main Level Sq. Ft.: 1,710

Upper Level Sq. Ft.: 774

Bedrooms: 4

Bathrooms: 3

Foundation: Basement

Materials List Available: Yes

Price Category: E

Upper Level Floor Plan

Copyright by designer/architect.

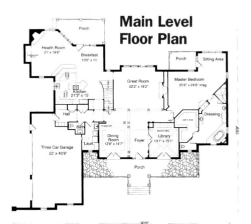

Main Level Floor Plan

Plan #161044

Dimensions: 90'6" W x 78'9" D

Levels: 2

Square Footage: 4,652

Main Level Sq. Ft.: 3,414

Upper Level Sq. Ft.: 1,238

Bedrooms: 4

Bathrooms: 3½

Foundation: Basement

Materials List Available: Yes

Price Category: I

Images provided by designer/architect.

Rear Elevation

Upper Level Floor Plan

Copyright by designer/architect.

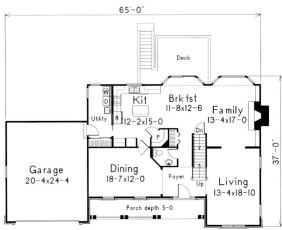

**Main Level
Floor Plan**

*Images provided by
designer/architect.*

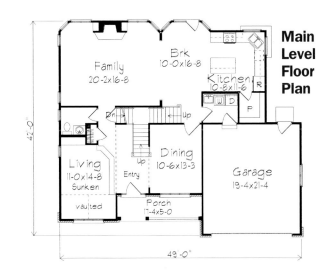

Upper Level Floor Plan

Copyright by designer/architect.

Plan #321059

Dimensions: 65' W x 37' D

Levels: 2

Square Footage: 2,521

Main Level Sq. Ft.: 1,375

Upper Level Sq. Ft.: 1,146

Bedrooms: 4

Bathrooms: 2½

Foundation: Basement

Materials List Available: Yes

Price Category: E

Plan #321050

Dimensions: 49' W x 42' D

Levels: 2

Square Footage: 2,336

Main Level Sq. Ft.: 1,291

Upper Level Sq. Ft.: 1,045

Bedrooms: 4

Bathrooms: 2½

Foundation: Basement

Materials List Available: Yes

Price Category: E

*Images provided by
designer/architect.*

**Main
Level
Floor
Plan**

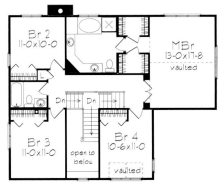

**Upper Level
Floor Plan**

*Copyright by
designer/architect.*

Images provided by designer/architect.

Plan #161037

Dimensions: 46' W x 59'4" D
Levels: 2
Square Footage: 2,469
Main Level Sq. Ft.: 1,462
Basement Level Sq. Ft.: 1,007
Bedrooms: 3
Bathrooms: 2½
Foundation: Slab
Materials List Available: No
Price Category: E

A brick-and-stone facade welcomes you into this lovely home, which is designed to fit into a narrow lot.

Features:

- Foyer: This entrance, with vaulted ceiling, introduces the graciousness of this home.

- Great Room: A vaulted center ceiling creates the impression that this large great room and dining room are one space, making entertaining a natural in this area.

- Kitchen: Designed for efficiency with ample storage and counter space, this kitchen also allows casual dining at the counter.

- Master Suite: A tray ceiling sets this room off from the rest of the house, and the lavishly equipped bathroom lets you pamper yourself.

- Lower Level: Put extra bedrooms or a library in this finished area, and use the wet bar in a game room or recreation room.

Kitchen

Main Level Floor Plan

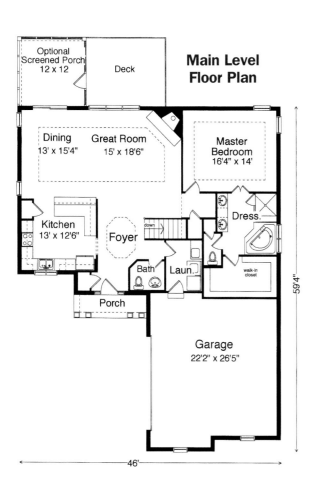

Optional Screened Porch 12 x 12

Deck

Dining 13' 15'4"

Great Room 15' x 18'6"

Master Bedroom 16'4" x 14'

Dress.

Kitchen 13' x 12'6"

Foyer

down

walk-in closet

Bath

Laun.

Porch

Garage 22'2" x 26'5"

59'4"

46'

Basement Level Floor Plan

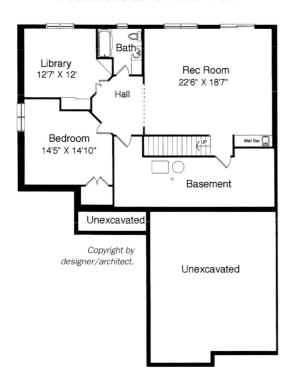

Library 12'7' X 12'

Bath

Hall

Rec Room 22'6" X 18'7"

Bedroom 14'5" X 14'10"

up

Wet Bar

Basement

Unexcavated

Unexcavated

Copyright by designer/architect.

Rear Elevation

Left Elevation

Right Elevation

Living Room

Main Level Floor Plan

Brk
9-6x
14-5

Kit
11-0x10-2

Family
20-4x16-10

Garage
21-5x25-5

Dining
14-6x14-3

Living
13-0x14-3

Dn

Up

Porch

R   P

W   D

38'-9"

60'-6"

Images provided by designer/architect.

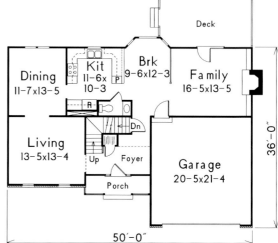

Br 4
12-2x11-1

Br 3
13-0x11-1

MBr
18-4x14-3

Br 2
13-0x12-2

Dn

L   L

Upper Level Floor Plan

Copyright by designer/architect.

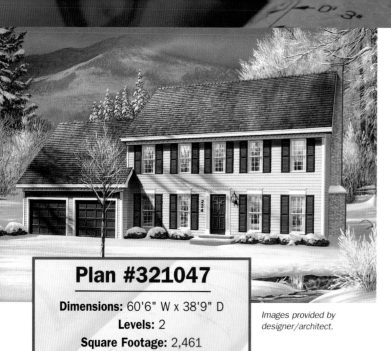

Plan #321047

Dimensions: 60'6" W x 38'9" D

Levels: 2

Square Footage: 2,461

Main Level Sq. Ft.: 1,252

Upper Level Sq. Ft.: 1,209

Bedrooms: 4

Bathrooms: 2½

Foundation: Basement

Materials List Available: Yes

Price Category: E

Main Level Floor Plan

Deck

Dining
11-7x13-5

Kit
11-6x
10-3

Brk
9-6x12-3

Family
16-5x13-5

Living
13-5x13-4

Foyer

Garage
20-5x21-4

Porch

Dn

Up

R

50'-0"

36'-0"

Images provided by designer/architect.

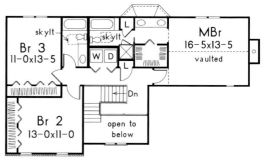

Upper Level Floor Plan

Copyright by designer/architect.

skylt

skylt

Br 3
11-0x13-5

MBr
16-5x13-5
vaulted

W   D

L

L

Br 2
13-0x11-0

open to below

Dn

Plan #321045

Dimensions: 50' W x 36' D

Levels: 2

Square Footage: 2,058

Main Level Sq. Ft.: 1,098

Upper Level Sq. Ft.: 960

Bedrooms: 3

Bathrooms: 2½

Foundation: Basement

Materials List Available: Yes

Price Category: D

Plan #131039

Dimensions: 50' W x 37' D

Levels: 2

Square Footage: 1,149

Main Level Sq. Ft.: 1,029

Lower Level Sq. Ft.: 120

Lower Level: Optional bonus area

Bedrooms: 1

Bathrooms: 1

Foundation: Basement, crawl space, or slab

Materials List Available: Yes

Price Category: C

Images provided by designer/architect.

Main Level Floor Plan

BATH · LIN · VAULTED DINING RM 11'-8" x 13'-0" · KITCHEN 12'-0" x 10'-0" · REF · PANT · DW

WICL · UTIL · DN · SNACK COUNTER · VAULTED GREAT RM 22'-4" x 13'-0"

VAULTED MSTR BEDRM 12'-6" x 16'-0" · RAIL · SL GL DRS · FIREPLACE · PORCH · SL GL DRS

W D

Lower Level Floor Plan

WORK SHOP 16'-2" x 9'-0" · CL · TWO CAR GARAGE 22'-0" x 23'-0"

GARAGE 12'-6" x 20'-0" · UP

COVERED PORCH

Copyright by designer/architect.

Plan #131049

Dimensions: 88'8" W x 59'2" D

Levels: 2

Square Footage: 2,837

Main Level Sq. Ft.: 2,152

Upper Level Sq. Ft.: 685

Bedrooms: 3

Bathrooms: 3

Foundation: Crawl space, slab, or basement

Materials List Available: Yes

Price Category: G

Images provided by designer/architect.

Main Level Floor Plan

DN · COVERED PORCH

10' HIGH STEPPED CLG MSTR BEDRM 13'-0" x 17'-0" · MSTR BATH · VAULTED GREAT RM 20'-0" x 17'-0" · BKFST RM 9'-0" x 11'-0" · 9' HIGH CLG · SL GL DRS

9' HIGH CLG OFFICE/ SITTING RM 15'-0" x 10'-0" · WICL · LIN · WICL · KITCHEN 14'-4" x 12'-0" · DW REF · DN

OPT FIREPLACE · BATH · DN TO OPT BSMT · UP

9' HIGH CLG LIVING RM/ GUEST RM 16'-0" x 12'-0" · UP · 2 STORY FOYER · 10' HIGH STEPPED CLG DINING RM 16'-0" x 12'-0" · LAUN RM · CL · UTIL RM · STOR

COVERED PORCH · DN · TWO CAR GARAGE 20'-0" x 20'-0" · W D

Upper Level Floor Plan

ATTIC · CL · CL · UPPER GREAT RM · ATTIC

BEDRM #3 16'-0" x 12'-0" · BATH · RAIL · DN · RAIL · WICL · BEDRM #2 16'-8" x 12'-0"

BALCONY

Copyright by designer/architect.

Plan #161034

Dimensions: 56' W x 53' D

Levels: 2

Square Footage: 2,156

Main Level Sq. Ft.: 1,605

Upper Level Sq. Ft.: 551

Bedrooms: 3

Bathrooms: 2½

Foundation: Slab

Materials List Available: No

Price Category: D

Images provided by designer/architect.

Multiple gables, a covered porch, and circle-topped windows combine to enhance the attractiveness of this exciting home.

Features:

- **Great Room:** A raised foyer introduces this open combined great room and dining room. Enjoy the efficiency of a dual-sided fireplace that warms both the great room and kitchen.

- **Kitchen:** The kitchen, designed for easy traffic patterns, offers an abundance of counter space and features a cooktop island.

- **Master Suite:** This first-floor master suite, separated for privacy, includes twin vanities and a walk-in closet. A deluxe corner bath and walk-in shower complete its luxurious detail.

- **Additional Rooms:** Two additional bedrooms lead to the second-floor balcony, which overlooks the great room. You can use the optional bonus room as a den or office.

Copyright by designer/architect.

Main Level Floor Plan

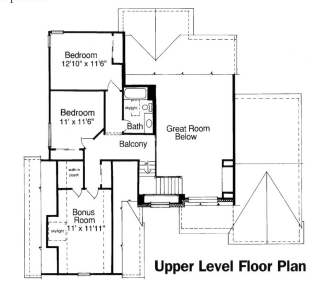

Upper Level Floor Plan

Photo provided by designer/architect.

Plan #151014

Dimensions: 70'2" W x 51'4" D
Levels: 2
Square Footage: 2,698
Main Level Sq. Ft.: 1,813
Upper Level Sq. Ft.: 885
Bedrooms: 5
Bathrooms: 3
Foundation: Crawl space, slab, optional basement for fee
Price Category: D

A comfortable front porch welcomes you into this home that features a balcony over the great room, a study, and a kitchen designed for gourmet cooks.

Features:

- Ceiling Height: 9 ft.
- Front Porch: Stately 12-in.-wide pillars form the entryway.
- Foyer: Open to upper story.
- Great Room: A fireplace, vaulted 9-ft. ceiling, and balcony from the second floor add character to this lovely room.
- Dining Room: Open to the kitchen for convenience.
- Kitchen: A large walk-in pantry, well-designed work areas, and eat-in bar make this room a treasure.
- Breakfast Room: Enjoy this spot that opens to both the kitchen and a large covered porch at the rear of the house.
- Study: This quiet room has French doors leading to the yard.
- Master Suite: This spacious area has cozy window seats as well as his and her walk-in closets. The master bathroom is fitted with a whirlpool tub, a glass shower, and his and her sinks.

Upper Level Floor Plan

Main Level Floor Plan

Copyright by designer/architect.

Plan #161051

Dimensions: 57'8" W x 58' D
Levels: 2
Square Footage: 2,484
Main Level Sq. Ft.: 1,710
Upper Level Sq. Ft.: 774
Bedrooms: 4
Bathrooms: 3½
Foundation: Slab
Materials List Available: Yes
Price Category: E

Images provided by designer/architect.

Upper Level Floor Plan

Main Level Floor Plan

Copyright by designer/architect.

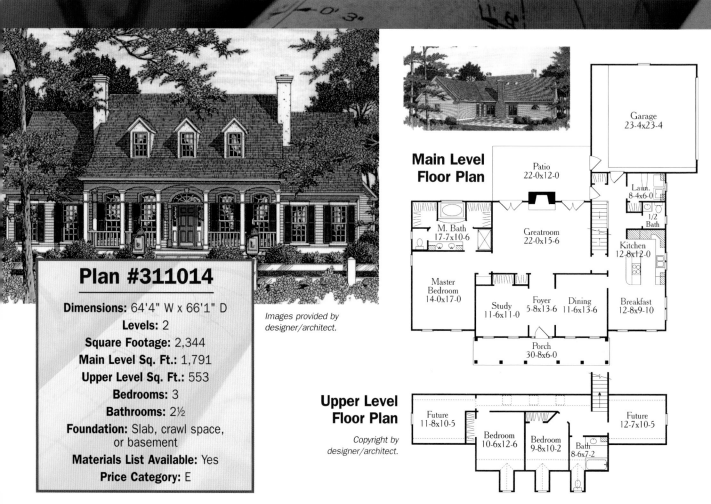

Plan #311014

Dimensions: 64'4" W x 66'1" D
Levels: 2
Square Footage: 2,344
Main Level Sq. Ft.: 1,791
Upper Level Sq. Ft.: 553
Bedrooms: 3
Bathrooms: 2½
Foundation: Slab, crawl space, or basement
Materials List Available: Yes
Price Category: E

Images provided by designer/architect.

Main Level Floor Plan

Upper Level Floor Plan

Copyright by designer/architect.

Main Level Floor Plan

Images provided by designer/architect.

Upper Level Floor Plan

Copyright by designer/architect.

Plan #271064

Dimensions: 76' W x 54' D

Levels: 2

Square Footage: 2,864

Main Level Sq. Ft.: 1,610

Upper Level Sq. Ft.: 1,254

Bedrooms: 4

Bathrooms: 2½

Foundation: Daylight basement

Materials List Available: No

Price Category: E

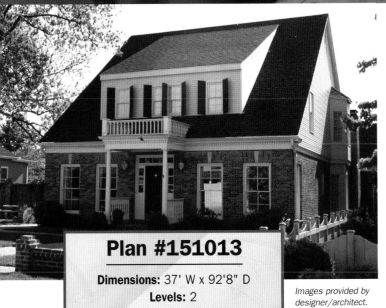

Plan #151013

Dimensions: 37' W x 92'8" D

Levels: 2

Square Footage: 2,618

Main Level Sq. Ft.: 1,865

Upper Level Sq. Ft.: 753

Bedrooms: 3

Bathrooms: 2½

Foundation: Crawl space or slab.
Optional basement foundation available for an additional $250.

Price Category: F

Images provided by designer/architect.

Upper Level Floor Plan

Copyright by designer/architect.

Main Level Floor Plan

Plan #151015

Dimensions: 72'4" W x 48'4" D

Levels: 2

Square Footage: 2,789

Main Level Sq. Ft.: 1,977

Upper Level Sq. Ft.: 812

Bedrooms: 4

Bathrooms: 3

Foundation: Basement, crawl space, or slab

Materials List Available: Yes

Price Category: F

Images provided by designer/architect.

Main Level Floor Plan

Upper Level Floor Plan

Copyright by designer/architect.

Plan #151025

Dimensions: 71' W x 55' D

Levels: 2

Square Footage: 3,914

Main Level Sq. Ft.: 2,291

Upper Level Sq. Ft.: 1,623

Bedrooms: 3

Bathrooms: 3

Foundation: Crawl space, slab; optional full basement plan available for extra fee

Materials List Available: Yes

Price Category: H

Images provided by designer/architect.

Main Level Floor Plan

Upper Level Floor Plan

Copyright by designer/architect.

Upper Level Floor Plan

Images provided by designer/architect.

Plan #161020

Dimensions: 60' W" x 50'4" D

Levels: 2

Square Footage: 2,082; 2,349 with bonus space

Main Level Sq. Ft.: 1,524

Upper Level Sq. Ft.: 558

Bedrooms: 3

Bathrooms: 2

Foundation: Basement

Materials List Available: Yes

Price Category: D

Main Level Floor Plan

Copyright by designer/architect.

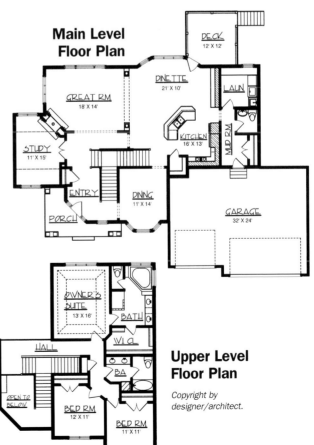

Main Level Floor Plan

Images provided by designer/architect.

Upper Level Floor Plan

Copyright by designer/architect.

Plan #271092

Dimensions: 68' W x 47' D

Levels: 2

Square Footage: 2,636

Main Level Sq. Ft.: 1,596

Upper Level Sq. Ft.: 1,040

Bedrooms: 3

Bathrooms: 2½

Foundation: Daylight basement

Materials List Available: No

Price Category: F

Plan #211108

Dimensions: 66' W x 66' D
Levels: 2
Square Footage: 2,954
First Level Sq. Ft.: 1,984
Second Level Sq. Ft.: 970
Bedrooms: 4
Bathrooms: 3½
Foundation: Slab, crawl space, or basement
Materials List Available: Yes
Price Category: F

Illustration provided by designer/architect.

- **Wet Bar:** This small wet bar is conveniently located between the kitchen and the family room.

- **Master Suite:** Retreat to this master suite, which features a gracious bath and a small sitting area.

This home is designed with the feel of a European cottage and will nestle nicely in any neighborhood.

Features:

- Ceiling Height: 8 ft.

- Living Room: This formal living room offers plenty of space for all kinds of entertaining and family activities.

- Eating Area: This eating area adjacent to the kitchen is the perfect spot for informal family meals, with its panoramic view of an intimate private courtyard through a graceful Palladian-style window.

- Family Room: Relax with the family in this cozy family room, which opens to the rear covered porch and the formal living room and dining room via pairs of French doors.

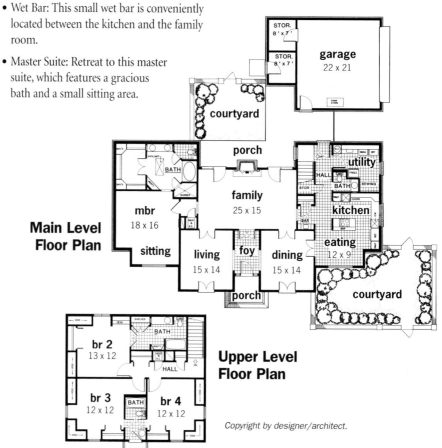

Main Level Floor Plan

Upper Level Floor Plan

Copyright by designer/architect.

Plan #281001

Dimensions: 54' W x 47' D
Levels: 2
Square Footage: 2,423
Main Level Sq. Ft.: 1,388
Second Level Sq. Ft.: 1,035
Bedrooms: 3
Bathrooms: 2½
Foundation: Basement
Materials List Available: Yes
Price Category: E

This stately manor appears larger than it is and is filled with amenities for comfortable living.

Features:

- Ceiling Height: 8 ft. unless otherwise noted.
- Foyer: The grand entrance porch leads into this spacious two-story foyer, with an open staircase and architecturally interesting angles.

- Balcony: This second story has a balcony that overlooks the foyer.
- Living Room: This delightful living room seems even more spacious, thanks to its sloped vaulted ceiling.
- Dining Room: This elegant dining room shares the living room's sloped vaulted ceiling.
- Kitchen: This beautiful kitchen will be a real pleasure in which to cook. You'll love lingering over morning coffee in the breakfast nook, which is located on the sunny full-bayed wall.
- Family Room: Relax in this roomy family room, with its 9-ft. ceiling.

Photo and Illustration provided by designer/architect.

**Main Level
Floor Plan**

**Upper Level
Floor Plan**

*Copyright by
designer/architect.*

Plan #161032

Dimensions: 75'8" W x 70'6" D
Levels: 2
Square Footage: 4,517
Main Level Sq. Ft.: 2,562
Finished Lower Level Sq. Ft.: 1,955
Bedrooms: 3
Full Baths: 2
Half Baths: 3
Foundation: Slab
Materials List Available: Yes
Price Category: I

Images provided by designer/architect.

The brick-and-stone exterior, a recessed entry, and a tower containing a large library combine to convey the strength and character of this enchanting house.

Features:

• Hearth Room: Your family or guests will enjoy this large, comfortable hearth room, which has a gas fireplace and access to the rear deck, perfect for friendly gatherings.

• Kitchen: This spacious kitchen features a walk-in pantry and a center island.

• Master Suite: Designed for privacy, this master suite includes a sloped ceiling and opens to the rear deck. It also features a deluxe whirlpool bath, walk-in shower, separate his and her vanities, and a walk-in closet.

• Lower Level: This lower level includes a separate wine room, exercise room, sauna, two bedrooms, and enough space for a huge recreation room.

Rear View

SMARTtip

Art Underfoot

Make a simple geometric pattern with your flooring materials. Create a focal point in a courtyard or a small area of a patio by fashioning an intricate mosaic with tile, stone, or colored concrete. By combining elements and colors, a simple garden room floor becomes a wonderful work of art. Whether you commission a craftsman or do it yourself, you'll have a permanent art installation right in your own backyard.

Main Level
Floor Plan

Deck

Deck

Hearth Room
19'10" x 17'7"

10' ceiling height

Master Bedroom
15'4" x 18'9"

9' ceiling height

Great Room
17'9" x 17'10"

9' ceiling height

Breakfast
11'7" x 9'6"
irregular

Kitchen
15'5" x 13'10"
irregular

Garage
13'8" x 20'

Dressing

Bath

Laun.

walk-in closet

Foyer

Dining Room
12' x 15'

Pantry

Two Car Garage
23' x 30'6"

Library
13' x 14'7"

Porch

Basement Level
Floor Plan

Rec. Room
15' x 17'2"

Bedroom
15' x 12'

Rec. Room
34'5" x 19'6"

stairs up

Bath

walk-in closet

Exercise
Room
9'7" x 15'3"

Unexcavated

Bedroom
16'6" x 13'

Bath

Wine Room

Sauna

Basement

Unexcavated

walk-in closet

*Copyright by
designer/architect.*

Rear Elevation

Kitchen

Kitchen

Living Room

Plan #111012

Dimensions: 43' W x 77' D

Levels: 2

Square Footage: 3,366

Main Level Sq. Ft.: 1,742

Upper Level Sq. Ft.: 1,624

Bedrooms: 4

Bathrooms: 3

Foundation: Basement

Materials List Available: No

Price Category: G

Illustration provided by designer/architect.

Main Level Floor Plan

Deck 25'8"x 9'
Porch 25'8"x 8'
Living 25'4" x 18'
Den 13'8"x 12'9"
Breakfast 16'6"x 10'
Kitchen 13'8"x 15'
Porch
Dining 13'8"x 12'
Bath
Bedroom 15'8"x 11'

Upper Level Floor Plan

Copyright by designer/architect.

Porch
Master Bedroom 20'x 18'
Master Bath
WIC
WIC
Utility
Porch
Bedroom 13'8"x 12'
Bath
Bedroom 15'8"x 11'

Plan #141020

Dimensions: 58' W x 40'4" D

Levels: 2

Square Footage: 3,140

Main Level Sq. Ft.: 1,553

Upper Level Sq. Ft.: 1,587

Bedrooms: 5

Bathrooms: 4

Foundation: Basement

Materials List Available: No

Price Category: G

Illustration provided by designer/architect.

Main Level Floor Plan

Sundeck 18-0 x 12-0
Guest Bdrm. 12-2 x 10-0
Two Story Family Rm. 18-8 x 15-4
Brkfst. 10-10 x 11-10
Kit. 12-6 x 14-0
Guest Bath
Cts
Pantry
Dbl. Garage 21-8 x 21-8
Living 11-4 x 13-4
Two Story Foyer 11-8 x 11-6
Dining 11-4 x 13-6
58-0
40-4
9-8

Upper Level Floor Plan

Copyright by designer/architect.

M. Bath
Two Story Family Rm.
Bdrm.4 13-2 x 11-8
Master Bdrm. 15-8 x 15-8
Bath 2
Bdrm.2 11-6 x 13-6
Two Story Foyer
Bdrm.3 11-6 x 13-8
Bath 3
Sitting 6-0 x 9-8

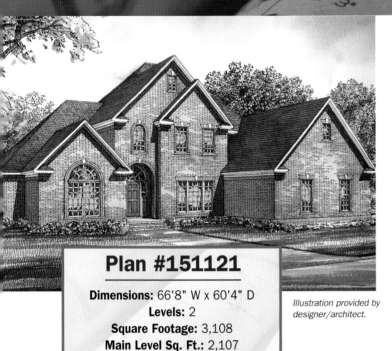

Plan #151121

Dimensions: 66'8" W x 60'4" D
Levels: 2
Square Footage: 3,108
Main Level Sq. Ft.: 2,107
Upper Level Sq. Ft.: 1,001
Bedrooms: 3
Bathrooms: 2½
Foundation: Crawl space, slab
(basement option for fee)
Materials List Available: Yes
Price Category: G

Illustration provided by designer/architect.

Upper Level Floor Plan

Main Level Floor Plan

Copyright by designer/architect.

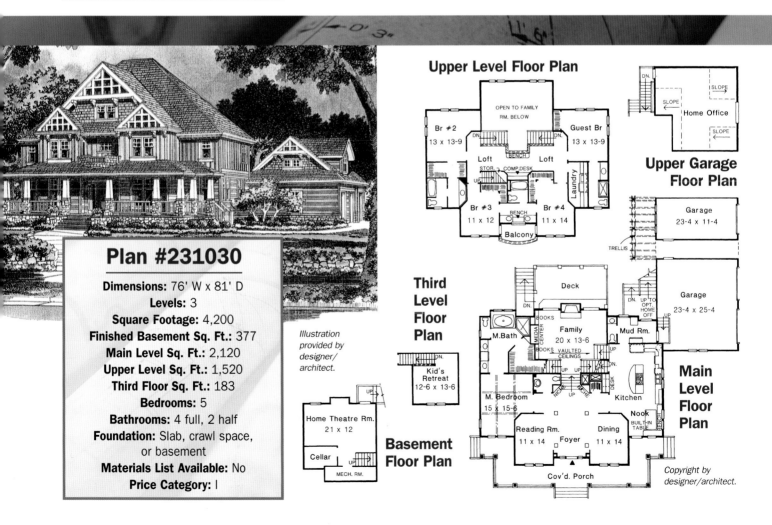

Plan #231030

Dimensions: 76' W x 81' D
Levels: 3
Square Footage: 4,200
Finished Basement Sq. Ft.: 377
Main Level Sq. Ft.: 2,120
Upper Level Sq. Ft.: 1,520
Third Floor Sq. Ft.: 183
Bedrooms: 5
Bathrooms: 4 full, 2 half
Foundation: Slab, crawl space,
or basement
Materials List Available: No
Price Category: I

Illustration provided by designer/ architect.

Upper Level Floor Plan

Upper Garage Floor Plan

Third Level Floor Plan

Main Level Floor Plan

Basement Floor Plan

Copyright by designer/architect.

Plan #331005

Dimensions: 85'11" W x 55'7" D
Levels: 2
Square Footage: 3,585
Main Level Sq. Ft.: 2,691
Upper Level Sq. Ft.: 894
Bedrooms: 4
Bathrooms: 3½
Foundation: Basement, crawl space, or slab
Materials List Available: No
Price Category: H

Images provided by designer/architect.

You'll love the stately, traditional exterior design and the contemporary, casual interior layout as they are combined in this elegant home.

Features:

- Foyer: The highlight of this spacious area is the curved stairway to the balcony over head.

- Family Room: The two-story ceiling and second-floor balcony overlooking this room add to its spacious feeling, but you can decorate around the fireplace to create a cozy, intimate area.

- Study: Use this versatile room as a guest room, home office or media room.

- Kitchen: Designed for the modern cook, this kitchen features a step-saving design, an island for added work space, and ample storage space.

- Master Suite: Step out to the rear deck from the bedroom to admire the moonlit scenery or bask in the morning sun. The luxurious bath makes an ideal place to relax in privacy.

Rear View

Main Level Floor Plan

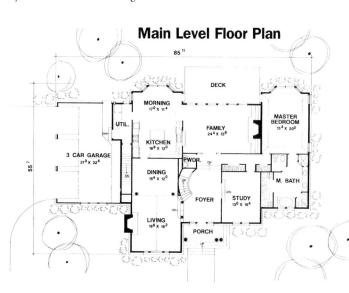

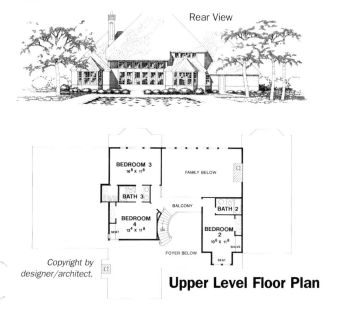

Upper Level Floor Plan

Plan #151012

Dimensions: 47' W x 94'1" D
Levels: 2
Square Footage: 3,730
Main Level Sq. Ft.: 2,648
Upper Level Sq. Ft.: 1,082
Bedrooms: 3
Bathrooms: 2½
Foundation: Crawl space or slab.
Optional full basement plan available
for extra fee.
Materials List Available: Yes
Price Category: H

Photo provided by designer/architect.

Amenities in this charmer include skylights over
the foyer and a built-in cedar storage chest.

Features:

- Living Room: Enjoy the vaulted ceiling and
warming fireplace in this gracious room.

- Den: A gas fireplace and built-in media center
and bookshelves add up to a relaxing space.

- Dining Room: 10-in. columns give formality
and built-in cabinets give practicality.

- Kitchen: Open to the morning room, the
kitchen has an island work area that's built
for efficiency.

- Morning Room: Enjoy the morning light
that streams through the bay window in
this room.

- Rear Covered Porch: Reach it from the
morning room, dining room, or master
bedroom.

Main Level Floor Plan

Upper Level Floor Plan

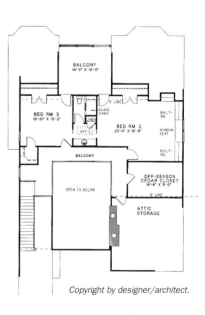

Copyright by designer/architect.

Plan #131031

Dimensions: 69'8" W x 48'4" D
Levels: 2
Square Footage: 4,027
Main Level Sq. Ft.: 2,198
Upper Level Sq. Ft.: 1,829
Bedrooms: 5
Bathrooms: 4½
Foundation: Crawl space, basement
Materials List Available: Yes
Price Category: I

Photos provided by designer/architect.

If you love dramatic lines and contemporary design, you'll be thrilled by this lovely home.

Features:

- Foyer: A gorgeous vaulted ceiling sets the stage for a curved staircase flanked by a formal living room and dining room.

- Living Room: The foyer ceiling continues in this room, giving it an unusual presence.

- Family Room: This sunken family room features a fireplace and a wall of windows that look out to the backyard. It's open to the living room, making it an ideal spot for entertaining.

- Kitchen: With a large island, this kitchen flows into the breakfast room.

- Master Suite: The luxurious bedroom has a dramatic tray ceiling and includes two-walk-in closets. The dressing room is fitted with a sink, and the spa bath is sumptuous.

Foyer

Breakfast Area

Butler's Pantry

Kitchen

Main Level Floor Plan

SL GL DRS

MAID'S RM 9' CLG 10'-0" x 12'-8"

BATH

LAUN RM

CL

KITCHEN 10'-8" x 17'-4"

ISLAND

FREZ

BKFST RM 9' CLG 10'-0" x 19'-4"

LOW WALL

FAMILY RM 9'-7" CLG SUNKEN 24'-0" x 19'-4"

CL

PANT

BUT'L PANT

LAV

DN

DN

DN

LIVING RM 9' CLG 17'-8" x 19'-8"

THREE CAR GARAGE 20'-0" x 30'-0"

DINING RM 9' CLG 16'-0" x 14'-0"

FOYER

CL

CL

PORCH

Upper Level Floor Plan

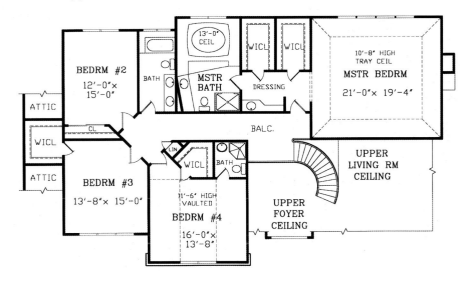

BEDRM #2 12'-0" x 15'-0"

13'-0" CEIL

BATH

MSTR BATH

WICL

WICL

DRESSING

MSTR BEDRM 10'-8" HIGH TRAY CEIL 21'-0" x 19'-4"

ATTIC

WICL

ATTIC

CL

BALC.

BEDRM #3 13'-8" x 15'-0"

LIN

WICL

BATH

BEDRM #4 11'-6" HIGH VAULTED 16'-0" x 13'-8"

UPPER FOYER CEILING

UPPER LIVING RM CEILING

Master Bedroom

Master Bathroom

Plan #181079

Dimensions: 60' W x 47'8" D
Levels: 2
Square Footage: 3,016
Main Level Sq. Ft.: 1,716
Upper Level Sq. Ft.: 1,300
Bedrooms: 6
Bathrooms: 4½
Foundation: Crawl space
Materials List Available: Yes
Price Category: G

Illustration provided by designer/architect.

Main Level Floor Plan

Upper Level Floor Plan

Copyright by designer/architect.

Plan #201126

Dimensions: 82'10" W x 54' D
Levels: 2
Square Footage: 3,813
Main Level Sq. Ft.: 2,553
Upper Level Sq. Ft.: 1,260
Bedrooms: 4
Bathrooms: 3½
Foundation: Crawl space, slab, or basement
Materials List Available: Yes
Price Category: H

Illustration provided by designer/architect.

Upper Level Floor Plan

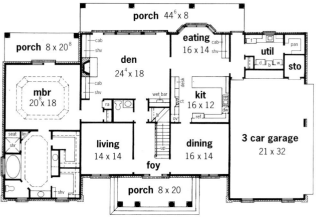

Main Level Floor Plan

Copyright by designer/architect.

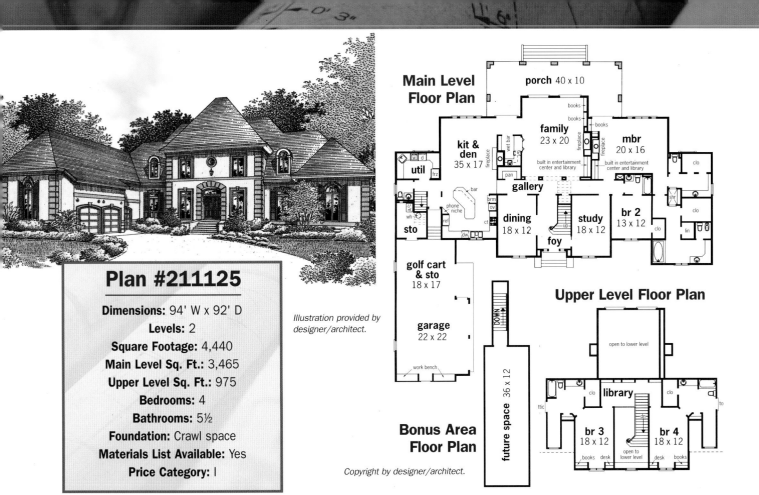

Plan #211125

Dimensions: 94' W x 92' D
Levels: 2
Square Footage: 4,440
Main Level Sq. Ft.: 3,465
Upper Level Sq. Ft.: 975
Bedrooms: 4
Bathrooms: 5½
Foundation: Crawl space
Materials List Available: Yes
Price Category: I

Illustration provided by designer/architect.

Main Level Floor Plan

porch 40 x 10

books
family 23 x 20
kit & den 35 x 17
util
wet bar
mbr 20 x 16
built in entertainment center and library
built in entertainment center and library
clo
sto
gallery
bar
dining 18 x 12
study 18 x 12
br 2 13 x 12
clo
clo
foy
lin
golf cart & sto 18 x 17
garage 22 x 22
work bench

Upper Level Floor Plan

open to lower level

DOWN

library
clo
clo
br 3 18 x 12
br 4 18 x 12
books desk
desk books
open to lower level

Bonus Area Floor Plan

future space 36 x 12

Copyright by designer/architect.

Plan #211127

Dimensions: 94' W x 71' D
Levels: 2
Square Footage: 5,474
Main Level Sq. Ft.: 4,193
Upper Level Sq. Ft.: 1,281
Bedrooms: 4
Bathrooms: 4 full, 2 half
Foundation: Slab, crawl space
Materials List Available: No
Price Category: I

Illustration provided by designer/architect.

veranda

sitting 16 x 12
den 16 x 12
breakfast 10 x 9
mbr 20 x 16
guest suite 14 x 13
family rm 26 x 22
kit
built-in entertainment
his clo
sto
3 car garage 29 x 22
computer room
her clo
library 20 x 16
foyer
dining 20 x 16
storage
receiving porch 50 x 8

Main Level Floor Plan

open to family room below

open to foyer below
bath
wic
wic
bath
attic
dress rm
dress rm
attic
desk
desk
br 3 17 x 16
study
br 4 17 x 16
down
up to attic

Upper Level Floor Plan

Copyright by designer/architect.

veranda

Plan #131025

Dimensions: 62'4" W x 65'10" D
Levels: 1½
Square Footage: 3,204
Main Level Sq. Ft.: 2,196
Upper Level Sq. Ft.: 1,008
Bedrooms: 4
Bathrooms: 4
Foundation: Basement, crawl space, or slab
Materials List Available: Yes
Price Category: H

Photo provided by designer/architect.

You'll appreciate the flowing layout that's designed for entertaining but also suits an active family.

Features:

• Ceiling Height: 8 ft.

• Great Room: Decorative columns serve as the entryway to the great room that's made for entertaining. A fireplace makes it warm in winter; built-in shelves give a classic appearance; and the serving counter it shares with the kitchen is both practical and attractive.

• Kitchen: A door into the backyard makes outdoor entertaining easy, and the full bathroom near the door adds convenience.

• Master Suite: Enjoy the sunny sitting area that's a feature of this suite. A tray ceiling adds character to the room, and a huge walk-in closet is easy to organize. The bathroom features a corner spa tub.

• Bedrooms: Each of the additional 3 bedrooms is bright and cheery.

Main Level Floor Plan

Upper Level Floor Plan

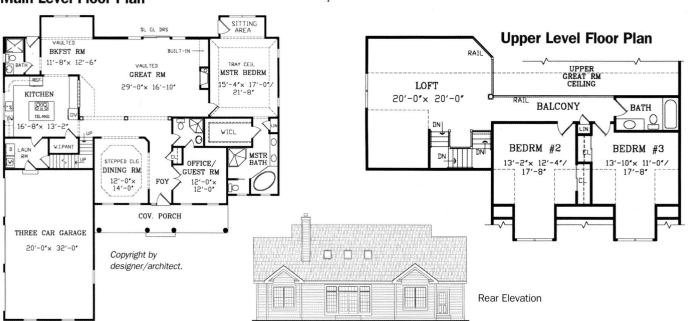

Copyright by designer/architect.

Rear Elevation

Plan #121026

Dimensions: 66'8" W x 76' D
Levels: 2
Square Footage: 3,926
Main Level Sq. Ft.: 2,351
Upper Level Sq. Ft.: 1,575
Bedrooms: 4
Bathrooms: 3 full, 2 half
Foundation: Basement
Materials List Available: Yes
Price Category: H

Plenty of space and architectural detail make this a comfortable and gracious home.

Features:

• Ceiling Height: 8 ft. unless otherwise noted.

• Great Room: A soaring cathedral ceiling makes this great room seem even more spacious than it is, while the fireplace framed by windows lends warmth and comfort.

• Eating Area: There's a dining room for more formal entertaining, but this informal eating area to the left of the great room will get plenty of daily use. It features a built-in desk for compiling shopping lists and recipes and access to the backyard.

• Kitchen: Next door to the eating area, this kitchen is designed to make food preparation a pleasure. It features a center cooktop, a recycling area, and a corner pantry.

• Lockers: You'll find a bench and lockers at the service entry and additional lockers in the laundry room next door.

Main Level Floor Plan

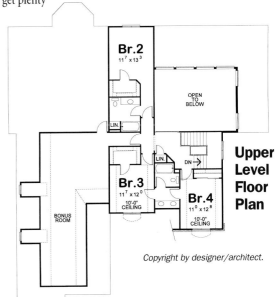

Upper Level Floor Plan

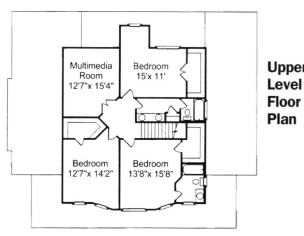

Images provided by designer/architect.

Plan #111002

Dimensions: 58' W x 59' D

Levels: 2

Square Footage: 3,266

Main Level Sq. Ft.: 2,036

Upper Level Sq. Ft.: 1,230

Bedrooms: 4

Full Bathrooms: 3½

Foundation: Aboveground basement

Materials List Available: No

Price Category: G

This design has every feature that you'll want in a home for a joyful family life.

Features:

- Ceiling Height: 10 ft.

- Front Porch: Stairs lead up to this wrap-around porch, where you can group rockers and a swing.

- Dining Room: This formal room opens from the foyer for the convenience of your guests.

- Study: French doors from the foyer open to this area, which could also serve as an office.

- Living Room: The French doors in this room lead to the screened-in porch at the rear of the house.

- Multimedia Room: On the second floor, this room is convenient to all three secondary bedrooms, so the children will love it.

- Master Suite: Two walk-in closets give a practical touch to this luxurious bedroom, and the two vanities, standing shower, and deluxe bathtub make you feel pampered by the bathroom.

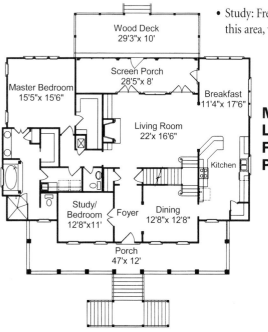

Main Level Floor Plan

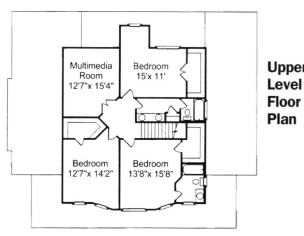

Upper Level Floor Plan

Copyright by designer/architect.

Kitchen

Living Room

SMARTtip

Woodstove Safety

A couple of issues need special emphasis with regard to stoves. The first is protecting children from contact burns. Several manufacturers make sturdy fireproof safety screens.

The second issue is making sure that logs are the right length to fit into the firebox. Once a log that's too long is popped into a hot stove, removing it safely can be tricky. Seasoned logs catch fire quickly. Nevertheless, should you insert a log that's too long in the stove, remove it immediately and transport it in a fireproof container (such as a metal ashcan) to a safe place outside: a gravel driveway, a sandbox, or a stone or concrete patio. Remember that a scorched log may be slowly burning, even if you can't see smoke. Dousing it with water from a bucket or garden hose will help.

Inadvertently closing a glass door on a slightly oversized log represents a whole set of hazards: broken glass, the need to remove the log, and a fire burning without a protective barrier between it and the combustibles in the room. If there are only embers in the firebox or the fire is low-burning and small, remove the log as described above and close what's left of the door. Open some windows, and let the fire burn down naturally. Then smother the embers with cold ashes from your ash bucket or with sand. If the fire is still crackling and sparking, create a fireproof barrier in front of the opening to prevent sparks from shooting onto combustible materials. (Possibilities for makeshift screens include metal cookie sheets or an all-metal window screen propped against the stove front.) Make sure the embers have burned out.

If there are shooting sparks and flames, get children out and call the fire department. While you wait, try to contain the flames in the firebox. (Throwing water on a fire is a last resort because of the steam and smoke that will result.) Don't cancel the SOS to the fire department even if it looks as if the flames are out.

www.ultimateplans.com   475

Plan #291013

Dimensions: 72' W x 75' D

Levels: 2

Square Footage: 3,553

Main Level Sq. Ft.: 1,830

Upper Level Sq. Ft.: 1,723

Bedrooms: 4

Bathrooms: 2½

Foundation: Basement

Materials List Available: No

Price Category: H

Main Level Floor Plan

Illustrations provided by designer/architect.

Copyright by designer/architect.

Upper Level Floor Plan

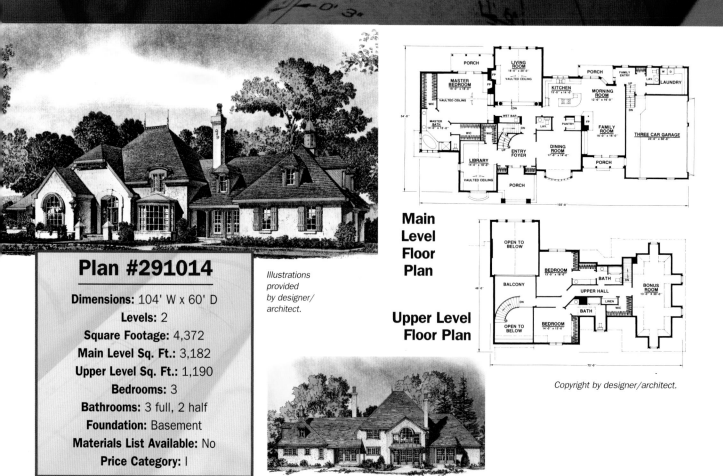

Plan #291014

Dimensions: 104' W x 60' D

Levels: 2

Square Footage: 4,372

Main Level Sq. Ft.: 3,182

Upper Level Sq. Ft.: 1,190

Bedrooms: 3

Bathrooms: 3 full, 2 half

Foundation: Basement

Materials List Available: No

Price Category: I

Illustrations provided by designer/architect.

Main Level Floor Plan

Upper Level Floor Plan

Copyright by designer/architect.

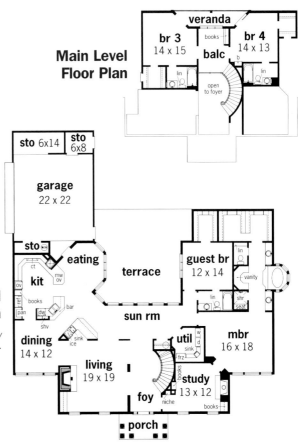

**Main Level
Floor Plan**

veranda

br 3
14 x 15

books

br 4
14 x 13

balc

b

lin

open
to foyer

lin

sto 6x14

sto
6x8

garage
22 x 22

sto
w/h

eating

kit

ct

ov

ref

pan

mw
ov

books

dw

shv

bar

terrace

sun rm

guest br
12 x 14

lin

vanity

lin

shr
seat

**Upper Level
Floor Plan**

*Copyright by
designer/architect.*

dining
14 x 12

sink
ice

util

sink

frz

mbr
16 x 18

living
19 x 19

foy

books

study
13 x 12

niche

books

porch

*Illustration provided by
designer/architect.*

Plan #211117

Dimensions: 74' W x 78' D

Levels: 2

Square Footage: 3,284

Main Level Sq. Ft.: 2,655

Upper Level Sq. Ft.: 629

Bedrooms: 4

Bathrooms: 4

Foundation: Slab

Materials List Available: Yes

Price Category: G

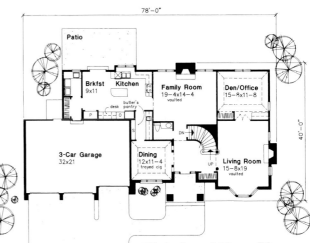

78'-0"

Patio

Brkfst
9x11

Kitchen

butler's
pantry

desk

Family Room
19-4x14-4
vaulted

Den/Office
15-8x11-8

40'-0"

3-Car Garage
32x21

Dining
12x11-4
trayed clg

DN

UP

Living Room
15-8x19
vaulted

Main Level Floor Plan

Br 3
15-8x11-6

open to below

shelf

M Suite
12-8x18-6

window seat

Br 4/
Sitting
11x10-6

shelf

DN

open to below

Br 2
15-8x13-4

**Upper Level
Floor Plan**

*Copyright by
designer/architect.*

*Illustration provided by
designer/architect.*

Plan #271032

Dimensions: 78' W x 40' D

Levels: 2

Square Footage: 3,195

Main Level Sq. Ft.: 1,758

Upper Level Sq. Ft.: 1,437

Bedrooms: 4

Bathrooms: 2½

Foundation: Basement

Materials List Available: No

Price Category: E

Plan #111011

Dimensions: 68' W x 49' D
Levels: 2
Square Footage: 3,292
Main Level Sq. Ft.: 2,862
Upper Level Sq. Ft.: 430
Bedrooms: 4
Bathrooms: 3½
Foundation: Crawl space, slab
Materials List Available: No
Price Category: G

If you're looking for a home where you can create a lovely and memorable lifestyle, this could be it.

Features:

- **Ceiling Height:** 10 ft.
- **Foyer:** This large area opens to the dining room and living room.
- **Dining Room:** You can decorate to enhance the slightly formal feeling of this room or give it a more casual atmosphere.
- **Living Room:** High ceilings and a fireplace make this room comfortable all year.
- **Office:** Use this office for a home business or as a place where family members can retreat for quiet time or solitary activities.
- **Kitchen:** This well-designed area has lots of counter space, an eating bar, and a door to the rear porch from the breakfast area.

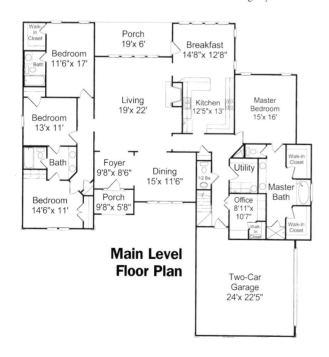

Main Level Floor Plan

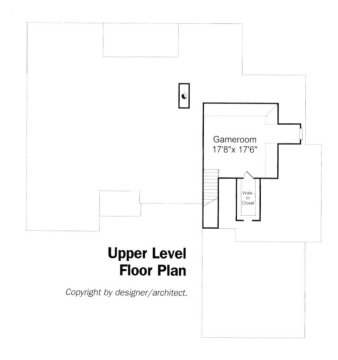

Upper Level Floor Plan

Copyright by designer/architect.

Dining Room

Rear Elevation

SMARTtip

Lead in Paint

Prior to the 1970s most paint contained lead, which is toxic to humans.

Lead poisoning symptoms include headaches, fatigue, disorientation, and in extreme cases, brain damage. Lead in paint has been banned, but many buildings still contain lead paint. Lead-paint-testing kits are available in many home centers. If you detect lead paint in your home, you should remove it. Because preparation for new painting work involves sanding and scraping, dangerous lead-laced chips and dust can be spread through the air and into your lungs. You should take the following common-sense precautions:

• Use drop cloths to catch paint chips, and then dispose of the chips. Vacuum and damp-mop the floor at the end of each workday.

• Wear a mask designed to filter out lead dust.

• Remove and wash work clothes every day. Shower and change before eating.

Children and fetuses are particularly susceptible to lead poisoning. You should keep children and pregnant women away from the work area until the work is completed. Have your children tested for lead levels, whether or not you are working with lead paint.

Living Room

Illustration provided by designer/architect.

Plan #211111

Dimensions: 66' W x 74' D

Levels: 2

Square Footage: 3,035

Main Level Sq. Ft.: 2,008

Upper Level Sq. Ft.: 1,027

Bedrooms: 4

Bathrooms: 3½

Foundation: Crawl space

Materials List Available: Yes

Price Category: G

Kids can be kids without disturbing the adults, thanks to the rear stair in this large family house.

Features:

- Ceiling Height: 9 ft. unless otherwise noted.

- Formal Living Room: This large formal living room is connected to the formal dining room and to the family room by a pair of French doors, making this an ideal home for entertaining.

- Wet Bar: This wet bar is neatly placed between the kitchen and the family room, adding to the entertainment amenities.

- Deck: Step out of the family room onto a covered porch that leads to this spacious deck and a breezeway.

- Master Suite: This master suite is isolated for privacy. The master bath is flooded with natural light from sky windows in the sloped ceiling, and it has a dressing vanity with surrounding mirrors.

- Secondary Bedrooms: All secondary bedrooms have bath access and dual closets.

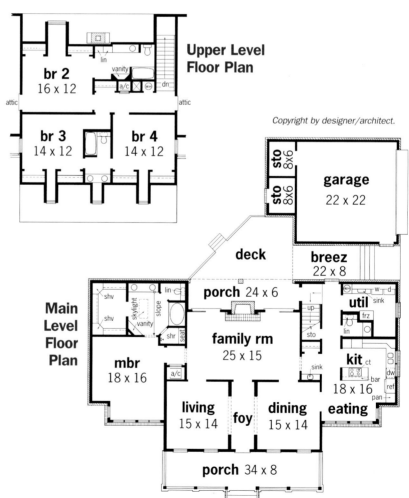

Copyright by designer/architect.

Plan #221025

Dimensions: 69'8" W x 72' D
Levels: 2
Square Footage: 3,009
Main Level Sq. Ft.: 2,039
Upper Level Sq. Ft.: 970
Bedrooms: 4
Bathrooms: 2½
Foundation: Basement
Materials List Available: No
Price Category: G

Illustration provided by designer/architect.

Designed to resemble a country home in France, this two-story beauty will delight you with its good looks and luxurious amenities.

Features:

• **Great Room:** You'll look into this great room as soon as you enter the two-story foyer. A fireplace flanked by built-in bookcases and large windows looking out to the deck highlight this room.

• **Dining Room:** This formal room is located just off the entry for the convenience of your guests.

• **Kitchen:** A huge central island and large pantry make this kitchen a delight for any cook. The large nook looks onto the deck and opens to the lovely three-season porch.

• **Master Suite:** You'll love this suite, with its charming bay shape, great windows, walk-in closet, luxurious bath, and door to the deck.

• **Upper Level:** Everyone will love the two bedrooms, large bath, and huge game.

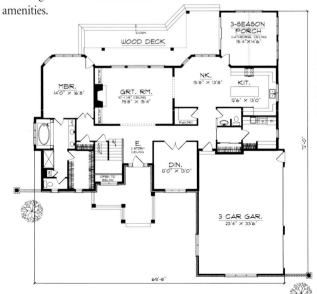

Main Level Floor Plan

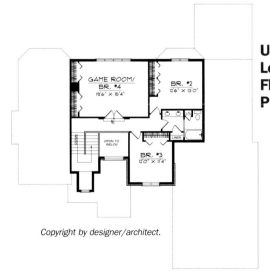

Upper Level Floor Plan

Copyright by designer/architect.

Plan #161029

Dimensions: 87' W x 82' D
Levels: 2
Square Footage: 4,470
Main Level Sq. Ft.: 3,300
Upper Level Sq. Ft.: 1,170
Bedrooms: 4
Bathrooms: 3 Full; 2 Half
Foundation: Slab
Materials List Available: Yes
Price Category: I

This gracious home is so impressive — inside and out — that it suits the most discriminating tastes.

Features:

- **Foyer:** A balcony overlooks this gracious area decorated by tall columns.

- **Hearth Room:** Visually open to the kitchen and the breakfast area, this room is ideal for any sort of gathering.

- **Great Room:** Colonial columns also form the entry here, and a magnificent window treatment that includes French doors leads to the terrace.

- **Library:** Built-in shelving adds practicality to this quiet retreat.

- **Kitchen:** Spread out on the oversized island with a cooktop and seating.

- **Additional Bedrooms:** Walk-in closets and private access to a bath define each bedroom.

Main Level Floor Plan

Copyright by designer/architect.

Upper Level Floor Plan

Rear View

Living Room

Living Room/Kitchen

Plan #161045

Dimensions: 57' W x 49'8" D

Levels: 2

Square Footage: 2,288

Main Level Sq. Ft.: 1,532

Upper Level Sq. Ft.: 545

Bedrooms: 4

Bathrooms: 2½

Foundation: Slab

Materials List Available: Yes

Price Category: E

Images provided by designer/architect.

Multiple gables, arched windows, and the stone accents that adorn the exterior of this lovely two-story home create a dramatic first impression.

Features:

- **Great Room:** With multiple windows to light your way, grand openings, varied ceiling treatments, and angled walls let you flow from room to room. Enjoy the warmth of a gas fireplace in both this great room and the dining area.

- **Master Suite:** Experience the luxurious atmosphere of this master suite, with its coffered ceiling and deluxe bath.

- **Additional Bedrooms:** Angled stairs lead to a balcony with writing desk and to two additional bedrooms.

- **Porch:** Exit two sets of French doors to the rear yard and a covered porch, perfect for relaxing in comfortable weather.

Main Level Floor Plan

Covered Porch 10' x 7'
Dining 14'2" x 11'
Kitchen 21' x 15'
pantry
Hall
Laun.
stairs up
Great Room 20'6" x 16'6"
Master Bedroom 13' x 14'7"
Foyer
Dress.
Bath
walk-in closet
linen
Two Car Garage 21' x 25'7"

57'

49'8"

Copyright by designer/architect.

Upper Level Floor Plan

Bedroom 14'2" x 11'3"
walk-in closet
Bedroom 16'8" x 10'9"
Bath
Balcony
desk
Great Room Below
Foyer Below
Bonus Room 13'2" x 17'
window seat

Rear Elevation

Rear Elevation

Plan #261001

Dimensions: 77'8" W x 49' D
Levels: 2
Square Footage: 3,746
Main Level Sq. Ft.: 1,965
Upper Level Sq. Ft.: 1,781
Bedrooms: 4
Bathrooms: 3½
Foundation: Basement
Materials List Available: No
Price Category: H

Images provided by designer/architect.

If contemporary designs appeal to you, you're sure to love this stunning home.

Features:

- Foyer: A volume ceiling here announces the spaciousness of this gracious home.

- Great Room: Also with a volume ceiling, this great room features a fireplace where you can create a cozy sitting area.

- Kitchen: Designed for the pleasure of the family cooks, this room features a large pantry, ample counter and cabinet space, and a dining bar.

- Dinette: Serve the family in style, or host casual, informal dinners for friends in this dinette with its gracious volume ceiling.

- Master Suite: A fireplace makes this suite a welcome retreat on cool nights, but even in warm weather you'll love its spaciousness and the walk-in closet. The bath features dual vanities, a whirlpool tub, and a separate shower.

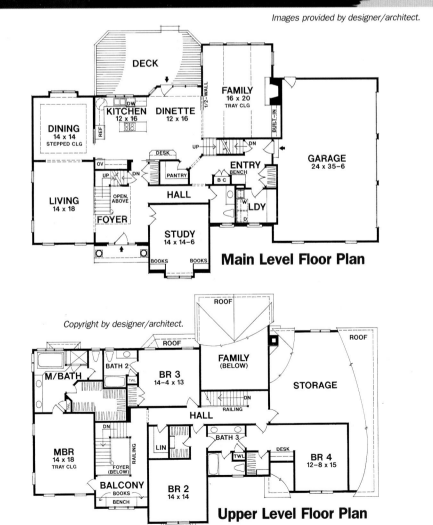

Copyright by designer/architect.

Main Level Floor Plan

Upper Level Floor Plan

Plan #151031

Dimensions: 60'2" W x 60'2" D
Levels: 2
Square Footage: 3,130
Main Level Sq. Ft.: 1,600
Upper Level Sq. Ft.: 1,530
Bedrooms: 3
Bathrooms: 3½
Foundation: Crawl space, slab
Materials List Available: Yes
Price Category: G

Photo provided by designer/architect.

If you love traditional Southern plantation homes, you'll want this house with its wraparound porches that are graced with boxed columns.

Features:

- Great Room: Use the gas fireplace for warmth in this comfortable room, which is open to the kitchen.

- Living Room: 8-in. columns add formality as you enter this living and dining room.

- Kitchen: You'll love the island bar with a sink. An elevator here can take you to the other floors.

- Master Suite: A gas fireplace warms this area, and the bath is luxurious.

- Bedrooms: Each has a private bath and built-in bookshelves for easy organizing.

- Optional Features: Choose a 2,559-sq.-ft. basement and add a kitchen to it, or finish the 1,744-sq.-ft. bonus room and add a spiral staircase and a bath.

Main Level Floor Plan

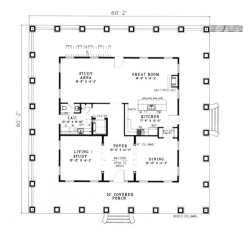

Upper Level Floor Plan

Copyright by designer/architect.

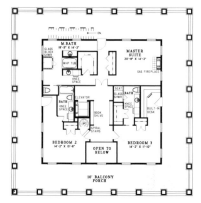

Basement Level Floor Plan

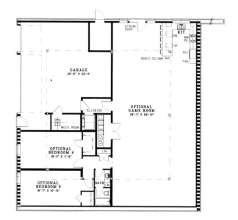

Optional Upper Level Floor Plan

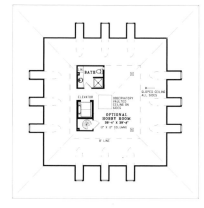

Plan #151020

Dimensions: 96'10" W x 75'10" D
Levels: 2
Square Footage: 4,532
Main Level Sq. Ft.: 3,732
Upper Level Sq. Ft.: 800
Bedrooms: 3
Bathrooms: 3
Foundation: Crawl space or slab; optional full basement plan available for extra fee
Materials List Available: Yes
Price Category: I

From the arched entry to the lanai and exercise and game rooms, this elegant home is a delight.

Features:

- Foyer: This spacious foyer with 12-ft. ceilings sets an open-air feeling for this home.

- Hearth Room: This cozy hearth room shares a 3-sided fireplace with the breakfast room. French doors open to the rear lanai.

- Dining Room: Entertain in this majestic dining room, with its arched entry and 12-ft. ceilings.

- Master Suite: This stunning suite includes a sitting room and access to the lanai. The bath features two walk-in closets, a step-up whirlpool tub with 8-in. columns, and glass-block shower.

- Upper Level: You'll find an exercise room, a game room, and attic storage space upstairs.

Rear View

Main Level Floor Plan

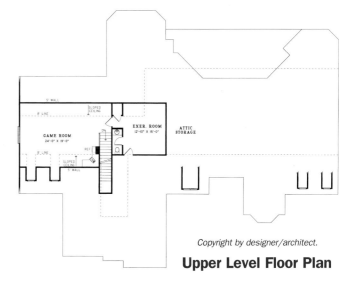

Upper Level Floor Plan

Plan #161036

Dimensions: 72'4" W x 65' D
Levels: 2
Square Footage: 3,664
Main Level Sq. Ft.: 2,497
Upper Level Sq. Ft.: 1,167
Bedrooms: 4
Bathrooms: 2½
Foundation: Slab
Materials List Available: No
Price Category: H

Images provided by designer/architect.

The traditional European brick-and-stone facade on the exterior of this comfortable home will thrill you and make your guests feel welcome.

Features:

- **Pub:** The beamed ceiling lends a casual feeling to this pub and informal dining area between the kitchen and the great room.
- **Dining Room:** Columns set off this formal dining room, from which you can see the fireplace in the expansive great room.
- **Library:** Close to the master suite, this room lends itself to quiet reading or work.
- **Master Suite:** The ceiling treatment makes the bedroom luxurious, while the whirlpool tub, double-bowl vanity, and large walk-in closet make the bath a pleasure.
- **Upper Level:** Each of the three bedrooms features a large closet and easy access to a convenient bathroom.

Main Level Floor Plan

Upper Level Floor Plan

Copyright by designer/architect.

Rear Elevation

Left Elevation

Right Elevation

Living Room

Kitchen

Dining Room

Living Room

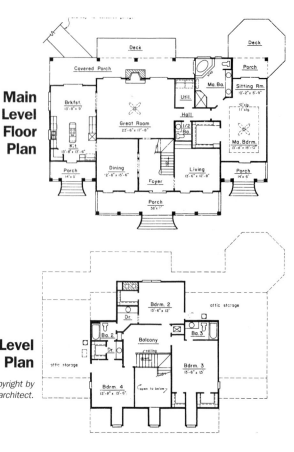

Main Level Floor Plan

Photo provided by designer/architect.

Upper Level Floor Plan

Copyright by designer/architect.

Plan #111036

Dimensions: 66' W x 47' D

Levels: 2

Square Footage: 3,149

Main Level Sq. Ft.: 2,033

Upper Level Sq. Ft.: 1,116

Bedrooms: 4

Bathrooms: 3½

Foundation: Pier

Materials List Available: No

Price Category: G

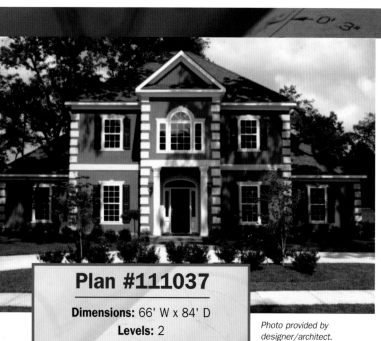

Main Level Floor Plan

Photo provided by designer/architect.

Upper Level Floor Plan

Copyright by designer/architect.

Plan #111037

Dimensions: 66' W x 84' D

Levels: 2

Square Footage: 3,176

Main Level Sq. Ft.: 2,183

Upper Level Sq. Ft.: 993

Bedrooms: 4

Bathrooms: 3½

Foundation: Slab

Materials List Available: No

Price Category: G

Plan #261003

Dimensions: 61'8" W x 58'4" D

Levels: 2

Square Footage: 2,974

Main Level Sq. Ft.: 1,569

Upper Level Sq. Ft.: 1,405

Bedrooms: 4

Bathrooms: 2½

Foundation: Basement

Materials List Available: No

Price Category: F

Images provided by designer/architect.

Main Level Floor Plan

Upper Level Floor Plan

Copyright by designer/architect.

Plan #261006

Dimensions: 73'10" W x 60' D

Levels: 2

Square Footage: 4,583

Main Level Sq. Ft.: 2,575

Upper Level Sq. Ft.: 2,008

Bedrooms: 4

Bathrooms: 3 full, 2 half

Foundation: Basement

Materials List Available: No

Price Category: I

Images provided by designer/architect.

Main Level Floor Plan

Upper Level Floor Plan

Copyright by designer/architect.

Plan #211074

Dimensions: 64' W x 89' D
Levels: 2
Square Footage: 3,486
Main Level Sq. Ft.: 2,575
Upper Level Sq. Ft.: 911
Bedrooms: 4
Bathrooms: 3
Foundation: Crawl space
Materials List Available: Yes
Price Category: G

This plantation-style home may have an old-fashioned charm, but the energy-efficient design and many amenities inside make it thoroughly contemporary.

Features:

- Ceiling Height: 9 ft.

- Porches: This wraparound front porch is fully 10 ft. wide, so you can group rockers, occasional tables, and even a swing here and save the rear porch for grilling and alfresco dining.

- Entry: A two-story ceiling here sets an elegant tone for the rest of the home.

- Living Room: Somewhat isolated, this room is an ideal spot for quiet entertaining. It has built-in bookshelves and a nearby wet bar.

- Kitchen: You'll love the large counter areas and roomy storage space in this lovely kitchen, where both friends and family are sure to congregate.

- Master Suite: It's easy to pamper yourself in this comfortable bedroom and luxurious bath.

Main Level Floor Plan

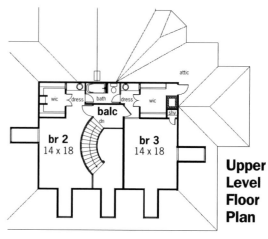

Upper Level Floor Plan

Plan #121061

Dimensions: 56' W x 52' D
Levels: 2
Square Footage: 3,025
Main Level Sq. Ft.: 1,583
Upper Level Sq. Ft.: 1,442
Bedrooms: 4
Bathrooms: 3 ½
Foundation: Basement
Materials List Available: Yes
Price Category: G

Photo provided by designer/architect.

This large home with a contemporary feeling is ideal for the family looking for comfort and amenities.

Features:

• Entry: Stacked windows bring sunlight into this two-story entry, with its stylish curved staircase.

• Library: French doors off the entry lead to this room, with its built-in bookcases flanking a large, picturesque window.

• Family Room: Located in the rear of the home, this family room is sunken to set it apart. A spider-beamed ceiling gives it a contemporary feeling, and a bay window, wet bar, and pass-through fireplace add to this impression.

• Kitchen: The island in this kitchen makes working here a pleasure. The corner pantry joins a breakfast area and hearth room to this space.

Main Level Floor Plan

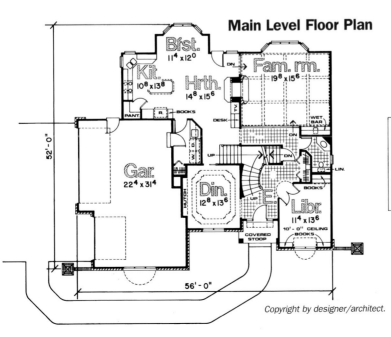

Copyright by designer/architect.

Upper Level Floor Plan

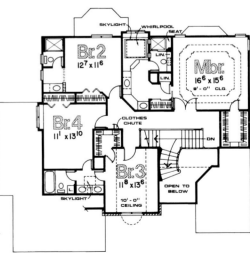

Plan #161035

Dimensions: 75' W x 64'11" D
Levels: 2
Square Footage: 3,688
Main Level Sq. Ft.: 2,702
Upper Level Sq. Ft.: 986
Bedrooms: 4
Bathrooms: 3½
Foundation: Slab
Materials List Available: No
Price Category: H

You'll appreciate the style of the stone, brick, and cedar shake exterior of this contemporary home.

Features:

• **Hearth Room:** Positioned for an easy flow for guests and family, this hearth room features a bank of windows that integrate it with the yard.

• **Breakfast Room:** Move through the sliding doors here to the rear porch on sunny days.

• **Kitchen:** Outfitted for a gourmet cook, this kitchen is also ideal for friends and family who can perch at the island or serve themselves at the bar.

• **Master Suite:** A stepped ceiling, crown moldings, and boxed window make the bedroom easy to decorate, while the two walk-in closets, lavish dressing area, and whirlpool tub in the bath make this area comfortable and luxurious.

Main Level Floor Plan

Upper Level Floor Plan

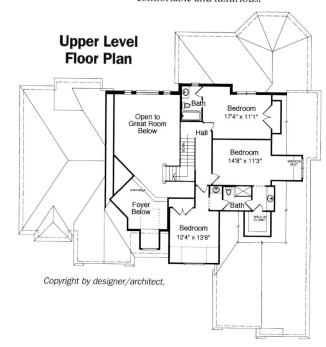

Copyright by designer/architect.

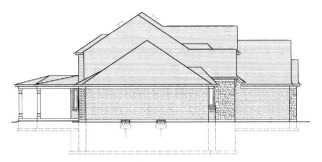

Left Elevation

Right Elevation

SMARTtip

How to Arrange Seating Around Your Fireplace

When the TV is near or on the same wall as the fireplace, you can arrange seating that places you at the best advantage to enjoy both. Position sofas and chairs in front of the fire, and remember that the distance between you and the TV should be at least three times the size of the screen.

Kitchen

Dining Room

Living Room

Master Bathroom

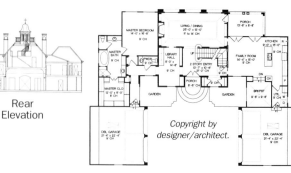

Main Level Floor Plan

Rear Elevation

Photo provided by designer/architect.

Copyright by designer/architect.

Upper Level Floor Plan

Plan #121049

Dimensions: 82' W x 60'8" D

Levels: 2

Square Footage: 3,335

Main Level Sq. Ft.: 2,054

Upper Level Sq. Ft.: 1,281

Bedrooms: 4

Bathrooms: 3½

Foundation: Slab

Materials List Available: Yes

Price Category: G

Plan #121096

Dimensions: 66' W x 58' D

Levels: 2

Square Footage: 3,611

Main Level Sq. Ft.: 1,857

Upper Level Sq. Ft.: 1,754

Bedrooms: 4

Bathrooms: 2½

Foundation: Basement

Materials List Available: Yes

Price Category: G

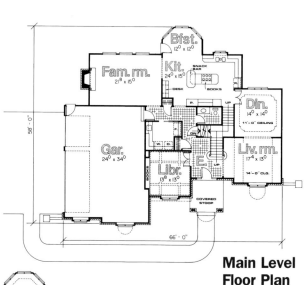

Main Level Floor Plan

Photo provided by designer/architect.

Upper Level Floor Plan

Copyright by designer/architect.

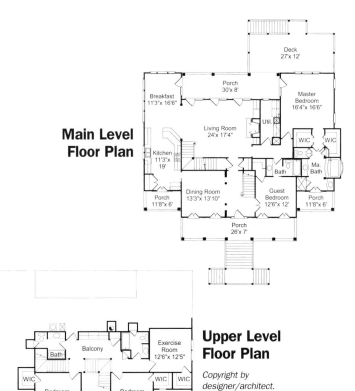

Main Level Floor Plan

Deck
27'x 12'

Porch
30'x 8'

Breakfast
11'3"x 16'6"

Master Bedroom
16'4"x 16'6"

Living Room
24'x 17'4"

Util.

WIC

WIC

Kitchen
11'3"x 19'

Bath

Ma. Bath

Dining Room
13'3"x 13'10"

Porch
11'8"x 6'

Guest Bedroom
12'6"x 12'

Porch
11'8"x 6'

Porch
26'x 7'

Plan #111038

Dimensions: 62' W x 67' D

Levels: 2

Square Footage: 3,223

Main Level Sq. Ft.: 2,213

Upper Level Sq. Ft.: 1,010

Bedrooms: 4

Bathrooms: 4

Foundation: Pier

Materials List Available: No

Price Category: G

Photo provided by designer/architect.

Upper Level Floor Plan

Bath

Balcony

Exercise Room
12'6"x 12'5"

WIC

WIC

WIC

Bedroom
13'6"x 12'6"

Open to Below

Bedroom
12'6"x 12'6"

Copyright by designer/architect.

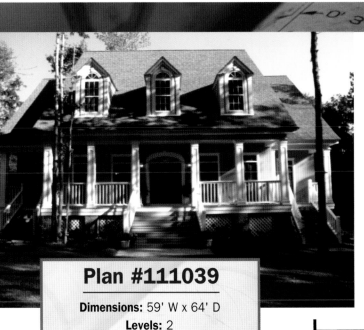

Plan #111039

Dimensions: 59' W x 64' D

Levels: 2

Square Footage: 3,335

Main Level Sq. Ft.: 2,129

Upper Level Sq. Ft.: 1,206

Bedrooms: 4

Bathrooms: 4

Foundation: Basement

Materials List Available: No

Price Category: G

Photo provided by designer/architect.

Main Level Floor Plan

Copyright by designer/architect.

Wood Deck
30'10"x 13'

Porch
30'5"x 8'

Breakfast
11'4"x 13'

Master Bedroom
16'4"x 16'4"

Living
21'6"x 17'2"

Util.

WIC

WIC

Kitchen
11'4" 18'4"

Bath

Ma. Bath

Dining
13'6"x 13'10"

Foyer

Study
13'8"x 12'

Porch

Porch

Porch
36'x 7'

Optional Lower Level Floor Plan

Storage
16'x 8'

Gameroom
21'3"x 17'

Two Car Garage
25'x 24'

Extra Storage
12'9"x 10'

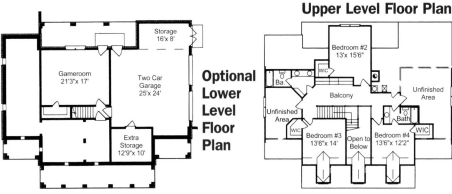

Upper Level Floor Plan

Bedroom #2
13'x 15'6"

Ba.

WIC

Unfinished Area

Balcony

Unfinished Area

WIC

Bedroom #3
13'6"x 14'

Open to Below

Bedroom #4
13'6"x 12'2"

Bath

WIC

Plan #121076

Dimensions: 64' W x 60'8" D
Levels: 2
Square Footage: 3,067
Main Level Sq. Ft.: 2,169
Upper Level Sq. Ft.: 898
Bedrooms: 4
Bathrooms: 3½
Foundation: Basement
Materials List Available: Yes
Price Category: G

You'll love the combination of formal features and casual, family-friendly areas in this spacious home with an elegant exterior.

Features:

• Entry: The elegant windows in this two-story area are complemented by the unusual staircase.

• Family Room: This family room features an 11-ft. ceiling, wet bar, fireplace, and trio of windows that look out to the covered porch.

• Living Room: Columns set off both this room and the dining room. Decorate to accentuate their formality, or make them blend into a more casual atmosphere.

• Master Suite: Columns in this suite highlight a bayed sitting room where you'll be happy to relax at the end of the day or on weekend mornings.

• Bedrooms: Bedroom 2 has a private bath, making it an ideal guest room, and you'll find private vanities in bedrooms 3 and 4.

Main Level Floor Plan

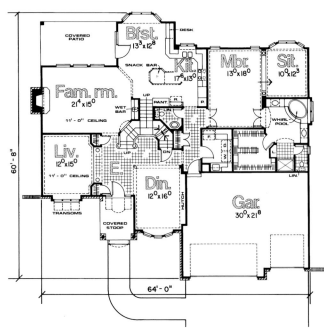

Upper Level Floor Plan

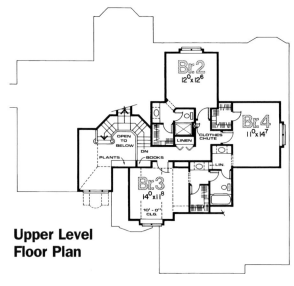

Plan #121081

Dimensions: 76'8" W x 68' D
Levels: 2
Square Footage: 3,623
Main Level Sq. Ft.: 2,603
Upper Level Sq. Ft.: 1,020
Bedrooms: 4
Bathrooms: 4½
Foundation: Basement
Materials List Available: Yes
Price Category: G

Photo provided by designer/architect.

You'll love this impressive home if you're looking for perfect spot for entertaining as well as a home for comfortable family living.

Features:

• Entry: Walk into this grand two-story entryway through double doors, and be greeted by the sight of a graceful curved staircase.

• Great Room: This two-story room features stacked windows, a fireplace flanked by an entertainment center, a bookcase, and a wet bar.

• Dining Room: A corner column adds formality to this room, which is just off the entryway for the convenience of your guests.

• Hearth Room: Connected to the great room by a lovely set of French doors, this room features another fireplace as well as a convenient pantry.

Main Level Floor Plan

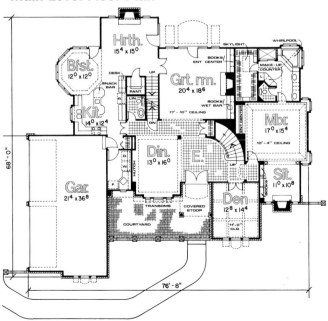

Upper Level Floor Plan

Copyright by designer/architect.

Plan #221023

Dimensions: 90'3" W x 65'8" D
Levels: 2
Square Footage: 3,511
Main Level Sq. Ft.: 1,931
Upper Level Sq. Ft.: 1,580
Bedrooms: 4
Bathrooms: 3½
Foundation: Basement
Materials List Available: No
Price Category: H

Images provided by designer/architect.

The curb appeal of this traditional two-story home, with its brick-and-stucco facade, is well matched by the luxuriousness you'll find inside.

Features:

• Ceiling Height: 9 ft.

• Family Room: This large room is open to the kitchen and the dining nook, making it an ideal spot in which to entertain.

• Living Room: The high ceiling in this room contributes to its somewhat formal feeling, and the fireplace and built-in bookcase allow you to decorate for a classic atmosphere.

• Master Suite: The bedroom in this suite has a luxurious feeling, partially because of the double French doors that are flanked by niches for displaying small art pieces or collectables. The bathroom here is unusually large and features a walk-in closet.

• Upper Level: You'll find four bedrooms, three bathrooms, and a large bonus room to use as a study or play room on this floor.

Main Level Floor Plan

FAM. RM.
22'4" × 17'0"

NK.
VAULT CEILING
11'0" × 10'0"

KIT.
18'8" × 13'6"

LIV.
10'-1 1/8" CEILING
14'4" × 18'6"

DEN
10'-1 1/8" CEILING
11'4" × 19'0"

BUTLER'S PANTRY

STOR.

3 CAR GAR.
22'0" × 43'4"

DIN.
13'0" × 15'0"

E.
2 STORY

90'-3"

65'-8"

Upper Level Floor Plan

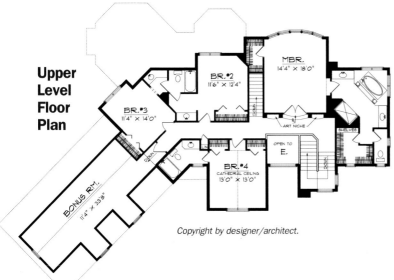

BR. #3
11'4" × 14'0"

BR. #2
11'6" × 12'4"

MBR.
14'4" × 18'0"

ART NICHE

SHELVES

BR. #4
CATHEDRAL CEILING
13'0" × 13'0"

OPEN TO E.

BONUS RM.
11'4" × 33'8"

Copyright by designer/architect.

Rear Elevation

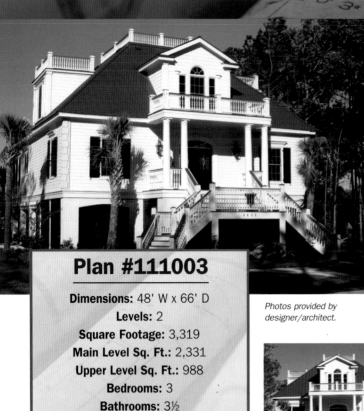

Plan #111003

Dimensions: 48' W x 66' D

Levels: 2

Square Footage: 3,319

Main Level Sq. Ft.: 2,331

Upper Level Sq. Ft.: 988

Bedrooms: 3

Bathrooms: 3½

Foundation: Pier

Materials List Available: No

Price Category: G

Photos provided by designer/architect.

Main Level Floor Plan

Copyright by designer/architect.

Master Bedroom 16'10"x 17'8"
Wood Deck 30'10"x 16'
Master Bath
Porch 17'7"x 12'
Breakfast 12'8"x 13'4"
Walk-In Closet
Family 17'6"x 20'6"
Kitchen 12'8"x 16'
Utility
½ Ba
Study 12'6"x 13'
Foyer
Dining 12'4"x 14'4"
Porch 18'x 8'

Upper Level Floor Plan

Balcony 17'5"x 10'
Bath
Playroom 13'11"x 12'1"
Dress
Bedroom 12'3"x 11'5"
Bath
Bedroom 12'3"x 11'5"
Library/ Office 11'5"x 12'1"

Plan #111035

Dimensions: 68'6" W x 74'7" D

Levels: 2

Square Footage: 3,064

Main Level Sq. Ft.: 2,143

Upper Level Sq. Ft.: 921

Bedrooms: 4

Bathroom: 3½

Foundation: Slab

Materials List Available: No

Price Category: G

Photo provided by designer/architect.

Main Level Floor Plan

Garage 22'6"x 24'6"
Covered Porch
Master Bedroom 17'2"x 16'4"
Living 22'2"x 18'
Bedroom 11'2"x 10'6"
Breakfast 12'6"x 10'
Dining 11'6"x 14'
Gameroom 13'6"x 15'6"

Upper Level Floor Plan

Copyright by designer/architect.

Bedroom 12'x 11'
Bedroom 11'x 16'
Bedroom 11'x 16'
Open to Below

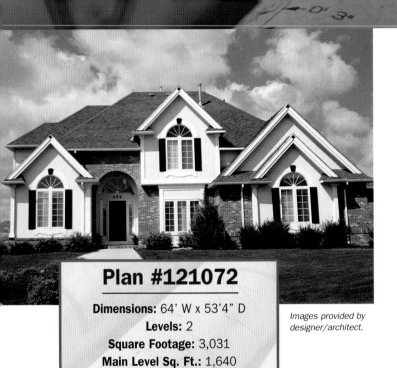

Plan #121072

Dimensions: 64' W x 53'4" D

Levels: 2

Square Footage: 3,031

Main Level Sq. Ft.: 1,640

Upper Level Sq. Ft.: 1,391

Bedrooms: 4

Bathrooms: 3½

Foundation: Basement

Materials List Available: Yes

Price Category: G

Images provided by designer/architect.

Main Level Floor Plan

Fam. rm. 19⁰ x 15⁰

Bfst. 12⁰ x 16⁰

Kit. 13⁰ x 13³

SNACK BAR

DESK

HUTCH

PANT

Den 12³ x 12⁷

Liv. 12⁰ x 13⁶

18'-0" CEILING

Din. 12⁰ x 15⁰

Gar. 21⁸ x 32⁸

COVERED STOOP

53'-4"

64'-0"

Upper Level Floor Plan

Copyright by designer/architect.

Mbr. 17⁰ x 15¹⁰
10'-0" CEILING

BUILT-IN DRESSER

Br 4 12⁰ x 13⁵

Br 2 13⁰ x 12⁰

LINEN

OPEN TO BELOW

w/P

GLASS BLOCK

LIN.

Br 3 12⁰ x 13⁰
17'-10" CEILING
10'-0" CEILING

Plan #261008

Dimensions: 68' W x 64'6" D

Levels: 2

Square Footage: 2,226

Main Level Sq. Ft.: 1,689

Upper Level Sq. Ft.: 537

Bedrooms: 4

Bathrooms: 3

Foundation: Basement

Materials List Available: No

Price Category: E

Images provided by designer/architect.

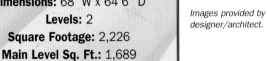

Main Level Floor Plan

WOOD DECK 22-3 x 22-8

DINETTE VAULTED CLG 14-6 x 10-2

WALL ABOVE

GREAT RM 20-6 x 15-4 VAULTED CLG

KITCHEN 13-6 x 11-0 WORK ISLAND

DW OV

3 CAR GARAGE 23-6 x 33-4

PANTRY

SHWR BATH 3

BENCH ENTRY

WALL ABV

BUILT IN SHLVS

WINDOW SEAT

OFFICE 11-0 x 13-6

BUILT IN SHLVS

FOYER

PORCH

BEDRM 4 11-4 x 11-0

Upper Level Floor Plan

Copyright by designer/architect.

GREAT ROOM BELOW VAULTED CLG

M BEDRM TRAY CLG 17-0 x 15-4

M BATH

HALL

BALC

BATH 2

W.I.C.

DN

LIN

BEDRM 2 11-0 x 13-6

W.I.C.

BEDRM 3 10-9 x 12-0

LND

STORAGE

Photos and illustration provided by designer/architect.

Plan #211076

Dimensions: 95' W x 90' D
Levels: 2
Square Footage: 4,242
Main Level Sq. Ft.: 3,439
Upper Level Sq. Ft.: 803
Bedrooms: 4
Bathrooms: 4 full, 3 half
Foundation: Raised slab
Materials List Available: Yes
Price Category: I

Build this country manor home on a large lot with a breathtaking view to complement its beauty.

Features:

- Foyer: You'll love the two-story ceiling here.

- Living Room: A sunken floor, two-story ceiling, large fireplace, and generous balcony above combine to create an unusually beautiful room.

- Kitchen: Use the breakfast bar at any time of the day. The layout guarantees ample working space, and the pantry gives room for extra storage.

- Master Suite: A sunken floor, wood-burning fireplace, and 200-sq.-ft. sitting area work in concert to create a restful space.

- Bedrooms: The guest room is on the main floor, and bedrooms 2 and 3, both with built-in desks in special study areas, are on the upper level.

- Outdoor Grilling Area: Fitted with a bar, this area makes it a pleasure to host a large group.

Kitchen

Kitchen

Main Level Floor Plan

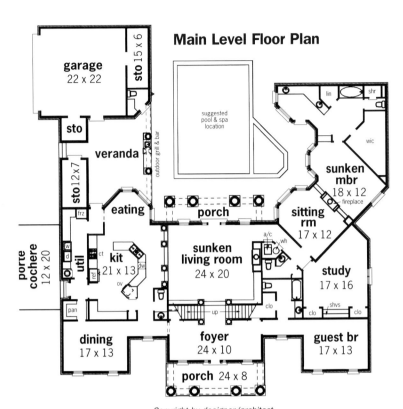

- garage 22 x 22
- sto 15 x 6
- sto
- veranda
- sto 12 x 7
- frz
- eating
- porte cochere 12 x 20
- util
- w / d
- ct
- ref
- pan
- kit 21 x 13
- dw
- ov
- suggested pool & spa location
- outdoor grill & bar
- porch
- sunken living room 24 x 20
- up
- a/c
- wh
- clo
- lin
- shr
- wic
- sunken mbr 18 x 12 — fireplace
- sitting rm 17 x 12
- study 17 x 16
- clo
- shvs
- clo
- dining 17 x 13
- foyer 24 x 10
- porch 24 x 8
- guest br 17 x 13

Copyright by designer/architect.

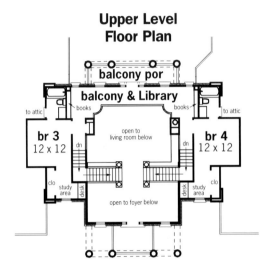

Master Bathroom

Upper Level Floor Plan

- balcony por
- balcony & Library
- to attic
- books
- books
- to attic
- br 3 12 x 12
- open to living room below
- br 4 12 x 12
- dn
- dn
- clo
- study area
- desk
- desk
- study area
- clo
- open to foyer below

Dining Room

Living Room

Plan #211077

Dimensions: 94' W x 68' D
Levels: 2
Square Footage: 5,560
Main Level Sq. Ft.: 4,208
Upper Level Sq. Ft.: 1,352
Bedrooms: 4
Bathrooms: 4 full, 2 half
Foundation: Slab, or crawl space
Materials List Available: No
Price Category: I

This palatial home has a two-story veranda and offers room and amenities for a large family.

Features:

- Ceiling Height: 10 ft.

- Library: Teach your children the importance of quiet reflection in this library, which boasts a full wall of built-in bookshelves.

- Master Suite: Escape the pressures of a busy day in this truly royal master suite. Curl up in front of your own fireplace. Or take a long, soothing soak in the private bath, with his and her sinks and closets.

- Kitchen: This room offers many modern comforts and amenities, and free-flowing traffic patterns.

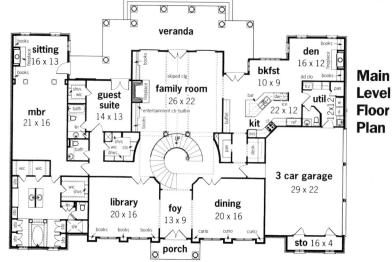

Main Level Floor Plan

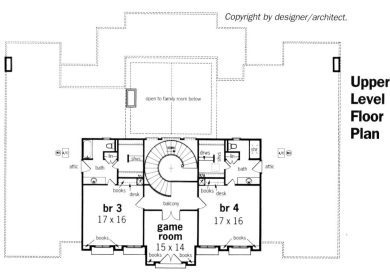

Upper Level Floor Plan

Plan #211075

Dimensions: 80' W x 84' D
Levels: 2
Square Footage: 3,568
Main Level Sq. Ft.: 2,330
Upper Level Sq. Ft.: 1,238
Bedrooms: 4
Bathrooms: 3½
Foundation: Crawl space
Materials List Available: Yes
Price Category: H

Photo provided by designer/architect.

The porte-cochere—or covered passage over a driveway—announces the quality and beauty of this spacious country home.

Features:

• Front Porch: Spot groups of potted plants on this 779-sq.-ft. porch, and add a glider and some rocking chairs to take advantage of its comfort.

• Family Room: Let this family room become the heart of the home. With a fireplace to make it cozy and a wet bar for easy serving, it's a natural for entertaining.

• Game Room: Expect a crowd in this room, no matter what the weather.

• Kitchen: A cooktop island and a pantry are just two features of this fully appointed kitchen.

• Master Suite: The bedroom is as luxurious as you'd expect, but the quarter-circle raised tub in the master bath might surprise you. Two walk-in closets and two vanities add a practical touch.

Main Level Floor Plan

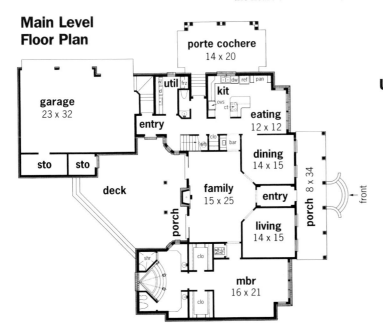

Upper Level Floor Plan

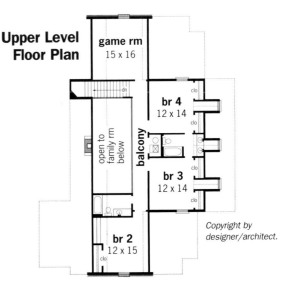

Copyright by designer/architect.

Plan #161033

Dimensions: 78'2" W x 74'6" D
Levels: 2
Square Footage: 5,125
Main Level Sq. Ft.: 2,782
Upper Level Sq. Ft.: 1,027
Optional Basement Level Sq. Ft.:
1,316
Bedrooms: 4
Bathrooms: 3½
Foundation: Slab
Materials List Available: Yes
Price Category: I

Images provided by designer/architect.

The dramatic design of this home, combined with its comfort and luxuries, suit those with discriminating tastes.

Features:

- **Great Room:** Let the fireplace and 14-ft. ceilings in this room set the stage for all sorts of gatherings, from causal to formal.

- **Dining Room:** Adjacent to the great room and kitchen fit for a gourmet, the dining room allows you to entertain with ease.

- **Music Room:** Give your music the space it deserves in this specially-designed room.

- **Library:** Use this room as an office, or reserve it for quiet reading and studying.

- **Master Suite:** You'll love the separate dressing area and walk-in closet in the bedroom.

- **Lower Level:** A bar and recreational area give even more space for entertaining.

Rear View

Main Level Floor Plan

Copyright by designer/architect.

Patio
22' x 18'

Dining Room
15'3" x 15'3"
9' ceiling ht.

Kitchen
20' x 15'4"

Master
Bedroom
14'6" x 15'4"

Great Room
21'5" x 27'8"
14' ceiling ht.

Library
15'6" x 15'2" irr.

Dressing

Laun.

Hall
9' ceiling ht.

Foyer
11' ceiling ht.

Music Room
14'9" x 12'2"
11' ceiling ht.

Porch

Three Car Garage
21' x 28'9"

Upper Level Floor Plan

Bedroom
12'10" x 12'10"

Bedroom
14'4" x 12'

Balcony
10'2" x 6'4"

Bath

Bedroom
17' x 12'

Sitting
Area
8'8" x 11'7"

Media
Room
12'7" x 15'

Billiards
19'6" x 22'3"

Hobby Room
14' x 16'5"

Bar
12' x 11'6"

Bath

Basement

Basement

Unexcavated

Unexcavated

**Optional Basement
Level Floor Plan**

Color Wheel Combinations

The color wheel is the designer's most useful tool for pairing colors. Basically, it presents the spectrum of pigment hues as a circle. The primary colors (yellow, blue, and red) are combined in the remaining hues (orange, green, and purple). The following are the most often used configurations for creating color schemes.

Dining Room

Living Room

Plan #161023

Dimensions: 71'8" W x 38'10" D

Levels: 2

Square Footage: 3,445

Main Level Sq. Ft.: 1,666

Mid Level Sq. Ft.: 743

Upper Level Sq. Ft.: 1,036

Bedrooms: 4

Bathrooms: 3½

Foundation: Slab

Materials List Available: No

Price Category: G

You'll love the versatility that the mixture of formal and informal spaces gives to this home.

Features:

• Dining Room: Let guests move from the formal dining room into the adjoining cozy hearth room.

• Hearth Room: Also situated close to the kitchen and breakfast room, the hearth room is a true center of this home. The fireplace, wood ceiling, and a recessed entertainment center add charm.

• Mid Level Wing: A computer area and 2 bedrooms highlight this separate space.

• Master Suite: A sitting area, fireplace, and dressing room attached to the master bath make this area a dream come true.

• Guest Room: This area includes a private bath and walk-in closet.

Images provided by designer/architect.

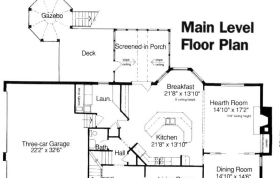

Main Level Floor Plan

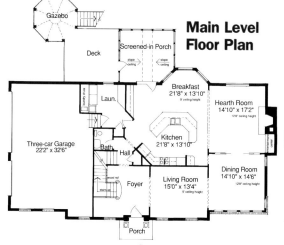

Upper Level Floor Plan

Copyright by designer/architect.

Living Room

Kitchen

Dining Room

Plan #151021

Dimensions: 75'2" W x 89'6" D
Levels: 2
Square Footage: 3,385
Main Level Sq. Ft.: 2,633
Upper Level Sq. Ft.: 752
Bedrooms: 4
Bathrooms: 4
Foundation: Crawl space, or slab
Materials List Available: Yes
Price Category: G

Photo provided by designer/architect.

From the fireplace in the master suite to the well-equipped game room, the amenities in this home will surprise and delight you.

Features:

- Great Room: A bank of windows on the far wall lets sunlight stream into this large room. The fireplace is located across the room and is flanked by the built-in media center and built-in bookshelves. Gracious brick arches create an entry into the breakfast area and kitchen.

- Breakfast Room: Move easily between this room with 10-foot ceiling either into the kitchen or onto the rear covered porch.

- Game Room: An icemaker and refrigerator make entertaining a snap in this room.

- Master Suite: A 10-ft. boxed ceiling, fireplace, and access to the rear porch give romance, while the built-ins in the closet, whirlpool tub with glass blocks, and glass shower give practicality.

Main Level Floor Plan

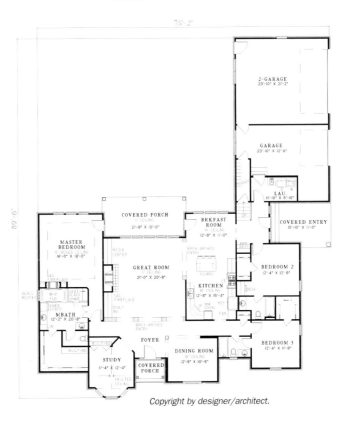

Copyright by designer/architect.

Upper Level Floor Plan

Plan #151026

Dimensions: 34' W x 66'8" D
Levels: 2
Square Footage: 1,574
Main Level Sq. Ft.: 1,131
Upper Level Sq. Ft.: 443
Bedrooms: 3
Bathrooms: 2
Foundation: Crawl space, slab; optional full basement plan available for extra fee
Materials List Available: Yes
Price Category: C

This French Country home gives space for entertaining and offers privacy.

Features:

- **Great Room:** Move through the gracious foyer framed by wooden columns into the great room with its lofty 10-ft. ceilings and gas fireplace.

- **Dining Room:** Set off by 8-in. columns, the dining room opens to the kitchen, both with 9-foot ceilings.

- **Master Suite:** Enjoy relaxing in the bedroom with its 10-ft. boxed ceiling and well-placed windows. Atrium doors open to the backyard, where you can make a secluded garden. A glass-bricked corner whirlpool tub, corner shower, and double vanity make the master bath luxurious.

- **Bedrooms:** Upstairs, two large bedrooms with a walk-through bath provide plenty of room as well as privacy for kids or guests.

Photo provided by designer/architect.

Main Level Floor Plan

Upper Level Floor Plan

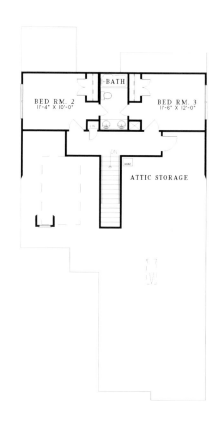

Copyright by designer/architect.

Plan #271025

Dimensions: 62' W x 57' D
Levels: 2
Square Footage: 2,223
Main Level Sq. Ft.: 1,689
Upper Level Sq. Ft.: 534
Bedrooms: 3
Bathrooms: 2½
Foundation: Basement
Materials List Available: Yes
Price Category: E

Photo provided by designer/architect.

This traditional home's unique design combines a dynamic, exciting exterior with a fantastic floor plan.

Features:

- **Living Room:** To the left of the column-lined, barrel-vaulted entry, this inviting space features a curved wall and corner windows.

- **Dining Room:** A tray ceiling enhances this formal meal room.

- **Kitchen:** This island-equipped kitchen includes a corner pantry and a built-in desk. Nearby, the sunny breakfast room opens onto a backyard deck via sliding glass doors.

- **Family Room:** A corner bank of windows provides a glassy backdrop for this room's handsome fireplace. Munchies may be served on the snack bar from the breakfast nook.

- **Master Suite:** This main-floor retreat is simply stunning, and includes a vaulted ceiling, access to a private courtyard, and of course, a sumptuous bath with every creature comfort.

Main Level Floor Plan

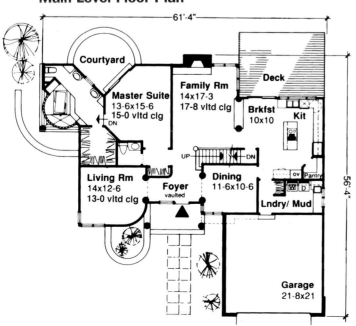

Upper Level Floor Plan

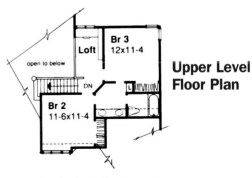

Copyright by designer/architect.

Plan #161031

Dimensions: 99'8" W x 68'8" D
Levels: 2
Square Footage: 5,381
Main Level Sq. Ft.: 3,793
Upper Level Sq. Ft.: 1,588
Bedrooms: 4
Bathrooms: 3½
Foundation: Slab
Materials List Available: Yes
Price Category: I

Images provided by designer/architect.

If you're looking for a compatible mixture of formal and informal areas in a home, look no further!

Features:

• Great Room: Columns at the entry to this room and the formal dining room set a gracious tone that is easy around which to decorate.

• Library: Set up an office or just a cozy reading area in this quiet room.

• Hearth Room: Spacious and inviting, this hearth room is positioned so that friends and family can flow from here to the breakfast area and kitchen.

• Master Suite: The luxury of this area is capped by the access it gives to the rear yard.

• Lower Level: Enjoy the 9-ft.-tall ceilings as you walk out to the rear yard from this area.

Entry

Rear View

Main Level Floor Plan

Copyright by designer/architect.

Bedroom
16'8" x 12'

Bath

Hall

Bedroom
16'8" x 12'

Laun.

Hearth Room   Breakfast
23' x 16' irr.

Kitchen
17'7" x 14'8"

Deck

Great Room
16' x 21'6"

Sloped Ceiling   Sloped Ceiling

Foyer

Master Bedroom
15'8" x 22"

tray ceiling

walk-in closet

Dressing

walk-in closet

Three Car
Garage
20' x 33'4"

Dining Room
13'6" x 15'3" irr.

Porch

Library
12'4" x 16'2" irr.

**Basement Level
Floor Plan**

Bedroom
12' x 10'

Rec Room
44'1" x 31'2" Irreg.

Bath

Bar

Unfinished Basement

Dining Room

Rear Elevation

Left Elevation

Right Elevation

Plan #181039

Dimensions: 38' W x 36' D
Levels: 2
Square Footage: 1,661
Main Level Sq. Ft.: 923
Upper Level Sq. Ft.: 738
Bedrooms: 3
Bathrooms: 1½
Foundation: Full basement
Materials List Available: Yes
Price Category: C

Illustration provided by designer/architect.

Main Level Floor Plan

Upper Level Floor Plan

Copyright by designer/architect.

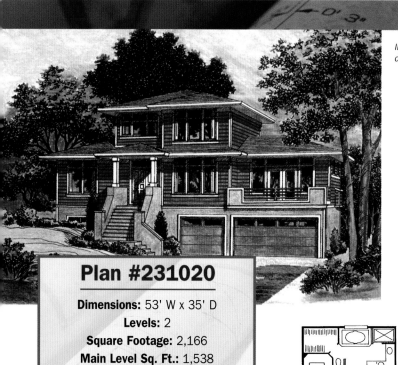

Plan #231020

Dimensions: 53' W x 35' D
Levels: 2
Square Footage: 2,166
Main Level Sq. Ft.: 1,538
Upper Level Sq. Ft.: 628
Bedrooms: 3
Bathrooms: 2½
Foundation: Slab, basement
Materials List Available: No
Price Category: D

Illustration provided by designer/architect.

Main Level Floor Plan

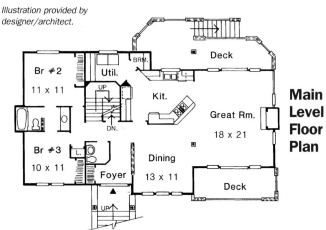

- Br #2 — 11 x 11
- Br #3 — 10 x 11
- Util.
- Kit.
- Great Rm. — 18 x 21
- Dining — 13 x 11
- Foyer
- Deck

Upper Level Floor Plan

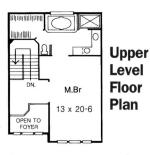

- M.Br — 13 x 20-6
- OPEN TO FOYER

Garage Level Floor Plan

- Shop — 13 x 13
- Garage — 31 x 27
- Unfin. Stor. — 13 x 15
- Unfin. Stor — 9-6 x 9

Copyright by designer/architect.

Plan #161027

Dimensions: 59'10" W x 37'4" D
Levels: 2
Square Footage: 2,388
Main Level Sq. Ft.: 1,207
Upper Level Sq. Ft.: 1,181
Bedrooms: 4
Bathrooms: 2½
Foundation: Slab
Materials List Available: No
Price Category: E

Double gables, wood trim, an arched window, and sidelights at the entry give elegance to this family-friendly home.

Features:

- Foyer: Friends and family will see the angled stairs, formal dining room, living room, and library from this foyer.

- Family Room: A fireplace makes this room cozy in the evenings on those chilly days, and multiple windows let natural light stream into it.

- Kitchen: You'll love the island and the ample counter space here as well as the butler's pantry. A breakfast nook makes a comfortable place to snack or just curl up and talk to the cook.

- Master Suite: Tucked away on the upper level, this master suite provides both privacy and luxury.

- Additional Bedrooms: These three additional bedrooms make this home ideal for any family.

Images provided by designer/architect.

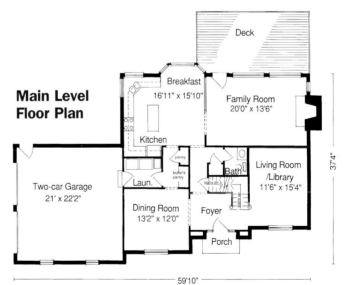

Copyright by designer/architect.

Photo provided by designer/architect.

Plan #121024

Dimensions: 60' W x 58' D
Levels: 2
Square Footage: 3,057
Main Level Sq. Ft.: 1,631
Second Level Sq. Ft.: 1,426
Bedrooms: 4
Bathrooms: 2½
Foundation: Basement
Materials List Available: Yes
Price Category: G

This distinctive home offers plenty of space and is designed for gracious and convenient living.

Features:

- Ceiling Height: 8 ft. unless otherwise noted.

- Foyer: A curved staircase in this elegant entry will greet your guests.

- Living Room: This room invites you with a volume ceiling flanked by transom-topped windows that flood the room with sunlight.

- Screened Veranda: On warm summer nights, throw open the French doors in the living room and enjoy a breeze on the huge screened veranda.

- Dining Room: This distinctive room is overlooked by the veranda.

- Family Room: At the back of the home is this comfortable family retreat with its soaring cathedral ceiling and handsome fireplace flanked by bookcases.

- Master Bedroom: This bayed bedroom features a 10-ft. vaulted ceiling.

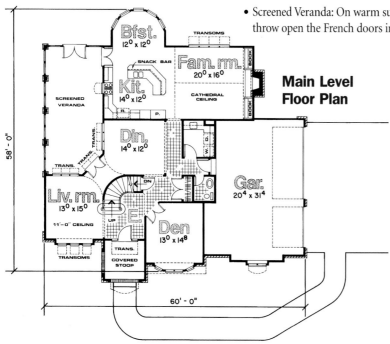

Main Level Floor Plan

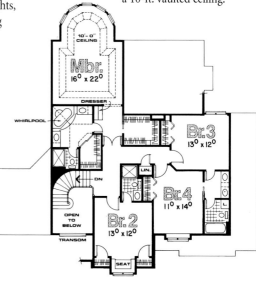

Upper Level Floor Plan

Copyright by designer/architect.

Plan #121020

Dimensions: 64' W x 46' D
Levels: 2
Square Footage: 2,480
Main Level Sq. Ft.: 1,369
Upper Level Sq. Ft.: 1,111
Bedrooms: 4
Bathrooms: 3
Foundation: Basement
Materials List Available: Yes
Price Category: E

Tapered columns and an angled stairway give this home a classical style.

Features:

- Ceiling Height: 8 ft.

- Living Room: Just off the dramatic two-story entry is this distinctive living room, with its tapered columns, transom-topped windows, and boxed ceiling.

- Formal Dining Room: The tapered columns, transom-topped windows, and boxed ceiling found in the living room continue into this gracious dining space.

- Family Room: Located on the opposite side of the house from the living room and dining room, the family room features a beamed ceiling and fireplace framed by windows.

- Kitchen: An island is the centerpiece of this convenient kitchen.

- Master Suite: Upstairs, a tiered ceiling and corner windows enhance the master bedroom, which is served by a pampering bath.

Main Level Floor Plan

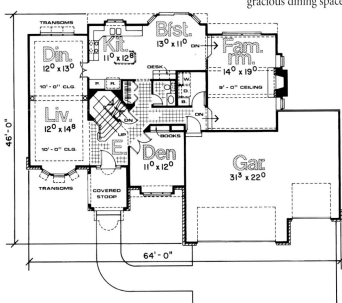

Upper Level Floor Plan

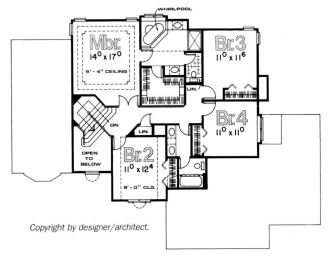

Plan #131033

Dimensions: 84'10" W x 48' D
Levels: 2
Square Footage: 2,813
Main Level Sq. Ft.: 1,890
Upper Level Sq. Ft.: 923
Bedrooms: 5
Bathrooms: 3½
Foundation: Crawl space, slab, or basement
Materials List Available: Yes
Price Category: G

Contemporary styling, luxurious amenities, and the classics that make a house a home are all available here.

Features:

- Family Room: A sloped ceiling with skylight and a railed overlook to make this large space totally up to date.

- Living Room: Sunken for comfort and with a cathedral ceiling for style, this room features a fireplace flanked by windows and sliding glass doors.

- Master Suite: Unwind in this room, with its cathedral ceiling, with a skylight, walk-in closet, and private access to the den.

- Upper Level: A bridge overlooks the living room and foyer and leads through the family room to three bedrooms and a bath.

- Optional Guest Suite: 500 sq. ft. above the master suite and den provides total comfort.

Images provided by designer/architect.

Main Level Floor Plan

Copyright by designer/architect.

Upper Level Floor Plan

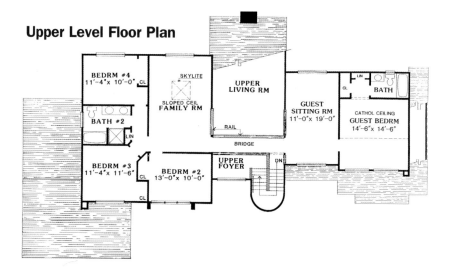

Entry

Living Room / Foyer

Living Room

Rear View

Photo provided by designer/architect.

Plan #121015

Dimensions: 52' W x 47'4" D
Levels: 2
Square Footage: 1,999
Main Level Sq. Ft.: 1,421
Upper Level Sq. Ft.: 578
Bedrooms: 3
Bathrooms: 3
Foundation: Basement
Materials List Available: Yes
Price Category: D

Hipped roofs and a trio of gables bring distinction to this plan.

Features:

- Ceiling Height: 8 ft.

- Open Floor Plan: The rooms flow into each other and are flanked by an abundance of windows. The result is a light and airy space that seems much larger than it really is.

- Formal Dining Room: Here is the perfect room for elegant entertaining.

- Breakfast Nook: This bright, bayed nook is the perfect place to start the day. It's also great for intimate get-togethers.

- Great Room: The family will enjoy gathering in this spacious area.

- Bedrooms: This large master bedroom, along with three secondary bedrooms and an extra room, provides plenty of room for a growing family.

- Attached Garage: The garage provides two bays of parking plus plenty of storage space.

Main Level Floor Plan

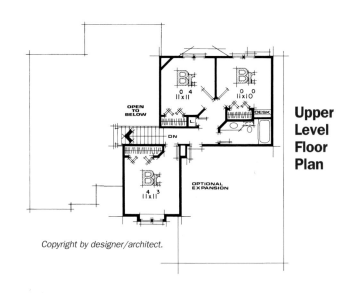

Upper Level Floor Plan

Copyright by designer/architect.

Plan #121031

Dimensions: 52' W x 51'4" D
Levels: 2
Square Footage: 1,772
Main Level Sq. Ft.: 1,314
Upper Level Sq. Ft.: 458
Bedrooms: 3
Bathrooms: 2½
Foundation: Basement
Materials List Available: Yes
Price Category: C

This home features architectural details reminiscence of earlier fine homes.

Features:

• Ceiling Height: 8 ft. unless otherwise noted.

• Foyer: This grand entry soars two-stories high. The U-shaped staircase with window leads to a second-story balcony.

• Great Room: You'll be drawn to the impressive views through the triple-arch

windows at the front and rear of this room.

• Kitchen: Designed for maximum efficiency, this kitchen is a pleasure to be in. It features a center island, a full pantry, and a desk for added convenience.

• Breakfast Area: This area adjoins the kitchen. Both rooms are flooded with sunlight streaming from a shared bay window.

• Master Suite: The stylish bedroom includes a walk-in closet. Luxuriate in the whirlpool tub at the end of a long day .

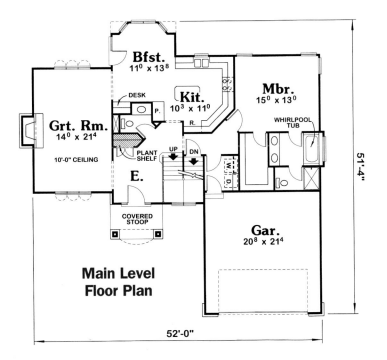

**Main Level
Floor Plan**

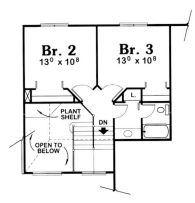

**Upper Level
Floor Plan**

Plan #321051

Dimensions: 69'8" W x 46' D

Levels: 2

Square Footage: 2,624

Main Level Sq. Ft.: 1,774

Upper Level Sq. Ft.: 850

Bedrooms: 4

Bathrooms: 2½

Foundation: Basement

Materials List Available: Yes

Price Category: F

Images provided by designer/architect.

If you're looking for a home that deserves to be called "grand" and "elegant," you will love this spacious beauty.

Features:

- **Entryway:** Two stories high, this area sets the tone for the whole house.

- **Great Room:** The 18-ft. ceiling in this room gives a bright and airy feeling that the three magnificent Palladian windows surely enhance.

- **Dining Room:** A classic colonnade forms the entry to this lovely bayed room.

- **Kitchen:** Designed for gourmet cooks who love efficient work spaces, this kitchen will delight the whole family.

- **Master Suite:** Relax in the comfort of this luxurious suite at the end of the day. You'll find walk-in closets, a large bay window, and plant shelves in the bedroom, as well as a sunken tub in the bathroom.

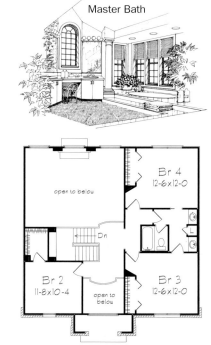

Master Bath

Main Level Floor Plan

Copyright by designer/architect.

Upper Level Floor Plan

Plan #231023

Dimensions: 72' W x 78'6" D
Levels: 2
Square Footage: 3,215
Main Level Sq. Ft.: 2,311
Upper Level Sq. Ft.: 904
Bedrooms: 3
Bathrooms: 2½
Foundation: Crawl space
Materials List Available: No
Price Category: G

Main Level Floor Plan

Illustration provided by designer/architect.

Upper Level Floor Plan

Copyright by designer/architect.

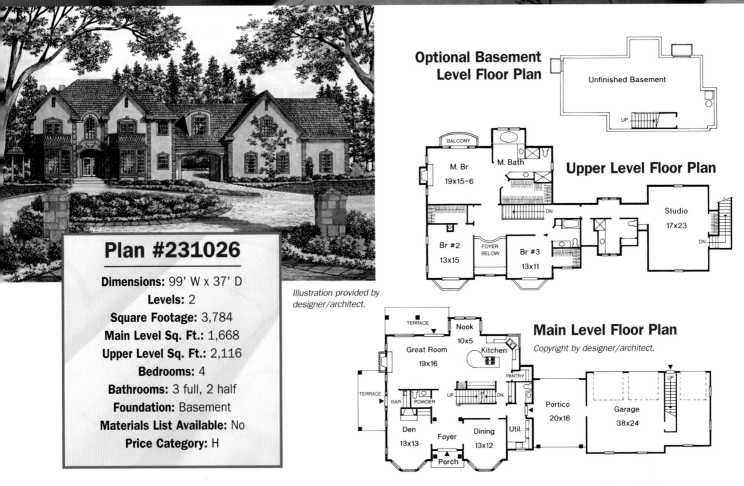

Plan #231026

Dimensions: 99' W x 37' D
Levels: 2
Square Footage: 3,784
Main Level Sq. Ft.: 1,668
Upper Level Sq. Ft.: 2,116
Bedrooms: 4
Bathrooms: 3 full, 2 half
Foundation: Basement
Materials List Available: No
Price Category: H

Optional Basement Level Floor Plan

Upper Level Floor Plan

Illustration provided by designer/architect.

Main Level Floor Plan

Copyright by designer/architect.

Plan #121029

Dimensions: 58'8" W x 54' D
Levels: 2
Square Footage: 2,576
Main Level Sq. Ft.: 1,735
Upper Level Sq. Ft.: 841
Bedrooms: 4
Bathrooms: 2½
Foundation: Basement
Materials List Available: Yes
Price Category: E

Photo provided by designer/architect.

This gracious home is designed with the contemporary lifestyle in mind.

Features:

- Ceiling Height: 8 ft. unless otherwise noted.

- Great Room: This room features a fireplace and entertainment center. It's equally suited for family gatherings and formal entertaining.

- Breakfast Area: The fireplace is two-sided so it shares its warmth with this breakfast area— the perfect spot for informal family meals.

- Master Suite: Halfway up the staircase you'll find double-doors into this truly distinctive suite featuring a barrel-vault ceiling, built-in bookcases, and his and her walk-in closets. Unwind at the end of the day by stretching out in the oval whirlpool tub.

- Computer Loft: This loft overlooks the great room. It is designed as a home office with a built-in desk for your computer.

- Garage: Two bays provide plenty of storage in addition to parking space.

Main Level Floor Plan

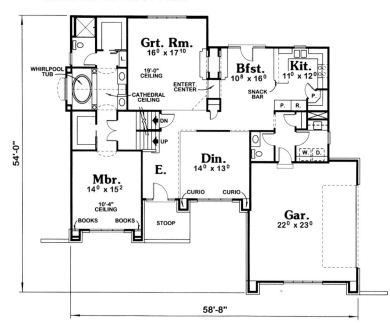

Upper Level Floor Plan

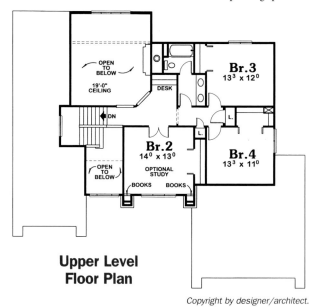

Copyright by designer/architect.

Plan #121025

Dimensions: 60' W x 59'4" D
Levels: 2
Square Footage: 2,562
Main Level Sq. Ft.: 1,875
Upper Level Square Footage: 687
Bedrooms: 4
Bathrooms: 2½
Foundation: Basement
Materials List Available: Yes
Price Category: E

Photo provided by designer/architect.

Dramatic arches are the reoccurring architectural theme in this distinctive home.

Features:

• Ceiling Height: 8 ft. unless otherwise noted.

• Foyer: This is a grand two-story entrance. Plants will thrive on the plant shelf thanks to light streaming through the arched window.

• Great Room: The foyer flows into the great room through dramatic 15-ft.-high arched openings.

• Kitchen: An island is the centerpiece of this highly functional kitchen that includes a separate breakfast area.

• Office: French doors open into this versatile office that features a 10-ft. ceiling and transom-topped windows.

• Master Suite: The master suite features a volume ceiling, built-in dresser, and two closets. You'll unwind in the beautiful corner whirlpool bath with its elegant window treatment.

Main Level Floor Plan

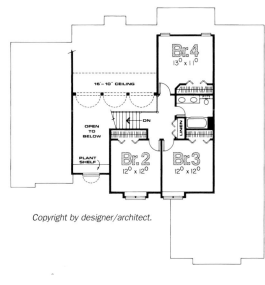

Upper Level Floor Plan

Copyright by designer/architect.

Plan #121017

Dimensions: 54' W x 50' D
Levels: 2
Square Footage: 2,353
Main Level Sq. Ft.: 1,653
Upper Level Sq. Ft.: 700
Bedrooms: 4
Bathrooms: 3
Foundation: Basement
Materials List Available: Yes
Price Category: E

The dramatic two-story entry with bent staircase is the first sign that this is a gracious home.

Features:

- Ceiling Height: 8 ft. except as noted.

- Great Room: A row of transom-topped windows and a tall, beamed ceiling add a sense of spaciousness to this family gathering area.

- Formal Dining Room: The bayed window helps make this an inviting place to entertain.

- See-through Fireplace: This feature spreads warmth and coziness throughout the informal areas of the home.

- Breakfast Area: This sunny area shares a see-through fireplace with the great room. It's the perfect place to start the day.

- Master Suite: Here are all the features you expect to find in large luxury homes. Wake up to tall, sloped ceilings, and enjoy the corner whirlpool, separate shower, and vanity. A large walk-in closet provides plenty of wardrobe storage.

Main Level Floor Plan

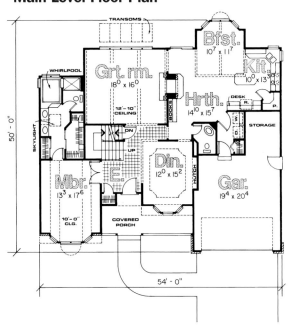

Upper Level Floor Plan

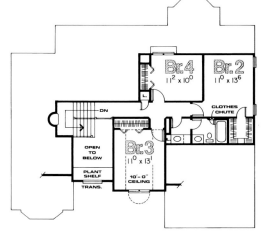

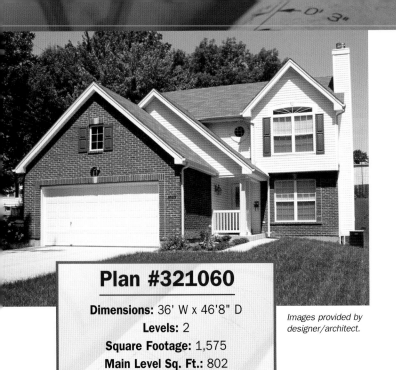

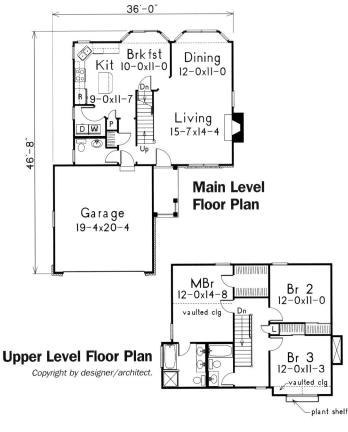

**Main Level
Floor Plan**

*Images provided by
designer/architect.*

Upper Level Floor Plan

Copyright by designer/architect.

Plan #321060

Dimensions: 36' W x 46'8" D

Levels: 2

Square Footage: 1,575

Main Level Sq. Ft.: 802

Upper Level Sq. Ft.: 773

Bedrooms: 3

Bathrooms: 2½

Foundation: Basement

Materials List Available: Yes

Price Category: C

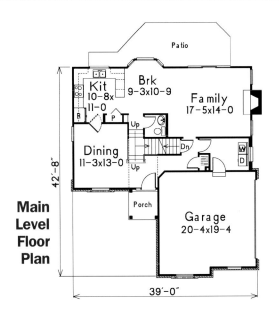

**Main
Level
Floor
Plan**

*Images provided by
designer/architect.*

**Upper Level
Floor Plan**

*Copyright by
designer/architect.*

Plan #321058

Dimensions: 39' W x 42'8" D

Levels: 2

Square Footage: 1,700

Main Level Sq. Ft.: 896

Upper Level Sq. Ft.: 804

Bedrooms: 4

Bathrooms: 2½

Foundation: Basement

Materials List Available: Yes

Price Category: C

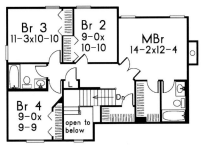

Plan #321057

Dimensions: 38' W x 39'4" D

Levels: 2

Square Footage: 1,524

Main Level Sq. Ft.: 951

Upper Level Sq. Ft.: 573

Bedrooms: 3

Bathrooms: 2½

Foundation: Basement

Materials List Available: Yes

Price Category: C

Images provided by designer/architect.

Main Level Floor Plan

Copyright by designer/architect.

Upper Level Floor Plan

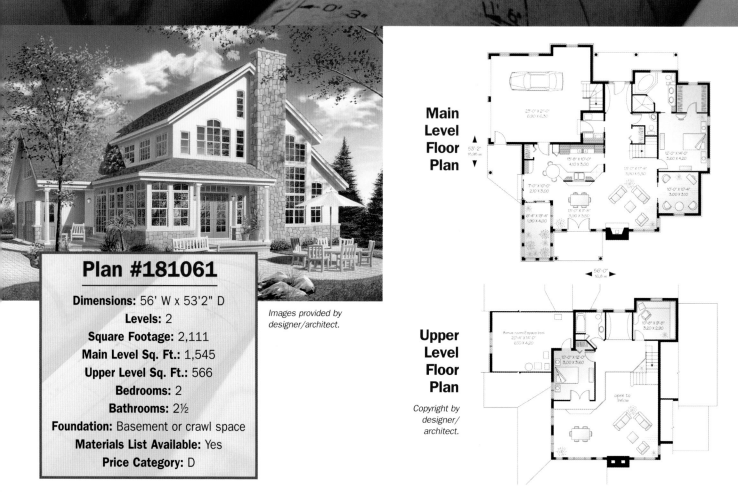

Plan #181061

Dimensions: 56' W x 53'2" D

Levels: 2

Square Footage: 2,111

Main Level Sq. Ft.: 1,545

Upper Level Sq. Ft.: 566

Bedrooms: 2

Bathrooms: 2½

Foundation: Basement or crawl space

Materials List Available: Yes

Price Category: D

Images provided by designer/architect.

Main Level Floor Plan

Upper Level Floor Plan

Copyright by designer/architect.

Plan #121021

Dimensions: 46' W x 48' D
Levels: 2
Square Footage: 2,270
Main Level Sq. Ft.: 1,150
Upper Level Sq. Ft.: 1,120
Bedrooms: 4
Bathrooms: 3
Foundation: Basement
Materials List Available: Yes
Price Category: E

Photo provided by designer/architect.

With its wraparound porch, this home evokes the charm of a traditional home.

Features:

• Ceiling Height: 8 ft.

• Foyer: The dramatic two-story entry enjoys views of the formal dining room and great room. A second floor balcony overlooks the entry and a plant shelf.

• Formal Dining Room: This gracious room is perfect for family holiday gatherings and for more formal dinner parties.

• Great Room: All the family will want to gather in this comfortable, informal room which features bay windows, an entertainment center, and a see-through fireplace.

• Breakfast Area: Conveniently located just off the great room, the bayed breakfast area features a built-in desk for household bills and access to the backyard.

• Kitchen: An island is the centerpiece of this kitchen. Its intelligent design makes food preparation a pleasure.

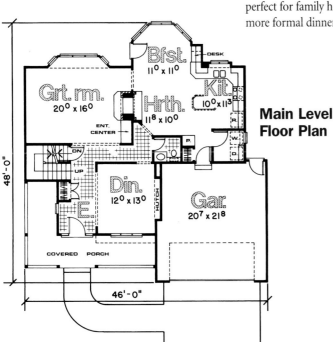

Main Level Floor Plan

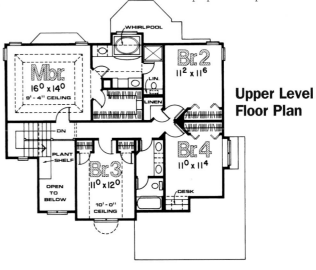

Upper Level Floor Plan

Copyright by designer/architect.

Plan #121045

Dimensions: 40' W x 48' D
Levels: 2
Square Footage: 1,575
Main Level Sq. Ft.: 787
Upper Level Sq. Ft.: 788
Bedrooms: 3
Bathrooms: 2½
Foundation: Basement
Materials List Available: Yes
Price Category: C

Photo provided by designer/architect.

This home is carefully laid out to provide the convenience demanded by busy family life.

Features:

• Ceiling Height: 8 ft.

• Family Room: This charming family room, with its fireplace and built-in cabinetry, will become the central gathering place for family and friends.

• Kitchen: This kitchen offers a central island that makes food preparation more convenient and doubles

as a snack bar for a quick bite on the run. The breakfast area features a pantry and planning desk.

• Computer Loft: The second-floor landing includes this loft designed to accommodate the family computer.

• Room to Grow: Also on the second-floor landing you will find a large unfinished area waiting to accommodate the growing family.

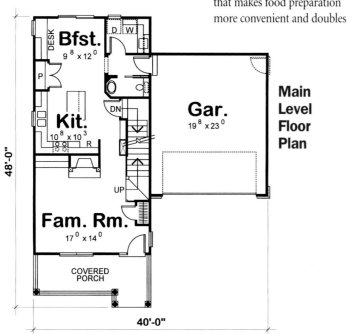

Main Level Floor Plan

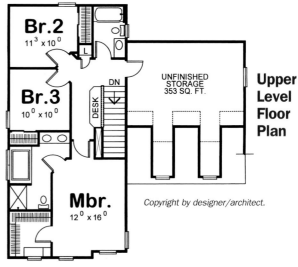

Upper Level Floor Plan

Copyright by designer/architect.

Plan #121035

Dimensions: 45'4" W x 38' D
Levels: 2
Square Footage: 1,471
Main Level Sq. Ft.: 716
Upper Level Sq. Ft.: 755
Bedrooms: 3
Bathrooms: 2½
Foundation: Basement
Materials List Available: Yes
Price Category: B

Photo provided by designer/architect.

This convenient and elegant home is designed to expand as the family does.

Features:

- Ceiling Height: 8 ft. unless otherwise noted.
- Family Room: An open staircase to the second level visually expands this room where a built-in entertainment center maximizes the floor space. The whole family will be drawn to the warmth from the handsome fireplace.
- Kitchen: Cooking will be a pleasure in this

bright and efficient kitchen that features an island and a corner pantry. A snack bar offers a convenient spot for informal family meals.

- Dining Area: This lovely bayed area adjoins the kitchen.
- Room to Expand: Upstairs is 258 sq. ft. of unfinished area offering plenty of space for expansion as the family grows.
- Garage: This two-bay garage offers plenty of storage space in addition to parking for cars.

Main Level Floor Plan

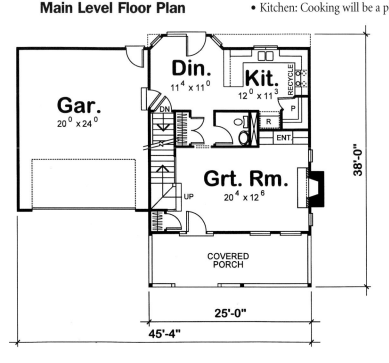

Upper Level Floor Plan

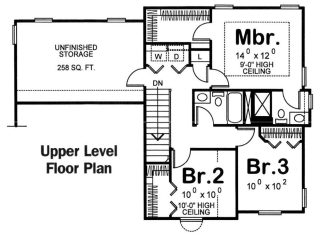

Copyright by designer/architect.

Plan #131030

Dimensions: 51' W x 41'10" D
Levels: 2
Square Footage: 2,470
Main Level Sq. Ft.: 1,290
Upper Level Sq. Ft.: 1,180
Bedrooms: 4
Bathrooms: 2½
Foundation: Crawl space, slab, basement, or walk-out basement
Materials List Available: Yes
Price Category: F

Photos provided by designer/architect.

Master Bedroom

Master Bathroom

Entry

If high ceilings and spacious rooms make you happy, you'll love this gorgeous home.

Features:

- Family Room: An 18-ft. vaulted ceiling that's open to the balcony above, a corner fireplace, and a wall of windows make this room feel special.

- Dining Room: This formal room, which flows into the living room, also opens to the front porch and optional backyard deck.

- Kitchen: A bright breakfast room joins with this kitchen and opens to the backyard deck.

- Master Suite: You'll smile when you see the 11-ft. vaulted ceiling, stunning arched window, and two walk-in closets in the bedroom. A skylight lets natural light into the private bath, with its spa tub, separate shower, and dual-sink vanity.

- Bedrooms: To reach these three charming bedrooms, you'll admire the view into the family room below as you walk along the balcony hall.

Main Level Floor Plan

OPT WOOD DECK

VAULTED CLG
FAMILY RM
18'-0" x 15'-0"

9' HIGH CLG
BKFST RM

9' HIGH CLG
DINING RM
12'-0" x 13'-4"

9' HIGH CLG
KITCHEN
18'-8" x 16'-0"

REF

LAV

W D

LAUN RM

PANT

DN

9' HIGH CLG
LIVING RM
13'-0" x 16'-6"

UP

STOR

TWO CAR GARAGE
21'-8" x 20'-0"

2 STORY
HIGH
FOYER

CL

COVERED PORCH

UP

Upper Level Floor Plan

SKYLITE

WICL

LIN

BEDRM #2
12'-0" x 11'-0"

UPPER
FAMILY RM

RAIL

MSTR
BATH

WICL

WICL

LIN

BATH #2

BALC

DN

CL

VAULTED CLG
MSTR BEDRM
13'-0" x 19'-0"

CL

UPPER
FOYER

BEDRM #4
10'-0" x 12'-0"

BEDRM #3
11'-4" x 12'-0"

Copyright by designer/architect.

Kitchen/Breakfast Area

Dining Room

Living Room

Kitchen/Breakfast Area

Plan #141014

Dimensions: 78' W x 38' D

Levels: 2

Square Footage: 2,091

Main Level Sq. Ft.: 1,362

Upper Level Sq. Ft.: 729

Bedrooms: 3

Bathrooms: 2½

Foundation: Basement

Materials List Available: Yes

Price Category: D

The wraparound front porch and front dormers evoke an old-fashioned country home.

Features:

- Ceiling Height: 8 ft. unless otherwise noted.

- Living Room: This spacious area has an open flow to the dining room, so you can graciously usher guests when it is time to eat.

- Dining Room: This elegant dining room has a bay that opens to the sun deck.

- Kitchen: This warm and inviting kitchen looks out to the front porch. Its bayed breakfast area is perfect for informal family meals.

- Master Suite: The bedroom enjoys a view through the front porch and features a master bath with all the amenities.

- Flexible Room: A room above the two-bay garage offers plenty of space that can be used for anything from a home office to a teen suite.

- Study Room: The two second-floor bedrooms share a study that is perfect for homework.

Illustration provided by designer/architect.

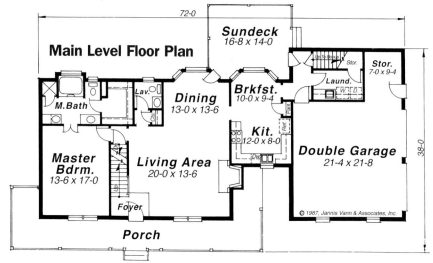

Main Level Floor Plan

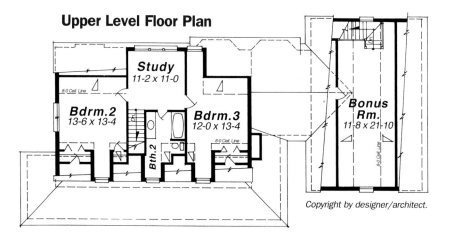

Upper Level Floor Plan

Copyright by designer/architect.

Plan #131041

Dimensions: 42' W x 45' D
Levels: 2
Square Footage: 1,679
Main Level Sq. Ft.: 1,134
Upper Level Sq. Ft.: 545
Bedrooms: 3
Bathrooms: 2½
Foundation: Crawl space, slab, or basement
Materials List Available: Yes
Price Category: D

Illustrations provided by designer/architect.

This rustic-looking two-story cottage includes contemporary amenities for your total comfort.

Features:

- **Great Room:** With a 9-ft.-4-in.-high ceiling, this large room makes everyone feel at home. A fireplace with raised hearth and built-in niche for a TV will encourage the whole family to gather here on cool evenings, and sliding glass doors leading to the rear covered porch make it an ideal entertaining area in mild weather.

- **Kitchen:** When people aren't in the great room, you're likely to find them here, because the convenient serving bar welcomes casual dining, and this room also opens to the p porch.

- **Master Suite:** Relax at the end of the day in this room, with its 9-ft.-4-in.-high ceiling and walk-in closet, or luxuriate in the private bath with whirlpool tub and dual-sink vanity.

- **Optional Basement:** This area can include a tuck-under two-car garage if you desire it.

Main Level Floor Plan

COVERED PORCH
37'-0" x 10'-0"

UP

KITCHEN
12'-8" x 14'-6"

MUD RM

MSTR BEDRM
12'-0" x 16'-0"

CLOS W/O BSMT

CLOS OR BUILT-IN

REF

CL

9'-4" HIGH STEP'D CEIL

DW

GREAT ROOM
14'/18'-0" x 26'-4"

DN

OV

P

UP

← OPT. GARAGE BELOW

BUILT-IN FOR T.V.

WICL

MSTR BATH

9'-4" HI CEIL

VAULTED FOYER

LAV

← HIGH WINDOW

COVERED PORCH
37'-0" x 8'-0"

UP

Upper Level Floor Plan

BATH

LIN

DN

BALC.

BEDRM #3
12'-0" x 11'-0"

CL

BEDRM #2
16'-4" x 11'-0"

CL

Copyright by designer/architect.

Great Room

Plan #121036

Dimensions: 42' W x 43' D
Levels: 2
Square Footage: 1,297
Main Level Sq. Ft.: 603
Upper Level Sq. Ft.: 694
Bedrooms: 3
Bathrooms: 2½
Foundation: Basement
Materials List Available: Yes
Price Category: B

This bright and cheery home offers the growing family plenty of room to expand.

Features:

• Ceiling Height: 8 ft. unless otherwise noted.

• Living Room: Family and friends will be drawn to this delightful living room. A double window at the front and windows framing the fireplace bring lots of sunlight that adds to the appeal.

• Dining Room: From the living room, you'll usher guests into this large and inviting dining room.

• Kitchen: A center island is the highlight of this attractive and well-designed kitchen.

• Three-Season Porch: This appealing enclosed porch is accessible from the dining room.

• Master Bedroom: A dramatic angled ceiling highlights a picturesque window in this bedroom.

• Bonus Area: With 354 sq. ft. of unfinished area, you'll never run out of space to expand.

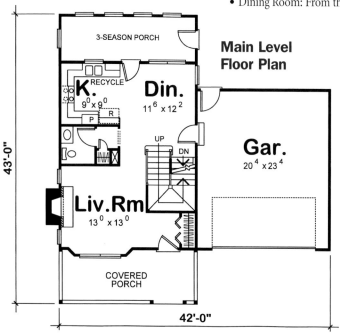

Main Level Floor Plan

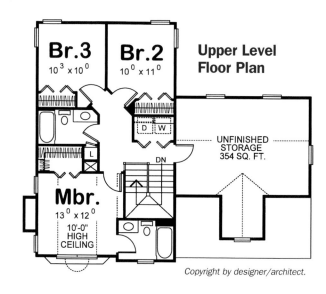

Upper Level Floor Plan

Plan #151028

Dimensions: 36' W X 69' D
Levels: 2
Square Footage: 2,252
Main Level Sq. Ft.: 1,694
Upper Level Sq. Ft.: 558
Bedrooms: 3
Bathrooms: 3
Foundation: Crawl space, slab; optional basement plan available for extra fee
Materials List Available: Yes
Price Category: E

Photo provided by designer/architect.

You'll love entertaining in this elegant home with its large covered front porch, grilling porch off the kitchen and breakfast room, and great room with a gas fireplace and media center.

Features:

- **Foyer:** A wonderful open staircase from the foyer leads you to the second floor.

- **Guest Room/Study:** A private bath makes this room truly versatile.

- **Dining Room:** Attached to the great room, this dining room features 8-in. wooden columns that you can highlight for a formal atmosphere.

- **Kitchen:** This cleverly laid-out kitchen with access to the breakfast room is ideal for informal gatherings as well as family meals.

- **Master Suite:** French doors here open to the bath, with its large walk-in closet, double vanities, corner whirlpool tub, and corner shower.

Main Level Floor Plan

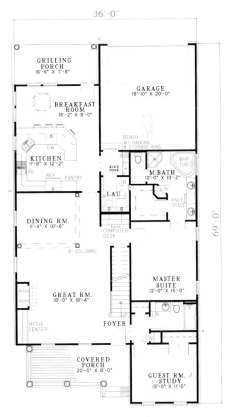

Copyright by designer/architect.

Upper Level Floor Plan

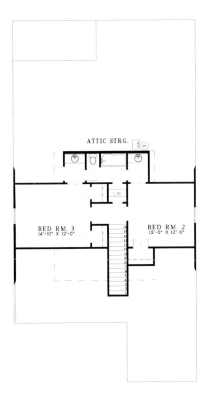

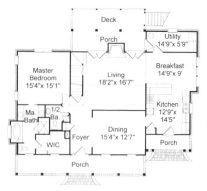

Main Level Floor Plan

Copyright by designer/architect.

Deck

Porch

Utility 14'9" x 5'9"

Master Bedroom 15'4" x 15'1"

Living 18'2" x 16'7"

Breakfast 14'9" x 9'

Ma. Bath

1/2 Ba.

Kitchen 12'9" x 14'5"

WIC

Foyer

Dining 15'4" x 12'7"

Porch

Porch

Plan #111009

Dimensions: 56' W x 49' D

Levels: 2

Square Footage: 2,514

Main Level Sq. Ft.: 1,630

Upper Level Sq. Ft.: 884

Bedrooms: 4

Bathrooms: 3½

Foundation: Basement

Materials List Available: No

Price Category: E

Photo provided by designer/architect.

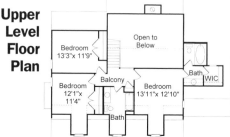

Upper Level Floor Plan

Bedroom 13'3" x 11'9"

Open to Below

Bedroom 12'1" x 11'4"

Balcony

Bedroom 13'11" x 12'10"

Bath

WIC

Bath

Basement Level Floor Plan

Future Gameroom 14'5" x 21'7"

Two-Car Garage

Main Level Floor Plan

Two Car Garage 21'2" x 21'1"

Patio

Porch

1/2 Ba

Storage

Master Bedroom 15' x 15'

WIC

Living 19'4" x 17'1"

Breakfast 13'8" x 10'7"

Ma. Bath

Bath

WIC

Kitchen 10'8" x 12'3"

Bedroom 12' x 11'7"

Dining 12' x 13'6"

Utility

Porch

Plan #111026

Dimensions: 66' W x 65' D

Levels: 2

Square Footage: 2,406

Main Level Sq. Ft.: 1,796

Upper Level Sq. Ft.: 610

Bedrooms: 4

Bathrooms: 4

Foundation: Crawlspace

Materials List Available: No

Price Category: E

Photo provided by designer/architect.

Open to Below

Bath

Balcony

Upper Level Floor Plan

Bedroom 12' x 11'7"

Bedroom 12' x 13'

Copyright by designer/architect.

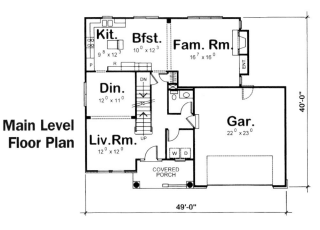

**Main Level
Floor Plan**

Kit.
9⁸ x 12³

Bfst.
10⁰ x 12³

Fam. Rm.
16⁷ x 16⁰

ENT

Din.
12⁰ x 11⁰

DN

Gar.
22⁰ x 23⁰

Liv.Rm.
12⁰ x 12⁰

UP

W D

COVERED
PORCH

40'-0"

49'-0"

**Upper Level
Floor Plan**

*Copyright by
designer/architect.*

Mbr.
12⁰ x 16⁶

9'-0" CEILING

BOOKS

Br.4
11⁰ x 10⁶

DN

L

Br.2
10⁰ x 11⁷

Br.3
11⁰ x 11⁰

Plan #121039

Dimensions: 49' W x 40' D

Levels: 2

Square Footage: 2,200

Main Level Sq. Ft.: 1,130

Upper Level Sq. Ft.: 1,070

Bedrooms: 4

Bathrooms: 2½

Foundation: Basement

Materials List Available: Yes

Price Category: E

*Photo provided by
designer/architect.*

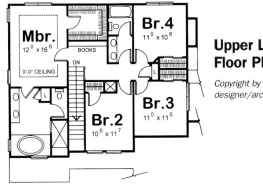

**Main Level
Floor Plan**

Mbr.
15⁰ x 13⁰
10'-0" CEIL.

Fam. Rm.
14⁶ x 15⁴

Bfst.
9⁴ x 11⁰

W
D

P

Kit.
13³ x 11²

R

DN

Gar.
19⁸ x 20⁴

UP

Den
10⁰ x 10⁶

COVERED
PORCH

47'-8"

40'-0"

**Upper Level
Floor Plan**

*Copyright by
designer/architect.*

OPTIONAL
EXPANSION

DN

L

Br.3
10⁰ x 10⁰

COMP.
AREA

Br.2
10⁰ x 10⁶

Plan #121099

Dimensions: 40' W x 47'8" D

Levels: 2

Square Footage: 1,699

Main Level Sq. Ft.: 1,268

Upper Level Sq. Ft.: 431

Bedrooms: 3

Bathrooms: 2½

Foundation: Basement

Materials List Available: Yes

Price Category: C

Plan #181151

Dimensions: 50' W x 46' D
Levels: 2
Square Footage: 2,283
Main Level Sq. Ft.: 1,274
Second Level Sq. Ft.: 1,009
Bedrooms: 3
Bathrooms: 2½
Foundation: Basement
Materials List Available: Yes
Price Category: E

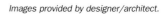

Images provided by designer/architect.

Multiple porches, stately columns, and arched multi-paned windows adorn this country home.

Features:

- Ceiling Height: 8 ft. unless otherwise noted.

- Great Room: The second-floor mezzanine overlooks this great room. With its soaring ceiling, this dramatic room is the centerpiece of a spacious and flowing design that is just as suited to entertaining as it is to family life.

- Dining Area: Guests will naturally flow into this dining area when it is time to eat. After dinner they can step directly out onto the porch to enjoy coffee and dessert when the weather is fair.

- Kitchen: This efficient and well-designed kitchen has double sinks and offers a separate eating area for those impromptu family meals.

- Master Bedroom: This master retreat has a walk-in closet and its own sumptuous bath.

- Home Office: Whether you work at home or just need a place for the family computer and keeping track of family finances, this home office fills the bill.

Main Level Floor Plan

17'-0" X 11'-8"
5,10 X 3,50

9'-8" X 8'-8"
2,90 X 2,60

21'-0" X 20'-8"
6,30 X 6,20

9'-0" X 10'-0"
2,70 X 3,00

10'-0" X 12'-0"
3,00 X 3,60

9'-8" X 9'-4"
2,90 X 2,80

12'-0" X 20'-8"
3,60 X 6,20

46'-0"
13,8 m

◄ 50'-0" ►
15,0 m

Upper Level Floor Plan

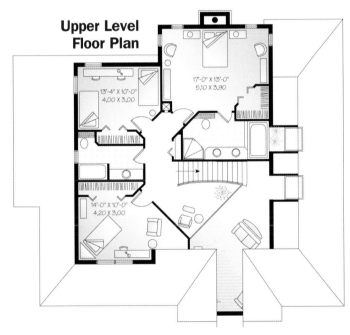

13'-4" X 10'-0"
4,00 X 3,00

17'-0" X 13'-0"
5,10 X 3,90

14'-0" X 10'-0"
4,20 X 3,00

Copyright by designer/architect.

SMARTtip

Coping Chair Rails

If the teeth of your rasp tend to break out thin edges of the cope, try wrapping the rasp with sandpaper to make fine adjustments.

Dining Room

Living Room

Master Bath

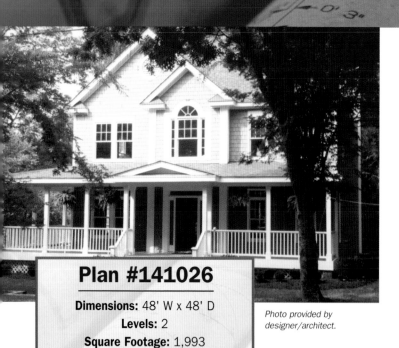

Main Level Floor Plan

Sundeck 17-6 x 13-6

Brkfst. 8-8 x 15-6

Kit. 11-10 x 10-0

Family 14-10 x 13-6

Dining 11-6 x 13-6

Lav

Living 13-6 x 13-6

Open Foyer 7-8 x 9-8

Ref

Pant

Cts

48-0

48-0

© 1995, Jannis Vann & Associates, Inc.

Plan #141026

Dimensions: 48' W x 48' D

Levels: 2

Square Footage: 1,993

Main Level Sq. Ft.: 1,038

Upper Level Sq. Ft.: 955

Bedrooms: 3

Bathrooms: 2½

Foundation: Basement

Materials List Available: Yes

Price Category: D

Photo provided by designer/architect.

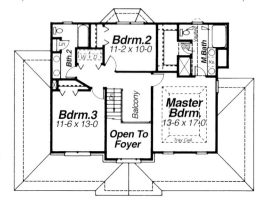

Bdrm.2 11-2 x 10-0

Bth.2

Lin

W D

M.Bath

Ks

Upper Level Floor Plan

Bdrm.3 11-6 x 13-0

Balcony

Open To Foyer

Master Bdrm. 13-6 x 17-0

Tray Ceil.

Copyright by designer/architect.

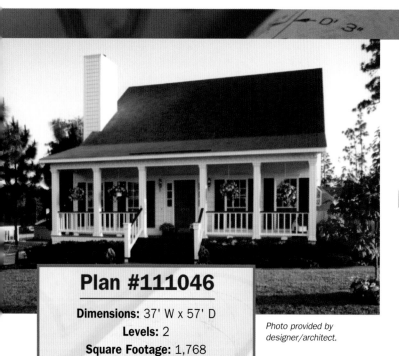

Plan #111046

Dimensions: 37' W x 57' D

Levels: 2

Square Footage: 1,768

Main Level Sq. Ft.: 1,247

Upper Level Sq. Ft.: 521

Bedrooms: 3

Bathrooms: 2½

Foundation: Crawl space

Materials List Available: No

Price Category: C

Photo provided by designer/architect.

Wood Deck 12'6"x 8'

Covered Porch 12'2"x 10'

Ext. Storage

Master Bath

WIC

Breakfast 11'10"x 9'6'

Utility

Master Bedroom 12'6"x 15'6'

1/2 Ba.

Kitchen 10'x 11'6'

Main Level Floor Plan

Living 14'4"x 17'6'

Dining 13'x 12'

Porch 32'x 5'

Bedroom 12'6"x 14'

Bedroom 10'6"x 13'2'

Balcony

Upper Level Floor Plan

Copyright by designer/architect.

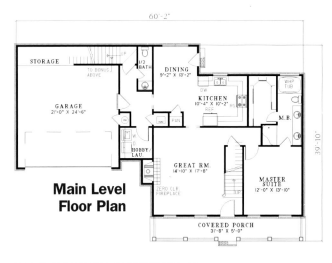

Main Level Floor Plan

Images provided by designer/architect.

Upper Level Floor Plan

Copyright by designer/architect.

Plan #151016

Dimensions: 60'2" W x 39'10" D
Levels: 2
Square Footage: 1,783;
2,107 with bonus
Main Level Sq. Ft.: 1,124
Upper Level Sq. Ft.: 659
Bonus Room Sq. Ft.: 324
Bedrooms: 3
Bathrooms: 2½
Foundation: Basement, crawl space, or slab
Price Category: C

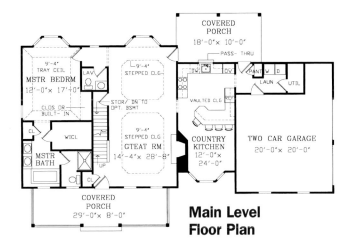

Main Level Floor Plan

Images provided by designer/architect.

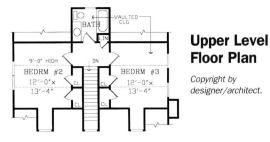

Upper Level Floor Plan

Copyright by designer/architect.

Plan #131043

Dimensions: 65'8" W x 43'10" D
Levels: 2
Square Footage: 1,945
Main Level Sq. Ft.: 1,375
Upper Level Sq. Ft.: 570
Bedrooms: 3
Bathrooms: 2½
Foundation: Crawl space, slab, or basement
Materials List Available: Yes
Price Category: E

Plan #131021

Dimensions: 60'0" W x 52'4" D
Levels: 2
Square Footage: 3,110
Main Level Sq. Ft.: 1,818
Upper Level Sq. Ft.: 1,292
Bedrooms: 5
Bathrooms: 2½
Foundation: Basement, crawl space, or slab
Materials List Available: Yes
Price Category: H

Photo provided by designer/architect.

Amenities abound in this luxurious two-story beauty with a cozy gazebo on one corner of the spectacular wraparound front porch. Comfort, functionality, and spaciousness characterize this home.

Features:

• Ceiling Height: 8 ft.

• Foyer: This two-story high foyer is breathtaking.

• Family Room: Roomy with open views of the kitchen, the family room has a vaulted ceiling and boasts a functional fireplace and a built-in entertainment center.

• Dining Room: Formal yet comfortable, this spacious dining room is perfect for entertaining family and friends.

• Kitchen: Perfectly located with access to a breakfast room and the family room, this

U-shaped kitchen with large center island is charming as well as efficient.

• Master Suite: Enjoy this sizable room with a vaulted ceiling, two large walk-in closets, and a lovely compartmented bath.

Rear Elevation

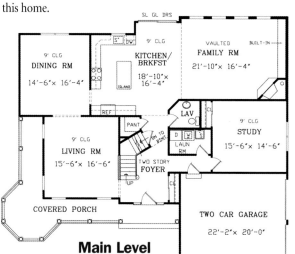

Main Level Floor Plan

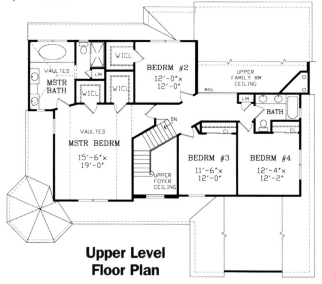

Upper Level Floor Plan

Copyright by designer/architect.

Plan #121047

Dimensions: 67'8" W x 57' D
Levels: 2
Square Footage: 3,072
Main Level Sq. Ft.: 2,116
Upper Level Sq. Ft.: 956
Bedrooms: 4
Bathrooms: 3½
Foundation: Slab
Materials List Available: Yes
Price Category: G

Photo provided by designer/architect.

A long porch and a trio of roof dormers give this gracious home a sophisticated country look.

Features:

- Ceiling Height: 8 ft. unless otherwise noted.
- Balcony: This balcony overlooks the entry and the staircase hall.
- Dining Room: Columns and a cased opening lend elegance, making this the perfect venue for stylish dinner parties.

- Family Room: A cathedral ceiling gives this room a light and airy feel. The handsome fireplace framed by windows is sure to become a favorite family gathering place.
- Master Bedroom: This architecturally distinctive bedroom features a bayed sitting area and a tray ceiling.
- Bedrooms: One of the bedrooms enjoys a private bath, making it a perfect guest room. Other bedrooms feature walk-in closets.

Main Level Floor Plan

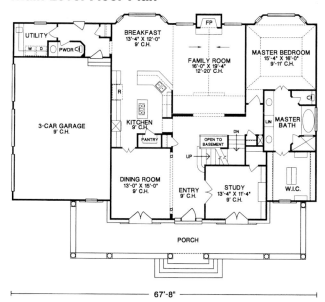

Upper Level Floor Plan

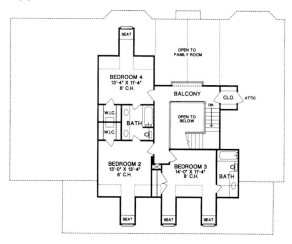

Copyright by designer/architect.

Plan #171017

Dimensions: 84' W x 54' D

Levels: 2

Square Footage: 2,558

Main Level Sq. Ft.: 1,577

Upper Level Sq. Ft.: 981

Bedrooms: 4

Bathrooms: 2½

Foundation: Slab, crawl space

Materials List Available: Yes

Price Category: E

Illustration provided by designer/architect.

Main Level Floor Plan

Upper Level Floor Plan

Copyright by designer/architect.

Plan #281003

Dimensions: 71' W x 35' D

Levels: 2

Square Footage: 2,370

Main Level Sq. Ft.: 1,252

Upper Level Sq. Ft.: 1,118

Bedrooms: 4

Bathrooms: 2½

Foundation: Full basement

Materials List Available: Yes

Price Category: E

Illustration provided by designer/architect.

Upper Level Floor Plan

Copyright by designer/architect.

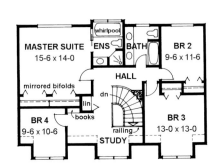

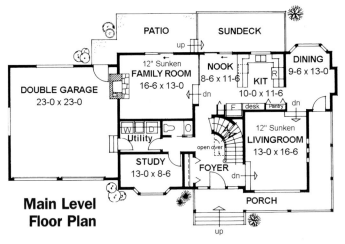

Main Level Floor Plan

Main Level Floor Plan

Plan #181034

Dimensions: 60' W x 44' D
Levels: 2
Square Footage: 2,687
Main Level Sq. Ft.: 1,297
Upper Level Sq. Ft.: 1,390
Bedrooms: 3
Bathrooms: 2½
Foundation: Full basement
Materials List Available: Yes
Price Category: F

Illustration provided by designer/architect.

Upper Level Floor Plan

Copyright by designer/architect.

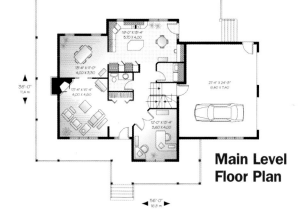

Main Level Floor Plan

Plan #181035

Dimensions: 56' W x 38' D
Levels: 2
Square Footage: 2,129
Main Level Sq. Ft.: 1,136
Upper Level Sq. Ft.: 993
Bedrooms: 3
Bathrooms: 2½
Foundation: Full basement
Materials List Available: Yes
Price Category: D

Illustration provided by designer/architect.

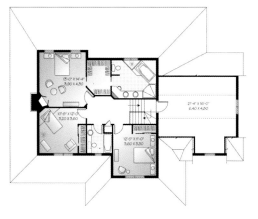

Upper Level Floor Plan

Copyright by designer/architect.

Plan #181047

Dimensions: 32' W x 24' D
Levels: 2
Square Footage: 1,458
Main Level Sq. Ft.: 768
Upper Level Sq. Ft.: 690
Bedrooms: 3
Bathrooms: 2½
Foundation: Full basement
Materials List Available: Yes
Price Category: B

Illustration provided by designer/architect.

Main Level Floor Plan

24'-0"
7,2 m

32'-0"
9,6 m

15'-0" X 11'-0"
4,50 X 3,30

12'-0" X 14'-0"
3,60 X 4,20

12'-0" X 11'-0"
3,60 X 3,30

Upper Level Floor Plan

Copyright by designer/architect.

12'-0" X 12'-0"
3,60 X 3,60

12'-0" X 9'-0"
3,60 X 2,70

12'-0" X 10'-0"
3,60 X 3,00

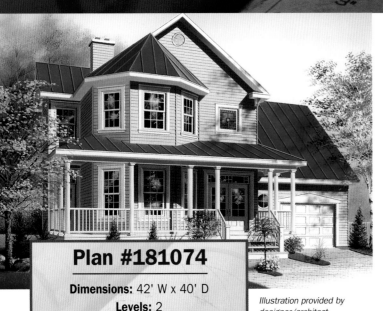

Plan #181074

Dimensions: 42' W x 40' D
Levels: 2
Square Footage: 1,760
Main Level Sq. Ft.: 880
Upper Level Sq. Ft.: 880
Bedrooms: 4
Full Baths: 2½
Foundation: Full basement
Materials List Available: Yes
Price Category: C

Illustration provided by designer/architect.

Main Level Floor Plan

40'-0"
12,0 m

42'-0"
12,6 m

20'-8" X 11'-4"
6,20 X 3,40

17'-0" X 11'-0"
5,10 X 3,30

15'-4" X 22'-8"
4,60 X 6,80

12'-8" X 15'-8"
3,80 X 4,70

Upper Level Floor Plan

Copyright by designer/architect.

13'-4" X 9'-0"
4,00 X 2,70

11'-0" X 11'-0"
3,30 X 3,30

15'-8" X 15'-4"
4,70 X 4,60

12'-8" X 15'-8"
3,80 X 4,70

Plan #121014

Dimensions: 52' W x 47'4" D
Levels: 2
Square Footage: 1,869
Main Level Sq. Ft.: 1,421
Upper Level Sq. Ft.: 448
Bedrooms: 3
Bathrooms: 2
Foundation: Basement
Materials List Available: Yes
Price Category: D

Photo provided by designer/architect.

This compact home is packed with all the amenities you'll need for a gracious lifestyle.

Features:

• Ceiling Height: 8 ft. except as noted.

• Great Room: A soaring ceiling and six tall transom-topped windows make this a light and airy spot for entertaining.

• Formal Dining Room: This elegant room is ideal for entertaining dinner guests.

• Breakfast Area: This sunny area shares a see-through fireplace with the great room. It's the perfect place to start the day.

• Master Suite: Here are all the features you expect to find in large luxury homes. Wake up to tall, sloped ceilings, and enjoy the corner whirlpool, separate shower, and vanity. A large walk-in closet provides plenty of wardrobe storage.

• Attached Garage: The garage provides two bays of parking plus plenty of storage space.

Main Level Floor Plan

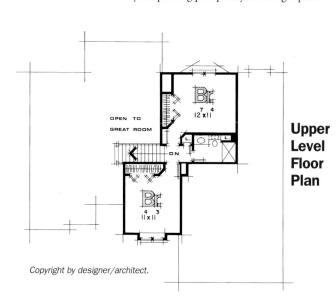

Upper Level Floor Plan

Copyright by designer/architect.

Plan #131029

Dimensions: 56'4" W x 46'6" D
Levels: 2
Square Footage: 2,936
Main Level Sq. Ft.: 1,680
Upper Level Sq. Ft.: 1,256
Bedrooms: 4
Bathrooms: 2½
Foundation: Crawl space, slab, or basement
Materials List Available: Yes
Price Category: G

This home is ideal if you love the look of a country-style farmhouse.

Features:

• Foyer: Walk across the large wraparound porch that defines this home to enter this two-story foyer.

• Living Room: French doors from the foyer lead into this living room.

• Family Room: The whole family will love this room, with its vaulted ceiling, fireplace, and sliding glass doors that open to the wooden rear deck.

• Kitchen: A beautiful sit-down center island opens to the family room. There's also a breakfast nook with a lovely bay window.

• Master Suite: Luxury abounds with vaulted ceilings, walk-in closets, private bath with whirlpool tub, separate shower, and dual sinks.

• Loft: A special place with vaulted ceiling and view into the family room below.

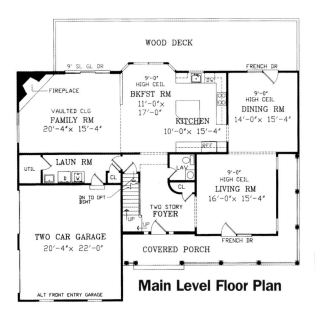

Main Level Floor Plan

Upper Level Floor Plan

Rear Elevation

Dining Room

Breakfast Area

Kitchen Island

Kitchen

Master Bathroom

Illustration provided by designer/architect.

Plan #181085

Dimensions: 56'4" W x 44' D
Levels: 2
Square Footage: 2,183
Main Level Sq. Ft.: 1,232
Second Level Sq. Ft.: 951
Bedrooms: 3
Bathrooms: 2½
Foundation: Basement
Materials List Available: Yes
Price Category: D

This country home features an inviting front porch and a layout designed for modern living.

Features:

- Ceiling Height: 8 ft.

- Solarium: Sunlight streams through the windows of this solarium at the front of the house.

- Living Room: Walk through French doors, and you will enter this inviting living room. Family and friends will be drawn to the corner fireplace.

- Formal Dining Room: Usher your guests directly from the living room into this formal dining room. The kitchen is located on the

other side of the dining room for convenient service.

- Kitchen: This generously sized kitchen is a delight, it offers a center island, separate eat-in area, and access to the back deck.

- Bonus Room: This room just off the entry hall can become a family room, a bedroom, or an office.

- Master Suite: Curl up by the corner fireplace in this master retreat, with its walk-in closet and lavish bath with separate shower and tub.

Main Level Floor Plan

Upper Level Floor Plan

Copyright by designer/ architect.

Plan #251008

Dimensions: 44'4" W x 73' 2" D
Levels: 2
Square Footage: 1,808
Main Level Sq. Ft.: 1,271
Upper Level Sq. Ft.: 537
Bedrooms: 3
Bathrooms: 2½
Foundation: Basement
Materials List Available: Yes
Price Category: D

Illustration provided by designer/architect.

An elegant front dormer adds distinction to this country home and brings light into the foyer.

Features:

• Ceiling Height: 9 ft. unless otherwise noted

• Front Porch: A full-length front porch adds to the country charm and provides a relaxing place to sit.

• Foyer: This impressive foyer soars to two stories thanks to the front dormer.

• Dining Room: This dining room has ample space for entertaining. After dinner, guests can step out of the dining room directly onto the rear deck.

• Kitchen: This well-designed kitchen has a double sink. It features a snack bar with plenty of room for impromptu meals.

• Master Bedroom: This distinctive master bedroom features a large-walk-in closet.

• Master Bath: This master bath features walk-in closets in addition to a double vanity and a deluxe tub.

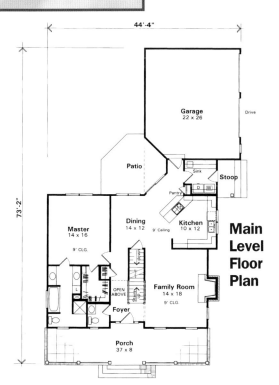

Copyright by designer/architect.

Main Level Floor Plan

Upper Level Floor Plan

Plan #181078

Dimensions: 58' W x 42'2" D

Levels: 2

Square Footage: 2,292

Main Level Sq. Ft.: 1,266

Upper Level Sq. Ft.: 1,026

Bedrooms: 4

Bathrooms: 2½

Foundation: Full basement

Materials List Available: Yes

Price Category: E

Illustration provided by designer/architect.

Main Level Floor Plan

Upper Level Floor Plan

Copyright by designer/architect.

Plan #181094

Dimensions: 50' W x 39' D

Levels: 2

Square Footage: 2,099

Main Level Sq. Ft.: 1,060

Upper Level Sq. Ft.: 1,039

Bedrooms: 4

Bathrooms: 2½

Foundation: Full basement

Materials List Available: Yes

Price Category: D

Illustration provided by designer/architect.

Main Level Floor Plan

Upper Level Floor Plan

Copyright by designer/architect.

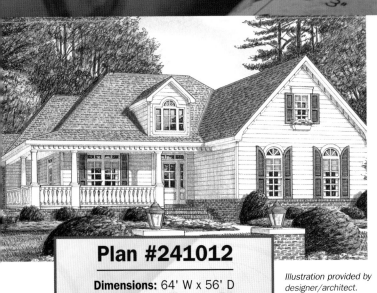

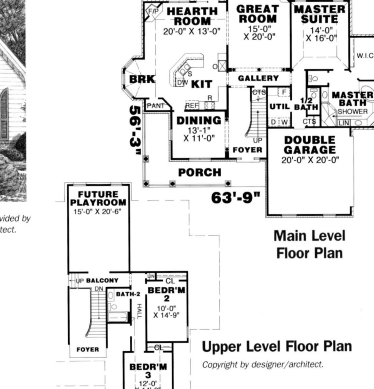

Plan #241012

Dimensions: 64' W x 56' D

Levels: 2

Square Footage: 2,743

Main Level Sq. Ft.: 2,153

Upper Level Sq. Ft.: 590

Bedrooms: 3

Bathrooms: 2½

Foundation: Slab

Materials List Available: No

Price Category: E

Illustration provided by designer/architect.

Main Level Floor Plan

Upper Level Floor Plan

Copyright by designer/architect.

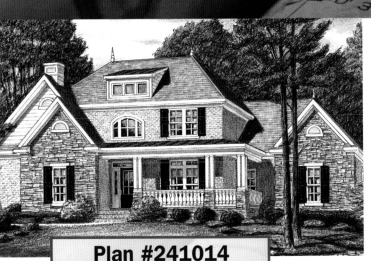

Plan #241014

Dimensions: 66'6" W x 55'6" D

Levels: 2

Square Footage: 3,046

Main Level Sq. Ft.: 2,292

Upper Level Sq. Ft.: 754

Bedrooms: 4

Bathrooms: 3

Foundation: Slab

Materials List Available: No

Price Category: G

Illustration provided by designer/architect.

Main Level Floor Plan

Upper Level Floor Plan

Copyright by designer/architect.

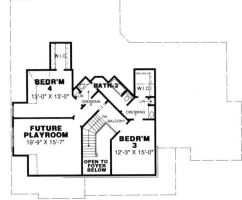

Plan #121016

Dimensions: 52' W x 47'4" D
Levels: 2
Square Footage: 2,594
Main Level Sq. Ft.: 1,322
Upper Level Sq. Ft.: 1,272
Bedrooms: 4
Bathrooms: 3
Foundation: Basement
Materials List Available: Yes
Price Category: E

Photo provided by designer/architect.

A huge wraparound porch gives this home warmth and charm.

Features:

• Ceiling Height: 8 ft. except as noted.

• Family Room: This informal sunken room's beamed ceiling and fireplace flanked by windows makes it the perfect place for family gatherings.

• Formal Dining Room: Guests will enjoy gathering in this large elegant room.

• Master Suite: The second-floor master bedroom features its own luxurious bathroom.

• Compartmented Full Bath: This large bathroom serves the three secondary bedrooms on the second floor.

• Optional Play Area: This special space, included in one of the bedrooms, features a cathedral ceiling.

• Kitchen: A large island is the centerpiece of this modern kitchen's well-designed food-preparation area.

**Main Level
Floor Plan**

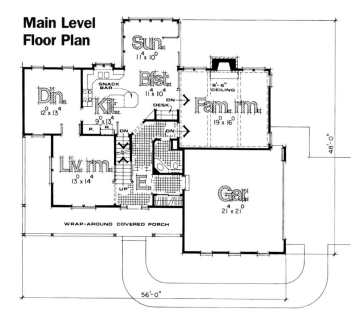

**Upper Level
Floor Plan**

Copyright by designer/architect.

Plan #121044

Dimensions: 40' W x 55'8" D
Levels: 2
Square Footage: 1,923
Main Level Sq. Ft.: 1,351
Upper Level Sq. Ft.: 572
Bedrooms: 3
Bathrooms: 3
Foundation: Basement
Materials List Available: Yes
Price Category: D

Photo provided by designer/architect.

The layout of this gracious home is designed with the contemporary family in mind.

Features:

• Ceiling Height: 8 ft. unless otherwise noted.

• Foyer: This elegant entry is graced with an open stairway that enhances the sense of spaciousness.

• Kitchen: Located just beyond the entry, this convenient kitchen features a center island that doubles as a snack bar.

• Breakfast Area: A sloped ceiling unites this area with the family room. Here you will find a planning desk for compiling menus and shopping lists.

• Master Bedroom: This bedroom has a distinctively contemporary appeal, with its cathedral ceiling and triple window.

• Computer Loft: Designed to house a computer, this loft overlooks the family room.

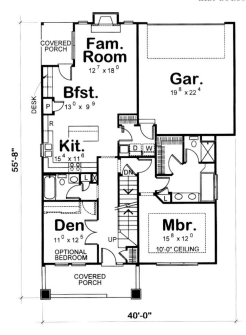

Main Level Floor Plan

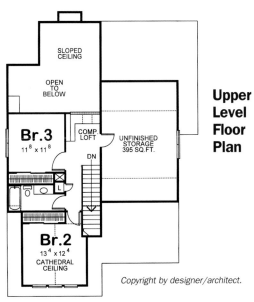

Upper Level Floor Plan

Copyright by designer/architect.

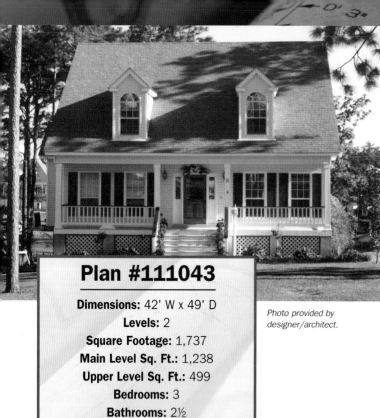

Main Level Floor Plan

Patio

Utility

Breakfast
8'10"x 11'5"

Living
20'6"x 14'

Kitchen
11'6"x 10'8"

1/2 Ba.

WIC

Dressing

Ba.

Dining
11'6"x 13'

Bedroom
16'6"x 13'6"

Porch
36'x 5'

Upper Level Floor Plan

Attic Storage

Open To Below

Bedroom
11'6"x10'

Balcony

Bath

Bedroom
11'6"x 11'4"

Attic Storage

Plan #111043

Dimensions: 42' W x 49' D

Levels: 2

Square Footage: 1,737

Main Level Sq. Ft.: 1,238

Upper Level Sq. Ft.: 499

Bedrooms: 3

Bathrooms: 2½

Foundation: Crawl space

Materials List Available: No

Price Category: C

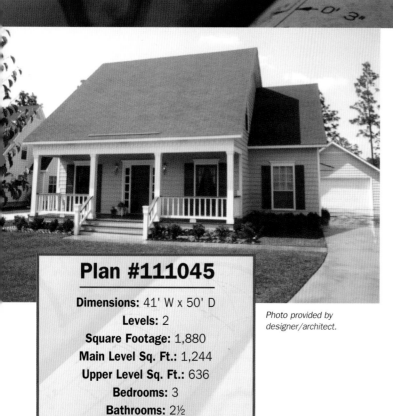

Deck

Main Level Floor Plan

Bedroom
12'6"x 15'

Living
14'6"x 17'6"

Breakfast
9'8"x 10'6"

WIC

Kitch.
9'8"x 11'1"

Dining
10'8"x 12'

Foyer

Porch

Open to Below

Bedroom
12'6"x 11"

Balcony

Bedroom
10'6"x 10'9"

Upper Level Floor Plan

Plan #111045

Dimensions: 41' W x 50' D

Levels: 2

Square Footage: 1,880

Main Level Sq. Ft.: 1,244

Upper Level Sq. Ft.: 636

Bedrooms: 3

Bathrooms: 2½

Foundation: Slab

Materials List Available: No

Price Category: D

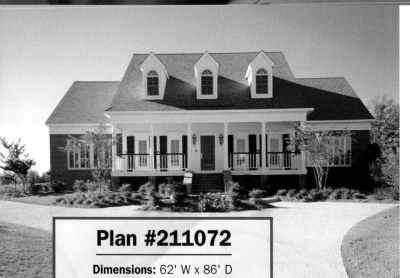

Plan #211072

Dimensions: 62' W x 86' D
Levels: 2
Square Footage: 3,012
Main Level Sq. Ft.: 2,202
Upper Level Sq. Ft.: 810
Bedrooms: 4
Bathrooms: 3½
Foundation: Crawl space,
optional basement
Materials List Available: Yes
Price Category: G

Photo provided by designer/architect.

Main Level Floor Plan

sto | sto | sto

garage
22 x 22

porch 18 x 6

util 14x9

bath 17 x 9

built-in entertainment ctr and library

family rm
25 x 16

kit 14x13

future space 28 x 12
sloped clg

built-in entertainment ctr and library

sitting
14 x 12

mbr
16 x 13

dining
16 x 12

eating
14 x 10

foy

porch 34 x 8

Upper Level Floor Plan

Copyright by designer/architect.

outline of lower level

sloped clg | sloped clg

br 4
11 x 12

attic space

balcony

attic space

br 2
13 x 13

br 3
13 x 12

open to lower level

hand rail

Plan #211073

Dimensions: 66' W x 80' D
Levels: 1½
Square Footage: 3,119
Main Level Sq. Ft.: 2,092
Upper Level Sq. Ft.: 1,027
Bedrooms: 4
Bathrooms: 3½
Foundation: Foundation: Crawl space,
optional basement
Materials List Available: Yes
Price Category: G

Photo provided by designer/architect.

Main Level Floor Plan

sto 11 x 6 | sto 11 x 6

3 car garage
22 x 30

deck
23 x 22

sunroom
23 x 10

util 12 x 12

mbr
16⁶ x 18⁶

family
25 x 15

kit 12 x 8⁶

study
14 x 15

foy 6 x 15

dining
14 x 15

eating
12 x 9

porch 34 x 8

br 4
16 x 12

to attic

dn

to attic

br 3
14 x 12

br 2
14 x 12

Upper Level Floor Plan

Copyright by designer/architect.

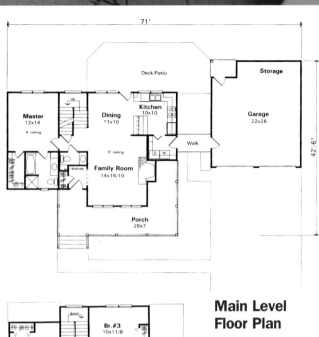

Plan #251007

Dimensions: 71' W x 42'6" D
Levels: 2
Square Footage: 1,597
Main Level Sq. Ft.: 982
Upper Level Sq. Ft.: 615
Bedrooms: 4
Bathrooms: 2½
Foundation: Basement
Materials List Available: Yes
Price Category: C

Illustration provided by designer/architect.

Main Level Floor Plan

Upper Level Floor Plan

Copyright by designer/architect.

Plan #251009

Dimensions: 57' W x 60' D
Levels: 2
Square Footage: 1,829
Main Level Sq. Ft.: 1,339
Upper Level Sq. Ft.: 490
Bedrooms: 4
Bathrooms: 2½
Foundation: Basement
Materials List Available: No
Price Category: D

Illustration provided by designer/architect.

Main Level Floor Plan

Upper Level Floor Plan

Copyright by designer/architect.

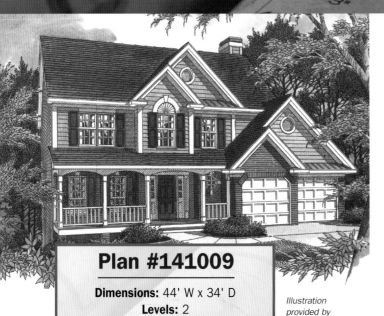

Plan #141009

Dimensions: 44' W x 34' D
Levels: 2
Square Footage: 1,683
Main Level Sq. Ft.: 797
Upper Level Sq. Ft.: 886
Bedrooms: 3
Bathrooms: 2½
Foundation: Basement, crawl space or slab
Materials List Available: No
Price Category: C

Illustration provided by designer/ architect.

Main Level Floor Plan

Sundeck 16-0 x 12-0
Brkfst. 8-0 x 9-6
Kitchen 9-4 x 11-8
Living Area 18-0 x 11-8
Stor. 5-6 x 12-0
Dining 11-0 x 13-4
Open Foyer 8-4 x 11-10
Double Garage 19-8 x 21-4
Porch

Upper Level Floor Plan

Copyright by designer/architect.

M.Bath
Bdrm. 3 13-0 x 9-6
Master Bdrm. 15-6 x 11-0
Open Foyer
Bdrm. 2 13-0 x 9-6

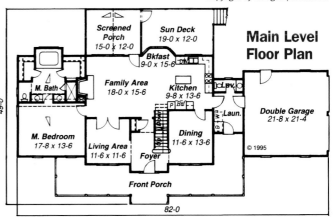

Plan #141017

Dimensions: 82' W x 50' D
Levels: 2
Square Footage: 2,480
Main Level Sq. Ft.: 1,581
Upper Level Sq. Ft.: 899
Bedrooms: 4
Bathrooms: 3½
Foundation: Basement, crawl space, or slab
Materials List Available: No
Price Category: E

Illustration provided by designer/ architect.

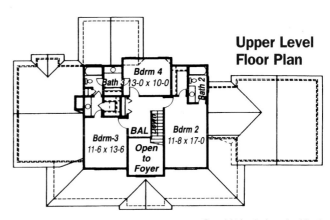

Upper Level Floor Plan

Bdrm 4 13-0 x 10-0
Bath 3
Bath 2
Bdrm-3 11-6 x 13-6
BAL Open to Foyer
Bdrm 2 11-8 x 17-0

Copyright by designer/architect.

Main Level Floor Plan

Screened Porch 15-0 x 12-0
Sun Deck 19-0 x 12-0
Bkfast 9-0 x 15-6
M. Bath
Family Area 18-0 x 15-6
Kitchen 9-8 x 13-6
M. Bedroom 17-8 x 13-6
Living Area 11-6 x 11-6
Foyer
Dining 11-6 x 13-6
Laun.
Double Garage 21-8 x 21-4
© 1995
Front Porch

Plan #151027

Dimensions: 37' W x 73' D
Levels: 2
Square Footage: 2,332
Main Level Sq. Ft.: 1,713
Upper Level Sq. Ft.: 619
Bedrooms: 3
Bathrooms: 3
Foundation: Crawl space, slab; optional basement plan available for extra fee
Materials List Available: Yes
Price Category: E

A traditional design with a covered front porch and high ceilings in many rooms gives this home all the space and comfort you'll ever need.

Features:

- Foyer: A formal foyer with 8-in. wood columns will lead you to an elegant dining area.

- Great Room: This wonderful gathering room has 10-ft. boxed ceilings, a built-in media center, and an atrium door leading to a rear grilling porch.

- Kitchen: Functional yet cozy, this kitchen opens to the breakfast area with built-in computer desk and is open to the great room as well.

- Master Suite: Pamper yourself in this luxurious bedroom with 10-ft. boxed ceilings, large walk-in closets, and a bath area with a whirlpool tub, shower, and double vanity.

- Second Level: A game room and two bedrooms with walk-thru baths make this floor special.

Photo provided by designer/architect.

Main Level Floor Plan

Upper Level Floor Plan

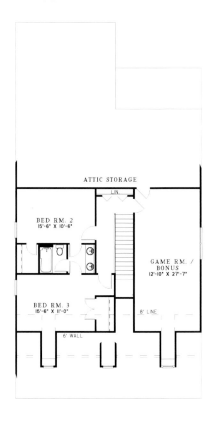

Copyright by designer/architect.

Plan #151029

Dimensions: 59'4" W x 74'2" D

Levels: 1½

Square Footage: 2,777

Main Level Sq. Ft.: 2,082

Upper Level Sq. Ft.: 695

Bedrooms: 4

Bathrooms: 2

Foundation: Crawl space, slab; optional basement plan available for extra fee

Materials List Available: Yes

Price Category: F

Photo provided by designer/architect.

This grand home combines historic Southern charm with modern technology and design. A two-car garage and covered front porch allow for optimum convenience.

Features:

- Foyer: This marvelous foyer leads directly to an elegant dining room and comfortable great room.

- Great Room: With high ceilings, a built-in media center, and a fireplace, this will be your

favorite room during the chilly fall months.

- Kitchen: An eat-in-bar with an optional island, computer area, and adjoining breakfast room with a bay window make a perfect layout.

- Master Suite: Relax in comfort with a corner whirlpool tub, a separate glass shower, double vanities, and large walk-in closets.

- Upper Level Bedrooms: 2 and 3 both have window seats.

Main Level Floor Plan

Copyright by designer/architect.

Upper Level Floor Plan

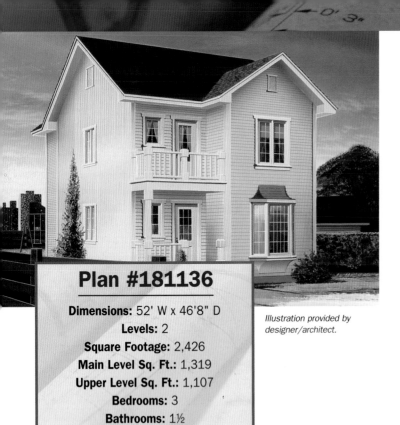

Main Level Floor Plan

32'-0"
9,6 m

9'-0" X 11'-4"
2,70 X 3,40

11'-8" X 10'-0"
3,50 X 3,00

11'-4" X 13'-4"
3,40 X 4,00

22'-0"
6,6 m

9'-0" X 10'-0"
2,70 X 3,00

11'-4" X 9'-8"
3,40 X 2,90

9'-4" X 6'-8"
2,80 X 2,00

11'-4" 10'-8"
3,40 X 3,20

Upper Level Floor Plan

Copyright by designer/architect.

Illustration provided by designer/architect.

Plan #181136

Dimensions: 52' W x 46'8" D

Levels: 2

Square Footage: 2,426

Main Level Sq. Ft.: 1,319

Upper Level Sq. Ft.: 1,107

Bedrooms: 3

Bathrooms: 1½

Foundation: Full basement

Materials List Available: Yes

Price Category: E

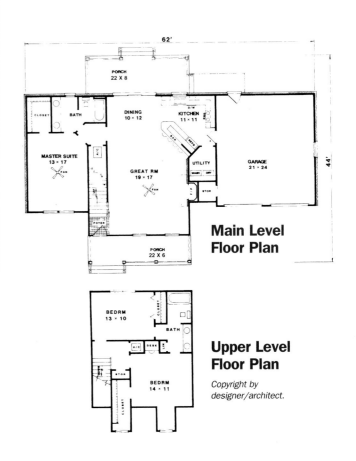

62'

PORCH
22 X 8

CLOSET | BATH

DINING
10 x 12

KITCHEN
11 x 11

MASTER SUITE
13 x 17

GREAT RM
19 x 17

UTILITY

GARAGE
21 x 24

STOR

FOYER

44'

PORCH
22 X 6

Main Level Floor Plan

BEDRM
13 x 10

CLOSET

BATH

DESK

STOR

BEDRM
14 x 11

CLOSET

Upper Level Floor Plan

Copyright by designer/architect.

Illustration provided by designer/architect.

Plan #171007

Dimensions: 62' W x 44' D

Levels: 2

Square Footage: 1,650

Main Level Sq. Ft.: 1,097

Upper Level Sq. Ft.: 553

Bedrooms: 3

Bathrooms: 2

Foundation: Slab, crawl space

Materials List Available: Yes

Price Category: C

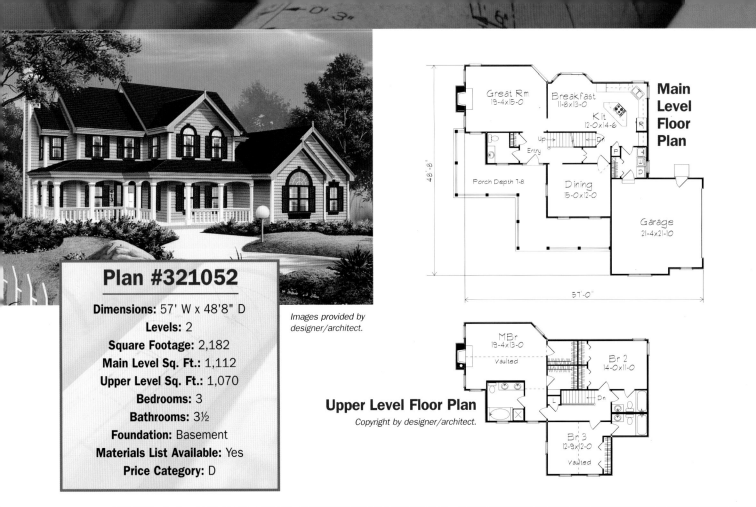

Plan #321052

Dimensions: 57' W x 48'8" D
Levels: 2
Square Footage: 2,182
Main Level Sq. Ft.: 1,112
Upper Level Sq. Ft.: 1,070
Bedrooms: 3
Bathrooms: 3½
Foundation: Basement
Materials List Available: Yes
Price Category: D

Images provided by designer/architect.

Main Level Floor Plan

Great Rm 19-4x15-0
Breakfast 11-8x13-0
Kit 12-0x14-6
Entry
Dining 15-0x12-0
Porch Depth 7-8
Garage 21-4x21-10

48'8"
57'-0"

Upper Level Floor Plan

Copyright by designer/architect.

MBr 19-4x13-0 Vaulted
Br 2 14-0x11-0
Br 3 12-9x12-0 Vaulted

Plan #141012

Dimensions: 44'4" W x 38' D
Levels: 2
Square Footage: 1,870
Main Level Sq. Ft.: 1,159
Upper Level Sq. Ft.: 711
Bedrooms: 3
Bathrooms: 2½
Foundation: Basement
Materials List Available: Yes
Price Category: D

Images provided by designer/architect.

Main Level Floor Plan

Sundeck 16-0 x 12-0
Brkfst. 10-6 x 7-6
Kit. 10-6 x 10-0
Dining 10-10 x 8-10
Lav.
W. D.
M.Bath
Living Area 20-6 x 13-6
Master Bedroom 17-6 x 14-6
Entry

6-0
38-0
44-4

Upper Level Floor Plan

Copyright by designer/architect.

Low Storage
Bth.2
Low Storage
Lin.
Bdrm.2 15-0 x 14-8
Bdrm.3 14-8 x 15-0
Low Storage
Low Storage

Plan #131027

Dimensions: 62'4" W x 53'6" D
Levels: 2
Square Footage: 2,567
Main Level Sq. Ft.: 2,017
Upper Level Sq. Ft.: 550
Bedrooms: 4
Bathrooms: 3
Foundation: Crawl space, slab, or basement
Materials List Available: Yes
Price Category: F

Images provided by designer/architect.

The features of this home are so good that you may have trouble imagining all of them at once.

Features:

- **Great Room:** Imagine a stepped ceiling, corner fireplace, built-media center, and wall of windows with a glass door to the backyard—in one room.
- **Dining Room:** A stepped ceiling and server with a sink add to the elegance of this formal room.
- **Breakfast Room:** Eat at the bar this room shares with the island kitchen, and admire the 12-ft. cathedral ceiling and bayed group of

8- and 9-ft. windows. Or go through the sliding glass door to the covered side porch.
- **Master Suite:** The bedroom has a tray ceiling and cozy sitting area, and a whirlpool tub, shower, and walk-in closet are in the skylighted bath.
- **Optional Study:** The private bath in bedroom 2 makes it ideal for a study or home office.
- **Bonus Room:** Enjoy the extra 300 sq. ft.

Breakfast Nook

Rear View

Great Room

Main Level Floor Plan

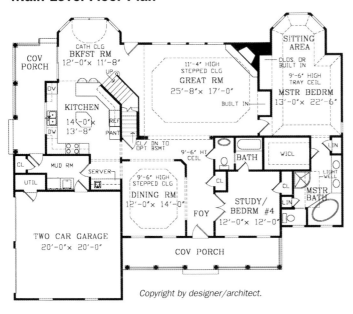

COV PORCH

CATH CLG
BKFST RM
12'-0"x 11'-8"

11'-4" HIGH STEPPED CLG
GREAT RM
25'-8"x 17'-0"

BUILT IN

SITTING AREA

CLOS. OR BUILT IN

9'-6" HIGH TRAY CEIL
MSTR BEDRM
13'-0"x 22'-6"

KITCHEN
14'-0"x 13'-8"

CL/DN TO OPT BSMT

9'-6" HI CEIL

BATH

WICL

LIN

LIGHT WELL

MUD RM

SERVER

UTIL

CL

9'-6" HIGH STEPPED CLG
DINING RM
12'-0"x 14'-0"

FOY

STUDY/ BEDRM #4
12'-0"x 12'-0"

MSTR BATH

TWO CAR GARAGE
20'-0"x 20'-0"

COV PORCH

Copyright by designer/architect.

Upper Level Floor Plan

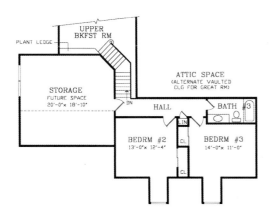

PLANT LEDGE

UPPER BKFST RM

STORAGE
FUTURE SPACE
20'-0"x 18'-10"

ATTIC SPACE
(ALTERNATE VAULTED CLG FOR GREAT RM)

DN

HALL

BATH #3

BEDRM #2
13'-0"x 12'-4"

BEDRM #3
14'-0"x 11'-0"

CL

LIN

CL

As with any skill, there is a right and a wrong way to paint. There is a right way to hold a brush, a right way to maneuver a roller, a right way to spray a wall, etc. Follow these basic professional tips:

Brushing vs. Rolling. Some painters insist that only a brush-painted job looks right. However, most painters will "cut in" the edges with a brush, and then finish the main body of a wall or ceiling using a roller. Brushing alone can be time-consuming, and it is typically reserved for architectural woodwork.

Using the Right Brush. Use the largest brush with which you are comfortable. Professional painters seldom pick up anything smaller than a 4-inch brush. Most homeowners will achieve good results using a 4-inch brush for "cutting in" and for large surfaces, and an angled 2½- to 3-inch sash brush for trim around windows and doors. Be sure, also, to use brushes that are appropriate for the type of paint being applied. Oil-based paints require a natural bristle (also called "China bristles"), while water-based paints are applied with a synthetic bristle brush.

Handling a Brush. Many people grip a paintbrush as if they were shaking someone's hand. It is better to grip a brush more like a pencil, with the fingers and thumb wrapped around the metal ferrule. This grip provides the hand and wrist with a wider range of motion and therefore greater speed and precision. If your hand cramps, switch hands or switch temporarily to the handshake grip.

Wiping Rags. Before you begin painting, put a dust rag in your pocket. This is helpful for clearing away cobwebs and dust before painting. It is also handy for wiping off paint drips before they have a chance to dry.

Paint Hooks. When working on a ladder, use a good-quality paint hook to secure the paint bucket to your ladder. Avoid makeshift hooks made with wire or coat hangers. Paint hooks are inexpensive and available at virtually all paint and hardware stores.

Plan #131046

Dimensions: 68' W x 57'6" D
Levels: 2
Square Footage: 2,245
Main Level Sq. Ft.: 1,720
Upper Level Sq. Ft.: 525
Bedrooms: 3
Bathrooms: 2½
Foundation: Crawl space, slab, or basement
Materials List Available: Yes
Price Category: F

You'll love the mixture of country charm and contemporary amenities in this lovely home.

Features:

• Porch: The covered wraparound porch spells comfort, and the arched windows spell style.

• Great Room: Look up at the 18-ft. vaulted ceiling and the balcony that looks over this room from the upper level, and then notice the wall of windows and the fireplace that's set into a media wall for decorating ease.

• Kitchen: This roomy kitchen is also designed for convenience, thanks to its ample counter space and work island.

• Breakfast Room: The kitchen looks out to this lovely room, with its vaulted ceiling and sliding French doors that open to the rear covered porch.

• Master Bedroom: A 10-ft-ceiling and a dramatic bay window give character to this charming room.

Main Level Floor Plan

Upper Level Floor Plan

Plan #101014

Dimensions: 52' W x 28' D
Levels: 2
Square Footage: 1,598
Main Level Sq. Ft.: 812
Upper Level Sq. Ft.: 786
Bedrooms: 3
Bathrooms: 2½
Foundation: Slab, crawl space
Materials List Available: No
Price Category: C

This lovely Victorian home has a perfect balance of ornamental features and modern amenities.

Features:

• Ceiling Height: 8 ft. unless otherwise noted.

• Foyer: An impressive beveled glass-front door invites you into this roomy foyer.

• Kitchen: This bright and open kitchen offers an abundance of counter space to make cooking a pleasure.

• Breakfast Room: You'll enjoy plenty of informal family meals in this sunny and open spot next to the kitchen.

• Family Room: The whole family will be attracted to this handsome room. A full-width bay window adds to the Victorian charm.

• Master Suite: This dramatic suite features a multi-faceted vaulted ceiling and his and her closets and vanities. A separate shower and 6-ft. garden tub complete the lavish appointments.

Main Level Floor Plan

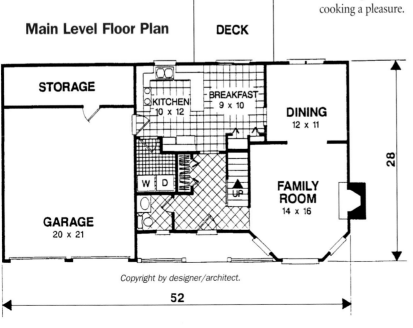

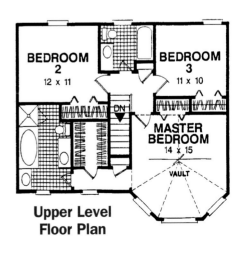

Upper Level Floor Plan

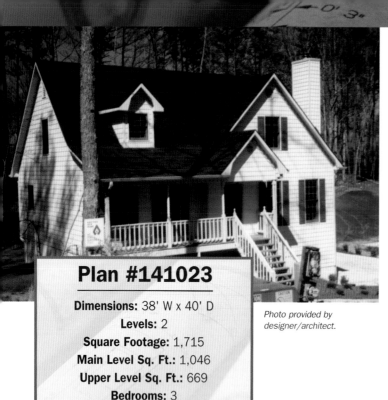

Plan #141023

Dimensions: 38' W x 40' D

Levels: 2

Square Footage: 1,715

Main Level Sq. Ft.: 1,046

Upper Level Sq. Ft.: 669

Bedrooms: 3

Bathrooms: 2½

Foundation: Basement

Materials List Available: Yes

Price Category: C

Photo provided by designer/architect.

Main Level Floor Plan

Deck 16-0 x 12-0

Breakfast

Kitchen 9-0 x 9-6

Dining Area 9-10 x 11-4

Bath

M. Bath

Living Area 18-0 x 13-6

Master Bedroom 15-6 x 13-6

© 1989

Porch

Upper Level Floor Plan

Copyright by designer/architect.

Bath

Bedroom 2 15-8 x 13-4

Bedroom 3 15-6 x 11-0

Plan #141024

Dimensions: 59' W x 46' D

Levels: 2

Square Footage: 1,732

Main Level Sq. Ft.: 1,128

Lower Level Sq. Ft.: 604

Bedrooms: 3

Bathrooms: 2½

Foundation: Basement

Materials List Available: Yes

Price Category: C

Photo provided by designer/architect.

Lower Level Floor Plan

Double Garage 19-6 x 23-4

Bdrm-2 11-8 x 11-6

Bedroom-3 12-6 x 11-6

Bth-2

Stor

Up

Furn

WH

© 1995

Copyright by designer/architect.

Main Level Floor Plan

Deck 50-6 x 12-0

M. Bdrm 12-2 x 16-0 w/ Bay

Dining 13-6 x 13-6 with Bays

Screen Porch 14-0 x 16-0

M.Bath

Great Room 17-10 x 19-0

Kitchen 11-6 x 12-0

Porch

Storage

Entry

Down

Porch

59-0

46-0

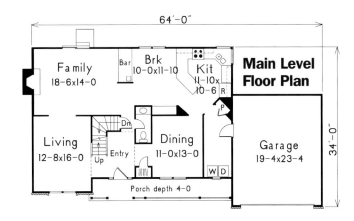

Main Level Floor Plan

64'-0"

Family 18-6x14-0

Bar

Brk 10-0x11-10

Kit 11-10x 10-6

Living 12-8x16-0

Entry Up Dn

Dining 11-0x13-0

Garage 19-4x23-4

34'-0"

W D

Porch depth 4-0

Plan #321041

Dimensions: 64' W x 34' D

Levels: 2

Square Footage: 2,286

Main Level Sq. Ft.: 1,283

Upper Level Sq. Ft.: 1,003

Bedrooms: 4

Bathrooms: 2½

Foundation: Basement

Materials List Available: Yes

Price Category: E

Images provided by designer/architect.

Upper Level Floor Plan

Br 4 10-2x 10-8

Br 3 11-7x10-8

MBr 12-8x15-11 vaulted

Dn L

open to below

Br 2 12-4x10-8

Copyright by designer/architect.

Plan #321055

Dimensions: 70' W x 40' D

Levels: 2

Square Footage: 2,505

Main Level Sq. Ft.: 1,436

Upper Level Sq. Ft.: 1,069

Bedrooms: 3

Bathrooms: 2½

Foundation: Basement

Materials List Available: Yes

Price Category: E

Images provided by designer/architect.

Main Level Floor Plan

70'-0"

Patio

Storage 13-6x10-6

D W

Kitchen 15-0x 14-8

Brk 9-0x 14-8

Family 20-6x14-8

sloped clg

40'-0"

Garage 23-4x25-0

P

Dining 12-9x14-2

Up Foyer

Dn

Living 12-9x14-2

Porch depth 6-0

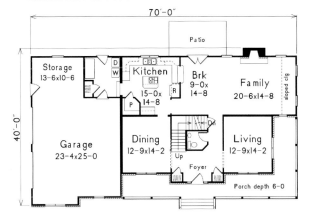

Upper Level Floor Plan

Copyright by designer/architect.

Br 2 12-6x11-6

MBr 12-9x18-0

Dn L

open to below

Br 3 12-9x12-0

Plan #131051

Dimensions: 64'4" W x 53'4" D

Levels: 3

Square Footage: 2,431

Main Level Sq. Ft.: 1,293

Upper Level Sq. Ft.: 1,138

Bedrooms: 4

Bathrooms: 2½

Foundation: Basement, crawl space, or slab

Materials List Available: Yes

Price Category: F

Gracious and charming with a wraparound front porch and a backyard terrace, this home also has a ready-to-finish third floor all-purpose room and a full bath.

Features:

- Main Level Ceiling Height: 8 ft.

- Family Room: A comfortable space for the entire family to gather, this delightful room can be warmed by a heat-circulating fireplace.

- Dining Room: A cozy dinette boasts a sliding glass door with access to a gorgeous backyard terrace with an optional calm reflecting pool.

- Kitchen: Adjoining the dining area, the kitchen offers plenty of storage and counter space. The laundry room and half-bath are nearby for convenience.

- Garage: The garage is tucked way back to keep it from intruding into the traditional facade.

Photo provided by designer/architect.

Main Level Floor Plan

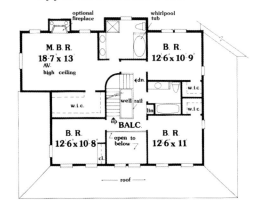

Rear Elevation

Upper Level Floor Plan

3rd Level Floor Plan

Copyright by designer/architect.

Plan #131024

Dimensions: 36' W by 54'4" D
Levels: 2
Square Footage: 1,635
Main Level Sq. Ft.: 880
Upper Level Sq. Ft.: 755
Bedrooms: 3
Bathrooms: 2 ½
Foundation: Basement, crawl space, or slab
Materials List Available: Yes
Price Category: D

Photo provided by designer/architect.

You'll love the combination of early-American detailing on the outside and the contemporary, open layout of the interior.

Features:

• Ceiling Height: 8 ft.

• Front Porch: Use this wraparound front porch as an extra room when the weather's fine.

• Living Room: Separated only by columns, the open arrangement of the living and dining rooms enhances the spacious feeling in this home.

• Family Room/Kitchen: This combination family room/country kitchen includes a large work island and snack bar for convenience.

• Master Suite: A tray ceiling creates a contemporary look in the spacious master bedroom, and three closets make it practical. A compartmented full bath completes the suite.

• Bedrooms: Two additional bedrooms share a second full bath.

• Attic: Finish the attic space that's over the garage for even more living space.

Main Level Floor Plan

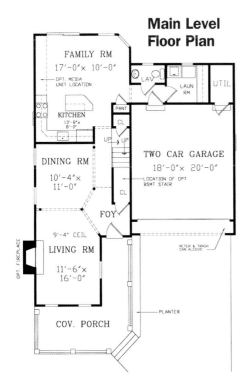

Upper Level Floor Plan

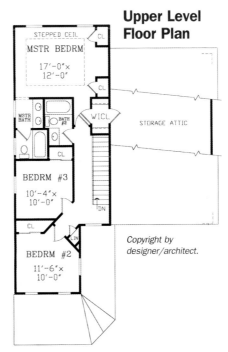

Copyright by designer/architect.

Rear Elevation

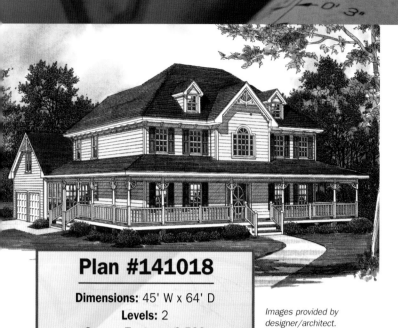

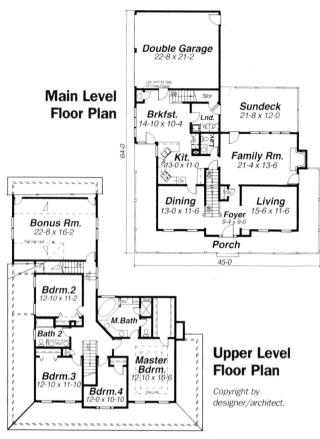

Main Level Floor Plan

Double Garage
22-8 x 21-2

Brkfst.
14-10 x 10-4

Sundeck
21-8 x 12-0

Kit.
13-0 x 11-0

Family Rm.
21-4 x 13-6

Dining
13-0 x 11-6

Living
15-6 x 11-6

Foyer
9-4 x 9-0

Porch

45-0

64-0

Images provided by designer/architect.

Bonus Rm.
22-8 x 16-2

Bdrm.2
12-10 x 11-2

M.Bath

Bath 2

Master Bdrm.
12-10 x 16-6

Bdrm.3
12-10 x 11-10

Bdrm.4
12-0 x 10-10

Upper Level Floor Plan

Copyright by designer/architect.

Plan #141018

Dimensions: 45' W x 64' D

Levels: 2

Square Footage: 2,588

Main Level Sq. Ft.: 1,320

Upper Level Sq. Ft.: 1,268

Bedrooms: 4

Bathrooms: 2½

Foundation: Basement, crawl space, or slab

Materials List Available: Yes

Price Category: E

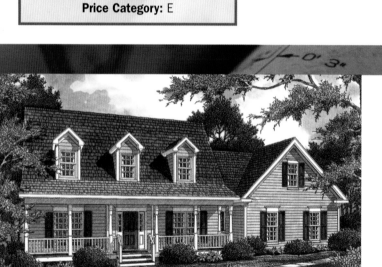

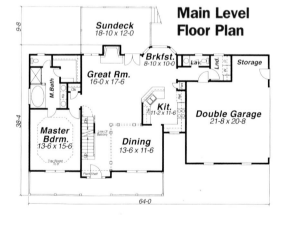

Main Level Floor Plan

Sundeck
18-10 x 12-0

Brkfst.
8-10 x 10-0

Storage

Great Rm.
16-0 x 17-6

M.Bath

Kit.
11-2 x 11-6

Double Garage
21-8 x 20-8

Master Bdrm.
13-6 x 15-6

Dining
13-6 x 11-6

9-8

38-4

64-0

Images provided by designer/architect.

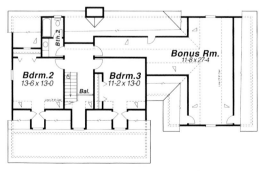

Upper Level Floor Plan

Bth.2

Bonus Rm.
11-8 x 27-4

Bdrm.2
13-6 x 13-0

Bdrm.3
11-2 x 13-0

Bal.

Copyright by designer/architect.

Plan #141013

Dimensions: 64' W x 38'4" D

Levels: 2

Square Footage: 1,936

Main Level Sq. Ft: 1,312

Upper Level Sq. Ft.: 624

Bedrooms: 3

Bathrooms: 2½

Foundation: Basement

Materials List Available: No

Price Category: D

Main Level Floor Plan

DECK 40'0" x 11'7"

SCREENED PORCH 11'10" x 11'7"

BREAKFAST 10'11" x 10'0"

MASTER BDRM 14'9" x 18'5"

FAMILY 19'0" x 17'0"

KITCHEN 13'10" x 13'2"

GARAGE 21'4" x 32'1"

LIVING 14'9" x 11'11"

ENTRY 11'7" x 14'5"

DINING 14'9" x 11'11"

49'-2"36'-4"

22'-0"

55'-8"

Images provided by designer/architect.

Plan #101020

Dimensions: 55'8" W x 49'2" D

Levels: 2

Square Footage: 2,972

Main Level Sq. Ft.: 1,986

Upper Level Sq. Ft.: 986

Bedrooms: 4

Bathrooms: 3½

Foundation: Basement

Materials List Available: No

Price Category: F

Copyright by designer/architect.

BEDROOM 4 14'9" x 13'0"

OPEN BELOW

MECHANICAL STORAGE 7'5" x 8'9"

BONUS ROOM 11'9" x 32'1"

BEDROOM 3 14'9" x 13'0"

OPEN BELOW

BEDROOM 2 14'9" x 15'5"

Upper Level Floor Plan

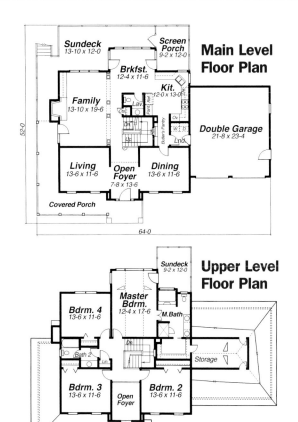

Sundeck 13-10 x 12-0

Screen Porch 9-2 x 12-0

Main Level Floor Plan

Brkfst. 12-4 x 11-6

Kit. 12-0 x 13-0

Family 13-10 x 19-6

Lav.

Double Garage 21-8 x 23-4

52-0

Butler's Pantry

Living 13-6 x 11-6

Open Foyer 7-8 x 13-6

Dining 13-6 x 11-6

Covered Porch

64-0

Plan #141016

Dimensions: 64' W x 52' D

Levels: 2

Square Footage: 2,416

Main Level Sq. Ft.: 1,250

Upper Level Sq. Ft.: 1,166

Bedrooms: 4

Bathrooms: 2½

Foundation: Basement

Materials List Available: Yes

Price Category: E

Illustration provided by designer/architect.

Sundeck 9-2 x 12-0

Upper Level Floor Plan

Master Bdrm. 12-4 x 17-6

Bdrm. 4 13-6 x 11-6

M.Bath

Bath 2

Storage

Bdrm. 3 13-6 x 11-6

Open Foyer

Bdrm. 2 13-6 x 11-6

Copyright by designer/architect.

Photo provided by designer/architect.

Plan #121037

Dimensions: 46' W x 47'10" D
Levels: 2
Square Footage: 2,292
Main Level Sq. Ft.: 1,158
Upper Level Sq. Ft.: 1,134
Bedrooms: 4
Bathrooms: 2½
Foundation: Basement
Materials List Available: Yes
Price Category: E

This convenient and comfortable home is filled with architectural features that set it apart.

Features:

• Ceiling Height: 8 ft. unless otherwise noted.

• Foyer: You'll know you have arrived when you enter this two-story area highlighted by a decorative plant shelf and a balcony.

• Great Room: Just beyond the entry is the great room where the warmth of the two-sided fireplace will attract family and friends to gather. A bay window offers a more intimate place to sit and converse.

• Hearth Room: At the other side of the fireplace, the hearth offers a cozy spot for smaller gatherings or a place to sit alone and enjoy a book by the fire.

• Breakfast Area: With sunlight streaming into its bay window, the breakfast area offers the perfect spot for informal family meals.

• Master Suite: This private retreat is made more convenient by a walk-in closet. It features its own tub and shower.

Main Level Floor Plan

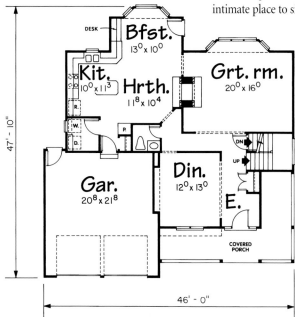

Upper Level Floor Plan

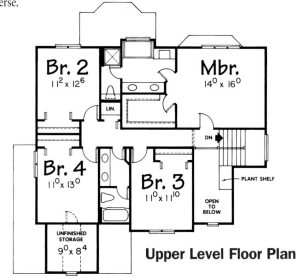

Copyright by designer/architect.

Plan #121083

Dimensions: 72' W x 45'4" D
Levels: 2
Square Footage: 2,695
Main Level Sq. Ft.: 1,881
Upper Level Sq. Ft.: 814
Bedrooms: 4
Bathrooms: 3½
Foundation: Basement
Materials List Available: Yes
Price Category: F

You'll love this home for its soaring entryway ceiling and well-designed layout.

Features:

- **Entry:** A balcony from the upper level looks down into this two-story entry, which features a decorative plant shelf.
- **Great Room:** Comfort is guaranteed in this large room, with its built-in bookcases framing a lovely fireplace and trio of transom-topped windows along one wall.

- **Living Room:** Save both this formal room and the formal dining room, both of which flank the entry, for guests and special occasions.
- **Kitchen:** This convenient work space includes a gazebo-shaped breakfast area where friends and family will gather at any time of day.

Main Level Floor Plan

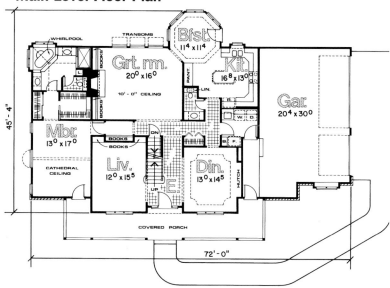

Upper Level Floor Plan

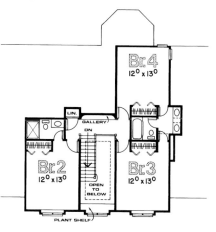

Photo provided by designer/architect.

Plan #211069

Dimensions: 58' W x 42' D
Levels: 1½
Square Footage: 1,600
Main Level Sq. Ft.: 1,136
Upper Level Sq. Ft.: 464
Bedrooms: 3
Bathrooms: 2
Foundation: Crawl space
Materials List Available: Yes
Price Category: C

Enjoy the large front porch on this traditionally styled home when it's too sunny for the bugs, and use the screened back porch at dusk and dawn.

Features:

• Living Room: Call this the family room if you wish, but no matter what you call it, expect friends and family to gather here, especially when the fireplace gives welcome warmth.

• Kitchen: You'll love the practical layout that pleases everyone from gourmet chefs.to beginning cooks.

• Master Suite: Positioned on the main floor to give it privacy, this suite has two entrances for convenience. You'll find a large walk-in closet here as well as a dressing room that includes a separate vanity and mirror makeup counter.

• Storage Space: The 462-sq.-ft. garage is roomy enough to hold two cars and still have space to store tools, out-of-season clothing, or whatever else that needs a dry, protected spot.

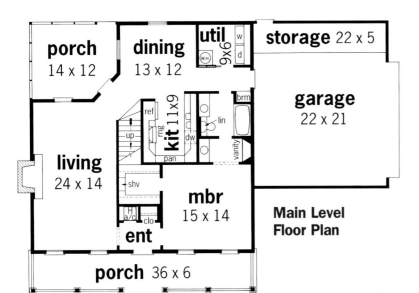

Main Level Floor Plan

Upper Level Floor Plan

Copyright by designer/architect.

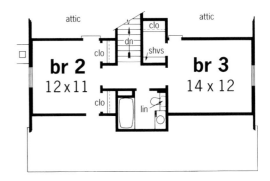

Photo provided by designer/architect.

Plan #121038

Dimensions: 54' W x 52' D
Levels: 2
Square Footage: 2,332
Main Level Sq. Ft.: 1,597
Upper Level Sq. Ft.: 735
Bedrooms: 4
Bathrooms: 2½
Foundation: Basement
Materials List Available: Yes
Price Category: E

Offering plenty of architectural style, this home is designed with the busy modern lifestyle in mind.

Features:

• Ceiling Height: 8 ft. unless otherwise noted.

• Family Room: The visual spaciousness of this stylish family room is enhanced by a cathedral ceiling and light streaming through stacked windows.

• Kitchen: This is sure to be a popular informal gathering place. The kitchen features a

convenient center island with a snack bar, pantry, and planning desk. The breakfast area is perfect for quick family meals.

• Master Suite: This peaceful retreat is thoughtfully located apart from the rest of the house. It includes a walk-in closet and a private bath.

• Bedrooms: Bedroom 2 has its own walk-in closet and private bath. Bedrooms 3 and 4 share a full bath.

Main Level Floor Plan

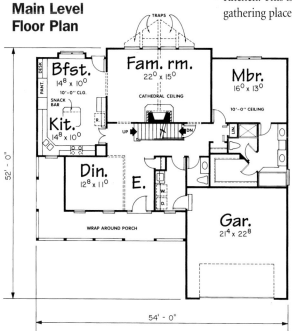

Upper Level Floor Plan

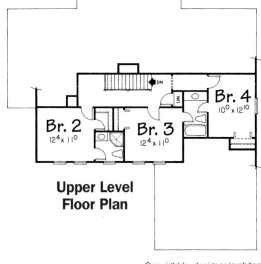

Copyright by designer/architect.

Plan #121040

Dimensions: 50' W x 48' D
Levels: 2
Square Footage: 1,818
Main Level Sq. Ft.: 1,302
Upper Level Sq. Ft.: 516
Bedrooms: 3
Bathrooms: 2½
Foundation: Basement
Materials List Available: Yes
Price Category: D

Offering plenty of architectural style, this home is designed with the busy modern lifestyle in mind.

Features:

• Ceiling Height: 8 ft. unless otherwise noted.

• Great Room: This is sure to be the central gathering place of the home with its volume ceiling, abundance of windows, and its handsome fireplace.

• Kitchen: This convenient and attractive kitchen offers a center island. It includes a snack bar that will get lots of use for impromptu family meals.

• Breakfast Area: Joined to the kitchen by the snack bar, this breakfast area will invite you to linger over morning coffee. It includes a pantry and access to the backyard.

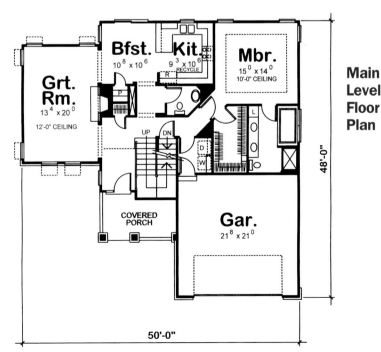

Main Level Floor Plan

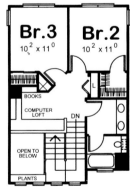

Upper Level Floor Plan

• Master Bedroom: This private retreat offers the convenience of a walk-in closet and the luxury of its own whirlpool bath and shower.

• Computer Loft: Designed with the family computer in mind, this loft overlooks a two-story entry.

Let Us Help You
Plan Your
Dream Home

Whether you've always dreamed of building your own home or you can't find the right house from among the dozens you've toured, our collection of ultimate home plans can help you achieve the home of your dreams. You could have an architect create a one-of-a-kind home for you, but the design services alone could end up costing up to 15 percent of the cost of construction—a hefty premium for any building project. Isn't it a better idea to select from among the hundreds of unique designs shown in our collection for a fraction of the cost?

What does Creative Homeowner Offer?

In this book, Creative Homeowner provides hundreds of home plans from the country's best architects and designers. Our designs are among the most popular available. Whether your taste runs from traditional to contemporary, Victorian to early American, you are sure to find the best house design for you and your family. Our plans packages include detailed drawings to help you or your builder construct your dream house. **(See page 584.)**

Can I Make Changes to the Plans?

Creative Homeowner offers three ways to help you achieve a truly unique home design. Our customizing service allows for extensive changes to our designs. **(See page 585.)** We also provide reverse images of our plans, or we can give you and your builder the tools for making minor changes on your own. **(See page 586.)**

Can You Help Me Stay on Budget?

Building a house is a large financial investment. To help you stay within your budget, Creative Homeowner can provide you with general construction costs based on your zip code. **(See page 586.)** Also, many of our plans come with the option of buying detailed materials lists to help you price out construction costs.

Is There Anything I Missed?

A typical construction crew consists of a number of skilled professionals. If you plan on doing all or part of the work yourself, or you want to keep tabs on your builder, we offer best-selling building and design books at attractive prices. (See our company Web site at www.creativehomeowner.com.) Our home-building book package covers all phases of home construction, from framing and drywalling to wiring and plumbing.

Our Plans Packages Offer:

All of our home plans are the result of many hours of work by leading architects and professional designers. Most of our home plans include each of the following.

Frontal Sheet

This artist's rendering of the front of the house gives you an idea of how the house will look once it is completed and the property landscaped.

Detailed Floor Plans

These plans show the size and layout of the rooms. They also provide the locations of doors, windows, fireplaces, closets, stairs, and electrical outlets and switches.

Foundation Plan

A foundation plan gives the dimensions of basements, walk-out basements, crawl spaces, pier foundations, and slab construction. Each house design lists the type of foundation included. If the plan you choose does not have the foundation type you require, our customer service department can help you customize the plan to meet your needs.

Roof Plan

In addition to providing the pitch of the roof, these plans also show the locations of dormers, skylights, and other elements.

Exterior Elevations

These drawings show the front, rear, and sides of the house as if you were looking at it head on. Elevations also provide information about architectural features and finish materials.

Interior Elevations and Details

Interior elevations show specific details of such elements as fireplaces, kitchen and bathroom cabinets, built-ins, and other unique features of the design.

Cross Sections

These show the structure as if it were sliced to reveal construction requirements, such as insulation, flooring, and roofing details.

Frontal Sheet

Floor Plan

Foundation Plan

Roof Plan

Cross Sections

Stair Details

Elevation

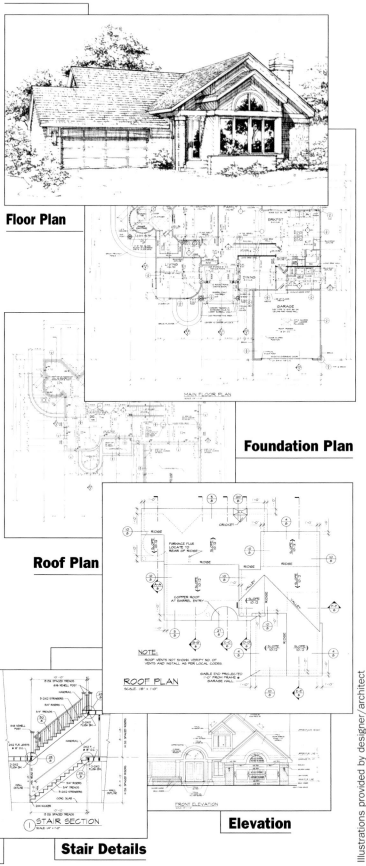

Illustrations provided by designer/architect

Customize Your Plans in 4 Easy Steps

1 **Select the home plan** that most closely meets your needs. Purchase of a reproducible master is necessary in order to make changes to a plan.

2 **Call 1-800-523-6789 to place your order.** Tell our sales representative you are interested in customizing your plan. To receive your customization cost estimate, we will send you a checklist (via fax or email) for you to complete indicating the changes you would like to make to your plan. There is a $50 nonrefundable consultation fee for this service. If you decide to continue with the custom changes, the $50 fee is credited to the total amount charged.

3 **Fax the completed checklist** to 1-201-760-2431 or email it to us at customize@creativehomeowner.com. Within three business days of receipt of your checklist, a detailed cost estimate will be provided to you.

4 **Once you approve the estimate,** a 75% retainer fee is collected and customization work begins. Preliminary drawings typically take 10 to 15 business days. After approval, we will collect the balance of your customization order cost before shipping the completed plans. You will receive five sets of blueprints or a reproducible master, plus a customized materials list if desired.

Modification Pricing Guide

Categories	Average Cost From...	To
Add or remove living space	Quote required	
Bathroom layout redesign	$120	$280
Kitchen layout redesign	$120	$280
Garage: add or remove	Starting at $400	
Garage: front entry to side load or vice versa	Starting at $300	
Foundation changes	Starting at $220	
Exterior building materials change	Starting at $200	
Exterior openings: add, move, or remove	$65 per opening	
Roof line changes	Starting at $360	
Ceiling height adjustments	Starting at $280	
Fireplace: add or remove	Starting at $90	
Screened porch: add	Starting at $280	
Wall framing change from 2x4 to 2x6	Starting at $200	
Bearing and/or exterior walls changes	Quote required	
Non-bearing wall or room changes	$65 per room	
Metric conversion of home plan	Starting at $400	
Adjust plan for handicapped accessibility	Quote required	
Adapt plans for local building code requirements	Quote required	
Engineering stamping only	Quote required	
Any other engineering services	Quote required	
Interactive illustrations (choices of exterior materials)	Quote required	

Note: *Any home plan can be customized to accommodate your desired changes. The average prices above are provided only as examples of the most commonly requested changes, and are subject to change without notice. Prices for changes will vary according to the number of modifications requested, plan size, style, and method of design used by the original designer. To obtain a detailed cost estimate, please contact us.*

Before Customization

After

Decide What Type of Plan Package You Need

How many Plans Should You Order?

Standard 8-Set Package. We've found that our 8-set package is the best value for someone who is ready to start building. Once the process begins, a number of people will require their own set of blueprints. The 8-set package provides plans for you, your builder, the subcontractors, mortgage lender, and the building department.

Minimum 4-Set Package. If you are in the bidding process, you may want to order only four sets for the bidding round and reorder additional sets as needed.

1-Set Study Package. The 1-set package allows you to review your home plan in detail. The plan will be marked as a study print, and it is illegal to build a house from a study print alone. It is a violation of copyright law to reproduce a blueprint without permission.

Buying Additional Sets

If you require additional copies of blueprints for your home construction, you can order additional sets within 60 days of the original order date at a reduced price. The cost is $45.00 for each additional set. For more information, contact customer service.

Reproducible Masters

If you plan to make minor changes to one of our home plans, you can purchase reproducible masters. Printed on vellum paper, an erasable paper that you can reproduce in a copying machine, reproducible masters allow an architect, designer, or builder to alter our plans to give you a customized home design. This package also allows you to print as many copies of the modified plans as you need for construction.

Mirror-Reverse Sets

Plans can be printed in mirror-reverse—we can "flip" plans to create a mirror image of the design. This is useful when the house would fit your site or personal preferences if all the rooms were on the opposite side than shown. As the image is reversed, the lettering and dimensions will also be reversed, meaning they will read backwards. Therefore, when ordering mirror-reverse drawings, you must order at least one set of right-reading plans. A $50.00 fee per order will be charged for mirror-reverse (regardless of the number of mirror-reverse sets ordered).

EZ Quote: Home Cost Estimator

EZ Quote is our response to one of the most frequently asked questions we hear from customers: "How much will the house cost me to build?" EZ Quote: Home Cost Estimator will enable you to obtain a calculated building cost to construct your new home, based on labor rates and building material costs within your zip code area. This summary is useful for those who want to know the total construction costs before purchasing sets of home plans. It will also provide a level of comfort when you begin soliciting bids from builders. The cost is $29.95 for the first EZ Quote and $14.95 for each additional one. Available only in the U.S. and Canada.

CompleteCost Estimator

CompleteCost Estimator is a valuable tool for use in planning and constructing your new home. It combines the detail of a materials list with line-by-line cost estimating. The result is a complete, detailed estimate—similar to a bid—that will act as a checklist for all the items you will need to select or coordinate during our building process. CompleteCost Estimator is only available for certain plans (please see Plan Index) and may only be ordered with the purchase of a set of home plans. The cost is $125 for CompleteCost Estimator.

Materials List

Available for most of our plans, the Materials List provides you an invaluable resource in planning and estimating the cost of your home. Each Materials List outlines the quantity, dimensions, and type of materials needed to build your home (with the exception of mechanical systems). You will get faster, more-accurate bids from your contractors and building suppliers—and avoid paying for unused materials. A Materials List may only be ordered with the purchase of a set of home plans.

Order Toll Free by Phone
1-800-523-6789
By Fax: 201-760-2431

Regular office hours are
8:30AM–7:00PM ET, Mon–Fri

Orders received by 3PM ET, will be
processed and shipped within two
business days.

Order Online
www.ultimateplans.com

Mail Your Order
Creative Homeowner
Attn: Home Plans
24 Park Way
Upper Saddle River, NJ 07458

Canadian Customers
Order Toll Free 1-800-393-1883

Mail Your Order (Canada)
Creative Homeowner Canada
Attn: Home Plans
113-437 Martin St., Ste. 215
Penticton, BC V2A 5L1

Before You Order

Our Exchange Policy

Blueprints are nonrefundable. However, should you find that the plan you have purchased does not fit your needs, you may exchange that plan for another plan in our collection within 60 days from the date of your original order. The entire content of your original order must be returned before an exchange will be processed. You will be charged a processing fee of 20% of the amount of the original plan set, the cost difference between the new plan set and the original plan set (if applicable), and shipping costs for the new plans. Contact our customer service department for more information. Please note: reproducible masters may only be exchanged if the package is unopened.

Building Codes and Requirements

At the time of creation, our plans meet the building code requirements published by the Building Officials and Code Administrators International, the Southern Building Code Congress International, the International Conference of Building Officials, or the Council of American Building Officials. Because building codes vary from area to area, some drawing modifications and/or the assistance of a professional designer or architect may be necessary to comply with your local codes or to accommodate specific building site conditions. We strongly advise you to consult with your local building official for information regarding codes governing your area.

Blueprint Price Schedule

Price Code	1 Set	4 Sets	8 Sets	Reproducible Masters	Materials List
A	$290	$330	$380	$510	$60
B	$360	$410	$460	$580	$60
C	$420	$460	$510	$610	$60
D	$470	$510	$560	$660	$70
E	$520	$560	$610	$700	$70
F	$570	$610	$670	$750	$70
G	$620	$670	$720	$850	$70
H	$700	$740	$800	$900	$70
I	$810	$850	$900	$940	$80

Shipping & Handling

	1-4 Sets	5-7 Sets	8+ Sets or Reproducibles
US Regular (7–10 business days)	$15	$20	$25
US Priority (3–5 business days)	$25	$30	$35
US Express (1–2 business days)	$40	$45	$50
Canada Reg. (8–12 business days)	$35	$40	$45
Canada Exp. (3–5 business days)	$50	$55	$60
Worldwide Exp. (3–5 business days)	$80	$80	$80

Note: All delivery times are from date the blueprint and package is shipped.

Order Form

Please send me the following:

Plan Number: _____

Price Code: _____ (see Plan Index)

Indicate Foundation Type: (see plan page for availability)
☐ Slab   ☐ Crawl space   ☐ Basement   ☐ Walk-out basement

Basic Blueprint Package | **Cost**
☐ Reproducible Masters $_____
☐ 8-Set Plan Package $_____
☐ 4-Set Plan Package $_____
☐ 1-Set Study Package $_____

☐ Additional plan sets:
☐ ___ sets at $45.00 per set $_____
☐ Print in mirror-reverse: $50.00 per order $_____
   ___ sets printed in mirror-reverse

Important Extras
☐ Materials List $_____
☐ EZ Quote for Plan #_____ at $29.95 $_____
☐ Additional EZ Quotes for Plan #s_____
   at $14.95 each $_____

Shipping (see chart above) $_____
SUBTOTAL $_____
Sales Tax (NJ residents add 6%) $_____

TOTAL $_____

Order Toll Free: 1-800-523-6789   By Fax: 201-760-2431
Creative Homeowner
24 Park Way
Upper Saddle River, NJ 07458

Name _____
(Please print or type)

Street _____
(Please do not use a P.O. Box)

City _____   State _____

Country _____   Zip _____

Daytime telephone (___)_____

Fax (___)_____
(Required for reproducible orders)

E-Mail _____

Payment   ☐ Check/money order *Make checks payable to Creative Homeowner*

☐ VISA   ☐ MasterCard   ☐ American Express Cards   ☐ DISCOVER

Credit card number _____

Expiration date (mm/yy) _____

Signature _____

Please check the appropriate box:
☐ Licensed builder/contractor   ☐ Homeowner   ☐ Renter

SOURCE CODE	CA901

Copyright Notice

Index

Index

Index

Index